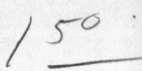

MILTON CROSS'
ENCYCLOPEDIA OF
THE GREAT COMPOSERS
AND THEIR MUSIC

MILTON CROSS'

Encyclopedia of the Great Composers and Their Music

MILTON CROSS

AND

DAVID EWEN

NEW, REVISED EDITION

Volume II

GARDEN CITY, NEW YORK

Doubleday & Company, Inc.

Contents

VOLUME II

Darius Milhaud • 505
Wolfgang Amadeus Mozart • 512
Modest Mussorgsky • 544
Jacques Offenbach • 558
Niccolò Paganini • 565
Serge Prokofiev • 572
Giacomo Puccini • 586
Serge Rachamaninoff • 598
Maurice Ravel • 609
Ottorino Respighi • 622
Nicholas Rimsky-Korsakov • 627
Gioacchino Rossini • 639
Camille Saint-Saëns • 652
Arnold Schoenberg • 664
Franz Schubert • 675

Robert Schumann • 698
Alexander Scriabin • 714
Dmitri Shostakovich • 725
Jean Sibelius • 738
Bedrich Smetana • 749
Richard Strauss • 758
Igor Stravinsky • 776
Peter Ilitch Tchaikovsky • 793
Ralph Vaughan Williams • 812
Giuseppe Verdi • 821
Heitor Villa-Lobos • 840
Richard Wagner • 847
William Walton • 882
Karl Maria von Weber • 888
Hugo Wolf • 897

PART III   *A Brief History of Music Since Bach*   909

PART IV   *Basic Works for the Record Library*
                   (With Recommended Recordings)   919

PART V   *The Anatomy of the Symphony Orchestra*   929

PART VI   *A Dictionary of Musical Forms*   935

PART VII   *A Glossary of Musical Terms*   951

                   A Select Bibliography   965

                   Index   979

Darius Milhaud

"One of the most facile and turbulent talents of our time has become one of the most completely calm of modern masters; . . . by adding . . . depth and penetration and simple humanity to his gamut, he has become the first composer of his country."
—*Virgil Thomson*

BORN: Aix-en-Provence, France, September 4, 1892.

MAJOR WORKS: *Orchestral Music*—Suite provençale; Protée—Symphonic Suite No. 2; Symphony No. 2; Symphony No. 3; Symphony No. 4; Symphony No. 6. ALSO: Le Boeuf sur le toit, La Création du monde, Le Train bleu, ballets; Orestes, Le Pauvre matelot, Christophe Colomb, Bolivar, operas; Symphony No. 1; Saudades do Brasil, for orchestra; 4 concertos for piano and orchestra; 2 concertos for cello and orchestra; 2 concertos for violin and orchestra; Concerto for Two Pianos and Orchestra; Le Bal martiniquais, for orchestra (also for two pianos); Symphonies Nos. 5, 7, and 8; Concerto for Harp and Orchestra; 18 string quartets; Scaramouche, Paris, for two pianos; 2 sonatas, for piano; 2 piano quintets.

HIS LIFE

WHEN Maurice Ravel died, in 1937, the leading position in French music passed to Darius Milhaud. His right to that position was not seriously questioned at that time, nor has it since been challenged. When Virgil Thomson visited Paris in 1945 he noted—in commenting on Milhaud's prolonged stay in America—that "all musical France hopes [for] the return of its master. . . . There is a vacancy in the center of the stage." Nor was that vacancy filled until 1947, when Milhaud (crippled by arthritis) returned home, at once to be officially appointed a member of the five-men committee to administrate his country's musical activities. Whether he is acclaimed (as he has so often been) or whether he is attacked (as he was in the early years of his career and once again in 1950, when his opera *Bolivar* was introduced in Paris), even his attackers would not now deny that he is the No. 1 composer of France.

His childhood in the Provence city of Aix was musical. "When I was a young boy, I played second violin in a quartet of my violin teacher, from 1905 to 1908. I was fascinated by the seventeen Beethoven quartets. When I was a student I decided that I would write eighteen."

After studying music with local teachers and at the College in Aix he entered the Paris Conservatory, in 1909. His teachers were some of the finest: Dukas in orchestral playing, Widor and Gédalge in composition. Under such admirable tuition his progress was rapid. He received prizes in violin playing, fugue, counterpoint, and composition. Two years after entering the Conservatory he started composing. First it was, modestly enough, some songs and piano pieces; after that, more ambitiously, his first opera, *La Brebis égarée.* World War I frustrated his ambition to compete for the Prix de Rome and brought his Conservatory training to a sudden and premature end.

Just before the war Milhaud had made a setting of Paul Claudel's *Connaissance de l'est.* This brought the then young and unknown composer to Claudel's attention. The friendship that soon developed between them was for Milhaud, as he later conceded, a decisive turning point.

In 1917 Claudel went to Brazil as the Ambassador from France, taking Milhaud with him to serve as attaché at the Legation. "We passed two years in this marvelous country in contact with the great tropical forest." During this time poet and musician worked together on several major undertakings. There was music for various tragedies by Aeschylus adapted by Claudel. There was the ballet *L'Homme et son désir.* Milhaud also wrote music independent of Claudel, notably the *String Quartet No. 4* and the score *Le Boeuf sur le toit,* for which Jean Cocteau wrote a ballet scenario *after* the music had been completed.

He was back in Paris in 1919 and came to more or less prominence a year later when the critic Henri Collet coined the name "The French Six" to describe collectively the work of six young composers, of whom Milhaud was one (see Honegger). As a member of this so-called school Milhaud began to enjoy publicity—and performances. His Second Orchestral Suite from *Protée* was introduced by the Colonne Orchestra on October 24, 1920. He collaborated with the other five members of "The Six" to produce the ballet score *Les Mariés de la tour Eiffel,* presented by the Ballets Suédois in Paris on June 19, 1921. His Sonata for Flute,

Oboe, Clarinet, and Piano was on the first program of the first concert of the International Society of Contemporary Music, which took place in Salzburg, Austria, on August 7, 1922. The youthful opera, *La Brebis égarée,* was seen at the Opéra Comique on December 15, 1923; the ballet *Le Train bleu* was seen at the Théâtre des Champs-Elysées on June 20, 1924.

There was, then, fame; but there was also notoriety. He was regarded as the most daring of "The Six," and the most unconventional, largely because of his "disreputable" excursions into the back streets of music: jazz, tango, and other music-hall and popular idioms. They called him "sensationalist," or "bluffer," or "vulgarian." But, praised or attacked, he continued to work hard with that extraordinary facility that has always characterized his career. The high quality of his best works silenced most attacks and all of the ridicule. In the early 1930s Boris de Schloezer could write: "Milhaud is, after Stravinsky, the most richly endowed and the most powerful musician of our times. He belongs to the race of great creators."

Milhaud's *Médée* was the last opera presented at the Paris Opéra just before the Nazi occupation during the early part of World War II. In the same year he arrived in this country. He had previously made several visits as pianist, conductor, and lecturer. This time he came because his native land was divided between Nazis and Vichyites and he would tolerate neither brand of fascism. He was appointed a faculty member of Mills College, in Oakland, California. In the mornings he taught composition. After that he could retreat to his beautiful home overlooking San Francisco Bay (which the College had built for him) and write his music. Many important works were completed in this country, including the opera *Bolivar,* two symphonies, several concertos, and chamber music.

Milhaud was crippled by a severe arthritis attack while still in America. He could now walk only by supporting himself on two canes; but most of the time he was confined to a wheel chair. His infirmity did not interfere with his activities as composer and teacher. He did not allow it to keep him from conducting the world *première* of his *Symphony No. 2* with the Boston Symphony on December 20, 1946 (or from repeating that performance at the Berkshire Music Festival in Tanglewood the following summer). He was wheeled to the conductor's stand and helped into another chair in front of the music stand, where he conducted his symphony from a seated position.

In 1947 he returned to his native land after a seven-year absence.

From then on he divided his year between France and the United States. In 1950 he became the center of a violent controversy in Paris, an aftermath of the *première* of his opera *Bolivar* at the Opéra on May 12 of the same year. Largely because of its excessive length (it required four hours for performance) a part of the audience expressed their resentment vocally. The admirers of Milhaud were just as audible. The controversy continued bitterly in the press in the days that followed. Milhaud made drastic cuts in his opera without changing its structure, however.

HIS MUSIC

MILHAUD's early development was influenced by three important French poets. The first of these was Francis Jammes, who wrote the text for Milhaud's first opera, *La Brebis égarée,* written while he was still a Conservatory student. Jammes's poetry led the young composer "out of the symbolists' fog and revealed to me a new world, to be captured merely by opening one's eyes." Milhaud was now able to rid himself of the Debussy spell which caught and transfixed so many of the younger French composers of that period. But he was still to find a manner of his own. Paul Claudel was the next milestone. "Claudel brought me on the threshold of an art that is alive, sane, ready to submit to the influence of the power that shakes the heart." The intense, passionate music he wrote for Claudel's adaptations from Aeschylus was in an individual vein; so were his works in an entirely different style, those that imitated the popular styles of North and South America. After his return to Paris, Milhaud befriended Jean Cocteau, even as did the other members of "The Six." In his own writing Milhaud was strongly affected by Cocteau's bent for wit and satire, by his alternation between "fresh-air realism" and absurdity and fantasia. In *Le Boeuf sur le toit,* Milhaud's style is at one with that of Cocteau; and this remains true even though Cocteau wrote his text after Milhaud had completed his score.

Milhaud has followed many different paths, but two are of particular importance. The first is that of popular idioms. This is the facile, charming, smart, and consummately skillful composer who earlier in his career wrote jazz, tangos, a shimmy, ragtime, and blues and who more recently found inspiration in popular folk tunes from eighteenth-century Provence or from present-day French West Indies. The other path brought Milhaud to ultramodern techniques. This is the composer who, even when he was still young, was one of the first to use polytonality both extensively and successfully. In his most ambitious operas and in his later symphonies and concertos Milhaud has used the fullest resources of modern music without sacrificing either lyricism or emotion.

ANALYTICAL NOTES

Orchestral Music. The *Suite provençale* is in Milhaud's lighter style. His melodic ideas originated in eighteenth-century Provence, some of them original with the Provençal composer André Campra (1660–1744). Milhaud completed his suite in 1936. It was immediately successful and almost at once became Milhaud's most frequently heard work. On two occasions it was used for stage productions at the festival of Orange, and it was interpolated into a Milhaud ballet at the Opéra Comique.

It is in eight short movements. In the first a folk melody is heard in full orchestra. A phrase from this melody becomes the subject for a fugal passage before the melody returns. The next part is given over first to a graceful tune in the strings, then to a livelier section. In the third movement the folk melody is set against a pronounced dance rhythm. The fourth is a folk dance in triple time. A theme for trumpets introduces the fifth section, but before it ends we hear a religious, almost mystical, song. The sixth is energetically rhythmic, while the seventh is a subdued song for the strings. The suite ends with a vigorous and sonorous finale, mostly for full orchestra; a virile return of the main theme concludes the work suddenly.

Protée—Symphonic Suite No. 2 is a much earlier work. In 1913 Claudel asked Milhaud to write some pieces of music for his recently completed satirical play about the love of an old man (Proteus) for a young girl. Milhaud produced some numbers for chorus and for orchestra. Three years later Milhaud adapted the score for a small orchestra in conjunction with a revival of the play. In 1919 a projected performance of *Protée* at the Theatre au Vaudeville, which did not materialize, made Milhaud adapt the score for large orchestra and add some new parts. Five sections from this last version form the *Suite*

No. 2. It opens with a gay and colorful overture, South American in character, emphasizing the tango-habanera rhythm. A fast prelude follows, culminating in a fugue for brasses. The next two sections are more poetic in atmosphere, the first being a gentle pastorale and the second a haunting nocturne. The suite concludes as it began, brilliantly and loudly.

The *Symphony No. 2,* written in 1944, was the first of two symphonies completed by Milhaud in this country. Milhaud provided each of the five movements with a descriptive tag to reveal its emotional content. The first is "Peaceful." The first theme, heard immediately in piccolo and flute, is serene; a more robust second theme is later presented by trumpet and the orchestra, but the first idea returns to bring the movement to a quiet close. This is followed by a scherzolike section called "Mysterious," in which the higher registers of the orchestra, harmonics in the violins, trills in flute and muted trumpet, are used with wonderful effect. In the third part, "Grieving," the main idea appears in the oboe, an idea described by the composer as "very expressive and of a sad and dramatic mood." Tranquillity returns in the fourth movement, as its caption, "With Serenity," reveals. The symphony concludes with an *"Allelouia"*—a fugue built out of the theme first projected by the full orchestra at the beginning of the work.

The *Symphony No. 3,* for soloists, chorus, and orchestra, came three years later. It was commissioned by the French government in 1945, soon after the liberation; the government wanted a setting of the *Te Deum* to commemorate that historic event. Instead of a *Te Deum,* Milhaud wrote a symphony with an original design. The first movement is for orchestra alone. The second uses chorus as well as orchestra, but the choral part is without a text. In the third movement the orchestra is once again used alone, while the fourth is a setting of the *Te Deum* for soloists, chorus, and orchestra.

The *Symphony No. 4,* like its immediate predecessor, was commissioned by the French government, this time to celebrate the centenary of the Revolution of 1848. While returning to France in 1947, aboard a freighter which made the journey from San Francisco to Le Havre in forty days, Milhaud sketched the entire symphony; the orchestration was completed on French soil. Each of the four movements has a descriptive title. The first, "Insurrection," is martial music emphasizing the brass and percussion instruments. An elegy entitled "To the Dead of the Republic" follows. The third movement, "The

Peaceful Joys of Liberty Regained," is dominated by a fugue. In the finale, "Commemoration," the martial character of the first movement is recalled, together with some of its themes, which are repeated, varied, and extended. The percussion instruments which introduce this movement also conclude it.

Symphony No. 6 (1955) was written on a commission from the Koussevitzky Foundation for the fiftieth anniversary of the Boston Symphony, which introduced it on October 7, 1955, under Charles Munch. There are two lyrical thoughts in the first movement (*Calme et tendre*), the first heard at once in the strings, and the second appearing later on in a fuller orchestra. The second movement is energetic, but it comes to a subdued ending. A highly emotional and melodic slow movement follows in three-part song form (*Lent et doux*), while the finale is more in the robust and rhythmically vital mood of the second movement opening.

Wolfgang Amadeus
Mozart

"Mozart, *l'angelo della musica!* . . . Who would dare to touch him without committing sacrilege?"

—*Rossini*

BORN: Salzburg, Austria, January 27, 1756.

DIED: Vienna, December 5, 1791.

MAJOR WORKS: *Operas*—The Marriage of Figaro; Don Giovanni; The Magic Flute. *Orchestral Music*—Symphony No. 35, in D major, "Haffner"; Symphony No. 39, in E-flat major; Symphony No. 40, in G minor; Symphony No. 41, in C major, "Jupiter"; Eine kleine Nachtmusik, for strings; Concertos in D minor (K.466), C minor (K.491), A major (K.488), B-flat major (K.595), for piano and orchestra; Concerto No. 4, in D major (K.218), for violin and orchestra; Concerto No. 5, in A major (K.219), for violin and orchestra. *Choral Music*—Requiem; Ave Verum. *Chamber Music*—6 "Haydn" quartets; 2 piano quartets; Quintet in A major, for clarinet and strings; Quintet in G minor, for strings; Sonatas in C major (K.296), G major (K.301), E minor (K.304), D major (K.306), F major (K.377), B-flat major (K.378), B-flat major (K.454), A major (K.526), for violin and piano. *Piano Music*—Sonata in A major (K.331); Fantasia and Sonata in C minor (K.475 & K.457); Sonata in D major (K.576); Sonata in F major (K.497), for four hands; Sonata in D major (K.448), for two pianos. ALSO: The Abduction from the Seraglio, Idomeneo, Cosí fan tutte, operas; masses, cantatas, motets, etc; other symphonies, concertos, chamber-music works, piano sonatas, etc.

HIS LIFE

SINCE the middle of the eighteenth century Mozart has been the yardstick by which to measure musical genius. To say of any prodigy that he is another Mozart is to suggest both great native power and great achievement. But though prodigies have arisen to earn the sobriquet of "another Mozart" by virtue of phenomenal talent, there has never really been a second Mozart. He is the musical genius *in excelsis,* unique, incomparable. What he accomplished in his childhood was matched and surpassed only by the achievements of full maturity. Those childhood exploits were, of course, the more spectacular, the more capable of inspiring wonder and awe among audiences; and they were, to be sure, breath-taking. But the accomplishments of his maturity were even more extraordinary: the quiet and swift dispatch with which he produced masterwork after masterwork in every form; the manner in which he arrived at perfection of style, structure, and musical expression.

The miracles of his childhood read like legends, yet they have all been substantiated. He was the son of Leopold Mozart, Kapellmeister at the court of the Archbishop of Salzburg. Herr Mozart was a respectable violinist, the author of a fine violin method, and a prolific composer. But he was no genius, and he knew it. As soon as he perceived signs of exceptional musical gifts in his son he was moved by the desire to create the boy in the image he himself would have liked to be.

At the age of three Wolfgang started to show more than passing interest in the harpsichord lessons given his older sister, Maria Anna (affectionately called Nannerl). He started experimenting at the keyboard, expressing delight whenever he arrived at a pleasing progression. Before long his father started teaching him the harpsichord; he was only four at the time. He learned his lessons more by instinct than by rote; he never seemed to have to be told what was right, but sensed it immediately. His ear was so sensitive that it could perceive when a violin was tuned an eighth of a note too low; and it could react so positively to unpleasant sounds that once, at the blast of a trumpet, he fainted with pain. He had an indelible memory and an infallible instinct. Hearing a melody once, he could reproduce it without an error. He could identify tones and chords blindfolded. Given a theme he could improvise for half an hour without repeating himself. He read a piece at sight the way others played it after hours of practice.

On one occasion a second violinist failed to report to Mozart's father's house to participate in a session of quartet music. The child took the place of the absent musician. Although he had never seen the music he filled in without apparent difficulty. To his father's amazement at this feat, he merely said, "Surely you don't have to study and practice to play *second* violin, do you?"

He started writing music as easily as he learned to play it. When he was five years old he wrote for the harpsichord two minuets, which have been preserved. He forthwith became ambitious. While still five, he filled his music paper with smudges, notes, and blots in an attempt to produce a concerto. It proved to be only an attempt, but he did complete a full-fledged sonata when he was seven and a symphony when he was eight.

Herr Leopold did not have to be told that a miracle was taking place in his household. Thenceforth his own musical endeavors were pushed to an insignificant background, as he concentrated exclusively on his son's development and career. When Wolfgang was six years old Herr Leopold decided to exhibit him to all of Europe. The whole Mozart family set forth on a tour. Wolfgang played for the Elector of Bavaria in Munich, where his performance was regarded as so extraordinary that word of his success reached Vienna. When the Mozarts arrived there they were immediately ordered to appear before the Empress Maria Theresa in Schönbrunn. Dressed in silk hose and a tight-fitting velvet jacket with puffed sleeves, with his hair carefully groomed, he sat at the harpsichord in Schönbrunn and played a concerto by Georg Christoph Wagenseil (1715-77). Wagenseil was present. At the child's request he turned the pages of the music; he could scarcely contain his tears. Then, at a dare, the miracle boy performed his tricks, feats of ear and memory. "You are a little sorcerer," said the Emperor, while the Empress kissed and fondled him. Little Mozart was showered with gifts.

The triumphs of Vienna whetted Herr Leopold's appetite. For the next three years he kept his wonder child traveling and performing. In Frankfort-on-the-Main his concert was advertised in the manner of a one-man circus show: "He will play a concerto for the violin, and will accompany symphonies on the harpsichord, the manual or keyboard being covered with a cloth, with as much facility as if he could see the keys; he will instantly name all the notes played at a distance, whether singly or in chords on the harpsichord or any other instrument, bell, glass, or clock. He will finally improvise as long as may be desired, and in any key, on the harpsichord and organ." One of those who heard him at this time was Goethe. "I was only fourteen years old," he wrote to Eckermann many years later, "but I see, as if I were still there, the little man with his child's sword and curly hair. . . . A phenomenon like that of Mozart remains an inexplicable thing."

The next major stop was Paris. In the palace of Versailles, as in

Schönbrunn, the boy Mozart was irresistible. To Baron von Grimm he was "so extraordinary a phenomenon that one finds it difficult to believe it unless one has seen him with one's own eyes and heard him with one's own ears." Only Madame Pompadour appeared aloof. When she turned her face away at his effort to kiss her he exclaimed, "Who is this that will not kiss me, when even my Empress kisses me?"

After having four of his violin sonatas published in Paris, Mozart proceeded to London and the court of George III. The royal Kapellmeister was Johann Christian Bach—son of the great Johann Sebastian, but at that time more famous than his late father. Bach fell in love with the child (as, indeed, did the whole court) and never tired of testing his powers and playing musical games with him. Mozart also gave several immensely successful concerts at the popular Vauxhall Gardens, usually in programs devoted entirely to his own works; here Mozart's first symphonies were played.

They were back in Salzburg in 1766, after an absence of more than three years. Mozart's genius had been acknowledged throughout all of Europe. Only the Archbishop of Salzburg remained skeptical. To test the boy's much-publicized genius, he had the boy locked in a room in the palace with the assignment to write an oratorio on a given text. Apparently the Archbishop was fully satisfied. He had the work performed and published. When one year later Herr Leopold applied for another leave of absence to embark on a new extended tour, the Archbishop did not withhold his blessings.

The Mozarts returned to Vienna for what they hoped would be a repetition of their onetime successes there. The impending marriage of the Archduchess Maria Josepha held promise of a profitable visit. Before they reached Vienna, however, a smallpox epidemic claimed the bride as a victim (Wolfgang himself was stricken and for nine terrible days was blind). When they finally arrived in Vienna the nobility was in mourning and in no mood to welcome them. Moreover, an eleven-year-old boy was not as prodigious seemingly as a five-year-old child. The Emperor did use his powerful office to get the boy a commission to write an opera. Wolfgang completed *La Finta semplice* with breathtaking speed. But the artists of the opera house (supported by Gluck) resented performing in an opera by a boy and saw to it that it never reached the stage. Wolfgang had to satisfy himself with a performance of another little opera, *Bastien und Bastienne,* at the home of Dr. Franz Anton Mesmer, a hypnotist whose name has been immortalized in the word "mesmerize."

They stayed in Salzburg a year before the old *Wanderlust* returned. This time Herr Leopold and Wolfgang set out for Italy. After the disappointments of Vienna, Italy was comforting balm. Everywhere he went Wolfgang was put to severe tests and everywhere he came through triumphantly. In Bologna they gave him a contrapuntal exercise that would take a master several hours to complete. He finished it in half an hour. The venerable Padre Martini (1706–84), one of Italy's most learned musicians, accepted him as an equal. In Naples, Wolfgang's exhibitions proved so startling that the superstitious were convinced that he derived his powers from the magic of a ring he wore on his finger. But his greatest triumph took place in Rome during Holy Week. Each year the *Miserere* of Gregorio Allegri (1582–1652) was performed by the papal choir. A papal decree forbade its performance anywhere else; and the only existing copy of the work was jealously guarded. Any attempt to reproduce the work in any form was punishable by excommunication. Mozart heard the performance; then, in the privacy of his rooms, he wrote down the entire complex contrapuntal score from memory. Word of this incredible achievement reached the Pope who, instead of excommunicating the boy, gave him the Cross of the Order of the Golden Spur.

Before he returned home Mozart was honored with election to a membership in the Accademia Philharmonica of Bologna, the long existing rule against anyone under twenty years of age being temporarily waived. He also received a commission from Milan to write a new opera. He returned to Italy in the winter of 1770 to assist at the rehearsals of that new opera, *Mitridate, Rè di Ponto*. "Before the first rehearsal," Herr Leopold wrote to his wife, "there was no lack of people to run down the music and pronounce it beforehand in satirical language to be something poor and childish, alleging that so young a boy, and a German to the bargain, could not possibly write an Italian opera and that, although they acknowledged him to be a great executant, he could not understand or feel the *chiaroscuro* required in the theater. All these people have been reduced to silence since the evening of the first rehearsal with small orchestra, and say not a word." When the opera was performed on Christmas Day 1770 the public responded with great enthusiasm. Contrary to all precedent, one of the soprano arias had to be encored. The opera proved so successful that it had to be given twenty performances.

The next few years in Mozart's life were a striking contrast to the excitement of the Italian triumphs. These years were spent almost entirely in his native city. A new Archbishop, Hieronymus von Colloredo, had come to Salzburg. He had little awareness of, or appreciation for, Mozart's genius. Although he gave him employment as virtuoso and composer, he paid him miserably and did not hesitate to treat him as just another lackey in his employ. Life was humdrum, particularly to one who had known the glamour of the outside world; the work was without stimulation; the company he had to keep at the court was vulgar and dissolute. And there was no recognition whatsoever for the masterpieces he was creating with such abundance: the five violin concertos, piano concertos, the two-piano concerto in E-flat major, the numerous string quartets, divertimentos and serenades (including the celebrated *Haffner* Serenade), and symphonies. Once in a while there was escape from the stifling atmosphere of Salzburg. In 1773 Mozart accompanied the Archbishop's entourage to Vienna and in December 1774 he went to Milan to supervise the production of his comic opera *La Finta giardiniera*.

More than ever before in his life Mozart felt the need to get away from Salzburg, to experience again the exhilaration of travel and the acclaim that usually came to him in the great music centers of Europe. More important still, he realized that, now that he was approaching maturity, he would have to find somewhere a profitable position. The Archbishop did not hesitate to let him go; in his eyes Mozart was just another court musician who could be easily replaced. But he did turn down Herr Leopold's request for a leave of absence. If Mozart was to embark on a new trip, he would have to go—and for the first time in his life—without his father. Herr Leopold recognized this bitter fact and had to reconcile himself to it.

In 1777, in the company of his mother, Mozart set forth for Paris. On the way they stopped off at Augsburg, where Mozart delightedly flirted with his little cousin, Bäsle, and at Mannheim, where he fell in love with Aloysia Weber. For a while he thought of running off to Italy with his beloved. Angry letters from Salzburg reminded him of his destination and mission; Mozart was still very much under the thumb of his father. Bidding an ardent farewell to Aloysia, he continued the journey to Paris, arriving there on March 23, 1778.

There he met fresh disappointments. There was no great interest in him now that he was no longer a prodigy but a mature musician. Baron von Grimm, once so effusive in his praises, could now complain bitterly that Mozart was "too confident, too little a man of action, too much ready to succumb to his own illusions, too little *au courant* with the ways that lead to success." All that came to Mozart were a few slight commissions and the offer of a humble job as organist at Versailles.

Disappointment was followed by tragedy: the sudden death of his mother. For the first time in his life Mozart was alone. He suddenly decided to return to Mannheim and marry Aloysia. When he arrived Aloysia did not at first recognize him, and when she did she let him know that her ardor had cooled during his absence. There was nothing for Mozart to do but obey the insistent commands of his father and return to Salzburg.

He had to fill a miserably paid post at the court of the Archbishop as organist and composer; the old-time boredom and indignities of life in Salzburg resumed. For two years Mozart squirmed and fidgeted and silently rebelled against his fate. A trip to Munich for a performance of his *opera seria, Idomeneo*—which took place on January 29, 1781—was welcome relief. And the success that met his new opera convinced him once and for all that he could no longer live in Salzburg. He had to free himself of his ties to the Archbishop, who treated him with the cold-blooded brutality of a feudal lord and continually subjected him to insults and humiliations.

The break came suddenly. The Archbishop had gone to Vienna to attend the funeral services of Maria Theresa and had sent a summons to Mozart in Munich to join him. In Vienna the Archbishop defiantly refused to allow Mozart to play at benefit concerts. This so infuriated the composer that the caution and patience Herr Leopold had been counseling with each letter were suddenly forgotten. He lost his temper; the Archbishop replied with vulgar insults. The final explosion took place soon after that, the provocation being the Archbishop's failure to give Mozart any notice of his decision to return to Salzburg. Mozart's letter to his father tells the story:

"A week ago, a footman appeared unexpectedly and told me I must be gone that instant. The others had all been warned of the day, but not me. So I threw everything into my trunks with all speed. . . . I arranged to leave by stagecoach on Wednesday . . . but as I could not collect the money still due me within that time, I postponed my journey till Saturday. When I presented myself this morning, the valet told me the Archbishop wished to place a packet in my charge to be carried with me. I asked if it were urgent. They told me, 'Yes, it is of the greatest importance.' 'Then,' said I, 'I am very sorry. I cannot have the privilege of serving his Grace for (on account of the afore-mentioned reasons) I do not leave before Saturday. I am not in the household, I live at my own expenses, and consequently, as is natural, I cannot travel till I have funds to enable me to do so—no one has the right to ask me to ruin myself.'

"As I came into his presence, his first words were: 'Well, when are you going, fellow?' 'I had intended going tonight but all the places are taken.' Then he began, without a pause for breath: I was the most slovenly fellow he knew; no one served him so ill as I; I had better leave today or he would write home and have my salary stopped. . . . At length my blood was boiling. I could no longer keep silence and said: 'Then is your Grace dissatisfied with me?' 'What! You would threaten me, would you? Oh, you idiot! There is the door! I will have no more to do with a wretch, do you hear?' At last I got a word in, 'Nor I with you!' 'Well, go!' And I, in going, said: 'This is final. Tomorrow you will have my resignation in writing.'"

Freed at last from his obnoxious tie with the Archbishop (and, coincidentally, from the domination of his father) Mozart settled in Vienna, ready to stand on his own feet for the first time in his life. He had no apprehensions about the future. He was not unknown in Vienna by any means. He was soon invited to the court to enter into a musical "duel" with one of the greatest pianists of the day, Muzio Clementi. Clementi played one of his own sonatas and Mozart extemporized a series of variations. The Emperor called it a draw, a fact which immediately placed Mozart on a par with the greatest virtuosos in Vienna, if not in all Europe. He was also receiving some recognition as a composer: the Emperor commissioned him to write a new opera, *Die Entführung aus dem Serail* (*The Abduction from the Seraglio*).

Despite the fact that Antonio Salieri, one of the most powerful musicians in Vienna, had put all sorts of obstacles in the way of its production, *The Abduction from the Seraglio*—through the intervention of the Emperor himself—was performed on July 16, 1782. Some of Salieri's cohorts had come to boo; but most remained to cheer. "The populace is quite crazy over this opera," Mozart wrote excitedly. "It does one good to hear such applause. . . . The people will hear nothing else, and the theater is constantly filled to the doors." The court was enchanted. Prince Kaunitz even said now that a genius like Mozart appeared "only once in a century."

Mozart did not doubt that a highly lucrative post at the court would soon come his way. Sure of himself and of his future as never before, he decided to get married. His choice was Constanze Weber—sister of

Aloysia, whom he had once loved and lost—and they were married on August 4, 1782.

But things did not go so well as he had hoped. The appointment he had expected was not forthcoming. At every turn he found himself obstructed—now by Salieri, who feared him as a formidable rival, now by the Emperor's niggardliness. His many admirers (and they now included the greatest composer in Vienna, Joseph Haydn) could effect little. He was tired of cooling his heels in the anterooms of Vienna; tired of giving lessons for a small and uncertain income; tired of waiting for fortune to strike.

Yet he was incapable of despair. While he waited for his moment (which was never to come!) he lived and sang and wrote and danced, always fashioning new beauty, always achieving still greater creative heights. Among the works he completed in 1782 (besides the opera *The Abduction from the Seraglio*) were three piano concertos, each a masterwork (F major, A major, and C major), the *Haffner* Symphony, in D major, and the C minor and D minor Fantasias for piano.

Mozart was delicately formed, short, slight of build. His head was a trifle too large for the body, and its most attractive feature was its crop of hair, of which he was as vain as a woman. There was something soft and effeminate about his face, which was almost always pallid. Only one element of strength did that face possess: the intense, piercing eyes.

He loved life with a passion that was sometimes painful. To a red coat, to a harlequin's costume for a masquerade, to dancing, to a game of billiards, or to even a new pair of lace cuffs he would bring almost the same kind of delirium that went into the shaping of his music. In all things he was the *Feinschmecker,* the *bon vivant.* But most of all he loved dancing, even more—his wife sometimes said—than music itself.

He loved people. With them he was gay, affable, alive, sometimes pensive, but never melancholy. On Sunday mornings his own house was filled with guests. There was gaiety, conversation, and punch which Mozart drank in great quantities. But always there was music, performed either by himself or by visiting musicians. Joseph Haydn would make an appearance. On one of these occasions Mozart deferentially placed before Haydn his newly composed quartets written in Haydn's honor. And then four musicians sat down to perform them for the first time. Haydn played the first violin; the well-known composer and favorite of the Emperor, Karl von Dittersdorf (1739-99), played the second violin; Mozart himself played the viola; while Mozart's friend Wanhal played the violoncello. When the quartets had been played

Haydn approached Leopold Mozart (then on a visit to Vienna) and said to him, "I tell you before God and as an honest man—your son is the greatest composer I know, either personally or by name."

In 1785 Mozart met the Abbé da Ponte, recently appointed poet to the imperial theater. Soon after this meeting Mozart proposed to Da Ponte that they collaborate on an opera, singling out Beaumarchais' *Le Mariage de Figaro* as a text. When they finally won the consent of the Emperor (given only when they promised to tone down Beaumarchais' revolutionary ideas) they set to work with a will and completed *Le Nozze di Figaro* (*The Marriage of Figaro*) in six weeks.

But once again Salieri became the spearhead of a faction determined to thwart Mozart and frustrate the *première* of his new opera. This faction plotted, and influenced musicians and singers. Salieri assured the performers that the music was unsingable and spurred them on to demand impossible alterations, which so enraged Mozart that he once threatened to withdraw his opera. But the Emperor intervened, and when the cast grew familiar with the music they underwent a change of heart. By the time the second rehearsal was called, singers and musicians were beside themselves with enthusiasm for the opera. "The players on the stage and in the orchestra were electrified," the singer Michael Kelly wrote after the second rehearsal. "Intoxicated with pleasure they cried again and again, and each time louder than the preceding one: 'Bravo! Bravo! Maestro! Long live the great Mozart!' Those in the orchestra beat the music stands incessantly with the bows of their violins, thus expressing their enthusiasm. It seemed as if this storm of applause would never cease. The little man returned thanks for the homage paid him by bowing repeatedly."

The Marriage of Figaro was performed at the Burgtheater on May 1, 1786. "The theater was packed," reported Michael Kelly, "and so many arias were repeated that the length of the opera was very nearly doubled. The Emperor himself expressed his delight."

But Salieri did not accept Mozart's victory with resignation. He fought back, with every means at his command. He had the Burgtheater present a charming and catchy little opera named *Una Cosa rara* with the express purpose of deflecting toward it much of the enthusiasm directed toward Mozart's opera. And he succeeded. *Una Cosa rara* became so successful and so talked about that Mozart's opera was thrown into the shade. It was withdrawn after only nine performances.

Mozart's total income from his opera was 450 gulden, hardly enough even to pay his debts. He was penniless, often forced to turn to his friends for aid. Every effort to get a well-paying position either at the court or at the palace of some nobleman came to nothing. The Emperor gave him nothing but his enthusiasm. This failure to acquire either the recognition he felt was due him or economic security, though a blow to his spirits, never affected the quality or quantity of his work. Soon after *The Marriage of Figaro* he completed a symphony, a piano sonata, two string quintets, and a piano concerto. He also began working on a new opera, *Don Giovanni,* the libretto of which was prepared by Da Ponte. Introduced in Prague on October 29, 1787, *Don Giovanni* took the city (always partial to Mozart) by storm. A contemporary journal reported: "Connoisseurs and artists say that nothing like this has been given in Prague. Mozart himself conducted, and when he appeared in the orchestra, he was hailed by a triple acclamation." And Mozart himself wrote: "Everything is being done to persuade me to remain here and write another opera. But I cannot accept the offer, however flattering."

Again he returned to Vienna, despite the insistent pleas that he remain in Prague. Perhaps he had received the news of the death of Gluck, which suddenly left vacant the post of chamber musician and court composer. Mozart was actually given that post; the Emperor could no longer ignore the hue and cry raised in Vienna over Mozart's pitiable circumstances. But with characteristic parsimony, the Emperor reduced the annual salary from 2,000 gulden to a miserable 800! Eight hundred gulden did not go far. Mozart was still reduced to the indignity of begging friends for loans, "at a suitable interest." His wife was ill and had to go to Baden for a cure. He himself was none too well. Mozart scarcely knew where to turn for help. During the next two years his situation grew increasingly worse.

At this darkest moment—when he seemed caught inextricably in the maze of his debts, illness, loneliness, and despair—Emanuel Schikaneder, an impresario, came to him with the request to write a German opera, *Die Zauberflöte (The Magic Flute)*. Mozart accepted eagerly. While he was working on the opera—in the middle of July, 1791—a mysterious stranger dressed in gray appeared at Mozart's home requesting that he compose a requiem. The fee was generous. One condition was imposed: Mozart must make no attempt to inquire the source of the commission. In reality the stranger was the messenger of Count von Walsegg, who habitually commissioned musical works which he later exhibited as his own. But to Mozart—oppressed by thoughts of death, harassed by illness and care—the mysterious stranger appeared like a messenger from the other world coming to ask him to write his own requiem. When *The Magic Flute* was completed, in September, Mozart set to work feverishly upon the other commission, which became more and more associated in his mind with his own death. "I cannot remove from my eyes the image of the stranger. I see him continually. He begs me, exhorts me, and then commands me to work. I continue, because composition fatigues me less than rest. Moreover, I have nothing more to fear. I know from what I feel that the hour is striking; I am on the point of death; I have finished before I could enjoy my talent. . . . I thus must finish my funeral song, which I must not leave incomplete."

But first there was the *première* of *The Magic Flute,* produced at Schikaneder's little theater, Auf der Wieden, on September 30, 1791. The Viennese public was at first cool to it. But succeeding evenings brought with them ever increasing approbation that was to persist for one hundred performances.

With the *première* off his mind Mozart could concentrate on his Requiem. He knew he was dying, that he was engaged in a race with death. Though racked with pain he did not abandon work. When he realized that his wasted strength made further work impossible, he explained to his pupil Süssmayer how the Requiem was to be completed. On evenings when he felt better he would hold his watch in his hand and point out to his friends the exact moment in which one of his favorite arias from *The Magic Flute* was being sung at the theater. It gave him pleasure to think that his opera was beginning to attract attention.

On December 4 he asked to be propped up in bed. Calling his friends close to him, he gave them the manuscript of his *"Lacrimosa,"* from the Requiem, and asked them to join him in singing it. In the middle he burst into tears. That night a priest administered extreme unction. At midnight Mozart said farewell to his family. Then he turned to the wall. When they touched him later they found he was dead.

The funeral was pitiful. It was a raw and cold day. A third-class burial, costing less than twelve gulden, had been arranged. The musical services at St. Stephen's were directed by Salieri—he who had for so long a time been such a ruthless enemy. The few friends did not, because of rain, follow the coffin to the churchyard of St. Mark's, and Mozart's wife was too prostrated by grief to attend the funeral at all. Alone and unmourned, Mozart's body was consigned to a pauper's grave. There was no tombstone or cross to mark the place! Some years later, when Constanze came to St. Mark's, she was unable to identify the spot where her husband had been buried.

HIS MUSIC

FOR A LONG TIME a great many music lovers and authorities on music were inclined to place a false evaluation on Mozart. They conceded that he had brought musical classicism to its ultimate development; that with perfection of form and technique he had arrived at a grace, refinement, and felicitousness of expression rarely found elsewhere. But they felt that his elegance was just veneer, that his beauty was just skin-deep. While Mozart was capable of enchanting and seducing his listeners—so they said—he was incapable of moving them profoundly. This idea was uppermost in the mind of the Viennese poet Richard Beer-Hoffmann when—in a monograph on Mozart—he insisted that the composer fell short of true greatness because he was incapable of expressing grief in his music. Such an idea is even propounded in the earlier criticisms of so passionate a Mozart enthusiast as the English critic W. J. Turner—although in a later work, *Mozart: The Man and His Works,* it is no longer seriously entertained.

It is quite true that a great deal by Mozart is delightful without being profound, brilliant without being poignant, charming without being unforgettable. He was extraordinarily abundant. Many of his works—particularly divertimentos, serenades, early symphonies, and so forth—are the kind of music that an efficient Kapellmeister can produce on short order, even though fresher in ideas, more ebullient in spirit, and more skillful in construction. It is music that is always a pleasure to listen to and is forgotten one moment later.

However, the greater Mozart—the Mozart of the best symphonies, quartets, operas, and concertos—is a profound artist as well as an aristocratic craftsman. The more intimate one becomes with Mozart the more does one become aware of his extraordinarily wide range. Gaiety and laughter and effervescent spirit are always identified with Mozart. But this is only a single facet of his personality. He has a deeper vein too, and that vein is found much more frequently than is generally suspected. A work such as the *Ave Verum* has radiant spirituality; the Requiem has an immense sorrow and incomparable poignancy and so does the slow movement of the *String Quintet in G minor;* there are nobility and grandeur in many of the arias of *The Magic Flute* and *Idomeneo;* both the D minor and the C minor concertos open with a depth of expression and touching accents of sorrow.

He was, then, a composer of many and varied moods. And, with that, he was also in his day a composer of daring and iconoclastic music. His *Quartet in C major* (K.465) is still known as the *Dissonant* Quartet because of the discords in the opening bar. The *Haydn* Quartets were so startling in their progressions and harmonic language that even Haydn was puzzled and finally had to say tolerantly, "If Mozart wrote it, he must have had good reason to do so." The first movement of the *Piano Concerto in C major* is so full of discordant suspensions and false relations that an analysis of the work by Eric Blom reads like the analysis of a twentieth-century piece of music.

For Mozart was indefatigable in searching out richer, deeper, and newer veins of musical expression. He was growing and changing all the time. That in the year of his death he could have written such works as the *Ave Verum, The Magic Flute,* the Requiem, the *String Quartet in E-flat major* and the *B-flat major Piano Concerto* is sufficient evidence that, despite the Alpine heights he had already scaled, he was still in the process of climbing when his life came to such a premature end.

ANALYTICAL NOTES

Operas. There are approximately twenty works by Mozart that can be classified as operas. Some are comic, others serious, while a work such as *Don Giovanni* combines both tragic and comic elements. Most of Mozart's operas are in the traditions of Italian opera accepted in his day. If they were not stifled by these traditions as were so many other eighteenth-century operas, it was only because of his incomparable gift for characterization and dramatic development together with his wit, noble feeling, and inexhaustible musical inventiveness. Two of his operas were set to German, instead of Italian, texts, laying the groundwork for German opera. The first was *The Abduction from the Seraglio,* the first German comic opera written by a great composer. Its parent was the German *Singspiel,* a kind of musical variety show with dialogue, which was popular among German and Austrian audiences in Mozart's day. The spoken dialogue and the tendency toward broad burlesque—integral elements of the *Singspiel*—are retained in *The Seraglio.* Mozart's second German opera, *The Magic Flute,* was also derived from the *Singspiel,* though in its grandeur and nobility it is also the precursor of German national opera.

Two of Mozart's greatest operas are unmistakably in the Italian style. Both have Italian texts by Lorenzo da Ponte. The first was *The Mar-*

riage of Figaro, a much diluted adaptation of Beaumarchais' bitter indictment of the tyranny, greed, and immorality of the nobility. Lorenzo da Ponte made his libretto a boudoir farce rather than a social document. Count Almaviva is an incorrigible philanderer. His many flirtations include one with the Countess's maid, Susanna, who is betrothed to the valet, Figaro. Hoping to trap her husband in one of his intrigues, the Countess prevails on the page, Cherubino, to disguise himself as a woman. At that moment the Count makes a hurried entrance into the Countess's boudoir, thus compelling Cherubino to escape through the window. The Count realizes that someone has been in the room and has escaped, and his jealousy is aroused. But this does not prevent him from pursuing his own intrigues. He threatens Susanna that he will compel Figaro to marry someone else if she does not become more ingratiating to him. Thus he manages to obtain a rendezvous with her in the garden at night. The Countess learns of this, exchanges clothing with Susanna, and proceeds to the rendezvous in Susanna's place. The Count makes love to the Countess, thinking she is Susanna. The Count also discovers Susanna (in the Countess's dress) making love to Figaro and is now sure that his wife is unfaithful. Eventually each one reveals his true identity. A general forgiveness takes place. The marriage of Figaro and Susanna now receives the Count's blessing.

For this comedy of amatory errors Mozart produced his most sparkling operatic score. It is a veritable geyser of the most wonderful melodies, duets, and ensemble numbers. It would be difficult to find another opera in which music, so spontaneous and effervescent, portrays so many different and subtle shades of emotion. The music passes through an entire catalogue of feeling: tenderness, mockery, irony, gaiety, anger, nostalgia, wistfulness, pathos, and burlesque. It would also be difficult to find another opera in which the score points up so mercilessly, and with such psychological penetration, the little foibles, human indiscretions, and idiosyncrasies of each character. For if there is any single department in which Mozart is truly incomparable, it is in his ability to delineate character in music.

The brisk little overture that prefaces the first act is infectious from beginning to end. The first theme is a fleet figure played softly by the strings in the opening measures; this is immediately followed by a subsidiary idea heard first in the woodwinds and after that in the full orchestra. The brisk pace continues to the second theme, which is a lyrical subject for the strings; and it progresses with *élan* to the vivacious coda.

In the first act, which takes place in the room assigned to Figaro and his bride-to-be, Figaro has two principal arias. In the first he explains mockingly to Susanna how easily he can handle his employer, the Count, *"Se vuol ballare."* Another note of mockery enters his second famous aria, as he comments on Cherubino's prospective entry into the army, *"Non più andrai."*

Two beautiful commentaries on love appear in the second act, set in the boudoir of the Countess. The Countess opens the act with her feelings about love in *"Porgi amor,"* while Cherubino, soon after this, offers his own tender interpretation of the meaning of love in *"Voi che sapete."*

In the third act (a hall in Almaviva's palace) the Countess presents one of Mozart's greatest arias, *"Dovo sono,"* in which she poignantly recalls days of the past when she was happy with the Count's love. In the concluding act, in the palace garden, we have Susanna's coquettish call of love to the Count, *"Deh vieni, non tardar."*

Don Giovanni, text by Lorenzo da Ponte, was the immediate operatic successor to *The Marriage of Figaro,* coming only one year later. The acclaim that attended the *première* of *Don Giovanni* in Prague must be regarded as a phenomenon. When commissioned to write it, after the great success of *Figaro,* Mozart was expected to produce another work with ebullience, light heart, and irony. That the Prague audience was not confused by the many alternating pages of dramatic power and light comedy in *Don Giovanni* speaks well for its perception. True, there is much in *Don Giovanni* that reveals the graceful hand and the light touch of *Figaro,* but this is incidental. The more significant parts of the opera are those in which the tragic element predominates: the scene of the duel, the death of the Commendatori, and Donna Anna's terrible grief in Act I; the final scene, in which the Don meets his inevitable doom. It is these moments of dramatic truth (together with those passages in which the music contributes subtle characterizations of Don Giovanni, Leporello, Zerlina, and Donna Anna) that an eighteenth-century audience could not expect to find in an opera. It is moments such as these that place *Don Giovanni* with the great operas of all time.

To understand the change of mood from comedy to tragedy it must be recalled that Mozart labeled his opera neither *opera buffa* nor *opera seria.* His designation was *dramma giocosa*—"gay drama." True artist that he was, Mozart was concerned first and foremost with the drama; the gaiety was only the trimming. And true artist that he was, Mozart synthesized the light and the shade with great astuteness. Only the brief epilogue—which Mozart used as a concession to opera-buffa tradition, and which he discarded in a later performance—is questionable in its artistic appropriateness, since a mood of comparative levity is injected immediately after the tremendous passion and power that accompany the Don's doom.

Don Giovanni is, of course, the famous lover of story and legend. In disguise he has come with his servant, Leporello, to the palace of the Commendatore to seduce the latter's daughter, Donna Anna, betrothed to Don Ottavio. Donna Anna's resistance, as she tries to uncover the identity of the Don, brings the Commendatore to the scene. The Don kills him and escapes. He next tries to win Donna Elvira. When he suddenly recognizes her as one of his old-time sweethearts, he makes a discreet exit, leaving his servant to make the necessary explanations. Don Giovanni is now attracted to Zerlina, who is being married to Masetto. At the wedding ceremony Leporello engages Masetto, while Don Giovanni works his charms on the bride. When Zerlina cries for help, the Don effects his escape by fighting his way through the crowd. But Don Giovanni's ruthless escapades are not to go unpunished. Leporello comes to him with the startling news that the marble statue of the Commendatore has spoken, promising to bring vengeance. Mockingly, Don Giovanni invites the statue to be his guest at supper that very evening. The statue comes. When Don Giovanni brazenly refuses to mend his dissolute ways, a pit of fire opens up and siezes him. The epilogue (frequently omitted) is a gay recital by Leporello of the Don's fate, and the joyous reaction of the other principal characters.

The overture opens with music of doom, foretelling the tragic fate eventually to befall Don Giovanni; this music is also heard in the dramatic closing scene. After thirty measures of this portentous mood, the music becomes lighter, portraying the capricious character of Don Giovanni and his merry escapades.

In the first scene of the first act, in the courtyard of the Commendatore's palace, the Commendatore is murdered by Don Giovanni and Donna Anna voices her terrible grief. The scene shifts to a square outside Seville. Leporello offers his celebrated Catalogue Song—*"Madamina, il catalogo e questo"*—in which he gaily enumerates the long list of Don Giovanni's amatory conquests to Zerlina. The next scene brings us to a country place near Don Giovanni's palace. Here the delightful love duet of Don Giovanni and Zerlina, *"La ci darem la mano,"* is heard, and after that Don Ottavio's glowing, rhapsodic song of love to Donna Anna, *"Dalla sua pace."* In the fourth scene (the garden in Don Giovanni's palace) Zerlina coyly pleads with the jealous Masetto to forgive her for showing interest in Don Giovanni, *"Batti, batti o bel Masetto."* The concluding scene of the first act, within the palace, opens with the ever popular Minuet.

The second act opens in front of Donna Elvira's house, where Zerlina is staying temporarily. Don Giovanni serenades Zerlina with the tender *"Deh, vieni alla finestra."* The scene changes to the garden of the Commendatore's palace, where Don Ottavio delivers one of the most exquisitely beautiful of all Mozart arias, the love song to Donna Anna, *"Il mio tresoro."* The next scene takes place in the graveyard, in front of the statue of the Commendatore, and is followed by a scene in the Commendatore's palace in which Donna Anna sings her flaming aria, *"Non mi dir,"* reassuring Don Ottavio of her love. The final scene—excluding the debatable epilogue—finds Don Giovanni at supper in a banquet hall in his palace. An orchestra is playing various tunes, including *"Non più andrai,"* from *The Marriage of Figaro.* "Ah," comments Don Giovanni, "I have frequently heard *that* tune!" When the Statue makes his appearance, the somber and ominous chords that opened the overture are heard. The Statue is greeted by Don Giovanni with a second theme from the overture. The inescapable doom that now awaits Don Giovanni takes place with some of the most dramatic music ever written by Mozart.

The Magic Flute differs from *Don Giovanni* in that it is first and foremost a comic opera, even though it has many pages of nobility and grandeur. It follows the *Singspiel* pattern of utilizing spoken dialogue instead of recitatives and—intended as a theatrical entertainment for the masses—of emphasizing broad comedy and burlesque, Oriental backgrounds and spectacle, so dear to the heart of the Viennese public. The character of the birdcatcher, Papageno, is one of the most delightful comic portraits in all Mozart; his antics and his comic search for a sweetheart belong to the Viennese popular theater rather than the opera house.

The plot, made up of so much confusion and nonsense, has often been critized severely. It was adapted by the impresario Emanuel Schikaneder from a story called *Lulu,* which he found in a collection of Oriental tales by Wieland. Much of the textual disorder in the opera was due to the necessity of both composer and librettist to change their opera completely while they were in the midst of writing it. A rival opera derived from the same source had in the interim appeared in Vienna, and it was a tremendous success. Obviously, it would have been foolhardy for Schikaneder to present another opera on the same subject. But he did not write a new libretto. He merely disguised the old one by making heroes into villains, and vice versa, and converting the whole into an allegory about Freemasonry, whose ideal was the "regeneration of humanity by moral means" (both Mozart and Schikaneder were Masons). Masonic ritual and symbolism were interpolated into the text. If the final result suffered from confusion and contradictions, this bothered neither composer nor librettist.

The story concerns the search by the Egyptian prince, Tamino, for Pamina, daughter of the Queen of the Night, imprisoned by a tyrant. To aid Tamino in this search, the Queen provides him with a magic flute which, when played, will carry him safely through dangers. She also instructs the birdcatcher, Papageno, to accompany him, presenting Papageno with magic chimes for protection. Tamino learns that Pamina is imprisoned by Sarastro, high priest of Isis—not a tyrant, but a man of high ideals. He has imprisoned Pamina to save her from her evil mother, whom he later destroys. Tamino and Pamina are now in love. But before they can marry they must be put through several tests. With the aid of Tamino's magic flute, they pass all the tests: those of unexplained silence, fire, and water. Tamino and Pamina are now ready to serve Isis. And Papageno has found a mate of his own in Papagena.

The overture opens with three majestic chords in full orchestra. (This is the only part of the overture repeated within the opera. These chords later preface the March of the Priests and Sarastro's aria, *"O Isis und Osiris."*) After a noble introduction the pace changes magically in the main section. There is a vivacious theme for the violins (the principal subject of the entire overture), which is treated fugally with brilliant effect. This theme is repeated by the orchestra, after which it is subjected to extended and effective development.

The score that follows is among the most varied produced by Mozart. Papageno's amusing little songs, with their simple folk-song character, are charmingly ingenuous; the lighthearted *"Der Vogelfänger bin ich ja"* is characteristic. In an altogether different vein are the Queen of the Night's two brilliant coloratura arias, with their fire and dramatic force. The first, *"Zum leiden bin ich auserkoren,"* appears in the first scene, while the second, *"Der hölle Rache kocht in meinem Herzen"* is heard in the third scene of Act II. Tamino's love song to Pamina, on seeing her picture for the first time, has affecting tenderness and beauty; it is the famous tenor aria *"Dies Bildnis ist bezaubernd schön"* in the first scene of Act I. The two great arias of Sarastro—*"O Isis und Osiris"* and *"In diesen heil'gen Hallen,"* both in Act II—have such majesty that

Bernard Shaw once called this the only music he knew that could be put into the mouth of God.

Orchestral Music. Mozart wrote his first symphony when he was eight years old. The last three were completed in 1788, three years before his death. Only a handful of his forty-or-so symphonies are in the permanent repertory. Those few are unqualified masterworks. With them the symphony took giant strides toward Beethoven from point of view of structure, instrumentation, musical expressiveness, and thematic growth. But the lesser Mozart symphonies, some of which are occasionally heard, also represent a world of enchantment. They are a continual source of joy for their vivaciousness and freshness, beauty of melody, beautiful proportion and balance, exquisite good taste. Because of the infrequency with which they appear on programs, these less familiar symphonies need not detain us. But they are distinguished examples of Mozart's aristocratic art. They include: the *Symphony No. 28,* in C major (1774); *Symphony No. 29,* in A major (1774); *Symphony No. 31,* in D major, "Paris," (1778); *Symphony No. 34,* in C major (1780); *Symphony No. 36,* in C major, "Linz" (1783); and *Symphony No. 38,* in D major, "Prague" (1786).

But the *Symphony No. 35,* in D major (K.385),* is one of Mozart's finest symphonies and one of the most popular. It was written in 1782 for Siegmund Haffner, son of the Salzburg burgomaster, for which reason the work is known as the *Haffner* Symphony.

There is only one principal theme in the first movement, an athletic subject heard immediately in the full orchestra. At the point where a second theme is ordinarily expected, this theme is repeated in a different key. But there is a subsidiary idea—a brief lyrical interlude for the violins, appearing after the first theme has been subjected to brilliant contrapuntal treatment. The slow movement has the gentle quality of a romanze. The delicate melody appears in the first violins without preliminaries. Midway in the movement there is a solemn interlude for the woodwinds, before the melody reappears. The minuet has characteristic Mozartean grace. The trio section, however, has a pastoral beauty not often encountered in symphonic minuets. The concluding

---

*Each of Mozart's works has an identifying number following the letter "K." Opus numbers started to come into use in Mozart's day, but Mozart did not employ this system. Considerable confusion arose after his death over the order and period of each of his works. To convert order out of chaos, the Viennese scholar Ludwig von Köchel prepared a catalogue of Mozart's works in 1862, in which Mozart's works were put in their proper chronological order. Since then, it has been the custom to identify each Mozart work with its place, or number, in the Köchel (or K.) catalogue.

movement (which, as Mozart specified in a letter, should be played as fast as possible) has a catlike agility. A soft, fleet melodic idea appears in the strings to open the movement. The second subject, also in the strings, is still nimble, but the pace is somewhat relaxed.

The *Symphony No. 39,* in E-flat major (K.543), is the first of three masterworks which were Mozart's valedictory in the symphonic form. All three were written in 1788, in the incredibly short period of six weeks, and they represent the culmination of Mozart's symphonic writing. All three are richer in emotional content, and more advanced in structural, harmonic, and thematic writing than any previous Mozart symphonies.

The *Symphony in E-flat major* begins with a dignified slow introduction made up of robust chords and scale passages. This introduction may fall pleasingly enough on our ears, but in Mozart's time it was daring music. Toward the conclusion of this section there is an iconoclastic dissonance (D-flat is set against C, which remains unresolved for a whole bar) as well as unusual harmonic progressions. The allegro part of the movement is introduced with a graceful melody in the violins, repeated by the basses. The second theme, shared by violins and clarinets, is also the very essence of grace and beauty. The slow movement is pure Mozartean song. The first melody has an almost religious character. It is presented immediately by the strings. After the woodwinds join in, the strings present a second effective lyrical idea. The third movement is one of Mozart's most famous minuets (except, of course, for the one in *Don Giovanni*). It begins robustly in the violins against chords in rest of the orchestra. The trio is a suave melody for the clarinets. The finale erupts in a happy spirit with an ebullient theme for violins alone. This theme, soon taken up by the entire orchestra, dominates the movement, which is Haydnesque throughout in its vivacity and mirth.

The *Symphony No. 40,* in G minor (K.550), begins with one of Mozart's most eloquent themes. It is a gentle, even sad, melody in the strings which opens up a breath-taking vista of beauty. Perhaps only a Mozart could proceed from this to a second lyrical idea and sustain the inspiration. This second theme is shared between oboe and clarinet on the one hand and the strings on the other. The development of these two themes parts company once and for all with eighteenth-century formalism. It is almost Beethovian in its enriched dramatic and expressive writing, in its emotional unrest and conflict. There is complete serenity in the second movement, which presents its first theme imitatively, first in the violas, then in second violins, and after that in the first violins. This theme evolves naturally into the second principal theme, in the first violins. The minuet has a stately theme for full orchestra, more vigorous than we usually find in this sedate courtly dance. The trio, however, introduces refinement with a pastoral melody shared between strings and woodwinds. The spirited finale is set into motion by an electrifying theme in the violins. This winged motion is arrested by the arrival of a graceful second subject in the first violins. But there is only a brief breathing space; the original vitality and fleet pace return.

The *Symphony No. 41,* in C major (K.551)—the last of this incomparable triptych—is best known as the *Jupiter* symphony. It is believed that the official christening of this symphony as "Jupiter" took place at a concert of the Royal Philharmonic Orchestra of London on March 26, 1821; that the name was concocted by the English pianist and publisher J. B. Cramer to describe the godlike perfection of the music. Another interpretation is that the name "Jupiter" was inspired by the dramatic opening chords of the first movement, whose impact is that of Jovian thunderbolts.

The first theme of the first movement is made up partly of these vigorous chords and partly of a soft answer in the strings. It is the opening strong figure, however, that is worked up with immense power before the delicate second theme emerges gracefully in the strings. The development, which begins with a change of key, is more in the dramatic vein of the opening chords than in the gentle character of the second theme. The principal melody of the beautiful slow movement is heard in muted strings. A theme for bassoon provides a transition to the second wonderful melody of this movement, in the oboes. The development here concerns itself primarily with the second theme, while the coda is largely devoted to the first. The minuet that follows is in the spirit of the eighteenth century, the graceful and flowing theme being given by the first violins. The trio contains a delightful dialogue between wind instruments and strings. The finale is the crown of the symphony. With phenomenal contrapuntal skill Mozart here fills the fugal form with radiance, eloquence, and power while building a structure of cathedral grandeur. This last movement, however, is not a fugue, as is sometimes erroneously believed; it is in the sonata form, utilizing fugal writing. It begins with a subdued and spiritual subject for violins alone; the first four notes come from an old church melody and were used by Mozart in other works. This theme is taken over by the orchestra and then given fugal treatment: second violins, first violins, violas, cellos, culminating in full orchestra. The second theme then appears in strings and woodwinds. The development begins with a repetition of the first theme and gives preference to dramatic fugal writing. A passage for two bassoons leads to the recapitulation. In the powerful coda, the first theme is once again subjected to broad fugal treatment.

Besides the symphonies, Mozart produced a library of orchestral music that includes divertimentos, serenades, nocturnes, cassations, and so forth. There is no clear structural difference between each of these categories. Eighteenth-century composers used these names indiscriminately for a light orchestral work in several movements (usually five) which was something of a crossbreed between the symphony and the suite. This type of work was usually a functional piece written on order for a garden party or other social functions of the nobility or to celebrate the name day of a nobleman.

The best loved in this group of compositions—and it is characteristic of the entire breed—is the serenade *Eine kleine Nachtmusik*. It was originally written for string quintet, but is most often heard today in performances by string orchestra. It is in four, instead of the usual five, movements. The first has the character of a march, with two principal themes and no development to speak of. The first theme is heard immediately; the second is more lyrical. A romanze follows. It is in the form of a rondo. The first section is in the three-part-song form in a decidedly sentimental vein. There are two additional sections, both lively, after each of which the sentimental melody is repeated. The minuet is bold and energetic, but with a delicate trio. The concluding movement is a breezy rondo, in Mozart's most infectious manner.

The concertos of Mozart are a world by themselves. There are more than twenty such works for the piano; many of them tower above the concerto literature of the period. The *Concerto in D minor* (K.466) and the *Concerto in C minor* (K.491) are works filled with somber moods and the turmoil of emotional upheaval. The first is filled with dramatic conflict, while the latter has a strong undercurrent of tragedy. The *Concerto in D minor* opens with an orchestral introduction in which the two principal themes are presented. The first, dark and dramatic, appears immediately; the second, more elegiac, is heard in oboes and bassoons. When the piano enters, at last, it is with a new episode, a gentle commentary. The piano then embarks on the two principal themes, enlarges them, and then engages the orchestra in developing them. The second movement is a romanze. The piano appears first, introducing a deeply felt, poetic melody. The orchestra joins in. The piano now gives the second main theme of the movement. Midway there comes an emotional outburst in the piano and woodwinds to destroy the placidity, which, however, returns with a repetition of the first melody. The finale is a rondo, the principal theme of which is restless; it is first heard in the piano and then taken over by the orchestra. After a transitional subject in the piano, the second theme arrives in the orchestra before being assumed by the solo instrument.

The dark and tragic character of the *Concerto in C minor* is immediately apparent in the orchestral introduction, which begins with a somber first theme for strings with poignant interpolations of chords in the woodwinds. The second theme in the strings is more elegiac than tragic. The piano enters with a new idea, a short and tender soliloquy, before the two themes are discoursed upon. In the development section the tragedy unfolds and grows majestically. The slow movement is in the form of a rondo. It begins with a sad, sweet song in three parts. The next two sections maintain this quiet and subdued pathos, and after each the sad, sweet melody of the opening is brought back. The finale has greater virility and somewhat more optimism. It consists of a theme and variations, the theme—proud, even heroic—being heard immediately in the orchestra.

The frequently performed *Concerto in A major* (K.488) is in a much more cheerful mood. The bright first theme appears immediately in the strings and is then repeated in the woodwinds. A transitional figure leads to the second theme in the first violins; the theme is repeated in bassoons and flute. The piano enters with the first theme, which is completed by the orchestra. After some embroidery and passage work, the piano recalls the second theme, which, when taken up by the orchestra, is given embellishments by the solo instrument. The second movement is, to Alfred Einstein, the "soul of the concerto." It is undoubtedly one of the most moving and passionate pages in all Mozart. It begins with a melancholy melody in the piano, to which the orchestra contributes an equally poignant countersubject. The piano returns with the first melody, against a light accompaniment, after which flutes and clarinets arrive with a new theme. All this material is worked out with great breadth and intensity, and frequently with pastoral beauty. But this excursion into melancholy is confined to the second movement. The finale arrives like an exclamation of joy, the merriment beginning with a delightful eight-bar theme first presented by the piano, then repeated by the entire orchestra. Many other ideas follow, most of them episodic, but the gaiety remains unclouded.

The *Concerto in B-flat major* (K.595) was Mozart's last piano concerto, written in the year of his death. His overwhelming debts and the illness of his wife combined to make this a trying period, but the concerto reveals nothing of his anxieties. As in the preceding concerto, in A major, gaiety is the prevailing mood.

The long orchestral introduction presents the principal thematic material. After a one-bar introduction, the first theme appears in the violins with comments by the wind instruments. This is followed by the second theme, also in the violins. The piano makes its entrance with an altered version of the first theme. After some passage work it enters upon the second theme. The development, which concerns itself primarily with the first theme, follows an orchestral *tutti*. The recapitulation is brought in by a statement of the first theme. The principal theme of the larghetto movement appears first in unaccompanied piano and then in the orchestra. The piano then extends this melody and presents a subsidiary idea. After an orchestral interlude, the piano presents a new important melody. Trills in the piano bring back the first principal theme. The concluding movement is a rondo. The first theme, full of spirit and animation, is given by the piano. After an orchestral interlude of twenty-five measures, a new episode appears in the piano before the second principal theme of the movement is announced. This material is treated throughout the movement with either witty or brilliant effects.

While, generally speaking, Mozart's concertos for the violin do not equal the piano concertos either in profundity of thought or originality of style, they include two works which are acknowledged masterpieces. The *Concerto No. 4,* in D major (K.218), written in 1775, begins with a bold theme in the orchestra that resembles a military fanfare. This is worked out orchestrally. The lyrical second theme is not heard until after the solo violin has made its appearance. There are other subsidiary ideas, briefly stated by either the violin or the orchestra. The development has brilliant virtuoso passages for the soloist, who also concerns himself with a cadenza before the closing eight-bar orchestral *tutti*. There are two important melodies in the second movement. The first is heard at once in the orchestra and is repeated by the violin. A change of key brings the second melody in the violin, supported harmonically by the orchestra. The concluding rondo movement begins with a graceful tune in the violin. After it has been repeated, the rhythm becomes livelier and the music gayer. A second section begins with a dialogue between the solo instrument and the first violins of the orchestra. There is a brief cadenza before the graceful first theme returns for the last time.

In the *Concerto No. 5*, in A major (K.219), also written in 1775, the orchestral introduction presents the two principal themes, both in the strings. When this introduction is finished there is a moment's pause, after which the solo instrument makes an unorthodox entry. It concerns itself not with any of the material already stated, but with a new, slow and reflective melody that is six bars long. Only when this melody has been completed does the violin take on the first theme vigorously. There are two subsidiary themes in the violin (the first has great depth of feeling) before it is concerned with the second theme. The development now proceeds along traditional lines. The slow movement is built out of two beautiful melodies, both heard in the opening orchestral introduction. The violin enters with the first soulful song, extends it, then takes up the second theme. The themes are then worked out simply and with a wealth of feeling and beauty. The concluding movement, like the first, receives unorthodox treatment. It begins with a delightful minuet, but instead of proceeding along the formal structural lines of a minuet it introduces, midway in the movement, a new passionate theme of Oriental personality; this new theme is in the Turkish style so often assumed by Mozart (as in the famous "Turkish March" of the *Piano Sonata in A major* and in parts of the opera *The Abduction from the Seraglio*). The minuet melody returns to conclude the movement in a graceful attitude.

There are a great many other concertos by Mozart for various instruments and combinations of instruments. Among the finest are: *Concerto in E-flat major*, for two pianos and orchestra (K.365); *Concerto in F major*, for three pianos and orchestra (K.242); *Concerto in B-flat major*, for bassoon and orchestra (K. 191); *Concerto in A major*, for clarinet and orchestra (K.622); *Concerto No. 1*, in G major, for flute and orchestra (K.313); *Concerto No. 2*, in D major, for flute and orchestra (K.314); *Concerto in C major*, for flute, harp, and orchestra (K.299). In this group there belongs also the *Sinfonia Concertante*, in E-flat major, for violin, viola, and orchestra (K.364), even though it is not officially designated as a concerto.

Choral Music. The Requiem was the last piece of music written by Mozart. He died before he could finish it, and it was completed by his pupil Süssmayer. The precise contribution of Süssmayer has long been subjected to controversy and doubt. Süssmayer himself (in a letter to the publisher Breitkopf & Härtel) claimed the lion's share of credit for this work. Musicological research, however, has convincingly proved that up to the last three sections he did little more than fill out the instrumentation. It is the last three sections—the *"Sanctus," "Benedictus,"* and *"Agnus Dei"*—that trouble the musical authorities. Not a single manuscript by Mozart has been discovered containing either this music or its sketches. Apparently they were written by Süssmayer. And yet these three parts not only equal but are in some respects superior to the music that preceded them. How could music of such grandeur and sublimity possibly come from one who produced nothing else in his life of lasting value? In this connection the German critic Marx made the following observation: "If these are not by Mozart, then it is a Mozart who wrote them."

What probably happened is that Mozart explained his intentions to Süssmayer so clearly and in such detail that the latter had no difficulty in putting down on paper Mozart's final conception. We have the evidence of Sophie Haibl, who was with the composer up to the time of his death, that "Süssmayer was at Mozart's bedside. The well-known Requiem lay on the quilt and Mozart was explaining to him how, in his opinion, he ought to finish it when he was gone."

About one point there can be no question. The Requiem is pure Mozart, and Mozart at his very greatest. The dramatic circumstances attending its writing have already been described in the composer's biography. These circumstances are important in understanding this music. The chilling awareness that he was dying, and that he was writing his own requiem, brought to his writing an other-worldly beauty and a depth of feeling unique even for Mozart.

The Requiem begins with quiet restraint, but already on an elevated plane, with a tender melody in the bassoons and basset horns against a soft string accompaniment. The voices enter in the eighth measure with a prayer for the dead: *"Requiem aeternam dona eis Domine."* This leads directly into an immense double fugue on *"Kyrie eleison"* and *"Christie eleison,"* a dramatic rather than poignant exhortation for mercy. The next two sections are forceful. The first, *"Dies Irae,"* brings us the turmoil of the sinner in the presence of final judgment. The second is the Judgment Day, announced by a theme in tenor trombone and followed by the solo quartet in *"Tuba mirum";* the vocal singing is throughout accompanied by the solo tenor trombone. The majestic music of *"Rex Tremendae Majestatis"* follows, the full chorus entering with the awesome cry of *"Rex"* after a brief orchestral introduction; a complete change of feeling arrives at the end with the supplication *"Salve me."* The *"Recordare"* opens with music of quiet and moving eloquence, but the music of the ensuing *"Confutatis"* is once again stormy, as we are made aware of the terrible fate of sinners; but a gentler atmosphere relieves the tensions with the supplication of female voices. In *"Lacrymosa"* we are in the presence of grief; this is one of the most touching pages in the entire work. Grief gives way to the somber music of *"Domine Jesu,"* which passes from gloom to terror. But the emotions grow calmer in the *"Hostias."* The majestic *"Sanctus"* culminates in a vital fugue on the word *"Osanna"* and proceeds to the serene beauty of the *"Benedictus."* The Requiem continues radiantly with the *"Agnus Dei,"* in which the soul has found peace at last. In the concluding portion, the *"Lux Aeterna,"* the music of the very opening of the Requiem is brought back to give a feeling of complete integration.

The familiar *Ave Verum* (K.618) is an independent choral which, like the Requiem, was written in the last year of Mozart's life. It is one of the simplest, and yet most poignant, pieces of music in choral literature. No analysis is required for this beautiful melody with its simple harmonic structure; its spiritual radiance and serenity cannot fail to touch the heart and exalt the spirit.

Chamber Music. Between 1782 and 1785 Mozart wrote a set of six string quartets which he dedicated to Joseph Haydn. They represent the peak in Mozart's string-quartet literature, which embraces more than twenty-five works, and they are the greatest string quartets written before Beethoven's *Rasoumovsky* group.

Mozart had completed more than a dozen string quartets before starting to work on the Haydn set. Some of these earlier works are characteristic of Mozart in the skill of their harmonic and even contrapuntal writing, the beauty and contrast of ideas, and the increasing subtlety and freedom with which his material is evolved. For nine years (1773–82) Mozart did not touch the string-quartet form at all. He returned to it to pay homage to Haydn with six towering masterworks that dwarf all his earlier string-quartet efforts. In these six quartets we find a Mozart more sober and reserved than in the earlier compositions; both the gaiety and the pathos are held in check. Mozart now becomes the impersonal commentator remarking on different emotions, but always without dramatics. In the objectivity of this music lies much of its great force—in its objectivity and in the amazing daring and newness of Mozart's technical means.

The *Quartet in B-flat major* (K.458) and the *Quartet in C major* (K.465) are most frequently played. The former is known as the *Hunt* Quartet because its opening theme has the quality of a hunting-horn call. (This suggestion of horn calls is further carried out in the passage that follows.) The first movement contains no other major theme, but merely a series of fragmentary ideas; the most expressive of these opens the development section. The opening hunting theme receives extended treatment in the coda. The minuet movement is gracious and is followed by a slow movement of profound beauty. The closing movement has Haydnesque vivacity; its main theme, presented by the first violin, is believed to have been derived from a folk song.

The *Quartet in C major* has been described as the *Dissonant* Quartet due to the cross relations in the opening measures, which give them an ambiguous tonality. The key of the work asserts itself forcefully after this introductory section has given way to the main body of the movement. As in the preceding *Quartet in B-flat major,* the slow movement brings us some of Mozart's most deeply moving lyricism, contrast being provided by subtle changes of meter. In the minuet that follows, the middle trio section has an intensity of feeling not usually encountered in Mozart's minuet movements. The finale has subdued gaiety that grows into exuberance only in the extended coda, which is built up from a brief theme borrowed from one of Mozart's own piano works.

The *Quartet in B-flat major* and the *Quartet in C major* are, respectively, the fourth and sixth works in the Haydn set. The first in the set is the *Quartet in G major* (K.387), outstanding for the vernal freshness and spontaneity of its first movement and the extraordinary contrapuntal skill of the finale, with its two fugal episodes. In the *Quartet in D minor* (K.421), the second in the set, there are many passages that must have sounded stark, forbidding, and new to eighteenth-century ears: the bold modulations and enharmonic changes in the first movement; the piquant pizzicato effect in the trio of the minuet. More conventional are the slow movement and the finale, the latter consisting of variations on a siciliana melody. The *Quartet in E-flat major* (K.428), the third of this group, alternates between the serenity and introspection of its slow movement and a prevailing mood of despair in the first movement and in the trio of the minuet. The fifth work is the *Quartet in A major* (K.464), which is structurally more integrated than the others. The second part of the opening theme is varied to become the main theme of the minuet, which in turn is recognizable in the opening measure of the slow movement; and the first theme of the first movement has a rhythmic similarity to the main theme of the finale. The strongest movement of the quartet is the third, an andante, a set of variations on a stately theme, the emotional pitch rising with each successive variation.

Mozart wrote two piano quartets, the first time that the piano was combined with three stringed instruments. The *Quartet in G minor* (K.478) came first, in 1785. It begins with a bold, short theme for the four instruments; but as the first movement develops the mood grows gentler and more poetic. The second movement has simple beauty, the main theme being announced at once by the piano; there is a more energetic second theme, stated first by the piano and answered by the strings. The concluding movement is a gay rondo.

The *Quartet in E-flat major* (K.493) followed one year later. Here the first movement is unorthodox in that the second theme is more important than the first; there is also a third principal idea before the exposition is concluded. The second movement is a gentle song, a dialogue between piano and strings. The concluding rondo, as in the preceding quartet, is infectiously gay and playful.

The most famous of all Mozart's quintets is the *Quintet in A major* (K.581), for clarinet and strings, written in 1789. Both main themes of the first movement have an elegiac character for which the dark colors of the clarinet are particularly suited; both themes, though, appear in the strings before the clarinet devotes itself to them. The melancholy deepens in the slow movement, in which the clarinet is the principal protagonist. The minuet has two trios, the first for the strings alone and the second in the character of a German peasant dance. The concluding movement consists of a short and delightful theme which is transformed by a series of variations.

Mozart wrote five string quintets (two violins, two violas, and cello). The *Quintet in G minor* (K.516), written in 1787, is both the greatest and the most tragic. W. W. Cobbett looks upon the work as a "struggle with destiny" and finds the music filled "with the resignation of despair." The first movement is tight-lipped in its pathos; both main themes have a strong undercurrent of melancholy, but the feeling is restrained throughout. The minuet movement that follows is one of the most sober pieces that Mozart wrote in that form; the opening minuet section fuses naturally and inevitably into the tender trio. It is in the slow movement that the tragic element is most prominent; to

Alfred Einstein, the musicologist, this movement is the prayer "of a lonely one surrounded on all sides by the walls of a deep chasm." The tragic element is still evident in the slow introduction to the finale; but in the ensuing allegro Mozart shakes himself loose of his depression and gives way to animated spirit. Henri Ghéon said that in this allegro part of the finale "Mozart had had enough . . . He knew how to cry . . . but he did not like to cry or to suffer for long."

Mozart wrote over forty sonatas for violin and piano. In his earlier sonatas the piano is the more important partner of the team, while the violin is usually assigned obbligato passages. It is only in his later works that the individuality and importance of each instrument is respected, each member of the team becoming an equal partner in the presentation and development of the musical ideas. The first of his mature violin and piano sonatas (but his twentieth in all) is the *Sonata in C major* (K.296), written in 1778; in the slow movement we have Mozartean lyricism at its purest and most seductive. Later sonatas that can be regarded as works of first importance include the following: *G major* (K.301); *E minor* (K.304); *D major* (K.306); *F major* (K.377); *B-flat major* (K.378); *B-flat major* (K.454); and *A major* (K.526). Of special interest are the theme-and-variations movement of the *F major Sonata,* the finale of the *D major Sonata* with its effective contrast of two sections in different tempos, the introspective and sometimes tragic mood of the *B-flat major Sonata* (K.378), and the personal musings of the slow movement of the *A major Sonata.* Although, generally speaking, Mozart may be less profound and less original in his violin sonatas than in his other great chamber-music works, he has filled these sonatas with such a wealth of lovable and ingratiating melodies that they never fail to enchant the listener.

Piano Music. Not even the most enthusiastic admirers of Mozart's seventeen piano sonatas will venture to say that they are of the stature of his greatest piano concertos. But they are important historically in solidifying and extending the sonata form; and a handful are pleasing aesthetically as well. The *Sonata in A major* (K.331) is famous and deserves to be. It begins in unorthodox fashion with a theme and variations, the pleasing little melody being subjected to six variations. The second movement is a minuet, in which the trio has such romantic feeling that we are almost at the threshold of the nineteenth century. The concluding movement is the most popular of all: the *"Alla turca"*—or "Turkish March"—in the pseudo-Turkish style in vogue in Vienna in the eighteenth century (a style used by Beethoven in his own

"Turkish March" from the *Ruins of Athens* and by Mozart in the *A major Violin Concerto* and the opera *The Abduction from the Seraglio*).

The *Fantasia and Sonata in C minor* are actually two separate works, written a year apart, and at first published separately (K.475 and K.457). The publisher Artaria issued them together in 1785, and it was known that Mozart himself was partial to having them played together as a single work. Today they are sometimes played separately and sometimes together. They are cut from the same emotional cloth and blend well. The fantasia is one of Mozart's greatest piano works, almost orchestral in its harmonic richness and color, and varied in its emotional content. It has five distinct sections (played, of course, without interruption), beginning on a tragic note and passing through dramatic and lyrical moods before returning to the original tragic feeling. In the first and last movements of the sonata, the dramatic character of the fantasia is emphasized, while the lyrical nature of the fantasia is found in the slow movement of the sonata.

The *Sonata in D major* (K.576) was Mozart's last piano sonata. The two themes of its first movement are in sharp contrast, the first being vigorous and the second tender. The slow movement has greater expressive beauty, tinged with a gentle sorrow. The finale has many brilliant passages, but is of exceptional interest for its ingenious contrapuntal writing.

Mozart also wrote a superb sonata for four hands, the *Sonata in F major* (K.497). The elevated mood of this work is immediately established in the majestic slow introduction to the first movement and achieves a great intensity in the slow movement, one of Mozart's finest examples of polyphonic writing for the piano. There is also the remarkable *Sonata in D major* (K.448), for two pianos. But where the sonata for four hands is majestic and intense, the two-piano sonata is lively, graceful, and filled with a happy spirit.

Modest Mussorgsky

> "He simply tried to translate into sound the soul's cries, which struck upon his ears from without or rose from within himself. In very truth, he trampled on the rules and crushed the life out of them by the sheer weight of his thought."
>
> —*Pierre d'Alheim*

BORN: Karevo, Pskov district, March 21, 1839.

DIED: St. Petersburg, March 28, 1881.

MAJOR WORKS: *Opera*—Boris Godunov. *Orchestral Music*—A Night on Bald Mountain (completed and orchestrated by Rimsky-Korsakov); Pictures at an Exhibition (orchestrated by Maurice Ravel); Prelude to Act I and Entr'acte from Khovantschina. *Vocal Music*—more than 75 songs, including "Song of the Flea" and the cycles Sunless, Nursery Songs, Songs and Dances of Death. ALSO: The Fair at Sorochinsk, Khovantschina, operas; piano pieces.

HIS LIFE

TWO PORTRAITS of Mussorgsky (one is verbal, the other pictorial) provide a striking study in contrasts. The first is by Borodin, who described the young Mussorgsky, then an army officer, as follows: "He was a true little dandy, a very handsome young officer looking like a picture in a tightly fitting uniform. His feet were small and finely turned. His hair was smoothly groomed, combed down and pomaded; his dainty hands chiseled. His manners were elegant and aristocratic. He spoke a little through his teeth, and interspersed his conversation with French expressions in a rather affected way. There was a certain air of foppishness about him, but well in moderation. His politeness and civility were out of the ordinary. The ladies liked him. He would sit down at the piano, and coquettishly throw his hands and then play very sweetly and gracefully some melodies from *Il Trovatore* and *La Traviata*. The ladies, buzzing around him, exclaimed: '*Charmant! Delicieux!*'"

The second is a painting by Repin, made in the last days of Mussorgsky's life. We now see a man unkempt and disheveled; the eyes are stark, even maniacal; the cheeks hollowed and discolored. We have only to look into those eyes to recognize that this is a picture not of a man ravaged by his last, fatal illness, but one who has arrived at the final stage of spiritual as well as physical disintegration. For, after his thirty-fifth year Mussorgsky was an alcoholic. Intoxication was his only avenue of escape from terrifying loneliness, morbidity, frustration, disappointment, poverty, and laziness.

This was the man who once had said: "Art is no mere play, and time is precious." But, then, Mussorgsky never regarded art as play, not even in the last, terrible years of his life. More than any of his famous colleagues—yes, more even than Borodin or Rimsky-Korsakov or Balakirev —he held steadfast to his mission as a nationalist composer; more than any of them he dedicated himself uncompromisingly to his ideals. His colleagues, whom he admired, might underestimate and depreciate him; they might, more often than not, regard him as a fumbling schoolboy. But he never lost faith in what he was trying to do, nor did he ever abandon his own way of doing it.

And time *was* precious to him. Fate never made it possible for him to devote all of himself to his music, as other composers could do. For the first twenty years he had to prepare for, and fulfill, the duties of a military career. He gave up his uniform for music. But five years later, and up to the last year of his life, he had to hold down a drab clerical position to keep from starving. Thus he was never able to acquire that background and training and musical *savoir-faire* that his colleagues possessed. Compared to them he was something of a musical illiterate. More important still, his composing had to be relegated to a secondary status in his life, to hours in the evening or during the week end, when he was not earning a living. And, as if this were not bad enough, there were his recurrent attacks of bad health (now delirium tremens, now a nervous breakdown, now even threats of insanity) to take still more of those precious few hours. That he could, in spite of his lack of time and frequent deflection of energy, produce some of the abiding monuments in Russian music, is testimony to his elemental, titanic creative force. For Mussorgsky was without doubt the greatest natural genius that Russian music produced. What he lacked in musical education and sophistication he could provide with his inborn powers.

He died in abject poverty. But he was born to wealth. His father was a prosperous landowner, the master of a forty-mile estate where Modest spent a happy childhood. We learn from an autobiographical fragment written (in the third person) in the last year of Modest's life: "Under the influence of his nurse, he became familiar with the old Russian tales. It was mainly his familiarity with the very spirit of the life of the people that impelled him to extemporize music before knowing even the most elementary rules of piano playing. His mother gave him his first piano lessons. When at the piano, he hated having to do as he was told. Nevertheless, he made such progress that at the age of seven he was able to play small pieces by Liszt; and at a party in his parents' home at the age of eleven, he performed in front of a large audience, a big concerto by Field. His father, who worshiped music, decided to develop his ability, and his musical education was carried on under Herke in St. Petersburg."

Yet Mussorgsky's father had no intention of raising a professional musician. For generations most of the Mussorgsky men had been members of the renowned Preobrazhensky Guards, which had originally been founded by Peter the Great. Modest was to carry on that tradition. He was entered in a fashionable school in St. Petersburg. One year after that he went to the Army Training Establishment, which made him ready for the Guards Cadet Academy. He was a sober young man, given to reading classic literature and studying German philosophy. The director of the Academy ridiculed these studious tendencies. (What use did an officer have for book learning?) He also encouraged the cadet to seek out the pleasurable diversions of wine and woman. Woman was never to be an important factor in Mussorgsky's life, except for his mother, whom he adored. But wine!—in the Academy, Mussorgsky was first directed toward the precipice from which he was in later years to hurl himself recklessly.

There was some preoccupation with music at the Academy. For four years Mussorgsky studied the piano privately with Anton Herke. He became a virtuoso, was popular with his classmates for his ability at both the piano and singing. Unfortunately he was given no training whatsoever in harmony, counterpoint, or theory. Despite this he started composing. His first opus was an *Ensign Polka* for piano which his teacher, Herke, arranged to have published. More ambitious was an opera based on Hugo's *Han d'Islande,* which never developed beyond fragmentary sketches. "Nothing could come of all this," Mussorgsky later commented about these apprentice attempts. "The composer was seventeen years old, and he knew nothing."

When he was graduated, in 1856, Mussorgsky joined the Pre-obrazhensky Regiment, dapper in his officer's uniform. A year later he was introduced to two composers with pronounced national leanings. One was Alexander Dargomyzhsky (1813–69), whose opera *Russalka*, produced in that same year of 1856, was a conscious attempt to proceed along the national lines marked out by Michael Glinka (1804–57) in *A Life for the Czar* and *Russlan and Ludmila*. The other was young Mily Balakirev (1837–1910), already fired by Glinka's ardor to produce a nationalist art. After 1861 Mussorgsky was to join actively with Balakirev and three other young Russian composers (Rimsky-Korsakov, César Cui, and Alexander Borodin) as a member of the national group thenceforth to be known as "The Russian Five" or "The Mighty Five" (see Rimsky-Korsakov).

Meanwhile, Dargomyzhsky and Balakirev stimulated Mussorgsky's latent creative interests and first aroused in him the ambition to write *Russian* music. Mussorgsky became Balakirev's pupil. The teacher led his pupil through the scores of Beethoven, Schubert, Schumann, and others in an effort to clarify the problems of theory and form. "Not being a theorist," Balakirev later explained, "I could not, unfortunately, teach Mussorgsky harmony as Rimsky-Korsakov teaches it now." These lessons, always irregular due to Mussorgsky's duties as an officer, came to a halt in the summer of 1858; after that, they were little more than extended conversations and exchange of ideas. Balakirev's teaching was valuable, to be sure, but it was incapable of filling in the yawning gaps in Mussorgsky's musical education.

In 1858 Mussorgsky suddenly decided to resign from military service to give himself up completely to music. Having freedom of movement, he started traveling in order to see more of Russia. A visit to Moscow, his first, was an overwhelming experience; it made him more conscious than ever of his Russian origin and made him increasingly proud of it. "All that is Russian is dearer and nearer to me." Mussorgsky was soon to make his debut as a composer. On January 23, 1860, Anton Rubinstein directed the first performance of the *Scherzo in B-flat major* with the Russian Music Society in St. Petersburg; it was well received.

But the Moscow visit was not altogether a happy experience. While there Mussorgsky suffered a nervous breakdown. Melancholia was followed by physical disorders. Mussorgsky himself explained the causes to

Balakirev as "youth, an immoderate capacity for enthusiasm, a strong, unconquerable desire for omniscience, exaggerated introspection, and an idealism that even goes as far as to take the dream for reality." But the immediate cause was a reading of Byron's *Manfred*. "I was so electrified by the suffering of that lofty spirit that I cried out: 'How I wish I were Manfred!' . . . Fate thought fit, apparently, to grant my wish. I became literally 'manfredized' for the time. My spirit slew my flesh! Now I must have recourse to every kind of antidote."

He went to the country for the summer and was well enough to undertake composing again. "Thank God, Mily, I am fully recovered," he wrote on October 8, 1860. "I am now putting all my musical peccadilloes in order. A new period of my musical life has begun." He started writing several orchestral works (including a symphony and sketches for a fantasy later to become *A Night on Bald Mountain*) and had a choral piece performed in St. Petersburg. The result was none too impressive and hardly gave warning of Mussorgsky's later development. No wonder that his colleagues regarded him as nothing but a dilettante, given to theorizing, ambitious plans, high ideals, but without either the talent or the equipment to accomplish anything. "Mussorgsky thinks he has accomplished a great deal for art in general and Russian art in particular," remarked Balakirev acidly to a friend.

In 1861 serfdom was abolished by an imperial ukase. Its effect was to impoverish Mussorgsky, who accepted this tragedy with good grace and without permitting it to affect his lifelong sympathy for and interest in the peasant. His colleagues wanted to help him out financially as best they could; if they did not respect his musical ability, they did not fail to like him personally. But Mussorgsky was too proud to become, suddenly, an object of charity. He sought employment. In 1863 he became a clerk at the Ministry of Transport. For seventeen of his eighteen remaining years he worked at his desk for a pittance. Time which should have belonged to music—he must have sensed that he did not have a long life before him, and he knew that he still had so much to learn and to accomplish—had to be consumed in the drab, dull clerical routines. A measure of relief from his drudgery was provided by the stimulation received from a group of intellectuals (none of whom were musicians) with whom he set up a co-operative communal existence. From this group, and from the friends they brought for evening discussions, Mussorgsky learned more of art, literature, politics, and philosophy. (Of "The Mighty Five," Mussorgsky was ever the most widely cultured, the best informed, and the most trenchant thinker.)

With the extension of his intellectual horizon came an expansion of his musical ambitions. He now wanted to write an opera of large dimensions, selecting for his text Flaubert's *Salammbô*. But, like so many other large ventures which he planned at this time, it was soon abandoned.

He appeared to have the endurance to complete only small projects. He preferred most of all the song form; its limited demands on his technique and concentration made it a grateful medium. He had written his first song in 1857. But between 1864 and 1865 there came the first of his little song masterpieces. "Night" and "The Peasant's Lullaby" revealed for the first time Mussorgsky's creative potential.

The death of his mother, in 1865, was a turning point. Mussorgsky began to lose control of himself. Physical deterioration began with an attack of delirium tremens; mental deterioration followed, with morbid depressions and overindulgence in drink. He had become such a burden on his comrades in the co-operative apartment that he was induced to set up home elsewhere, with his brother. But, as if in compensation, there was at the same time a strengthening of creative powers. His musical thinking grew ever more original, ever more daring. His production now included many poignant songs (such as *"Hopak"*), his first complete major composition, *The Destruction of Sennacherib,* for chorus and orchestra (text from Byron's *Hebrew Melodies*), and the first draft of *A Night on Bald Mountain* (which he never completed, but which was heard after Mussorgsky's death in Rimsky-Korsakov's orchestration and with his finishing touches).

In 1868 he started writing an opera on Gogol's *The Marriage,* in which he made his first important experiments with musical realism and a new kind of melody patterned after the inflections of human speech. He managed to write only one act, then abandoned the opera because a new project had captured his imagination. This time his enthusiasm carried him through two years of the most intense application, excitement, concentration, and dedication. In 1870 he completed his first opera—and it was his masterwork: *Boris Godunov*. He submitted it to the Imperial Theater in St. Petersburg which, puzzled by its strange form and still more unorthodox style, turned it down. Mussorgsky set about to revise his opera along a more orthodox pattern, introducing some formal arias and a love scene, both of which had been noticeably lacking in the original version. Resubmitted, the opera was turned down a second time. Three scenes from the opera, however, were heard at the Imperial Theater in St. Petersburg on February

17, 1873, due to the efforts of Mussorgsky's friends. The performance made enough of an impression to induce the Imperial Theater to present the opera in its entirety. That event took place on February 8, 1874. The audience was responsive, but the critics and the professional musicians were devastating. Hermann Laroche, a leading critic in St. Peterburg, referred to its "coarseness and cacophony." Even Mussorgsky's colleagues of "The Mighty Five" failed to understand or appreciate what he was trying to do, or to perceive how he had succeeded. César Cui wrote a denunciatory review; Rimsky-Korsakov was upset by the opera's "clumsiness and illiteracy"; Balakirev expressed pointed and sacrastic opinions about the opera in public.

This reaction to what he knew was his life's work did not help Mussorgsky's worsening physical and mental condition. The death of one of his closest friends in the summer of 1873, the painter Victor Hartmann, had also had its effect. Whatever sense of personal dignity Mussorgsky might have had was now gone. He sold his furniture to pay for his drinks, wore beggar's clothes, and often returned to his rooms after a period of dissipation to find himself locked out because he had not paid the rent. Friends would search for him and find him in rags, in the most disreputable company, stupefied by intoxication. The amazing side to this otherwise disagreeable story was that Mussorgsky could still function as a composer, and with no decrease in his creative powers. Between periods of mental confusion and physical orgies, he was able to produce some of his finest songs (including the cycles *Sunless* and *Songs and Dances of Death*), the opera *Khovantschina,* and the piano suite *Pictures at an Exhibition.*

In 1879 the singer Daria Leonova induced Mussorgsky to tour Southern Russia in joint concerts. He went because he needed the money and because he felt the trip might do him good. It exhilarated him—for a while. After his return to St. Petersburg he went from bad to worse. He had to give up his civil service position in 1880 and—he who had once been so proud!—live on the bounty of intimate friends. On one occasion he had to go to one of them with tears in his eyes, saying that if help was not forthcoming he would have to beg in the streets.

He was seized by a fit one evening at the home of a friend. He had to be committed to the hospital, where his sickness was diagnosed as apoplexy. To the last he demanded, then begged for, cognac. He died a week after his forty-second birthday. There is some evidence to point to the fact that in the last weeks of his life Mussorgsky suffered periods of insanity. He was buried in the Alexander Nevsky Cemetery in St. Petersburg. There were tributes from several musical institutions; and there was silent grieving by the four remaining members of "The Mighty Five."

HIS MUSIC

THE IDEAL of "The Russian Five" to create a great national art was fully realized by Mussorgsky. To this day *Boris Godunov* remains one of the greatest of all folk operas. All his other important works stem from the Russian soil and the Russian people. But Mussorgsky's achievements do not rest there. He was a great and original force; he was an innovator; he opened for music new sluices of expression.

What he accomplished can perhaps be most readily understood in terms of what he tried to do. And what he tried to do is most clearly set forth in his own words: "The quest for artistic beauty for its own sake is sheer puerility—is art in its nonage."

Mussorgsky rejected the old concepts of beauty in music—neat symmetry, proportion, and balance; pleasing sounds; elegant forms—in search for *truth*. Truth to him meant identifying music with everyday life and having it express everyday people. "The goal of the artist should be to study the most subtle features of human beings and of humanity in the mass. To explore and conquer these unknown regions, and find therein a health-giving pabulum for the minds of all men, that is the duty and the joy of joys."

The all-important medium for arriving at musical truth was the "melodic recitative," the new kind of melody he evolved after the pattern of human speech. "I foresee a new kind of melody which will be the melody of life. With great pains I have achieved a type of melody imitating that of speech. Someday, all of a sudden, the ineffable song will arise, intelligible to one and all. If I succeed, I shall be a conqueror in art—and succeed I must!"

This new kind of melody was both the spine of his songs and the integral element of his operas. "What I want to do is to make my characters speak on the stage as they would in real life, and yet write music which will be thoroughly artistic." That melody was his means with which to break down the artificiality of operatic expression and to arrive at a greater realism. "If you forget all operatic conventions and admit the principles of musical discourse carried out in all simplicity, then *The Marriage* is an opera. If I have succeeded in rendering the straightforward expression of thoughts and feelings as it takes place in ordinary speech, and if my rendering is artistic and musicianly, then the deed is done."

This necessity to seek out the truth at all costs impelled him frequently to do the unexpected and the unorthodox. He avoided carefully planned transitions, indulged in unusual chord sequences, used primitive rhythms, and went back to the modal scales and part writing of old Russian polyphonic music. Ugly sounds, awkward writing, inept instrumentation, and unschooled harmonizations abound in his works. These are due mostly to negligence or ignorance; but sometimes they are calculated effects. Soon after Mussorgsky's death, his colleague Rimsky-Korsakov set himself the task of removing the imperfections of Mussorgsky's scores, disregarding the composer's own statement: "With whatever shortcomings my music is born, with them it must live if it is to live at all." It was a formidable achievement and one which made possible the wide acceptance of Mussorgsky's music. But the peasant dressed up in civilized clothes often has the appearance of being in disguise. Rimsky-Korsakov's sophistication does not always harmonize with Mussorgsky's primitivism.

ANALYTICAL NOTES

Opera. *Boris Godunov* is the work of a courageous genius. Only a composer completely dedicated to artistic truth would have dared to undertake writing it. In using a text based on *Czar Boris,* Mussorgsky was challenging czarist authority. His adaptation of Pushkin's drama did not hesitate to emphasize the rising surge of rebellion among the common people against Godunov. A theme such as this was not likely to be regarded with favor in high places, which were bent on keeping the people subjugated to czarist rule.

But it took even greater courage to shape a new kind of opera. Mussorgsky was not at all interested in following the accepted pattern of formal arias and duets, tender love scenes, picturesque dances, and theatrical scenes—all pleasing to eye and ear. He was bent on creating a mighty drama of the Russian people; he sought to penetrate the Russian soul. What concerned him first and foremost was the psychological torment of Boris. Thus Boris is the central figure of the opera, and his inner conflicts and anguish are its central theme. The love interest is negligible (in the original version it did not exist at all). Mussorgsky was also concerned with the Russian people as Boris' antagonist. The people, then, play the second principal role in the opera. Mussorgsky's sympathetic treatment of the lower strata of Russian society makes *Boris Godunov* the first proletarian opera.

In his music Mussorgsky reflected the life of the Russian people with such directness and force that he is described as a realist. His melodies, imitating the inflections of Russian speech, lean toward authenticity and force rather than beauty of sound. Rhythm, harmony, and orchestral color are used, often with brutal strength, to interpret the conflicts of Boris with himself and those of the people against Boris. Mussorgsky imitated stylistic traits of Russian folk and church music to impart a national flavor to his score; he also used materials from Polish dances for his Polish scene. The demands of the play dictated the kind of music he wrote. On the one hand he could be down to earth, as in his portrait of the dissolute monk, Varlaam; on the other, he could be ecclesiastical, as in the prayers of the people.

The theme of Mussorgsky's opera is, of course, a page of Russian history. Boris Godunov becomes Czar by murdering Dmitri, heir to Czar Feodor. Twelve years later the monk Gregory spreads the rumor that Dmitri is alive. He—the monk—aspires to appear as Dmitri, avenge the murder, and take over the throne. The people believe in the false Dmitri and rally around him to overthrow Boris. Haunted by the dread that the dead Dmitri has risen from the grave, Boris loses his mind. He dies, after bidding his son farewell and pointing to him as his successor.

A brief prelude is built out of a theme of unmistakably Russian character, presented first by bassoon and English horn. The theme, as it passes to different instruments, grows and expands in sonority. When the climax is reached, the curtain rises on the first scene of the first act, a public square in front of a monastery near Moscow. The people have come to plead with Boris to become Czar, now that Dmitri is dead. The big moment of the first act comes in the third scene, set in the square between two cathedrals in Moscow. It is the Coronation of Czar Boris. Tolling bells bring on a pageant full of pomp and splendor. A folk hymn is intoned by the people. Boris then addresses them, promising to work for their good, invoking them to pray with him.

The first scene of the second act is in an inn at the Lithuanian border. Gregory is on his way to Moscow to achieve his self-appointed mission to pose as Dmitri; he has come to the inn with two companions. One of them, Varlaam, sings a stirring drinking song, "In the Town of Ka-zaan." The next scene, in Boris' palace, is climaxed by the Czar's mono-logue and hallucinations. Giving way to his torment and doubts, Boris falls on his knees and gives a dramatic exposition of his accomplish-ments, "I Have Attained Power." He then falls on his knees and is ter-rorized by the vision of Dmitri's ghost.

The second scene of Act III begins with a charming polonaise, danced by the Polish gentry in the palace of Marina, Gregory's beloved. In this scene we get the only love music of the entire opera, the duet of Marina and Gregory, "O Czarevitch, I Entreat You."

The closing scene of the opera is perhaps the most moving of all. Boris tenderly bids farewell to his son, Feodor ("Farewell, My Son, I Am Dying"), whom he designates as his successor. Outside the palace the people chant a prayer for their dying Czar. Bells ring out as the councilors enter solemnly. Boris breathes his last, and the curtain de-scends. Lawrence Gilman once pointed out that it is in a scene such as this—Boris' poignant farewell to his son—that the opera rises to its greatest heights. "The immense pitifulness, the sorrowing tenderness, the fathomless compassion of Mussorgsky's music are among the pre-cious heritages of our time. There is nothing at all like it in the whole stretch of the art as it has come down to us. . . . It is not in the somberly splendid moments of *Boris Godunov* that Mussorgsky is greatest; nor even in those moments that imprison the clutching horror of the Mac-beth-like hallucination scene, in which the tortured Boris grovels before the specter of the murdered Dmitri. It is when he is simplest, most in-timate, most quietly compassionate that he is to be most treasured; when he voices an immemorial sorrow, an ageless grief, as in the scene between the dying Boris and his son."

It is important to remember that there are many different versions of *Boris Godunov*. There is, first of all, Mussorgsky's original score, which was seen at the première performance in 1874. After Mussorgsky's death, Rimsky-Korsakov took it upon himself to edit Mussorgsky's works and reorchestrate them. Refined, polished, and manicured, *Boris Godunov* was presented in 1904 in St. Petersburg and made a deep im-pression. Still a different version of the opera was seen in St. Petersburg in 1908. For, by then, Rimsky-Korsakov had subjected his own revision to revision, trying to be truer to Mussorgsky's original intentions by re-storing sections previously deleted. It is this adaptation that has since circled the globe and become known; and it is this adaptation that you are likely to see when you attend a performance of *Boris*.

On February 26, 1928, Mussorgsky's original and unedited score was revived at the Bolshoi Theater. A year and a half later American audiences had an opportunity to acquaint themselves with it when Leopold Stokowski and the Philadelphia Orchestra presented it in a concert version. But though critical opinion was agreed that, as originally conceived, *Boris Godunov* had an elemental power and a dramatic impact which were negated by Rimsky-Korsakov's refinements, Mussorgsky's original version has returned to its earlier obscurity, and the Rimsky-Korsakov version continues to be heard.

Orchestral Music. The orchestral fantasy *A Night on Bald Mountain* (which Rimsky-Korsakov completed, edited, and orchestrated) is a musical picture of the Witches' Sabbath which, according to Russian legend, takes place on Bald Mountain near Kiev at the stroke of midnight on St. John's Eve. The printed score contains the following program: "A subterranean din of unearthly voices. Appearance of the Spirits of Darkness, followed by that of Tchernobog, the Black God. The Black Mass. The Revelry of the Witches' Sabbath, interrupted from afar by the bell of a little church, whereupon the spirits of evil disperse. Dawn breaks."

An eerie, supernatural atmosphere is immediately created by quivering violins (in the upper register), cries by the woodwinds, and a loud and somber theme in the trombones and bassoons. Soon there comes a Russian dance in the violins and clarinets, first soft and light-footed, then growing in intensity until the orchestra becomes a riot of rhythm and color. The excitement spends itself; a quieter mood prevails. Against murmuring strings there arises a delicate dance melody in the woodwinds. But the passions are once again aroused. We hear a veritable dance orgy. The madness stops short suddenly. Soft bells toll; it is the voice of the church. The violins chant a poignant strain. A pastoral tune follows in the clarinet, heralding the dawn. Peace and serenity return to Bald Mountain.

Pictures at an Exhibition was written as a suite for the piano. It is sometimes heard in this form at piano recitals (there is an excellent recording by Vladimir Horowitz for RCA Victor). But the work is most familiar to concertgoers as an orchestral composition. Many fine transcriptions exist, but the one generally regarded as the best (and the one most likely to be heard) was made by Maurice Ravel on a commission from the conductor, Serge Koussevitzky.

The work was the result of a posthumous exhibition of paintings by Mussorgsky's dear friend Victor Hartmann, which took place in St.

Petersburg in 1874. The various sections are tonal representations of different Hartmann paintings as seen through the eyes of the composer. The work begins with the "Promenade," showing Mussorgsky walking through the halls of an exhibition. The "Promenade" is a broad Russian melody—for the brass in the Ravel transcription. The strings join in, at which moment the composer stops at the first picture: "Gnomes." The deformed little creature (it is said this picture was intended by the artist as a decorative design for a toy nutcracker) is recreated in hesitant rhythms. The "Promenade" theme returns briefly, slower and more subdued. The composer pauses before "The Old Castle." A beautiful melody appears first in the bassoon, then in saxophone, against strings; it evokes a picture of a medieval castle. Once again the "Promenade" theme is heard (in trumpet, then trombone and tuba), bringing the visitor to a picture of the "Tuileries," the famous gardens of Paris; music of light texture, with gay rhythms, describes the children at their play and possibly their nurses in gossip. We progress immediately to the next picture, "Bydlo," a Polish oxcart. The robust but halting rhythm for solo tuba suggests the awkward movement of the cart. The "Promenade" in a minor key brings on "The Ballet of the Unhatched Chickens." This capricious design for a stage setting inspired Mussorgsky to produce some of his most realistic and witty writing, as the chirping and the moving of the little chickens in their shells are recreated with brilliant effects. "Samuel Goldenberg and Schmuyle" is a portrait of two Polish Jews (without anti-Semitic malice), one rich and powerful, the other poor. Goldenberg appears in a pompous progression in the basses; Schmuyle in an abrupt subject for muted trumpets. The themes are combined as the two men enter upon a heated discussion. Realism returns in "The Market Place at Limoges," as the gossiping of housewives doing their shopping is suggested in fluttering thematic phrases and leaping rhythms. The "Promenade" theme becomes somber, heavy, with a touch of the ecclesiastical, in the "Catacombs." But lightness returns in "A Hut on Fowl's Legs," with ideas strongly suggesting Russian folk songs. The music reaches toward a grandiose climax in the concluding portrait, "The Great Gate at Kiev" (a monument Hartmann had planned in the city of Kiev). With luxuriant orchestration, punctuated by the tolling of bells, a sonorous and majestic ending is promulgated.

Khovantschina, successor to Boris Godunov, is represented on the stage only in rare revivals. But two orchestral excerpts are part of the symphonic repertory. The first is the Prelude to Act I, a landscape pic-

ture which Mussorgsky entitled "Dawn on the Moskva River." We get
a nostalgic picture of early dawn in Moscow. The prelude begins with a
beautiful and intensely national melody which is then given five variations. These variations were intended (in the opinion of Oskar Riesemann) to reproduce the tendency of Russian singers to vary the melody
of their song with each succeeding stanza. The second orchestral excerpt is the Entr'acte, heard before Act IV, Scene 2. This, too, is a landscape—this time of the bleak and vast expanses of the Siberian plains.
The principal melody of the Entr'acte is a funereal song for solo
trumpet and violins which comes immediately after quivering, dirgelike
introductory phrases in the doublebasses, cellos, and bassoons.

Vocal Music. Mussorgsky was one of Russia's greatest composers of
songs. Unorthodox in all things, he could be expected to be unconventional as a song writer. Unlike most other song composers, he avoided
romantic subjects such as love and nature. In his music the emphasis
was never on lyricism. The goal of patterning the melodic line after the
inflections of speech is as evident in his songs as in his operas. Most of
his songs are declamations, declamations of great strength and impact.
The text was the thing. To meet the needs of the word, Mussorgsky
utilized unusual rhythms, changing meters, abrupt modulations, distorted harmonies, and strange cadences. The result is a product far different from, say, the songs of Schubert and Brahms; but that does not
mean that the effect is less great.

There are many different veins in Mussorgsky's songs. His flair for
satire, irony, and wit is evident in many of them. American audiences
are probably most familiar with a gem such as "Song of the Flea" (from
Goethe's *Faust*), with its mocking criticism of aristocracy. His satire
grows knife-edged in such songs as "Gathering Mushrooms" and
"Pride." There are realistic songs, too, such as "The Love Song of an
Idiot" and "The Goat"; simple folk songs, as in the treasurable cycle of
childhood days, *Nursery Songs;* dramatic songs such as the four *Songs
and Dances of Death;* and sensitive, delicate songs such as the *Sunless*
cycle.

Jacques Offenbach

"The Mozart of Champs-Elysées."
—Rossini

BORN: Cologne, Germany, June 20, 1819.
DIED: Paris, October 4, 1880.
MAJOR WORKS: *Operas*—The Tales of Hoffmann. ALSO: Orpheus in the Underworld, La Belle Hélène, La Vie parisienne, comic operas.

HIS LIFE

Hᴵˢᵀᴼᴿʸ, partial as it is to repetition and coincidence, must have smiled pleasurably each time the operatic idol of Paris, Giacomo Meyerbeer, stepped into his second-row seat in Offenbach's Bouffes Parisiens to attend a performance of an Offenbach operetta. And it must have chuckled at the fitness of things when an operetta such as Offenbach's *Ba-ta-clan* mocked at Meyerbeer's pretentious style. For the careers of Meyerbeer and Offenbach followed a single pattern. Both were German by birth. Both were Jews. Both had come to Paris young and unknown, their destinies still to be decided. Both made assumed names immortal. Both were to become symbolic of French music in the nineteenth century: Meyerbeer as one of the first great figures in the evolution of French grand opera, Offenbach as one of the creators of the French operetta.

Offenbach's father, a synagogue cantor named Isaac Judah Eberst, had come from the city of Offenbach. So often was he referred to as "Isaac der Offenbacher" that one day he decided to assume the name of "Offenbach." He married and settled in the Jewish quarter of Cologne, where he taught singing and various instruments, wrote some religious tracts, and tried creating poetry. Later he filled the post of cantor in one of Cologne's synagogues.

His seventh child, and second son, early showed that he would carry on the musical traditions of the family. When Jacques was six he started studying the violin, and at eight he began to write little songs. He had to study the cello secretly because his parents thought that instrument too strenuous for a child of delicate health. One day he startled his family by filling the cello seat in a family performance of a Haydn quartet when the regular cellist failed to make an appearance. From then on he concentrated on the cello. He also became a member of a family trio which went from one restaurant to another, and to the various cafés, giving impromptu concerts.

The cantor recognized that his son was meant for a future more important than that of café musician. He therefore took him to Paris to enter him in the Conservatory. But that august institution had a rule against foreigners; only a decade earlier it had denied admittance to the prodigy Franz Liszt for that very reason. But the cantor would not accept this decision as final. He badgered Cherubini, the director, at least to listen to Jacques; possibly to get rid of the persistent man, Cherubini consented. Jacques played a difficult work at sight with such fluency and self-assurance that Cherubini admitted the boy to the Conservatory.

The cantor's stout effort to get his son into the Conservatory was unfortunately misspent. Jacques was not happy there, avoided his classes, and after a single year left the Conservatory for good. He found employment in the orchestra of the Opéra Comique. An uncontrollable disposition for pranks brought him into frequent trouble with the authorities, who imposed so many fines on him that he often drew no salary whatsoever. During this period he continued his studies privately: the cello with Norblin and composition with Jacques Halévy, composer of *La Juive*. He did some composing, mostly popular dances. The first of these, a waltz entitled *Rebecca*, attracted unfavorable criticism from *Le Ménestral* because it adapted a synagogical melody for popular usage. "Why is it absolutely necessary to burlesque melodies sanctified by religious observance in a wanton waltz?" the critic inquired. "Nowadays it is necessary at all costs to be original."

He gave up the orchestra post to further his career both as cello virtuoso and as composer. For a while he did much better as performer than creator. He played in fashionable *salons,* then began concertizing publicly and with ever increasing success. But his popular pieces did not make much of an impression, while some music he wrote for a variety entertainment at the Palais Royale was a fiasco.

In 1850 Offenbach became the musical director of the Comédie française, a post he held for five years. "It was then that the idea came to me of starting a musical theater myself, because of the continued impossibility of getting my work produced by anybody else," he noted in an autobiographical fragment. "I said to myself that the Opéra Comique was no longer the home of comic opera, and that the idea of really gay, cheerful, witty music—in short, the idea of music with life in it—was gradually being forgotten." He had already given some evidence of his capacity to write in a witty and satirical vein. In 1846 he had written a broad burlesque on a symphonic ode of Félicien David which glorified the desert and which had achieved quite a vogue in Paris that year. Offenbach's satire, which was privately presented in a *salon,* sent the audience into guffaws. But others, more in a position to further his career, were far less appreciative of his gifts. His indefatigable attempts to get a hearing at the Opéra Comique came to naught; managers of the leading musical theaters were inaccessible.

The dream of starting his own theater was realized in 1855 with the Bouffes Parisiens. The theater opened on the evening of July 5, 1855, with a musical entertainment that included a satire on beggars, *Les deux aveugles,* text by Jules Moinaux, music by Offenbach. The piece caught the fancy of the Paris public; it became the rage of the season. Offenbach began writing numerous other satirical pieces—he completed more than twenty-five farces, satires, and *bouffonneries* within the next three years! It was due to their immense popularity that the Bouffes Parisiens became an institution in Paris, the first place to go when one visited Paris.

Offenbach's fame grew by leaps and bounds. His music was sung in the streets and played at the opera balls. He was the favorite son of the boulevards. His melodies—one might even say, his pince-nez, side whiskers, and dapper and vividly colored clothing—were symbolic of Paris of the Second Empire. It was a period of political repression, censorship, and infringment on personal liberties. The secret police penetrated into the private lives of citizens to uncover and report any visible signs of discontent. It was the better part of valor to avoid politics and to concern oneself with less dangerous pastimes: love, petty gossip, dancing, the good life. The pursuit of pleasure was a passion encouraged by the ruling powers. The courtesan occupied a place of dignity in the life of the *grand monde.* The Parisian of the Second Empire made a fetish of luxurious living, aping the splendor of the Emperor Napoleon III and the Empress Eugénie. The Parisian wanted to laugh, be amused, to flee from anything that approached the serious and the controversial. The theater, that sensitive social barometer, reflected these existing tendencies. Taking the lead of court entertainments, which set the standard for lavishness and frivolity, the theater went in for gaiety, levity, tongue-in-cheek mockery.

The period found its own reflection in Offenbach's operettas. The lighthearted vivacity of his melodies was the pulse and beat of the Second Empire. The satirical texts—now mocking at pretentions and attitudes, whether those of Meyerbeer or those of rulers; now chuckling at petty intrigues, whether amatory or political—provided their audiences with a convenient safety valve for pent-up steam.

In 1858 Offenbach's triumphs had pyramided into *Orpheus in the Underworld,* the greatest of his operettas. *Orpheus* was not an immediate success—most of the audience and critics found little amusement in a satire about Olympian gods—and it might soon have been relegated to Offenbach's less happy ventures. But destiny intervened. Destiny assumed the form of Jules Janin, a powerful critic, who suddenly hurled a Jovian critical thunderbolt at the operetta. He accused *Orpheus* of blasphemy; it was, as he piously put it, "a profanation of holy and glorious antiquity." The vehemence of his attack piqued the curiosity of a sensation-loving public. It had to flock to the Bouffes Parisiens to see for itself what had motivated the criticism. Before long the operetta was selling out at each performance. It became the thing to see, to discuss, to quote, and to dance to. In short, it was the vogue. People began boasting of the number of times they had seen it. The Offenbach melodies—the waltzes, galops, quadrilles—were heard and played everywhere. And the exciting and naughty cancan—that audacious dance that mocked at the pretentions of an entire era—became a veritable disease. *Orpheus* could have run indefinitely to capacity audiences. Only the fatigue of the performers closed the operetta after 228 performances.

The success of *Orpheus* brought Offenbach great personal rewards. Largely due to that operetta, his application for French citizenship was finally endorsed and the ribbon of the Legion of Honor was bestowed upon him. It brought him wealth as well as fame. He bought a beautiful summer villa, appropriately entitled Villa d'Orphée. His lavish entertaining at the rue Lafitte became the talk of social Paris.

By 1861 Offenbach had given up his own theater. He kept on writing new operettas for other managers, with no decline either in quality or success. *La Belle Hélène* came in 1864, *Barbe-Bleue* and *La Vie parisienne* in 1866, *La Périchole* in 1868.

But after 1870 Offenbach's success began to disintegrate, even as did the Second Empire itself. In 1872, in an effort to revive the glory of the Bouffes Parisiens, he took over the direction of the Gaîté Theater. He spent money recklessly on his productions, and after being involved in several disastrous failures, was faced with overwhelming deficits. He needed most of all another *Orpheus in the Underworld* to rehabilitate his fortune. But both he and the times were incapable of realizing another *Orpheus*. Two lavish pantomimes on texts by Sardou were an unsatisfactory substitute. The theater went into bankruptcy and the company had to be liquidated. In May 1875 Offenbach called his company together, explained the situation, and said sadly, "You will be paid to the very last sou, my children. I may have been careless, but I am not dishonorable." As a partial payment of his debts, he allocated all his property and his royalties for the next three years to his creditors. The rest of his debts would be paid from the proceeds of an American tour.

During that American visit, which took place in the spring of 1876, Offenbach conducted semipopular orchestral concerts at Gilmore's Gardens in New York and at the Philadelphia Centennial Exposition. His own music, and his personality, dominated these affairs. For Offenbach was not much less popular in America than he was in Paris, London, or Vienna. Several of his operettas had been successfully produced in New York. His melodies were known everywhere. His visit was, consequently, a personal triumph—and the last he was to experience.

"In France I became Offenbach again." Such was the concluding line of his impressions of the American trip. But he was the old Offenbach no more. Physically he was a sick and wasted man. He sensed that he did not have long to live. For the first time he regretted having wasted his time and talent on the frivolities of operetta. If he continued writing operettas, it was only because he needed money. The old verve, the old joy were gone—and for these reasons, no doubt, his operettas were not successful. Only a single ambition was left: to write a serious opera and to see that opera produced.

He led the life of a recluse as he worked on his first—and his last—serious work, *The Tales of Hoffmann*. He completed it; only his will seemed to sustain him. "There is nothing left of him," his physician said. "His body is completely exhausted." Turning his score over to the director of the Opéra Comique, who had accepted it, Offenbach urged that the performance take place without delay. "I have not much time left," he added quietly. But as production difficulties delayed the *première,* it became apparent that Offenbach would lose his race with death. He was dying and he knew it. One day his friends helped him to get to the Opéra Comique so that he might, at least, hear parts of his opera rehearsed.

He did not live to hear his opera. While glancing through the manuscript of his opera, on October 4, 1880, he had a fatal attack of suffocation. Four months later the *première* of *The Tales of Hoffmann* was one of the great events, and one of the great successes, of the musical season.

HIS MUSIC

THE GENIUS of the French operetta, a form and a tradition which Offenbach helped to establish, need not concern us in these pages. The operettas, for all their melodic delights and exquisite subtleties of wit and satire, belong in the theater rather than the opera house; their delightful overtures, even that of *Orpheus in the Underworld,* are for the repertory of *salon* ensembles rather than symphony orchestras.

But, like the proverbial comedian whose life's ambition it is to act in *Hamlet,* Offenbach always aspired to produce a serious work of art. He did realize that ambition in the last years of his life and with his very last work—realized it with such complete success that it became apparent that had he chosen to dedicate himself to the opera, instead of to the operetta, he would have been one of its truly great practitioners. *The Tales of Hoffmann* had no historic role to play in the evolution of opera. But it is a work of imagination and originality, a source of some wonderful music—a justified bid for immortality.

ANALYTICAL NOTES

Opera. *The Tales of Hoffmann* is an adaptation by Jules Barbier and Michel Carré of several of the eerie and fantastic tales of E. T. A. Hoffmann. Each of the three acts concerns one of Hoffmann's bizarre love affairs. The first is with Olympia, a mechanical doll; the second, with Giulietta, the dupe of a magician; the third, with Antonia, victim of consumption, who sings herself to death. The entire play is set in a strange, half-real world which—to be artistically valid—calls for music of the utmost grace, refinement, lightness of touch, and fantasy. Offenbach, genius of the operetta, was not out of his element in undertaking this assignment. The "Mozart of the Champs Elysées" was able to produce sensitive and diaphanous music which was completely in the spirit of the fantastic play.

There are only a few bars of orchestral prelude. In the prologue that precedes the first act, the poet Hoffmann is in the taproom of a Nuremburg tavern. He tells a group of students that, as a result of three disastrous episodes, he is through with love for good. He then proceeds to tell his friends the story of each affair.

The first act takes place in the drawing room of the scientist Spalanzani. Spalanzani and his friend Coppelius have created a mechanical doll, Olympia, which seems so human that Hoffmann, from a distance, falls in love with her. When Hoffmann comes to pay court to her, the doll sings him a beautiful song, *"Les Oiseaux dans la charmille"* (better known as "The Doll Song"). More in love with her than ever, Hoffmann dances deliriously with her, only to learn at last, and with broken heart, that she is not real.

The second act, which takes place in the gallery of Giulietta's palace in Venice, opens with one of the most celebrated pages in all opera, the "Barcarolle" (*"Belle nuit, O nuit d'amour"*), sung as a duet by Giulietta and Hoffmann's friend Nicklausse. Hoffmann falls in love with Giulietta without knowing that she is the victim of a magician, to whom she returns while taunting Hoffmann for his advances.

Hoffmann's last love, Antonia, is the theme of the third act. Antonia is suffering from consumption and must never sing again. But by conjuring the ghost of Antonia's mother, a magician contrives to get Antonia to sing for the last time. Her song, one of the most poignant arias in the opera, is *"Elle a fui la tourterelle."* Antonia dies in her father's arms, to Hoffmann's great grief.

There is an epilogue: we are back in the taproom of a tavern in Nuremburg; the students leave after hearing Hoffmann's tales; the Muse of Art comes to console the poet; Hoffmann then falls dead.

Niccolò Paganini

"Paganini is one of those artists of whom it must be said: 'They are because they are and not because others were before them.' "

—*Berlioz*

BORN: Genoa, October 27, 1782.
DIED: Nice, Sardinia (now France), May 27, 1840.
MAJOR WORKS: *Orchestral Music*—Concerto in D major, for violin and orchestra. *Violin Music*—24 caprices. ALSO: Witch's Dance, Perpetual Motion, Carnival of Venice, for violin and piano; La Campanella (second movement of Concerto in B minor, for violin and orchestra).

HIS LIFE

WHETHER or not Niccolò Paganini was the greatest violin virtuoso of all time, a statement that appears repeatedly in his biographies, he was certainly the most adulated musical performer of his generation. Franz Schubert, hearing Paganini at a concert, exclaimed, "I have heard an angel sing." Rossini was in awe of him. Meyerbeer followed him from one recital to another, sometimes from one city to another, unable to get enough of Paganini's playing. Castelli, a Viennese dramatist, described him as the "God of the violin." Berlioz considered him "unique in his kind."

He was not only the toast of all Europe. He was a legend in his own time. His fabulous technical command of his instrument was no legend, however. Nor was it legend that no audience on the face of Europe failed to succumb to a kind of spell in the presence of his musical exploits and his personal dynamism. He had acquired permanent possession of his Guarnerius violin after borrowing it for a single concert;

the lender begged Paganini to keep it, as it would have been sacrilegious for anybody else to put a finger on it after Paganini. He won his equally treasured Stradivarius violin in a wager, by playing a technical piece of music at sight which musicians insisted nobody could perform even after preparation.

Not only his playing, but also his cadaverous appearance on the stage, aroused terror and awe. His pale, long-drawn face with its hollow cheeks, his thin lips that seemed to curl into a sardonic smile, and the piercing expression of his eyes (which were like flaming coals) gave him a diabolic appearance. The rumor was circulated that he was a son of the devil. Some people crossed themselves if they were accidentally touched by him. At one time Paganini was forced to publish letters of his mother to prove that he had had human parents! The word was then spread that the G string of his violin was made from the intestines of a murdered mistress. At any rate, he aroused fear as well as adulation. In Paris he was called Cagliostro. The Irish circulated the report that he had reached their land on the legendary *Flying Dutchman*. In Prague they referred to him as the original "wandering Jew."

But despite his diabolical appearance and the suspicions about his origins, he was worshiped wherever he came. *"Paganini fara sentire il suo violino,"* was an announcement calculated to bring shudders of anticipatory delight in all parts of Europe. Women pursued him; his name was often linked with amatory adventures in high places. "I am neither young nor handsome," he said when he was at the height of his fame. "On the contrary, I am very ugly. But when women hear my music, my melting tones, they begin weeping and then I become their idol, and they lie at my feet."

Paganini's father, who worked in a shipping firm in Genoa, raised his son to be a genius. Despite a frail constitution, weakened by an early attack of measles that almost proved fatal, Niccolò was subjected to a severe regimen and relentless discipline. The father, aware that he had a prodigy on his hands and eager to capitalize on this development, kept the boy at his practicing with a rod that was seldom spared. The child made phenomenal progress under his teachers, Giovanni Servetto and Giacomo Costa. When he was eight, he played a Pleyel Concerto in a Genoa church with such success that he was thenceforth in great demand for local social functions. At nine, he made an official debut in a Genoa concert auditorium, introducing his own taxing variations, *La Carmagnole*. By the time he was thirteen, he was known throughout his native city as the "wonderchild."

Some additional study took place in Leghorn with Ferdinando Paër, and in Parma with Alessandro Rolla, after which Paganini undertook his first extended concert tour. He played in most of the large cities of Lombardy to ever increasing acclaim, particularly for renditions of his own highly intricate and electrifying pieces. Later he would devote his concerts exclusively to his own music and transcriptions.

His mounting success and financial independence made him break forever the tyrannical hold that his father had had on him. Seventeen years old, completely self-assured, aware of his native gifts, Paganini was on his own. Freed for the first time of supervision, he began giving free rein to two passions—women and gambling—to which he was thenceforth to be addicted.

He disappeared from the public eye at about the turn of the century. It is generally believed that he became the lover of a proud Tuscan noble lady and that for a few years he lived with her at her château. He appears to have abandoned the violin temporarily, concentrating his virtuoso and creative gifts on the guitar. But after three years he returned to Genoa—and to the violin. He studied, played, and composed with renewed industry. In 1805 he reappeared on the concert stage, and from 1805-13 he combined concert work with filling a Kapellmeister post for the Princess of Lucca.

He had enjoyed great success up to this time; but it was only a suggestion of the triumphs yet to come. The story is told that at a concert in Leghorn a series of mishaps threatened to make a fiasco of his performance. When a string of his violin snapped in an intricate passage, the audience began expressing derision. But when Paganini continued playing the piece on three strings instead of four, the derision turned to wonder and awe. The incident taught Paganini a lesson in virtuoso-audience relationship that he never forgot. Thenceforth, to win enthusiasm, he would not hesitate to resort to trickery and device. It was believed that he often used worn strings so that he might complete his performance on three, even two, strings when some of them snapped. In any case, the breaking of strings was not an infrequent accident with him. The trick of playing on less than four strings soon gave him the idea of writing works entirely for a single string, such as his exciting *Fantasia on the G String* (after Rossini's *Mosè in Egitto*).

With a concert appearance in Milan in 1813, he emerged as the greatest violinist of his day and the most worshiped. So sensational was this performance that he was compelled to give thirty-six more concerts. For the next decade and a half he confined his appearances to Italy. His increasingly bad health—he was suffering from cancer—compelled him to take frequent rest cures and made him hesitant to leave his country on long and trying voyages. But within Italy his fame achieved fabulous proportions. It was at this time that Meyerbeer followed him wherever he played. "Where our powers of thought end, there Paganini begins," he said. "Imagine the most astounding effects that can be produced from a violin, and dream of the most extravagant prodigies that can be performed with the bow and with melody. Paganini knows how to surpass all your imaginings with his realities."

When Paganini finally left his country to perform in other parts of Europe, he was a myth coming to life. Anticipation for his appearances achieved new heights. His first stop was Vienna, in 1828, and at his first concert (on March 28) "the audience was hypnotized," as the *Theatrezeitung* reported. "Never has an artist caused such a great sensation within our walls." For the next few weeks, people spoke of nothing but Paganini. The Viennese poet Grillparzer wrote a rhapsody in his honor. Pretzels, rolls, sweets, and gloves were named after him. A good billiard shot became a "Paganini coup." The Theatre-an-der-Wien presented a theatrical piece inspired by him.

Other music centers in Europe followed the lead of Vienna in his worship. First he performed extensively throughout Germany. Robert Schumann wrote: "Paganini is the turning point in the history of virtuosity." "One takes fright, one laughs, one is reduced to despair over the most hazardous tricks of technique," Karl Friedrich Zelter wrote to Goethe after hearing Paganini in Berlin. In 1831 Paganini arrived in Paris, preceded not only by glowing reports of his triumphs but also by rumors, both true and false, about his personal conduct. He dispatched a fiery letter to *La Revue musicale* denying (1) that he had spent eight years in prison, (2) that he had murdered his mistress, and (3) that whenever he played the devil stood at his elbow to direct him. Then he settled down to the business of giving concerts and unleashing a whirlwind of homage and adulation. "What a man! What a violin! What an artist! Heavens!" gasped Franz Liszt, who suddenly found for himself a new goal. Rossini was quoted as saying, "I wept only three times in my life. The first time was when my earliest opera failed. The second time was at a boating party when a truffled turkey fell into the water. The third time was when I first heard Paganini play."

It did not seem possible, but England and Scotland outdid even Vienna and Paris in acclaiming him. His tour there netted him the equivalent of $85,000, the largest sum that any performing artist had earned up to this time on a single trip. Henry Chorley, one of England's leading critics wrote: "Paganini is a solitary man in his art."

Back in Italy, he purchased a beautiful estate near Parma. Although suffering increasingly from poor health, he continued to make concert appearances. He amassed a fortune, but lost some of it in a regrettable investment in a fashionable Paris gambling house named "Casino Paganini." Worry and heartbreak over this reverse affected his health seriously. He suffered from intense weariness. He started coughing. By 1838 he had lost his voice completely. He went to Nice for a rest cure —but he neither rested nor was cured. In the last hours of his life he improvised feverishly on his violin, defying his rapidly waning strength.

Because he had refused to accept the final sacrament, Paganini's body lay for a long time in its coffin, first in Nice and then at Villefranche, before being allowed burial in holy ground. The townspeople of Nice and Villefranche used to say that every night they heard the sounds of a ghostly violin emanating from that coffin. Legend followed Paganini until the very end.

HIS MUSIC

PAGANINI intended his music primarily as a showcase for his phenomenal technique. It is filled with the most dazzling and electrifying effects, in which technical complexity is glorified for its own sake without much regard for sound musical values. His pieces present charming melodic ideas and effective harmonies which have been praised by such composers as Berlioz and Schumann. But the interest is largely centered on pyrotechnics. The digital feats called for by this music make the severest demands on the virtuosity of a performer. But when Paganini's music is played well, it has sure-fire audience appeal.

His greatest importance rests in his extension of the horizons of violin technique. No one before him resorted so extensively—and with such variety and brilliance—to harmonics, simultaneous pizzicato and bow passages, double and triple stops, variety of bowing, passages in tenths, and so forth. Suddenly the violin realized colors, dynamics, and effects it had not possessed before; and music for the violin appears to have acquired a set of wings capable of soaring to formerly inaccessible stratospheres. Indeed, modern violin technique can be said to have originated with Paganini. He made possible the writing of the great violin concertos of the nineteenth century as well as the production of Romantic and modern literature for the violin.

ANALYTICAL NOTES

Orchestral Music. The *Concerto in D major* is the only one of Paganini's three concertos to survive. Of the other two, only a single excerpt is heard: the Rondo à la clochette movement of the *Concerto in B minor;* this movement, better known as *La Campanella* (named after the bell-like effects of the music), is performed either as a violin solo or as a transcription for piano by Franz Liszt.

The first movement of the *Concerto in D major,* while in the traditional sonata form, is a kind of a fantasia in which ideas are presented episodically and then worked out with bravura passages for the solo violin. It begins with an extended orchestral introduction that is spirited, tuneful, and infectious in the vein of Rossini. In this introduction the main melody of the entire movement is heard in the strings, a beautiful, expansive flight of lyricism almost operatic in character. When the orchestral introduction ends, the solo violin enters with a bold declamation, then proceeds on technical exploits before taking over the main melody. The entire movement alternates between bravura writing and pleasing Italian lyricism.

The slow movement is believed to have been inspired by the acting of the Italian tragedian Demarini in an emotionally wrought scene in which, as a prisoner, he falls on his knees and prays to God to end his life. A dramatic orchestral introduction precedes the entrance of the solo instrument in a deeply moving and highly emotional melody. The finale is an excursion in gaiety and good spirits, and once again calls for the fullest resources of violin virtuosity.

Most frequently, the concerto is heard in the adaptations of either August Wilhelmj or Fritz Kreisler. In these versions only the first movement is presented. The material of this movement is telescoped and the orchestration modernized. But there has been an increasing tendency on the part of many violinists—notably Yehudi Menuhin and Zino Francescatti—to present the concerto as Paganini wrote it.

Violin Music. The twenty-four Caprices for unaccompanied violin comprise Paganini's magnum opus. The collection has been aptly described as a lexicon of the Paganini technique. A caprice (in the present-day meaning of the term) is a short piece of instrumental music, often in quick tempo, which goes in for surprises or whimsical effects of rhythm, modulation, dynamics, color, and so forth. Paganini conceived the caprice as an exercise for solo violins; each piece utilizes a recurrent melodic motive which is allowed freedom of growth within a flexible form. His caprices traverse the techniques of arpeggios, tremolo, staccato, octave passages, double and triple stops, harmonics, double-stop trills, and so forth. But musical interest is not sacrificed. These caprices contain so much "fantasy and poetical romance" that their aesthetic value is no less than their pedagogic value. Brahms esteemed them so highly that he was led to the excessive statement that "Paganini's genius for composition was fully equal to his genius for the instrument."

Among the most often heard are: *Caprice No. 9,* in E major, called *"La Chasse"* because of its hunting theme in double stops; *Caprice No. 13,* in B-flat major, sometimes referred to as *"Le Rire du diable"* due to its mocking descending theme which some imaginative listeners interpreted as a devil's chuckle; and *Caprice No. 24,* in A minor, a theme and variations. The last is particularly celebrated, in its own right and also because its theme provided the subject for Brahms's *Variations on a Theme of Paganini* and Rachmaninoff's *Rhapsody on a Theme of Paganini.*

Robert Schumann and Franz Liszt transcribed some of these caprices for piano, while several other composers (including a contemporary Italian named Mario Pilati) have provided them with piano accompaniment.

Serge Prokofiev

"Prokofiev's creative work is among the most original and valuable which the Russian art of this century has produced."
—*Leonid Sabaneyev*

BORN: Ekaterinoslav, Ukraine, April 23, 1891.
DIED: Moscow, March 4, 1953.
MAJOR WORKS: *Orchestral Music*—Classical Symphony; Symphony No. 5; Symphony No. 6; Concerto No. 3 for Piano and Orchestra; Concerto No. 1 for Violin and Orchestra; Peter and the Wolf; Lieutenant Kije. *Choral Music*—Alexander Nevsky, cantata. ALSO: The Love for Three Oranges, War and Peace, operas; On Guard for Peace, oratorio; The Age of Steel, L'Enfant prodigue, Romeo and Juliet, Cinderella, Stone Flower, ballets; Symphonies Nos. 2, 3, 4, 7; Concertos Nos. 1, 2, 4, 5 for Piano and Orchestra; Concerto No. 2 for Violin and Orchestra; Concerto for Cello and Orchestra; Scythian Suite; Overture on Hebrew Themes, for clarinet, string quartet, and piano; 3 sonatas for violin and piano; 2 string quartets; 8 sonatas, Visions fugitives, Sarcasmes, Suggestion diabolique, for piano.

HIS LIFE

PROKOFIEV's position in Soviet music changed several times between 1917 and his death in 1953. He left his native land a half year after the Bolshevik Revolution of October–November 1917. Until then he had associated himself closely with the new regime and was honored by it. Indeed, a "Prokofiev Week" was celebrated in Petrograd in 1918. In the same year Prokofiev expressed the wish to go to America on a concert tour. The People's Commissar gave his consent, saying, "You are a revolutionary in music and we are revolutionaries in life. We ought to work together. But I will not stand in your way." Prokofiev left Petrograd on May 7, 1918, ostensibly for a short absence. But he had no intention of returning.

But, in 1933, Prokofiev decided to go back. For some time he had become increasingly sympathetic to Soviet ideology. He had even written a ballet, entitled *The Age of Steel,* interpreting Soviet life. "I had not grasped the significance of what was happening in U.S.S.R.," he said at the time. "I did not realize that the events there demanded the collaboration of all citizens—not only men of politics, but art as well."

Having become a world figure in music, Prokofiev—the prodigal son —was welcomed home with open arms. He was, in word and deed, the true Sovietist. He expressed contempt for Western musical thought. ("The ordinary subject matter of the West now repels me.") He used his music to propagandize Soviet ideals and interpret Russian history and culture in Soviet terms. He became one of the leading composers of the land, the recipient of numerous public honors and government favors. And to the world outside the Soviet Union, he represented the fruition of the highest ideals of Soviet art.

At the height of his fame and creative powers, Prokofiev was suddenly, and without warning, hurled down from his seemingly unassailable position. On February 10, 1948, the Central Committee of the Communist Party announced the adoption of a new music policy. The motivation had been the *première* of *Great Friendship,* a new Soviet opera by Vano Muradeli (1908-   ), whose cacophony had aroused to anger many Communist officials, including Stalin himself. These officials, headed by A. A. Zhdanov, demanded a new orientation on the part of Soviet composers—away from modernism, or cerebralism, and toward a musical expression which was easily assimilable and which drew its styles and techniques from the Russian past. The public resolution of February 10 vigorously denounced some of the leaders in Soviet music—not only Prokofiev, but also Khatchaturian, Shostakovich, Nikolai Miaskovsky (1881-1950), and Vissarion Shebalin (1902-   ) —for "decadent tendencies" in their thinking. The official phrase, thenceforth to become a kind of battle cry in the press, was "decadent formalism." The thing condemned in these composers was (in the words of the resolution) "the negation of the basic principles of classical music; a sermon for atonality, dissonance, and disharmony, as if this were an expression of 'progress' and 'innovation.' "

The indictment against Prokofiev was specific: "Prokofiev's creative style was formed to a considerable extent during his years in the West, where the external novelty of his manner pleased the narrow, bourgeois circle of aesthetes, for whom he wrote his music. His musical language corresponded perfectly to the subject matter of his works at that time. Later, when he was confronted with the reality of Soviet thematics, there opened a break between his technical devices and the content of his music. The most vivid characteristics of Prokofiev's art are ridicule and grotesque. For that reason, Prokofiev was unable to reflect the greatness of our people. The unfeeling essence of his music is alien to our reality."

At a meeting of Soviet musicians in Moscow, one week after the indictment, Prokofiev hotly exclaimed to a fellow musician, "They should stick to politics, and leave music to musicians!" But it became increasingly evident that this new trend was not a passing one, but that it had become part of a new cultural attitude. Prokofiev, therefore, wrote a long and detailed apology to Tikhon Khrennikov (1913-   ), head of the General Assembly of Soviet composers: "Elements of formalism were peculiar to my music as long as fifteen or twenty years ago," he said with as much dignity as a groveling position would permit. "Apparently the infection was caught from contact with some Western ideas." He concluded that in all his future composition he intended taking a new direction: toward melody, simplicity, polyphony, and folk idioms. "In my new opera, *A Tale of a Real Man,* I intend to write trios, duets, and contrapuntally developed choruses for which I will make use of some interesting northern Russian folk songs. Lucid melody, and as far as possible, a simple harmonic language are elements which I intend to use in my opera."

However, *A Tale of a Real Man,* when completed, did not please the authorities. The opera was condemned by Khrennikov for its "modernistic and antimelodic style." Prokofiev had to make a more studied attempt to placate the powers. He wrote an oratorio, *On Guard for Peace,* which condemned the Western "warmongers" and sounded a hymn of praise to the Soviet "international peace movement." He also wrote a vocal-symphonic suite, *Winter Bonfire,* which (like the oratorio) adopted the realistic and pleasing style demanded by the new Soviet aesthetics.

Both of these works were responsible for bringing Prokofiev the Stalin Award in 1951. Obviously, his position was regained. To emphasize still further the return of Prokofiev to the good graces of the authorities, the government conducted a special concert of Prokofiev's music to celebrate his sixtieth birthday on April 23, 1951.

Prokofiev, too ill to attend the concert, heard the performance and the rousing demonstrations that followed over the radio.

His mother, a fine pianist, introduced him to music by playing for him continually when he was a child. His early experiences were described in an autobiographical article: "One day, when mother was practicing exercises by Hanon, I went up to the piano and asked if I could play my own music on the two highest octaves of the keyboard. To my surprise, she agreed, in spite of the resulting cacophony. This lured me to the piano. Soon I began climbing up to the keyboard all by myself and would try to pick out some little tune. One such tune I repeated several times, so that mother noticed it and decided to write it down.

"My efforts at that time consisted of either sitting down at the piano and making up tunes which I could not write down, or sitting at the table and drawing notes which could not be played. I just drew them like designs, like other children drew trains and people, because I was always seeing notes on the piano stand. One day, I brought out my papers covered with notes and said: 'Here, I've composed a Liszt rhapsody.' I was under the impression that a Liszt rhapsody was a double name of a composition like sonata-fantasia. Mother had to explain to me that I couldn't have composed a Liszt rhapsody because a rhapsody was a form of composition, and Liszt was the name of a composer who had written it. Furthermore, I learned that it was wrong to write music on a staff of nine lines without any divisions, and that it should be written on a five-line staff with division into measures. I was greatly impressed by the way in which mother wrote down my Indian Galop and soon, with her help, I learned something about how to write music. I couldn't always get my thoughts into notes, but I actually began to write down little songs which could be played."

By the time he was twelve years old, he had written the words and music of two operas (*The Giant,* performed privately by his cousins on an uncle's estate, and *The Feast During the Plague*), fragments of a third opera, a set of twelve piano pieces, a symphony for four hands, and sundry other items. He brought some of this music to Taneiev. "You must develop a more interesting harmony," Taneiev told him. "Too much of your music employs a tonic, dominant, and subdominant." But Taneiev recognized creative talent and advised Prokofiev to begin intensive study.

When Prokofiev was thirteen, he entered the St. Petersburg Conservatory. He remained there ten years, studying with Rimsky-Korsakov, Tcherepnin, and Liadov. He wrote numerous works, many of them ambitious in form and treatment. These included his first published works: *Piano Sonata No. 1* (Op. 1); *Four Etudes,* for piano (Op. 2); *Suggestion diabolique,* for piano (Op. 4); *Sinfonietta* (Op. 5); two choral works (Op. 7); two songs (Op. 9); *Concerto No. 1* for Piano and Orchestra (Op. 10); an opera, *Magdalene* (Op. 13); and *Ballade,* for cello and piano, (Op. 15).

Much of this music, written while he was still a student, had unorthodox chords, tonalities, and melodies. Some of his teachers were horrified at the kind of music he was writing. When the *Piano Concerto No. 1* was played for the first time, at a concert of the St. Petersburg Conservatory, Alexander Glazunov—professor and composer—cupped his hands over his ears to drown out the sounds. Then he could stand it no longer and fled from the hall. Even Taneiev—he who had once criticized Prokofiev for being too conventional—was shocked. "I have merely followed your advice, master," Prokofiev told him when the teacher grumbled at the boy's liberties. "I proceeded to develop a more interesting harmony—even as you had advised me."

The story is told that when an early scherzo for four bassoons by Prokofiev was introduced in Russia, the cacophony was so awful that a wit in the audience shouted, "Let's run for it. They are going to shoot." Maxim Gorky, hearing Prokofiev's song "The Ugly Duckling" remarked, "He must have written it about himself."

In the spring of 1914 Prokofiev was graduated with diplomas in composition, piano, and conducting. He also won the honored Rubinstein Prize for his Second Piano Concerto, though the more conservative professors objected violently to its advanced technique.

Soon after leaving the Conservatory, Prokofiev went on a holiday to London, where he met Diaghilev, impresario of the Ballet Russe. So impressed was Diaghilev by the young composer, that he commissioned him to write the music for a ballet. Meanwhile, World War I began in Europe. As the only son of a widow, Prokofiev was exempt from military service; he could devote himself to composition.

The ballet which Prokofiev was writing for Diaghilev was on the ancient race of the Scythians and their gods. Diaghilev did not like the theme; he felt it unsuitable for ballet treatment. Prokofiev was so taken with his subject that, as Diaghilev did not want it, he decided to write an orchestral suite around it. The *Scythian Suite* (*Ala and Lolly*) was heard for the first time in St. Petersburg, Prokofiev conducting, on January 29, 1916. Audience and critics alike were antagonistic to Prokofiev's modern style.

The *Scythian Suite* was responsible for a minor scandal in Moscow, involving the critic Leonid Sabaneyev. It had been scheduled for an earlier performance. But as the orchestra was not ready, the piece was postponed virtually at the last moment. Sabaneyev, however, did not know of the postponement, nor had he taken the trouble to attend the concert. Instead he wrote a violent review attacking the work. This review appeared in the newspapers the following morning, even though the Prokofiev work had not been played. The additional fact that the only copy of the score was in Prokofiev's hands provided proof that Sabaneyev could not possibly have known a note of the *Scythian Suite* when he wrote his review. This incident, which exposed the critic so cruelly, created a furor in Russian music circles and did much to aid the young composer's reputation.

If Diaghilev did not take to the theme of the Scythians, he did approve another subject which engaged Prokofiev at this time. In Russian folk lore, Prokofiev came upon a whimsical tale of a buffoon. He used it as a text for the ballet *Chout*. Because of the war, it was not produced at this time. But on May 17, 1921, the Ballet Russe introduced it in Paris with outstanding success.

Other important works were completed during this period, including two which are still regarded as fully representative of Prokofiev's maturity: the *Concerto No. 1* for Violin and Orchestra and the *Classical* Symphony.

Prokofiev was becoming increasingly impatient with the new regime in Russia and the restrictions it placed on the free creative spirit. The idea of undertaking an American tour, with funds provided by the publishing house of Serge Koussevitzky, presented a convenient avenue of escape. Prokofiev's American debut took place in New York City on November 20, 1918, in a piano recital featuring some of his own works. The critics liked his playing, but were intolerant of his modernism. His music was described by our critics as "Bolshevism in art" and "Russian chaos" and an "orgy of dissonant sounds." "If this is music," remarked one New York critic, "I am inclined to prefer agriculture." To another critic, Prokofiev's music "evoked visions of a charge of mammoths on some vast immemorial Asiatic plateau."

He was somewhat better received in Chicago. More important, he received an important commission there: Italo Campanini, impresario of the Chicago Opera, contracted for him to write a new opera for the company. Unfortunately, when Prokofiev finished his new opera—*The Love for Three Oranges*—Campanini found it too difficult to perform. Not until two years later, when Mary Garden took over the direction of the Chicago Opera, was it heard: on December 30, 1921. It was a failure and was never again heard in its entirety until November 1949, when it was successfully revived by the New York City Opera Company.

Prokofiev now made his home in Paris, leaving it each year for an extended period to make concert appearances in Europe and the United States. All this while he continued writing major works. The ballet *Le Pas d'acier* (*The Age of Steel*) was introduced in Paris by the Ballet Russe on June 8, 1927, and scored a triumph when performed in London. The Boston Symphony introduced his *Symphony No. 4*, written in 1930 to commemorate the fiftieth anniversary of that organization. The *Piano Concerto No. 5* was heard in Berlin, while two new ballets—*Le Fils prodigue* and *Sur le Borysthène*—were produced by the Ballet Russe and the Paris Opéra respectively.

And then Prokofiev decided to go home. From then on, his music was influenced by Soviet ideology and was written tailored for specific Soviet needs. For the films he wrote *Lieutenant Kije* and *Alexander Nevsky*—the first adapted into an orchestral suite, the latter revised and expanded into a cantata. For children, he wrote ingratiating songs and the symphonic fairy tale *Peter and the Wolf*.

When the Nazi hordes invaded the Soviet Union in 1941, Prokofiev was living in a suburb of Moscow working on the ballet *Cinderella*. Prokofiev immediately dedicated himself to the war effort, writing military marches and anti-fascist popular songs. "But soon events assumed such gigantic and far-reaching scope," he told an interviewer, "as to demand larger canvases." The *Symphonic Suite: 1941* was his first serious work to reflect the impact of the war. But works of greater importance and more ambitious stature followed. In 1942 came his *Piano Sonata No. 7*, sometimes known as the *Stalingrad* Sonata because its power and grandeur reflect the heroism that turned the tide of Stalingrad. With this sonata, Prokofiev won the Stalin Prize for the first time. Two years later came the *Symphony No. 5*, Prokofiev's return to the symphonic form after fourteen years. The symphony was extraordinarily successful both in the Soviet Union and the western world. But the most ambitious work born in those years of war was the opera *War and Peace*, a work of epical concept. In five acts, and utilizing sixty characters, the opera was of such proportions that it required two evenings for performance. The libretto, prepared by Myra Mendelson (who later became Prokofiev's second wife), was devoted exclusively to the Napoleonic invasion of Russia, a subject that had suddenly acquired new significance and meaning during World War II.

Prokofiev was a levelheaded, practical man, precise, punctual, and efficient. He looked and behaved like a successful American business man. His method of writing music (as reported in *Time* Magazine) provided an illuminating insight into his personality: "He composes with the cold matter-of-factness of a mathematician, and keeps stacks of copybooks in which he hoards themes for future compositions. He jumps from bed to jot one down; they occur to him while taking walks, and especially while riding trains. . . . When he has saved up enough scraps of melody, he works out an idea for a large composition to use them in. . . . He works regularly between the hours of ten and noon every day."

Prokofiev died in Moscow of a cerebral hemorrhage on March 5, 1953. His last major works included the Seventh Symphony, the Second Cello Concerto, and the ballet, *The Stone Flower*. The *première* of the ballet at the Bolshoi Theater on March 7, 1959, shattered the classical traditions of the company with the performance of a work so modern in style and idiom.

HIS MUSIC

PROKOFIEV himself provided us with an admirable analysis of his evolution as a composer and of his style, in the April 1941 issue of *Sovietskaya Musica:*

"The principal lines which I followed in my creative work are these: The first is classical. . . . It assumes a neoclassical aspect in the sonatas and concertos, or imitates the classical style of the eighteenth century as in the Gavottes, the *Classical* Symphony, and, in some respects, the Sinfonietta.

"The second is innovation, the inception of which I trace to my meeting with Taneiev, when he taunted me for my rather 'elementary harmony.' At first this innovation consisted in the search for an individual harmonic language, but later was transformed into a desire to find a medium for the expression of strong emotions as in the *Scythian Suite,* the *Symphony No. 2,* etc. . . . This innovating strain has affected not only the harmonic idiom, but also melodic inflection, orchestration, and stage technique.

"The third is the element of the toccata, or motor element, probably influenced by Schumann's Toccata, which impressed me greatly at one time. This element is probably the least important.

"The fourth element is lyrical. It appears at first as lyric meditation, sometimes unconnected with melodies . . . but sometimes is found in long melodic phrases, as in the opening of the First Violin Concerto. . . . This lyric strain has for long remained in obscurity, or, if it was noticed at all, then only in retrospection. And since my lyricism has for a long time been denied appreciation, it has grown but slowly. But at later stages I paid more and more attention to lyrical expression.

"I should like to limit myself to these four elements, and to regard the fifth element, that of the grotesque, which some critics try to foist on me, as merely a variation of the other characteristics. In application to my music, I should like to replace the word grotesque by 'Scherzo-ness,' or by three words, giving its gradations: 'jest,' 'laughter,' mockery.' "

ANALYTICAL NOTES

Orchestral Music. The *Classical* Symphony, Prokofiev's first symphony, was a conscious attempt on the part of the composer to write within the structural dimensions and with the self-imposed limitations of instrumentation of the eighteenth-century classical symphony of such a composer as Mozart; or, to put it another way, it was an attempt to approximate how Mozart would have written a symphony had he lived in the twentieth century. Each of the four movements is epigrammatic in its brevity, given to pellucid writing, old-world grace, and a bright-faced wit.

The main theme of the first movement is vivacious. It enters, without any preliminaries, in the strings. Also without ado, the second theme appears in the strings, a subject with quixotic two-octave leaps against an ingenuous bassoon accompaniment. Both the development and recapitulation are straightforward and unsophisticated.

A tender little tune in the strings, against an insistent accompaniment, starts the second movement. The woodwinds offer a subsidiary idea, but the main melody soon reappears after an unconventional and arresting modulation.

The third movement is a gavotte, in place of the minuet traditional with classical symphonies. But like the minuet, the gavotte is an old-world dance, full of courtly grace. Its spirited main theme is set forth vigorously; the dance melody moves forward with athletic stride. The middle part of the movement is in a more pastoral vein, with the theme first in the woodwinds, then in the strings. When the gavotte melody returns, it is played with delicacy.

A vigorous chord sets forth the main theme of the finale. The theme itself is played quietly and is fleet music with quicksilver mobility. Two more ideas appear, the first in the woodwinds and the second in solo flute.

The *Symphony No. 5*, in B-flat major, came twenty-six years after the *Classical* Symphony. Both works were written in periods of war. The *Classical* Symphony, born during World War I, can be regarded as an escape from the grim realities of war into the serenity of a remote past. There is no escape in the Fifth Symphony, child of World War II. The composer now comes into direct grips with the world around him. The music is intensely contemporary in spirit, form, and color. In the large sweep of its lyricism, in the power of its rhythmic momentum and sonorities, in the vibrancy of its orchestral and harmonic colors it is music expressing a period of crisis. But it emerges from that crisis proud of spirit and strong of flesh to become—as the composer said he intended—a testament of "the spirit of man."

The first movement has spaciousness of architectonic design to make room for expansive lyrical ideas. The two principal themes are marked by contrast of rhythm (the first is in triple time, the second in duple) as well as temper. Alternation between a subdued introspection and passionate struggle is prevalent throughout the movement. But the long and involved coda is in an exultant mood, and as the brilliant chord brings the movement to a close we realize that the spirit has triumphed.

The second movement has the character of a scherzo. In the first section the principal idea is passed from one woodwind instrument to the next. The middle part of the movement resembles the scherzo-trio, with the theme in the clarinet. When the opening section returns, it is subjected to variation.

The third movement is in a tragic vein. The melody that we hear at once in the woodwinds, and which is soon passed on to the strings, is intensely emotional. The gloom deepens, the tensions mount as the tragedy becomes uncontrolled. But a lighter section soon arrives to provide a welcome respite. The respite is brief, and the tragic mood is back with us.

The finale opens in a tranquil vein with a subject for divided cellos and basses. After this subject has been evolved fully, a second theme appears in the clarinet. Both ideas are then worked out at great length, frequently with animation and in the light vein that Prokofiev liked to refer to as "scherzoness." As the movement draws to its conclusion, the music becomes more and more agitated, even savage. The propulsion is not retarded until the eruption of the final brilliant chord.

The *Symphony No. 6,* in E-flat minor, was completed three years after the Fifth. It was heard for the first time in Moscow on October 10, 1947, just four months before the 1948 attack on Prokofiev by the Central Committee. After that attack the symphony was more or less officially proscribed.

The first movement was described by Prokofiev as "of agitated character . . . lyrical at times and austere at others." Its two themes are studies in contrasts. The first is in a fast dance rhythm; the second is slow and lyrical. Agitation comes in the development of these ideas, austerity in the transitional material to the second movement. The entire first movement has pronounced tragic implications. The second, designated by the composer as "brighter and full of song," is filled with ingratiating lyric ideas. Particularly interesting are a theme for horns and, later on, a soulful passage for the violins. The third movement, in a humorous, even satirical, attitude, has the character of a dance. But the gaiety is not sustained; midway there is a brief return to the somber feelings of the first movement.

Prokofiev wrote five concertos for piano and orchestra. The best of these—one of the finest of all his works—is the *Concerto No. 3,* in C major. It was written between the years of 1917 and 1921, but was the outgrowth of themes accumulated over a long period, one of them jotted down as far back as 1913.

There is a slow introduction, with its main idea in the clarinets, before the allegro part of the first movement emerges. When it does, the principal theme is heard at once in the piano. This theme is allowed extended treatment. Chords in the piano and a descending scale in the orchestra bring on the second theme, in the woodwinds, lighter in character and more expressive in feeling. The piano takes over, embellishes this second idea, and leads the way to a climax. Earlier material is now brought back with force and brilliance. An exciting crescendo brings an end to these activities.

The second movement consists of a theme (immediately stated by the orchestra) and five variations. Prokofiev himself analyzed these variations: "In the first . . . the piano treats the opening theme in quasi-sentimental fashion and resolves into a chain of trills, as the orchestra repeats the closing phrase. The tempo changes to allegro for the second and third variations, and the piano has brilliant figures, while snatches of the theme are introduced here and there in the orchestra. In Variation Four the tempo is once again andante, and the piano and orchestra discourse on the theme in a quiet and meditative fashion. Variation Five is energetic. . . . It leads without pause into a restatement of the theme by the orchestra, with delicate chordal embroidery in the piano."

A satiric subject for bassoon and plucked strings brings on the finale. The second theme is a long lyric passage for the woodwinds, to which the piano replies caustically. A development of these ideas leads to an increase of sonority and generation of motor power until the movement is brought to a conclusion with stirring effect.

The *Concerto No. 1,* in D major, for violin and orchestra, was completed in 1913. It opens with an expansive, gentle melody for the solo violin. The melody fully stated, there follow glistening bravura passages for the violin. The opening melody then returns in the flute, around which the solo violin embroiders delicate passages. The second movement is in a capricious mood; the leaping figures and mocking accents are in Prokofiev's recognizable satiric manner. A lyric passage in the solo violin begins the closing movement. This is now worked out with great virtuosity and brilliant effects. The violins then bring back the tender opening melody of the first movement, while the solo violin trills out the same melody an octave higher.

Peter and the Wolf, the delightful orchestral fairy tale for narrator and orchestra, is surely the most popular of Prokofiev's shorter works. It was written to illustrate for children the instruments of the orchestra. As Prokofiev explains in the remarks made by the narrator before the tale begins, each of the characters is represented by a different instrument: the bird, by a flute; the duck, by an oboe; the cat, by a clarinet in the low register; the grandfather, by a bassoon; the wolf, by three horns; Peter, by a string quartet; the shooting of the hunters, by the kettledrums and the bass drums. But Prokofiev also assigns a specific descriptive little motif to each character—presented in the preface when each of the instruments make its appearance; the different melodies appear and reappear throughout the work, like Wagnerian *leitmotifs,* to identify the characters involved in the story.

The story is a simple fairy tale about a boy named Peter who, despite his grandfather's warning, goes out into the meadow. There he confronts a wolf, captures it with a stout rope, then proudly marches off with it to the zoo.

Lieutenant Kije, suite for orchestra, was adapted by the composer from a score for a film of the same name produced in Leningrad in 1933. The film was a satire on Czarist stupidity. Nicholas I misreads a military report and concocts the name of a fictitious officer named Kije. His aides, dreading to inform their ruler that he has made a mistake, have to contrive the existence of Kije, make of him a hero, and then expediently kill him off for good.

Prokofiev's music carries out the satirical nature of the story. It indulges in Prokofiev's natural bent for grotesquerie and is consistently whimsical and witty. The suite comprises five sections. The first, "The Birth of Kije," describes the creation of Lieutenant Kije in the minds of the Czar's aides. It begins with an off-stage fanfare for cornet. Military music for drum and fifes gives a mock character to the proceedings. A pseudo-sentimental "Romance" follows, originally intended as a song for baritone, but more usually heard as a solo for tenor saxophone. The next section, "Kije's Wedding," combines the bravado of a soldier with the sentimentality of a lover. "Troika," the fourth part, consists of a lusty tavern song, once again originally intended for voice and once again usually assumed by one of the wind instruments. In the concluding section, "Burial of Kije," the lieutenant is disposed of. Fragments of melodies from the other movements recall his career. The sound of a muted trumpet melts into space to end both Kije's stay in this world and the suite.

Choral Music. *Alexander Nevsky,* a cantata for mezzo-soprano, chorus, and orchestra, is one of Prokofiev's most significant choral works. Like the *Lieutenant Kije* Suite, it started out as a score for the motion pictures. In this instance, the film (directed by Serge Eisenstein) was a powerful historical drama concerned with the defense of Novgorod against the invasion of the Knights of the Teutonic Order in 1242. Headed by Prince Alexander Nevsky, who created a large militia to supplement his army, the Russians met the foe on the icy waters of Lake Chud and inflicted a terrible defeat on the invaders.

The cantata, an adaptation of the finest pages from the film score, is made up of seven tonal pictures. The first, "Russia Under the Mongolian Rule," is for orchestra alone. The music is somber and depressive; the era of oppression and desolation under the Tartar rule is here described. This is followed by a section for chorus and orchestra entitled "Song About Alexander Nevsky." This is an exultant hymn of praise to the hero. "The Crusaders in Pskov" follows; choral music in a Gregorian mode utilizes an orchestral background of ominous chords. We have now a picture of the false crusaders, the Teutonic Knights. Midway is heard an elegiac interlude for orchestra: Russian grief at the losses suffered from the Germans. In the fourth part, "Arise Ye Russian People," a resounding song rings out urging the Russians to drive out the foe. "The Battle on the Ice" presents a realistic picture of the clash of the Russians and the Teutonic Knights on Lake Chud. There are two themes to suggest the opposing armies. The choral theme originally heard in "The Crusaders in Pskov" portrays the Knights, while a virile folk melody describes the Russians. More and more prominently does the Russian melody emerge from the labyrinth of the orchestration, to point to the victor. The sixth portrait, "Field of the Dead," is for mezzo-soprano and orchestra. It is a moving, but at the same time fiery, threnody of a Russian girl for her beloved, fallen in battle. Chorus and orchestra join in the concluding part, "Alexander's Entry into Pskov," a mighty, resplendent song of praise to the hero of Lake Chud for his famous victory.

Giacomo Puccini

"Perhaps the best measure of his outstanding qualities is that since his death nobody has succeeded in writing an opera that commands universal allegiance."

—*Francis Toye*

BORN: Lucca, December 22, 1858.
DIED: Brussels, November 29, 1924.
MAJOR WORKS: *Operas*—La Bohème; Tosca; Madama Butterfly.
ALSO: Manon Lescaut, The Girl of the Golden West, La Rondine, Gianni Schicchi, Turandot, operas.

HIS LIFE

GIACOMO PUCCINI's profession was preordained. For generations the Puccinis had held respectable music posts in the town of Lucca. The first of the musical Puccinis, who was also named Giacomo, was a composer of church and opera music who had been appointed musician to the Republic of Lucca in 1739. For three generations after that the musical traditions thus established were passed on. It was taken for granted, then, that Giacomo should follow suit.

When his father died, two of the posts he had held—that of choirmaster and organist at the San Martino Church, and that of teacher at the Collegio Ponziano—were reserved for the boy who, at that time, was only six years old. That he might possibly outgrow such provincial positions by the time he was old enough to assume them, or that he might want to turn them down, was never seriously entertained. All the Puccinis had been humble musicians who had been satisfied with their lot in Lucca. It was casually assumed that Giacomo would be no different from his ancestors.

At that, Puccini might have been satisfied to continue where his father left off had he not, late in his boyhood, heard a performance of Verdi's *Aida.* That performance took place in Pisa, thirteen miles from Lucca. Verdi was then the great man of Italian opera, the venerated Maestro; and *Aida,* his latest opera, had been introduced first in Cairo, Egypt, then at La Scala in Milan with tumult and shouting, and with a success extraordinary even for the great Verdi. Puccini was determined to get to Pisa and hear the much discussed and highly praised masterwork. He made the trip (both ways) on foot. What he heard affected him more deeply than any piece of music up to that point. It may be that the opera composer was born that evening in Pisa. In any case, Puccini must have known then that he would aspire to a future that held out greater promise than the posts of small-town teacher and choirmaster.

He was a talented boy, and he loved music. But he was also irresponsible and mischievous. At the Seminary San Michele he was frequently the cause of, and even more often the participant in, any trouble that developed among the boys. In singing class he often sang wrong notes, more out of sheer indifference to the task at hand than out of ignorance. As the youthful organist in San Pietro, in Somaldi, he scandalized the priests by interpolating opera arias in his improvisations.

There were a few people in Lucca who sensed that he had latent and undeveloped gifts. A great-uncle provided Puccini with the financial support, supplemented by a small subsidy from Queen Margherita, to go to Milan for further music study.

Puccini came to Milan in the fall of 1880, successfully passed the entrance examinations, and became a pupil at the Conservatory. His teachers included two famous composers, Antonio Bazzini (1818–97) and Amilcare Ponchielli (1834–86), the latter already celebrated for *La Gioconda.* Puccini was an excellent student. For his final examination he wrote a promising *Capriccio sinfonico,* for orchestra, which, when performed at a Conservatory concert, was highly praised. This initial taste of success tempted Puccini into assuming that he was meant to be an orchestral composer. But his teacher, Ponchielli, thought otherwise. He urged Puccini to turn to the theater. In fact, he had a specific assignment in mind: a one-act opera for a competition then being conducted by the publishing house of Sonzogno. Ponchielli even arranged with a friend to provide the libretto. To meet the deadline, the opera had to be written in such haste that Puccini did not even have time to make a copy of the score for himself.

That opera, *Le Villi,* did not win the prize, which went to another unknown young composer. (Puccini did not even receive mention.) But the powerful musician and critic, Arrigo Boïto (1842–1918)—composer of the opera *Mefistofele* and later the librettist of Verdi's *Otello* and *Falstaff*—was so impressed by Puccini's work that he raised a fund to subsidize its performance. That event took place at the Teatro dal Verme in Milan on May 31, 1884. *Le Villi,* to the surprise of its composer, was an immense success. La Scala accepted it for the following season. Ricordi published it. He did more than that; he commissioned Puccini to write a second opera and gave him an advance of 300 lire a month for two years. *Edgar,* the second opera, was introduced at La Scala on April 21, 1889, and was a failure, due mainly to a very poor libretto. But there were many enthusiastic words for Puccini's music. Ricordi did not lose faith in his find.

The period between his graduation from the Conservatory and the *première* of *Edgar* was one of intense poverty and physical deprivation. Most of the time Puccini lived on beans (he was to detest beans for the rest of his life!) and raw onions. Had it not been for the fact that a Milan restaurant, The Aida, permitted him to run up a bill for extended periods, there were times when he might have starved. One of the first things Puccini did after getting his thousand-lira advance from Ricordi was to rush to The Aida. There he ordered a sumptuous meal, then proudly demanded all his back bills, which he paid off. "That was for me the greatest, the most memorable satisfaction."

His financial problems were no less pressing after *Edgar.* In 1890 he wrote to his brother, then in South America: "I am terribly hard up, and I don't know how I can go on.... I'm piling up debts. Presently the crisis will come and then, God help me!" He even entertained the idea of joining his brother in South America. "I am sick of this eternal struggle with poverty!" he wrote him vehemently.

Fortunately, Puccini did not leave Italy; he did not have to. Less than three years after his pathetic communications to his brother, Puccini was a successful and established composer. The opera that suddenly lifted him from his abyss was *Manon Lescaut,* which—like Massenet's celebrated *Manon,* which it followed by almost a decade—was based on the novel of Abbé Prévost. Its *première* in Turin on February 1, 1893, was a triumph. The *Gazetta del Popolo* described how the audience was "stunned and overcome by emotion." And the *Corriere della Sera* reported: "*Manon* is the work of the genius, conscious of his powers, master of his art, a creator and perfecter of it. *Manon* can be ranked among the classical operas. Puccini's genius is truly Italian. His song is the song of our paganism, of our artistic sensualism. It caresses us and becomes part of us."

La Bohème came next. Puccini had long been attracted to Henri Murger's novel. And the Bohemian life was not unfamiliar to a young musician, whether the setting be Paris or Milan; Puccini had even belonged to a young Bohemian club of writers, artists, and musicians. The news (which came to him casually in a conversation) that a fellow composer, Leoncavallo, was also writing an opera on the same story only meant that Puccini would have to work faster and make a stronger attempt to identify himself in the public eye with that text. Puccini's *La Bohème* was introduced on February 1, 1896, at the Teatro Regio in Turin, Arturo Toscanini conducting, more than a year before Leoncavallo's opera. Strange to say, in view of its later popularity and its general acceptance as one of Puccini's greatest and most lovable works, *La Bohème* was not at first successful. The first-night audience was apathetic at best, while the critics were hostile. Carlo Bersezio of *Stampe* regarded the music as having been hurriedly written "with very little labor of selection and polishing." He then added with quiet self-assurance: "*La Bohème,* even as it leaves little impression on the minds of the audience will leave no great trace upon the history of our lyric theater." Not until a third production of the opera took place in Palermo was *La Bohème* acclaimed for the first time; on that occasion the death scene had to be repeated in its entirety. From then on, and in all the opera theaters of the world, *La Bohème* took its place among the great works of the repertory. Poor Leoncavallo!—the immense and universal success of Puccini's opera could only mean that his own *La Bohème* would be doomed, a fact which he recognized and which made him bitter to the end of his days.

The competition among Italian opera composers for good librettos was further revealed in the almost discreditable maneuvering which enabled Puccini to write *Tosca.* From the time he had seen Sarah Bernhardt in the Sardou drama, Puccini had recognized its operatic possibilities. The desire to write the opera was finally arrived at after *La Bohème.* An obstacle presented itself in the fact that one of Puccini's librettists, Luigi Illica, was preparing *Tosca* for another Italian composer, Alberto Franchetti (1860–1942), who had acquired the operatic rights. Puccini, Illica, and the publisher Ricordi then engaged in a

Machiavellian intrigue to convince Franchetti that *Tosca* was the worst possible choice for operatic treatment and to tear up his contract. When they had succeeded in this, Puccini set to work—but not before convincing Sardou himself that he was the man for the play. Puccini visited Sardou in Paris, had dinner with him, then sat at the piano to play for Sardou. He had as yet written none of the *Tosca* score, so he played passages from his other operas, allowing the dramatist to infer they were meant for his play. Sardou was so delighted with the music he heard that he gave Puccini his blessing.

Tosca was seen for the first time at the Teatro Costanzi in Rome on January 14, 1900. The word had spread that Puccini's enemies planned attending the *première* to throw a bomb on the stage. A great deal of apprehension preceded that performance, but the theater was nevertheless crowded. Except for a ten-minute delay in beginning, the performance progressed without disturbance. *Tosca* was received with only passing approval. Like its predecessor, *La Bohème, Tosca* was to wait for approval; and like *La Bohème,* it did not have to wait long. In less than five years it was well on its way toward present-day popularity, having been performed with remarkable success in Paris, London, New York, and other important music centers.

With the arrival of the twentieth century, Puccini's place in operatic music was secure. Verdi died in 1901, but even before his death it was apparent that Puccini had become his legitimate successor. Puccini was now honored, feted, and universally performed. He was both famous and wealthy. Already he was very much the *grand seigneur:* ever meticulously dressed and dapper, his mustache neatly trimmed, his hat at a provocative angle. He was a gourmet, he liked fine wines and cigarettes, and he adored beautiful women. "I am almost always in love," he once conceded. His diversions included hunting in the vicinity of his beautiful Florentine villa at Torre del Lago and driving his high-powered car.

For all his great success, and for all the luxuries and beauty with which he continually surrounded himself, he was given to intense melancholy. His published letters are punctuated with parenthetical remarks such as this one: "I am a poor, unhappy man, discouraged, old, abject, nothing!" Or this one: "I am going to sleep so as not to be tortured with thinking." What went on in him all the time was a titanic struggle with his conscience, feverish doubts that attended everything he wrote. He was rarely sure of himself as an artist, rarely confident that what he was producing was as good and as original as it ought to be.

When he said of Wagner that "beside him we are all mandolin players," he was expressing not only great reverence for a master but also uncertainty about himself.

On the night of February 25, 1903, Puccini and his family were being driven in his car by his chauffeur. Missing a curve, the car dived about fifteen feet over an embankment; it hit a tree and overturned. Miraculously, neither his wife nor son, both of whom were thrown out of the car, suffered injuries. But Puccini was pinned under the car—only the circumstances that the car was partly supported by the tree and that he was lying in a hollow depression in the ground saved his life. At that, he was almost asphyxiated by the gasoline fumes. His right tibia was fractured. The next eight months was a period of intense physical suffering, notwithstanding which Puccini kept on working virtually without interruption. He was engaged in the writing of *Madama Butterfly,* and he completed the opera even while enslaved to an invalid's chair and in frequent pain.

Madama Butterfly came to La Scala on February 17, 1904, directed by Campanini. Almost with the rise of the curtain, a vocal attack against Puccini and the new opera became audible in the theater. During the evening the attack developed in intensity. The next morning the news vendors shouted through the streets of Milan: "The Fiasco of Maestro Puccini." Puccini's reaction was: "This is the best opera I have ever written, and the most modern."

Many explanations have been forthcoming for this failure. Some have said that the absence of a striking tenor aria in the first act, combined with the fact that the second act was much too long, irritated the audience. Others feel that a Japanese setting and a Japanese heroine were too exotic for operagoers. Still others insist that composers envious of Puccini's great success and fame secretly arranged a cabal against him to destroy the new opera.

For one of the few times in his life Puccini was sure of himself, convinced that he had created his finest work. Nevertheless, he immediately withdrew it from the Scala repertory, even though the management was willing to continue performing it. One other great musician had faith in *Madama Butterfly:* Arturo Toscanini. Toscanini told Puccini he would be willing to conduct the opera in South America if the composer made some necessary alterations. Originally presented in two acts of uneven length, the opera was now recast in three. One or two objectionable arias were deleted; others, more lyrical, were interpolated. The tenor part was somewhat extended.

But before Toscanini could play the new version in South America, it was heard in Brescia, on May 28, 1904. It was a major triumph. There were so many encores in the second act that it was interrupted four times. Puccini took ten curtain calls. After that, *Madama Butterfly* was acclaimed wherever heard; and it was heard in all of the world's major opera houses.

In 1907 the Metropolitan Opera House invited Puccini to New York to supervise rehearsals of *Madama Butterfly*, about to be performed for the first time at that opera house. Puccini arrived on the day they were performing his *Manon Lescaut*. He was rushed from the pier to the opera house; the first scene was in progress when he was seated in the directors' box. When the lights went on after the first act, his presence was detected. The musicians sounded a fanfare; the audience rose to its feet. "I have never seen anything like it," he said, obviously touched. The first performance of *Madama Butterfly* took place on February 11; it was a sensation.

America made such a deep impression on Puccini that he suddenly expressed the wish to write an opera with an American background. "If I could get a good western libretto," he said at the time, "I would undoubtedly write the music for it." While attending the Broadway plays, he came upon such a libretto. It was *The Girl of the Golden West*, adapted by David Belasco from a Bret Harte story. Puccini liked the play, and the Metropolitan Opera commissioned him to write the opera. He did not complete it until three years later. In 1910 he returned to the United States, and on December 10 attended the world *première* of his latest work. It was a gala affair. The brilliant cast included Caruso, Destinn, and Amato; Toscanini conducted. The audience, which included Puccini, was among the most glamorous ever to attend a Metropolitan *première*. Everybody acclaimed the opera. But *The Girl of the Golden West* never became a permanent favorite with the opera public.

During the next decade Puccini completed *La Rondine* (an opera in a lighter vein) and a trilogy of one-act operas which included *Il Tabarro, Suor Angelica,* and *Gianni Schicchi.* He was working on his last opera, *Turandot,* when a throat ailment, from which he had been suffering for some time, was diagnosed as cancer. He underwent a serious operation in Brussels which appeared to be successful. But a fatal heart attack followed. Even while suffering great pain, and on the threshold of death, Puccini worked intensively on the last pages of his score. He never completed *Turandot,* a task that was left to another Italian composer, Franco Alfano (1876–   ).

The news of his death reached Rome while a performance of *La Bohème* was taking place. The performance was immediately interrupted. After the grim announcement, the orchestra struck up the music of Chopin's Funeral March, as the audience stood silently in homage to the dead master.

HIS MUSIC

PUCCINI was not a creator of grand canvases in the manner of Verdi or Wagner. He himself once said: "The only music I can make is that of small things." He aimed at poignant dramas in which the characters are human, subjected to the same emotional storms and stresses as everyday human beings. He wanted most of all to touch the heart. No one can deny that he did this, probably with incomparable success.

He had a sense for the theater that was almost infallible. His dramatic instinct was so sure that rarely did he fail to achieve the effect or emotion for which he was striving.

If his music often lacked genuine depth and originality, it had nevertheless a tender vein of lyricism, bittersweet in character, which was his own. Even his recitatives had a lyric character. To this gift he added a mastery of orchestral technique and a consummate knowledge of writing for the voice.

He was incapable of Wagner's grandeur or Verdi's nobility. But he did produce poignant works of art which are unfailing in their ability to delight and enchant audiences with their beauty and intense feelings.

ANALYTICAL NOTES

Operas. *La Bohème* is an opera without big scenes, immense climaxes, or eye-filling spectacles. Its simplicity and its realism may have been the reasons why it did not impress its first-night audience. It is a human story that emphasizes the little joys, sorrows, conflicts, and misunderstandings of human beings. The music, filled with Puccini's most tender and affecting lyricism, evolves and grows out of the characters rather than the situations. Many of the famous melodies, besides being self-sufficient as beautiful arias, are subtle characterizations of the people who sing them, as for example Mimi's aria in Act I and Musetta's waltz in Act II. Skillfully, these melodies recur through the opera with slight variations to throw ever new light on different facets of their personalities.

The story is built around four Bohemians in Paris whose lives are a continual struggle for existence. One is the poet Rodolfo, who is in love with Mimi; another, the painter Marcello, is involved with Musetta. Love, like life, is not without complications. Rodolfo's intense jealousy brings about a rupture of his affair with Mimi. Mimi becomes ill, fatally so, and is brought to Rodolfo's attic, where the lovers are finally reconciled. But it is too late.

In the first act, set in the attic room of the four Bohemians, we have two principal arias following in succession. First there is Rodolfo's famous narrative, *"Che gelida manina,"* in which he speaks about himself to Mimi, whom he has just met. She replies with an autobiographical description of her own, *"Mi chiamano Mimi."* The scene ends with the ardent love duet *"O soave fanciulla."*

The second act—outside Café Momus in the Latin Quarter—is festive. It is Christmas Eve. There is gaiety and bustle. Musetta, in the company of a wealthy beau, has eyes only for her temporarily estranged lover, Marcello. With her consummate art at coquetry, she sings an infectious waltz to taunt the heartsick Marcello, *"Quando m'en vo soletta per la via."*

The next act brings us to a snow-covered square on the outskirts of the city. Both Rodolfo and Mimi realize they have come to the parting of ways. Poignantly, Mimi bids farewell to her lover in the moving aria, *"Donde lieta usci."* Marcello and Musetta are also in trouble again. The quartet *"Addio, dolce svegliare"* reflects the different emotional responses of the two pairs of lovers: Rodolfo and Mimi are parting sadly and in pain; Marcello and Musetta, with fire and defiance.

The concluding act takes place again in the attic of the four Bohemians. Rodolfo and Marcello are pining for their lost loves, expressing their feelings in the beautiful duet *"O Mimi, tu piu."* Musetta arrives with the sad news that Mimi is terribly sick. Indeed, Musetta has brought her back to the attic. Tenderly, Mimi is placed on Rodolfo's bed. The death scene—the duet of Mimi and Rodolfo, *"Sono andati"*—arrives as the tragic climax of the opera.

Tosca, which followed *La Bohème,* is wine of a different vintage. It is strange, indeed, that Puccini should have taken such an immediate interest in Sardou's play, which exploited every possible dramatic device to inflict horror and shock on audiences. Up to *Tosca,* Puccini had preferred writing music for dramas rich with human values, dramas deriving their impact from sensitive and tender emotions. In *Tosca* he has blood-and-thunder drama. It is the lurid action, rather than characterization, that is important.

Man of the theater that he was, Puccini wrote for *Tosca* a far different score from that for *La Bohème.* The three violent chords which open the opera, in place of a formal overture, immediately set the mood for the conflicts and horrors to follow. The emotional discords—the violence of death and suicide, the harrowing spectacle of physical torture—are conveyed in music that is cogent, even violent, instead of tender and compassionate. One writer remarked that the music in the torture scene becomes so realistic that it even suggests the smell of blood!

Floria Tosca, a celebrated singer in early nineteenth-century Rome, is loved passionately by Baron Scarpia, chief of police. But her love lies elsewhere, with the painter Cavaradossi. Tosca and Cavaradossi fall into Scarpia's hands when they become involved in political intrigue by helping Angelotti, a political prisoner, to escape. In an attempt to uncover Angelotti's hiding place, Scarpia subjects Cavaradossi to physical torture, with Tosca in the next room listening to her beloved's anguished shouts. When Tosca can tolerate the ordeal no longer, she offers herself to Scarpia in exchange for Cavaradossi's freedom. He agrees joyfully. But Tosca kills him. When she discovers that her lover has been executed, she commits suicide by jumping into the Tiber.

In the beginning of the first act, in the Sant' Andrea Church, Cavaradossi sings a hymn to Tosca's beauty as he is painting her image on canvas, *"Recondita armonia."* After Tosca arrives, he joins her in a passionate love duet, *"Non la sospiri la nostra casetta."* Later on, against the background music of *"Te Deum"* sung as part of the church service, Scarpia joyfully anticipates the doom he is planning for his hated rival.

The great soprano aria *"Vissi d'arte"* comes in the second act, which is set in Scarpia's palace. Here Tosca bemoans her fate, wondering why she should be subjected to the humiliation of Scarpia's lustful love when she has led the good life, devoted to art, the church, and charity.

The terrace of Castel' Sant' Angelo, where Cavaradossi is imprisoned, is the setting for the concluding act. Church bells announce the approach of dawn. In one of the most moving arias of the opera, Cavaradossi bids farewell, both to his art and to the woman he loves, in *"E lucevan le stelle."*

Madama Butterfly, whose action takes place in Japan, inevitably called for an exotic score. Obviously, Puccini could not completely discard his Italian identity, and on more than one occasion the Italian mannerisms of his musical writing are incongruous with the stage action. But he did succeed in realizing an atmosphere and mood not found in his other operas. He evoked again and again the Oriental world of cherry blossoms and geisha girls. He did this by means of altered harmonies and piquant suspensions. In no other opera, up to this point, had he been so experimental in his harmonies. This harmonic originality—together with occasional excursions into the Oriental pentatonic scale and his sometimes unusual instrumental and rhythmic effects—creates an authentic background against which his heroine moves to her doom. The impact of the tragedy is emphasized by the closing shrieking chords.

For all its attempts at authenticity, even naturalism, *Madama Butterfly* is most outstanding for its lyricism. Several of Cio-Cio-San's arias, including the justly famous *"Un bel dì, vedremo,"* are among Puccini's finest.

Before it became an opera, *Madama Butterfly* was a successful stage play, adapted by David Belasco from a story of John Luther Long. The central theme concerns the tragic love of an American naval lieutenant, Pinkerton, for a Japanese geisha girl, Cio-Cio-San. For him, she renounces her gods and her family. When Pinkerton must leave Japan for naval maneuvers, she is convinced that he will return to her and she abruptly rebuffs the advances of a wealthy Japanese suitor. But when Pinkerton returns, he is accompanied by an American wife. Discovering that, during his absence, Cio-Cio-San has given birth to his son, Pinkerton is seized by remorse. Cio-Cio-San commits hara-kiri, after bidding her son farewell. Pinkerton finds her dead and is grief-stricken at the tragedy.

The "Japanese marriage" of Pinkerton and Cio-Cio-San (Madama Butterfly) takes place in the first act, at Pinkerton's home in Nagasaki. Pinkerton describes his reaction to the geisha girl in *"Amore o grillo."* But the American consul, Sharpless, cannot regard this affair as lightly as does Pinkerton, recognizing the possible dire consequences. The chatter of girlish voices is heard, and above it soars the love song of Cio-Cio-San, *"Spira sul mare."* The marriage ceremony takes place. Its gaiety is suddenly shattered by the abrupt arrival of Butterfly's uncle, who denounces her vehemently. She is consoled by Pinkerton, and the act ends with their ecstatic song of love, *"Viene la sera."*

Three years pass. Pinkerton has gone away, but he has promised to return. Within her house Butterfly sings about her faith in her husband's promise in what is surely one of the greatest and most popular soprano arias in operatic literature, *"Un bel dì, vedremo."* Suddenly a cannon shot announces the arrival of an American warship. Through her telescope Butterfly recognizes Pinkerton's ship. He has come back! Joyously, she and her servant gather cherry blossoms to decorate the house, singing the delightful flower duet, *"Tutti i fior."* Night falls. Butterfly waits for Pinkerton.

The scene remains unchanged in the final act. Morning has come, bringing Pinkerton and, with him, his American wife. Realizing that the moment has come for him to confess to Cio-Cio-San that he has married someone else, Pinkerton bids a tender farewell to all the happiness he has known in this house, *"Addio fiorito asil."* When Butterfly enters and sees an American woman with Pinkerton, she recognizes the terrible truth immediately. After all the others have left, she bids her son a frenzied farewell, *"Tu, tu, piccolo iddio."* She blindfolds the child and, withdrawing behind a screen, commits hara-kiri. Pinkerton enters, calling to her.

Serge Rachmaninoff

> "Rachmaninoff endures the sight of the dark aspects of Russian life, of all life—but rather as the seer than as the rebel."
>
> —*Arthur Farwell*

BORN: Onega, Novgorod district, April 1, 1873.

DIED: Beverly Hills, California, March 28, 1943.

MAJOR WORKS: *Orchestral Music*—Concerto No. 2, for piano and orchestra; Concerto No. 3, for piano and orchestra; Rhapsody on a Theme of Paganini, for piano and orchestra; Symphony No. 2; The Isle of the Dead, tone poem. *Piano Music*—Prelude in C-sharp minor; Prelude in G minor. ALSO: Symphonies Nos. 1 and 3; The Bells, choral symphony; Concertos Nos. 1 and 4, for piano and orchestra; Symphonic Dances; Moments musicaux, preludes, Etudes tableaux, 2 sonatas, for piano; "In the Silent Night," "Lilacs," "Vocalise," "The Island," "Maiden Fair," and other songs.

HIS LIFE

THERE is an old Russian proverb which Rachmaninoff sometimes quoted in self-criticism. It says, "If you hunt two hares at once, how sure can you be that you will catch a single one?"

Rachmaninoff hunted not two but three hares at once. He was a composer, a concert pianist, and a conductor. Following three careers simultaneously is a complicated process. As he once confided to a friend, "When I am concertizing I cannot compose. When I feel like writing music I have to concentrate on that; I cannot touch the piano. When I am conducting I can neither compose nor play concerts. . . . I have to concentrate on any one thing I am doing to such a degree that it does not seem to allow me to take up anything else."

Yet Rachmaninoff was able to find a workable formula for hunting three hares. And he caught them all. Besides being one of the most successful and highly regarded composers of his time, he was also one of the most formidable pianists of the twentieth century. And to conducting he brought authority, instinct, and musicianship.

A career such as this, so richly productive in three branches of musical activity, is unique in contemporary music. As a child, Rachmaninoff gave unmistakable indications of his immense talent. He had perfect pitch, a retentive memory, a pronounced aptitude for the piano. He was still an infant when his mother started teaching him the elements of music. By the time he was four, he was already quite an adept performer. His father had planned that all his sons would follow military careers, but he was astute enough to make an exception in the case of Serge. When the Rachmaninoff estates in Onega went into bankruptcy, the family moved on to St. Petersburg, in 1882, where Serge entered the Conservatory. He was a brilliant, but also indolent, student. He hated studies and practicing, and evaded both when he could. He often played truant from his classes. Only his ability to assimilate effortlessly what was taught to him in class enabled him to keep stride with his fellow students.

His grandmother, completely confident of the boy's ability, decided that a change of scene would be worth while. She saw to it that Serge lived and studied with Nikolai Zverev in Moscow. Zverev was a severe taskmaster who subjected the boy to an exacting daily routine devoted not only to music but to languages, literature, and history. He was also a sympathetic, understanding, and tactful human being, who knew how to excite the boy's musical interests and spur him on to greater activity. Rachmaninoff made extraordinary progress under his master and was soon entered in the Moscow Conservatory. But his natural tendency to shirk work brought him into continual conflict with his teachers, none of whom, however, doubted his gifts. One of them, Taneiev, had to resort to diplomatic maneuvers to get Rachmaninoff to do his lessons. He would send a special messenger to Rachmaninoff's house with the day's lessons; the messenger was instructed not to return until she had Rachmaninoff's completed homework in her hands. "Once or twice I was caught," Rachmaninoff later recalled. "But the third time I gave orders to say that I was out, so she was obliged to leave the manuscript paper."

Despite his lackadaisical, disinterested attitude, Rachmaninoff was one of the brightest lights of the Conservatory, continually the recipient of praise and of honors. At one of his examinations he played his own *Song Without Words* for a jury including Tchaikovsky. The master gave him the highest possible rating. In 1892 Rachmaninoff won the gold medal for piano playing and the faculty voted unanimously to place his name on the Honor Roll.

While still a student, he was already making his mark as a composer. In 1892 he published a set of five piano pieces (Op. 3). One of these was the *Prelude in C-sharp minor,* whose success was so immediate that Rachmaninoff's name became a household word. This prelude is still one of Rachmaninoff's most often heard pieces of music; its continued popularity once tempted Ernest Newman to refer to the piece as "It." It has had a sensational sale throughout the world, but as Rachmaninoff failed to copyright it, he earned almost nothing from this fantastic success.

Rachmaninoff also completed a one-act opera, *Aleko,* good enough to be accepted for performance by the Bolshoi Theater on May 9, 1893. Everybody praised it highly, most of all the great Tchaikovsky himself.

But despite this early and easily acquired success, Rachmaninoff was still to have a bitter taste of failure. The *Symphony No. 1,* which he at first regarded with the confidence and enthusiasm of youth, was introduced in St. Petersburg on March 27, 1897, at a Belaiev concert directed by Glazunov. The performance was so miserable that parts of the work were unrecognizable. But as he listened to the *première* of his symphony, its many defects—which could not possibly be ascribed to an inadequate performance—struck him with sledge-hammer impact. Embarrassed, he fled from the auditorium. For hours he wandered, a stunned man, on the Nevsky Prospekt, trying to lose himself in the crowds. Suddenly he recalled that his friends were giving him a supper that evening and that they would be concerned over his unexplained absence. With supreme effort he made his way to the affair. The warm greetings and the sincere congratulations did not reassure him. "The despair that filled my soul would not leave me. My dreams of a brilliant career lay shattered. My hopes and confidences were destroyed." The critics did not help matters, either. César Cui wrote: "If there were a Conservatory in hell, Rachmaninoff would gain first prize for his symphony, so devilish are the discords he has dished up for us."*

---

*This symphony has had a curious history. After that first performance, the score disappeared mysteriously and for many years was considered (even by Rachmaninoff himself) completely lost. But soon after Rachmaninoff's death a copy of a two-piano transcription was suddenly uncovered in the Soviet Union. This stimulated the search

"There are serious illnesses and deadly blows from fate which change a man's character," remarked Rachmaninoff. "This was the effect of my own Symphony on myself. When the indescribable torture of this performance had at last come to an end, I was a different man."

His overwrought condition was the prelude to a complete nervous breakdown. His grandmother, with whom he now stayed in Novgorod, tenderly ministered to him and helped bring about physical recovery. But, back in Moscow, he was still a victim of violent depressions and stultifying inertia; there were times when he was in a kind of mental stupor. He subjected himself to psychotherapeutic treatment at the hands of a celebrated Moscow physician named Dr. Dahl, who effected cures through the powers of autosuggestion. Dr. Dahl kept working on Rachmaninoff's shattered will and self-confidence. "You will compose again. You will write a piano concerto. You will write with great facility." Dr. Dahl kept repeating these sentences. Somehow, in some way, Rachmaninoff found himself. He set to work with a will and found, as Dr. Dahl had insisted he would, that writing came easily. He completed the *Piano Concerto No. 2*—to this day one of his best-loved works—and dedicated it to Dr. Dahl. On October 27, 1901, Rachmaninoff himself introduced the concerto with the Moscow Philharmonic. It was a triumph.

The Second Piano Concerto marked Rachmaninoff's return both to music and to success. He became conductor of opera at the Moscow Grand Theater and before long was acknowledged one of the finest of the younger Russian conductors. He gave piano recitals. And he kept on writing music, principally a great many pieces for the piano, and a Sonata for Cello and Piano. He was soon one of the most celebrated musicians in Moscow. His apartment became a favored gathering place for leading musical and intellectual Muscovites. His future being filled with promise, he married his sweetheart, Natalia Satin, on April 29, 1902.

Before several years had passed, the increasing pressure of his activities as conductor and pianist, combined with an expanding social life, denied him the solitude and relaxation he needed for creative work. He decided to leave Moscow, and with his wife and daughter he settled in

---

for the original score. Orchestral parts were found in the library of the Leningrad Conservatory. In the fall of 1945 the *Symphony No. 1* received its second performance, being revived after almost half a century. It was now acclaimed. The American *première* took place on March 19, 1948, in an all-Rachmaninoff program commemorating the fifth anniversary of his death, directed in Philadelphia by Eugene Ormandy.

Dresden. There, in 1907, he wrote two major works: the *Symphony No. 2* and the tone poem, *The Isle of the Dead*.

In Germany he completed arrangements to tour the United States for the first time. He returned to Moscow to prepare for that trip by working with fantastic devotion on his piano playing and by writing a new piano concerto (his third) expressly for the tour. His first American appearance took place on November 4, 1909, in a recital at Smith College in Northampton. Three weeks later he gave the world *première* of his *Concerto No. 3,* with the New York Symphony Society under Walter Damrosch. For the rest of that tour he appeared, on different occasions, as either composer and pianist, or composer and conductor, widely acclaimed in whatever capacity he appeared.

Rachmaninoff next returned to the United States not only for a concert tour, but also to find a new home. The year was 1918. When war had come to Russia, Rachmaninoff had stood ready to help by giving concerts for soldiers and refugees. Some relief from the sufferings of the time came to him in composition, though he found he could produce little that satisfied him. Then came the Revolution, which found him deep at work revising his *Piano Concerto No. 1,* written many years earlier. "I sat at the writing table or piano all day without troubling about the rattle of machine guns and rifle shots."

But he could not disregard permanently the "anarchistic upheaval" outside his study. He did not understand the new order arising in his country. Everywhere he saw death and destruction. The excesses of the ardent revolutionists filled him with disgust. Russia was his country no more; the old world he had known had disintegrated. He knew he would have to find a new home.

He left Russia in December 1917, crossing the Russian-Finnish border. He stayed in Scandinavia almost a year, replenishing his depleted resources by giving concerts. Then, in 1918, he was back in the United States for the second time. Thenceforth he was to spend most of his time in America, touring extensively and establishing his winter home on Riverside Drive, in New York. Summers were spent at first in Clairefontaine, near Paris, and after 1932 at a beautiful villa on Lake Lucerne, Switzerland. Almost pathetically, he tried to make wherever he was a little corner of Russia. He remained faithful to the language, the food, the customs, and the holidays of his native land. At his villa the atmosphere of a Russian estate was carefully simulated. But it was at best synthetic. Away from Russia, which he could never hope to see again, he always felt lonely and sad, a stranger even in lands that were ready to be hospitable to him. His homesickness assumed the character of a disease as the years passed, and one symptom of that disease was an unshakable melancholy.

He did not stop writing music. His works, some completed in Switzerland and others in this country, included: *Symphony No. 3; Concerto No. 4,* for piano and orchestra; *Rhapsody on a Theme of Paganini; Symphonic Dances.* Most of his activity was concentrated on concert appearances; he was one of the major musical figures, and one of the largest drawing cards, on the American concert stage. The thirtieth anniversary of his first appearance in America was ceremoniously celebrated in 1939. In Philadelphia there took place a cycle of three concerts in which Rachmaninoff appeared as composer, conductor, and pianist—conducting most of his major works, then passing his baton on to Eugene Ormandy when he took his place at the piano to play three of his concertos. Later that year a single commemorative concert was heard in Carnegie Hall; once again Rachmaninoff filled a triple role by conducting his own *Symphony No. 3* and appearing as piano soloist in his *Concerto No. 2.*

His health was beginning to give way, in spite of which he continued his concert work. For the next three summers he tried rehabilitating himself after the stress of the concert season by living quietly in seclusion on Long Island Sound. But the changing weather was affecting him more painfully than ever. Temporarily giving up his concert activity, he turned to the sunshine of California, acquiring a small house in Beverly Hills. "This is my last home on earth," he said. "Here I will die." Conscious that he did not have much longer to live, he wanted—more than anything else—to make one more tour of the United States. In spite of his increasing weakness he made intensive preparations for that tour, which began on February 8, 1943. It did not progress very far. Rachmaninoff was stricken in New Orleans. He was brought back to his California home for the last time. Just before he died he kept insisting that there was music being played somewhere near by. Assured that no music was being sounded, he replied sadly, "Then it is in my head." Less than two months after the first concert of his farewell tour he was dead.

HIS MUSIC

RACHMANINOFF—whose youthful *Symphony No. 1* was so violently attacked in 1897 for its dissonance—became the leading figure of the conservative group of Russian composers. Where Tchaikovsky had left off, he carried on. It was as if the modernism of such men as Stravinsky and Prokofiev, and the mysticism of Scriabin, had made no impression on Russian music. Rachmaninoff was not concerned with new paths; the old ones brought him where he wanted to go. He believed in the importance of a well-sounding melody. He once wrote to a friend: "I intend to 'sing' a melody on the piano as singers do, and to find a suitable accompaniment which would not drown out the theme." He believed in expressing in his music deeply felt emotions. In an interview he said: "I try to make music speak simply and directly that which is in my heart at the time I am composing. If there is love there, or bitterness, or sadness, or religion, these moods become part of my music, and it becomes either beautiful or bitter or sad or religious." The new formulas, principles, and techniques, to which so many of his contemporaries were addicted, were not for him. He explained: "I am not a composer who produces works to the formulae of preconceived theories. Music, I have always felt, should be the expression of a composer's complex personality; it should not be arrived at cerebrally, tailor-made to fit certain specifications."

He aimed at the production of Russian music, not by assuming a specific method (as the nationalist Russians did) but merely by being himself. "I am a Russian composer, and the land of my birth has inevitably influenced my temperament and outlook. My music is the product of my temperament and so it is Russian music; I never consciously attempt to write Russian music, or any other kind of music." He was not a new voice in Russian music. But being able to convey beauty and sentiment with sincerity and overpowering effect, he does not fail to touch the heart.

ANALYTICAL NOTES

Orchestral Music. The *Concerto No. 2,* in C minor, for piano and orchestra (like the piano concertos of Grieg and Tchaikovsky) has become a perennial favorite not only with virtuosos and concert audiences but also with the public at large. It has been heard in numerous motion pictures, including Noel Coward's *Brief Encounter,* and one of its principal melodies was adapted into the popular-song hit "Full Moon and Empty Arms." It is easy to understand the immense and sustained popularity of this concerto. It has an inescapable emotional effect, with its wealth of warm-blooded melodies, the force of its exciting and passionate utterances, and the drama of its climaxes and contrasts. It begins in a dramatic vein: nine unaccompanied chords in the piano, increasing in sonority, precede the entrance in the strings of the first theme, which is broad and rhapsodic, against arpeggios in the piano. This theme becomes increasingly passionate. Then the second theme—yearning, of feminine tenderness—appears in the piano. A loud statement of the first theme brings on the development. In this part an altogether new idea makes an appearance; it is a vigorous marchlike section, first heard in the orchestra, which gains strength and is sounded with full force and ringing chords in the piano. The recapitulation begins with a return of the first main theme. The coda, evoked softly with staccato strings, ends vigorously.

In the second movement we have the genius of Russian song. This is Rachmaninoff at his most beguiling. A nocturnal song emerges from the flute (and after that, from the clarinet) out of a broken chord in the piano. Soon the piano takes up the melody, while the violins assume the broken-chord accompaniment. The middle section of the movement brings on livelier material. A brief cadenza for the piano restores the starry and poetic mood of the opening section.

Introductory material for orchestra and for the piano precedes the entrance of the first theme of the finale. This is heard in the piano, prefaced by rising chords; it has a vigorous, martial character. The theme, worked out with frequent bravura passages for piano, is succeeded by a second idea, more broadly lyrical in style and more nostalgic in mood. It is found first in oboe and violas supported by clarinets and horns, then elaborated by the piano. This beautiful melody is given prominent attention throughout the rest of the movement. It is sensuously projected by violins and flute (and after that taken up by the piano) following a brief fugato section. And after a short cadenza for the piano, the melody returns majestically in full orchestra, against powerful chords in the piano.

The *Concerto No. 3,* in D minor, for piano and orchestra, written for the composer's first tour of America, came eight years after the Second Piano Concerto. Two introductory measures for orchestra prelude the first theme of the first movement: a Slavic theme for the piano, accompanied by strings and bassoon. This idea is soon repeated by horn and violas, as the piano provides interesting passages in the background. The second theme enters very softly in the strings and is answered by the piano, which soon works out this new material with great intensity and expansive feelings. In the development these ideas are elaborately transformed, while the piano is permitted to indulge in brilliant virtuoso passages. The development concludes with an extended cadenza for the piano. Unlike most cadenzas, this one is accompanied: flute, oboe, clarinet, and horn take turns in interpolating snatches of the first Slavic theme. This first theme, repeated by the piano with string accompaniment, brings on the recapitulation, which is concluded with a passing suggestion of the second theme.

The second movement is a brooding and sentimental intermezzo made up of two basic melodies. The first is stated by the woodwinds and repeated by strings. It is worked out in great detail, by both the orchestra and the solo instrument, before the second melody is heard in clarinet and bassoon against a waltz rhythm in the strings.

A forceful figure in triplets given by the piano, in the third measure, is the first of two principal ideas in the finale. The second idea, divided by piano and strings, comes after energetic chords in the orchestra. In the development there is a scherzando passage, evolved from the second theme of the first movement. There are other reminiscences of the first movement before a pianissimo phrase in the piano leads to a vigorous recapitulation of the two ideas of the finale.

The *Rhapsody on a Theme of Paganini* was Rachmaninoff's last work for piano and orchestra. It came in 1934, seven years after the *Concerto No. 4,* in G minor (though the latter was revised in 1938). The theme is that of the Paganini *Caprice No. 24.* It it faintly suggested in the nine-measure orchestral introduction, but is heard in its entirety in the violins in the first variation. Twenty-three other variations follow, each brief, with contrasting style and moods; the Paganini theme is often transformed with considerable harmonic and rhythmic subtlety, but its identity is rarely lost. Other thematic ideas are occasionally interpolated. In the seventh and tenth variations we hear the melody of the *"Dies Irae"* in the piano, while the orchestra offers alterations of the Paganini theme as background. The *"Dies Irae"* melody returns fortissimo in brass and strings in the last variation, this time to have the piano dilate forcefully on the Paganini theme. A culminating point is reached with a powerful chord for piano and orchestra, after which the piano brings the work to an end with a final vigorous recollection of the Paganini subject.

The *Symphony No. 2,* in E minor, is the most celebrated of Rachmaninoff's three works in the symphonic form. The first movement begins with an extended largo section. The composer seems to plumb the very depths of his thoughts and feelings, speaking with an emotional intensity and passion that remind us of Tchaikovsky. Forceful chords break the somber and introspective mood. The main theme of the ensuing allegro emerges in lower strings, clarinets, and bassoon. This theme is elaborated, after which the second theme, more relaxed than the first, begins in the wind instruments and is continued by descending strings. This second idea is worked up to a pitch of excitement. But a long diminuendo follows, pointing to a restatement of the first theme by solo violin; this marks the beginning of the development, in which the first theme plays the major role. The coda concludes this movement with vigor and brilliance.

The second movement is in the three-part form of the traditional scherzo. The two main themes of its first section are a vigorous idea for the horns and a more subdued one for the violins. The trio is introduced by a forceful chord. It has a marchlike character, and prominent use is made of the brass and some percussion. In the third part there is not only a restatement of the two main ideas of the first section but also an extended fugue that grows into a monumental climax.

The slow movement follows. The violins present the principal melody, a beautiful and strongly felt theme. Other ideas soon follow, including a poignant subject for clarinet and a third theme shared by oboes and violins. Before long we are reminded of the theme of the introductory largo in the first movement. It is first presented contrapuntally with one of the themes of the slow movement, and then, toward the close of the movement, appears by itself.

The finale begins with a theme for full orchestra that has athletic vigor and powerful drive. The energetic mood is maintained until a diminuendo is realized. Plucked notes in the bass, descending the scale, bring on a quixotic march in the wind instruments. The powerful first theme is brought back, and after that a lyrical octave passage for the strings. There is a quick backward glance at main themes of the first and third movements before the symphony evolves to a resounding conclusion.

The tone poem, *The Isle of the Dead,* is an attempt to translate into music both the subject and the mood of Arnold Böcklin's painting of the same name, which Rachmaninoff saw in a Leipzig gallery in 1906. The painting presents a grim island of towering cliffs and ominous black cypresses. A small boat is quietly proceeding toward the island, carrying a flag-draped coffin before which stands a mourner, his head bent, dressed in ghastly white. The whole effect of the painting is one of terrifying stillness.

The tone poem begins with a quiet undulating figure in the cellos suggesting the lapping of the waters on the shore of the island. This figure is repeated persistently throughout the work by different instruments. There soon rises a solemn theme for horn, and the gloom becomes intensified with the poignant voice of a solo violin and a mournful subject for divided strings. Suddenly there comes the suggestion of the medieval hymn *"Dies Irae"* in the cellos. The *"Dies Irae"* theme is developed into a powerful climax. The grief is spent, and we are once again back in the awful silence; the materials with which the tone poem began return to restore an atmosphere of tranquillity and an ominous feeling of doom.

Piano Music. As Rachmaninoff was one of the great piano virtuosos of his day, it was to be expected that: (1) he would write a great many pieces for his instrument; (2) they would show a consummate command of the resources of the piano; and (3) he would confide to these smaller forms some of his most intimate thoughts.

Within his small pieces we sometimes find little mood pictures, passing thoughts or feelings spoken with touching simplicity, with poignancy of lyric expression: the *Moments musicaux* (Op. 16), for example. We also have little dramas, so vivid in their musical expressiveness that the temptation is to find in them some extramusical meaning: the preludes.

Rachmaninoff's preludes are among the finest, and most consistently inspired, of his smaller works for piano solo. The *Prelude in C-sharp minor*—the second of five preludes gathered in Op. 3—is by all odds the most famous piece of music written by Rachmaninoff. It has telling theatrical effect: the majestic procession of chords (now light, now dark) followed by an emotionally disturbed middle section; then the effective return of the solemn chords. The *Prelude in G minor* (Op. 23, No. 5) is also popular. Here the agitation comes in the first and third parts, the music of which suggests war and the marching of soldiers; the middle part is a nostalgic interlude.

Maurice Ravel

"Ravel rules an enchanted world made up of children, gods, fairies, tender animals, turbulent puppets. It is the kingdom of Ariel."

—*Roland-Manuel*

BORN: Ciboure, France, March 7, 1875.

DIED: Paris, December 28, 1937.

MAJOR WORKS: *Orchestral Music*—Rapsodie espagnole; Alborada del gracioso (also for piano); Daphnis et Chloé—Symphonic Fragments, two series; Mother Goose Suite (also for piano duet); La Valse; Boléro; Concerto for the Left Hand; Concerto in G major, for piano and orchestra. *Piano Music*—Pavane pour une Infante défunte (also for orchestra); Jeux d'eau; Valses nobles et sentimentales (also for orchestra); Le Tombeau de Couperin (also for orchestra). ALSO: L'Heure espagnole, one-act opera; L'Enfant et les sortilèges, opera; Daphnis et Chloé, ballet; Tzigane, for violin and orchestra; Quartet in F major; Introduction and Allegro, for harp, string quartet, flute, and clarinet; Miroirs, Sonatina, Gaspard de la nuit, for piano.

HIS LIFE

THE TENDENCY of Paris to instigate and nurse artistic scandals was responsible for bringing attention to Maurice Ravel. He was involved in two major musical scandals. The first took place in 1905, after Ravel had made a fourth unsuccessful attempt to gain the Prix de Rome. By 1905 Ravel had written such highly esteemed works as the *Quartet in F major* and the *Pavane pour une Infante défunte* (*Pavane for a dead Infanta*), for piano. This fact was well known by a group of outraged musicians, who felt that Ravel surely deserved a Prix de Rome and that the judges had been guilty of partiality toward less gifted composers and prejudice toward Ravel. Romain Rolland was one of those who wrote heatedly to the director of the Conservatory:

"Ravel is not only a student of promise; he is already one of the out-standing of the younger masters of our school, which does not have many such. . . . I cannot understand why one should persist in keeping a school in Rome if it is to close its doors to those rare artists who have originality—to a man like Ravel."

Rolland had sounded the tocsin; the battle was on. So much heat was generated in the newspapers and pamphlets—as everybody in Paris took sides—that Théodore Dubois, director of the Paris Conservatory, was compelled to resign.

This controversy was by no means forgotten when, in 1907, Ravel suddenly found himself once again a center of storm. On January 12 there took place at a concert of the Société nationale the *première* of Ravel's *Histoires naturelles*. The work amused a few, but outraged a great many. In his criticism, Pierre Lalo accused Ravel of plagiarizing Debussy. It was not hard for him to make out a good case for his argu-ment. Ravel had been invading Debussy's impressionist territory and, like Debussy, had shown a tendency toward exotic scales and old modes. But, most damning of all, Ravel wrote numerous works whose titles suggested similar works by Debussy. Ravel wrote a *Rapsodie espagnole* (just as Debussy had written an *Ibéria*), a piano set entitled *Miroirs* (to approximate Debussy's *Images*), and *Jeux d'eau* (in opposition to Debussy's *Reflets dans l'eau*). Other critics soon echoed Lalo's senti-ments; a minor incident was being inflated into a major scandal.

There were other writers to rush to Ravel's defense—such men as Jean-Aubry, Calvocoressi, and Laloy. They showed that the similarities between Ravel and Debussy were superficial, while the stylistic dif-ferences were profound. They pointed out that Ravel's intellectualism was opposed to Debussy's sensuousness; Ravel's sense for classical order and symmetry was different from Debussy's frequently amorphous structures; that Ravel's virility and wit was a world apart from Debussy's refinement. They conceded that Ravel had been influenced. But an imitator—never!

When the smoke of battle cleared, Ravel, far from being discredited, was famous. His personality dominated the Paris musical scene. His music was sought after, and *premières* of his works became events of first importance. Yet his career had only begun. In 1907 he was only thirty-two years old and had been out of the Conservatory less than three years.

He was born in 1875 in the Basque region of France, where for gen-erations his mother's family had been fishermen or sailors. She had met her husband, a Swiss engineer, in Spain. They were married in 1874 and intended settling in Paris. But pregnancy impelled her to return and live with her family in Ciboure, at least until the child was born. When the child was only a few months old, the family moved to Paris, which was to remain Ravel's home until the end of his life.

"From my early childhood," Ravel recalled in later life, "I was interested in music. My father, much better educated in this art than most amateurs are, knew how to develop my taste and to stimulate my enthusiasm at an early age." Ravel's first teacher was Henri Ghys (who achieved fame with a musical trifle, *Amaryllis*); in Ghys's diary, Ravel's first lesson was carefully entered for the date of May 31, 1882. Before long, Ravel could play the piano well enough to collaborate with his father in duets. At this time he also received some harmony instruction at the Lycée from Charles-René, for whom he wrote several piano pieces which impressed the teacher greatly.

Having successfully passed his entrance examinations in 1889, Ravel entered the Conservatory, where he was to remain for the next fifteen years. His principal teachers were Gédalge, Pessard, Charles de Bériot, and Fauré. One of his fellow students was Ricardo Viñes, later famous as a concert pianist and as an interpreter of Ravel's piano works. To Viñes, the boy Ravel looked like "a young page from Florence, with a stiff and cautious gait, and serious manner. . . . His Basque face was delicate, with a clear profile, rising from a slender neck and narrow shoulders."

Ravel was a brilliant student at the Conservatory. Gédalge later went so far as to declare him the most remarkable counterpoint student he had ever had. The admiration of his teachers suggests that Ravel could respect, master, and submit to the classical rules of the classroom. But this does not mean that his curiosity was not piqued by unorthodox harmonies and techniques. In his first years at the Conservatory he met Erik Satie, whose rebellious ideas and unorthodox music impressed him profoundly. One day Ravel startled his teachers and fellow pupils by playing Satie's *Gymnopédies*. Pessard told him: "You had better leave such trash strictly alone!"

He became infected with the spirit of adventure that prevailed among the younger Parisian composers. His first compositions, two songs and the *Sérénade grotesque* for piano, were markedly influenced by Satie. So was Ravel's first published piece, *Menuet,* which Roland-Manuel described as a "conflict between scholastic severity and bold exploration."

In March 1898 Ravel entered the class of Gabriel Fauré. Fauré could be sympathetic to Ravel's restless search for new expression and could encourage him in his experiments. Under Fauré's sympathetic guidance, Ravel began writing with greater independence. Meanwhile, on March 5, 1898, there took place the first performance of a work by Ravel: *Sites auriculaires,* for two pianos, introduced at a concert of the Société nationale by Ricardo Viñes and Mademoiselle Dron. The performance went badly; the music failed to make any sort of impression. (The first movement of this suite, Habanera, was later orchestrated by Ravel to become a section of his famous *Rapsodie espagnole.*) The following year Ravel conducted the overture to *Shéhérazade* at a concert of the Société nationale; this performance was also a failure.

In 1899 Ravel wrote the first of his famous works: the poignant *Pavane pour une Infante défunte,* introduced by Ricardo Viñes at a concert of the Société nationale in 1902. This marked the end of Ravel's first creative period, that of apprenticeship. When Viñes introduced the *Pavane,* he coupled it with another piano piece of Ravel, the *Jeux d'eau,* to this day one of Ravel's most celebrated piano compositions. Both pieces were well received. But what may be regarded as Ravel's first triumph came in 1904, when the Heyman Quartet introduced his *Quartet in F major.* For the first time, critics stood read to apply the word "masterpiece" to one of Ravel's works.

At about this time Ravel associated himself with several other progressive musicians in a group that called itself the *"Société des apaches."* These musicians (they included Ravel, Viñes, and Maurice Delage among the earliest members; Florent Schmitt, Roger-Ducasse, Manuel de Falla, and Stravinsky among the later ones) adopted the name *"apaches"* to signify their endorsement of artistic lawlessness. What they actually sponsored was not lawlessness, but innovation and experiment. They apotheosized Claude Debussy, then at the height of his fame. They promoted the music of "The Russian Five," which, at the time, was still unknown in Paris. The Russian music proved a powerful stimulant to Ravel, just as Debussy was a decisive influence.

We have already seen how, involved in two publicized scandals, Ravel developed from an important composer into a famous one. As if to justify his newly won status, he proceeded to produce one major work after another. In 1907, the year in which he was vindicated of the charge of imitating Debussy, he completed the *Rapsodie espagnole* and the effervescent one-act comedy *L'Heure espagnole.* One year after that came *Ma mère l'oye* (*Mother Goose* Suite) and the *Gaspard de la nuit.* In 1911 the *Valses nobles et sentimentales* appeared, while in 1912 there took place the *première* of his most important work up to then, the ballet *Daphnis et Chloé.*

Daphnis et Chloé was commissioned by Serge Diaghilev, guiding genius of the Ballet Russe. When the impresario first heard the score (the composer played it for him on the piano), he was extremely disappointed in the music. He even thought of abandoning the ballet altogether, but was finally dissuaded by the publisher, Durand.

At last, after many delays, *Daphnis et Chloé* was seen at the Théâtre Châtelet on June 8, 1912; Nijinsky and Karsavina were the principal dancers. The audience cheered the new ballet, which was beautifully mounted and presented. The critics were divided on the merits of Ravel's score. Gaston Carraud thought the music rhythmically weak; Pierre Lalo considered it of second-rate inspiration. But others were rhapsodic.

With the outbreak of World War I, Ravel tried to enlist in the army, but was rejected because of his delicate constitution. He then made an effort—no more successful—to get into the air corps. Finally he was taken for the motor convoy. He served at the front, where his experiences had a shattering effect on him both physically and emotionally.

Soon after the war Ravel bought a beautiful villa in the Ile-de-France section of France: Montfort l'Amaury. That villa, "Belvedere," was to be his home for the rest of his years. In semiseclusion he continued producing works of importance, notably the "choreographic poem" *La Valse* and the opera *L'Enfant et les sortilèges* (*The Child and the Magic Spirits*).

Ravel, now regarded as the foremost composer in France, visited the United States for an extended concert tour early in 1928. Everything about America impressed him greatly: jazz music in Harlem; motion pictures at the Roxy Theater; skyscrapers; mechanical gadgets. His first American appearance took place in Boston, on January 12, when he directed the Boston Symphony in a program of his music. He gave thirty-one performances in all; wherever he went he was acclaimed.

In the same year Ravel was commissioned by the dancer Ida Rubinstein to write a work for her. That ballet was destined to be Ravel's greatest success: *Boléro.* When Ida Rubinstein introduced it in Paris on November 20, 1928, she completely captivated the audience. *Boléro* became an immediate favorite on symphony programs. On November 14, 1929, it received its first American performance at a concert of the New York Philharmonic-Symphony, Toscanini conducting. The demonstration that followed was tremendous. "This debut made *Boléro* an American craze," noted the critic Pitts Sanborn. It was heard and reheard at concerts of most of the American orchestras. Six different recordings appeared simultaneously. Before long the radio appropriated it. *Boléro* was adapted for jazz bands, for every possible combination of instruments, for two pianos, for harmonica. It was used in a Broadway revue and in a cabaret. One company paid Ravel a fabulous sum for the film rights, believing it to be some sort of opera; to his dying day Ravel could not get over the wonder of having been paid so handsomely for the use of a word which, after all, was common property.

Ravel's last important works were two concertos for the piano—one was for the left hand alone—which were completed in 1931. His last composition was a set of three songs for voice and piano, *Don Quichotte à Dulcinée;* they had been commissioned by a motion-picture company for a projected film of Don Quixote, starring Chaliapin, but they were not used.

In the fall of 1932 Ravel suffered an accident in a Paris taxi. His injury was at first considered minor, but within a few months he revealed alarming symptoms: he lost powers of co-ordination. The doctors disagreed in their diagnoses. For a long time Ravel suffered intense pain together with partial paralysis. In 1935 a trip to Spain and Morocco temporarily exhilarated him. But, back in Paris, his melancholia and physical disability grew rapidly worse. The doctors finally decided on a brain operation, which took place in a private hospital in Paris on December 19, 1937. Ravel never regained consciousness; he passed away quietly nine days later.

He had never married. After 1917, when his mother died, he had no one to whom he could be completely attached. His biographer, Madeleine Goss, remarked that in his loneliness he concentrated all his affection on his villa, "Belvedere," which became "mother, wife, and child to him . . . the only real expression of his entire life." He had decorated it himself and liked nothing better than to exhibit it to visitors. He lived there with his solicitous *bonne,* Madame Reveleau, and a family of Siamese cats. He shared with Debussy a veritable passion for these animals. They were with him continually, on his lap when he was relaxing and even on his table when he was working. He was as devoted to them as if they were his children, and continually reported their welfare to his friends in his letters.

There was something childlike about the way he would romp and play with them, or would try to make himself understood by speaking to them in "cat language." (He insisted that cats understood him, just as he understood them.) In his lighter moments he always gave the impression of a boy who had never grown older. He had a boyish sense of fun: in the way he would suddenly interrupt a serious conversation by tossing his head to one side and emitting a bird cry; in the way he would imitate a seasick Chinese by covering an orange with a napkin and then squeezing it; in the way he would participate with friends in adolescent games. Roland-Manuel, the French musician and lifelong friend and biographer of Ravel, summed up his personality as follows: "He had more frankness than elegance; more courtesy than cordiality; more sociability, more humor than abandon; more devotion to friendship than indulgence in camaraderie. And more ingenuousness than anything else."

HIS MUSIC

THERE are several veins in Ravel's music. One of these is Spanish. Having been born on the border of Spain, Ravel had a lifelong fascination for Spanish music, dance, and geography, and some of his finest works (*Rapsodie espagnole, Alborada del gracioso, L'Heure espagnole*) reflect the Spanish scene with remarkable authenticity and vividness. A second vein is the satiric. His wit could be infectious, his satire knife-edged, as in the *Histoires naturelles, L'Heure espagnole,* and *L'Enfant et les sortilèges*. A third vein is waltz music, the Viennese waltz particularly, which Ravel tried to recreate in his own individual way in such pieces as *La Valse* and *Valses nobles et sentimentales*. A fourth vein is that of fantasy, the fantasy of children and animals, in which he revealed a seductive charm: *Mother Goose* Suite, and *L'Enfant et les sortilèges*. Finally, there was his impressionistic vein, his partiality toward sensitive and delicate tone pictures drawn with the most refined and exquisite strokes: *Daphnis et Chloé, Quartet in F, Miroirs,* and so forth.

Whatever vein he chose to tap, Ravel was always the master. His extraordinary compositorial technique had an almost virtuoso quality, as he used rhythm, instrumentation, melodic development, harmonic color, and counterpoint with stunning effect. Elegance of style was, consequently, combined in him with true inspiration and a variety of idiom.

ANALYTICAL NOTES

Orchestral Music. The *Rapsodie espagnole,* completed in 1907, was Ravel's first successful work for orchestra. It is in four sections. The first, *"Prélude à la nuit,"* has a recurrent figure of four descending notes, first heard in muted strings, then assumed by other instruments. This becomes the background for two main Spanish melodies, the first for clarinets in octaves and the second for strings in thirds. The *"Malagueña"* that follows presents its characteristic dance melody in 3/8 time first in the bassoons and then in muted trumpets. Against this is set an impelling rhythm in the basses. There is a slow middle section, an improvisation for solo English horn. In the *"Habanera"* that follows, the rhythm of the dance is set forth by the clarinets. Fragments of Spanish melodies appear and disappear; the most important of these is played *espressivo* by the woodwinds. With *"Féria"* the *Rapsodie* comes to an exciting end. This section begins softly and nebulously. Muted trumpets suggest the main theme, which is worked up into an immense climax. A beautiful Spanish subject for English horn follows, and after that a recollection of a thematic idea from the first section. The *Rapsodie* is now built up to its conclusion with overpowering sonorous effect and dazzling brilliance of orchestral color.

Alborada del gracioso is another of Ravel's famous orchestral works in the Spanish style. Ravel wrote it originally (1905) for piano; it was the fourth of a set of five pieces for the piano entitled *Miroirs.* He orchestrated it in 1912. The name gives a clue to the musical content. *"Alborada"* suggests a Spanish "morning song" or "morning serenade." *"Gracioso"* is a jester.

Plucked strings and harp suggest strumming guitars. A Spanish dance theme is hinted at first by the oboe, then by the English horn; the melody finally emerges in full orchestra. A vital interplay of rhythm and instrumental color follows. A slow section soon provides contrast: first an improvisation for bassoon; then a solemn, even dramatic, declamation for strings. All the melodic ideas are briefly quoted as the music alternates between languor and voluptuousness. The work ends in a riot of colors and uninhibited rhythms.

The music to *Daphnis et Chloé* is Ravel's masterpiece. For concert purposes, Ravel adapted the ballet score into what he called "two series" of "orchestral fragments." The Second Series (or suite) is one of the landmarks of twentieth-century orchestral music.

The following specific program appears in the published score of the Second Series: "No sound but the murmur of rivulets fed by the dew that trickles from the rocks. Daphnis lies stretched before the grotto of the nymphs. Little by little the day dawns. The songs of birds are heard. A far-off shepherd leads his flock. Another shepherd crosses the back of the stage. Herdsmen enter, seeking Daphnis and Chloé. She appears, at last, encircled by shepherdesses. The two rush into each other's arms. Daphnis observes Chloé's crown. His dream was a prophetic vision; the intervention of Pan is manifest. The old shepherd, Lammon, explains that Pan saved Chloé in remembrance of the nymph, Syrinx, whom the god loved.

"Daphnis and Chloé mime the story of Pan and Syrinx. Chloé impersonates the young nymph wandering over the meadow. Daphnis appears as Pan, and declares his love for her. The nymph repulses him; the god becomes more insistent. She disappears among the reeds. In desperation he plucks some stalks, fashions a flute and plays on it a melancholy tune. Chloé comes out and imitates by her dance the accents of the flute.

"The dance becomes more and more animated. In mad whirlings Chloé falls into the arms of Daphnis. Before the altar of the nymphs he swears on two sheep his fidelity. Young girls enter; they are dressed as bacchantes, and shake their tambourines. Daphnis and Chloé embrace tenderly. A group of young men come on the stage.

"Joyous tumult. A general dance. Daphnis and Chloé."

The Second Series is in three sections: "Daybreak," "Pantomime," and "General Dance." The thematic material is frequently fragmentary and episodic, but the total effect of sensual lyricism is not sacrificed. In translating his program, Ravel depends on the resources of the impressionist art for color and atmosphere, and it is in these two facets that this music is so remarkable. His orchestral palette is amazing for the variety and subtlety of its hues; he uses orchestral sonority with the most consummate virtuosity.

The less frequently heard First Series is also in three sections: "Nocturne," "Interlude," and "Warlike Dance." Its program is as follows: "A little flame suddenly burns on the head of one of the statues. The nymph comes to life and leaves her pedestal. Others descend, come together, and begin a slow and mysterious dance. They see Daphnis, bend over him, and dry his tears. Reanimating him and leading him to the rock, they invoke the god Pan. Little by little the form of the god assumes definite shape.

"Daphnis kneels in supplication. All is dark. Behind the scene voices are heard, far off at first. And now there is a dim light. The pirates' camp is disclosed. There is a bold cast; the sea is in the background, with rocks to the right and left. . . .

"The pirates, laden with booty, run to and fro. Torches are brought, which at last throw a strong light on the stage."

The *Mother Goose* Suite is a happy excursion into the ingenuous, but vividly imaginative, world of childhood. Ravel wrote it at first as a suite for piano duet in 1908 for two of his children friends; and two child pianists gave its first performance. Recognizing that his little score had musical value, Ravel converted it into a ballet in 1912. The orchestral suite came out of this ballet score. It is in five sections. In the first, "Pavane of the Sleeping Beauty," the principal melodic idea grows out of a phrase for flute, horns, and violas heard at the very beginning. This is slow and tender music, only twenty measures long. The second part, "Hop o' My Thumb," carries the following quotation from one of the tales of Charles Perrault: "He believed he would easily find his path by the means of bread crumbs which he had scattered wherever he had passed. But he was very much surprised when he could not find a single crumb; the birds had come and eaten everything up." Quivering muted strings suggest the sinuous path; above this is heard the voice of a solo oboe. Chirpings of birds are simulated to provide a touch of realism to the picture. "Laideronnette, Empress of the Pagodas" also carries an illustrative quotation: "She undressed and entered her bath. Immediately the Pagodas and Pagodins began to sing and play on various instruments." This section has a marchlike character, and the exotic creatures are musically reproduced with an engaging touch of fantasy. "The Conversations of Beauty and the Beast" follows. The dialogue is represented by a solo clarinet (for Beauty) and a doublebassoon (for the Beast). Later on, as the music develops, Beauty is represented by solo flute, solo oboe, and solo violin. The movement ends with the ringing sounds of the cymbals, signifying the end of the witch's spell. The concluding section of the suite, "The Fairy Garden," depicts the awakening of Sleeping Beauty by the Prince. The principal subject is a tender melody for strings.

La Valse and *Boléro* apotheosize orchestrally the dances of two different countries: Austria and Spain. These two works, perhaps the most frequently heard of all Ravel's music, reveal Ravel's striking compositorial virtuosity.

In *La Valse* we see Ravel's consummate skill in transmuting a theme;

a waltz is evolved from an embryo into a vibrant living organism. Out of an orchestral haze, the hint of the waltz appears, first in the bassoons, then in the other woodwinds, slowly acquiring shape in the strings and oboe. The waltz unfolds, grows, and expands until the full orchestra becomes a delirium in 3/4 time. Dissonant chords bring the mad whirling to a sudden end. The waltz as it now appears is no longer gay and abandoned, but with overtones of despair: Ravel was writing this music in 1920, and the Vienna of old was Vienna no more.

Ravel termed *La Valse* a "choreographic poem." He intended his music to interpret the following brief text, which appeared in his published score: "Whirling clouds give glimpses, through rifts, of couples waltzing. The clouds scatter little by little. One sees an immense hall peopled with a twirling crowd. The scene is gradually illuminated. The light of chandeliers bursts forth fortissimo. An imperial court, about 1855."

Boléro is an exercise in instrumentation and sonority. It is a long and gradual crescendo of approximately seventeen minutes' duration. And it consists of a single theme in two sections (the first section heard in flute, then in clarinet; the second heard in bassoon, then in clarinet). Different combinations of instruments take over the theme literally; each time the theme reappears, the sonority grows. All the while, a side drum punctuates the bolero rhythm. A tremendous momentum is realized as the orchestral colors grow brighter and brighter and the sounds louder and louder. Finally the full force of the orchestra is used to thunder out the final statement of the theme with titanic strength.

The two piano concertos Ravel completed in 1931 were his last major productions. Ravel regarded them as his most important works. The *Concerto for the Left Hand,* which came first, is in a single movement. It begins with an introductory section in which the two principal themes are heard, the first in the contrabassoon, the other in the horns; these two themes are later altered to make up a jazz section. After these ideas have been built up by the orchestra with great power and intensity, the piano arrives with savage chords and embarks upon a kind of rambling and improvisatory dissertation. A cadenza becomes the climax of this part. A more lyrical and restful section follows. This, too, is brought to a climactic point after which we get the jazz section. The subdued setting of the introduction is returned, but the concerto ends vigorously.

The *Concerto in G major,* for piano and orchestra, was written (as Ravel explained) in the spirit of Mozart and Saint-Saëns. Ravel set himself the task of producing gay and witty music which would bring out the personality of the piano. The first movement is in this happy spirit, with occasional borrowings from jazz. The first theme, almost capricious in its mood (heard in the piccolo), sets the tone of levity that prevails throughout the movement. This is followed by a sustained song, presented by the piano before being taken over by the orchestra. The extended lyric line reminds some Ravel experts of a Bach arioso. In the finale we return to the gaiety of the first movement. Against a syncopated rhythm in the piano, the orchestra presents a "blues" melody. The spirit of jazz renders an irresponsible attitude to the entire proceedings, which never falter in their wit and youthful verve.

Piano Music. The best-known of Ravel's pieces for the piano are two which he wrote early: *Pavane pour une Infante défunte,* and *Jeux d'eau,* completed in 1899 and 1901 respectively. With these two items, Ravel gave the first evidence of his creative potentialities. And he helped introduce a new technique of producing sonorities and colors for the piano (particularly in the uppermost register) which influenced even Debussy in all his later writing for the piano.

The *Pavane pour une Infante défunte** is a tender elegy for a dead Infanta (not, for a dead infant!), the pavane being a slow court dance of great dignity which probably originated in Spain. This piece is sometimes heard in Ravel's own orchestration, though more familiar in its original piano version.

The *Jeux d'eau* is a vividly realistic piece inspired (as Ravel revealed) "by the sound of water and the music of fountains, cascades, and streams."

The *Valses nobles et sentimentales* was written in 1911; two years later Ravel transcribed it for orchestra. The work is a set of seven waltzes and an epilogue played without pause. The point of departure was Schubert, whose waltzes Ravel admired greatly. But in the refinement and sensitiveness of its harmonic language, the restraint of its rhythmic motion, and the undercurrent of irony the *Valses* are more recognizably French than Viennese.

In *Le Tombeau de Couperin,* Ravel paid homage to the celebrated seventeenth-century French composer of harpsichord music: François Couperin-le-Grand (1668–1733). It is a suite of six seventeenth-century forms and dances. The first two movements consist of a prelude and fugue. Three dances follow. The first is a forlane, a dance in 6/8 time

---

*In 1939 this was adulterated into a popular American song hit, by Peter DeRose, Bert Shefter, and Mitchell Parish: "The Lamp Is Low."

which resembles the old gigue and which originated in Venice, where it was a favorite with gondoliers. A classic French minuet follows. After this comes a rigaudon, a spirited Provençal dance in 2/2 or 2/4 time. The concluding movement is a toccata.

The music preserves the tranquillity and grace of an old world; but the style is still recognizably Ravel's. Modern techniques of melodic, harmonic, and rhythmic writing are still exploited—as, for example, in the closing bar of the stately minuet, which concludes with an unresolved discord. But there is no feeling of incongruity or anachronism, so harmoniously are the old and the new blended.

In 1920 Ravel transcribed *Le Tombeau de Couperin* for orchestra. In this version, only four movements remain—the fugue and toccata being omitted.

Ottorino Respighi

"Respighi is in the front rank of those composers who have brought about a renovation of symphonic music in Italy."

—*G. A. Luciani*

BORN: Bologna, July 9, 1879.

DIED: Rome, April 18, 1936.

MAJOR WORKS: *Orchestral Music*—Fountains of Rome; Pines of Rome. ALSO: The Sunken Bell, opera; Old Airs and Dances for the Lute, transcribed for orchestra; Concerto Gregoriano, for violin and orchestra; Concerto in the Mixolydian Mode, for piano and orchestra; The Birds, orchestral suite; Roman Festivals, symphonic poem; Toccata, for piano and orchestra.

HIS LIFE

IT IS said: "Italy was the cradle of instrumental music; and she has been in the cradle ever since."

But at the turn of the twentieth century, a school of younger Italian composers aspired to restore the long-lost traditions of Italian instrumental music, which had been established by such old masters as Arcangelo Corelli (1653–1713), Domenico Scarlatti (1685–1757), Antonio Vivaldi (c.1680–1741), Giuseppe Tartini (1692–1770), and so on. For centuries afterwards, Italian composers had canalized their finest energies into the opera at the expense of symphonic and chamber music. The younger Italians of the early twentieth century sought to achieve a renascence of Italian instrumental music by redirecting these energies into every branch of musical creation. Ottorino Respighi stood in the vanguard of this movement.

Ottorino's grandfather was a violinist and organist in a Bologna church, while his father taught the piano at the Liceo Musicale in the same city. His father early introduced him to the elements of piano playing. When Ottorino was twelve years old—and had by this time given proof of being able to carry on the musical traditions of the family —he was entered in the Liceo. He stayed there eight years, studying the violin with Federico Sarti and composition with Luigi Torchi and Giuseppe Martucci; he was graduated in 1899 with a diploma in violin playing.

To extend his musical horizon, Respighi left Italy to travel and study. Soon after his *Symphonic Variations* was performed at the Bologna Liceo (the first time a work of his was heard publicly) he went to Russia, got a job as violist in the orchestra of the St. Petersburg Opera House, and studied composition with Rimsky-Korsakov. He obtained his diploma in composition with an orchestral work, *Prelude, Chorale, and Fugue*. Two years after coming to Russia he went to Berlin. There he completed his study of composition with Max Bruch.

Between 1903 and 1908 Respighi appeared on the concert stage as a violin virtuoso and as a violist in the Mugellini Quintet. In his composition, he was growing increasingly ambitious. After his *Concerto for Piano and Orchestra* had been introduced in Bologna in 1902, he started work on his first opera, *Re Enzo,* which he completed in 1905 and which was introduced in the same year with moderate success in Bologna. A *Notturno,* for orchestra, was performed in New York City on January 6, 1905, and some of his songs were published in 1906.

During 1908 and 1909 Respighi taught the piano in a private school in Berlin. After that he returned to Italy, to become one of the more dynamic figures among the younger Italian musicians. He became professor of composition at the Santa Cecilia Academy in Rome in 1913. Three years after that he toured Italy extensively as a conductor in programs of his own works. He also achieved his first major success as a composer. On March 11, 1917, his symphonic poem *Fontane di Roma* (*Fountains of Rome*) was introduced by the Augusteo Orchestra in Rome, Antonia Guarnieri conducting. It was instantly acclaimed. Toscanini conducted it three times the following year and helped to make it one of the most successful orchestral works of the younger Italian school. Other major successes followed in later years. His opera *Belfagor* was seen at La Scala in Milan in 1923. One year after that, Bernardino Molinari directed the Augusteo Orchestra of Rome in the world *première* of *Pini di Roma* (*Pines of Rome*), Respighi's best-known work. Indicative of Respighi's leading position in Italian music was his appointment, in 1923, as director of the Santa Cecilia Academy, by the unanimous vote of a commission which had been created by the Italian government.

In the winter of 1925 Respighi visited the United States for the first time. He made his first American appearance, as a pianist, on December 31, with the New York Philharmonic Orchestra, in his *Concerto in the Mixolydian Mode*. That season he appeared with many other major American orchestras. He was to return to America on several other occasions. In 1928 he attended the American *première* of his opera *La Campana sommersa* (*The Sunken Bell*) at the Metropolitan Opera House in New York. In 1929 he toured the country in performances of his own works, and in 1932 he attended the world *première* of *Maria Egiziaca* (*Mary of Egypt*), given by the New York Philharmonic under Arturo Toscanini.

In 1925 Respighi resigned his post as director of Santa Cecilia so that he could concentrate on composition and his concert tours. But he continued teaching higher composition there for several years after that. Important performances of his works in all parts of the musical world now placed him with the major composers of his time. In 1927 the Hamburg Opera introduced *The Sunken Bell* and the Boston Symphony under Koussevitzky gave the first performance of his *Vetrate di chiesa* (*Church Windows*). In 1929 Arturo Toscanini gave the world *première* of *Feste Romane* (*Roman Festivals*) in New York City.

In 1932 Respighi was nominated to the Royal Academy of Italy. Four years later he was stricken by a heart attack. Though confined to bed, he worked on the orchestration of his last work, a one-act opera, *Lucrezia*. He died with his opera virtually completed; it was finished by his widow and introduced at La Scala on February 24, 1937. As the most famous Italian composer of the period, Respighi was given an impressive funeral, attended not only by Italy's foremost musicians, but also by the King and Premier Mussolini. A funeral Mass by Palestrina was sung by the Augusteo Choir. His remains were transferred to his native city of Bologna in 1937, when the municipality, with elaborate ceremony, buried him with the great men of Bologna's past.

HIS MUSIC

THE MUSIC of Respighi has a double face, one side of which looks to the past and the other to the future. Most of his works, and those he himself regarded most highly, belong to the past. They are the creations of a neoclassicist who was partial to old modes, plain chants, and classical forms. He produced a violin concerto, the melodic material of which was derived from Gregorian chants. He used the mixolydian mode for a piano concerto, the doric mode for a string quartet, and various ecclesiastical modes for *Church Windows*. In line with this tendency to reach into the past are other works such as the *Old Airs and Dances for the Lute,* which he adapted for modern orchestra, and the orchestral suite *The Birds,* based on the music of such old masters as Jean-Phillipe Rameau (1683-1764), Bernardo Pasquini (1637-1710), and Jacques de Gallot (seventeeth century).

But it is not for his neoclassical music that he is remembered. His survival in our concert halls is due primarily to those symphonic poems interpreting different facets of Roman life: primarily, *Fountains of Rome* and *Pines of Rome,* and, incidentally, *Roman Festivals.* Here he is of the vibrant present, utilizing the fullest resources of contemporary harmony and orchestration to arrive at vivid pictorialism and, occasionally, at realism.

ANALYTICAL NOTES

Orchestral Music. *Fountains of Rome* came first, in 1916. The composer's intent was to portray four Roman fountains at the time of day when their character was at one with their setting. He realizes a set of four nature pictures. The four movements are played without interruption. The first, "The Fountain of Valle Giulia at Dawn," is a landscape picture describing, as the composer explains, cattle "passing and disappearing in the fresh, damp mists of a Roman dawn." Snatches of pastoral melodies are heard in various woodwind and brass instruments. The tempo quickens, then the oboe presents an intriguing melodic idea which is repeated by the clarinet. The pastoral mood returns. There is a slight pause, after which we hear the loud call of horns above trills in the orchestra. We have come to the second section, "The Fountain of the Triton in the Morning." A dance melody is heard in flutes, clarinets, and harps. The violins bring in still another dance tune. A spirit of jubilation prevails. "Naiads and Tritons come running up pursuing each other and mingling in a frenzied dance between the jets of water." A solemn theme, "borne on the undulations of the orchestra," describes the "Fountain of Trevi at Midday." The solemn theme passes from the woodwinds to the brass and grows triumphant and full of pomp. It is the passage of Neptune, chariot-drawn by sea horses. As the procession passes, the music decreases in sonority, and the section ends with the call of horns and trumpets. "The Fountain of the Villa Medici at Sunset" begins with a tender melody in the flute and English horn, suggesting the soft glow of sunset. "The air is full of the sound of tolling bells, birds twittering, leaves rustling." An expressive idea is given to the violins against harp glissandos. Other thematic episodes occur in the flute, the horn, and the violins. The opening melody now reappears, first in the violins, then more delicately in the flute. "All dies peacefully into the silence of the night."

Pines of Rome succeeded *Fountains* by eight years. If *Fountains* is a series of nature portraits, *Pines of Rome* consists of memories and nostalgic thoughts which Roman landscapes evoke in the composer. Like its predecessor, *Pines* is in four movements which are played without pause. "Pines of the Villa Borghese" opens with vivacious music. Snatches of tart melodies heard in the woodwinds and brass suggest the playing of children—now in a game which is the Italian equivalent of "Ring-around-a-rosy," and now in one imitating soldiers. The music grows dissonant, and suddenly a different mood is upon us. Against a dark background of lower strings there rises a solemn theme. The scene shifts to "Pines Near a Catacomb," a picture of grim, stately pine trees leading to the entrance of a catacomb. The peace of this scene is realized with muted and divided strings and muted horns. A religious hymn rises from the orchestra and fades away. "Pines of the Janiculum" are illuminated by the light of a full moon. There is a solo for the clarinet. Soon we hear the voice of a nightingale against a tremulous background of strings. The nightingale's song is reproduced by means of a phonograph recording. In "Pines of the Appian Way" the mist of dawn settles over the countryside. A compelling, inexorable rhythm is sounded. Trumpets blare. The music grows overpowering, its colors coruscate. The orchestral forces gather and hurl their strength into one of the mightiest crescendos in orchestral literature. It is a vision of past glories: the army of the Consul advances in triumph to the Capitoline Hill.

Nicholas Rimsky-Korsakov

"In the course of time, he gave the world a treasury of nationalistic musical art, and an army of pupils each of whom was able to reflect no little glory upon the master."

—*M. Montagu-Nathan*

BORN: Tikhvin, Novgorod district, March 18, 1844.

DIED: St. Petersburg, June 21, 1908.

MAJOR WORKS: *Orchestral Music*—Scheherazade, suite; Capriccio espagnol; Russian Easter Overture. ALSO: Le Coq d'or (The Golden Cockerel), Sadko, Sniegurotchka (Snow Maiden), operas; Symphonies Nos. 1 and 3; Antar Symphony; Concerto for Piano and Orchestra.

HIS LIFE

RIMSKY-KORSAKOV was the dean of the national school of composers known as "The Russian Five" or "The Mighty Five." He did not found that school; that distinction goes to Mily Balakirev (1837–1910). Others, like Mussorgsky, had greater native talent than he. But as the finest and best-schooled theoretician of the group, he was its most influential member; and his music embodies the principles and ideals of that group more completely and more successfully than that of his colleagues.

It required the pioneer efforts of still another composer, of an earlier period, to lay the foundations for "The Russian Five." That composer was Michael Glinka (1804–57). But for Glinka, "The Russian Five" might never have arrived at its basic aesthetics nor received that vital stimulation needed to realize those aesthetics within important works of music. His two operas—*A Life for the Czar* and *Russlan and Ludmila*—derived their texts from Russian history and legend, with backgrounds and characters unmistakably Russian. As early as 1840, Prosper Mérimée recognized the individual character of Glinka's art. "It is more than an opera," he said of *A Life for the Czar.* "It is a national epic. . . . Poetically and musically, it is a faithful account of all that Russia has suffered and sung." In both of these operas (and in his orchestral fantasy *Kamarinskaya*) Glinka either carried over the spirit of Russian folk song and dance or quoted actual folk tunes.

Glinka was the inspiration for the national school which Balakirev helped found. César Cui (1835–1918), himself one of the original members of "The Five," described how the group originated: "In 1856, two young musicians, passionately devoted to art, met in St. Petersburg. . . . One of them was Balakirev, and the other was the author of these pages. Some little time afterwards they were joined by Rimsky-Korsakov, Borodin, and Mussorgsky. Thus a little circle was formed of friends drawn together by a common enthusiasm for music. These informal meetings gave rise, from that time on, to the most interesting debates, which ranged conscientiously over the whole of the then existing literature of music. . . . In this way, the little brotherhood ended by acquiring fixed convictions, and by forming criteria, which they applied to a number of questions in the realm of art that frequently lay far outside the current ideas of the public and press. While each member of the group retained his own characteristics and capacity, an ideal common to all soon began to be sharply defined, and an effort was made to imprint it on their compositions."

The ideal "common to all" was to produce a basically Russian art. Once and for all, these composers wanted to shake themselves loose from the French and German influences to which Russian music had been subservient for so long a time. They wanted an art no longer imitating that produced elsewhere, but one so indigenous that its Russian source could never be doubted.

They arrived at several elementary procedures. In writing operas, they would use Russian subjects, while striving for greater realism and truth. Their music was to be derived from, or influenced by, the styles and idioms of Russian folk songs and dances and old Russian church music. The spirit of the Russian people, the backgrounds of Russia's geography, the essences of its culture—these were to pervade every bar of music they would write.

Rimsky-Korsakov moved within the orbit of Mily Balakirev in 1861, when he was only seventeen years old. Up to then he had had a haphazard musical training, virtually no lessons in theory and very little disciplined piano instruction. He did not even entertain the ambition of embarking on a musical career. He was already a midshipman at the Naval Academy, where he was preparing to follow a family tradition of entering the Navy. The sea was no less a passion with him than it was for so many other members of his family, some of whom had been, or were to be, admirals. Before Nicholas was entered in the Navy School, in his twelfth year, he had voraciously read books about the sea, built model ships, memorized and quoted nautical terms.

But he had also been drawn to music from earliest childhood. There was a good deal of music making in the Rimsky-Korsakov home, to which the child responded. He wrote in his autobiography: "I was not fully two years old when I clearly distinguished all the tunes that my mother sang to me. Later, when three or four years of age, I beat a toy drum in perfect time, while my father played the piano. Often my father would suddenly change the tempo and rhythm on purpose, and I at once followed suit. Soon afterwards, I began to sing quite correctly, whatever my father played, and often I sang along with him. Later on, I myself began to pick out on the piano the pieces and accompaniments I had heard him perform and, having learned the names of the notes, I could from an adjoining room recognize and name any note of the piano." He started studying the piano with local teachers when he was eight years old, and when he was nine he began composing even though he was completely innocent of harmony and theory.

There had been indications that, raw though he was, Rimsky-Korsakov was good material for Balakirev's nationalist cause. Of all the music taught him in his boyhood, he was most excited by several excerpts from Glinka's *A Life for the Czar*. Later on, he went to the opera and was impressed by such works as *Lucia di Lammermoor* and *Der Freischütz*. Once again it was a performance of *A Life for the Czar* that had the profoundest effect on him. Other works by Glinka "dazzled him," and he soon regarded *Russlan and Ludmila* as "the best opera in the world." He bought piano scores of Glinka's music and delighted in orchestrating the works or transcribing parts for different groups of instruments. He even organized a choral group at the Navy School and directed it in passages from Glinka's operas.

There were other ways, too, in which he had shown an intuitive response to Russian music. Of the earliest musical impressions he had received, the most vivid had been—not the formal opera arias he heard at home or the piano music he was taught—but the folk songs which an eccentric uncle sang to him continually. He also derived his greatest musical enjoyment in listening to ecclesiastical Russian music in a nearby monastery and to Russian folk songs and dances played by a band of musicians employed on his father's estate.

Balakirev accepted Rimsky-Korsakov with open arms; he had been searching for a convert. He introduced the young man not only to his own concepts about Russian music, but also to the last quartets of Beethoven and the works of Berlioz, in an effort to extend his musical horizon. He had Rimsky-Korsakov attend the Saturday meetings where the Balakirev disciples played and discussed their own and each other's music. He also led him to an appreciation of Russian literature and philosophy.

Balakirev soon had Rimsky-Korsakov attempting a symphony—despite his primitive technique in composition!—painstakingly guiding his student, bar by bar. But that symphony had to wait some years before being completed. In April 1862 Rimsky-Korsakov's naval schooling ended. He was required to go on a world cruise. In the fall of that year Rimsky-Korsakov set sail on the *Almaz* on a two-and-a-half-year voyage that, in 1864, brought him to the United States. In 1865 the *Almaz* was back in its home port. By then Rimsky-Korsakov had given up all thoughts of music. "I had become an officer dilettante, who sometimes enjoyed playing or listening to music. But all my dreams of artistic activity had completely flown away. Nor did I regret them."

But when Rimsky-Korsakov was stationed in St. Petersburg, which happened soon after his return, he naturally gravitated back to the Balakirev circle. Its enthusiasms infected him anew. He began studying the piano with greater intensity. He also returned to, and completed, his long neglected symphony. Balakirev thought enough of the work to present it, at a concert of the Free Music School, as a worthy representative of his nationalist group. Cui's report on that performance, which took place on December 19, 1865, follows: "The audience listened to the symphony with growing interest. After the Andante and Finale the composer was called to the stage, and when he appeared—a naval officer, a young man of twenty-one—all who believe in a great future for our music . . . got up as one man and hailed the young beginner composer with thunderous applause." Cui goes on to say: "Rimsky-Korsakov has written the first Russian symphony."

The success of his symphony was all the stimulation Rimsky-Korsakov needed to continue composition with renewed industry. During the next three years he produced some songs, an *Overture on Three Russian Themes*, a *Fantasia on Serbian Themes*, a symphonic poem,

Sadko (not to be confused with his later opera of the same name), and the earliest work of his that is still sometimes heard, the *Antar* Symphony. By 1868 his canvas grew more ambitious; he began his first national opera, *The Maid of Pskov* (which, however, he did not complete until 1872). His fame was growing, too. *Sadko* (the symphonic poem) was well received when it was introduced by the Music Society under Balakirev in 1867, and it scored a major triumph when—in a revised version—it was reintroduced in 1869. After that second performance Borodin wrote to his wife that "the public was enraptured." And even the critic-composer Alexander Serov (1820–71), ever a bitter opponent of "The Russian Five," could write: "Rimsky-Korsakov . . . gifted with enormous talent . . . glitters amid his unfortunate entourage like a diamond."

For all his production in ambitious forms, and for all his growing success, Rimsky-Korsakov was still a novice at the business of writing music. What he had done up to now, and what he was now doing, was achieved more through instinct and trial-and-error procedures than by science; for Rimsky-Korsakov knew practically nothing about harmony, counterpoint, or theory. He was, therefore, astounded to find the director of the St. Petersburg Conservatory asking him, in 1871, to assume the position of professor of composition and instrumentation. He knew his own limitations better than anybody else. "At the time, I could not harmonize a chorale properly, had never written a single contrapuntal exercise in my life, and had only the haziest understanding of strict fugue. I didn't even know the names of the augmented and diminished intervals or the chords. . . . In my compositions I strove after correct part-writing and achieved it by instinct and by ear. My grasp of the musical forms . . . was equally hazy. Although I scored my own compositions colorfully enough, I had no adequate knowledge of the technique of the strings, or of the practical possibilities of horns, trumpets, and trombones."

He hesitated about accepting a position for which he was so obviously unqualified. But his colleagues spurred him on, and he finally decided to take the plunge. (He did not have to resign his naval commission.) For a while he had to rely on generalities and bluff to carry him through those knotty problems which he himself did not understand. But at the same time he started studying theory from the ground up, not only from textbooks, but also by unashamedly attending the Conservatory classes. He was further aided by his wife, Nadejda (whom he married in 1872), who was a soundly trained musician. A supreme will carried him through those difficult years until he became not only a thoroughly schooled theoretician, and a master in certain fields of musical technique, but also one of the greatest and most adulated teachers the Conservatory ever had.

The Maid of Pskov, finally completed, was seen at the Marynsky Theater in St. Petersburg on January 13, 1873. It was a great success. The composer had to take more than a dozen curtain calls. So great was the curiosity toward the new opera, that it was given ten performances. The government authorities did not fail to remark Rimsky-Korsakov's growing prestige. They relieved him of the necessity of wearing a naval uniform and created for him the special civilian post of Inspector of Naval Bands. The salary was munificent; no less important, the position enabled Rimsky-Korsakov to learn instrumentation firsthand, from the dais of a band conductor. He had never conducted before—that would not dissuade him from trying!—but he was able to learn the technique rapidly. In 1874 he directed a choral-orchestral concert, in which he introduced his Third Symphony. He made such a fine impression with the baton that he was soon asked to take over the direction of the Free Music Society. He conducted these concerts for seven years; later on, from 1886 to 1900, he was the conductor of the Russian Symphony Concerts, also in St. Petersburg.

Rimsky-Korsakov was now beginning to draw away from two of his colleagues of "The Mighty Five." More and more sure of himself, he began to resent Balakirev's attempt to dominate him and to direct his work. Besides, after 1872, Balakirev—who had shown a weakness for superstition and fortunetellers—yielded to a religious mania which took him away from music completely; Rimsky-Korsakov had little sympathy for this startling change. His relations with Mussorgsky (with whom he had lived in a single room in 1871) were also becoming more distant. Mussorgsky resented Rimsky-Korsakov's increasing concern with technique and musical scholarship. When Rimsky-Korsakov, directing his first concert with the Free Music Society, neglected the works of "The Five" and concentrated on the classical works of the past, Mussorgsky convinced himself that his friend was betraying the nationalist ideal. Cui and the critic Stassov (the latter had from the beginning been the spokesman for the group) were also getting cool toward Rimsky-Korsakov. Only Borodin remained close to him and sympathetic with what he was doing. "A lot of people are up in arms because Korsakov has turned back and taken to the study of musical antiquity," he wrote a friend. "But that doesn't worry me. It's quite understandable. Korsakov developed in just the opposite way from me. He began with Glinka . . . and, being surfeited . . . it's only natural that he should turn to a field which is unknown to him and which still has the interest of novelty."

But Rimsky-Korsakov was not betraying the cause; he was merely going through a transitional phase in which he filled in the yawning gaps in both his technique and musical knowledge. Between 1875 and 1877 he completed a monumental collection, *One Hundred Russian Folk Songs,* an all-important attempt to organize and present in modern dress the best examples of Russian folk music. He also devoted himself to a tremendous labor of love: editing the operas of Glinka. These two activities indicated that the old nationalist ardor had not died within him. They also helped lift Rimsky-Korsakov out of his intense preoccupation with technique and theory. Between 1878 and 1881 he wrote two new operas, *May Night* and *Snow Maiden,* both of which were Russian to the core. He also conducted four concerts for the Free Music Society which propagandized the works of "The Five," including as they did the *premières* of Borodin's "Polovtsian Dances" from *Prince Igor,* two excerpts from Mussorgsky's opera *Boris Godunov,* and several parts of his own *May Night.* And when Mussorgsky died, in 1881, Rimsky-Korsakov unhesitatingly assumed the thankless and Gargantuan assignment of editing, revising, and orchestrating (and, wherever necessary, completing) Mussorgsky's most important works, including *Boris Godunov.* He did the same service for Borodin's *Prince Igor.* Yes, Rimsky-Korsakov was still faithful and dedicated to the principles of "The Five."

But the old order was disintegrating. Mussorgsky was dead, and Borodin died in 1887. Balakirev was beginning to live in isolation, to devote himself more and more to religious meditation and prayer, and to divorce himself from his former colleagues. Cui, too, now had little traffic with the remaining living members of "The Five."

And a new group was arising to fill the vacuum created by the passing of "The Five." Rimsky-Korsakov was its musical leader; the powerful publisher Belaiev, its patron. Younger men, mostly ex-students of Rimsky-Korsakov, gathered around him and were inspired by him. Such men as Anatol Liadov (1855–1914), Anton Arensky (1861–1906), Michael Ippolitov-Ivanov (1859–1935), and Alexander Glazunov (1865–1936) now represented the rising generation of nationalists, continuing toward those "new shores" first pointed out by Balakirev and his disciples.

Like the calm before the storm, the years of Rimsky-Korsakov's most fruitful production were preceded by a quiescent period. In the early 1880s he was most occupied with his editing duties. But the creative spark burst again into flame in 1887. First there came the *Capriccio espagnol,* followed one year later by the *Russian Easter* Overture and one year after that by the *Scheherazade* Suite. In 1890 he completed the opera *Mlada.*

Before the *première* of *Mlada,* which took place on November 1, 1892, Rimsky-Korsakov was attacked by an overpowering physical weariness. He lost all interest in work and developed a distaste for composing. The *première* of *Mlada* buoyed his spirits, but only temporarily. Fatigue was soon followed by lapses of memory, then by peculiar sensations in his head. The official diagnosis was "neurasthenia cerebrospinalis," necessitating a complete cessation of musical activity. "We have sunk into a kind of mental torpor," he wrote his son. "We live from day to day and speak not of the future. . . . I can do absolutely nothing in these days. The greater part of the time I pace from one corner of the room to another, or sit and smoke endlessly."

But still another stretch of creative fertility was before him. In 1894 he wrote a new opera, to a fairy tale by Gogol, *Christmas Eve.* As if suddenly revitalized, he proceeded to write many operas, some of them his finest: *Sadko,* in 1896; *Mozart and Salieri,* in 1897; *The Czar's Bride,* in 1898; *Czar Saltan,* in 1900; *The Invisible City of Kitezh,* in 1906; and his last and most famous opera of all, *Le Coq d'or (The Golden Cockerel),* in 1907.

In 1905 a revolutionary fever infected the youth of St. Petersburg, brought on largely by Russian reserves in the Japanese war. The students of the Conservatory were no exception. Because he sided with these students, and vehemently opposed the repressive measure against them, Rimsky-Korsakov was summarily dismissed. As an additional rap on his knuckles, the government authorities forbade performances of his works for two months. A wave of indignation followed. Alexander Glazunov and Anatol Liadov, two of the Conservatory's highly esteemed professors, resigned in protest. Letters of sympathy came to Rimsky-Korsakov from individuals and cultural organizations in all parts of Russia. The protests mounted to such a pitch that the authorities decided a retreat was in order. They ordered a reorganization of the Conservatory, made Glazunov its director, and reinstated Rimsky-Korsakov.

In 1907 Rimsky-Korsakov was invited to conduct some of his own works in a festival of Russian music in Paris. This was his last public appearance. On April 23, 1908, he suffered a heart attack. It was the beginning of the end. He was too ill to attend the marriage of his daughter on June 17 of the same year. Four days after that he was dead.

HIS MUSIC

ITS NATIONAL identity is, of course, the predominating trait of Rimsky-Korsakov's music. He brought to full realization the ideals of "The Five"—and, it should be added, with sophistication, technical assurance, as well as brightness of spirit, variety, and radiance. His music can never deny its Russian origin. The melodies are often in the style of the Russian folk song. Harmonies are often derived from the old scales of Russian church music. His instrumentation has Russian brilliance and splendor; and, since he was an incomparable master of orchestration, clarity is never sacrificed.

He is most often heard in such orchestral works as the *Scheherazade* Suite, the *Capriccio espagnol,* and the *Russian Easter* Overture. But, though much more rarely performed, his operas find him in his most original and personal vein. From his operas, we hear most often such popular items as the "Hindu Chant" from *Sadko* and the "Hymn to the Sun" from *Le Coq d'or.* The operas themselves, fine and original as they are, are virtual strangers to the opera stage.

But in his best operas he evokes a world far removed from the realism of Mussorgsky or the Oriental barbarism of Borodin. It is a world, as Gerald Abraham remarks so aptly, "half-real, half-supernatural, a world as limited, as distinctive and as delightful as the world of Grimm's fairy tales and as Alice's Wonderland. It is a world inextricably confused with the fantastic, naïveté with sophistication, the romantic with the humorous, and beauty with absurdity."* With its piquant rhythmic and harmonic effects, tender Russian lyricism, blazing vividness of color, and quixotic moods, his scores—particularly those for *Sadko* and *Le Coq d'or*—are completely in harmony with the delightfully fantastic texts.

Masters of Russian Music, by M. D. Calvocoressi and Gerald Abraham. New York: Alfred A. Knopf, Inc., 1936.

ANALYTICAL NOTES

Orchestral Music. *Scheherazade,* suite for orchestra, is based on unrelated episodes in *The Arabian Nights.* In his published score, the composer added the following explanatory paragraph: "The Sultan Schahriar, convinced of the faithlessness of women, had sworn to put to death each of his wives after the first night. But the Sultana Scheherazade saved her life by diverting him with stories which she told him during a thousand and one nights. The Sultan, conquered by his curiosity, put off from day to day the execution of his wife, and at last renounced entirely his bloody vow."

Two themes are used to integrate the four movements of the suite. The first is a robust Sultan theme, which opens the first movement. The other is a tender violin solo, in triplets, which recurs throughout the work to represent Scheherazade spinning her wondrous tales to the enraptured Sultan.

The first movement, "The Sea and Sinbad's Ship," opens with the Sultan theme in unison brass with woodwinds and strings. Quiet chords in the brass bring on the Scheherazade theme in the solo violin against harp arpeggios. A fast section appears, with undulating arpeggio figures describing the swell of the sea, above which appears the Sultan theme. One other important theme is heard, first in solo flute, then in oboe and the clarinet; it may be said to represent Sinbad's ship.

The Scheherazade theme in the solo violin introduces the second movement, "The Tale of Prince Kalender." The tale begins with a theme in solo bassoon, which is taken over by different instruments with increasing animation. Now there comes a section brilliant with Oriental colors and dynamic with barbaric rhythms.

The third part, "The Young Prince and the Princess," is a haunting love song. The voice of the Prince is heard first, in a tender passage for the violins. The Princess then responds with a theme in the clarinet. Later on, a rhythmic background by triangle, tambourine, cymbals, and snare drum adds a piquant effect to this love music. Scheherazade's soliloquy ends this section.

The strong theme of the Sultan introduces the concluding movement, "The Festival at Bagdad; the Sea; the Ship Founders on the Rocks." The Scheherazade theme soon follows. Then comes a dazzlingly vivid scene, rhythmically and sonorously alive, describing the festival at Bagdad. But there is a sudden change, as we are carried out into a disturbed and vengeful sea. The ship is thrown to its doom against a rock surmounted by the bronze statue of a warrior. The commotion subsides. The tender melody of Scheherazade is back for the last time. She has finished her recital and has won over the Sultan.

The *Capriccio espagnol* (*Spanish Caprice*) derives most of its effect from brilliant orchestration. The composer himself explained: "The change of timbres, the felicitous choice of melodic designs and figuration patterns, exactly suiting each kind of instrument, brief virtuoso cadenzas for solo instruments, the rhythm of the percussion instruments, etc., constitute here the very *essence* of the composition and not its garb."

The five movements are played without pause. The first is an "*Alborada,*" or "morning song." The two principal themes appear in full orchestra. Arpeggios for violin lead to the "Variations" movement. After the horn gives forth the theme, five brief variations ensue. A solo for flute brings on a return of the opening "*Alborada,*" though in a different pitch and orchestral raiment. The fourth part is called "Scene and Gypsy Song." After a roll in the side drum, there appear five cadenzas. A harp glissando sets the stage for a gypsy song in the violins. This song grows in intensity and drama and comes to a whirlwind climax. The concluding movement, "*Fandango Asturiano,*" begins at once with a rhythmic theme for the trombones. A subsidiary idea follows in the woodwinds. The pace grows hectic. But the mood of the opening part is restored with a recollection of the "*Alborada.*"

The *Russian Easter* Overture is based on themes of the Orthodox Greek Church. A lengthy, slow introduction presents the two principal melodies. The first is the ecclesiastical theme "Let God Arise," heard in the woodwinds. After a cadenza for solo violin, the second hymn is presented by the solo cello, "An Angel Cried Out." "The gloomy colors" of this slow movement "seemed to depict the Holy Sepulcher that had shone with ineffable light at the moment of the Resurrection," explained the composer. The first theme is now repeated antiphonally by trombones and strings. After a second cadenza for solo violin, the main body of the overture unfolds, as both main themes are presented and elaborated. Trumpet blasts and horn calls bring on a subsidiary section. But the two principal melodies are brought back, the second before the first, and separated by a recitative for trombone which sounds like the chanting of a priest. The two themes are once again developed. A brilliant and triumphant coda, realized with overwhelming power and vividness of color, brings up the picture of the cathedral and the altar. A statement of the second theme in trombones and strings brings the overture to a triumphant close.

Gioacchino Rossini

"The only creator of truly comic music."
—*Franz Werfel*

BORN: Pesaro, Italy, February 29, 1792.
DIED: Passy, France, November 13, 1868.
MAJOR WORKS: *Operas*—The Barber of Seville; William Tell.
Orchestral Music—Overtures to L'Italiana in Algeri, Semiramide, La
Gazza ladra. ALSO: L'Italiana in Algeri, Semiramide, La Gazza ladra,
La Cenerentola, operas; Stabat Mater.

HIS LIFE

In his thirty-seventh year Rossini completed his thirty-eighth opera,
William Tell. He was at the height of his fame, unquestionably
the most celebrated and most widely performed opera composer
in the world. He was also at the height of his creative powers.

He was to live for another thirty-nine years. Yet never again was he
to write an opera. What made him stop short while he was still in full
stride? There are many explanations offered for this phenomenon.
Some of them came from Rossini himself. But none seems to satisfy.

Had his inspiration begun to fail? Maybe so. But Rossini had never
counted exclusively on inspiration. For years he had produced one
work after another cut to specification (often with the precision of a
skilled mechanic). He was not likely to be suddenly silenced for lack
of inspiration.

Had he decided to indulge his notorious indolence? He was now
wealthy and could afford to do so. But then, the many anecdotes and

legends about his laziness always fail to ring true; it is hard to conceive of a lazy man writing four or five operas a year.

Had he grown bitter at the failure of *William Tell,* and did this bitterness bring on creative atrophy? Hardly likely! Rossini's career up to *William Tell* had been studded with magnificent failures as well as successes, and he could take both in his stride.

Did he (as some have suggested) resent the soaring fame of Meyerbeer in Paris, and refuse to share the limelight with anybody? Once again—hardly likely. Rossini's position, in 1829, could not be assailed by any competitor, and he knew it. Beyond that, by the time Meyerbeer became a reigning favorite in Paris (his first French opera was seen in 1831 and his second in 1836), Rossini had been silent for almost a decade.

There are still other explanations: Rossini's neurasthenia; his inability to find adequate singers; his sense of futility at working in a period of political turmoil. Each is less satisfying than the other. Whatever the explanation, Rossini's refusal to write operas for almost four decades, with the stages of the world clamoring for them, is a unique episode in music history.

But then, Rossini's biography is rich with unusual incidents. He was born in a leap year, on February 29. And he died on Friday the thirteenth—he who all his life had been intensely superstitious! These two unusual days of birth and death were the boundary lines of a life that continually refused to follow a normal pattern.

It was not an orthodox boyhood, for example. His father was an ardent republican and Francophile who frequently tangled with the authorities. Because of his political sympathies, he was deprived of his posts as town trumpeter and inspector of public slaughter houses and on several occasions was even imprisoned. After his release, he and his wife earned their living by traveling from one opera house to another; the father played the horn in the orchestra, while the mother sang. This nomadic existence meant that their son had to be entrusted to the care of his grandmother. The boy was left to himself, allowed to run wild. He was given only a token education. Attempts to impose discipline on him were, at first, futile. He was twice apprenticed to a blacksmith and once to a butcher, but on each occasion was soon given up as incorrigible.

But he did show an unmistakable aptitude for music. Having a beautiful voice, he was sometimes called upon to sing in the church. By the time he was twelve, he was already the proud composer of some songs and opera arias, and could play the cembalo, horn, and viola. But the only music instruction he had received up to this time was some unsatisfactory cembalo lessons from a teacher who could play the instrument with only two fingers. He also received some coaching in singing from a local priest, who was the first to introduce the boy to the music of Haydn and Mozart.

His parents set up a permanent home again and reclaimed their son; they could finally attend to his musical education. In 1804 the family settled in Bologna. There Gioacchino was enrolled at the Liceo Musicale; at first he studied the cello, and after that he studied counterpoint with Padre Mattei. Mattei was a fanatic about textbook rules, subjecting his students to a severe and inflexible routine. Rossini's rebellion against this taxing discipline expressed itself in so complete an absorption with the scores of Haydn and Mozart that his master soon dubbed him *"Il Tedeschino"* ("The Little German"). But notwithstanding his rebellion, he was an excellent student. He received a gold medal in counterpoint and was selected by the school authorities to write a cantata.

He did not complete his schooling at the Liceo, but only because family financial difficulties demanded that he provide some help. In 1810 he had to start thinking of making a living. He had already earned some money as a cembalist and chorus master in some of the smaller theaters in or near Bologna. He was ready to return to these duties. But chance provided him with an opportunity to compose professionally. An opera house in Venice was scheduling a bill of five one-act operas by local composers. One of these operas did not materialize. Rossini's friend, a singer, convinced the manager to call on the young composer for the fifth attraction. With a dispatch that was soon to be characteristic, Rossini completed his opera, *La Cambiale di matrimonio,* in three days' time. It was seen on November 3, 1810, bringing Rossini forty dollars and some welcome appreciation.

He set to work writing operas with a will. His second, presented in Bologna in 1811, was also liked, but it was soon suppressed by the authorities because of its indecent libretto. Three operas were produced in 1812. Then Rossini achieved his first major success with *La Pietra del paragone,* introduced at La Scala in Milan in 1812 and performed fifty times during its first season. It also won for its composer exemption from the army, because the recruiting officer had seen the opera and had instantly become a Rossini admirer. An even greater success came in 1813 to *Tancredi,* based on Voltaire's work of the same name.

Tancredi, Rossini's first attempt at serious opera (all the others had been comedies), retained its popularity in Europe for many years. Its principal aria, *"Di tanti palpiti"* (the finest love song he was to write), spread like a contagious disease. On one occasion the Venetian law court had to order its citizens to desist from singing, humming, and whistling it continually! And less than three months after *Tancredi,* Rossini gave his public still another major triumph, the comic opera *L'Italiana in Algeri.*

Only three years out of the Conservatory, Rossini was the idol of Venice and the most famous opera composer in Italy. That a young man, not yet twenty-two, should already have written ten operas, two of them extraordinarily popular, was in itself calculated to arouse the admiration of the Italian opera world. But Rossini was also extraordinarily handsome, a young man of great personal charm and wit, and the hero of many widely publicized love escapades. Venetians worshiped him.

In 1815 Domenico Barbaja, the most powerful opera impresario in Italy, engaged Rossini to direct his two opera theaters in Naples and to write for each a new opera each year. Rossini's first opera for Naples, *Elisabetta,* was a fittingly resplendent vehicle for the glamorous and strikingly beautiful prima donna Isabella Colbran, Barbaja's mistress. This was the first of several operas he was to write for Colbran, including the powerful tragedy *Otello* (one of his greatest successes) and a comic adaptation of the Cinderella tale, *La Cenerentola.* It was not long before Colbran's favorite composer became her lover; Barbaja apparently was ready to accept the inevitable stoically.

On a temporary leave of absence from Naples, in the winter of 1815, Rossini went to Rome to write and help produce two new operas. The first was a trifle written in haste; it met the unhappy fate it deserved. With his second opera, Rossini hoped to make amends. He adapted Beaumarchais' play *Le Barbier de Séville* into an opera which he originally entitled *Almaviva, ossia l'inutile percauzione* and for which he wrote music in his freshest and brightest comical vein. However, when presented at the Teatro di Torre Argentina on February 20, 1816, *Almaviva* was received with very little cordiality. The opera lovers of Rome resented Rossini's use of a text already treated operatically by their idol, Giovanni Paisiello (1740–1816). (Paisiello himself had engaged a special claque to create a disturbance.) Several unfortunate accidents in staging and performance further aroused the audience. Rossini took the fiasco calmly enough, left the theater and went to bed; when one of the singers visited him to console him, she found that he was fast asleep. But at the second performance (which Rossini refused to attend) things went much better. Paisiello's professional claque was no longer present. The opera proceeded smoothly and profited from the interpolation of a new beautiful serenade. The audience liked it. The performance after that was given an ovation. *The Barber of Seville* (as it was soon rechristened) had begun its triumphant career as the greatest of all opera buffa and the one most admired universally. The fame of the twenty-four-year-old Rossini was now embracing all of Europe.

The next six years saw the production of no less than sixteen operas, some of them triumphs, other fiascos. Rossini had risen as high as an opera composer could in Italy. In 1822 he left Venice (stopping off at Bologna to marry his mistress, Isabella Colbran) and proceeded to Vienna. There three Rossini operas were presented. Before long, the entire city (including the powerful Metternich) was singing and humming the airs of Rossini. "So long as I have money for the Italian opera," wrote the philosopher Hegel after seeing one of the Rossini operas, "I shall not leave Vienna." The great Beethoven, generally aloof toward visitors, welcomed Rossini warmly and expressed his sincere affection for *The Barber of Seville*. He is reputed to have advised Rossini to write nothing but opera buffa.

Rossini remained in Vienna four months. Shortly before his departure, a benefit night was arranged for him at the Kärntnerthor Theater. Those who could not get into the theater (several thousand admirers) swarmed outside. Rossini heard of the crowd and decided to arrange an impromptu concert on the balcony. Arias from *Elisabetta* and *Zelmira* were sung by the leading members of the cast. Rossini himself joined in by singing the *"Largo al factotum"* from *The Barber of Seville*. The music went on until two in the morning.

Rossini left Vienna, but not before he had written a parting song, *"Addio ai Viennesi."* Back in Venice, he wrote a new opera, *Semiramide,* which was introduced with immense success on February 3, 1823, and for a long time after that was regarded as his greatest work. But the man who had met hero worship in Vienna, and who within the year of 1823 had had twenty-three of his operas performed in different (and remote) places of the world, was no longer satisfied with Venice. He was off again, first to London, where he received a tremendous welcome—even from George IV himself. And in 1824 he arrived in Paris to become the director of the Théâtre Italien. He expected his stay to be temporary. But he remained in Paris on and off for the rest of his life.

Besides directing the Théâtre Italien for two years, Rossini presented two serious works at the Opéra: *Le Siège de Corinthe* in 1826, and a new adaptation of an old opera, *Moïse,* in 1827. Charles X gave a practical demonstration of his admiration for Rossini. He gave the composer a contract calling for five new operas during the next ten years, each opera to bring the composer 15,000 francs; at the expiration or lapse of the contract he was to be awarded an over-all pension for life of 6,000 francs a year.

The opera *William Tell* was the first completed by Rossini under this new arrangement. He considered it his *chef-d'oeuvre.* Seen at the Opéra on August 3, 1829, it was extravagantly acclaimed by the critics and leading French musicians. But the public did not like it: the libretto was poor; the opera was much too long; and it had too many dull stretches.

William Tell was Rossini's operatic swan song. After that came what has so aptly been described as "the great renunciation": Rossini would write no more for the stage. During the next four decades all Rossini produced was some sacred music (including a single masterpiece, the *Stabat Mater*), some songs, and a few piano trifles, one or two with quixotic titles.

The twenty years following *William Tell* were among the most difficult of his life. First he became embroiled in a long and difficult legal battle with the French government over his contract with Charles X, which had been prematurely terminated by the July Revolution. After five years of prolonged court battles, Rossini won at least one point, but that on a technicality: his annual pension was to be continued, but the order for the five new operas was to be considered abrogated.

Legal entanglements were at times accompanied, and then succeeded, by violent attacks of neurasthenia. The slightest emotional disturbance was enough to induce hysterics. A train ride in 1836 (Rossini's first) so terrified him that he fainted and had to be carried off. The death of a friend brought on a prolonged illness. At one time he was on the verge of a complete mental collapse. For one period, in Florence, he was virtually bedridden for several years, tortured by insomnia and inability to digest his food.

But the man who had renounced his art was not yet ready to reject life. He had acquired a mistress in 1832, Olympe Pélissier, a bewitching courtesan who had already numbered among her lovers many men of high station and reputation. The pair's devotion and tenderness for each other remained untarnished by years of intimacy. Fifteen years after their first meeting (and two years after the death of Rossini's wife) they were quietly married.

In 1855 Rossini returned to Paris after a long absence in Italy. He had not been forgotten. Thirteen years earlier, in 1842 (while the composer was in Italy), there had taken place the first Rossini *première* in thirteen years: the *Stabat Mater*. It was presented with éclat, and its performance recalled some of the great Rossini triumphs of former years. The critics and musicians described it as the most notable choral work since Haydn's *The Creation*. For days the public spoke of little else but Rossini's music.

Back in Paris—his body and nerves magically revitalized by a cure in Baden—Rossini was a dominating figure in the social and cultural life of the city. His apartment on the rue de la Chaussée d'Antin and his summer villa in nearby Passy became as brilliant scenes of festive entertainments as could be found. There was no musician who, on arriving in Paris, did not aspire to perform at a Rossini gathering; there was none so high in public life who did not cherish an invitation to one. The great and the near great came to his Saturday evenings as much to see the great man of Italian opera, to talk to him, and possibly to be the first to hear a delectable witticism, as to rub elbows with, say, a Liszt, or a Wagner, or a Clara Schumann, or an Adelina Patti.

Rossini's wit was now quoted as widely as the airs of his most famous operas were hummed. There was the time a young composer came calling at the rue de la Chaussée d'Antin apartment to play for him two new compositions. Rossini listened to the first, then said quickly, "I like the other one better." There was the time when, as a guest of George IV, he accompanied the singing of his royal host at the piano. Despite the many errors perpetrated by the monarch, Rossini kept on playing as if nothing had happened. After the performance the king congratulated Rossini on his tact. "Sire," he said, "it is my duty to accompany you—even to hell."

Once as a dinner guest he ate a magnificent meal with great gusto; for he loved good food and had an immense appetite. "When will you dine with us again?" the hostess asked him politely over the liqueur. Rossini smacked his lips and said, "Right away, if you wish, madam!"

He could be witty even at his own misfortunes. For some time it had been the custom at the Paris Opéra to present the overlong *William Tell* in a truncated version, much to the composer's chagrin. Told once that the Opéra planned presenting the second act of that opera at a gala evening, Rossini shouted, "Surely not the whole of it?"

Rossini remained the regal host to the very end of his life. The last of his Saturday evenings took place on September 26, 1868. Only two weeks later he suffered a heart attack; other complications followed. The Pope, aware that Rossini was dying, sent a special nuncio to Paris to administer extreme unction. Rossini was, at first, buried in the cemetery of Père Lachaise in Paris. But, at the request of the Italian government, his body was removed and transferred to Florence, where it was reburied in the Church of Santa Croce.

HIS MUSIC

THERE was so much of the hack in Rossini that it is sometimes difficult to remember that he was also a genius. He wrote abundantly because he was blessed with facility and spontaneity. But he was also ready to accept third-rate music when the first-rate would cost him pain and effort. He was always looking for the short cut. He continually plagiarized himself, interpolating material in new operas that he had used earlier. He produced *Maometto II,* a new opera, for Paris by the simple expedient of taking one of his old scores and adapting it *in toto* to a new libretto. Even such an integrated masterwork as *The Barber of Seville,* which never falters in its mirth and infectious charm, was made up of something old, as well as something new. The overture had been previously used for two different operas, while five major numbers were lifted from five other operas, including such celebrated arias as the serenade, *"Ecco ridente in cielo,"* and *"La Calunnia."* In *La Cenerentola* he not only used sections from other operas, but even called upon another composer to write two additional numbers; for the *première* of *The Barber of Seville* he did not hesitate to allow the principal tenor, Manuel García, to introduce an aria of his own creation. And the man who could borrow from himself was not above borrowing from others as well. We find the lovable minuet from Mozart's *Don Giovanni* at the end of *L'Italiana in Algeri.* *"Zitti, zitti,"* from *The Barber of Seville,* is obviously the plowman's song from Haydn's *The Seasons.* The resemblance between the Allegretto of Beethoven's Eighth Symphony and an excerpt from Act II of *Le Comte Ory* is more than coincidental.

He once said: "Give me a laundry list and I will set it to music." He never hesitated to write music to order, ready (like a tailor) to fit it to any required size or shape. An important aria was sometimes produced with the range of a specific singer in mind, to enhance the strong points of her singing and to disguise her weak points. There was the case of the contralto who could produce an excellent middle B-flat. In *La Pietra del paragone* he wrote an aria for her in which she could concentrate on that note, while the orchestra carried the melody. The specific needs of a theater, as well as a singer, always found him ready to recast his material in a more functional mold.

Yet, for all his lack of artistic scruples, for all his haphazard working methods, he was able to produce an unblemished masterwork such as *The Barber of Seville*. He had the gift of melody—the birthright of every great Italian composer—and with it a sublime sense for comedy. His music has laughter, effervescence, mockery, sentimentality, and burlesque.

He was also a great innovator who expanded and enriched the technique of operatic writing. He paid attention to his orchestra in a way no other Italian of his day did, introducing colors, instruments, and effects which enhanced the dramatic or comic expressiveness of his music. Already in his first opera, *La Cambiale di matrimonio,* he was so concerned with his orchestral writing that the singers complained they were being slighted. Another of his early operas, *La Pietra del paragone,* introduced an orchestral effect he was thenceforth to use with consummate skill and with which his name is associated: the extended crescendo. This device had such an impact on its public that, when heard for the first time, it was instrumental in making the opera a success.

Rossini was responsible for other innovations. In his early operas he already made elaborate use of the alternation of a slow section (cavatina) and a fast one (cabaletta), which later composers were to utilize extensively. In *Elisabetta* he wrote out—for the first time—the cadenza passages for his arias, rather than leaving them to the whim and fancy of the singer; he also started here the practice of accompanying his recitatives by strings instead of merely the cembalo.

ANALYTICAL NOTES

Operas. *The Barber of Seville* is the standard by which all opera buffa were thenceforth to be measured; to this day it is one of the greatest of them all. In the best traditions of that form, it abounds in irrepressible gaiety—laughing at most of its characters, at the intrigues, and even at the absurdities of the opera-buffa technique of that day. But it has also the magic of lyricism, now tender and wistful, now vivacious, now satirical, now subtly pointing up some facet of a character or a situation. But to some of Rossini's contemporaries, *The Barber* was not sufficiently melodious. This is because Rossini alternated sentimental and emotional arias with patter songs in which—for the sake of subtle characterization, or satiric overtones, or realism—he enlisted tempo, dynamics, or rhythm (rather than lyricism) to serve his artistic ends. His contemporaries were not accustomed to such subtleties, and so they did not altogether comprehend them at first hearing.

The two plays of Beaumarchais which inspired Rossini (*The Barber* and *The Marriage of Figaro*) centered around the character of the versatile barber Figaro, who boldly laughed at and put up to ridicule the foibles and weaknesses of the aristocracy. Count Almaviva enlists the aid of Figaro to further his courtship of the lovely Rosina. The barrier to his suit is Bartolo, Rosina's guardian, who wants her (and her dowry) for himself. In order to gain admission for Almaviva into Bartolo's house, Figaro has him disguise himself first as a drunken soldier, then as Basilio, the music teacher. Bartolo tries to frustrate the love affair by telling Rosina that her lover is unfaithful. Eventually the Count is able to convince Rosina of the truth. Wile and strategy combine to bring about their marriage in Bartolo's absence. Faced with a *fait accompli,* Bartolo accepts the situation gracefully—particularly since the Count is quite willing to forgo the dowry.

The brisk and vivacious little overture sets the mood for the play so wonderfully that it is perhaps wisest to forget that Rossini originally wrote it for several other operas, two of them tragedies. It begins with a slow introductory section in which the principal melody is a suave tune for violins against pizzicato strings and which ends with four chords. The main part begins with a saucy theme for strings, doubled by piccolo. Another piquant melody appears later on, first in the oboe and clarinet, then in the horn. The exposition ends with a characteristic Rossini crescendo. The two main themes are repeated, then the overture ends with a merry coda.

The first scene of the first act takes place in a street in Seville. We hear Count Almaviva singing a beautiful serenade to the accompaniment of mandolins, "*Ecco ridente in cielo.*" Figaro appears and embarks on his celebrated monologue, "*Largo al factotum.*" In this scintillating patter song he tells of his many and varied occupations, which bring him into different homes and make him such a useful instrument for promoting the intrigues of young lovers. After Figaro has promised to help Almaviva in his suit for Rosina, the Count sings a second poignant love song to Rosina, *"Se il mio nome."*

The second scene, in Bartolo's house, opens as Rosina reads a love letter from Almaviva. She expresses her agitation in the finest and best-loved aria of the opera, *"Una voce poco fa."* Basilio, the music teacher, who suspects that Almaviva is pursuing Rosina, is ready to use slander as a means of discrediting him. He expatiates on the power of slander in *"La Calunnia."* Bartolo, too, is suspicious of his ward. In a florid aria, *"A un dotter della mia sorte,"* he warns her not to trifle with a man of his position.

The second act also takes place in Bartolo's house. Disguised as the music teacher, Count Almaviva comes to give Rosina a singing lesson. He enters with a greeting of mocking politeness, *"Pace e gioia."* During the lesson it is customary for the prima donna to interpolate arias of her own choice, Rossini's original aria having been lost after the *première*. (Some of the songs introduced into the Lesson Scene by leading sopranos of the past and present include "Home Sweet Home," Alabiev's "The Nightingale," and Arditi's *"Il Bacio."*) Having planned to elope, Almaviva and Rosina express their rapture in the duet *"Ah quel colpo."* Then, with Figaro, they suggest the necessity for quiet and haste, *"Zitti, zitti, piano, piano."* But the marriage can take place then and there without elopement, as a notary and witnesses are at hand. Bartolo, returning home to find Rosina and Almaviva married, accepts his fate with resignation. The opera ends as the chorus sings *"Amor e fede eterna."*

In *William Tell* we have a different Rossini—no longer the genius of the comic, but a composer who wrote with symphonic breadth and who was principally concerned with the dramatic and poetic content of his music. Sobriety, seriousness of purpose, pageantry, and melodrama represent Rossini in a less familiar, and less lovable, vein. But while *William Tell* is inconsistent in its material, is much too long (without cuts it would require six hours for performance), and contains many dull and arid stretches, it is, nevertheless, a masterpiece. Rossini's gift for melody is never purer or more varied than in two or three of its finest arias. His harmonic and orchestral writing was never more daring. His big dramatic scenes and his scenes of pomp were an inspiration to Meyerbeer, soon to emerge with the first of his French grand operas. Wagner even conceded that, with its ambitious symphonic writing, it pointed in the direction of the music drama.

To this day, the overture is *William Tell's* crowning glory, Rossini's most ambitious attempt at symphonic writing. It is sometimes described as a miniature symphonic poem because of its complete success in realizing both programmatic and poetic writing. It begins with the beautiful slow section in which the main theme in the cellos and basses depicts the rise of the sun over the Swiss mountains. A fast section follows, the full orchestra presenting a storm from its inception to its culmination. Another slow part comes, by way of contrast. Here we have a pastoral scene, in which the English horn presents a gentle Swiss mountain melody. Trumpet fanfares bring on the Swiss soldiers, and the overture ends with the exciting *brio* music which in our day of radio and television has become inextricably associated with the exploits of The Lone Ranger.

The finest vocal pages in *William Tell* (and among the best by Rossini) include: the coloratura aria *"Sombre forêt,"* an apostrophe to the simple, idyllic life, sung by Gessler's daughter, Matthilde, in Act II, Scene 1; the aria of her lover, Arnold, in his farewell both to her and his dreams of love, in Act III, Scene 1, *"Pour notre amour";* and Arnold's paean to home and country, in Act IV, Scene 1, *"Asile héréditaire."* The dance *"Passo a Sei"* (*"Dance in Six"*), in Act I, and the ballet music in Act III, Scene 2, are also of outstanding musical interest.

Orchestral Music. The delightful overtures from other Rossini operas have remained favorites with concert audiences, even though the operas themselves are almost never seen. *L'Italiana in Algeri* (*The Italian Woman in Algiers*) was one of Rossini's early comic-opera triumphs; it took Venice by storm in 1813. The overture begins with a slow section. Softly plucked strings culminate suddenly in a loud chord, after which we hear a brief tune in the oboe. The main body comes after a typical Rossini crescendo. The first subject is a gay tune for the woodwinds, punctuated by chords in the strings. The second melody is also pert and carefree. It comes in the oboe after the first melody has been developed. Both themes return, and the overture ends with another effective Rossini crescendo.

Semiramide, a tragic opera set in ancient Babylonia, came a decade after *L'Italiana.* The overture begins with a crescendo in which a brisk figure for the strings grows from pianissimo to fortissimo. A stately and dignified melody then appears in four horns and is soon elaborated by the woodwinds with an accompaniment of plucked strings. A loud and dramatic outburst by the orchestra, followed by a soft transitional passage for the woodwinds, brings the opening crescendo back briefly. We have come to the allegro part of the overture, which starts with a bouncing, chattering melody for the strings and continues with a second jaunty idea for the woodwinds. A long Rossini crescendo of tremendous effect brings this part of the overture to an end. Both main themes of the fast section are repeated. A crescendo brings a pulse-quickening conclusion.

The overture to *La Gazza ladra* (*The Thieving Magpie*) begins in a military manner with two rolls in the side drum. The full orchestra loudy presents the main melody, a vigorous march which is worked out briefly. The drum rolls, a brief crescendo, and five chords end this part of the overture. The allegro section contains two basic melodies: a glistening and delicate theme for the strings and a piquant subject shared by woodwinds and strings. As with other Rossini overtures, an exciting culmination is realized with a crescendo.

Camille Saint-Saëns

"He brings into the midst of our present restlessness something of the sweetness and clarity of past periods, something that seems like fragments of a vanished world."

—*Romain Rolland*

BORN: Paris, October 9, 1835.
DIED: Algiers, December 16, 1921.
MAJOR WORKS: *Orchestral Music*—Symphony No. 3, in C minor; Danse macabre, tone poem; The Carnival of Animals, suite for two pianos and orchestra; Concerto No. 2, in G minor, for piano and orchestra; Concerto No. 3, in B minor, for violin and orchestra; Concerto No. 1, in A minor, for cello and orchestra. *Opera*—Samson et Dalila. ALSO: Concerto No. 2, in A minor, for violin and orchestra; Concertos Nos. 4 and 5, for piano and orchestra; Le Rouet d'Omphale, Phaëton, La Jeunesse d'Hercule, tone poems; Jota aragonese, Rapsodie auvergne, Suite algérienne, for orchestra; Symphony No. 2, in A minor; Introduction and Rondo capriccioso, for violin and orchestra; Havanaise, for violin and orchestra (also violin and piano); Christmas Oratorio; Requiem; Septet; 2 sonatas for violin and piano; 2 sonatas for cello and piano; 2 piano trios; 2 string quartets; bagatelles, etudes, valses, fugues, for piano.

HIS LIFE

CAMILLE SAINT-SAËNS was the exception to the general rule that composers must undergo a long and bitter period of struggle before arriving at recognition. He began his musical career as a prodigy who was the object of too much attention for his own good. At twenty-two he was a musician of established position: the organist at the Madeleine, one of the great churches of Paris; the composer of two symphonies, both already performed and one having won an important prize. Berlioz called him "one of the greatest musicians of our epoch," and Anton Rubinstein regarded him as "the greatest organist in the world." Liszt was both a friend and an ardent admirer. Hans von Bülow complained to a friend that Germany possessed no musician comparable to Saint-Saëns (except, he added wryly, "you and me"). When Saint-Saëns was elected a member of the Institut in 1881, one of the speakers said: "If it were necessary to characterize Saint-Saëns in a few words, we should call him the best musician in France." And when, on October 27, 1907, Saint-Saëns was present at the unveiling of his own statue in the foyer of the Dieppe Opéra, he had lived long enough to find that he had become a classic.

There were some disappointments—of course. His two attempts to win the Prix de Rome were fruitless: the first time he was regarded as too young, and the second time as too successful. Then there was the long and trying wait to get his opera, *Samson et Dalila,* performed in France. But these setbacks represented only minor defeats in a predominantly triumphant career.

His people were of humble station. His father, a successful government employee in the Ministry of the Interior who had come from Normandy peasant stock, died when Camille was only three months old. The child was sent to a baby farm in the country until his second year. When he was brought back to Paris, his mother and a great-aunt assumed the responsibility of raising a prodigy.

For the signs were there—immediate, unmistakable. As an infant, Camille revealed an extraordinary sensitivity to musical sounds. A beautiful tone made his face shine; a discord brought an expression of pain. At two-and-a-half, he was taught the piano by his great-aunt. When he completed his first exercise book within a month, both his mother and great-aunt decided to stop the lessons for fear of overtaxing him. The child made such a scene ("I cried like a lost soul," he later explained) that they had to continue teaching him. At three, he was taught the elements of musical notation. By the time he was five, he was composing songs and piano pieces. One of these was dedicated to the famous artist Ingres, who responded by presenting the boy with a beautiful medallion on which was painted a likeness of Mozart. It bore the following inscription: "To M. Saint-Saëns, charming interpreter of this divine artist."

He showed his phenomenal talent, and uninhibited enthusiasm, in many different ways. While still four-and-a-half, he made an appearance as pianist in a performance of a Beethoven sonata for violin and piano. He took a score of a Grétry opera and read it fluently at sight.

Given the full orchestral score of Mozart's *Don Giovanni,* in his sixth year, he read it through with as much facility and delight as if it were a fairy tale.

A more intensive period of study was begun when he was seven, with Camille-Marie Stamaty (piano) and Pierre Maleden (theory). On May 6, 1846, Saint-Saëns gave a recital in the Salle Pleyel, performing an exacting program that included two concertos (by Mozart and Beethoven) and sundry other works. Such was his technical assurance and musicianship that some critics already hailed him as a virtuoso of the first rank.

The temptation to exploit him was great. But both his mother and great-aunt recognized the danger of launching his career too early. They wisely decided to forgo the concert stage for further musical training. In 1848 Saint-Saëns entered the Paris Conservatory. In the organ class of Benoist he won first prize in 1851. As a composition pupil of Halévy, he completed an *Ode to Sainte-Cecile* which won a prize and was performed on December 26, 1852. He failed, however, to get the Prix de Rome, largely because he was only seventeen years old at the time.

He left the Conservatory in 1853. Despite his youth, he was already able to enter the ranks of the professional musician. His *Symphony No. 1* was played that year in Paris, and to arouse curiosity in it was presented anonymously as the work of a German composer. It was well received. When Charles Gounod discovered that Saint-Saëns was its composer, he impressed on the young musician his responsibility to use his native gifts properly in order to develop into "a great master." During the same year, Saint-Saëns also acquired his first post, as organist at the Church Saint-Merry.

Between his twenty-first and twenty-second year several important things happened, bringing him forcefully to the fore of the younger French musicians. For one thing, he acquired one of the most important organ posts in Paris, at the famous Madeleine Church, which he held for twenty years. His performances there placed him with the finest organ virtuosos of the day. Famous musicians visiting Paris soon made it a practice to stop off at the Madeleine and hear him play; they included Clara Schumann, Robert Franz, Pablo de Sarasate, Anton Rubinstein, and many others. Besides establishing himself as an organist, he brought further attention to himself as a composer by winning first prize for his *Symphony No. 2* in a contest of the Société Sainte-Cecile. The symphony was heard in 1857 in Paris and enjoyed a huge success.

Energy, drive, and versatility—thenceforth to characterize his activities—led him in many different directions. As pianist for Princess Mathilde, he once urged her to use her influence in getting him a commission for writing an opera, whereupon she exclaimed, "He plays the organ at the Madeleine, and the piano for me. Does not that content him?" However, a man of Saint-Saëns' restless intellect and prodigious capacity for work needed many channels through which to direct his energies. It was not long before he entered upon other duties. He resumed his long interrupted career as concert pianist, touring extensively both in solo concerts and in performances of his piano concertos (the first of which, completed in 1858, he performed in 1865). He conducted, particularly his own works. He edited the music of some of the masters. He wrote theoretical treatises. In 1861 he became professor of the piano at the Ecole Niedermeyer. And ten years later he helped found (and subsequently he helped direct) the Société nationale, which was dedicated to the performance of music by French composers.

And even this prolific and highly varied musical endeavor did not completely satisfy him. He studied astronomy, physics, and natural history. He wrote books on philosophy, literature, painting, and the theater. He produced poetry and a play. He wrote critical essays. He had a gift for caricature. He read classical literature omnivorously, mastered several languages, and revealed a vigorous curiosity for archaeology.

Fortunately, his immense culture (virtually unique among composers) and his amazing musical scholarship (regarded with awe by some of the greatest musicians of the time) brought on neither arrogance nor stuffiness. It is true that he made acidulous remarks, which he used with deadly effect in puncturing the stupid, the egotistic, and the poseur. But, as Philip Hale wrote, "He was faithful to friends, appreciative of certain rivals, kindly disposed toward young composers, zealous in practical assistance as well as in verbal encouragement. A man that knew the world and sparkled in conversation; fond of society; at ease and on equal terms with leaders in art, literature, fashion."

He had a wonderful capacity for fun. While on a visit to Russia, he happened to be on the stage of the empty hall of the Moscow Conservatory with Tchaikovsky and Anton Rubinstein. Suddenly he began pirouetting across the stage like a lithe ballerina. His distinguished colleagues entered into the spirit of the thing. Rubinstein sat at the piano and played ballet music, while Tchaikovsky joined Saint-Saëns in the dance. All his life he had a fine gift for mimicry. At one of his famous Monday-evening musicales he might delight his guests by wearing an outlandish costume and impersonating Marguerite in Gounod's *Faust;* or he would sit at the piano and parody an early Italian opera; or, with extravagant gestures, enact a scene from Offenbach's *La Belle Hélène.*

After 1871 Saint-Saëns' creative work began assuming greater importance. In 1871 he completed *Le Rouet d'Omphale,* with which the Lisztian concept of the tone poem entered French orchestral music. He also completed his first comic opera, *La Princesse jaune,* which was presented by the Opéra Comique on June 12, 1872. His first serious opera, *Le Timbre d'argent,* was given by the Théâtre Lyrique on February 23, 1877. Meanwhile he had completed his operatic masterpiece, *Samson et Dalila.* The opera managers in Paris unanimously turned it down as too severe in style, too serious in approach, too Wagnerian in idiom. But the opera found a champion in Franz Liszt, who arranged for its *première* in Weimar on December 2, 1877. It was a triumph. Not until thirteen years later was *Samson et Dalila* seen in Paris. But by then it had been seen and acclaimed in almost every important European city.

In February 1875 Saint-Saëns married Marie-Laure Truffot. It was the prelude to tragedy. Three years later his oldest child fell out of the window and was killed; a second child died suddenly only a few weeks after that. Before that fatal year was over, Saint-Saëns decided that he could no longer live with his wife. On a vacation with her, he disappeared early one morning. At first it was thought he had met with an accident, and an intensive search was made. A few days later, however, his wife received a formal note from him to the effect that he would never return to her.

During the next quarter of a century—despite the intensification of his industry in his many musical and extramusical occupations—he produced one new work after another with extraordinary rapidity. In this period he completed five operas, fifteen major orchestral works (including two symphonies and four concertos), thirteen large chamber-music works, more than a dozen choral works, more than twenty compositions for the piano, as well as various works for the theater and for the organ.

At the same time he started traveling extensively, thenceforth a favorite pastime. He visited virtually every country in the world, some of them several times. Occasionally, when on vacation, he would assume a fictitious name and occupation so that his privacy might not be violated. He turned up as Charles Sannois in the Canary Islands one time, and on another occasion as a Dutch diamond merchant in Ceylon. This insatiable wanderlust kept him continually on the move. He came to the United States: the first time, in 1906, he gave concerts as far west as Chicago; the second time, in 1916, he represented the French government at the Panama Exposition and led the *première* of his *Hail California*. In his eighty-first year he toured South America. And when he was eighty-five he went on a concert tour of Algiers and Greece.

On August 6, 1921, he performed some piano pieces in Dieppe, after which he announced quietly, "Seventy-five years ago I played for the first time in public. Today I have played for the last time." Two weeks later he directed his last orchestral concert. That winter, spent in Algiers, was devoted to composition. He died there suddenly, in his eighty-sixth year. His body was brought back to Paris, where it was buried with pomp and lavish eulogies.

HIS MUSIC

SAINT-SAËNS once wrote: "The artist who does not feel completely satisfied by elegant lines, by harmonious colors, and by a beautiful succession of chords does not understand the art of music."

Here, in brief, we have not only the essence of his musical aesthetics, but also the essence of his music. His works have clarity, proportion, balance, and precision within well-defined structures; above everything else, they *sound* well. He made a fetish of correctness. It is said that when, in his old age, he came upon some pieces written when he was a child, he was overjoyed to find that the form and technique were so correct. On the other hand, he rejected experiments, excessive emotions, and any philosophic implications. His best works have a crystalline beauty whose surface is not disturbed by passion. And though he was the French apostle of the Lisztian tone poem—in which form he produced several programmatic works—he was essentially the high priest of absolute music.

He had an incredible technique, exquisite taste, and incomparable glibness. He could write pieces in imitation of other composers with remarkable accuracy, from the sixteenth-century harpsicord composers to Wagner and Verdi. He was just as successful in recreating the musical styles and idioms of other lands. Among his works we find an Egyptian concerto, an Algerian suite, a Breton rhapsody, Persian songs,

Russian or Arabian caprices, and Portuguese barcarolles. He even traveled back in time by producing dance music of the sixteenth and seventeenth centuries, and preludes and fugues of the eighteenth.

Obviously this is not an artist in search of originality or individuality. Had he not been so consummate a master of his technique —had he not combined technique with elegance of style, purity of writing, and impeccable good taste—he would surely not have survived. His best works may not excite the listener or move the heart, but they do make for pleasurable listening.

ANALYTICAL NOTES

Orchestral Music. The *Symphony No. 3*, in C minor (with organ), is the last of five Saint-Saëns symphonies. Today it is known as the Third Symphony because the composer had previously discarded two earlier works in that form and removed them from the catalogue of his works. The *Symphony No. 3* was completed in 1886, the year of Franz Liszt's death. The fact that the work is also dedicated to Liszt has led to the often repeated, but erroneous, belief that it is a memorial to him. History provides evidence to the contrary: Saint-Saëns' symphony was introduced in London on May 19, 1886; Liszt did not die until more than two months later.

The composer himself provided what has since become the definitive analysis of the work: "The symphony is divided in two parts. . . . Nevertheless, it includes practically the traditional four movements: the first, checked in development, serves as an introduction to the Adagio, and the Scherzo is connected, after the same manner, with the Finale. . . .

"After an introduction Adagio of a few plaintive measures, the string quartet exposes the initial theme, which is somber and agitated. The first transformation of this theme leads to a second motive, which is distinguished by greater tranquillity; after a short development, in which the two themes are presented simultaneously, the second motive appears in characteristic form, for full orchestra, but only for a short time. A second transformation of the initial theme includes now and then the plaintive notes of the introduction. Varied episodes gradually bring calm, and thus prepare the Adagio. The extremely peaceful and contemplative theme is given to the violins, violas, and cellos, which are supported by organ chords. This theme is then taken by clarinet, horn, and trombone, accompanied by strings divided into several parts. After a variation (in arabesques) performed by the violins, the second transformation of the initial theme appears again, and brings with it a vague feeling of unrest, which is enlarged by dissonant harmonies. These soon give way to the theme of the Adagio performed this time by some of the violins, violas, and cellos, with organ accompaniment and with a persistent rhythm of triplets presented by the preceding episode. This first movement ends in a coda of mystical character. . . .

"The second movement begins with an energetic phrase which is followed immediately by a third transformation of the initial theme in the first movement, more agitated than it was before, and into which enters a demoniac spirit that is frankly disclosed in the Presto. Here arpeggios and scales on the piano, swift as lightning, are accompanied by the syncopated rhythm of the orchestra, and each time they are in a different tonality. This badinage is interrupted by an expressive phrase (strings). A recapitulation is followed by a second Presto, which at first is apparently a repetition of the first Presto; but scarcely has it begun before a new theme is heard, grave, austere (trombone, tuba, double-basses), strongly contrasted with the eerie music. There is a struggle for mastery, and this struggle ends in the defeat of the restless, diabolical element. A new phrase rises to orchestral heights, soaring as in the blue of a clear sky. After a vague reminiscence of the initial theme of the first movement, a Maestoso announces the approaching triumph of the calm and lofty thought. The initial theme of the first movement, wholly transformed, is now exposed by divided strings and piano (four hands) and repeated by the organ with the full strength of the orchestra. Then follows a development built in a rhythm of three measures. An episode of tranquil and pastoral character (oboe, flute, English horn, clarinet) is twice repeated. A brilliant coda, in which the initial theme by a last transformation takes the form of a violin figure, ends the work."

Saint-Saëns wrote four symphonic (or tone) poems in emulation of Franz Liszt. The most popular is the *Danse macabre*, written in 1874. The poem by Henri Cazalis, on which it is based, tells of Death playing a dance tune on his violin on a wintry midnight. Through the cold darkness, white skeletons come dancing, their bones rattling as they dance. The cock crows. The dancing comes to a sudden halt and the skeletons disperse.

It is not difficult to follow this program in Saint-Saëns' music. The striking of midnight is heard at once in the harp. This is followed by

Death tuning his violin. Suddenly we hear the dance melody in the flute. The music grows frenetic as the skeletons go through their demoniac dance; the rattling of their bones is suggested by a xylophone. Strains of the *"Dies Irae"* are suddenly interpolated and merge with the dance melody. The pace grows faster and faster. Suddenly the crowing of the cock (in the oboe) sounds the coming of dawn. The skeletons disperse, and the dance melody vanishes into space.

The Carnival of Animals, a suite for two pianos and orchestra, is subtitled "a grand zoological fantasy." The composer regarded the work as a lark, written exclusively for his own entertainment. He neither permitted it to be published nor performed while he was alive (though he did sanction a single private performance for his friends). The composition is an ingratiating excursion into wit and satire. One amusing feature is its characterization of the various animals; another is the malicious interpolation of musical quotations.

The suite begins with the "Introduction and Royal March of the Lion." Rumblings of sound portray the lion, and his march is prefaced by an impressive fanfare. Next the calls of "Hens and Cocks" are imitated, the cackle of the hens in the piano and strings and the voice of the cocks in the clarinet. "Mules" is exclusively for two pianos, played without any change of rhythm or dynamics. It is believed that in this part Saint-Saëns wished to satirize those meticulously correct pianists who depend more on their technique than on musicianship. In "Tortoises," Saint-Saëns quotes briefly two melodies from Offenbach's *Orpheus in the Underworld.* One of these is played at a plodding pace by all the strings in unison. In "The Elephant" a cumbersome melody in a solo doublebass is set against a waltz rhythm in the piano. With more malice than wit, Saint-Saëns quickly introduces a theme from Berlioz' *The Damnation of Faust.* "Kangaroos" is played by the two pianos. The halting rhythms are meant to suggest not only the hesitant movement of these animals, but also the exchange of gossip that is likely to take place between concertgoers during a performance. In "Aquarium" a pure melody in flute and violin describes the fish, and arpeggios in the piano depict the water. "Personages with Long Ears" brings us intervallic skips with a short rest to imitate the kicking of the mule, while in "Cuckoo in the Woods" the voice of the bird is imitated by the clarinet, punctuating a delightful melody in the pianos. "Aviary" emulates not only the voices of birds, but their movement through space. "Pianists" now enter the zoo of Saint-Saëns; the composer here ridicules "the awkward performance of beginners." In "Fossils," Saint-

Saëns once again indulges in quotation, this time from Rossini's *The Barber of Seville,* from two old French folk songs, and from his own *Danse macabre.* "The Swan" is the most celebrated movement of the entire suite. A beautiful, serene melody for the cello simulates the majestic movement of the swan. This is the only part of the entire work that the composer allowed to be published and performed in his lifetime. It was also made popular in one of Pavlova's most celebrated ballets. In the "Finale" all the characters return to take a final bow.

Saint-Saëns wrote five concertos for piano and orchestra. The *Concerto No. 2,* in G minor, written in 1868, is heard most often. It begins with a long fantasia for the solo piano. When the orchestra finally makes its appearance, it brings the first theme, a forceful subject. The piano replies with an expressive lyrical passage, before proceeding with brilliant virtuoso music, frequently electrifying in movement and rhythm. A climax is reached with a return of the robust first theme in the orchestra against octaves in the piano.

The second movement is a scherzo. (The concerto does not have a slow movement.) The kettledrums set forth an exciting rhythm, after which the piano presents the first theme, which is vivacious and rhythmic. The second theme is heard in unison violas, cellos, and basses against a rhythmic background in the piano.

The third movement is an exciting presto. The first theme has the character of a whirling, leaping Italian folk dance. After a brief transition in the piano, we get the second energetic subject, which begins with trills in the piano, against woodwinds and horns, and continues as a virile dialogue between piano and strings. The impetuous motion of this presto is temporarily arrested with an impressive short chorale in woodwinds and horns against trills in the piano.

The *Concerto No. 3,* in B minor, for violin and orchestra, is the last and most famous of the composer's violin concertos. The violin introduces the passionate first theme, accompanied by strings and timpani. There are some virtuoso passages for the solo instrument before the second main idea of the movement arrives. Both the development and the coda pay particular attention to the first theme.

In the second movement there are three measures of introduction before the violin offers a barcarolle kind of melody. This melody is elaborately worked out before the solo instrument loudly presents the second theme. Both themes are then recalled. The coda makes effective use of arpeggio passages in harmonics by the solo violin.

Soloist and orchestra share the recitative that introduces the finale.

After two bars of rhythmic accompaniment, the solo instrument offers the first theme. The second theme, also in the solo violin, arrives without delay. There is still another idea—a kind of chorale for muted strings, supported by woodwinds and solo violin. After some development of earlier material, the chorale theme returns in trumpets and trombones, with the second theme soon bringing the movement to its end.

Saint-Saëns wrote two concertos for cello and orchestra. The more popular is the *Concerto No. 1,* in A minor, which is played without any pause between movements. The principal theme, which has great sobriety, is heard at once in the cello. After being developed by the cello and taken over by the orchestra, it is succeeded by a second theme, tranquil and expressive, in the solo cello. There is an agitated section marked by pyrotechnical passages for the cello. Brief recollections of the two main themes preface an entirely new section, in which a graceful minuet-like dance subject is given by muted strings against a countertheme in the cello. This part is concluded with a cadenza for the solo instrument. Repetition of old material alternates with interpolations of episodic new ideas. After the first theme has returned forcefully in the violins, the orchestra is presented in a vigorous *tutti* passage. An altogether new subject for the solo cello forms the concluding coda.

Opera. *Samson et Dalila* is the only opera by Saint-Saëns which has survived. It is good theater and excellent spectacle, with music of great emotional intensity and vivid atmospheric colors. Nowhere did Saint-Saëns surpass the sensual beauty of his two beautiful arias for Delilah, the famous "Spring Song" and the even more celebrated aria *"Mon coeur s'ouvre à ta voix,"* ("My Heart at Your Sweet Voice"). This is French melody at its lyrical best. The effectiveness of the score comes not only from its fine French melody, but also from the successful exploitation of exotic Hebrew chants and the languorous rhythms and harmonies of Oriental music.

The reason it took so long for *Samson et Dalila* to be performed in Paris was—so the managers said—that it had a forbidding severity of musical style and that it was too strongly influenced by Wagner. The latter accusation is the more curious of the two. In its scenes of pageantry, sumptuous bacchanal, and in its humble subservience to operatic formulas, *Samson et Dalila* embodies many of the evils of French grand opera against which Wagner fought so bitterly.

When *Samson et Dalila* was first heard in England, it was presented as an oratorio, without scenery or costumes, because a century-old law forbade the representation of Biblical or religious themes on the stage. *Samson et Dalila* has since been performed in both its operatic and oratorio versions, and with equal success.

The familiar Biblical story was adapted by Ferdinand Lemaire. Before the curtain rises, a chorus of Israelites are heard lamenting their bondage to the Philistines, *"Dieu, d'Israël."* As the curtain rises on a public square in the city of Gaza, the Israelites are still bemoaning their fate, entreating their God to deliver them. Samson appears, to console them with a fiery promise that the day of liberation will soon be at hand, *"Arrêtez, O mes frères."* Inflamed by his words, the Israelites promise to follow his leadership, raising their voices with his in a spirited battle song, *"Israël romps ta chaine!"* Samson kills Abimelech, leader of the Philistines, who are then put to flight by the Israelites. The High Priest of the Philistines hurls a mighty curse at Samson and his people. The triumphant Israelites sing a hymn of joy. Meanwhile, Delilah and her maidens emerge from the nearby temple to welcome the victors. Seductively, Delilah tries to win the heart of Samson by singing to him a sensual "Spring Song," *"Printemps qui commence."*

In the second act, Delilah awaits Samson at her house. Passionately she calls on love to help her in winning him, *"Amour, viens aider ma faiblesse."* After Samson arrives, she woos him ardently with her ecstatic song, *"Mon coeur s'ouvre à ta voix."* He is now a helpless victim of her beauty and his passion, and as a victim he reveals to her the source of his great power: the locks of his hair. Delilah has his hair cut and calls to the Philistines to take him away to his doom.

The third act is divided into two scenes. In the first, Samson—blind, shorn of his hair, and chained—cries out to God for mercy. But he is soon led to his final fate. The scene changes to the Temple of Dagon, where Samson's ruin is celebrated by the Philistines with pomp and festivity. A sumptuous bacchanal takes place. Accompanied by taunts and derision, Samson is bound between two pillars that support the temple roof. His prayer to God for a brief return of strength is suddenly answered. As the Philistines engage in their ecstatic worship of the god Dagon, Samson brings down the mighty pillars and the temple roof on the Philistines and destroys them as well as himself.

Arnold Schoenberg

> "His greatness is incontestable. So is his loneliness. Who could be companion to this genius?"
>
> —*Paul Stefan*

BORN: Vienna, September 13, 1874.
DIED: Brentwood, California, July 13, 1951.
MAJOR WORKS: *Orchestral Music*—Verklärte Nacht (Transfigured Night), for string orchestra; Theme and Variations for Orchestra. ALSO: Die glückliche Hand, drama with music; Von Heute auf Morgen, one-act opera; Erwartung, monodrama; Pierrot lunaire, melodrama for recitation and chamber orchestra; Gurre-Lieder, for soloists, chorus, and orchestra; A Survivor from Warsaw, for narrator, men's chorus, and orchestra; Kammersymphonie; Five Pieces for Orchestra; Concerto for String Quartet and Orchestra; Concerto for Violin and Orchestra; Concerto for Piano and Orchestra; Ode to Napoleon, for recitation, piano, and string orchestra; 4 string quartets; Moses und Aron, biblical drama.

HIS LIFE

WHEN Arnold Schoenberg celebrated his seventy-fifth birthday, in September 1949, the occasion was not neglected by the world of music. As one of the dominating figures in the music of the twentieth century—by virtue of the twelve-tone system, a technique which he brought into being and which has had a profound influence on the musical thinking of our times; and by virtue of the often imaginative, original, and powerful music he wrote over a period of five decades—Arnold Schoenberg could hardly be ignored.

Commemorative all-Schoenberg concerts, covering a wide span of his creative activity, took place in different parts of the country. A part of its season's activity was allocated by the New Friends of Music, in New

York City, to Schoenberg's chamber music. A cycle of the four Schoenberg string quartets was presented, and these and several other major Schoenberg works were recorded. Several major orchestras included at least one Schoenberg work on their programs.

In the face of this homage (which, incidentally, does not take into account the numerous tributes paid to the composer, in forms other than public performances), Schoenberg maintained, toward critics and the music public in general, the aggressive and defiant attitude of the misunderstood genius.

There was, for example, the letter he wrote to James Fassett, the commentator for the New York Philharmonic-Symphony Orchestra radio broadcasts, when that organization included a portion of the *Gurre-Lieder* as a birthday tribute. Schoenberg thanked the orchestra for the performance of a work written so many years before. But he also expressed the hope that on his hundredth birthday the orchestra might get around to playing one of his more recent compositions. Schoenberg had evidently forgotten that the New York Philharmonic had given the world *première* of his *Ode to Napoleon,* written in 1942, and that the New York Philharmonic had more recently performed his 1944 *Theme and Variations.*

In April 1947 the American Academy and the National Institute of Arts and Letters conferred on Schoenberg a Special Award of Distinguished Achievement, carrying with it a cash prize of $1,000. By this gesture the American Academy honored Schoenberg for his notable contributions to American musical life. In a strangely worded letter Schoenberg acknowledged his gratitude, but he also hurled a bitter tirade against all those who continually misunderstood and vilified him. "I never understood what I had done to them to make them as malicious, as furious, as cursing, as aggressive," Schoenberg wrote. He concluded his letter by expressing the belief that part of the award should have gone to his lifelong opponents, whose vicious attacks were really responsible for his growing fame and acceptance. *"They* were the ones who really helped me."

A year and a half later, Schoenberg sent another bitter letter—this time to the editor of the *Saturday Review of Literature.* He was attacking Thomas Mann for taking advantage of "my literary property" in the novel *Doctor Faustus.* The principal character of Mann's novel is a composer who employs the twelve-tone system. Another composer would surely have been gratified to find a technique of his invention utilized as the basis of a novel by one of the world's great writers. But to Schoenberg—haunted by feelings of persecution—this represented not flattery but a personal attack. He was upset at the "consequences of ascribing my creation to another person which, in spite of being fictitious, is represented as a living man." And he foresaw the awful possibility of an encylcopedist of the year 2060 attributing "my theory" to Thomas Mann! It is, to say the least, a strange hurt that Schoenberg was nursing. It seems stranger still when one realizes that Mann had included the following unequivocal statement as an explanatory note in the first edition of his novel: "It does not seem supererogatory to inform the reader that the form of musical composition delineated in Chapter XXII, known as the twelve-tone or row system, is in truth the intellectual property of a contemporary composer and theoretician, Arnold Schoenberg. I have transferred this technique in a certain ideational context to the fictitious figure of a musician, the tragic hero of my novel. In fact, the passages of this book that deal with musical theory are indebted in numerous details to Schoenberg's *Harmonielehre.*"

The catalogue of grievances that Schoenberg compiled against the world of music is familiar to all those who knew him. The critics, he said, did not understand him, the general public did not like him, and many who should have known better were inclined to regard him more as a great innovator and theoretician than as a creative artist. Besides, he felt, his works were not performed often enough; and those of his works that were performed did not represent his art in all its maturity, for they belonged to a creative past long since rejected by him.

Yet Schoenberg was by no means an unsung prophet. There are few contemporary writers on music who have not, for a long time now, considered him one of the major creative forces of our day, or who have denied him the right to stand with the half dozen of our most important composers. Nicolas Slonimsky went so far as to say that Schoenberg has succeeded in establishing "the first rational system of new composition since the fugue," while in a review Virgil Thomson described one of Schoenberg's provocative compositions, *Five Pieces for Orchestra,* as "among the most celebrated works of our century."

The general music public also came to appreciate him in an ever increasing measure. The day when a Schoenberg work used to unleash storms in the concert auditorium is long past. In recent years, reactions to Schoenberg's works have been unquestionably enthusiastic—and the works heard have represented not only the Schoenberg of the distant past, but also his much more recent works. Such an emphatic success was scored by the *Theme and Variations* that, between 1944 and 1948, it was performed by virtually every great American orchestra. A Schoenberg concert presented in September 1949 by "Evenings on the Roof," in Los Angeles, could not accommodate all those who wanted to attend. And, as if to prove that this was by no means a local phenomenon, an overflowing house in New York heard the all-Schoenberg concert sponsored, in November 1949, by the International Society for Contemporary Music.

For the last three decades of his life, Schoenberg knew the adulation of disciples who derived from him their inspiration and strength, who paid him that highest of all tributes—imitation. Schoenberg has seen many famous composers, in many different parts of the world, adopt his technique as the basis of their art: Alban Berg and Anton Webern (1883–1945) in Vienna of the 1920s; Ernst Křenek (1900–) among Viennese composers who settled in this country; Luigi Dallapiccola (1904–) from Italy. There have been major composers who, while not embracing his theory completely, nevertheless have utilized it on occasion for specific artistic effects, as Béla Bartók did in his Violin Concerto.

It may be true that Schoenberg was not the most frequently performed of contemporary composers; and it may also be true that some of his contemporaries—several of lesser stature—were more successful. Unfortunately, it is not always possible for every composer to get the precise share of recognition that is his due. But, on the other hand, Schoenberg—in the last decade of his life—was far from being a much maligned and neglected genius.

His victory was, of course, not an easy one. The role of the prophet and pioneer is a lonely one in a conformist society. For many years Schoenberg stood virtually alone against a hostile world. The intensity of his struggle inevitably created bitternesses within him. In the early years his wounds were real.

The battles that raged around him began virtually at the dawn of his career and continued for many years. He began studying the violin at the Realschule in Vienna, which he attended for six years. Although he began composing early, learned to play the cello by himself, and frequently participated with his friends in chamber-music performances, he did not arrive at the decision to become a professional musician until his sixteenth year. At that time, following the death of his father, he showed one of his compositions to the eminent Viennese composer and teacher Alexander Zemlinsky (1872–1942). Zemlinsky saw so much talent there that he immediately assumed the role of guardian to the boy. He gave him a job as cellist in the Polyhymnia Orchestra, which he then directed. He also taught him counterpoint (the only formal instruction Schoenberg ever received), introduced him into a musical circle of friends, and always stood ready to provide him with the benefits of his experience and wisdom. After several years Schoenberg completed a string quartet, which became his first work to receive a public performance. The reaction to it was noncommittal. But some songs, heard in Vienna in 1900, aroused hostility. "And from that time on," Schoenberg remarked, "the scandals never ceased."

Schoenberg's most important work during this apprentice period was the *Verklärte Nacht* (*Transfigured Night*), completed as a sextet in 1899 but transcribed for chamber orchestra in 1917. In 1900 Schoenberg started work on his most ambitious composition up to that time, the *Gurre-Lieder*, a vast setting of a cycle of poems by Jens Peter Jacobsen for soloists, chorus, and orchestra. Schoenberg here utilized such immense musical forces that in writing down his score he had to order manuscript paper of a special size. Most of the *Gurre-Lieder* was completed by the end of 1901, but Schoenberg did not get around to orchestrating it, and making a last revision, until a decade later. Meanwhile, he completed a symphonic poem, *Pelleas und Melisande,* the *Quartet in D minor,* and the *Kammersymphonie.*

He was also attending to the prosaic business of earning a living. In 1901 he married Mathilde Zemlinsky, the sister of his friend and teacher. To support himself and his wife he had to do a great deal of hack work. He orchestrated numerous operettas (he once estimated that in this period he produced about six thousand pages of such orchestrations). He led a cabaret orchestra in Berlin, to which city he had come soon after his marriage. More gratifying by far was his post as teacher at the Stern Conservatory, which he had acquired through the recommendation of Richard Strauss.

He was back in Vienna in July 1903, devoting himself to composing and teaching. He was growing more and more individual, more and more daring in his writing, as he began to renounce the traditional concepts of harmony and tonality. It was at this time that he started gathering around him students who believed as he did and who were influenced by his trenchant intellect, individual theories, and the originality of his music. Those students, who included Alban Berg and Anton Webern, became his passionate disciples and were soon to establish a new school of composition embodying Schoenberg's principles and ideas. Schoenberg was also acquiring a few allies among the powerful musicians of Vienna, notably Gustav Mahler, the great composer and conductor, and Guido Adler, the professor of music history at the University of Vienna.

On January 26, 1905, Schoenberg directed the *première* of his symphonic poem, *Pelleas und Melisande,* at a concert of the Society of Creative Musicians. Neither the audience nor the critics disguised their hostility to this music. Ludwig Karpath epitomized the Viennese reaction with the following stinging sentence in *Die Signale:* "One deals here with a man either devoid of all sense or who takes his listeners for fools." When the Rosé Quartet introduced the *Quartet in D minor,* on February 15, 1907, the hostility to Schoenberg had grown to such proportions that a riot developed in the concert hall. Thereafter, for the next decade or so, every performance of a new Schoenberg work provoked the audience to laughter, derision, or shouts and hisses of disapproval, and sometimes even started fist fights and ugly brawls. There was a disturbance in London when the *Five Pieces for Orchestra* was performed there in 1912. The critic of the London *Daily Mail* described the music "as scrappy sounds and perpetual discord," while the reviewer for the *Daily News* expressed heartfelt sympathy for the composer who, by his own admission, had depicted his own experiences in this music. A little more than a month after that, Berlin heard the world *première* of *Pierrot lunaire.* There was hysteria in the audience; blows were exchanged; one woman fainted. "If this is music," wrote Otto Taubmann in the *Börsen Courier,* "then I pray my Creator not to let me hear it again." Some years later, reverberations of this concert were still felt; in a Berlin court, one of the men of that audience brought suit against another for assault. A prominent physician testified that the music had been so nerve-racking as to arouse strange neuroses.

The *Gurre-Lieder* was the exception to the existing rule that Schoenberg's works be violently attacked. When it was introduced in Vienna under the direction of Franz Schreker, on February 23, 1913, it made a profound impression. The final chorus, "Behold the Sun!" had such an impact that the audience rose to its feet and remained standing until the end. The ovation after that was thunderous. Schoenberg refused to acknowledge the acclaim, leaving the concert hall hurriedly while the audience was clamoring for his appearance on the stage. "For years those people who cheered me tonight refused to recognize me," he remarked bitterly in explaining his attitude. "Why should I thank them for appreciating me now?"

But the great success of the *Gurre-Lieder* did not mean that Schoenberg had finally won his battle with his audiences. Far from it! Only one month later a performance of his *Kammersymphonie* provoked a riot. A dispatch to the *Musical Courier* tells the story: "If this concert was intended to be a 'memorable occasion' it surely succeeded, for it occasioned the greatest uproar that has occurred in a Viennese concert hall. . . . Laughter, hisses and applause continued throughout a great part of the actual performance. . . . The dispute almost became a riot. The police were sought after and the only officer who could be found actually threw out of the gallery one noisemaker who persisted in blowing on a key for a whistle. But this policeman could not prevent one of the composers from appearing in the box and yelling to the crowd: 'Out with the trash!' Whereat the uproar increased. Members of the orchestra descended from the stage and entered into the spirited controversy with the audience."

During World War I, Schoenberg served in the Austrian army. It was at this time that he began formulating the technique with which his name is associated: the twelve-tone system. He did not begin writing in this revolutionary manner until 1922, but after that the technique dominated his musical thinking and for a long time completely governed his writing.

From the end of World War I to the rise of the Nazi government in Germany, Schoenberg divided his activities between Berlin and Vienna. In Berlin he assumed the chair in the Prussian Academy of Arts vacated by the death of Ferruccio Busoni (1866-1924). In Vienna he divided his activities between teaching and composing. More and more, he drew sharply away from audiences, critics, public performances, and the world of music outside his own intimate circle of friends, pupils, and disciples. He founded in Vienna the Society for Private Performances which—since it barred all critics and admitted only those who were sympathetic—allowed for a more favorable climate in which his works, and those of his followers, could be heard. No longer did he seek performances elsewhere; sometimes he went out of his way to discourage them. He almost never attended a concert at which his works were played, and his works were heard on few occasions. Possibly as a carryover from the past, he avoided public performances of his works up to the end of his life.

And yet there were signs that his position in contemporary music— if not actually his works—was being appreciated. In 1924 the occasion of his fiftieth birthday was celebrated at the Vienna Town Hall with a speech by the Mayor of the city and a performance by the chorus of the

Vienna State Opera. The Viennese music magazine *Anbruch* devoted an entire issue to him, and his disciples published a book about him.

When the Nazis assumed power in Germany, Schoenberg disassociated himself completely from Berlin and came to the sad decision that he could remain in Europe no longer. The racial persecution in Germany also sent him back into the Hebrew faith, which he had abandoned through conversion to Christianity; he was officially reinstalled as a member of the Jewish faith in a ceremony in a Paris synagogue on July 24, 1933.

He came to the United States late in 1933, conscious that he had come here for good. (He became a citizen on April 11, 1941.) For a while he conducted some classes at the Malkin School of Music in Boston. Then he settled permanently in Los Angeles and taught first at the University of Southern California and after that at the University of California, from which he retired in his seventieth year. After that he taught privately, generally gathering around him a class of about eight pupils. He gave up all teaching only one month before his death.

As a composer, he was highly productive. Some of his most ambitious works were written in this country, including the *String Quartet No. 4,* two concertos (one for violin, the other for piano), the *Theme and Variations for Orchestra,* the *Ode to Napoleon,* and *A Survivor from Warsaw.* These and other important works received performances throughout the country—particularly when his seventieth and seventy-fifth birthdays were celebrated—and usually with considerable enthusiasm on the part of audiences. In any event, the disturbances and hostilities of the 1910s and 1920s became things of the past. But the bitterness of his early struggles, unfortunately, remained with him to the very end. When he died, at his home in Brentwood, California, in his seventy-seventh year, he still nourished the conviction that he was a much misunderstood and much unappreciated composer.

HIS MUSIC

SCHOENBERG began as an ardent disciple of the Wagnerian music drama and as a faithful son of German post-Romanticism. In the years closing the nineteenth century, the young musicians of Vienna gathered at the Café Landtmann, opposite the Burgtheatre, to discuss the latest aesthetic theories. Schoenberg, just past his twenty-second birthday, shared the then current passion for *Tristan und Isolde* and for the blend of intellectualism and romanticism found in Brahms. These enthusiasms left their imprint on his early music. The string quartet which he wrote in 1897 was the kind of music that Vienna of the late 1890s liked to hear, romantic and expressive. In the two major works that followed—the famous *Verklärte Nacht* and the less popular *Pelleas und Melisande*—there is an increasing richness of harmonic texture, a greater plasticity of formal construction, and a growing inventiveness in melodic elaboration. But the writing is still, for the most part, in a traditional vein.

But it was not long before Schoenberg began to feel constrained by traditional forms and techniques, and to react against romanticism and Wagnerism. After the *Quartet in F-sharp minor,* completed in 1908, he refused for many years to use a key signature, in order to give his tonality greater freedom. He began to seek simplicity and economy; he began to experiment with new sounds. Two major works revealed this growing tendency toward severity of style, austerity of melodic writing, conciseness of form, avoidance of tonality and consonance: the *Five Pieces for Orchestra* and *Pierrot lunaire.*

He soon realized that this complete rebellion against the past only led to anarchy. His precise, mathematical mind felt the need for some kind of order, a new order. Thus, over a period of years, he evolved a system of his own which filled his need for freedom of movement while at the same time imposing on him a certain degree of discipline. That system was the twelve-tone technique. Schoenberg thenceforth built his works out of twelve arbitrary tones arranged in a definite order, each tone equal in importance to the others, no tone being repeated until the others had been used. This formula resulted in music that was ugly and brutal in sound, seemingly disorganized, and without an element of human feeling.

Up to the time he settled in this country, Schoenberg remained fanatically true to his system. But as he grew older, the artist grew more mellow. In some of his works he no longer used the twelve-tone technique at all, while in others it appeared only intermittently. He no longer concerned himself exclusively with musical abstractions completely divorced from human experience, but tried to make his music reflect the world around him. Most important of all, he now tried to bring even to his atonal writing a warmth of feeling and romantic expression.

But even the later works, for all their power and originality, do not fall easily on the ear. This is not the kind of music that can acquire great popular appeal. But its influence on the evolution of modern musical thinking has been profound.

ANALYTICAL NOTES

Orchestral Music. *Verklärte Nacht* (*Transfigured Night*) is music of Schoenberg's youth; in its romantic ardor, passionate glow, and emotional intensity it is essentially the music of youth. It is most familiar in the transcription for chamber orchestra made by the composer from the original sextet version.

It was inspired by a poem of Richard Dehmel, which Henry E. Krehbiel summarized as follows: "Two mortals walk through a cold, barren grove. The moon sails over the tall oaks, which send their scrawny branches up through the unclouded moonlight. A woman speaks. She confesses a sin to the man at her side; she is with child, and he is not its father. . . . She had thought herself blessed, but now life had avenged itself upon her, by giving her love of him she walked with. She staggers onward, gazing with lack-lustre eye at the moon which follows her. A man speaks. Let her not burden her soul with thoughts of guilt. . . . Together they are driving over chill waters, but a flame from each warms the other. It, too, will transfigure the little stranger, and she will bear the child to him. For she has inspired the brilliant glow within him and made him, too, a child. They sink into each other's arms. Their breaths meet in kisses in the air. Two mortals wander through the wondrous moonlight."

The work can be divided into two separate sections, the first concerned with the woman's confession of sin and the second with the man's forgiveness. A slow and highly atmospheric introduction describes the walk through the darkness of a grove at the beginning. It is also used to link the two sections, and it returns a last time at the end of the tone poem.

The music of the tone poem is a sensitive and delicate nocturnal picture in which themes appear episodically; the effect of the work as a whole comes from the harmonic colors and the sensuous moods. The shimmering moonlight, the tender walk, the quiet confession, and the gentle forgiveness are all caught in music that passes from sensuousness to radiance, from otherworldly tranquillity to intensity. The music arrives at a climactic point with a violin solo in the upper register against delicately plucked chords—a vision of the transfigured night. Radiant love music follows. Soon the theme of the transfigured night and the love music become contrapuntally enmeshed. A crescendo is a final outburst of passion, but the tone poem ends on a tranquil note with a repetition of the opening introduction.

The *Theme and Variations for Orchestra* is the only one of Schoenberg's later works to acquire wide acceptance. This is because it is the only one of his mature compositions to be consistently tonal (the prevailing key is G minor), to indulge in romantic harmonic writing, and to adopt a traditional concept of form. Schoenberg wrote it in 1943 for band, intending it for school use. One year later he transcribed it for symphony orchestra. After its *première* by the Boston Symphony Orchestra under Serge Koussevitzky, on October 20, 1944, it was performed by most of the major American orchestras, and usually with great success.

The theme is a twenty-one-bar march. In the seven variations that follow, harmonic and thematic germs of the march are used to produce new themes. The first two variations are in an accelerated tempo, the first variation evolving logically from the march, while the second variation grows naturally out of the first. The third variation is a slow song; the fourth is in a waltz rhythm; and the fifth is an inverted canon. The sixth is fast, turbulent, and with a fugal character. The concluding variation has the semblance of a chorale prelude. In the finale, ideas previously presented, though frequently in altered form, are treated contrapuntally.

Franz Schubert

"He has strains for the most subtle thoughts and feelings, nay even for the events and conditions of life; and innumerable as are the shades of human thought and action, so various is his music."
—*Robert Schumann*

BORN: Vienna, January 31, 1797.
DIED: Vienna, November 19, 1828.
MAJOR WORKS: *Orchestral Music*—Symphony No. 8, in B minor, "Unfinished"; Symphony No. 9, in C major; Incidental music to Rosamunde. *Chamber Music*—Quartet in A minor; Quartet in D minor, "Death and the Maiden"; Quintet in C major, for strings; Quintet in A major, for piano and strings, "Die Forelle"; Trio in B-flat major, for piano and violin, and cello; Trio in E-flat major, for piano, violin, and cello. *Piano Music*—Moments musicaux; Impromptus; Sonata in C minor, Sonata in A major, Sonata in B-flat major (posthumous). *Vocal Music*—More than 600 songs, including "Gretchen am Spinnrade," "Erlkönig," "Hark, hark, the Lark," "Die Forelle," "Der Tod und das Mädchen," "Ave Maria," "Ständchen," "An die Musik," and so forth; song cycles, Die schöne Müllerin, Die Winterreise, Schwanengesang. ALSO: Symphonies Nos. 1 through 7; Masses; other string quartets, piano sonatas, songs, and so forth.

HIS LIFE

Franz Schubert's father was a simple man who neither over-estimated his own modest ability nor allowed himself the luxury of entertaining ambitions beyond his limited reach. For a few years he was a parish schoolmaster in the Lichtenthal suburb of Vienna. From his frugal earnings (a single florin a month for each child in his class) he was able to save enough to purchase the schoolhouse (which he was thenceforth to use for his living quarters as well): a modest investment bringing a modest income. His station remained humble; but he knew his place and was satisfied with it. Before buying the school, he had married a cook; they brought children into the world without delay. And if he had no great ambitions for himself, he also had none for his children. He wanted them to become schoolmasters too—as upright, hard-working, and self-respecting as he was.

He was early given testimony that his son Franz had exceptional talent for music. Probably incapable of believing that any son of his could be a genius—or governed by a sound practical sense which told him that a self-supporting teacher was better off than a starving musician—he never allowed himself to be deflected from the goal of making his son a teacher. Not that he was unmusical himself. He was a good amateur cellist, encouraged music making at home, and often joined his children in performances of chamber music.

In keeping with the musical interests of the whole family, the child Franz was soon taught music. His father gave him some lessons on the violin, and before long the two were playing duets. His brother Ferdinand taught him the piano. In a few months Franz had outdistanced his brother completely and had quietly announced that he preferred thenceforth to proceed on his own; Ferdinand had to concede that there was not much more he could teach his brother. Schubert was then placed in the hands of the parish choirmaster, Michael Holzer, who taught him singing and thorough bass, as well as something about the organ and viola. After Schubert had been with Holzer a short period, the old man said, "He seems to know each lesson perfectly before I can begin explaining it to him."

In 1808 the Vienna newspapers announced that two vacancies among the Imperial Chapel choirboys were to be filled by examination. Those selected would be given free tuition, board, and lodging at the School of the Imperial and Royal Court Chapel while being trained for the choir. Holzer was eager to have Schubert apply; the boy would get the kind of musical instruction his great talent required. And Schubert's father agreed to the plan only because he felt that such an education was excellent preparation for the teaching profession.

Schubert presented himself at the Chapel School for examination; he wore a long gray smock which encouraged several of the other candidates to refer to him as "the miller's boy." Always shy and timid, he grew flustered. But when the examiners—one of whom was the celebrated Antonio Salieri (1750–1825), dean of Viennese musicians—gave him trial pieces to sing, he performed with such assurance and sound musicianship that he was accepted without hesitation.

Life at the school was not easy. The rooms were never heated; often they were insufferably cold. The food was both poor and scarce. Schubert would send appealing letters to his brother asking for a few extra coins a month to enable him to buy an apple or some bread to supplement his inadequate diet. But there were compensations; and, for all his physical deprivations, Schubert was comparatively happy. There was music all the time. Besides composing, what he liked best of all was to play in the orchestra. Each evening, for an hour and a half, the students were guided through the works of Haydn, Mozart, and Beethoven. The experience of getting to know this music was a continual source of excitement. Schubert described Mozart's overture to *The Marriage of Figaro* as "the most beautiful in the whole world." Playing Mozart's *Symphony in G minor* was a revelation; "you could hear the angels sing," he said. The slow movements of Haydn's symphonies moved him greatly. But his most profound admiration—even awe—was reserved for the great Beethoven.

His teachers were greatly impressed by the effortless way in which he learned everything taught him. One day Ruzička exclaimed, "I can't teach him anything else, he's learned it all from God himself!" He was then put into Salieri's class. Before long Schubert submitted to his teacher an extended song called *"Hagars Klage."* Salieri said, "You can do everything, for you are a genius."

He did not make friends easily. He was too withdrawn, diffident, and timid. Yet a few boys were attracted both to the softness of his nature and to his phenomenal talent. They befriended him and immediately became touchingly sympathetic and devoted. One of these was Josef von Spaun—for the rest of his life one of Schubert's dearest friends and greatest admirers. In his memoirs, Spaun recalled how he was first drawn to Schubert: "The tiny fellow did not seem at ease in that institution, for he was always serious and not very friendly. As he was already rather proficient on the violin, he was taken into the small orchestra. . . . I was the leader of the second violins. Little Schubert stood behind me and fiddled, looking over my shoulder. Very soon, I noticed that the little musician far surpassed me in rhythmic surety. This aroused my interest and made me realize with what animation the lad, who otherwise seemed quiet and indifferent, gave himself up to his impression of the beautiful symphonies which we did. Once I came upon him alone in the music room, sitting at the piano which his tiny hands could already play very passably. He was just then trying over a Mozart sonata, and said that he liked it very much, but found

Mozart difficult to perform well. Under my friendly encouragement, he played me a minuet of his own invention. He was shy and red with shame; but my approval made him happy. The lad confided to me that he often secretly wrote his thoughts down; but Father mustn't know about it; for he was dead set against his son's devoting himself to music. After that I sometimes slipped him music paper."

Now that Spaun provided him with music paper, Schubert wrote continually. He completed several chamber-music works, a nonet, some choral pieces, a great deal of piano music, songs, and (in his final weeks at the Court Chapel School) a symphony.

Schubert's voice broke in 1813. Most students were compelled to leave the Chapel School when their voices broke. But Schubert might have remained on a scholarship if he had consented to make up a deficiency in mathematics. But he had grown tired of school life. He returned to his father's house. Expediency dictated that he yield to his father's wish and become a teacher, and for two reasons: first, because teaching exempted him from military service; second, because he had to think of making a living. He completed a preparatory course at the St. Anna Normal School, and in the fall of 1814 assumed a teaching post at his father's school.

He hated teaching and the schoolroom, was incapable of maintaining discipline, and was completedly uninterested in the studies he had to teach. For two years he slaved at the schoolmaster's desk. On two occasions he tried freeing himself by applying for musical posts, but on both occasions he was rejected.

But his occupation could not dam the irrepressible creative stream. In the classroom, while the pupils were scribbling in their notebooks, he wrote music. Most of his evenings and some of his nights were consumed in composition. In 1814 he completed his first opera, his first Mass, two string quartets, and many smaller pieces for piano and for voice—including his first undisputed masterpiece, the song *"Gretchen am Spinnrade."* During the year of 1814 he also had one of his works performed publicly for the first time. The *Mass in F major* was heard at the Lichtenthal church on October 16, under his own direction, and was repeated ten days later at a different church. The venerable Salieri attended this second performance, embraced the young composer, and said, "You are a worthy pupil, and you will do me great credit."

The year of 1815 was even more fruitful: two symphonies, two Masses, one opera, four operettas, four sonatas, pieces for the piano, several small choral works, and 146 songs (including *"Erlkönig"*).

He wrote with a rapidity that was incredible. One movement of a quartet was completed in less than five hours. He wrote sometimes six, sometimes eight, songs in a single day—*"Gretchen am Spinnrade"* and *"Erlkönig"* were produced at a single sitting each.

Schubert's boyhood friend Spaun revealed how the *"Erlkönig"* was written. "One afternoon, Mayrhofer and I called on Schubert. . . . We found him all aglow, reading *'Der Erlkönig'* out of a book which he carried several times to and fro across the room. Suddenly, he sat, and in the shortest possible time the magnificent ballad was put down on paper. As Schubert had no piano, we ran with it to the Chapel School; and there that evening, the *'Erlkönig'* was sung . . . and received with enthusiasm. Ruzička . . . then played it through effectively without voice. He was so appreciative and the composition moved him deeply. When some of the hearers criticized a recurrent dissonance, Ruzička sounded it on the piano and explained how necessarily it mirrored the text; more than that, how beautiful it was and how happily it was resolved."

The above quotation mentions the name Mayrhofer. Johann Mayrhofer, an official in the censor's bureau but a poet by avocation, had joined the widening circle of Schubert's friends. Schubert had written the music for one of his poems, *"Am See,"* and from that moment on they were fast friends. The other new and close friends included Franz von Schober, the restless dilettante and aristocrat, drawn to the composer after hearing some of his songs. And then there was the famous singer Johann Vogl, certainly the most celebrated of this group. All of these men clung to Schubert up to the time of his death. They gave him the only full measure of appreciation he was destined to receive, and his only happiness. Characteristic of their attitude toward Schubert was a remark by Vogl—he who could be so haughty and domineering. "We must all bend the knee before Schubert's genius," he once said when Schubert kept him waiting. "If he does not come, we must creep after him on our knees."

Schubert had had enough of the classroom. In 1816 he broke once and for all with the teaching profession, preferring uncertainty and poverty to classroom drudgery. He went to live with his friend Schober and gave himself up completely to his music. Thenceforth he would reside first with one friend, then with another, usually dependent on their generosity for his livelihood.

It was often a Bohemian kind of existence. Schubert and his friends were, primarily, a happy-go-lucky group, given to evening parties, gaiety, café discussions, and the drinking of wine. When one had money, everybody ate well and drank. When money was scarce, they consoled themselves with their capacity for having innocent fun. At the homes of his friends there were merry evenings which soon came to be known as "Schubert evenings." Vogl would sing the *lieder;* Schubert would play some of his piano works. There would also be feasting and dancing. Frequently a light mood would prevail. Schubert would amuse his friends with parodies at the piano, or would perform a piece of music, with mock seriousness, through the teeth of a comb. After such a session they would sometimes go to the café for wine and discussions on art, literature, and music; then they would proceed to the next café, until half the night was gone.

His friends have left us vivid accounts of his daily life in their midst. Anselm Hüttenbrenner wrote: "Every day at six in the morning, Schubert seated himself at his writing desk and composed without a break till one o'clock in the afternoon, smoking a few small pipes. If I came to see him in the morning, he would play to me what he had already composed and wait to hear my opinion. If I praised any song especially, he would say: 'Yes, that was a good poem; and when one has something good the music comes easily—melodies just stream from one, so that it is a real joy.'" After work, there would be a session at the café. Schubert would drink a cup of coffee (or wine, or punch, if money was free), and smoke for several hours. "When the blood of the vine glowed in him, he did not rant, but moved into a quiet corner to give himself up to a comfortable frenzy. A smiling tyrant who, if possible, would destroy something—glasses, for instance, or a plate or a cup—he would sit there and grin and contract his eyelids so that his eyes became very small."

His friends did not consider him "of very striking appearance." Eduard Bauernfeld even described him as "a lump of fat." To Hüttenbrenner he was "short, somewhat corpulent, with a full round face, but with eyes so sparkling that they revealed at once the inner fire. His brow had an agreeable curve. Because of his nearsightedness, he always wore eyeglasses." (Schober also revealed that very often Schubert slept with his eyeglasses so that, on awakening in the morning, he could begin composing without a moment's delay!) "He never concerned himself with his dress, and he detested going into higher society because it necessitated careful dressing. In short, he found it impossible to discard his spoiled frock coat for a black suit. To bow or scrape or cringe in society was odious to him, and to be flattered for his genius disgusted him."

In the summer of 1818 Schubert was engaged as music tutor at the summer estate of Count Esterházy in Zelész, Hungary. It was a pleasant enough experience (even though Schubert was treated as a servant). But he was homesick for Vienna and his friends, and was glad to be back with them that fall. (In 1824 he spent a second summer at Zelész as music tutor, this time to fall in love with one of the Esterházy daughters.)

By 1820 he had written more than five hundred works embracing every branch of composition. Of these only the *Mass in F major,* in 1814, and a single song, in 1819, had been heard publicly. But hope of recognition came in 1820. The Kärntnerthor Theater, instigated by Vogl, commissioned Schubert to write music for *Die Zwillingsbrüder*. Shortly after this, the Theatre-an-der-Wien followed suit, by asking for a score for *Die Zauberharfe*. Performance in two of Vienna's greatest theaters provided an opportunity to reveal his powers.

The *Zwillingsbrüder* (with Johann Vogl singing the two principal roles) was produced on June 14, 1820. The entire Schubert clique turned out to witness what it hoped would be his first triumph. "I sat beside Schubert in the last row of the gallery," wrote Hüttenbrenner. "He was quite pleased that the operetta was being received with loud applause. All the solos and scenes in which Vogl took part were clapped vigorously. At the end, Schubert was called, but he refused to come before the curtain because he had on an old shabby overcoat. I took off my black tail coat and tried to persuade him to put it on, and to present himself to the audience, which would have been a good thing for him. But he was too irresolute and bashful. As the calls became more and more persistent, the producer at last had to appear before the curtain and announce that Schubert was not in the house."

The audience liked the operetta; but the critics did not. The Vienna correspondent of the *Dresdener Abendzeitung* wrote that "the public received the operetta as if it were a masterpiece, which, of course, it was not." The *Wiener Sammler* found that Schubert's arias were "somewhat antiquated and many unmelodious." The critical reaction spelled doom. The *Zwillingsbrüder* was withdrawn after only six performances.

But Schubert could look forward to the first performance of *Die Zauberharfe* on August 19. Once again his hopes soared, and once again he was disappointed. The critics were still destructive. "It is much too long, ineffective, and fatiguing," wrote the critic of the *Leipzig Allgemeine Musikalische Zeitung.*

Such solace as Schubert could derive from the failure of his two stage works came from his first major publication. The *"Erlkönig"* was sung publicly by Johann Vogl on March 7, 1821, and received such a thunderous ovation that a few of Schubert's friends decided to publish it and some of Schubert's other songs at their own expense. A hundred subscribers were found—and, at long last, Schubert's Op. 1 made an appearance in Vienna.

But the failures at the Viennese theaters were followed by others. His incidental music to Wilhelmine von Chézy's *Rosamunde* was heard in 1823 and was accused of being "bizarre." The critic added: "On this occasion he got too much applause. May he never have to deplore getting too little." He had also written an opera called *Alfonso und Estrella,* which he brought to the notice of Karl Maria von Weber, composer of the famous *Der Freischütz.* Weber glanced hurriedly at the manuscript and (perhaps remembering a disparaging remark Schubert had made about him) said abruptly, "First puppies and first operas should be drowned."

Disappointment, frustration, and continual defeat—these were not all that harassed Schubert. There was also his intense poverty and, with it, the ravages of a venereal disease from which he was to suffer on and off for the rest of his life. Perhaps inevitably, he succumbed to desolation. "Picture to yourself," he wrote at this time to a friend, "a man whose health can never be re-established, who from sheer despair makes matters worse instead of better; picture to yourself, I say, a man whose most brilliant hopes have come to nothing, to whom proffered love and friendship are but anguish, whose enthusiasm for the beautiful threatens to vanish entirely, and then ask yourself if such a condition does not represent a miserable and unhappy man. . . . Each night when I go to sleep I hope never again to awaken, and every morning reopens the wounds of yesterday."

There would be respite from gloom in the company of his dear friends in the café and at their social gatherings. But when the merriment was over, and Schubert returned to his rooms, morbidity once again overwhelmed him. He could no longer make light of the fact that he was unknown, a failure, dependent on charity. "My days are spent in sorrow's laden ban," he wrote pathetically in a poem in which he tried to unburden his soul.

But neither his immense despair nor even his illness could stifle his creativeness. The ability was still there, together with a continual strengthening of his powers. While he was confined to the hospital, in 1823, tortured by pain, he began the settings for his song cycle *Die schöne Müllerin*. It was in the midst of frustration and spiritual anguish that he wrote the deathless springtime of music known as the *Unfinished* Symphony.

From this time on, and up to the end of his life, Schubert became subject to increasing melancholy and violent physical attacks. Once in a while—though none too often—there was happiness. One such period took place in the summer of 1825, when he took a long walking trip through Upper Austria with Vogl. They visited mutual friends, performed some of Schubert's latest works, and enjoyed the beautiful countryside. But always an even deeper despair succeeded these brief moments of happiness.

The death of Beethoven, in 1827, was a terrible blow. Although it is unlikely that Schubert ever came into personal contact with the master (the testimony on this point is conflicting), he had from boyhood on worshiped him from a reverent distance. "Who can ever hope to follow him?" he once said after hearing a concert of Beethoven's music. Beethoven was not altogether unaware of Schubert's existence. Just before his death he went through some Schubert songs which had been brought to his attention. "Surely," he said, "there is a divine spark of genius in this Schubert!"

But the giant was dead; and Schubert mourned his death as he had mourned no other person. Schubert carried one of the torches at Beethoven's funeral, and after Beethoven had been buried, he proposed a toast at a nearby tavern to the one who would be the first among them to follow Beethoven to the grave. From that moment on, he had one crowning ambition: to be buried next to Beethoven.

During this sad year of 1827 he was to write the tragic song cycle *Die Winterreise,* so full of the foreboding of death. Death and the heartbreak of tragedy were to weave their themes through his last works: the wonderful *C major String Quintet;* the three posthumously published piano sonatas; the *Mass in E-flat major;* the song cycle *Schwanengesang.*

He was to have one taste of success in this last year of his life. On March 26, 1828, the Musikverein of Vienna gave a concert, the entire program devoted to Schubert's works. It seemed that at last Vienna had awakened to his presence. The concert took place before "more people than the hall had ever been known to hold." The enthusiasm for Schubert's music was overwhelming. His day—his friends insisted —was at hand.

But he was sick, mortally sick. In September he was living with his brother in a suburb of Vienna, still making ambitious plans for the future: large works to be written; the study of counterpoint to be undertaken with a recognized master. Even while he lay dying, he was busily correcting the proofs of *Die Winterreise*. He wrote to Schober on November 12: "For eleven days I have neither eaten nor drunk anything. I am tottering from the chair to the bed and vice versa. . . . Whenever I eat anything, I promptly throw up. Do be kind and help me in this desperate condition by sending me some books. I have read Cooper's *The Last of the Mohicans, The Spy, The Pilot,* and *The Pioneers*. In case you have any other books by this author, I beg you to leave them for me at the café with Bogner's wife."

Six days later he became delirious. He babbled endlessly, mostly to inquire if he were lying next to Beethoven. He died in the afternoon of November 19, and two days after that the funeral train set out from Kettenbrückengasse, where Schubert had died, to the Church of St. Joseph. Here Schubert's *Pax Vobiscum* was sung to words by Schober. Schober recited a last poetic farewell, and the body was committed to earth—as near to Beethoven's grave as could be arranged.

Each of Schubert's friends spent that evening alone. Mayrhofer secluded himself in his rooms in the Wipplingerstrasse (where he had lived with Schubert) to write a poem, *Secret Remembrance to the Memory of Schubert*. Bauernfeld noted in his diary: "The most honest soul, the finest friend! I wish I were lying there instead of him!" The painter Schwind, then in Munich, wrote to Schober: "Schubert is dead, and with him all that was brightest and most beautiful in our life."

It was unusually quiet that evening at Bogner's café. When one of the patrons remarked on the strange absence of the Schubert clique, Herr Bogner answered, "Haven't you heard the news? Franz Schubert, the little musician, was buried today."

A few months later a monument was erected on Schubert's grave containing the following epitaph by the poet Grillparzer: "Music has here entombed a rich treasure, but still fairer hopes."

So little music by Schubert had been published or performed when he was alive that, at the time of his death, the music world was completely unaware of how much he had accomplished. For years, most of

Schubert's manuscripts (containing some of the most inspired music ever conceived) lay neglected or completely forgotten on dusty closet shelves, and in disorganized bundles. Their discovery by several different musicians, and over a period of many years, represents one of the most dramatic episodes in musical history.

The first discovery of a Schubert masterwork came a decade after his death. Robert Schumann, who knew some of Schubert's music and admired it, decided—during a visit to Vienna in 1838—to pay a call on the composer's brother, Ferdinand. Ferdinand showed Schumann a ragged package of Schubert manuscripts which had been lying in a disordered state on a shelf, untouched since the composer's death. Schumann browsed through them, then stopped short as he came upon the great *Symphony in C major,* the Ninth. He knew instantly what a prize had fallen into his hands. He sent a transcript of the work to the publishers Breitkopf and Härtel, urging its publication. He sent another copy to Felix Mendelssohn, then the conductor of the Gewandhaus Orchestra in Leipzig. He himself wrote a piece in his magazine proclaiming the importance of his discovery. "No symphony has made such a strong impression on us since the days of Beethoven," he announced. Schumann's devoted efforts bore immediate fruits in the publication of the symphony and its performance by Mendelssohn on March 21, 1839.

The world *première* of the *Unfinished* Symphony—which took place almost half a century after the work was written—was also made possible by an act of discovery. In this case, the discoverer was the Viennese conductor Johann Herbeck.

In 1860 one of Schubert's friends, Joseph Hüttenbrenner, wrote Herbeck urging him to perform something by his brother, Anselm, then living in Graz. There was bait to catch the interest of the conductor: Hüttenbrenner revealed that Anselm possessed "a treasure in Schubert's *B minor Symphony,* which we put on a level with the great *Symphony in C major,* his instrumental swan song, and any one of the symphonies by Beethoven."

It took Herbeck five years to do something about this piece of information. In 1865 Herbeck planned an all-Viennese program, and his desire to introduce a new work by Schubert sent him to Graz. Coyly he told Hüttenbrenner of his desire to perform one of his works. Then, having won over Anselm's interest, he added that he was also interested in something new by Schubert. The old man opened up a huge chest and pointed to a pile of manuscripts. Herbeck rummaged through them—and came upon the *Unfinished* Symphony. He had it copied, and on December 17, 1865, he introduced it to the world in Vienna.

This phenomenal find so excited two young Englishmen that they decided to set off for Vienna in search of some more Schubert gold; their immediate goal was to recover the long lost music to *Rosamunde*. One of these Englishmen was the musicologist George Grove, subsequently the editor of the celebrated *Dictionary of Music and Musicians;* the other was Arthur Sullivan, his fruitful collaboration with W. S. Gilbert still in the future. Their first stop in Vienna was at the publishing house of Spina. Spina turned them over to a Dr. Schneider who, he said, had many Schubert manuscripts. Schneider dumped one package of Schubert manuscripts after another into the laps of the two young English musicians, who thus stumbled upon Schubert's Symphonies Nos. 1, 2, 3, 4, and 6!

Still in search of *Rosamunde,* Grove and Sullivan prevailed on Spina to allow them to browse about in his manuscript collection. One decrepit bundle yielded about sixty Schubert songs, forty of them completely unknown. But still no sign of *Rosamunde!* Grove and Sullivan then returned to Schneider's house to intensify their search. Grove tells the rest of the story: "Might I go into the cupboard and look for myself? Certainly—if I had no objection to being smothered with dust. In I went. After some search, during which my companion kept the doctor engaged in conversation, I found, at the bottom of the cupboard, and in its furthest corner, a bundle of music books two feet high, carefully tied round, and black with the undisturbed dust of nearly half a century.... We were ... vociferous ... when we dragged out the bundle into the light and found that it was actually neither more nor less than what we were in search of.... For it was the part-books of the whole of the music in *Rosamunde,* tied up after the second performance, in December 1823, and probably never disturbed since." Besides the *Rosamunde,* they recovered a trio, a Stabat Mater, and many more songs. So excited did the young musicians become with their find that, midway in their hunt, they stopped short and played a game of leapfrog around the room.

HIS MUSIC

FRANZ SCHUBERT was the first musical voice of the Romantic movement, which swept over all of Europe in the first years of the nineteenth century. Romanticism had affected Beethoven strongly. But not until Schubert did the flood tide of that movement inundate all of music. Romanticism brought an altogether new concept of musical form, which now became completely elastic and servant to the idea. Schubert might at times function within the familiar boundaries of the symphony, the sonata, and the string quartet. But in his songs and smaller pieces for the piano, he succeeded in having his idea shape and mold the form. Romanticism gave birth to lyric poetry; as part of this development, Schubert gave birth to the *lied,* the German art song. Romanticism stressed the poetic idea, emphasized the personal element, made a fetish of beauty—even as Schubert did so instinctively and spontaneously.

The expression of beauty, the sustained poetry, the deeply personal element are found in other Romantic composers. But if Schubert is unique, it is for other qualities.

There is about a Schubert work the radiant joy of creation. Nothing betrays the pangs of birth pains, for the simple reason that those pains did not exist. We know the way Schubert worked. His masterworks came all in one piece. He did not labor over details, or work out an idea or an effect fastidiously the way other composers did. He rarely revised. Everything flowed naturally and without obstruction—not only his copious ideas and his warm sentiments, but even his frequently novel effects, his poignant modulations and striking transitions, an unexpected harmony, a breath-taking progression. He wrote only for his own delight and according to his own conscience; that delight shines in every page. He wrote easily and quickly; his best music has the ingratiating quality of spontaneity.

His music has what George Eliot once described as "mighty youth." It has freshness, optimism, fullness of heart, buoyancy, vibrancy, sentimentality, excitement—qualities of youth. It has a kind of youthful charm that ingratiates itself coyly, bewitches the listener, seduces him. (No one can be more lovable than Schubert.) It has a youthful kind of innocence about it, which does not depend for its effect on sophistication or passion.

His greatest gift was melody. The abundance of his lyricism, its incomparable beauty, its rich-textured poetry remain without parallel in music. He himself said that he no sooner got one idea on paper than several others started crowding into his consciousness. Melodic ideas haunted him all the time, one more wonderful than the other. Almost any kind of stimulus was enough to inspire a soaring lyric flight. In his songs and in the shorter piano pieces—which he could write in a single burst of inspiration with reliance on his unfailing melodic invention—he was the incomparable master.

But in his larger works he had serious technical shortcomings. (He achieved miraculous effects more through instinct than through design!) He did not have the power to enlarge and develop his thematic material, preferring either to present new ideas or to repeat old ones in different keys or with different instrumentation. His use of the variation form was often ingenuous, with the most obvious alternations. His contrapuntal technique was notoriously weak. Many of his large works suffer seriously from such faults, and it is due to these faults that so much of what he wrote (particularly the operas) is in permanent discard.

Yet he was not exclusively a miniaturist. The composer of the *Unfinished* and C major Symphonies, the *Forelle* and C major Quintets, the A minor and *Death and the Maiden* Quartets, the Piano Trios in B-flat and E-flat was a creator in great designs. Here his inspiration was unfailing. He used his melodic gift with such richness, expressiveness, and variety that not for a moment do we get a feeling of artistic frustration.

ANALYTICAL NOTES

Orchestral Music. The *Unfinished* Symphony, in B minor, is Schubert's Eighth, even though it was written when the composer was only twenty-five. It is his first masterwork in the symphonic form, and one of the most popular symphonies of all.

The description "unfinished" refers, of course, to the fact that it has only two, instead of the traditional four, movements. Schubert actually sketched out more than a hundred measures of a third-movement scherzo and orchestrated nine of them. But he never completed it and never began a fourth movement. Although he lived another six years and wrote another symphony, he never attempted to provide his *Unfinished* Symphony with its two complementary movements. It may well be that in the first two movements he realized such a consistently high level of inspiration, such perfection of integration between style and form that even he was incapable of providing other music worthy of them.

It begins with a solemn introductory theme rising from the basses and cellos. A quiet running figure in the violins is the background for a sweet, melancholy tune for oboe and clarinet. Winds join in. For a brief period the mood becomes somewhat disturbed, but several loud chords bring this phase to an end. A more peaceful atmosphere now prevails. Against syncopated chords in violas and clarinets, the cellos present one of the most beautiful melodies found in symphonic literature. The violins repeat it more tenderly. Suddenly the music becomes stormy and tragic. But the second melody, wonderfully treated in the strings and woodwinds, restores the calm. The development, which is mostly intense and agitated, is brought in with the solemn introductory theme, while the recapitulation returns with the sweet, melancholy tune in oboe and clarinet against the running figure in the violins. In the coda, the introductory theme is worked out with great emotional force.

The first movement contains both quiet melancholy and agitated tragedy. But the second movement is music of the most fragile loveliness, its gentle serenity untouched by emotional conflict. There are two principal melodies, each Schubertian in its effeminate softness and breathless beauty. The first is heard at once in the violins, while a descending scale is plucked out by the basses as a background. There is a passing moment of strength, with vigorous accents in the strings and a strong theme for trombones and woodwinds. The opening melody reappears. We now hear the second melody, an exquisite idyl, given by the clarinet against a syncopated figure in the strings. This second melody soon acquires force in full orchestra. But the pastoral character of the movement as a whole is maintained as both main themes are brought back, sometimes in wonderful but easily recognizable transformations.

The *Symphony in C major* is chronologically Schubert's ninth and last symphony, having been written in the last year of his life. Due to the fact that it was published before the *Unfinished,* it is sometimes designated as *Symphony No. 7.* It is a work of greater structural design than the *Unfinished,* with a wider gamut of expression. It has such impressive dimensions that it is customarily referred to as the "Great C major Symphony," while Robert Schumann referred to its "heavenly length."

A long introduction to the first movement is dominated by a dignified theme which is first given softly by the horn and then tenderly repeated by the woodwinds. A stormy crescendo leads to the main body of the movement, which begins with a strong, rhythmic theme divided between strings and woodwinds. This is worked out with considerable vigor before the second theme—more deft and graceful than the first—is heard in oboes and bassoon. There is still a third important subject, arising out of the involved texture of the development of the second theme: a majestic melody for the trombones. These ideas are developed with a passion, intensity, heroic breadth, and dramatic interest that we associate more with Beethoven than with Schubert— and that emphasizes how immense was Schubert's growth as a symphonic composer and how far he might have gone had he lived. The movement ends with a powerful surge toward, and a magnificent restatement of, the theme of the introduction.

If the first movement contains much to remind us of Beethoven, the second is pure Schubert. Several introductory bars lead to a song for oboe, soon joined by clarinet. The arch of this melody grows more spacious. A more vigorous idea is interpolated by full orchestra before the melody is repeated. A second broadly lyrical section now appears in the strings; it is quietly introspective, gentle, and lovable as only Schubert could be. At the conclusion of this part, mysterious calls in the trumpet are sounded, which Schumann described as "descended from another sphere." Earlier material is recalled, and with it a new passage so strikingly beautiful as to be almost painful: an exquisite chant for the cello (while other strings provide a pizzicato background) in which is joined the plangent voice of the oboe in a countertheme. All these melodies are reviewed, and the movement ends on a note of sublimity with a final recall of the eloquent duet of cello and oboe.

The scherzo begins with a strongly accented theme (like an Austrian peasant dance) shared by strings and oboe. This grows into a more suave, waltzlike melody for the strings, with a countersubject in the cellos. Still another dancelike theme is prominent: a graceful subject heard first in the flute and then carried on by oboe and violins. All this material is elaborated upon before the arrival of the trio. In the trio the main theme is heralded by a repeated "E" in the horns; the theme itself, for the woodwinds, has the character of an Austrian folk song. After the trio, the entire scherzo section is recalled.

The finale begins with an outburst of demoniac energy. There is a vigorous outcry in the full orchestra, followed by an ebullient triplet figure in the strings. This is the basic material of the introductory section, but the rhythm of the triplet figure appears and reappears throughout the rest of the movement and gives it much of its motor energy. The first principal theme, however, is a flowing figure for the oboes. The second theme, preceded by four "Ds" in the horns and presented by the woodwinds, has for its accompaniment a throbbing background of the introductory triplet figures. In the development section, the four horn notes that prefaced the second theme are used to set powerful forces into action. All the thematic ideas of the movement are brought back in the recapitulation.

From the incidental music that Schubert wrote in 1823 for the play *Rosamunde,* only three pieces have survived: the overture; the ballet music; and the third entr'acte. But the *Rosamunde* Overture that is heard today is not the one that was used in 1823; it is one that Schubert had written three years earlier for *Die Zauberharfe.* It begins with a stately slow section. After some preliminary chords, a graceful melody is given by oboe and clarinet. The first theme of the allegro part is a sprightly tune for the first violins. After a vigorous workout of this theme, a beautiful second melody appears in the woodwinds.

The enchanting, and characteristically Viennese, ballet music is deservedly popular, particularly the second dance, in G major, which is also famous in Fritz Kreisler's charming transcription for violin and piano. The beautiful song for strings which is heard in the third entr'acte (B-flat major) is the same melody used by Schubert for the slow movement for his *A minor Quartet* and in the *B-flat major Impromptu* for piano.

Chamber Music. Schubert wrote fifteen string quartets, as well as two quintets, two piano trios, an octet, and various lesser works. Not all of this music is of the first rank, but an amazingly high average is attained.

Some of Schubert's string quartets are second-rate. A few are interesting for flashes of Schubertian genius. But two are not only among Schubert's greatest and most consistent masterworks, but among the finest in the entire literature for the string quartet.

The *Quartet in A minor* (1824) begins with one of those bittersweet melodies that are the exclusive property of Schubert. This wonderful song in the first violin, against a gently swaying figure in the second, is in the class of his finest *lieder*. A forceful transitional theme leads to a second melody, which continues in the melancholy vein of the opening theme. In the development, Schubert devotes himself exclusively to the first theme.

The main melody of the slow movement was one of Schubert's favorites. He used it again as an entr'acte in *Rosamunde* and another time as a piano impromptu. Once again we are in the presence of incomparable lyrical genius. H. L. Mencken once wrote that a melody such as this was the convincing proof of the existence of God.

The minuet begins unorthodoxically with a single phrase in the lower register of the cello, repeated by the other strings. Out of this phrase, the minuet melody evolves naturally. It is a song of sadness and sweetness which we do not ordinarily associate with the minuet. The elegiac mood prevails in the trio. But if the minuet is unexpectedly melancholy, the finale realizes in its happy spirit the expectations of the listener. It begins with a lively Hungarian dance theme. The personality of the Hungarian folk song and the drive of Hungarian folk rhythms are prominent throughout the movement.

The *Quartet in D minor* (1826) is subtitled *"Der Tod und das Mädchen"* (or "Death and the Maiden"), because Schubert used part of his own famous *lied* in the second movement. But the presence of death can be detected in the other three movements too. The quartet was written after a period of illness and despair. The thought of death was uppermost in Schubert's mind at the time, and it penetrated every pore of his music. Few of his chamber-music works have so unified an atmosphere—funereal and dramatic moods prevailing in all four movements. The first begins with a defiant phrase which W. W. Cobbett interpreted as a struggle with death; the element of struggle is prominent in the first theme that follows. There is, however, a feeling of resignation in the second theme.

Schubert used only the second half of his song "Death and the Maiden" in the second movement: the exhortation of death, rather than the earlier frantic appeal of the maiden. In the quartet, the melodic idea of the song becomes a starting point for a new song, which—after its complete statement—is subjected to five variations. The scherzo opens vigorously, but the trio is once again permeated with sadness. There is a febrile atmosphere in the finale, which begins with a breathless tarantella theme. The subsidiary theme is a solemn declamation for the four instruments in which there is an echo of Schubert's song *"Erlkönig"*—still one more suggestion of a struggle with death.

The shadow of death hovers even more darkly over the *Quintet in C major,* for strings (two violins, viola, and two cellos). It was Schubert's last chamber-music work, written in the final year of his life and probably in his very last months (the exact date is unknown). Nowhere did he give voice to such pathos as in the first three movements of this quintet. The first movement begins with the swelling of dynamics, on a single note, from piano to forte, out of which grows the tender but emotionally restrained first theme. The high point of this movement, how-ever, is the second theme—a fully developed elegy first given by the somber voices of the two cellos before being repeated more passionately by the higher strings. This tight-lipped sorrow is carried over in the wonderful song that unfolds in the first section of the second move-ment; the background for this song is a relentless beat of deep plucked notes in the cello. But in the section that follows the grief becomes un-controlled: the first violin and first cello present a new melancholy melody against a savage and tortured accompaniment. There is an at-tempt to escape from this gloom in the succeeding scherzo, which at one point sounds like hunting music. But the middle trio is an outright dirge, so charged with pain that some writers believe that Schubert had here written his own requiem. The finale is made up of several dance tunes, some of them Hungarian in style; and it ends in an almost mis-chievous vein. The immense sorrow of the first three movements has given way to a reaffirmation of life.

The *Quintet in A major*—better known as *Die Forelle,* or *Trout,* Quintet—has none of the emotional intensity or profound melancholy of the preceding work. It was written in 1819, while Schubert and his friend Vogl were on a happy vacation in Upper Austria. One of Schu-bert's hosts, in Steyr, suggested that he some day incorporate the lilting song *"Die Forelle"* in a large chamber-music work. Schubert complied —by sitting down at once and writing out the string parts and later playing the piano part from memory.

The work is unusual in several ways. It is the first important work in music to use a piano and four strings, thereby originating the piano quintet. Its instrumentation is unique, calling for a piano, violin, viola, cello, and doublebass. And it is in five, instead of the usual four, move-ments.

Every measure of this ebullient score—so abundant with delightful melodies—betrays Schubert's exhilaration at the time he wrote it. The first movement and the slow movement that follows are filled with buoyant, deeply felt themes, one succeeding another in a joyous proces-sion. There is little attempt at thematic development, and (in the first movement) the transitional material is labored. But the melodies are all filled with such beauty that the first two movements never fail in their enchantment. The third and fifth movements are in the vein of Aus-trian peasant dances, while in the fourth movement we hear the song *"Die Forelle"* with five variations.

Schubert wrote his two great piano trios in the year 1827. In both, the finest movement is the slow one. In the *Piano Trio in B-flat major* the slow movement is a tranquil, moody song in the cello, soon taken up by the violin. The slow movement of the *Trio in E-flat major* has greater emotional depth. It is a funeral march—the elegiac melody being presented by the cello against a marchlike accompaniment in the piano. (Schubert repeats this theme in the last movement.)

Piano Music. Schubert's larger piano works (with solitary exceptions) are greater in parts than in the whole. But he was the consummate master in the shorter forms, the finest of which are consistent masterpieces. In writing these smaller pieces, Schubert was both the inspirer and the precursor of such Romantic composers as Schumann and Mendelssohn. Schubert originated the form of the *"Moment musical,"* which, as its name implies, is a brief musical thought. Some of the *Moments musicaux,* such as the two in the key of A-flat major, are tender and introspective, and the one in F minor is among the most popular of all Schubert piano pieces. Schubert wrote six of these items, each a treasure, and collectively described as "tidbits for the musical epicure," by Ernest Hutcheson.

Another short form for piano in which Schubert was successful was the impromptu, a kind of brief improvisation. He did not invent the form, but was the first to make it popular with Romantic composers for the piano. Schubert wrote eight impromptus. An impromptu is constructed in several distinct sections, as, for example, the *Impromptu in E-flat major,* in which a forceful trio is preceded and followed by a delightful and gay theme in flowing triplet figures. One of the most famous is the *Impromptu in B-flat major,* which uses the beautiful melody also found in the *Quartet in A minor* and in the incidental music to *Rosamunde.* In this impromptu, the presentation of the melody is followed by five variations.

Although Schubert wrote about twenty sonatas for the piano, he was rarely at ease wandering within this more spacious structure. Many of his sonatas are filled with wonderful musical thoughts which more than compensate for structural weaknesses and for the frequent lack of interest in the development of his ideas. But the three sonatas that he wrote in the last year of his life—C minor, A major, and B-flat major, all published posthumously—can be accepted without reservation. They are among Schubert's greatest works, combining that moving intensity of musical expression and that epical conception of design which we find in the works of his last two years. There is more than happy lyricism here; there is profound human experience.

Each of the three sonatas is on a different emotional level. The *Sonata in C minor* has (particularly in the first movement) the torrential drive and the leonine strength of Beethoven. (No other of the three sonatas opens with such a show of force.) As the first movement expands beyond the expressive second theme, the drama is heightened with exciting modulations. The *Sonata in A major* is the most tragic of the three works. Its greatest movements are the second and the fourth, the second with its sustained pathos and the fourth with its cumulative power. The *Sonata in B-flat major* is of heroic cast. Once again, Schubert is greatest in the slow movement. We have here a long sweep of melody—thirteen bars long before Schubert stops to catch his breath, and then twelve more bars of answer—which brings to this movement an epical design.

Vocal Music. It can be said that the *lied* (German art song) as we know it today was born on October 19, 1814, the day on which Schubert set to music *"Gretchen am Spinnrade,"* the text taken from Goethe's *Faust*. This does not mean that the great composers before Schubert did not write songs. Bach, Haydn, Mozart, and Beethoven all wrote secular songs. On occasion—as when Mozart wrote *"Das Veilchen"* and when Beethoven wrote *"Adelaide"* and the cycle *An die ferne Geliebte*—they produced excellent songs. But, after all, the song was a stepchild with these composers, who showered their favors on the larger instrumental, stage, or choral forms. They hardly scratched the surface of the artistic potentialities of the song form, and for a very good reason: the stimulation for the *lied,* German lyric poetry, did not flower until the beginning of the nineteenth century.

"Gretchen am Spinnrade," written when Schubert was only seventeen years old, brought into existence an altogether new concept of the song as an art form. *"Gretchen"* was a drama in miniature, an artistic partnership involving poem, melody, and accompaniment in equal responsibility. Musical realism entered boldly; the whirring of Margaret's spinning wheel (in the piano) as she sings of her love. Poem and melody become one, the melody always concerned with the subtlest suggestion of the poem. The lyric line grows in its excitement, even as does Margaret's emotion as she muses about her beloved—culminating ecstatically with the interval of a fourth as she speaks of his kiss. At the same time, the whirring of the spinning wheel stops short. But it soon resumes its motion—and the music describes the individual rotations of the wheel until it finally gathers momentum and is put into sustained motion.

The writing of such a song as *"Gretchen am Spinnrade"* by a boy, and with no precedent to guide him, is surely one of the phenomena in musical history and one of its miracles. No less miraculous was the writing of *"Erlkönig"*—the poem once again by Goethe—one year later. The *lied,* born with *"Gretchen,"* suddenly developed to maturity with *"Erlkönig,"* its destiny now preordained. The process of "through composition" (what the Germans call *"Durchkomponieren"*)—in which the melody is transformed with each change in thought or mood of the poem, instead of being automatically repeated with each stanza—was never before used with such mastery and integration. Every musical resource was used to build up and heighten the mighty drama: the futile struggle of the child, dying in his father's arms, and the implacable Erl King. The storm rages in the piano accompaniment as the melody tells now of the father's poignant concern, now of the child's terror, and now of the beguiling, tempting calls of the Erl King and his daughters. In the closing measures, the melody becomes a recitative— and the accompaniment passes into dissonance—as the child dies in his father's arms.

Schubert wrote almost six hundred songs after *"Erlkönig."* The facility with which he produced masterpieces is as amazing as his fecundity. The writing of "Hark, hark, the Lark" is typical of the almost effortless way in which he worked. At a café, he happened to be thumbing through Shakespeare's *Cymbeline,* when the poem struck his eye. He took the menu, drew some staves on the back, and proceeded to write the song from beginning to end; and he never returned to it for revision.

Poetry could always stir him that way, bad poems as well as good. He was never at a loss to find the precise musical equivalent for every thought, every feeling, every atmospheric suggestion in each poem he put to music. The frivolous play of a fish in water, on the one hand, or the awful sense of the funereal in death's call to a maiden are caught rhythmically in *"Die Forelle"* and *"Der Tod und das Mädchen."* There was no mood or feeling that could not find itself echoed in his inexhaustibly varied melodies, whether it be the religious (*"Ave Maria"*), the lighthearted (*"Auf dem Wasser zu singen"*), or the ecstatic (*"An die Musik"*).

Besides his individual songs, Schubert wrote several song cycles. A cycle consists of a group of songs tied together by a single theme or mood. *Die schöne Müllerin* is made up of twenty songs from lyrics by Müller. In these songs, the miller passes from the joy of living to disillusion and suicide. Among the memorable songs in this group are: *"Das Wandern,"* in which the miller speaks buoyantly of the exhilaration of a wanderer's life; *"Wohin,"* in which he asks the brook for a destination; *"Ungeduld,"* in which he voices the fever of his love for the maid of the mill; *"Der Müller und der Bach,"* in which, rejected by his beloved in favor of a hunter, he seeks consolation from the brook; and the final song, *"Des Baches Wiegenlied,"* in which the brook soothes him with a gentle song as it receives him in its arms.

Die Winterreise is a cycle of twenty-four songs on poems by Wilhelm Müller. It was written in the bleak year of 1827, the year of Beethoven's death and a year of great personal suffering and despair for Schubert. All the gloom that was in his heart at that time—this, and his feeling that death was imminent—was transferred into these melancholy songs. Probably nothing in song literature matches these in heartbreak; to Newman Flower they represent an "epic in sadness."

The cause of the poet's overwhelming grief is his frustration in love, and in these poems he is forever seeking a peace that does not come. The cycle begins in a somber vein with the pessimism of *"Gute Nacht."* Other lugubrious, but eloquent, songs follow, the most notable being: *"Der Lindenbaum," "Rückblick," "Frühlingstraum," "Die Post," "Das Wirtshaus,"* and *"Der Leiermann."*

Schubert's last song cycle was the *Schwanengesang,* fourteen songs on lyrics by Rellstab (the first seven), Heine (the next six), and Seidl (the last one). Some of Schubert's greatest and most famous songs are found in this group, among them: *"Liebesbotschaft," "Ständchen"* (one of the most popular of all love songs), *"Die Stadt,"* the highly atmospheric *"Der Doppelgänger,"* and *"Am Meer."*

Robert Schumann

"In his own field, Schumann is lonely, incomparable. No composer has whispered such secrets of subtle and ravishing beauty to a receptive listener."

—Philip Hale

BORN: Zwickau, Germany, June 8, 1810.
DIED: Endenich, near Bonn, July 29, 1856.
MAJOR WORKS: *Piano Music*—Etudes symphoniques; Carnaval; Fantasiestücke (Op. 12); Fantasie in C major; Scenes from Childhood; Album for the Young. *Orchestral Music*—4 symphonies; Concerto in A minor, for piano and orchestra; Concerto in A minor, for cello and orchestra; Overture to Manfred. *Chamber Music*—Quintet in E-flat major, for piano and strings; 3 string quartets. *Vocal Music*—Dichterliebe, song cycle; Frauenliebe und Leben, song cycle; "Die beiden Grenadiere," "Die Lotosblume," "Der Nussbaum," "Widmung," and other songs. ALSO: Genoveva, opera; Quartet in E-flat major, for piano and strings; 3 piano trios; 2 sonatas for violin and piano; Davidsbündlertänze, Toccata, Paganini Etudes, Kreisleriana, romances, novelletten, arabeskes, humoreskes, Albumblätter, 3 sonatas, for piano; Liederkreis, song cycle; and so forth.

HIS LIFE

IT WAS Schumann's fate to gain nothing important in life without a fierce, and sometimes tortured, struggle. His first major goal was music, but (as he said) he had to go through a "twenty years' war between prose and poetry—between law and music" before he could finally give himself up completely to it. His mother stubbornly insisted that he become a lawyer. For many years he had to plod through law studies, which he detested, while his heart was elsewhere.

Literature was an early interest. His father was an author, publisher, and a lover of books. As a child, Robert wrote dramatic sketches. When he was fourteen he read the Greek classics and the early Romantic poets. One year after that he formed a little society among his friends to read and discuss literature. He wanted to become a poet. "I possess imagination, but I am not a profound thinker," he wrote in self-evaluation when he was seventeen. "Whether I *am* a poet—for I cannot become one—posterity must decide." He added: "The strange thing is that where my feelings make themselves most strongly felt I am forced to cease being a poet; at such times I can never arrive at adequate ideas."

He began the study of the piano when he was six years old, and almost immediately started writing music. A piano recital by Ignaz Moscheles was a powerful stimulant, making him study harder than ever and sending him into varied musical activities. He gathered eight of his musical friends into a little orchestra, which he directed. He played piano duets with a neighbor: arrangements of symphonies by Beethoven, Haydn, and Mozart. A second great musical influence was the songs of Schubert, brought to his attention in his adolescence. His infatuation with Schubert made him once again return to musical activity with passionate dedication, after a period in which literature had engaged his enthusiasm.

His father ignored neither his son's enthusiasm nor his talent. At one time he tried (though unsuccessfully) to get Karl Maria von Weber to give the boy instruction and direction. It was tragic, indeed, that Schumann's father should have died at this point; had he lived, the first of Schumann's intense struggles would have been avoided. For Schumann had to pass on to the rule of his mother—a stubborn, strong-willed, unimaginative woman. She had set her heart on his becoming a lawyer, and dismissed his musical and literary enthusiasm as the indiscretion of youth. When Schumann completed the course of study at the Gymnasium, in his eighteenth year, she sent him to the University of Leipzig for law study. He worked at these studies as best he could, though he hated them, and found relief by attending the Gewandhaus concerts, associating with musical friends, and continuing the study of the piano with a gifted Leipzig teacher, Friedrich Wieck. This division of energy between a duty he detested and an avocation he adored was a nervous strain that brought on a violent attack of melancholia. But through his music and an invigorating holiday tour of Germany he was able to avoid serious consequences.

He decided on a change of scene and continued his law study in Heidelberg. He neglected law for music even more than before. Slowly he arrived at a major decision. On November 11, 1829, he wrote to his mother: "If ever I were to have achieved anything in the world, it would have been in music. From the first I have had within me a powerful drive toward music, and without overrating myself, the creative spirit as well." About eight months later, his decision became fully crystallized. "I have . . . arrived at the conviction," he wrote to his mother, "that with work, patience, and a good master, I shall be able within six years to challenge any pianist. . . . Besides this, I also possess imagination, and perhaps aptitude, for individual creative work." From Friedrich Wieck in Leipzig came a similar letter of glowing confidence in Schumann's musical ability: Wieck promised Frau Schumann that, in three years' time, he would make Schumann into one of the greatest piano virtuosos of the day. Reluctantly, Frau Schumann gave her consent: Schumann could return to Leipzig and prepare himself for a musical career.

Schumann brought back from Heidelberg a draft of his first serious attempt at composition, *Theme and Variations on the Name Abegg,* for piano. (Countess Pauline Abegg was a young lady Schumann met at a sumptuous gathering in Mannheim. Wanting to write and dedicate a musical work to her, he translated the letters of her name into the musical notes "A, B, E, G, G" and made up a theme out of those notes.) This work was followed by two other pieces for the piano: *Papillons* and *Toccata.* His main interest, however, was not composition but the piano: he wanted to become, as Wieck had said he could, a great virtuoso. He took a room in the house where Wieck lived and, with intense application, set himself the goal of mastering the piano as no one had done before him. Intensive study with Wieck and indefatigable practicing were not enough; he had to devise a new method for making his fourth finger as flexible as the others, by keeping it rigid and extended while the others continued functioning. This artificial position did not bring on flexibility, but it induced paralysis. The doctors could do nothing to relieve the condition. To his great horror, Schumann suddenly had to accept the awful truth that his virtuoso career was over, even before it had begun.

But Schumann would not succumb to despair. If he could not be a concert pianist, he could still write music. He changed teachers—the theorist Heinrich Dorn replacing Friedrich Wieck—and he began working on a symphony and the *Paganini* Etudes. And yet, he did not make this transition from pianist to composer without inner doubts and turmoil.

He gave way to fits. For a long time he lapsed into intermittent periods of overwhelming depression.

There was relief in work—hard work—and in several different fields of music. Toward the end of 1833 Schumann helped organize a musical society called the Davidsbündler. Just as David had attacked and defeated the Philistines, so these young Davids aspired to shatter Philistinism in music—to uncover shams and to raise the banner of high ideals and standards. "Let us not be mere idle lookers on," they said. "Let us set to work to make things better, so that the poetry of art shall be restored to its place of honor." The organization needed a voice through which to spread their ideas. Schumann helped create such a voice, the *Neue Zeitschrift für Musik,* the first issue of which appeared on April 3, 1834. The life of the Davidsbündler was brief, but its ideals were carried on boldly for the next decade by the magazine under Schumann's editorship. It became one of the finest journals of its kind in the world, a powerful influence in German music. Something of its importance in fighting for the best interests of music can be measured by the fact that it was in this journal, and in pieces by Schumann, that the genius of such composers as Chopin and Brahms was loudly proclaimed to the world at a time when these men were still in their apprenticeship, unknown and obscure.

Work helped to restore his emotional equilibrium—work, plus the increasing self-assurance and the growing feeling of creative power that came with the writing of the *Etudes symphoniques* and the *Carnaval,* for the piano. But a new crisis was at hand, and it was the severest of his life. Before becoming a professional musician he had had to win a bitter "twenty years' war." But he had to engage in an even fiercer life-and-death struggle before he could finally realize his second great ambition: to marry the woman he loved, Clara Wieck, daughter of his onetime teacher.

The love affair of Robert Schumann and Clara Wieck was surely one of the most beautiful and most celebrated in all music biography; but it was also one of the most tempestuous and tortured. When Schumann first met Clara, she was only nine years old and he was eighteen. The shy and introverted little girl at first made very little impression on him. But before long he could not fail to remark and admire her phenomenal growth as a pianist (her father was raising her to be a concert artist) and to be excited by the way she played his *Papillons* and other early pieces. A more personal interest developed. He took to playing childish games with her, reading stories to her—and finding, to his surprise, that he derived considerable pleasure from these activities. He could not fail to note the emptiness around him when Clara was away. As for Clara, from her twelfth year she worshiped Schumann—reservedly, undemonstratively, but completely.

She was sixteen, and he twenty-five, when they recognized that they were in love. Clara was about to leave with her father for a concert tour, and Schumann came to say good-by. She escorted him down the stairs. At the bottom, Schumann turned to say a last farewell. He looked into Clara's eyes and impulsively took her in his arms and kissed her. "I thought I should faint," Clara later confessed. "Everything went black before my eyes."

But Friedrich Wieck had no intention of encouraging the love affair. On the contrary, he was to use every means at his command—foul as well as fair—to destroy it. For he would allow nothing and no one to stand in the way of Clara's career, which was already promising so much. And even if he favored a marriage, he would certainly not accept an indigent and neurotic young composer as a son-in-law.

He stoutly forbade Clara ever again to meet or communicate with Schumann, and sent her off to Dresden. When Schumann followed her there, and Clara received him, Wieck's fury grew so violent that he threatened then and there to kill him. For the next fifteen months Clara and Robert Schumann had no way of contacting each other; but their love never wavered, nor did they ever lose their determination to marry as soon as Clara came of age and could defy her father.

From then on, Friedrich Wieck used lies and deceit to poison Clara against Schumann. He could be cruel, even sadistic, in his studied efforts to break their spirit through separation, which sometimes was so painful to the lovers that it seemed it could no longer be endured. Occasionally they managed to meet quickly and surreptitiously, exchange a few words, and hurry away with the shame and fear of those committing a terrible crime. Sometimes they managed to exchange clandestine notes.

The cruel affair dragged on for four years. Clara went on one of her extensive (and increasingly successful) concert tours. After that Schumann was away: in Vienna, a visit made memorable by his discovery of the long forgotten and dusty manuscript of Schubert's great *Symphony No. 9*, in C major. They managed to exchange ardent notes. "Some day my turn will come," Schumann would write. "Then you will see how much I love . . . you!" Or again: "I will never forsake you!" And Clara wrote in reply: "I say to you again that my love knows no bounds. If you wanted my life today, I would give it up."

There was only one course left open to them: the law courts. Schumann finally brought suit against Friedrich Wieck to compel him legally to permit the marriage to take place. After many trying, ugly months of trial, Schumann won his case, and on September 12, 1840, he and Clara were married at last. "This has been the loveliest and most important day of my life," Clara wrote in her diary. "Now begins a new existence, a beautiful life, a life wrapped up in him whom I love more than myself and everything else."

The agony and heartbreak of those years of tempestuous courtship were later to exact a heavy toll from Schumann. But first there were wonderful years of happiness, and wonderful years of musical creation. Clara and Robert grew immeasurably and were deepened by their intimacy—she to become the greatest woman pianist of her generation; he, one of the greatest of all Romantic composers. Almost from the beginning of their marriage, Schumann found a new reservoir of creative vigor. He was no longer satisfied merely to write piano music. In 1840 he turned to vocal music, and after that to orchestral and chamber music. In three years' time he completed thirty major works, most of them of the first rank.

Those who knew Schumann described him as moderately tall, built lithely, with a face round, full, and effeminately soft. "I can still see the quiet face," wrote Frederick Niecks, "the protruding lips (as if he were whistling), and the absorbed, absent look." Schumann was self-centered, usually deeply in thought. Even in the company of friends he would appear to be alone, sitting somewhat apart from the rest of the crowd, little conscious of what was happening near him. When he was alone in the café, he would take the table nearest the distant wall and, turning his back to the rest of the room, would whistle or talk to himself. He liked to visit the café, to drink wine there and read the newspapers. He found its atmosphere stimulating to the resolution of any compositorial problems perplexing him. He never visited any one café frequently. Something would always occur to annoy him—either excessive noise, or the brusqueness of a waiter, or the thick smoke. He would then change his allegiance to a different café until that, too, displeased him.

He was absent-minded, often leaving the café without paying his bill and (like Beethoven) sometimes even trying to pay a bill without having consumed anything. Those waiters who knew him would send his unpaid bills to Clara, so that they might not disturb him as he left, weighted down by his thoughts. Others sometimes trusted his honest face and expected him to return with the payment at a later hour.

For a while he was active in different capacities: as a composer; as the editor of the *Zeitschrift;* and as a teacher of the piano and composition at the newly founded conservatory in Leipzig. But he was not well. He was once again experiencing nervous disorders and melancholia. He suffered from a mysterious itching of the skin. He found it hard to work or to concentrate. In 1844 he had to give up all his activities except composing and he was forced to seek a change of scene. He went to Dresden, where he lived for a while in quiet and seclusion, and completed such masterworks as his piano concerto and the *Symphony in C major*. His health improved—though not the general state of his mind—and by 1850 he was well enough to accept a post as conductor in Düsseldorf. But he was not a good conductor to begin with; and his growing nervousness, irritability, and even lapses of memory now made him a very poor one. He gave up the post in 1853, after a special committee from the orchestra discreetly suggested to him that he husband his strength by devoting himself only to composition.

"The night is beginning to fall," Schumann wrote in a letter to Joachim. The signs of impending tragedy were there, though Clara preferred to dismiss them. He heard voices and musical sounds that tormented him endlessly. His depressions deepened. He would say that the dead masters visited him to dictate melodies to him. Some consolation came in his friendship with the young Brahms, whose genius he recognized immediately. But he was a doomed man, and he knew it. "My music is silenced," he wrote sadly. One cold rainy winter evening, while a carnival was being celebrated in the streets, he slipped out of his house and tried to commit suicide by jumping into the Rhine. He was rescued and taken back home. A week later he was confined to an insane asylum near Bonn. He was kept there for two years—Clara stayed away to avoid upsetting him—a victim of strange fantasies and terrifying noises.

Just before he died, Clara visited him; he had grown so old and haggard that for a moment she did not recognize him. "He smiled at me and put his arms around me with great difficulty, for he had almost lost control of his limbs. Never shall I forget that moment. I would not give up that embrace for all the treasures on earth." He died in her arms and one day later was buried in the Bonn cemetery.

HIS MUSIC

SCHUMANN's practice was to concentrate on a single branch of composition at a time. Up to 1840 he devoted himself to music for the piano. The year of his marriage to Clara was a year of song, no less than one hundred and forty being written at that time. In 1841 he turned to the orchestra, completing his First Symphony, the *Overture, Scherzo, and Finale,* and the first draft of the *Symphony in D minor.* One year after that came his chamber music: three string quartets; the celebrated Piano Quintet; and the *E-flat major Piano Quartet.*

He was greatest in his piano music, which he filled with the most imaginative flights of fancy and whimsey and the widest possible range of moods. To this music he brought not only the most adroit use of rhythm and harmony and a profusion of lyrical ideas, but also a wealth of polyphonic writing. In the Romantic tradition, he preferred loosely knit and flexible structures, which he filled with poetic allusions. He evolved a new form for the piano: a large structure made up of many smaller parts tied together by an integrating poetic idea.

Next to his piano music, his greatest achievements came in the song form. In this field he was truly Schubert's successor, in his ability to conceive of melody, poem, and accompaniment as a single and inextricable unity, in the wonderful expressiveness of his lyricism, and in his sensitive response to every nuance of the poetic phrase.

He was less at ease in the larger forms. Like Schubert, he tended to rely too greatly on lyricism at the expense of development and transformation. He did not have the skill to build large architectonic structures, and in the science of orchestration he was noticeably deficient. Yet, his deeply poetic nature, his humanity, his warm and radiant feeling for lyric beauty are compensatory. What the best of his larger works lack in organizational and structural astuteness, they more than make up for in inspiration.

ANALYTICAL NOTES

Piano Music. With the *Etudes symphoniques* and *Carnaval,* completed between 1834 and 1835, Schumann made his first bid for greatness. The *Etudes symphoniques* may have been inspired by the first set of Chopin etudes (Op. 10), published in 1833. However, Schumann's work is not a consecutive number of different etudes in the Chopin vein, but an integrated work consisting of a theme and twelve variations. The theme is a soft, but stately, melody which was not original with Schumann; he appropriated it from the father of his onetime sweetheart, Ernestine von Fricken. The variations follow without any break. In this composition Schumann arrived at a new concept of variation technique, one which was to influence Brahms profoundly. Schumann no longer felt bound to retain the identity of his original melody in each variation. Indeed, the melody itself is not necessarily the source of each variation. A single phrase from that melody, a turn in the accompaniment, a rhythmic and harmonic fragment was enough to arouse Schumann's imagination. Such an element becomes the basis of new music (now dramatic, or lyrical, or romantic, or wistful, or majestic) which often has only a subtle or intangible relation to the original theme. The final variation opens with a forceful subject taken from a romantic opera of Heinrich Marschner (1795—1861).

Carnaval is subtitled "little scenes on four notes," the four notes being "A, E-flat, C, B." These notes had a special significance for Schumann. He had written the work for Ernestine von Fricken at the time he was in love with her. Ernestine lived in the Bohemian town of Asch. In German notation, the letters *S* (or *Es*) is "E-flat" and *H* is "B"; thus the four letters of "Asch" can be translated into four notes of the musical scale. Coincidentally, the letters *A-S-C-H* are also the only musical notes in Schumann's name. All this intrigued Schumann (who enjoyed such anagrammatic games). He introduced these four notes, in three permutations, throughout *Carnaval*.

Carnaval is made up of many little pieces, each picturesquely titled, strung together by the central idea of a carnival. The first, *"Préambule,"* bring up the picture of a gay carnival. Characterizations of two characters from the *commedia dell' arte* follow: *"Pierrot et Arlequin."* The third piece is an elegant and nostalgic little dance entitled *"Valse noble."* This is followed by two sketches which together constitute a self-portrait. The first sketch, *"Eusebius,"* reveals Schumann as a poetic dreamer, while the second, *"Florestan,"* shows Schumann as the energetic fighter for ideals. (Eusebius and Florestan were pen names used by Schumann in his pieces for the *Zeitschrift für Musik*.) A flirtatious girl now makes an appearance in *"Coquette,"* and her advances receive the proper response in *"Réplique."* The piece entitled *"Sphinxes"*—which provides two different anagrams of "Asch"—is usually omitted in performance. *"Papillons"* (not to be confused with

Schumann's Op. 2 of the same name) is an airy description of butterflies. *"Chiarina,"* Italian for "little Clara," was Schumann's pet name for Clara Wieck (to whom he was already being drawn) and is her portrait. This is followed by two more portraits: *"Chopin,"* which simulates the style of a Chopin nocturne, and *"Estrella,"* inspired by Ernestine von Fricken. The joy of reunion is found in *"Reconnaissance,"* while *"Pantalon et Colombine"* refers to two characters familiar in Italian comedies. *"Valse allemande"* is a second brief excursion into dance music. *"Paganini"* has a melody for the right hand that might have been written for the violin, and is followed by a repetition of the *"Valse allemande."* There is passion in *"Aveu,"* and *"Promenade"* is an infectious waltz. The brief and turbulent *"Pause"* follows. The concluding section is called *"Marche des Davidsbündler contre les Philistins."* It opens with a heroic theme symbolizing the stalwart champions of the highest ideals in art; the Philistines are characterized in a trivial little waltz melody, the theme of which is the *Grossvater Tanz,* favorite of German middle-class families a century ago.

The two contrasting facets of Schumann's personality found in the *"Eusebius"* and *"Florestan"* sections of *Carnaval*—the gentle dreamer and the forceful doer—dominate the *Fantasiestücke* (Op. 12). There are eight items in this work, alternating from gentle to energetic moods. It begins tranquilly with a picture of the night, *"Des Abends,"* only to become passionate in *"Aufschwung."* A gentle note of questioning enters into *"Warum."* The piece called *"Grillen"* goes in for whimsey, and *"In der Nacht"* is feverishly restless. *"Fabel"* is a ballad in a light and good-humored vein, a pleasing contrast to the passionate storms of *"Traumeswirren."* In the concluding piece, *"Ende vom Lied,"* we have both Eusebius and Florestan. "In the end," Schumann wrote to Clara about this finale, "it all resolves itself into a jolly wedding. But at the close my painful anxiety about you returned; so that it sounds like wedding and funeral bells comingled."

The *Fantasie in C major,* dedicated to Franz Liszt, is surely one of Schumann's greatest piano works. It has epic character throughout; and nowhere else did Schumann write with such passion and grandeur. These lines by Friedrich August Wilhelm von Schlegel appear in the published score as the composer's clue to its inner message: "There is one gentle note for the secret listener through all the tones that sound in earth's fitful dream."

The first movement begins passionately, but midway there comes a gentle lyrical interlude (subtitled *"Im Legendenton"*). The tempestuous mood of the opening comes back to dispel the grief. Schumann wrote as follows to Clara about this magnificent movement: "I do not think I ever wrote anything more impassioned than the first movement. It is a profound lament about you." The second movement is a march with heroic stride and a proud spirit. The concluding movement is poignant slow music. In Frederick Niecks's description, "a pure stream of beatific melody flows through this meditation."

Schumann wrote two albums of piano pieces for children, familiar to all young students. One of these is the *Kinderscenen* (*Scenes from Childhood*), written in 1838. Ten years later Schumann completed two sets of pieces entitled *Album für die Jugend* (*Album for the Young*). Schumann decided to write the *Kinderscenen* when Clara Wieck said one day that in many ways he resembled a child. He wrote thirteen pieces in which a mature artist looks at and describes the world of a child; the most famous of these is the ever popular *Träumerei*. The two sets of the *Album für die Jugend*—forty-three pieces in all—comprise music of a different character. What we have here is simple music intended for performance by children while discussing subjects close to the child's heart.

Orchestral Music. The *Symphony No. 1,* in B-flat major—Schumann's first ambitious work for the orchestra—is known as the *Spring* Symphony. A couplet by Adolph Böttget was Schumann's initial inspiration: "Oh, follow, follow on the run, for the valley blooms with the spring."

The slow introduction to the first movement begins with a call for horn and trumpet which, in a quicker tempo, becomes the first principal theme of the ensuing allegro section. The second theme, prefaced by four measures in two horns in octaves, follows at once in clarinets and bassoons. There is still a third idea—a vigorous staccato subject ascending the scale—before the exposition is concluded.

The freshness and the romance of the vernal season is found in the exquisite larghetto movement that follows. A wonderful song is first heard in divided violins. Later it unfolds radiantly in the cello, and after that is taken over by the oboes and horns. In the final measures of this movement, a phrase is hinted at which immediately becomes the brisk and strongly accented theme of the scherzo; a countertheme of Schubertian loveliness appears in the woodwinds. This movement has two trios, with the scherzo section reappearing after each. The finale begins with a jubilant upsurge in the full orchestra. A graceful dance melody soon engages the violins and becomes the principal idea of the movement. But Schumann had no intention of engaging in a frivolous attitude. "I was thinking rather of the passing of spring," he explained, and as the movement progresses we become increasingly conscious of an autumnal sadness that pervades the music in spite of the vivacity of the principal theme.

Not springtime, but bleak winter is found in Schumann's *Symphony No. 2*, in C major. He wrote it during 1845 and 1846, at a time when he was suffering from physical and mental disorders. He used to say that he was tormented by the piercing sound of trumpets in the key of C in his head. And these trumpets are heard in the impressive slow introduction of the first movement, which opens with a solemn theme for brass, a motto subject for the entire work. The woodwinds present a lighter theme before the tempo quickens and the sonority swells, and the allegro section emerges with a vigorous first theme in the orchestra. Schumann himself explained that this theme represented a struggle between his body and mind. But before long a gentler subject appears, to relieve the tension. The development of both themes follows. A pedal point in the horns and basses leads to a restatement of the first theme. In the coda, the motto theme of the introduction reappears brilliantly in the trumpets.

The scherzo begins with a vivacious theme in sixteenth notes for the violins, an outburst of happy spirits. There are two trios—the first, a melody in triplets shared by strings and woodwinds; the second, a subdued meditation for strings and woodwinds—after each of which the ebullient scherzo melody returns.

The third movement, an adagio, is one of those passionate, yet melancholy, songs for which Schumann was so famous—but of a spiritual beauty which not even Schumann equaled elsewhere. The song is heard immediately in the strings, but the oboe and the bassoon soon join in. After a passing interlude in the strings with horn and trumpet accompaniment, the radiant song returns.

A rising subject brings on the finale. At once the stirring first theme appears in full orchestra. A second theme (for strings and woodwind), derived from the beautiful adagio, and a third subject (for the oboe) are of a more exalted character. The symphony ends with an exultant exclamation of the motto theme by the brass.

The *Symphony No. 3*, in E-flat major, completed in 1850, is in five, instead of the usual four, movements. Schumann intended it as a picture of Rhenish life, and consequently it has come to be known as the *Rhenish* Symphony. The first movement has two contrasting themes.

It begins in an exuberant vein, with a joyous subject in full orchestra. The reflective second theme is introduced by oboe and clarinet. The main theme of the second movement, which we hear in cellos and violas, was derived from an old German song; the trio gives prominence to a melody in horns and other winds. The third movement is a romanza, with clarinets and bassoons singing a graceful tune against an accompaniment of violas, followed by a second pleasing melody in the first violins and flutes. Next comes the ecclesiastical music of the fourth movement, known as the "Cathedral Scene." Trombones and horns here present the stately subject, which is a fragmentary idea rather than a fully realized theme; this idea becomes the foundation for an elaborate and dignified contrapuntal structure. In the concluding movement, Schumann has set a Rhenish festival to music. There is prevailing gaiety in the thematic material, but former subjects are also brought back. Toward the end of the movement we hear quoted the stately music of the "Cathedral Scene."

The *Symphony No. 4,* in D minor, was actually Schumann's second. He had written it in 1841, before those in C major and E-flat major. Dissatisfied with it, he put it aside and numbered his next symphony (C major) as the Second. In 1851 he reorchestrated the *Symphony in D minor* and designated it as the Fourth. It is a more unified work than the other three. Each movement passes so fluidly into the next that the work almost seems to be in a single movement with varied sections. Important thematic ideas recur throughout the work, while an arpeggio figure (with which the symphony opens) is used as a motto theme.

There is a slow introduction to the first movement. The melancholy theme of this introduction (heard in violas and second violins) becomes a subsidiary theme in the second movement. The main body of the first movement is introduced by an ascending figure in the first violins, flutes, and oboes, which, extended, becomes the forceful first theme (first violins). A second lyric theme appears in the first violins. The second movement is a romanza, beginning with an elegiac melody in oboes and cellos against plucked strings, and continuing with a repetition of the melancholy theme first heard in the first-movement introduction. In a later repetition of the melancholy melody, a solo violin weaves an exquisite fabric around it. The scherzo movement has a strongly rhythmic theme, while its trio is, by contrast, diaphanous in texture and graceful in style. A slow transition, which hints at phrases heard in previous movements and which emphasizes the brass, leads to the finale. It begins with a powerful marchlike subject, which is the main theme of the first movement in a major key. There is a frolicsome second theme. A free fantasia section follows. The coda, with which the symphony comes to a joyous and exciting conclusion, is made up of fresh material.

The date of the *Concerto in A minor* for piano and orchestra is given as 1845. But the first movement was written four years earlier as an independent composition for piano and orchestra, entitled *Fantasie*. It is for this reason that the first movement is a fantasia in structure. After an introductory chord in the orchestra, the piano begins with a defiant three-bar declamation. A poetic melody is given by the wind instruments and taken over by the piano. The theme is then enlarged and transformed so extensively that it may be regarded as a second theme, while serving as a development of the first. A fantasia section follows, profuse with thematic ideas, with rapid changes of tempo, tonality, and rhythm. An extended cadenza for the solo piano grows logically out of preceding material and leads to a coda which makes use of the main theme. The second movement, an intermezzo, begins with a graceful staccato melody shared between piano and strings. A high point is reached with a flowing sentimental song for the cellos against arpeggios in the piano. After a return of the graceful staccato melody, there is a brief recollection of the first melody of the first movement, leading without pause to the finale. A bold and brilliant theme is proclaimed by the solo piano. Subsequently, a soft, syncopated theme appears in the strings. A short fugato passage, based on the first bold theme, leads to a free fantasia in which new thematic ideas are introduced. The concluding section brings back both principal themes.

Schumann's *Concerto in A minor* for cello and orchestra, his only cello concerto, is in the same key as his Piano Concerto. The three movements are played without interruption. In the first movement, the broadly lyrical first theme is given by the solo cello after four introductory measures in the orchestra; and the second theme appears first in the orchestra, before the soloist elaborates on it. Over plucked strings, the cello provides the transition to the slow movement, which presents the elastic and expressive melody (also in the solo cello), the spine of the second movement. A quickening of tempo, a six-measure passage for the cello, and the finale enters with a passionate subject. This movement is more vivacious than dramatic and has many lively, capricious passages for the solo instrument.

In 1848 Schumann wrote an overture and fourteen numbers as incidental music for Byron's *Manfred*. Only the overture remains; it is the most famous of Schumann's shorter orchestral works. It begins with three dramatic, syncopated chords for full orchestra. A slow introduction follows, in which a savage theme for oboe portrays Manfred's disturbed spirits. In the main part of the overture, an agitated idea in the violins suggests Manfred's struggle. This is developed before a second theme—plaintive and tender—appears as Astarte's consoling voice. Both themes are worked out with intensity, another picture of Manfred's torment. The turmoil passes. Three chords in the trumpets bring on a more subdued atmosphere. Earlier material is now recalled; the overture ends quietly with a gentle passage telling about Manfred's death.

Chamber Music. The *Quintet in E-flat major,* for piano and strings (which came in Schumann's "chamber-music year" of 1842), is his greatest chamber-music work. It has historical importance, besides aesthetic interest, because it was the first important work in musical history for the combination of piano and conventional string quartet. A vigorous opening subject evolves naturally into a mobile melody. It is followed by a gentle second theme: a duet for cello and viola. The second movement is captioned "in the style of a march." The lugubrious character of the music points to the possibility of its being a funeral march. The march theme appears in the first violin after a three-measure descending phrase in the piano. This march music is succeeded by a melody for the violin in which the melancholy atmosphere grows more poignant. After a return of the march theme, there appears an agitated section. The movement concludes with a return of the melancholy second theme before the march subject reappears. An ascending E-flat major scale passage is the main idea of the scherzo which follows. There are two trios, after each of which the scherzo theme reappears. The powerful finale is constructed mostly out of the dynamic subject with which it opens. In this movement there is extended polyphonic writing, climaxed by a giant double fugue based on the main themes of the first and fourth movements.

Schumann wrote only three string quartets. But all three came within a few weeks' time, in 1842. They are, respectively, in the keys of A minor, F major, and A major. The first and third Quartets, in A minor and A major, have moody introductions to the first movements. In both works, the adagio movements—with the eloquence and emotional depth of their principal melodies, followed by a change of mood to agitation—are the most impressive. The second, the *Quartet in F major,* is more youthful and optimistic in spirit than the other two, particularly in the vivacity of its finale. The third, the *Quartet in A major,* employs an original thematic device, emphasizing certain intervals in each of the four movements: fifths and fourths in the first movements; the fourths in the second; sevenths in the third; and descending sixths in the finale.

Vocal Music. In the realm of the *lied,* Schumann was an undisputed monarch, the first of Schubert's legitimate successors. His great strength lay in his incomparable sympathy for and understanding of the poetic text. He had been both a passionate enthusiast of poetry and something of a lyric poet himself. The written word affected him as it did no other composer, not even Schubert, and he directed every musical resource at his command to serve it. To catch every line and shadow of the poet's mood and feelings, he would frequently venture into unorthodox practices. In the famous *"Ich grolle nicht,"* he was impelled to abandon his usually warm and singable lyricism for the more stark declamation. The ending of *"Im wunderschönen Monat Mai"* is a half-cadence—carrying over in the music the half-answered question of the poem. Many of Schumann's songs have extended piano epilogues, to round out the mood, and at times Schumann introduced material that did not appear in the song. Other songs have bold harmonies, startling modulations, and unusual treatment of the voice, as Schumann sought restlessly to penetrate to the essence of the poem.

One of Schumann's most popular songs is the effective ballad *"Die beiden Grenadiere"* (*"The Two Grenadiers"*), but much more characteristic of his great and subtle song art are such individual songs as *"An meinem Herzen," "Die Lotosblume," "Der Nussbaum,"* or *"Widmung."* He also produced several outstanding song cycles. The *Dichterliebe* includes sixteen songs to poems by Heine, among the best-known of which are the opening one, *"Im wunderschönen Monat Mai,"* the sixth, *"Im Rhein, im heiligen Strome,"* the seventh, *"Ich grolle nicht,"* and the fifteenth, *"Aus alten Märchen winkt es." Frauenliebe und Leben* comprises eight songs to lyrics by Chamisso, the most beautiful being the second and third, *"Er, der Herrlichste von allen"* and *"Ich kann's nicht fassen,"* inspired by his recent marriage to Clara Wieck.

Alexander Scriabin

"In his mind, art was but a means of achieving a higher form of life."

—*Boris de Schloezer*

BORN: Moscow, January 6, 1872.
DIED: Moscow, April 27, 1915.
MAJOR WORKS: *Orchestral Music*—Symphony No. 4, "Poem of Ecstasy"; Symphony No. 5, "Prometheus." *Piano Music*—10 sonatas; 85 preludes; 24 etudes. ALSO: Concerto for Piano and Orchestra; Symphony No. 3, "The Divine Poem"; mazurkas, impromptus, waltzes, and so forth, for the piano.

HIS LIFE

IN THE last ten years of Scriabin's life he was a man dedicated to a vision. No longer was he concerned with writing good music—the ideal of his youth and early manhood. No longer was he interested in writing music weighed down by philosophical or metaphysical concepts—as he had done in the *Divine Poem,* the *Poem of Ecstasy,* or *Prometheus.* He wanted now to bring to life a monumental world philosophy such as no musician—and few of other professions—had ever conceived. He aspired to propound, as he said, a new Gospel to replace the old.

He called his vision the "Mystery" and made it nothing less than the summation of man's history from the dawn of time to the final cataclysm. His "Mystery" would call upon music, poetry, drama, and the dance—as well as colors, perfumes, and a new kind of language made up of sighs and exclamations—to express what up to then had been inexpressible. His "Mystery," he felt, would be the last will and testament of a dying civilization.

The more he planned and dreamed, the more ambitious did his scheme grow. He would perform his "Mystery" in India, in a special globular temple at the side of the lake. The audience would be "worshipers" who, seeing his vision, would yield to a "supreme final ecstasy."

He believed implicitly that once his "Mystery" had been projected there would come the inevitable cataclysm. When World War I began, Scriabin was seized with a wonderful joy, for he was sure that this was the form the cataclysm would assume. This, he said, would be the purifying force to make the world ready for his mighty "Mystery." And in the brave, new world emerging from the ruins of the old, he—Scriabin—would appear as the true Messiah, "to sound the final chord of our race, reuniting it with the Spirit."

He spoke, dreamed, and planned for ten years. At one time he provided himself with some of the necessities for living in the Orient (including a sun helmet). On another occasion he procured from a travel agency all the essential information about travel to, and accommodations in, India. As for the writing of the "Mystery," Scriabin succeeded only in completing the text and a few musical sketches for a preamble, which he entitled *"Propylaea"* (Propylaea, the entrance to the Acropolis in Athens, became for Scriabin a symbol for the initiation into the arts and religion). The rest of his time was consumed in planning and talking. His grandiose concept was finally brought to an unrealized end by his death.

The "Mystery" was the ultimate goal of a route he had been pursuing since 1900. From the beginning of the twentieth century, he had been gravitating more and more to mysticism. First he associated himself with a mystic group called The Philosophical Society and was profoundly moved by its doctrines. Then he embraced philosophy and became a passionate reader of Nietzsche, before very long even identifying himself with the Superman. From philosophy he turned to theosophy.

All the while, he sought to make his music express his ever deepening mysticism, burdening it with vague and often bombastic metaphysical programs and trying to make it speak cosmic ideas. In the *Divine Poem* he tried to trace the evolution of the human spirit through pantheism to the affirmation of the divine ego. In the *Poem of Ecstasy* his theme was the joy of creative activity, the ecstasy of unrestricted achievement. In *Prometheus* he described the struggle of man against the cosmos—man being endowed with the creative will, through a divine spark which Prometheus gave him.

Many were confused not only by his pretensions and involved ideas, but also by the amorphous forms and the vague writing of his music. Rimsky-Korsakov once said of him: "He's half out of his mind." But a wave of Scriabinism swept over musical Russia in the first part of the twentieth century. Those who believed in him regarded him as a prophet and looked upon his music as a revelation. To the critic Boris Schloezer, the first six notes of the *Poem of Ecstasy* caught the "essence of the creative spirit." One of the Scriabinites who attended a rehearsal of the *Poem of Ecstasy* described how "excitement reigned. Perfect strangers who happened to get into conversation quarreled warmly or shook each other's hands in delight. Sometimes there were even more unrestrained scenes of agitation and enthusiasm."

What manner of man was this, who could pass from music with metaphysical concepts to the serious planning of the fabulous "Mystery"? He was known to be an eccentric. He would go without a hat (at a time when such a practice was unheard of) because he thought it would prevent depilation; in Paris, children would follow him in the streets chanting a refrain about the man without a hat. He was a hypochondriac, in dread of drafts, given to taking quack medicines, usually in doses larger than those prescribed, and always wearing gloves as a precaution against germs. He was neurotically afraid of being alone, even when composing. And yet, paradoxically, he kept himself aloof from everybody. The Russian critic Sabaneyev noticed "the awful distance" Scriabin kept from those who surrounded him, a distance which had "the effect of placing a gap of some millions of kilometers between himself and those he was talking to" and which he used as a protection from "intrusions upon his psychology."

He had to be a super-egoist, given to self-glorification, even self-adoration, and tremendously affected by his creations. Sabaneyev has given us a vivid picture of the way he listened to his own music. "He sometimes lowered his face rather strangely, his eyes closed. His appearance expressed an almost physiological enjoyment. He would open his eyes and look upwards as if wishing to fly; but in tense moments of the music he breathed violently and nervously, sometimes gripping his chair with both hands. I have seldom seen a composer's face and figure so mobile while listening to his own music. It was as if he could not constrain himself to conceal the profound experiences he derived from it."

He also was a man of intense feelings, given to excessive emotional demonstrations. He had been that way all his life. As a child he showed his affection for the piano by kissing it, as if it were an animated being, and by expressing anguish when it was repaired, tuned, or moved. Somewhat later, as a Chopin enthusiast, it was not enough for him to play Chopin continually, to talk about Chopin, even to imitate Chopin; he had to take Chopin's music and sleep with it under his pillow.

His father, Nicholas, was a law student who, at the age of twenty-one, fell in love with and married an aspiring young concert pianist, Liubov. From the time they got married, matters went from bad to worse for them. First, Nicholas had to give up law study to support his wife as best he could. When she became pregnant, he had to call on his father for charity. Things were further complicated by Liubov's sickness after she had given birth to Alexander. Instead of returning to the concert stage, as she had hoped and planned, she had to go to southern Tyrol for her health. A few months after getting there, she died of tuberculosis.

Alexander, therefore, had to be entrusted to the care of a grand-mother and an aunt. They doted on him. He was pampered, petted, and spoiled. Continually they hovered over him to protect him from danger and illness. He was not allowed to play with other children, and after a while he appeared perfectly satisfied to depend on them for company. One or the other was always with him, until he was incapable of being alone. He was fourteen before he went out in the street unaccompanied, but after that he required someone to go with him wherever he went. His oversolicitous grandmother and aunt also laid the foundations for his later hypochrondria.

When he was five years old he was taken to an opera. It made such an impression on him that he built his own little theater, performing dramas (first Gogol's *The Nose* and then pieces of his own composition) by assuming all the roles. He was also highly musical. Without taking a single lesson, he was able to play on the piano a tune he had just heard played by a military band. He also made attempts at learning to play the guitar and violin, but it was the piano that appealed to him most. He was always playing, usually spontaneous improvisations. Yet when an attempt was made to give him formal instruction, he resisted strongly. His early musical education was, consequently, aimless and undisciplined. He could not even read music for a long time. But when Anton Rubinstein heard him play (Scriabin was seven at the time), he said: "Everything will come out in time. Let the child develop in freedom."

By his own wish, he entered the Military School in 1882, with the intention of making the army his career. He was an all-around excellent student, usually at the head of his class. He was also popular with his classmates, whom he frequently entertained at the piano. It was not long before Scriabin started a systematic study of the piano, with G. E. Conius. "He was a puny boy, pale, short, looking younger than he was," Conius wrote. "He knew his notes, scales, and keys. With weak fingers he played cleanly and fluently. He learned things quickly, but, probably owing to his weak physique, his performance was always ethereal and monotonous." Later on, Scriabin studied theory with Taneiev and advanced piano with Zverev. He was Zverev's favorite, often called upon to perform for Zverev's friends at his Sunday evening musicales.

By this time Scriabin had given up all thought of the army. In 1888 he entered the Moscow Conservatory to prepare for a career as a professional musician. His teachers included Safonov, Taneiev, and Arensky. In the piano class, Safonov set up Scriabin as a model for the other students. But Scriabin was much less happy in his counterpoint and theory studies. He took advantage of Taneiev's easygoing temperament by avoiding homework and sometimes even the classes. Arensky had no use for Scriabin whatsoever; the boy was too intransigent, too inflexible, too determined on doing things his own way.

Fired with the ambition of becoming a great pianist, Scriabin worked so hard on technique that he abused his right hand and paralyzed some of its muscles. It was the opinion of the physician that he would never recover sufficiently to embark on a virtuoso's career. Nevertheless, Scriabin continued to work passionately on finger exercises until some of his old flexibility returned. In competing for the gold medal at the Conservatory, his right hand was still afflicted, notwithstanding which he won the prize.

Piqued that certain favors given to a friend and fellow student, Rachmaninoff, were not also tendered to him, Scriabin left the Conservatory in a huff without taking his final examinations in composition. He started concertizing, despite the fact that his hand had not as yet recovered completely. "When playing in public," it was reported, "he would point to his right hand as if asking for indulgence." Nevertheless, he played exceptionally well and was well received. Among those who attended Scriabin's recital in St. Petersburg in 1894 was the powerful publisher Belaiev. Scriabin's pianism and, even more, Scriabin's pieces for the piano (which he played at all his recitals) made Belaiev sit up and take notice. He decided to take the young musician under his wing. He offered to publish everything Scriabin wrote, at the same time managing his concert appearances. The first of Scriabin's tours under Belaiev took place in 1896, with concerts in Russia, Berlin, Paris, Brussels, Amsterdam, and The Hague. He was a great success, both as pianist and composer. So impressed was Belaiev with this reaction, and so convinced of his protegé's genius, that he soon arranged a special annual prize of between 500 and 1500 rubles to be paid secretly to Scriabin over a period of a few years. Not until after Belaiev's death did Scriabin uncover the identity of his benefactor.

In 1897 Scriabin married Vera Ivanova, a gifted pianist fresh out of the Conservatory. After her marriage, Vera appeared in concerts devoted to the works of her husband. But she soon decided to relegate her own career to the background in order to devote herself more completely to her husband and their children. Supporting a wife and child was a financial hardship. Scriabin had to take a teaching post at the Conservatory, where he remained for five years. He never liked teaching, and continually resented the fact that it absorbed time he preferred to give over to his composing.

And he was growing increasingly ambitious in his music. From the writing of numerous smaller pieces for the piano he graduated (in the year of his marriage) to a concerto for piano and orchestra. It was heard in Odessa on October 23, 1897, with the composer at the piano and Safonov conducting. Three years later he finished his first symphony, whose choral ending was intended as a religious glorification of art. "I still have something to say!" he exclaimed confidently to a friend after the symphony had been performed. "If my health will permit me, I will still show them what I can do!" Gargantuan ideas were formulating in his mind, giving him neither peace nor rest. Not only was he thinking in terms of larger symphonic structures, but—in line with his growing bent for mysticism—he wanted to fill these structures with philosophic ideas never before spoken in music.

This new tendency become increasingly evident in his third symphony, subtitled the *Divine Poem*. Completed in 1903, it was introduced two years later in Paris under Nikisch. It attracted much attention and much provocative discussion. This was followed, in 1908, by the fourth symphony, the *Poem of Ecstasy*. When Rachmaninoff, Rimsky-Korsakov, and Glazunov heard Scriabin play parts of the work at the piano, they were puzzled and confused. The first performances of the *Poem of Ecstasy,* in New York and St. Petersburg, in 1908 and 1909 respectively, won some converts to Scriabin's mysticism, but also many skeptics. The Belaiev publishing house gave it the second Glinka Prize.

Scriabin's personal life was undergoing a radical change. In or about 1902 he met and fell in love with a young pianist, Tatiana Schloezer (sister of the critic, Boris), who brought Scriabin two things he needed most: youth and adoration. In her eighteenth year she heard one of Scriabin's works. "It was the strongest impression of my life. After that I wanted to play nothing but Scriabin. I dreamed of seeing the composer." She met him and, for a brief period, even studied with him. From then on she abandoned her own musical ambitions for the single aim of understanding "*his* compositions better." She seemed to know and love every note Scriabin wrote. And Scriabin, in turn, came to depend on her undisguised adulation and humble reverence.

In 1904 Scriabin left Russia to live with his family in Switzerland, enabled to do so by a generous annuity from a patron-friend. Tatiana followed, and lived near by. Matters, of course, had to come to a head. One day Scriabin told his wife he had to leave her for good. "I have to make a sacrifice for the sake of my art," was the way he put it. In short, he felt he could no longer live and function without Tatiana. Vera accepted her fate stoically, though she would never give him a divorce. They continued to communicate politely with each other after the separation, and Vera later devoted herself passionately to spreading the gospel of Scriabin's piano music in recitals throughout Europe.

Scriabin visited the United States in the winter of 1906, making his debut as soloist with the Russian Symphony Orchestra in New York. A tour followed. But when Tatiana came to join him, a minor scandal developed. To avoid unpleasantness with the government authorities on the issue of moral turpitude, Scriabin and his common-law wife left the country quietly without completing the tour.

In 1908 Scriabin acquired a new and powerful patron (Belaiev having died four years earlier). He was the young and brilliant conductor Serge Koussevitzky, who supplemented his activities with the baton by founding and directing his own publishing house devoted to Russian composers and Russian music. Both as conductor and as publisher,

Koussevitzky needed to promote a highly publicized and provocative new composer. He knew at once that Scriabin answered all the specifications. And Scriabin, in turn, needed a publisher. It was a happy partnership, even if it was not destined to last long. Koussevitzky not only accepted Scriabin's works for publication, but provided him with a generous annual income to enable him to work on his "Mystery."

In 1910 Scriabin traveled with Koussevitzky and his orchestra down the Volga, appearing eleven times as soloist in his own piano concerto. Not long after that, conductor and composer came to the parting of ways. Each was headstrong, temperamental, and individualistic; each was convinced of his own genius and importance. A break was inevitable—but Koussevitzky never relaxed his efforts in propagandizing Scriabin's music, first in Russia and then in the western world.

On March 15, 1911, Koussevitzky directed the world *première* of Scriabin's last major work for orchestra, *Prometheus,* which was a kind of preliminary study for the "Mystery," since it merged colored lights and music. The colors were dispensed with in Koussevitzky's *première* performance. The concert was a *succès de scandale.* "The majority of the audience was puzzled," wrote Yuri Engel in the *Musical Contemporary*. "A minority of the listeners applauded ardently. But some hissed. And in the press, along with the eulogies, there were many sharp attacks on Scriabin."

Scriabin was appearing in London when a severe pain in the upper lip developed into a furuncle. This furuncle was healed without medical intervention, and Scriabin was able to continue with his concerts. When he was back in Moscow a small carbuncle grew on his upper lip. Scriabin was sure that it would heal just as the furuncle had. But fever developed, and before long gangrene covered his entire face. Several incisions were made on the face, but the infection continued. "Suffering is necessary," Scriabin said a few days before his death. "It is good. I have a sense of well-being in suffering." On April 26, 1915, the situation grew grave. He lost consciousness, was given the supreme unction, and died on the morning of April 27.

HIS MUSIC

SCRIABIN at first wore the mantle of Chopin, and wore it with dignity. He wrote many smaller pieces for the piano, as well as sonatas, which are Chopinesque in their elegance of form, delicacy of mood, poetic sensitivity of style, and melodic felicity. He is the foremost composer of piano music to emerge in Russia.

The influence of Chopin was succeeded by that of another master: Richard Wagner. Scriabin's orchestral music derived its harmonic and instrumental texture, its passion and ecstasy, its striving for the grandiose and the grandiloquent from Wagner's music dramas. Besides this, Scriabin's concept of the "Mystery" originated in Wagner's synthesis of the arts.

As he drew within the orbit of mysticism, he shed the influence of other composers and evolved his own complex language. His thinking grew increasingly ambiguous; his style achieved a kind of nebulous state; his ideas became episodic; his tonality acquired complete freedom. Perhaps his greatest individuality rested in his harmony, the spine of which was the so-called "Mystery" chord of his own invention—"C, F-sharp, B-flat, E, A, D"—derived from the upper harmonics inaudible to ordinary musicians but closer to the ideal world of subtler overtones.

ANALYTICAL NOTES

Orchestral Music. Scriabin wrote five symphonies, the last three of which are essentially tone poems. The third symphony is entitled the *Divine Poem;* the fourth symphony is the *Poem of Ecstasy;* and the fifth symphony is *Prometheus.*

The *Poem of Ecstasy* is Scriabin's most successful work for orchestra. Like the other two tone poems, it has an involved and frequently ambiguous metaphysical program. The work as a whole describes the "ecstasy of untrammeled action, the joy of creative activity." The music is built out of five leading theosophic motives: (1) Motive of Yearning, in the flute; (2) Motive of Protest, in muted trombones; (3) Motive of Apprehension, in muted horns; (4) Motive of Will, in the trumpet and (5) Motive of Self-Assertion, in the trumpet, the central idea of the entire work.

Prometheus, Scriabin's last work for orchestra, came two years after the *Poem of Ecstasy.* Scriabin's plan here was to combine colored lights with music. He invented a special color-keyboard, which projected colors on a screen to synchronize with the music. Koussevitzky eliminated the colors when he introduced *Prometheus* in Moscow, but in 1915 Modest Altschuler played the work in New York as Scriabin had intended it. The effect did not come off. The color images proved too distracting to allow for concentration on the music. *Prometheus* has since been heard without color accompaniment.

The program is also an obscure glorification of creative action. Prometheus gives the fire of heaven to human beings. The nobler of mankind are inspired by it to creative activity, while the baser use it only for evil. The conflict of good and evil is set forth, culminating in the ecstatic triumph of the creative will and the blending of the human with the divine.

A solo piano is used to represent man, as distinguished from the cosmos (the full orchestra). Originally the score also called for a wordless chorus at the end of the work, but this is usually dispensed with. A "Mystery" chord introduces the first of several important themes; it is heard in the horns. A second important idea is heard in the trumpet, representing the assertion of the creative will. A third subject, in the piano, characterizes the joy of life.

Piano Music. Scriabin's voluminous writings for the piano include ten sonatas. Up to his fourth sonata, he uses a two-movement structure made up of an introduction and the main body of the sonata. The sonatas that came after that are all in a single movement, while all sonatas after the sixth are without key signatures. The *Sonata No. 4,* in F-sharp major, is characteristic of the earlier works. Its two main themes have programmatic implications; the first is intended as desire and the second represents anguish. Among the later sonatas, which grow increasingly complex in technique, nebulous in structure, and elusive in thought, the finest is the *Sonata No. 9.* It opens in a mysterious atmosphere. Four ideas are then heard in rapid succession and are worked out with mastery. The sonata ends in the same mysterious vein with which it began.

Besides his sonatas, Scriabin produced many preludes, etudes, mazurkas, impromptus, waltzes, and so forth. The eighty-five preludes and the twenty-four etudes are the cream of this crop. The best are among the finest miniatures in piano literature. The preludes are filled with poetic and introspective moods that remind us of Chopin, of which the prelude, Op. 11, No. 15 is a notable example. But in such preludes as the Op. 11, No. 14, or the Op. 27, No. 1, Scriabin realizes a passionate intensity and force that express his own temperament rather than that of Chopin.

The Scriabin etudes are essentially dramatic cameos. The etudes Op.

8, Nos. 2 and 3 have a breadth and rhapsodic feeling that make us think of Brahms rather than Chopin. As was the case with Scriabin's other piano works, the style becomes more original and rarefied as the etudes progress in opus numbers. The last three etudes, gathered in Op. 65, utilize bold progressions and unorthodox melodies.

Dmitri Shostakovich

"It is my deepest feeling that there has never been a composer since Beethoven with such tremendous appeal to the masses."
—*Serge Koussevitzky*

BORN: Leningrad, September 25, 1906.
MAJOR WORKS: *Orchestral Music*—Symphony No. 1; Symphony No. 5; Symphony No. 7; Symphony No. 9; Symphony No. 10; Symphony No. 11; Concerto for Piano, Trumpet, and String Orchestra; Concerto for Violin and Orchestra. ALSO: Symphonies Nos. 6 8, 12; Ballet Suite No. 1, for orchestra; The Age of Gold, The Bolt, ballets; Lady Macbeth of Mzensk, opera; Song of the Forest, oratorio; 2 cello concertos; Quintet for Piano and Strings; 7 string quartets; Sonata for Cello and Piano; Trio in E minor; 2 sonatas, 24 preludes and 24 preludes and fugues for piano.

HIS LIFE

SHOSTAKOVICH's career as the most publicized and most provocative composer in the Soviet Union has been meteoric. He rose as high as any musician could in the Soviet Union, only to fall into sudden disgrace. He was able to recover his high station, once again to become an object for honor and admiration, but only to be discredited a second time. These fluctuations in Shostakovich's fortunes have had little relation to the quality or kind of music he was writing. He was only—as Nicolas Slonimsky pointed out—"the barometer of political current in the Soviet music. Whenever the line changes, Shostakovich is made the prime target of either praise or vehement denunciation."

Shostakovich's parents were musical. His father was an amateur pianist and singer, while his mother was a graduate of the Leningrad Conservatory. The first realization that their son was unusually gifted in music came in his fifth year, when he was taken to a performance of

Rimsky-Korsakov's opera *Czar Saltan.* The next day the child sang several of the important arias for the family. As his mother did not believe in teaching children music early, she delayed his first lessons until his ninth year. Almost immediately he revealed an unusual tendency to associate images with musical sounds. One chord represented to him stars; one passage was "somebody looking out of the window." He was almost always at the piano, and his progress was so rapid that his mother soon realized the need for more professional instruction. She enrolled him in the Glasser Music School; during the first year in that school he wrote his first composition, *Theme and Variations* for the piano.

He was only ten years old at the time of the revolution. "Hard times soon set in," his mother recalled. "Petrograd was hemmed in by the enemy and tormented by famine." Despite these hardships, Shostakovich's musical education was not allowed to be interrupted. The spirit of the revolution affected his musical writing, however, and he produced such pieces as the *Hymn to Liberty* and the *Funeral March for the Victims of the Revolution.*

In 1919 Shostakovich entered the Leningrad Conservatory, where his teachers included Nikolaev (piano) and Maximilian Steinberg (composition). His development was rapid. The other students thought so well of him that they created a special delegation to petition Glazunov, director of the Conservatory, to increase Shostakovich's food rations. Glazunov said: "Academicians' rations are not intended for youngsters of thirteen, but this is an exceptional case. The boy's gifts are phenomenal, comparable to Mozart's. I would willingly give up my own rations in his favor."

In his first Conservatory year he wrote a set of eight piano preludes, following this with his first published work, *Three Fantastic Dances.* These, and his earlier piano pieces, appeared prominently on his programs when he gave piano recitals in and out of the Conservatory. Simon Barere (later a world-famous piano virtuoso) recalled vividly Shostakovich's fine piano performances at the Conservatory and the profound impression they had made on him. The reviewers were also enthusiastic. The first review he ever received appeared in a Leningrad newspaper: "He played . . . with a clarity of artistic intention that showed him to be a musician who deeply feels and understands his art. Shostakovich's compositions . . . are fine examples of serious musical thought."

This was a difficult time for Shostakovich. The revolution made the situation trying for everybody, but Shostakovich had troubles of his own. His poverty was intense, his father having died and his mother's income as a secretary being hardly enough to provide for the family's needs. Besides, Shostakovich was suffering from tuberculosis of the lymphatic glands, which made it necessary for him to visit a sanatorium. But his studies continued and so did his creative work.

For a while he tried to help support his family by playing the piano in a motion-picture theater. But he did not keep the job. As his wife subsequently revealed: "An American comedy was being shown. . . . Every time certain scenes were flashed on the screen, the piano was silent, and the audience heard the piano player burst into laughter and enjoying the antics of the comedian. For this unseemly behavior, the administration decided to part company with the youthful pianist."

In his nineteenth year Shostakovich completed his *Symphony No. 1,* presenting it as his graduation piece at the Conservatory. It was heard in Leningrad under Nicolas Malko on May 12, 1926, and was well liked. A few months later the symphony was performed in Moscow, where it enjoyed even greater success. "It is a symphony," wrote the Moscow *Evening Radio,* "which reflects all that a composition can give of the most important in the artist."

In 1927 Shostakovich competed in an international pianists' contest in Warsaw, in which he won honorable mention. On his way home he stopped off in Berlin, where he met the famous conductor Bruno Walter. Walter expressed interest in Shostakovich's *Symphony No. 1* and offered to give it its first performance outside the Soviet Union. That performance, in Berlin under Walter, marked the beginning of the symphony's international fame. Leopold Stokowski introduced it in the United States on November 2, 1928, and after that its appearance on symphony programs everywhere was frequent. To this day it is Shostakovich's most popular work.

Having left the Conservatory, Shostakovich was ready to enter the professional ranks. But first, as he was quoted some years later in *La Revue musicale* as saying to an interviewer, "it was necessary for me to overhaul a great part of the musical baggage I had acquired. I understood that music was not a combination of sounds disposed in this or that order, but an art capable of expressing, by proper means, the most diverse ideas and sentiments. This conviction I did not acquire without pain. It suffices to say that during the year 1926 I did not write a single note, but from 1927 I have never ceased to compose."

In the spring of 1927 he was commissioned by the Soviet government to write a symphony commemorating the tenth anniversary of the October Revolution. With this work, Shostakovich assumed for the first time the role of a *Soviet* composer, his music thenceforth serving to express the ideologies of his country and addressing itself to the Soviet masses. Here is the way he himself explained it: "I cannot conceive of my future creative program outside of our socialist enterprise, and the aim which I assign to my work is that of helping in every way to enlighten our remarkable country." And on another occasion he said: "There can be no music without an ideology. . . . Lenin himself said that 'music is a means of unifying broad masses of people' . . . Even the symphonic form . . . can be said to have a bearing on politics. Good music . . . is no longer an end in itself but a vital weapon in the struggle."

Neither the *Symphony No. 2* ("To October") nor the *May Day* Symphony that followed it were successful. Shostakovich decided to exploit a new vein: satire. On January 12, 1930, his satirical opera *The Nose* (based on the story by Gogol) was introduced in Leningrad. While the Association of Proletarian Composers condemned the opera as decadent and bourgeois, Shostakovich's position was not seriously affected. He produced a second satirical work—the ballet *The Age of Gold*—which won first prize in a competition conducted throughout the country for a ballet on a Soviet theme. *The Age of Gold,* seen in 1930, was also a failure, but only because its libretto was complicated and confused; Shostakovich's music was highly praised. Two excerpts from the score have survived and remained popular: the "Polka" and the "Russian Dance," the former intended as a satire on the Geneva Peace Conference.

By the middle 1930s Shostakovich was regarded as one of the most promising composers in the Soviet Union. His increasing significance brought him many commissions for music for films and stage productions. In a more serious vein, he produced several works of pronounced originality: the ballet *The Bolt,* produced in Leningrad in 1931; a set of twenty-four preludes for the piano, written between 1932 and 1933; and the Concerto for Piano, Trumpet, and String Orchestra, completed in 1933.

With his position in Soviet music solidified, and his significance in the cultural life of the Soviet Union accepted, there took place the first major crisis of his life. It was brought on by his opera *Lady Macbeth of Mzensk,* which he completed in 1932 and which was first seen in Leningrad on January 22, 1934. The curious fact is that *Lady Macbeth of*

Mzensk was an immense success at first. It was praised by the critics extravagantly and for two years it played to packed houses. In 1935 it was also performed in Cleveland and New York. In and out of the Soviet Union, it was regarded as the finest opera to come out of that country.

Then—suddenly and without warning—came the attack. On January 28, 1936, *Pravda* published an article entitled "A Pandemonium Instead of Music." Shostakovich's opera—after two years of success!—was suddenly discovered to be "crude, primitive, vulgar." "The music quacks, grunts, growls, suffocates itself in order to express the amatory scenes as naturalistically as possible. . . . The composer, apparently, does not set himself the task of listening to the desires and expectations of the Soviet public. He scrambles sounds to make them interesting to formalist-aesthetes, who have lost all good taste."

When this violent attack was followed by an equally devastating attack on Shostakovich's new ballet, *The Limpid Stream* ("the composer," said the editorial, "apparently has only contempt for our national songs"), it appeared that Shostakovich was through. For more than a year the foremost Soviet musicians were either contemptuous of him or avoided him completely.

But with amazing resilience Shostakovich bounced back into favor. There took place on November 21, 1937, the *première* of his *Symphony No. 5*, in conjunction with festivities commemorating the twentieth anniversary of the Soviet Republic. After that performance there was an ovation. The critics, so long apathetic to Shostakovich, were ecstatic in their reviews. Andrei Budyakovsky wrote, in the Moscow *Daily News,* that this was a "work of great depth, with emotional wealth and content, and is of great importance as a milestone in the composer's development."

This formidable success was followed by others. In 1940 Shostakovich won the Stalin Prize for his Quintet for Piano and Strings. Once again he was among the most highly honored of Soviet composers. He was soon to achieve an even greater prestige: after the invasion of Russia by the Nazis, he became a national hero.

He tried three times to join the Red Army and was turned down. He remained in Leningrad, joining the fire-fighting brigade at the Conservatory. His major activity was the writing of a symphony that would express the turbulent times. When the Soviet government was forced to leave Moscow for its temporary capital on the Volga, Kuibyshev, Shostakovich accompanied it. He completed his *Symphony No. 7* there; and there it was introduced on March 1, 1942. Diplomats, Red Army officers, high Soviet officials, and representatives of the American military and diplomatic corps were all present. Samuel Samosud, the conductor, described how the excited ovations that followed the performance "assumed the proportions of a powerful demonstration of patriotism." And one of the Russian writers who was present prophesied that the finale "will be played in Red Square by an orchestra of five thousand on the day of our victory." Intended as a reflection of the country and its people during the siege of Leningrad, the Seventh Symphony became a vibrant testament of the times, a powerful force for morale, a shattering weapon in the war effort. It brought Shostakovich the Stalin Prize for the second time.

The first performance of the Seventh Symphony outside of the Soviet Union took place in London on June 29, 1942. The audience rose to its feet and cheered wildly. Immediately there developed a spirited rivalry among American conductors for the privilege of performing it for the first time in the Western Hemisphere. That distinction went to Arturo Toscanini. The score was photographed on microfilm in Kuibyshev and rushed by plane and automobile to New York by way of Teheran and Cairo. In New York it was transferred into a musical score of 252 pages by a staff of photographers. Toscanini's performance took place on July 19, 1942, over the network of the National Broadcasting Company. One month later the symphony received its first concert performance at the Berkshire Music Festival, with Serge Koussevitzky conducting. The following autumn every major orchestra in the United States performed it. A writer for *Life* remarked wryly that it was almost an act of treason not to be enthusiastic about this symphony. In any case, enthusiasm was not lacking anywhere.

The *Symphony No. 8*, which was heard in Moscow on November 4, 1943, was not received kindly by the leading Soviet critics. Nor were Soviet officials more generously disposed toward the *Symphony No. 9*, heard in Leningrad on November 3, 1945. They found that this new symphony contained "ideological weakness" and insisted that it was poor reflection of Soviet life and thought. This was a storm warning. The storm itself did not occur until February 10, 1948. At that time the Central Committee of the Communist Party attacked some of the leading Soviet composers for their "formalism" and "subservience to bourgeois decadence" and "cerebralism" (see biography of Prokofiev). In this attack Shostakovich was not spared.

Shostakovich did not hesitate to make a public confession of his "guilt." He said he was ready to atone for his musical sins. Taking to heart the new aesthetic principles set forth by the authorities, he started writing music which would meet with government approval. And it was not long before he was restored to the good graces of the authorities.

In March 1949 he was one of seven members of a committee sent to the United States to represent the Soviet Union at the Cultural and Scientific Conference for World Peace held in New York. This, his first visit to the United States, did not receive the welcome it deserved. But the international tensions of the times were not altogether responsible. Always surrounded by Soviet officials, Shostakovich was denied contact with our press, musicians, and musical organizations. From the discreet distance at which he was kept, he made a poor impression. On the stage at the conference, he usually appeared bored by the proceedings. Shostakovich hoped to tour the United States after that, but was prevented from doing so by the State Department. In the fall of 1959, however, Shostakovich paid a second visit to the United States under happier auspices, making a one-month tour of principal cities and attending performances of his works.

If there was still some doubt about Shostakovich's position in Soviet music, it was completely dispelled during that same year. On November 26, 1949, there took place the *première* of his oratorio, *Song of the Forest,* in praise of the Stalin reforestation plan, which won the Stalin Prize. In 1956 he received the Order of Lenin on the occasion of his fiftieth birthday. Two years later, as the recipient of the Finnish Sibelius Prize, he turned over the cash award of $22,000 to the Finnish Soviet Friendship Association.

Shostakovich has always been a man of excessive enthusiasms. When a musical work engages him, he is so excited by it and so completely engrossed in it that he becomes oblivious to everything around him— people, noise, and personal discomfort. "The door of the room where he works is usually open," his wife revealed in an interview, "and often the children romp around in his room. Sometimes Galya climbs on to his knees while he is composing. . . . While Dmitri was finishing the final bars of the Seventh Symphony, for instance, friends who had come in were chatting and joking in the room where he sat." His wife further explains: "Once the work is finished, he cools off, only to warm up again and become entirely absorbed with the next work."

He has the same kind of intensity about his diversions. "He is a great sports fan. Heat or cold, rain or snow—there was not one soccer, ice hockey, or boxing match he would miss. . . . He once instituted a special 'debit-credit ledger' in which he could diligently enter all games won or lost by all the soccer teams during the current sports season. From various towns, soccer players keep Dmitri fully posed on the 'situation.' "

His wife has also revealed that one of Shostakovich's distinguishing characteristics is "his extraordinary, almost bureaucratic conscientiousness and scupulousness in whatever he may be engaged. Whenever the Conservatory fire-fighting brigade of which he was a member was barracked, he punctiliously obeyed all regulations and flatly refused repeated suggestions that special allowances be made for him. If antityphoid vaccinations are announced, he is sure to be among the first to arrive. At concerts, he arrives before the cloakroom attendant, and always turns up ahead of time for duty at the Composers' Union. He is always afraid of being late."

HIS MUSIC

SHOSTAKOVICH has been a provocative figure outside the Soviet Union as well as in it. His music has been extravagantly praised and just as extravagantly denounced. The significant point is that both the praise and the condemnation are justified. For when Shostakovich is good, he is very good; and when he is poor, he is awful. At his best, his craftsmanship is superb. His lyricism is engaging. His rhythmic drive is cogent. He can be noble, witty, and ironic with equal effect. But at his worst, he is imitative, blatant, and given to clichés. The sad thing is that the good and the bad are not only found in different works, but also in the very same composition.

However, after subtractions are made, Shostakovich still remains an important composer, the creator of several distinguished pieces of music. He is at his best in the First, Fifth, and Ninth Symphonies, the Concerto for Piano, Trumpet, and String Orchestra, the Piano Quintet, the Second String Quartet, works which are likely to remain representative of the finest musical creation of our time.

ANALYTICAL NOTES

Orchestral Music. The *Symphony No. 1* was a work of Shostakovich's youth, having been written when he was only eighteen. It is filled
with youthful verve, exuberance, intensity, and abandon. The introduction to the first movement presents a theme in two sections, the first in
muted solo trumpet and the second in the bassoon. The clarinet picks
up this idea against a pizzicato figure in the cellos. A brief pause separates the introduction from the allegro. The main theme, which is almost martial, is soon heard in the clarinet. The second principal theme
of the movement is, on the other hand, elegiac, with a Tchaikovsky-like
wistfulness; it appears first in the flute against plucked strings and is
then appropriated, in turn, by the clarinet, horn, and bassoon. The
music now becomes agitated. Although the storm is momentarily
broken by a return of the elegiac melody, the feverish mood prevails.
But the tranquillity comes back at the end of the movement with a
repetition of the introduction in a slightly altered form.

The second movement is a scintillating scherzo, fleet in movement,
capricious in tone. The main theme appears in the strings in the fourteenth measure and is immediately repeated boisterously by the piano.
The theme of the middle trio is found in two flutes. After the opening
theme reappears in the bassoon, a huge climax is created, with the trio
theme played forcefully by the brass and the main theme played in
strings, woodwinds, and piano.

The vigor of the preceding sections now gives way to a tender lento
movement. A sad mood is immediately created by a poignant solo for
oboe against tremolo strings. The mood grows increasingly melancholy
as the main melody of the movement is played pianissimo by strings;
the intrusion by the oboe, five measures later, further intensifies the
pathos. This oboe theme is soon taken over loudly by the brass, and a
forceful climax is built up. When the opening idea reappears in the
solo violin, the grief once more becomes subdued. The movement ends
softly and plaintively in divided strings.

A crescendo in the side drum brings on the finale without a pause.
After a loud measure, there comes an extended brooding section. The
main body of the finale is music of dramatic contrasts and whirlwind
motion. It is introduced by a lively theme for clarinet, which is repeated
and developed and then culminates in a powerful climax. Violin glissandos in the upper register introduce the second theme, which appears

first loudly in strings and woodwinds, then dies down in sonority until it is heard softly in a solo violin against tremolo strings and after that in solo horn. After a restatement of the first theme in flute and clarinet, the entire orchestra becomes engaged in a tremendous climax, punctuated by fanfares for the trumpets. Descending chromatic scales in the woodwinds, strings, and piano bring on another immense climax. The passions have now been dissipated. A solo for kettledrum alternates between very loud and very soft passages. A solo cello gently recalls the second theme. A last outburst of energy and an acceleration of pace bring the symphony to an exciting finish.

The next two symphonies, which were failures when introduced, are rarely heard. The Fourth Symphony aroused such hostility among the members of the orchestra during rehearsals that Shostakovich withdrew it and never allowed it to be performed. But the *Symphony No. 5,* completed in 1937, is one of Shostakovich's masterpieces. The youthful ardor of the First Symphony is replaced by the breadth and the vision of maturity. This is music of spacious design and eloquent expression. The first movement immediately engages a broad and dramatic subject, presented antiphonally between low and high strings. Out of this theme, a more placid melody is evolved in the violins. After a dissonant climax, we hear the second main theme of the movement in violas against an insistent rhythmic background in cellos and basses; this is as dramatic and as spacious as the first theme. A powerful subject for horns, set against a rhythmic figure in lower strings and piano, brings on the development section. The music now grows excitable, as both themes are transformed into frequently powerful and exultant statements. But the concluding section of the movement has greater sobriety.

The second movement is dance music in Shostakovich's most ingratiating satiric vein. A vigorous theme in waltz time is presented loudly by cellos and doublebasses. Another waltz melody is infectiously introduced by the woodwinds. Various delightful episodes follow, each brief and pleasingly lyrical. The movement ends with a repetition of the opening material.

The levity of the second movement is succeeded by one of the most soulful pages of music by Shostakovich. It begins with an expressive melody for the violins which is continued in divided strings. A new idea emerges in the flute, with harp accompaniment, but it is only a fleeting thought. A much more substantial subject appears in the oboe over tremolos in the violins. The clarinet and the flute take it over in turn, before it is subjected to development. The tensions are now increased and the music becomes passionate as the first theme is presented loudly by the strings. A forceful climax is built up, but the placid and introspective mood of the opening page is revived before the movement concludes.

The finale enters with an uncontrolled burst of energy. A powerful march, whose Russian identity is unmistakable, is given by the brass instruments against vigorous accents by the kettledrums. This idea assumes increasing importance until a storm is let loose. The dynamics and instrumental colors of the orchestra are now fully exploited. But a more subdued and slower middle section is a welcome respite; it recalls some of the more lyrical episodes of the preceding movements. The march music returns with ever increasing power and grandeur to carry the symphony to its triumphant resolution.

The *Symphony No. 7,* the so-called *Leningrad* Symphony, was born during World War II in the first year of the Nazi invasion of the Soviet Union. The composer expressed here the spirit of the citizens of Leningrad during the siege. There is no mistaking the martial character of the music. The first movement was intended as a "requiem in memory of the heroes who sacrificed their lives so that justice and reason might triumph." The opening theme, played in unison by strings and bassoons, represents the spirit of Leningrad. The second theme, a sinister march, speaks for the Nazi invaders. In the development section the Nazi theme grows in power and sweeps relentlessly and with increasing sonority through the orchestra. But the Leningrad theme rises from the background of the orchestra and finally overpowers the Nazi march. The music mourns the Soviet dead (bassoon solo over plucked chords in the strings), and a muted trumpet against a muffled military drum repeats the Nazi march for the last time.

Shostakovich explained that the next two movements were an intermezzo. "They confirm life in opposition to war. I tried to express the thought that art, literature, and science must advance in spite of war." The second movement is a scherzo, with a middle section that recalls briefly the martial character of the symphony, while the third movement is lyrical and emotional, with an almost religious feeling. There is no pause between this slow movement and the finale, the transition being a roll in the timpani. This movement, said Shostakovich, "is dedicated to our victory.... The victory of light over darkness, wisdom over frenzy, lofty humanism over monstrous tyranny." Like the development of the first movement, the finale is a monumental march which grows in momentum and gains in tonal strength until it becomes well-nigh overpowering. Three trombones in unison revive the first theme of the opening movement. Now transformed into a mighty paean to victory, this Leningrad theme is the symphony's final, exultant declaration.

The *Symphony No. 9,* written in 1945, brought Shostakovich into conflict with the Soviet authorities, who regarded it as cerebral music. Nevertheless, it is one of Shostakovich's most lovable pieces of music. In comparison to such works as the Fifth and Seventh Symphonies, it is simple and economical in design, lucid in its writing, filled with bright melodies, and overflowing with good spirit and even merriment. It is in five movements, the last two played without interruption. Drollery alternates with introspection to provide variety of pace and mood. Drollery is found in the first, third, and fifth movements. The first is consistently jovial and ironic; the third is a fleet-footed presto, whose flight is uninterrupted; the finale has elements of naïveté and broad comedy. Introspection comes in the second and fourth movements. The second is a long and involved meditation, emphasizing the woodwinds, while the fourth is a gentle intermezzo, highlighting an improvisational melody for the bassoon.

The *Symphony No. 10,* in E minor (1953), won the New York Music Critics Award after its American *première* in 1954. The symphony is lyric. Two significant melodies appear in the first movement, the first in the clarinet after a fifty-measure slow introduction, and the second in the flute. Energy is temporarily released in the short second-movement scherzo, but lyricism is again emphasized in the slow movement which opens with a folk song in strings in imitation, and continues with a brooding nocturne for horn solo accompanied by pizzicato strings. An exotic tune for oboe solo introduces the finale which thereafter recalls material from the scherzo, the slow movement, and finally a motive from the first-movement introduction.

Symphony No. 11, in G minor (1957), is subtitled "1905" and commemorates the fiftieth anniversary of the Revolution of that year. Much of the musical material has martial character, with brass fanfares and percussion effects continually prominent. Other materials, of a more lyric character, are derived from Russian folk songs and songs of the 1905 Revolution.

The Concerto for Piano, Trumpet, and String Orchestra belongs with Shostakovich's earlier works, having been written in 1933. Its instrumentation is one of its most original features: it is scored for strings and a single trumpet.

After an introductory trumpet call, the principal theme of the first movement appears in the piano. It is then discussed by the strings, and by piano and orchestra. A transitional theme in the violin brings both a change of tempo and the second major theme, also in solo piano. The themes are worked out in lively fashion, sometimes with an occasional excursion into burlesque. The recapitulation section enters with a return of the first theme in the violins.

The second movement begins with a melody in the violins against a ground bass. The piano enters with a trill and answers with a subsidiary theme unaccompanied. After an intensification of tempo and sonority, culminating in a dynamic climax, the first theme returns in the trumpet and is brought to a conclusion by the piano.

The third movement serves as a prelude to the finale; it includes two brief cadenzas for the piano, one of them accompanied. The finale itself begins with a short piano passage which leads to the first theme in the violins. The burlesque mood so lightly suggested in the first movement is now given free play as one gay episode follows another, the trumpet assuming a major role in these drolleries. A detailed cadenza for the piano is succeeded by a sprightly coda, in which the bright voice of the trumpet is heard up to the very end.

The Concerto for Violin and Orchestra (1955) was written for the Soviet violinist, David Oistrakh, who introduced it in both the Soviet Union and the United States. The first movement is a poetic nocturne, the main melody appearing in the solo violin against a bassoon accompaniment. An airy, vivacious scherzo is succeeded by a Passacaglia constructed from an ostinato figure in cellos and basses. The finale enters without pause with an ironic tune in orchestra. After that the music of the finale is filled with brilliant orchestral effects and pyrotechnical passages for the solo instrument.

Jean Sibelius

"Sibelius reveals a fresh and unsuspected beauty in the old,
whereas most modern composers seek to discover a familiar
beauty in the new."

—*Cecil Gray*

BORN: Tavastehus, Finland, December 8, 1865.
DIED: Järvenpää, Finland, September 20, 1957.
MAJOR WORKS: *Orchestral Music*—Symphonies Nos. 1, 2, 4, and
7; Concerto for Violin and Orchestra; En Saga; The Swan of
Tuonela; Finlandia; Tapiola. ALSO: Symphonies Nos. 3, 5, and 6;
Pohjola's Daughter, Belshazzar's Feast, Valse Triste, for orchestra;
Voces Intimae, for string quartet; sonatinas, short pieces, for piano;
songs.

HIS LIFE

AMERICA recognizes Sibelius as a great composer, one of the greatest
of our time. But in his native Finland he was much more than
that. He was a national hero. The Finnish government issued
stamps bearing the picture of Sibelius, an unprecedented honor for a
living composer. In 1940 a campaign was launched in Finland to erect
a statue of him for his diamond jubilee; the project was dropped only
when Sibelius wrote to a newspaper urging his friends to desist. Rarely
before has a composer meant so much to his country as Sibelius does.
He is the voice of Finland, its symbol. Those who have visited Finland
know what a unique position he occupied. The children in the streets
know his name and sing his melodies; they speak of him with the awe
which, in other lands, is usually reserved for athletes or military heroes.
The older people (not necessarily music lovers) honor his name and
speak it with reverence.

He is Finland in music; and he is Finnish music. The ideal to create music that echoed and vibrated with the overtones of his country's culture, people, geography, and lore came to him in the closing decade of the nineteenth century. He had just returned to his native land from Germany and Austria, where he had completed his music study. At that time Finland was suffering oppression at the hands of its Russian rulers. The ruthless despotism of Nicholas II robbed the Finnish government of its sovereignty and the Finnish people of freedom. Patriots were imprisoned; newspapers were suppressed. This attempt to crush the Finnish people inevitably aroused their patriotism. Underground movements arose to carry on the messages of truth and freedom, to keep alive the spark of national pride and dignity. The spirit of the times infected Sibelius, who now wished to have his music express love of his country and pride in its cultural and historic traditions. He reread the Finnish epic poem the *Kalevala* avidly. "Golden gifts do I not ask for"—so runs one of the lines in the *Kalevala*—"and I wish not for thy silver, only bring me back to my country." Sibelius was brought back to his country when he produced the first of his Finnish works, a five-movement symphonic poem, *Kullervo,* based upon an episode from the *Kalevala,* introduced in Helsingfors on April 28, 1892, under the composer's direction. *Kullervo* was a great success, for it spoke in music what the Finnish people did not dare to express in words. And Sibelius had found his direction as a composer.

The son of a regimental doctor, Jean Sibelius was born in the small Finnish town of Tavastehus. He was a sensitive child who was drawn to beauty in all forms: art, books, music, and nature. In his fifth year he started experimenting with consonant harmonies at the piano, and four years later he began formal study. From the beginning he was more interested in improvisation than in formal exercises. He wrote his first piece of music when he was ten years old: a duet for violin and cello called *Drops of Water,* in which plucked strings imitated the sound of dripping water.

He was enrolled in the Finnish Model School when he was eleven. One of his fellow students later recalled how shy and introspective he was: "Jean found it difficult to sit still during lessons and listen to things that did not interest him. He sat, buried in thought, and would be quite absent-minded, when questioned suddenly. On such occasions, our beloved headmaster would look at him reproachfully and say with a deep sigh: 'Good gracious, again Sibelius is in another world!'"

Sibelius started studying the violin with Gustav Levander when he reached his fifteenth year, and at that time his ambition was to become a virtuoso. But his interest in the creative phase of music had not diminished. He studied by himself all the texts he could find in the library; getting some knowledge of theory and form, he wrote several chamber-music works including a trio and a piano quartet.

After being graduated from the high school, Sibelius attended the Helsingfors University to specialize in law. Music had come to mean so much to him that he neglected his law studies to concentrate on musical activities, including further study at the Musical Academy. After a year at the University he received his parents' blessings to concentrate entirely on music study. He now made notable progress with such sympathetic teachers as Ferruccio Busoni (at that time a professor at the Helsingfors Academy) and Martin Wegelius.

Adolf Paul, later a novelist and playwright, was Sibelius' fellow student at the Academy. He left us the following impressions of the young music student: "He did not seem to dwell on this earth. His nature was delicate and impressionable; his sensitive imagination found outlet in music at the slightest provocation. His thoughts always strayed, his head was always in the clouds, and he continually expressed such original and bizarre ideas that his friend and most faithful protagonist, Robert Kajanus, said pointedly that in his normal mood he was like the rest of us drunk."

On a scholarship from the Musical Academy, Sibelius went to Berlin in 1889 to study with Albert Becker and after that to Vienna to complete his studies with Karl Goldmark and Robert Fuchs. In 1891 he was back in his native land; from this time on he devoted himself to the writing of Finnish music. One year after his return he married Aino Järnefelt. After a honeymoon in Karelia (a section of Finland glorified in one of his orchestral works) he settled in Helsingfors, earning his living by teaching theory at the Musical Academy and the orchestral school of the Philharmonic Society, and playing the violin in a string quartet. It was at this time that he completed the first of his famous tone poems, *En Saga,* with which national Finnish music can be said to have emerged. *En Saga* was followed by the *Karelia* Suite and by the *Four Legends,* the latter inspired by the *Kalevala* and centered around the Finnish hero Lemminkäinen. But the most stirring and the most celebrated work by Sibelius was *Finlandia,* written in 1899. Sibelius' fame had grown so great with his first national works that, in 1897, he had become the first Finnish composer ever to be voted an annual grant by the Senate. This grant enabled him to give up all teaching duties and to concentrate on composing.

In 1899 Sibelius completed his First Symphony, and it was introduced in Helsingfors on April 26, 1899, under Robert Kajanus. The Second Symphony was written in Italy during 1901; it was first heard in Helsingfors in March 8, 1902. The next five Sibelius symphonies came between the years of 1907 and 1924. For more than two decades the rumor was circulated that an Eighth Symphony was being completed, but it is now certain that little more than random sketches exist.

In 1901 Sibelius suffered from a disease of the ear which threatened to bring on total deafness. He became increasingly morbid; it was at this time that he wrote his highly popular *salon* piece, *Valse Triste*. Fortunately, complete recovery took place. But in 1908 Sibelius was again afflicted, this time by a malignant growth in the throat at first diagnosed as cancer. It took thirteen operations to relieve him of his terrible pain and to remove the anxiety over possible cancer. No doubt the music completed at this time reflected Sibelius' physical and emotional upheaval: the elegiac and often melancholy Fourth Symphony and the intensely personal string quartet which he entitled *Voces Intimae* (*Intimate Voices*).

Sibelius visited the United States in 1914, invited by Carl Stoeckel, a music patron, to participate in the Norfolk Festival of Music conducted by the Lichfield County Choral Union. Sibelius directed a concert of his music on June 4, 1914, at the Music Shed in Norfolk, Connecticut— his American debut. "During the last fifteen years," wrote Henry E. Krehbiel in his review, "I have felt three times that I was confronted by genius . . . and lastly when by the courtesy of Carl Stoeckel I had the privilege of hearing Jean Sibelius of Finland direct nine of his old and new compositions."

The era of World War I, and the revolution in Russia, which had violent repercussions in Finland, was a critical one for the composer. Shortly after Finland declared its independence of Russian domination, civil war broke out between the "Red Guard" revolutionists and the "White Guard." Murder (Sibelius' brother, a physician, was a victim), terror, and hooliganism spread throughout Finland. The authorities did not permit Sibelius to leave his villa, but even there the composer was not completely safe. On two occasions the Red Army descended on him, subjecting his house to an intensive search and throwing its members into an uproar.

When the war was over, and a normal life was once again possible, Sibelius undertook an extensive tour of Europe, conducting concerts of his works in Norway, Sweden, and Italy. He had become not only a national idol, but a composer recognized internationally as the greatest symphonist since Brahms. His last known work was completed in 1929. After that Sibelius withdrew from the world scene to become something of a legend. Not even his most intimate friends learned whether he was writing any music.

Despite his immense fame, Sibelius was always a simple man who derived his keenest pleasures from nature. The gardens of Villa Ainola (his home since 1904), a walk in the nearby forests, a peaceful respite at the lake near his house—these, through the years, provided him with the relaxation and inner peace he always required for fruitful work. Before World War II, he sometimes enjoyed visiting the tavern in Järvenpää, indulging in small-town talk with neighbors while drinking schnapps and smoking cigars. After the war he was virtually a recluse.

He was always fastidious about his appearance. When he left his villa, it was to visit his tailor in Helsingfors. He combined meticulousness in his choice of clothes with a passion for comfort. His custom-made suits were sewed a size larger than necessary to give him freedom of movement, and he always wore collars that fitted loosely around the neck. His shoes were made by hand in Berlin.

His massive bald head was evidence of his vanity. When he was forty years old, his first gray hairs appeared. Rather than provide visible proof that he was growing older, he shaved his head and kept it shaved. He resented the thought that he might be an old man and always tried to provide evidence that he was young and vigorous.

During World War II the false rumor was spread that he was destitute and starving. His government pension and the food he could raise on his own grounds were adequate to serve the needs of his family. He suffered only as every patriotic Finn did when the Soviets attacked his land. Often when the Soviet planes zoomed over his villa he would rush outdoors and raise a defiant fist at them.

After the war he kept pretty much to himself; he discouraged visitors. He still allowed himself the luxury of drinking expensive cognac and smoking the finest cigars. His contact with the world outside the Villa Ainola was maintained mostly by means of his radio, through which he was able to hear much of the new music being written and occasionally performances of his own works. He died in his villa on September 20, 1957.

HIS MUSIC

As a music student in Berlin and Vienna, Sibelius wrote several large works (including an octet and an orchestral overture) which were derivative from Brahms and Tchaikovsky. But it was not long before he evolved his own idiom. When, at the close of the century, he became the musical voice of Finland, he completely and permanently broke all ties with German and Russian Romanticism. A work such as *En Saga,* completed in 1892, was in the image of the later symphonies, in its broad and wind-swept themes, its vigorous rhythms that were primitive and strong, its bleak harmonies, and its rugged sonorities. After *En Saga,* the personality of Sibelius' music was unmistakable. His austere, solitary, and frequently pastoral moods contrasted with wild and brilliant outbursts of color and passion are the Finnish landscape and sagas in musical tones. So completely does this music realize the temperament of its country that it is often believed that Sibelius utilizes actual folk melodies; but the materials Sibelius uses are always his own.

He is at his greatest and most individual in his symphonies. In the first two, he still wears borrowed clothing. But with each succeeding work he becomes increasingly personal, his speech becomes more and more concentrated and exalted, his form gains greater compactness. The goal becomes economy and simplicity. He leans toward epigrammatic ideas and fragments of themes (rather than spacious melodies), which he builds up with monumental power.

He belongs more to the late nineteenth century than to our own day. While he was successful in freeing himself from the influence of Brahms and Tchaikovsky, he has always remained a romantic. He has never concerned himself with the new concepts of melody, harmony, and tonality that arose throughout the world. The conventional techniques and idioms were serviceable. Yet there can never be any question of his originality: his music could have come from no one else.

ANALYTICAL NOTES

Orchestral Music. The first two Sibelius symphonies have never lost their popularity. They do not have much subtlety of expression. They are Russian in their overindulgence in dramatic statements, Slavic in their haunting, poignant melodies of peasant energy. They wear the heart on the sleeve. But what they lack in subtlety, they make up in dramatic effect. They have an overwhelming emotional impact.

The *Symphony No. 1,* in E minor, begins with a brooding introduction in which a melody for clarinet is prominent. A dramatic theme for strings brings on the allegro section. After a secondary subject for the woodwinds, a climax is reached with the orchestra thundering the opening allegro theme. We now hear the second main theme of the movement, a reflective melody for two flutes. The development is mostly stormy, and the movement ends in an agitated mood.

The second movement is nostalgic music in folk character. The main melody, given by muted violins and cellos, resembles an expressive Finnish folk song. Another tranquil idea is presented by the woodwinds. An outburst by the full orchestra temporarily shatters the mood, but a solo cello leads to a return of the original atmosphere.

The barbaric rhythmic drive of the first part of the scherzo is put into motion with a figure stated forcefully by two kettledrums. This whole first part has demoniac energy, but the reflective trio is a welcome contrast. The basic melody of this trio is a poignant subject for flute.

The opening section of the finale brings back the poignant theme of the first-movement introduction, but now touched with tragedy. A hint of a new theme appears in the lower strings before the woodwinds present it fully. There is a wind-swept surge in the orchestra. The second theme, broad and lyrical, now appears in the strings, the percussion providing a rhythmic background. A fugato based on the first theme prefaces a second climax, the peak of which is a powerful restatement of the first theme. The second theme now passes to different groups of the orchestra and is succeeded by a passionate, even turbulent, coda.

The *Symphony No. 2,* in D major, is neither the best of Sibelius' symphonies nor the most representative. But concert audiences have been most partial to it. It is not difficult to understand why. It is theatrical, emotionally demonstrative, and punctuated with powerful climactic surges. It has an overpowering impact.

In the first eight measures the violins present a pulsating figure which becomes the accompaniment for the first theme, soon heard in oboes and clarinets. This theme has a bucolic character. Eight measures in plucked strings lead to the second theme, in the woodwinds. This second theme is worked out in detail in the development, in which various new episodes are interpolated briefly. A brief pause separates the development from the recapitulation, the latter beginning with a restatement of both main themes, the first by the woodwinds and the second by the brass.

The slow movement begins with rumblings in the kettledrums. The lower strings bring a figure soon to become the accompaniment to the mournful first theme for bassoons. The mood then becomes animated, and a loud climax is built up. We next hear in the strings a beautiful second theme which resembles a simple folk melody. Before the movement ends in a powerful outburst, both themes are recalled as a pronounced dramatic atmosphere is created.

The first theme of the scherzo is a sprightly subject for the violins. The rhythm of this theme becomes a background for the second subject, in flute and bassoon. In the trio there is a delightful melody for the oboe. The ideas of both the opening section and the trio are repeated. The last movement follows without pause. Strings, soon supplemented by trumpet, are engaged in the bold first theme. An idea for flutes and bassoons leads to the second theme, heard first in the oboe and then in other woodwind instruments. These two ideas are worked out forcefully, as a powerful climax is worked up. In the recapitulation, the main theme appears in the strings while the second theme is given by the trumpet and answered by the oboe. The main theme becomes an exultant proclamation in the coda.

There is much more restraint in the *Symphony No. 4,* in A minor, written a decade after the Second Symphony. The vivid dramatics and stirring passions of the first two symphonies are replaced by a gentle sorrow, introspection, and poetic feeling. Emotional sobriety and asceticism are combined with a compact structure, economy of orchestration, and brevity of ideas. The first movement acquires much of its effect from its austerity. There is a rumbling theme in the lower strings in a six-bar introduction; the intervallic structure of this motive becomes the germinal idea for the entire movement. A mournful song then appears in the cello. As other strings join in, this melody becomes a dirge. But the second theme, introduced by a brass fanfare, has the autumnal beauty and resignation of a Brahms melody; it appears in the strings. All this material is repeated, with some enlargement, but without dispelling the elegiac character of the music.

The second movement is brief. It begins in a quasi-whimsical attitude with a lighthearted tune in the oboe. The violins take over the melody. But a later episode in the oboe and clarinet brings on a feeling of despair. Even when the whimsical tune returns it is no longer lighthearted, but sinister.

The largo brings back the meditation of the first movement. It opens with a pastoral idea in the flute, which is continued by the clarinet. The main theme is vaguely suggested in the horns before the cellos give it in its entirety. This is the most lyrical subject not only of this movement but also of the entire symphony. It grows in beauty and intensity when it reappears—first in the strings in octaves, then in the strings supplemented by woodwinds and brass. In the coda there is an episodic idea in bassoons and clarinets which, when developed, becomes the introductory theme of the finale. Tolling bells herald the arrival of the principal thematic material of this movement. The ideas are stated briefly and hurriedly: one is a fanfare, another a declamation, a third a chorale. There is no development to speak of. The recapitulation section repeats earlier material dramatically. But the tension is always controlled and finally subsides into a gentle benediction for the strings.

The *Symphony No. 7,* in C major, is Sibelius' last symphony. It is in a single movement. It begins with an air of mystery. A rumbling in the kettledrums brings on an ascending figure in the strings. A more expressive second subject appears in divided strings. After a hymn-like declamation for solo trombone there is a quickening of pace. A scherzolike section develops. This is followed by a return to the slow tempo of the beginning, with a restatement of the hymn for trombone, soon repeated with increasing grandeur by the rest of the brass. Once again there is a change of pace and mood. A succession of ideas leads to a monumental climax. When the tempo of the opening is brought back, the hymn is recalled by the brass with grandiose effect. Another immense climax is built up, after which the unaccompanied strings take on an emotional subject. The flute and bassoon enter with a last poignant reflection. There is a forceful crescendo and a dramatic finish.

The Concerto for Violin and Orchestra, completed in 1903 and revised in 1905, stands between the Second and Third Symphonies. The rhapsodic first movement passes from sentimental and romantic effusions to bold and vigorous statements. It is filled with warm and ingratiating melodies. The first theme is a passionate and extended song, heard immediately in the violin. The second theme, more restful, also appears first in the violin, after an orchestral interlude. The second movement is a sentimental poem—one of Sibelius' most romantic pages. After a five-measure introduction for the woodwinds, the solo violin enters with a tender melody against a dark background of chords in the horns and bassoons. When the melody later passes into the orchestra, the solo violin decorates it with a subtle lacework of tones. The finale is a strong-fibered rondo made up of two important themes. Timpani and basses project a strong rhythm in the first four measures. The solo violin then embarks on a bold theme. The second subject, strongly tinged with national colors, is soon heard in the violins and cellos. Striking virtuoso passages for the violin and two forceful orchestral *tutti* maintain the brilliant character of the movement. In the coda, the violin indulges in pyrotechnical octave passages against an accompaniment recalling the main theme.

With the tone poem *En Saga*—Sibelius' first major orchestral work— Finnish national music arrived at artistic significance. A horn call rises above tremolos and arpeggios in muted, divided strings. The principal theme, after being hinted at, appears fully in the bassoons against arpeggios in muted, divided strings. After this theme has been developed by the brass, a lyrical idea arrives briefly in the violin. The second principal theme appears after a dramatic climax has been built up by the brass; this theme is given by the violas. There is still a third important idea, in the strings. All this material is developed with theatrical effect. After an immense climax, there is a brief emotional respite as the music acquires a pastoral character. One of the most striking passages of the entire work is now heard in solo clarinet, accompanied by chords in muted strings and soft rolls by the cymbals. Still another tremendous climax erupts, built up out of the first theme, before the music subsides for the last time into tranquillity.

The Swan of Tuonela was originally one of four orchestral pieces found in the suite *Four Legends*. Like the other three legends, it was inspired by the Finnish epic poem the *Kalevala*. The following succinct program note appears in the published score: "Tuonela, the land of death, the hell of Finnish mythology, is surrounded by a broad river with black waters and rapid current, on which the Swan of Tuonela floats majestically, singing." The sad and majestic swan melody is heard at the beginning of the tone poem as a solo for English horn, accompanied by muted strings and drum rolls. A muted horn soon takes over a fragment of this swan melody with telling effect. A climax of great power is slowly evolved, followed by a breath-taking pianissimo. The swan melody appears quietly for the last time, as the violins imitate the flapping of the swan's white pinions by rapping the backs of the bows on the strings.

Finlandia is the most famous of all Sibelius' national works. To the outside world, during the past five decades, it has been the forceful and eloquent voice of the land and its people. The powerful chords in the brass that open the work seem to speak of a strong-fisted defiance toward oppressors. We now hear the tender choir of woodwinds and a beautiful melody for strings, bringing a supplication for peace and freedom. There is the storm and stress of struggle in the fiery allegro section that follows, as the opening brass chords repeat defiance. But a vigorous theme for strings injects the note of optimism. The woodwinds now present the most famous melody of the work. It is peaceful and exalted, speaking for the good life where truth and freedom prevail. The strings take over the melody. A dramatic climax follows, thundering out the inevitable triumph of a people that would be free.

Tapiola is a scenic tone picture of Finland. It does not describe the composer's emotional response to the beauties of his land, but it attempts to catch the very soul, the spirit, the essence of the brooding Finnish forests. For Tapio, who gave the tone poem its name, was the ancient forest god of Finland. The following four lines, which appear in the published score, provide the clue to the atmosphere of the music:

> Widespread they stand, the Northland's dusky forests,
> Ancient, mysterious, brooding savage dreams;
> Within them dwells the Forest's mighty God,
> And wood-sprites in the gloom weave magic secrets.

The entire work is built out of a single theme, which is heard in the strings after a soft drum roll. The subsidiary ideas are variations of this melody which, throughout the highly atmospheric piece of music, grows, swells, changes color and character, and evolves into an elaborate network of sound.

Bedřich Smetana

"Smetana is more than a mere musician: he is one of the chief builders of modern Czech civilization, one of the chief creators of Czech culture."

—*Vladimir Helfert*

BORN: Litomischl, Bohemia, March 2, 1824.
DIED: Prague, May 12, 1884.
MAJOR WORKS: *Opera*—The Bartered Bride. *Orchestral Music*—The Moldau (Vltava), tone poem. *Chamber Music*—Quartet No. 1, in E minor, "From My Life." ALSO: Dalibor, Libussa, operas; Wallenstein's Camp, From the Fields and Groves of Bohemia, tone poems; Trio in G minor; String Quartet No. 2, in D minor.

HIS LIFE

Music assumed importance in Bohemia's cultural life for the first time with Bedřich Smetana. He has been called the father of Bohemian national music. More than that, he created Bohemian music as we know it today. He laid the foundation upon which a mighty structure was subsequently to arise with the music of such composers as Dvořák, with the performances of Prague's great orchestras and opera houses, and with the instruction in its excellent music schools.

Although his father was a splendid amateur musician and he himself gave early demonstration of phenomenal talent, Smetana did not receive any formal training for many years. He apparently learned music by assimilation and trial and error. Before long he could play both the violin and the piano. He was only five when he participated with his father and two other musicians in a performance of a Haydn quartet, and only six when he made his debut as pianist by playing a transcription of an Auber overture at an entertainment honoring Emperor Francis I of Austria. Still without systematic instruction, he started composing when he was eight.

But his academic education was not neglected. Between his seventh and fifteenth years he attended German schools (as was then the custom in Bohemia) in Neuhaus, Iglau, and Deutschbrod. He was then enrolled in a Prague school, and in 1840 he transferred to a school in Pilsen. He was always preoccupied with musical activity, often at the expense of his academic studies. He made frequent appearances as pianist at the homes of rich music lovers. And he kept on writing music, sometimes—significantly enough in view of his later national tendencies—in the rhythms of Bohemian dances. "With God's help and grace, I will be a Mozart in composition and a Liszt in technique," he wrote ambitiously in his diary on January 23, 1843. He wanted more than anything else to devote himself completely to music. But he was nineteen years old before he could realize this ambition. He had fallen in love with Katharina Ottilie Kolař, with whom he had been playing piano duets. It was she who encouraged him to concentrate on music, and it was her mother who arranged for a fine piano teacher in Prague, Joseph Proksch, to give him lessons. Smetana went to Prague in 1843 virtually penniless. For the first time he was given intensive instruction, and he combined his study with writing pleasing pieces for the piano. He supported himself by giving piano lessons. Not until he was made music teacher for the family of Count Leopold Thun, in 1844, was he relieved of the financial problems that had overwhelmed him since his arrival in Prague. He stayed with Count Thun for four years.

Oppressed by the meager musical activity in Prague, he soon expressed an ambition to establish a musical school where young Bohemian musicians could be trained. In 1848 he finally received an official permit to found a school of music, the first important one in Prague. The year of 1848 was important to Smetana for still another reason. By writing several revolutionary pieces of music, he became involved in the unsuccessful movement seeking to overthrow an oppressive regime. This brief excursion into political activity had important repercussions later on, for it awakened a national consciousness in him for the first time.

On August 27, 1849, Smetana married his lifelong sweetheart, Katharina. One year later, he obtained a profitable post as official pianist for Ferdinand I, former Emperor of Austria, then residing in Prague. He wrote several ambitious works between 1850 and 1855. One of these was a large orchestral composition celebrating the marriage of Emperor Francis Joseph in 1854: the *Triumphsymphonie*, which quoted the Austrian national anthem. Another was the elegiac *Trio in G minor*, inspired by the death of his four-year-old daughter in 1855.

Smetana left Bohemia in 1856, to settle for a five-year period in Göteborg, Sweden. His continued brooding over the death of his daughter had dictated a change of scene. In Göteborg he found many influential friends and made important connections. He gave piano recitals, taught extensively, and conducted the newly organized Göteborg Philharmonic. In 1859 he returned to Prague because the northern climate did not agree with his wife's delicate constitution. She died en route. The following year he married a second time and was back in Sweden resuming his varied and profitable activities. During the five-year period there he completed several orchestral works, including three tone poems obviously influenced by Liszt: *Richard III, Wallenstein's Camp,* and *Hakon Jarl.*

He was back in Prague in the fall of 1861. On his return, he found an aroused national consciousness and was influenced by it. From this time on, he worked with passionate dedication to develop the musical culture of his country. He soon assumed direction of a choral society and took charge of a new school; he became a music critic, vigorously promoting the cause of Bohemian music; he helped found the Society of Artists; he was vigorous in encouraging the activities of the Provisional Theater (which opened in 1862), and in helping form and direct the Philharmonic Society; in 1869 he founded a dramatic school for the Bohemian Theater in Prague, and became its director in 1873.

He, therefore, led the way in many different senses. Almost single-handed he helped bring about a flowering of musical activity in Prague. He also led the way in the writing of national music. In 1863 he completed the first national Bohemian opera ever written, *The Brandenburgers in Bohemia.* It was presented on January 5, 1866, under his own direction. There was great enthusiasm, for it echoed and glorified the prevailing national feeling. But it was not a good opera (it had a particularly poor libretto) and it was thrown into discard by the tremendous success of Smetana's next work, the comic folk opera *The Bartered Bride.* Introduced on May 30, 1866, it was a major triumph after its third performance. Smetana soon completed two other fine national operas, both based on Bohemian legends: *Dalibor* in 1868 and *Libussa* in 1871.

In 1874 Smetana began suffering from severe headaches. These were soon followed by deafness. At first he merely complained of hearing a continual whistling in his ears "like the A-flat major chord in the first inversion in the high treble." Then he heard buzzing and roaring "as though I were standing under a waterfall." Finally: "I hear absolutely nothing, not even my own voice. . . . Concentration with me is impossible. I hear my own piano only in fancy, not in reality. I cannot hear the playing of anybody else, not even the performance of a full orchestra in opera or in concert. I do not think it is possible for me to improve. I have no pain in the ear, and my physicians agree that my disease is none of the familiar ear troubles, but something else, perhaps a paralysis of the nerves and the labyrinth. And so I am wholly determined to endure my sad fate in a calm and manly way as long as I live."

He remained deaf for the rest of his life. But this tragedy did not limit his musical activity. On the very first day on which he became deaf he conceived the main theme of the first of six national tone poems which, collectively entitled *My Country (Ma Vlast)*, comprise Smetana's greatest orchestral monument to nationalism. These tone poems took him five years to complete, all written when he was no longer capable of hearing a sound. The entire cycle was performed for the first time on November 2, 1882, at a concert for the composer's benefit. The audience realized—as Smetana's friend V. V. Zeleny wrote—that this work was his "greatest poetic deed, as well as the proudest glorification with which an artistic spirit had ever celebrated his country."

Besides *My Country,* Smetana wrote several operas (including *The Kiss,* which was an immense success when introduced in 1876) and his autobiographical string quartet, in E minor, to which he himself gave the title "From My Life." He was also able to make several personal appearances, giving a recital in 1880 to commemorate the fiftieth anniversary of his debut as pianist and conducting the one hundredth performance of *The Bartered Bride,* in 1881, the latter event a great personal triumph.

His last opera was one of his greatest disappointments. *The Devil's Wall,* first heard in 1882, was a fiasco that broke his heart. The third performance was intended as a benefit for the composer. But the attendance was so poor that the pitiful sum turned over to Smetana was a humiliation. "I shall write nothing more," he exclaimed. "No one wants to hear from me!"

He suffered a nervous breakdown late the same year. He defied the orders of his physicians—and his own vow—by working on his second string quartet. As he labored, he gave in to violent depressions and mental disturbances. On one of the pages of this quartet he wrote, almost as if in apology, "Composed in a state of disordered nerves."

His mind snapped in 1883. He had to be confined in an insane asylum, where he died one year later.

HIS MUSIC

IN 1924 there took place throughout the then new republic of Czechoslovakia (and formerly the much-oppressed Bohemia) the centenary celebration of Smetana's birth. There was no village or hamlet too small or too remote to pay tribute in one form or another. For Smetana —through his musical glorification of the national spirit, ideals, traditions, and heritage—was perhaps more responsible than any other cultural figure for bringing about the final creation of a free Czechoslovakian state. To Jan Lowenbach, Smetana "by his artist's intuition . . . became a precursor of the scholarly researches in Czech history and ideology of later days. In this he was one of the advance guard which aided the founder of the Republic of Czechoslovakia to bring to fulfillment his national program." Paul Stefan put it differently: "He is the standard bearer and symbol of the history and liberation of his people."

In Czech music, his figure assumes even greater stature than it does in Czech history. It is impossible to conceive of Czech music without him, so inevitably do composers such as Dvořák, Joseph Suk (1874-1935), and the contemporary Bohuslav Martinu (1890-   ) evolve out of Smetana. Smetana was the first to demonstrate how Bohemian folk melody and dance can be artistically serviceable, how these folk elements can be fused with a modern approach to structure, harmony, and thematic construction, to become the spine of a great musical art. He sang of his country with a freshness of viewpoint and with the excitement of a lover. He sang romantically and lyrically so that, in listening to him, we, too, get to know the Bohemia of old.

ANALYTICAL NOTES

Opera. *The Bartered Bride* is one of the earliest of all national operas, and to this day it is one of the best. The story is a rich slice of Bohemian village life, made colorful with festivals, dances, peasant costumes, and a performance by a visiting theatrical troupe. It has the ingratiatingly ingenuous quality of a folk tale. Smetana's score is also piquant with folk flavors. His songs and dances imitate the style of Bohemian folk music so successfully that the entire score seems to spring from the very bosom of his country. It is an excursion into innocent merriment made by one who never loses his love or fascination for his subject.

Marie is in love with Hans, but her parents want her to marry Wenzel, the idiot son of wealthy Micha. The marriage broker, responsible for this unhappy match, bribes Hans to renounce Marie. Hans is willing to do this, but with the specific understanding that the contract must say that Marie is to marry the son of Micha. Marie, heartbroken that Hans has renounced her for money, is ready to marry Wenzel, if only out of spite. What she does not know—what all who are involved soon learn—is that Hans is a long-lost son of Micha and can, consequently, marry Marie and keep his bribe too.

The overture, built out of several subjects from the opera, is full of gaiety. It begins briskly. The robust first theme appears in unison strings and woodwinds against a sustained chord in the brass and a roll of the kettledrums; this is the theme of the marriage contract. The melodic germ of this theme becomes the basis of a fugal passage, which culminates in a vigorous restatement of the complete theme. A secondary idea now appears in the orchestra, later to become a countersubject for the first theme. A more tender episode follows in the oboes, expressing Marie's sorrow. The overture ends gaily with a return of the first theme.

The curtain rises on the village square, where a feast day is being celebrated. The chorus is heard in a joyous paean to spring, "See the Buds Burst on the Bush." We soon hear Marie's tender aria to Hans, "Gladly Do I Trust You," followed by one of the lyrical high lights of this first act, the poignant duet of Hans and Marie, "With My Mother." The first of several famous dances in the popular vein is heard at the close of the act. It is a polka, in which all villagers participate.

The second act, which takes place in the village inn, opens with a robust male drinking chorus. When the village girls come into the inn, they join the men in the second of the opera's familiar folk dances, the furiant. The idiot, Wenzel, appears on the scene when the dance is over and the villagers have dispersed. His highly amusing stuttering song, "Ma-ma-mamma dear," reveals that he is as slow of tongue as of mind. Later in the act, the marriage broker tries to convince Hans to renounce Marie by telling him, in the mocking and cynical air "Everyone Praises His Own Girl," that each must play the game of love for what it is worth. He has a rich girl for Hans. In the vivacious duet "I Know One Who Has Money Galore," he tells Hans of her many worldly possessions, which Hans reviews quickly in his own mind. But he is true to Marie. His moving aria, one of the most beautiful in the opera, exultantly anticipates his eventual union with her, "How Is It Possible?"

In the third act, a traveling troupe of performers is entertaining the villagers in the square outside the inn. The acrobats put on a demonstration to the music of the ever popular "Dance of the Comedians." The heartbreaking pathos of Marie's great aria about her beloved's betrayal, "How Strange and Dead," is a striking contrast to the festivities of the opening scene. In the duet "My Dearest Love, Just Listen," Hans tries to make explanations, but Marie stubbornly refuses to listen. But all turns out well in the end. The opera ends with the chorus joyously hailing bride and groom.

Orchestra Music. *The Moldau* (*Vltava*) is the second of a set of six national tone poems glorifying Bohemia and collectively entitled *My Country* (*Ma Vlast*). The following program appears in the published score: "Two springs pour forth their streams in the shade of the Bohemian forest, the one warm and gushing, the other cold and tranquil. . . . The woodland brook, chattering along, becomes the river Moldau. . . . It flows through dense woods amid which the joyous sounds of the chase resound, and the call of the hunter's horn is heard ever nearer and nearer. It flows through verdant meadows and lowlands, where a marriage feast is being celebrated with song and dance. At eve, in its glimmering wavelets, wood nymphs and naiads hold revels, and in these waters many a fortress and castle are reflected which bear witness to the bygone splendor of knight-errantry and to martial fame vanished with days of yore. At the rapids of St. John, the stream spreads onward, winds through cataracts, cleaves a path for its foaming torrent through the rocky gorge into the wide river bed in which it rolls on, in majestic calm, toward Prague, where, welcomed by time-honored Vysehrad, it disappears from the poet's gaze far on the horizon."

The tone poem begins with a strain in the flute against pizzicato chords in the strings. The ebb and flow of the waters is reproduced in the strings. Above this there rises a beautiful folk melody in violins and woodwinds to describe the course of the Moldau. We soon hear the hunting calls in the horns. When the calls die down, a vigorous peasant dance erupts in the orchestra. After this, we hear in the flutes the revels of nymphs and naiads. There is a brief episode for the winds preceding the return of the beautiful Moldau melody. The river gathers momentum as the whole orchestra builds up a stirring climax. But tranquillity succeeds this powerful surge as the river quietly flows toward Prague and disappears into the horizon.

Chamber Music. The *Quartet No. 1*, in E minor, is autobiographical, as its name, "From My Life," suggests. The composer has provided his own program to the music. "The first movement depicts the love of art in my youth, the romantic supremacy, the inexpressible yearning for something which I could not clearly define, and also a kind of warning of future misfortune." There is an intense, descending theme for viola, following the opening dramatic chord, which suggests the "warning of future misfortune." This theme is heard throughout the work and integrates it. The second theme of the first movement is a tender, lyrical effusion in the best traditions of Romantic music; it depicts "the love of art in my youth, the romantic supremacy."

The second movement, a polka, "brings to memory the joyful days of my youth when I composed dance music . . . and was known as a passionate lover of dancing." The lively polka theme is heard after several introductory bars. The slow movement "recalls the bliss of my first love for the girl who afterwards became my faithful wife." The predominating theme in this movement is a beautiful love melody touched with pathos.

The closing movement describes "the discovery that I could treat the national element in music, and my joy in following this path until the catastrophe overwhelmed me, the beginning of my deafness with the prospect of so wretched a future." This movement begins with gay folk tunes and lively folk rhythms. There are two main themes, the first of Bohemian character, the other Russian. In the coda, a high "E" is sounded by the first violin over a tremolo of the second violin, viola, and cello. "The long-drawn-out note," Smetana explained, "is the fatal whistling in my ear in the highest registers that in 1874 announced my deafness. I permitted myself this little joke, such as it is, because it was so disastrous to me." After this sustained high note, we hear brief quotations of earlier themes: the passionate first theme and the lyrical second theme of the first movement, and the love song of the third. The quartet ends in a somber mood.

Richard Strauss

"This composer, make no mistake about it, is an authentic lord of tone, amazing in the range and richness and expressiveness of his art."

—*Lawrence Gilman*

BORN: Munich, June 11, 1864.
DIED: Garmisch-Partenkirchen, Bavaria, September 8, 1949.
MAJOR WORKS: *Orchestral Music*—Don Juan; Death and Transfiguration; Till Eulenspiegel's Merry Pranks; Thus Spake Zarathustra; Don Quixote; A Hero's Life. *Operas*—Salome; Elektra; Der Rosenkavalier. *Vocal Music*—"Allerseelen," "Zueignung," "Morgen," "Wiegenlied," "Traum durch die Dämmerung," "Ständchen," "Cäcilie," "Ruhe, meine Seele," and other songs for voice and piano.
ALSO: Ariadne auf Naxos, opera; Burleske, for piano and orchestra; Sinfonia domestica; An Alpine Symphony; 2 concertos for horn and orchestra; Concerto for Oboe and Orchestra; Metamorphosen, for twenty-three solo strings; Sonata for Violin and Piano.

HIS LIFE

IN THE 1860s, in Munich, the name of Franz Strauss was associated with one of the finest horn players in the city, but also with one of the bitterest enemies of Richard Wagner. Wagner had come to the city during that period to help prepare the world *première* of *Tristan und Isolde*. The orchestra included some of the finest Munich instrumentalists, and Franz Strauss played first horn. He made no attempt to conceal his contempt for Wagner's music. While one rehearsal was still in progress, he rose from his seat and angrily left the orchestra pit, muttering under his breath (but loud enough for Wagner to hear him) that he refused to play such outlandish music. On one occasion he played a horn passage with particularly beautiful tone and phrasing. Wagner remarked that anybody playing a piece of music so beautifully could not possibly dislike it intensely; Strauss answered heatedly that the way he played had nothing whatsoever to do with the way he liked the music. In Munich, most of the intrigues and cabals that mushroomed against Wagner gravitated around the personality of Herr Strauss. When, in 1883, the conductor, Hermann Levi, announced to his orchestra the sad news that Wagner had just died, every man rose in silent homage except Strauss.

All this fierce antagonism to Wagner's music, which remained with Franz Strauss to his dying day, would hardly require detailed comment here, but for one paradoxical fact. Herr Strauss's son, Richard, was to become one of Wagner's most passionate advocates and most brilliant interpreters. What is more, Franz Strauss lived long enough to see this come to pass.

Franz Strauss married Josephine Pschorr, daughter of a wealthy Munich brewer. Richard was their first born—their only son and the elder of two children. He was a *wunderkind*. His mother started teaching him the piano when he was four years old. He did so well that his father began to take a hand in the child's music education. In his sixth year Richard wrote a delightful polka for the piano and a song inspired by the singing of children around a Christmas tree. He was always scratching little melodies on paper. When he started going to school, he wrapped his books in notepaper so that he could continue this practice in the classroom.

It was apparent that he gravitated naturally to music. Franz Strauss was, of course, ready to encourage and develop this tendency, but he also wanted his son to get a comprehensive academic education. From childhood, Strauss's music training went hand in hand with his academic schooling. When he finished elementary school, he was sent to high school, where he remained until his eighteenth year. He also studied the violin, piano, harmony, counterpoint, and instrumentation.

Already his works were being performed. Two choral pieces were heard at a student concert at the Gymnasium. In 1880 a concert singer included three of his songs in one of her recitals in Munich. A year later, one of his teachers, Benno Walter, gave the first performance of Strauss's *Quartet in A major* with three other instrumentalists. In March 1881 there took place the most important of these performances, that of his *Symphony in D minor* under the direction of Hermann Levi.

In 1882 Strauss was graduated from high school. He entered the

University of Munich, intending to get a degree. But after a full year at the University he decided to specialize in the study of music. He left the University and went to Berlin to attend a performance of his *Overture in C minor*. His presence there stimulated his publisher, Eugen Spitzweg (Strauss's music had been published as early as 1881), to send some of his piano pieces to one of Germany's most influential musicians, Hans von Bülow, then the conductor of the Meiningen Court Orchestra. Hans von Bülow wrote to Spitzweg: "I thoroughly dislike them. I miss the youthful spirit in them. He is no genius but only a talent, of the sort that takes sixty to make a bushel." But apparently he liked other things by Strauss, and in 1882 performed in Meiningen Strauss's *Serenade for Thirteen Wind Instruments*. He now thought so well of Strauss that he called the young composer to Meiningen and had him compose several new works for his orchestra. One was a Concerto for Horn and Orchestra; another, a *Suite for Thirteen Wind Instruments*. Strauss himself directed the suite, and with complete assurance and competence even though he had been denied rehearsals.

Hans von Bülow appointed Strauss his assistant in 1884. Strauss's career as a conductor was launched; it was eventually to become hardly less lustrous than his career as a composer. This was a busy time for Strauss. He conducted the Meiningen Orchestra frequently (he soon succeeded Hans von Bülow as principal conductor). He sometimes appeared as solo pianist. And he wrote one large work after another. One of the most significant was the *Symphony in F minor,* which received its world *première* in the United States on December 13, 1884, Theodore Thomas conducting. A piano quartet won the first prize of the Berlin Tonkünstlerverein.

By this time Strauss's musical values were beginning to change. When, in his boyhood, he heard *Tristan und Isolde* for the first time, he echoed his father's bitter denunciation of Wagner. But a few hearings of *Tristan* and acquaintanceship with *Die Walküre* revealed to him Wagner's genius in a kind of blinding flash. Thenceforth he worshiped only one musical god.

Wagner's music not only made him re-examine his musical thinking, it forced him to re-evaluate the music he had thus far written, made him dissatisfied with it. During this period of transition he became an intimate friend of one of the men in his orchestra, Alexander Ritter, who was a poet and philosopher as well as a musician. Ritter was a true believer in the Wagnerian faith (he had married Wagner's niece), and it was his belief that as a composer Strauss had to carry the Wagner torch if he aspired to greatness. Ritter spoke endlessly of the modern composer's necessity to desert absolute music for the dramatic and the programmatic, to free himself completely from the choking limitations of classical form and German Romantic style. He pointed out, as examples for emulation, not only the Wagnerian music drama but also the Liszt tone poem. "His influence was in the nature of a storm-wind," Strauss confessed. "He urged me on to the development of the poetic, the expressive in music, as exemplified in the works of Liszt, Berlioz, and Wagner."

After a brief visit to Italy, in 1886, Strauss wrote the first work in which he parted company with the musical past and in which he set off into the future. It was a symphonic fantasy, *Aus Italien.* Flexibility of structure was now combined with realistic writing—even dissonance—in his pictures of Italian life. Introduced in Munich on March 2, 1887, under the composer's direction, *Aus Italien* was hissed; it was regarded as noisy, ugly, and confusing. Hans von Bülow, commenting on this score, wrote: "Does my age make me reactionary? I find that the clever composer has gone to the limits of tonal possibilities (in the realm of beauty) and, in fact, has even gone beyond these limits without real necessity."

Despite the fiasco of *Aus Italien,* Strauss had no intention of turning back. He was—the public reaction notwithstanding!—sure of himself and convinced of his destiny. Besides, he enjoyed becoming the subject of discussion and controversy. In 1887 he wrote his first tone poem, *Macbeth.* During the next decade he produced the works with which his international fame (and notoriety) was established—works which startled and shocked the world and put their composer in the role of "bad boy of music." These works consisted of six tone poems which are among Strauss's finest and most popular orchestral works: *Don Juan,* in 1888; *Tod und Verklärung (Death and Transfiguration),* in in 1889; *Till Eulenspiegels lustige Streiche (Till Eulenspiegel's Merry Pranks),* in 1895; *Also sprach Zarathustra (Thus Spake Zarathustra)* and *Don Quixote,* in 1897; *Ein Heldenleben (A Hero's Life),* in 1898. During the same period he also produced some of the finest songs written since those of Schubert and Schumann. The first set of eight songs (including *"Allerseelen"* and *"Zueignung"*) came in 1882–83. Before the century ended he had written such gems as *"Morgen," "Traum durch die Dämmerung,"* and *"Wiegenlied."*

Strauss invaded still another field of musical composition, that of opera. His first opera, *Guntram,* seen in 1894, was a failure; so was the second, *Feuersnot,* in 1901. But it was not long before Strauss brought into the theater the daring and the iconoclastic thinking of his tone poems. He revived the scandals that had stormed and raged around his name in the 1890s by writing *Salome,* seen in Dresden on December 9, 1905, and following it with *Elektra,* introduced in Dresden on January 25, 1909. The music world recoiled with horror from the realism of text and music; but eventually it was to recognize both operas as masterworks.

While Strauss was developing as one of the greatest (and one of the most provocative) composers of his time, he was also gaining significance as a conductor of first importance. In 1886 he left Meiningen to become third Kapellmeister of the Munich Opera. From 1889–94 he was court conductor in Weimar. In 1898 he received one of the most important musical posts in all Europe when he was appointed musical director of the Berlin Royal Opera, a post he retained for a dozen years. He used his strong position in German music and his far-reaching influence to establish the Genossenschaft Deutscher Tonsetzer —a kind of trade union of German composers—which, for the first time, made possible the collection of a royalty from every performance of a contemporary work by a major orchestra or opera house.

Early in 1904 Strauss paid his first visit to the United States. He came with the Wetzler Orchestra, directing it in concerts of his own works. His first American appearance took place in New York City on February 27, 1904. After Hermann Wetzler had directed *Thus Spake Zarathustra,* Strauss was brought to the platform to acknowledge the bows. "The orchestra received him with a fanfare," reported Richard Aldrich in *The New York Times,* "and there was prolonged and vociferous applause that kept him bowing his acknowledgements for several minutes." Strauss then directed *A Hero's Life.* One month later, on March 21, 1904, Strauss led the same orchestra in New York in the world *première* of his most recent work, *Sinfonia domestica,* a musical autobiography which, Strauss explained, illustrates "a day in my family . . . partly humorous." The three subjects of a triple fugue were meant to represent, he said, "papa, mama, and baby."

Beginning with the twentieth century, Strauss completely dominated German music. He was the recognized dean of German composers. To the end of his life, he was esteemed a master who had become a classic in his own lifetime. Music lovers of the world made pilgrimages to his beautiful villa in Garmisch, in the Bavarian Alps, to pay him tribute. Whenever he appeared on the conductor's platform, the audience rose in admiration and respect. The city of Vienna presented him with grounds cut from the park of the imperial Belvedere Palace so that he might live in that city four months a year. He kept his position in world music even though his creative powers began to disintegrate and even though, after World War I, he produced nothing to equal the passion and the originality and the genius of his early tone poems, operas, and songs.

When the Nazis first came to power, Strauss became a loyal subject of Hitler. He accepted the position of President of the Third Reich Music Chamber. He was in full support of the program of purging German music of Jewish or "unwholesome" influences. When Bruno Walter was hurriedly removed from his post as musical director of the Leipzig Gewandhaus Orchestra, Strauss substituted for him. Strauss was in full agreement with the Nazi powers in proscribing the music of Paul Hindemith. He conducted in Bayreuth when Toscanini would not come.

But this honeymoon with the Nazis was of brief duration. He came into direct conflict with the officials when he insisted on collaborating with the Jewish author Stefan Zweig on the opera *Die schweigsame Frau* (*The Silent Woman*). As his position grew more untenable, Strauss resigned his official position in 1935 and went into seclusion at Garmisch. During World War II, he lived mostly in Switzerland.

When the American army occupied Bavaria, they found Strauss at his villa in the Bavarian Alps, still occupied with composition. One of his works was *Metamorphosen,* a study for twenty-three solo strings, subtitled "In Memoriam" and intended as a dirge for crushed Germany. By special army dispensation, Strauss was allowed to keep his villa and continue his creative work without interference. Some time later he was brought to trial before an American denazification court and was completely exonerated of Nazi affiliation.

The war over, Strauss returned to active participation in music—despite his old age—by visiting London in 1947 and conducting a concert of his own music at a Strauss festival. His eighty-fifth birthday, in 1949, was celebrated throughout the entire world and came just a few months before he died at the Bavarian villa. Less than three years after his death, his last opera, *Die Liebe der Danae,* received its world *première* at the Salzburg Festival, on August 14, 1952.

Strauss was a man of extensive cultural background, well versed in arts other than music and particularly well read and well informed in history, science, and philosophy. A genial, pleasant companion at all times, he had an ingratiating wit and a healthy capacity for enjoying life. He liked drinking beer, playing cards, and, earlier in life, indulging in dancing and sports.

His wife was a singer by the name of Pauline de Ahna, whom he married in 1894. Practical, supremely efficient, and something of a shrew, she dominated him completely. She arranged his social engagements, planned his day, advised him on business affairs, and sent him off each day to do his composing as a mother might send a child to his homework. She guarded the family purse strings rigorously and meted out to him a regular allowance. When she did not like what he did—and this went for his music as well as for his behavior—she demolished him with crushing remarks, which he accepted meekly.

Those who knew him well did not have much respect for the man, however much they might admire his music. He was notoriously vain, ever jealous of anybody who might be a rival, and small in all his business dealings. He was psychopathically parsimonious, bickering over pennies as if fortunes were involved. "The sad part of it," once commented the famous conductor Franz Schalk, "is that he's not putting it on, but it's the real man." He often tried to supplement the allowance his wife gave him by playing the card game skat, at which he was uniquely adept; he even played with the musicians in his orchestra, who could little afford the losses he inflicted on them. Yet he insisted that they play with him. In Bayreuth, in 1933, some of the musicians suffered such severe losses that Winifred Wagner had to reimburse them before they consented to play in the orchestra.

HIS MUSIC

RICHARD STRAUSS is a phenomenon in contemporary music in that his best works belong to his earlier period, while his weakest and least original ones were produced in his later years. In the tone poems, songs, and operas written between 1885 and 1910, Strauss was a genius; of that there can be little question. There were things in these works to startle, as well as to marvel at: his bold use of dissonance; his amazing excursions into realism; his fantastic orchestral virtuosity; his use of new special instruments, such as the wind machine or thunder machine, to simulate sounds of nature; his flexibility in adapting structure to the requirements of his ideas; his passion, even sensuality. But this music was cause for wonder as well as shock. These early works were filled with pages of majestic, poetic, inspired music which burst on the closing nineteenth century like a blinding flash of sunlight. There were some indiscretions, such as his occasional pomposity and inflated orchestration, his sentimentality and oversensuousness, his willingness at times to use shopworn materials. But there were also such grandeur of speech, dramatic power, intensity of emotion, and originality of concept that here, surely, was the dawn of a new era in orchestral, vocal, and operatic music.

But after the opera *Der Rosenkavalier* (*The Cavalier of the Rose*), completed in 1910, disintegration began to take place. Strauss was destined to live another four decades and to write many works in virtually every form. But the flame that burned so hot in his earlier compositions had become subdued. Gone were the onetime elemental passion, irresistible force, the power and fury of genius. In their place came technical adroitness, cleverness, wit, and sophistication—poor substitutes for the original commodity. Strauss was still a master of technique, still a composer of infectious charm. But cleverness and skill had to do the work of inspiration. As the years passed, Strauss's works grew more and more labored. Momentarily there were flashes reminiscent of his onetime power; but the flashes refused to erupt into a sustained flame. He started repeating little mannerisms that once had made him controversial and successful. In some of his last works—concertos for oboe and for horn—he completely reverted to the style of his apprenticeships, when he had been an admirer and imitator of Brahms. And in his last opera, *Die Liebe der Danae,* he imitated Wagner, just as he had done in his first opera. Creatively he was returning to the womb.

ANALYTICAL NOTES

Orchestral Music. *Don Juan* was Strauss's second tone poem, written in 1888, one year after *Macbeth*. It was inspired by a poem of Nicholas Lenau about which the composer said: "My *Don Juan* is no hot-blooded man eternally pursuing women. It is the longing in him to find a woman who is to him incarnate womanhood, and to enjoy, in the one, all the women on earth, whom he cannot possess as individuals. Because he does not find her, although he reels from one to another, at last Disgust seizes hold of him and this Disgust is the Devil that fetches him." As Strauss refused to provide a specific program for his music, the above quotation might serve as a substitute. It is known, however, that Strauss intended portraying Don Juan's ardor in pursuing his ideal, the beauty and charm of the woman he sought, and his ultimate disillusion and disgust.

The tone poem begins with a passionate upward surge of the strings, suggesting Don Juan's ardor. This is followed by a tender strain in the strings—the lover's longing. There is a third, heroic theme in the horns, portraying Don Juan himself. Several subsidary ideas describe some of the love episodes, the most important being a beautiful love song first heard in the oboe and then repeated by the clarinet. These ideas are brought to a high emotional pitch, in which the orchestral forces are let loose in an outburst of color and sound; Don Juan's sensual pursuits have degenerated into debauchery. A shattering dissonant chord is followed by prolonged silence. There is a shudder in the orchestra (as the tone poem comes to an end), telling of Don Juan's ultimate disgust and disillusion.

Death and Transfiguration came one year later. Its program is a poem by Strauss's friend Alexander Ritter. It is interesting to remark, however, that while the tone poem appears to be a literal, even realistic, adaptation of this poem, the latter was written *after* the music. A condensed summary follows: "In the little room, dimly lighted by only a candle end, lies the sick man on his bed. But just now he has wrestled despairingly with Death. Now he has sunk exhausted in sleep. But Death does not long grant sleep and dreams to his victim. Cruelly he shakes him awake, and the fight begins afresh. Will to live and power of Death! What frightful wrestling! Neither bears off the victory, and all is silent once more. Sunk back, tired of battle, sleepless, as in fever-frenzy the sick man now sees his life pass before his inner eye. First the morning red of childhood. Then the saucier play of youth, till he ripens to the man's fight, and now burns with hot lust after the higher prizes of life. Cold and sneering, the world sets barrier upon barrier in the way of his achievement. And so he pushes forward, so he climbs. Then clangs the last stroke of Death's iron hammer, breaks the earthly body in twain, covers the eye with the night of death. But from the heavenly spaces sounds mightily to greet him what he yearningly sought for here: deliverance from the world, transfiguration of the world."

Though played without pause, *Death and Transfiguration* is in four sections. The first, described as "Sleep, Illness, Revery," is a slow introduction. It opens with a syncopated theme in the second violins and violas symbolizing Death. We soon hear a tender melody in the oboe, as the dying man recalls the happy days of youth. An agitated section follows, interpreted as "Fever and Struggle with Death." Violent chords point the way to a mighty crescendo. The Death motive appears. A Herculean struggle now takes place in the full orchestra, fortissimo, after which the dying man succumbs to his terrible weariness. The beginning of the transfiguration theme is now heard in trombones, cellos, and violas. The third part—"Dreams, Childhood Memories, and Death"—is atmospheric, as the dying man yields to his reveries and visions. Once again he recalls his youth, then his manhood struggles. The violent battle with Death ensues. Ascending harmonies register the dying man's last protests. Harp and tam-tam sound his defeat; he passes from life. The final part, "Transfiguration," begins with a majestic rendition of the transfiguration theme in the horns. Briefly, the man's childhood is recalled; but it is the transfiguration motive that is dominant. The theme grows richer in texture, more passionate in feeling. At last it is heard in the trumpet against sensuous strings, then taken over by the strings against arpeggios in the harp. Now all is peaceful, for we have come to the transfiguration and deliverance.

There was a hiatus of more than five years before Strauss produced his next tone poem, *Till Eulenspiegel's Merry Pranks*. The source of inspiration was a famous old German legend about an incorrigible rogue. Strauss's program is an adaptation of this legend. But in the legend the rogue manages to escape fatal punishment, while Strauss relentlessly sends him to the gallows.

The tone poem begins with a simple melody which seems to say, "once upon a time there was a rogue by the name of Till Eulenspiegel." A saucy theme in the French horn tells of his bent for mischief and is developed with considerable gusto. There arrives an impudent phrase in the small clarinet to bring Till on the scene; the shrill voice of this instrument suits the character of Till well. Both themes—the one for French horn, describing his mischievous nature, and the other in the small clarinet, symbolizing Till himself—reappear throughout the work. The disturbances now begin in earnest. Flutes, oboes, and clarinets speak for the women gathered in the market place. A solemn theme describes Till on his horse. A crash of the percussion, and Till has wrought disaster and induced panic. Now there is a dignified and pious theme to reveal that Till has put on holy vestment. He expresses holy thoughts, but the rascal is betrayed by the saucy clarinet theme. A glissando in the violin, and Till has torn off his holy garb. Now glowing love music speaks of Till in love. He is rejected; fortissimo horns in unison describe his rage. He forgets his anger when a group of Philistines arrive and he can mock them. A moment later he can indulge in a peasant dance with the girls of the village. And so his escapades continue. But soon there is a drum roll. Till is being brought to justice. There develops a somber march. Till is not afraid; his saucy theme is heard shrilly above the march music. But the march soon smothers Till's impudent voice. A descending major-seventh interval in the bassoons, horns, trombones, and tuba announces his final doom. The opening melody of the tone poem is brought back in an altered and extended form. Once upon a time there was a rogue by the name of Till Eulenspiegel. . . .

Thus Spake Zarathustra was completed in 1896. Strauss explained: "I did not intend to write philosophical music or portray Nietzsche's great work musically. I meant to convey by means of music an idea of the development of the human race from its origin, through the various phases of evolution, religious as well as scientific, up to Nietzsche's idea of the Superman." Strauss also explained that he had attempted to "embody the conflict between man's nature as it is and man's metaphysical attempts to lay hold of his nature with his intelligence—leading finally to the conquest of life by the release of laughter."

The composition is made up of several sections played without interruption. First there is a majestic introduction: Zarathustra's invocation to the dawn. A proclamation for the trumpet grows into powerful chords in the orchestra. A crescendo works up into an immense climax for full orchestra and organ. In the first part, "Of the Dwellers in the World Behind Us," prominent use is made of the Gregorian Credo in the horns. "Of Great Yearnings" follows with a Gregorian Magnificat in the organ. In "Of Joys and Sorrows," a rich-textured melody in second violins, oboe, and horns speaks of human passions. "Song of the Grave" has a passionate theme for the oboe. "Of Science" contains a canonic imitation in fifths, to represent the solution of life's riddle through science. "The Convalescent" develops the science theme with contrapuntal amplifications. "Dance Song" is a sweeping waltz melody —man's pursuit of earthly joys. There are twelve strokes of the bell to announce the arrival of midnight and the concluding section, "The Song of the Night Wanderer."

Don Quixote, completed in 1897, was subtitled by the composer "fantastic variations on a theme of knightly character." But it is made up of three parts: an introduction, the theme and variations, and a finale.

Throughout the work, Don Quixote is represented by a solo cello; his squire, Sancho Panza, appears first in tenor tuba and bass clarinet and subsequently in the solo viola.

The introduction finds the aging Don, fascinated in his study of chivalric lore, losing his mind and determined to set forth as a knight in seach of adventure. An opening subject in the woodwinds, followed by an expressive melody in the strings, ends in unrelated chords. Confusion sets in in the orchestra (just as it does in Don Quixote's brain). There are frighteningly dissonant chords—and we realize that Don Quixote has lost his mind.

The second part begins with the compassionate and mock-heroic theme of Don Quixote in solo cello, followed by the more comic, even satiric, portrait of Sancho Panza in tenor tuba and bass clarinet. Ten variations follow. The first describes the adventure with the windmills. Inspired by his concept of the Ideal Woman (who appears in a beautiful melody in violins and woodwinds), the Don proceeds to attack windmills, which appear to him as giants. The Don is unseated by the sails. Next comes his battle with the sheep. Muted brass simulate the bleating of sheep who come down the road. To the Don, the sheep are the army of Emperor Alifanfaron. He attacks and disperses them. Don Quixote and Sancho Panza now discourse on chivalry, entering into a heated dispute during which the Don loses his temper and angrily silences his squire. We next hear a melody of religious character in bassoons and muted brass. The knight and his squire come upon a band of pilgrims. To the Don, these pilgrims are robbers whom he must attack. He is beaten by the pilgrims, who leave him senseless on the ground and proceed on their way, chanting as they go. While Sancho sleeps, Don Quixote dreams about his Ideal Woman, who is represented first by a bass and then by an extended melody in the solo cello, with the interpolation of a cadenza for strings and harp. The pair now come upon three peasant girls. Determined to have some fun at the expense of Don Quixote, Sancho tries to convince him that the ugliest of the three is the Ideal Woman. The tender melody of the Ideal Woman is satirized by oboes and tambourine. Next the knight and his squire are astride a wooden horse, imagining they are flying through space. In this variation, Strauss introduces a "wind machine," to bring greater realism to the flight. An empty boat now assumes special significance for the Don. He insists that it was sent him by supernatural powers to bear him off for new adventures. A barcarolle melody in the orchestra tells of their voyage. But the boat capsizes, and the pair have to struggle to the shore. A pious tune in the woodwinds and horn expresses their thanks for their safety. After this the Don mistakes two monks for magicians who are abducting a princess. He attacks them and is victorious. But in the final variation the Don meets his final defeat. A townsman, disguised as the Knight of the White Moon, engages him in battle in order to rid him once and for all of his grandiose illusions. Badly defeated, the disillusioned Don returns home to resume his onetime calling as shepherd. A pastoral melody in the English horn informs us of the Don's sad intention to become a shepherd again, while simplification of the instrumental and harmonic texture indicates that order and reason have replaced his former insanity.

The finale tells of Don Quixote's death. His theme, in the cello, becomes poignantly sad—for he now realizes the folly of his onetime exploits. He dies peacefully. Consonant chords bring his biography to an end in an atmosphere of complete serenity.

A Hero's Life, written in 1898, was the last of these famous tone poems. The composer intended here the portrait of a hero, beset by adversaries and surrounded by intrigues. Overcoming his enemies and surmounting all obstacles, he is able to build a new and better world. It is not difficult to find in such a program Strauss's own career. With more vanity than wit, he identifies himself with his hero; his own struggles and victories are those of his protagonist. And in summing up the achievements of his hero, Strauss does not hesitate to quote from some of his most famous works.

The tone poem is in six uninterrupted sections. In the first, the hero is presented in the opening measures with a powerful theme for strings and horns. Different facets of the hero's personality—his strength of will and purpose, idealism, pride, and ambition—are revealed as this theme is worked out with all of Strauss's wonderful harmonic and contrapuntal equipment. The next part introduces the hero's adversaries, their malice and cunning revealed in the petty chattering of the woodwinds. The hero protests in a quiet theme for muted cellos and basses reinforced by clarinets, bass clarinet, and later horns. But a fanfare in the brass arouses the hero to battle. A vigorous section follows, suddenly interrupted by a tender melody in the violins: a profile of the hero's beloved. In the third part, the love music of the hero and his beloved unfolds with wondrous beauty. The beloved appears in a solo violin, which at turns becomes playful, coquettish, and affectionate. Then the entire orchestra erupts into a sensual, ecstatic song of love. A flourish in the trumpets brings on the fourth part, the music becoming agitated as a battle scene is being described. Victory in this battle enables the hero, in the fifth section, to embark on his missions of peace. The hero here summarizes his achievements in times of peace. A motive identified with "works of peace" appears in the trumpet. Before long we hear fragments from other Strauss's works, as Strauss—stepping into the role of the hero—reviews his own career: thematic reminiscences from *Don Juan, Death and Transfiguration, Don Quixote,* the song *"Traum durch die Dämmerung,"* *Macbeth* and *Guntram.* In the concluding part the hero, satisfied with his achievements, takes leave of the world. The hero's departure is spoken of in a tranquil and beautiful melody for the strings. A solo violin brings back the image of the hero's beloved. The hero's soul takes flight as the solo violin embarks on a wonderful melody, spiritual and exalted. The hero theme appears for the last time, now solemn. It is developed into an overwhelming climax, but after this the music becomes funereal as the hero is laid to rest.

Operas. *Salome* outraged the morals of an entire generation of opera lovers. The text of Oscar Wilde, about Salome's sensual love for John the Baptist and climaxed by the distasteful spectacle of her dance before his head, was not likely to be accepted with quiet tolerance in the first years of the twentieth century. Strauss's music matched the Wilde play in sensuality, decadence, and eroticism. With his lavish orchestration, the erotic suggestions of his tortuous melodies and impulsive rhythms, and his suggestive characterizations, Strauss was, in his own way, as offensive to his contemporaries as was Wilde to his.

Present-day audiences no longer react unfavorably to the Salome theme or to the suggestiveness of Strauss's music. They are, instead, usually spellbound before a work of immense artistic importance. Never before had Strauss shown such orchestral virtuosity; never before had he been so daring in the sweep of his melodies and rhythms, or so rich in his harmonic language. He caught the essence of the Wilde play in music that never digresses from its artistic purpose but moves with inexorable logic—and shattering dramatic impact—to the climax of Salome's dance and her final apostrophe.

The story, of course, originated in the Scriptures. Salome, daughter of Herodias, is in love with the prophet John the Baptist, who repels her. King Herod asks Salome to dance for him, offering as compensation the granting of any wish. Salome dances her celebrated "Dance of the Seven Veils," then demands her payment: the head of John. Her wish is granted: the prophet is decapitated; his head is brought to Salome on a tray. Salome dances before the head lasciviously. Herod is so shocked by this demonstration that he orders Salome's death.

The "Dance of the Seven Veils" is not only the most famous part of the opera, but is also frequently heard as an independent piece of music at symphony concerts. The music begins with demoniac rhythms and brief, but intense, outcries. The agitation subsides. The first dance theme, sensual and sinuous, appears in viola and flute. The moods become now passionate, now languorous, now exotic, now even tender, as Salome's body weaves and gyrates through a lascivious dance. A second dance melody appears in the strings—slower and more sensual than the first. Then the music grows more and more savage—all restraint is gone. A shattering climax erupts in full orchestra. A trill in the woodwinds combined with tremolos in the strings suggests the final movements of the dance. The music rushes precipitately to its conclusion.

It would seem impossible in music to go beyond the sensuality of this dance; yet Strauss succeeded in doing it. When Salome addresses the head of John with glowing passion, this is the climactic point of the opera; Salome's lust for John is expressed in an exultant apostrophe beginning with the words, *"Ah! Du wolltest mich nicht deinen Mund küssen lassen!"*

There is even greater realism in Strauss's next opera, *Elektra*. To the sometimes sordid, frequently frenzied drama, Strauss brought a score in which shrieking arias, violent discords, and piercing orchestral sounds yield imitative effects which are a musical equivalent for the turbulent emotions of the text. Elektra, with her mad lust for vengeance, and the corrupt Klytemnestra are as vividly delineated in the music as in the play. The result is an artistic entity of compelling strength, one with an irresistible effect on the listener. Yet not everything in Strauss's music is neurotic and hypertensioned, though most of it is. There are some pages of sensitive beauty, including for example, Elektra's meeting with Orestes.

The opera marked the beginning of Strauss's long and successful collaboration with the Austrian poet Hugo von Hofmannsthal. Von Hofmannsthal's adaptation of the Sophocles drama emphasizes the more lurid character of the tragedy. Klytemnestra and her lover are responsible for the death of King Agamemnon. Her lover now rules in place of the dead king, and Klytemnestra has humiliated her daughter, Elektra, by making her live and act like a servant. Elektra hates her mother and lives only to destroy her and avenge her father's death. When Elektra hears the false news that her brother, Orestes, who had escaped, is dead, she entreats her sister to join her in her act of vengeance. But Orestes is not dead; he has returned. When he vows to avenge his father, Elektra's ecstasy knows no bounds. Orestes kills both his mother and her lover. Excited by this retribution, Elektra gives way to a mad, triumphant dance which ends in her death.

In *Der Rosenkavalier,* completed two years after *Elektra* and its immediate successor, Strauss sought a radical change of mood and pace. He now wanted to write a comic opera in the vein of Mozart, which—though gay and light of heart—would succeed in traversing the gamut of emotions from sentimentality to burlesque and from wistfulness to satire. Hugo von Hofmannsthal satisfied Strauss's ambition by producing one of the finest librettos in all opera, vivid in characterization, rich in dramatic incidents, spiced with intrigues, yet full of compassion and humanity. Such a book was a challenge, and Strauss met it successfully by writing his most lovable, varied, and infectious score and some of his most inspired music.

The play is set in the Vienna of Empress Maria Theresa, and the action centers around the dignified and sympathetic character of the Feldmarschallin, the Princess von Werdenberg. In the first act we are in her sumptuously furnished apartment. Young Octavian is on his knees making love to her. There is an intrusion with the abrupt arrival of her cousin, the fat, lecherous, comical Baron Ochs. Octavian quickly disguises himself as a maid, and it is not long before the Baron flirts with "her" and tries to arrange an intimate supper appointment. The Princess, meanwhile, attends to her morning interviews and is entertained by an Italian tenor singing a beautiful aria in the traditional Italian style, *"Di rigori armato il seno."* Before he leaves, the Baron imparts to the Princess the purpose of his visit. He wants her to have a silver rose dispatched to his prospective bride, Sophie, daughter of the wealthy Faninal. She has Ocatavian deliver it. Then, when alone, she sadly contemplates her advancing age, her vanishing beauty, and the futility of loving one so young as Octavian. This contemplation by the Princess is surely one of the most poignant and most moving pages of music in twentieth-century opera; it is the monologue beginning with the words *"Was erzürn' ich mich denn?"*

In the second act, Octavian comes to Faninal's house to present the silver rose to Sophie. On meeting, they fall in love. When left alone, they exchange ardent expressions of tenderness in the fervent love duet

"Mit Ihren Augen voll Thränen." The Baron catches them, challenges Octavian to a duel, and suffers a mere scratch; but he moans and rumbles as if he had been fatally wounded. Wine helps restore the good humor of Baron Ochs, and he sings the snatch of a waltz melody, *"Ohne mich."* Octavian now contrives to have a note reach the Baron— apparently from the "maid" with whom he had flirted at the Princess' apartment—arranging for a rendezvous. The Baron's happy spirits now find expression in the infectious waltz tune, as he chants *"Ohne mich, ohne mich, jeder Tag dir so bang"* and, after that, *"Mit mir, mit mir, keine Nacht dir zu lang."*

Baron Ochs's rendezvous with Octavian (disguised as a maid) takes place in the third act in a private room of a disreputable hotel. Octavian tortures the Baron by continually eluding his amorous advances. Octavian also arranges little pranks. Faces appear at the window until the Baron thinks he is losing his mind. Then a woman with a brood of children bursts into the room to accuse the Baron of being their father. In the ensuing commotion the Princess, Sophie, and her father arrive. Only then does the Baron realize how he has been duped by Octavian. In an exquisite trio—one of the finest ensemble numbers in the entire opera—the Princess magnanimously renounces Octavian and allows him to follow his new love, *"Hab' mir's gelobt, ihn lieb zu haben."* Sophie and Octavian are now free to express their love openly, and they do so in a fervent duet, *"Ist ein Traum, kann nicht wirklich sein."*

Vocal Music. Strauss wrote almost one hundred and fifty songs. A few came at the end of his life; but his masterpieces were created early, and one of their most engaging traits is their youthful ardor, intensity, exuberance, and freshness. These early songs, though written long before the famous operas, already reveal traits that made Strauss so successful in the theater: his mastery of writing for the voice; his artistic concern over accompaniments; his sensitive response to a given text; his feeling for atmosphere; his pronounced dramatic sense; his gift for writing a mobile, aristocratic melody.

He published his first collection of songs before his twentieth birthday. As this set includes the fervent and intense *"Allerseelen"* and the exquisitely lyrical *"Zueignung"*—to this day among his most popular songs—it is obvious that he arrived at greatness in the song form earlier than in other media. Between this first group and the collection of five songs published in 1899, Strauss produced his finest songs. His gift for the long, sustained melody, elegant in workmanship and charged with feeling, is found in such songs as *"Morgen"* and *"Wiegenlied."* Effective atmospheric writing distinguishes *"Traum durch die Dämmerung,"* Strauss's own favorite among his songs. Gaiety and the joy of life appear in the lovable *"Ständchen,"* while, on the other hand, a song such as *"Ruhe, meine Seele"* has caught the pain of heartbreak. In *"Cäcilie"* we have the soaring, ecstatic expression which is perhaps Strauss's most identifiable attribute in his early songs. His emotional span, then, is elastic—and this elasticity together with his craftsmanship and the distinct personality of his style have put him in the company of the greatest of *lieder* composers, with Schubert, Schumann, Brahms, and Hugo Wolf.

Igor Stravinsky

"He is a liberator. More than anyone else he has freed the musical thought of today."

—*Erik Satie*

BORN: Oranienbaum, Russia, June 17, 1882.

MAJOR WORKS: *Orchestral Music*—Suites from The Fire-Bird, Petrouchka, The Rite of Spring, Card Party (also ballets); Symphony in Three Movements; Capriccio, for piano and orchestra; Concerto in E-flat major, for chamber orchestra, "Dumbarton Oaks"; Concerto in D major, for chamber orchestra, "Basel." *Choral Music*—Oedipus Rex, opera-oratorio; Symphony of Psalms. ALSO: Renard, Mavra, The Rake's Progress, operas; Pulcinella, Apollon Musagète, The Fairy's Kiss, Perséphone, Orpheus, ballets; Mass; Les Noces, "choreographic scenes"; Cantata on Anonymous Elizabethan Songs; Symphonies of Wind Instruments; Symphony in C major; Concerto for Piano and Orchestra; Concerto for Violin and Wind Instruments; Danses concertantes, for chamber orchestra; Ode, Four Norwegian Moods, Scènes de ballet, for orchestra; 2 concertos for unaccompanied piano; Sonata, for piano; Agon, ballet; Canticum sacrum; Threni, for soloists, chorus and orchestra.

HIS LIFE

As STRAVINSKY's father was the leading bass of the St. Petersburg Opera (he created the role of Varlaam in Mussorgsky's *Boris Godunov*), the boy's early life was rich with musical associations and experiences. He was nine years old when he started learning the piano. From the time he acquired a degree of fluency, he improvised—at the expense of formal practice—much to the chagrin of his teachers and parents, who felt he was wasting his time. He was also unusual in the way he liked to spend hour after hour in his father's study, browsing through his library of opera scores; as he had a great facility for reading music, he came to know many of the operas well. Before long, his father took him to the opera house. His first hearings of Glinka's *A Life for the Czar* and *Russlan and Ludmila*—both of which he had already come to "love to distraction"* from the score— probably did more to shape his future than any other single influence. He himself regards a first hearing of Tchaikovsky's music in a living performance—the *Pathétique* Symphony, played in memory of the composer, who had just died—as "the beginning of my conscious life as artist and musician."

His parents, however, had no intention of making him a professional musician. Igor was sent to local schools for academic studies, which he detested and in which, as he himself confessed, he was singularly inept. The monotony of school was relieved by music: spasmodic study at the piano; attendance at orchestral concerts and recitals. But the schooling had to continue. After completing preliminary studies, Stravinsky entered the University of St. Petersburg to study law. During this period he succeeded in convincing his parents that he should study music more intensively. He engaged a tutor for harmony lessons, which he disliked, "perhaps owing to the pedagogical incompetence of my teacher, perhaps to the deficiency of the method used, and perhaps— and this is most likely—to my inherent aversion to any dry study." He found much more satisfaction in counterpoint, which he started learning by himself from a textbook and which fascinated him from the very beginning.

In the summer of 1902, while vacationing in Germany, Stravinsky met Rimsky-Korsakov, then spending the summer in Heidelberg. For the master he played a few pieces he had recently written, without making much of an impression. Rimsky-Korsakov advised Stravinsky to continue his law studies, but also urged him to acquire a more comprehensive knowledge of harmony and counterpoint through formal study.

Stravinsky's father died that year. Igor did not leave the University, still unconvinced of his musical ability. But he did spend a great deal of time on music study and musical interests. He moved in a circle of musicians and absorbed their conversation and discussions. He took every opportunity to visit and talk with Rimsky-Korsakov, whose household was open to him due to the fact that the master's son was Stravinsky's friend and fellow student at the University. He also joined

*Quotations by Stravinsky, unless otherwise identified, are from *Stravinsky: An Autobiography*. New York: Simon and Schuster, 1936.

a music society which gave performances of contemporary French chamber music, his first contact with the French style of such composers as Franck and Debussy, which impressed him greatly. He also worked on his compositions, completed a full-fledged piano sonata. He showed it to Rimsky-Korsakov, who did not hesitate to dissect it analytically. For the first time, Rimsky-Korsakov found something in Stravinsky worth encouraging, and he accepted him as his pupil in instrumentation.

By the time Stravinsky had completed his course of study at the University, in 1905, he no longer hesitated about the course he would pursue. He rejected law for good and married his cousin, who encouraged him in his music work. Carefully led by his teacher, Rimsky-Korsakov, he wrote two large works: the *Symphony in E-flat major* and *Le Faune et la bergère,* the latter a suite for voice and orchestra on three poems of Pushkin. Rimsky-Korsakov saw to it that both works were performed. The symphony, introduced in St. Petersburg on January 22, 1908, was the first Stravinsky work to be heard publicly.

Still another orchestral work, *Fireworks,* was written to commemorate the imminent marriage of Rimsky-Korsakov's daughter. Stravinsky dispatched it to his master at his country place as a surprise gift. The package came back unopened; Rimsky-Korsakov had died a few days earlier.

Fireworks and another new orchestral work, *Scherzo fantastique,* were performed at a Siloti concert in St. Petersburg in 1909. This concert suddenly changed Stravinsky's future. Among those who attended was the fabulous Serge Diaghilev, dilettante of the arts—"master painter who never painted," as his biographer, Arnold L. Haskell, wrote of him, "a master musician who never wrote or played, a master dancer who never danced or devised the steps of a ballet." At that time Diaghilev was in the process of organizing the Ballet Russe, as whose director he would soon become world-famous. Listening to both *Fireworks* and *Scherzo fantastique,* Diaghilev sensed that here was a composer who could make important contributions to the Ballet Russe.

As a first assignment, Diaghilev commissioned Stravinsky to orchestrate two Chopin pieces for a ballet, *Chopiniana.* The ballet *Chopiniana,* with the two Stravinsky orchestrations, was seen during Diaghilev's first season in Paris on June 2, 1909. Diaghilev liked Stravinsky's work and was ready to entrust him with a major project. For some time he had been planning a ballet on the subject of an old Russian legend about the Fire-Bird. He had asked Anatol Liadov (1855–1914) to write the music, but Liadov was incorrigibly lazy and dilatory about completing assignments. Tired of waiting for the score, Diaghilev decided to turn the job over to Stravinsky.

Stravinsky worked on his music for a year, usually aided by Fokine, who had prepared the scenario. "They worked very closely together, phrase by phrase," wrote Lincoln Kirstein in his biography of Fokine. "Stravinsky brought him a beautiful cantilena on the entrance of the Czarevitch into the garden of the girls with the golden apples. But Fokine disapproved. 'No, no!' he said. 'You bring him in like a tenor. Break the phrase where he merely shows his head on his first intrusion. Then make the curious swish of the garden's magic horse's return, and then, when he shows his hand again, bring in the full swing of the melody.'"

Stravinsky completed his score in May 1910, and on June 25 *L'Oiseau de feu* (*The Fire-Bird*) was presented at the Paris Opéra with Fokine, Madame Fokina, and Karsavina as the principal dancers. The settings were designed by Bakst and Golovine; and the conductor was Gabriel Pierné. It was an instantaneous success. On the opening night Debussy rushed backstage to embrace Stravinsky. *The Fire-Bird* became the triumph of the Diaghilev season and for the first time brought the name of Stravinsky to the attention of the music world. Diaghilev now depended on him for his most important ballet score for the following season.

Stravinsky preferred for his next subject a theme lighter in mood than *The Fire-Bird*. He had no scenario in mind, but he started writing the music for a composition which—for lack of a more suitable title—he called *Konzertstück*. He knew the music he was writing lent itself for ballet treatment, but a subject somehow eluded him. He has described how, for hours, he would walk along the edge of the Lake of Geneva, whistling to himself different fragments from his latest work, exhausting his imagination for a descriptive theme or title. An idea finally arrived when he least expected it, bursting upon his consciousness suddenly. This was *it,* he knew with finality: he would call his new composition *Petrouchka,* after the pathetic puppet so often seen at Russian fairs. When Diaghilev heard Stravinsky play this new work, and was told about the Petrouchka theme, he was hardly less enthusiastic than Stravinsky. He envisioned Nijinsky as Petrouchka, capering to the dynamic rhythms of Stravinsky's satirical music.

Petrouchka was seen in Paris on June 13, 1911, with Nijinsky and Karsavina as principal dancers, and it surpassed the success of *The*

Fire-Bird. Stravinsky was now recognized as one of the most vital and original figures to emerge in music since Debussy. His next ballet score was, consequently, awaited with considerable anticipation. It was *Le Sacre du printemps* (*The Rite of Spring*), which he had been planning for almost two years, since before he started work on *Petrouchka*. As he explained: "One day, when I was finishing the last pages of *L'Oiseau de feu* in St. Petersburg, I had a fleeting vision which came to me as a complete surprise, my mind at the moment being full of other things. I saw in imagination a solemn pagan rite: sage elders, seated in a circle, watched a young girl dance herself to death. They were sacrificing her to propitiate the god of spring. Such was the theme of the *Sacre du printemps*. I must confess that this vision made a deep impression upon me and I at once described it to my friend, Nicholas Roerich, he being a painter who had specialized in pagan subjects. He welcomed my inspiration with enthusiasm, and became my collaborator in this creation. In Paris, I told Diaghilev about it, and he was at once carried away by the idea."

Much has been written about the *première* of Stravinsky's *The Rite of Spring* at the Théâtre des Champs Elysées, in Paris, on May 29, 1913. Much more will continue to be written, not only because the work is one of the towering landmarks in twentieth-century music, but also because the first performance was one of the greatest scandals in contemporary music.

Carl van Vechten described the events of that evening in his book *Music after the War:* "A certain part of the audience, thrilled by what it considered to be a blasphemous attempt to destroy music as an art, and swept away with wrath, began very soon after the rise of the curtain to whistle, to make catcalls, and to offer audible suggestions as to how the performance should proceed. Others of us who liked the music and felt that the principles of free speech were at stake bellowed defiance. The orchestra played on unheard, except occasionally when a slight lull occurred. The figures on the stage danced in time to music that they had to imagine they heard, and beautifully out of rhythm with the uproar in the auditorium. I was sitting in a box in which I had rented one seat. Three ladies sat in front of me, one young man occupied the place behind me. He stood up during the course of the ballet to enable himself to see more clearly. The intense excitement under which he was laboring, thanks to the potent force of the music, betrayed itself presently when he began to beat rhythmically on the top of my head with his fists. My emotion was so great that I did not feel the blows for some time. They were perfectly synchronized with the music."

He might have added other interesting details. Hardly had the performance begun when Camille Saint-Saëns rose in his seat, made a bitter remark about the music, and left the theater with indignation. The critic André Capu yelled at the top of his lungs that the music was a colossal fraud; the Austrian ambassador laughed loudly in derision; the Princesse de Pourtalès left her box exclaiming, "I am sixty years old, but this is the first time that anyone dared to make a fool of me!" One lady reached out into the adjoining box and slapped the face of a man who was hissing; her escort arose, cards were exchanged, and a duel was arranged. A society lady rose majestically in her seat and spat in the face of one of the demonstrators. All the while, Maurice Ravel was shouting the word "genius"; another French composer and critic, Roland-Manuel, had the collar torn from his shirt because he defended the music, and he kept that collar as a precious memento ever after. Claude Debussy, pale and overwrought, was pleading with the audience around him to be silent and listen to the music. Backstage, Stravinsky held on to Nijinsky to prevent him from jumping into the audience and engaging in a fist fight with the obstreperous demonstrators.

The Rite of Spring shook the world of music to its very foundation. Stravinsky's growing boldness in dispensing with traditional harmonic, rhythmic, and melodic concepts—evident first in *The Fire-Bird* and increasingly apparent in *Petrouchka*—had grown in his latest score into outright anarchy, or so it appeared in 1913. With *The Rite of Spring,* Stravinsky became the most provocative, publicized, and fiercely discussed figure in music.

Disregarding both the great praise and the extravagant abuse that now were poured on him, Stravinsky continued fearlessly writing in the unorthodox style that had crystallized in *The Rite of Spring*. He produced equally unconventional music in *Le Chant du rossignol* (*The Song of the Nightingale*) and *Les Noces* (*The Wedding*). *The Song of the Nightingale* appeared in two different versions: as a symphonic poem, it was introduced in Paris on December 16, 1917, with Ernest Ansermet conducting; and as a ballet, it was presented by the Ballet Russe at the Paris Opéra on February 2, 1920. *Les Noces*—described by the composer as "Russian choreographic scenes"—was given by the Ballet Russe in Paris on June 13, 1923.

Meanwhile, Stravinsky had broken permanently with the land of his birth. In 1919 he moved his family to the outskirts of Paris (subsequently he took an apartment in the heart of Paris) and applied for French citizenship. For the next fifteen years France was his adopted country and Paris his permanent home. From then on, he was to be more French than Russian. And he was thenceforth to write music in an altogether new vein, his style becoming strictly classical where it had formerly been revolutionary. In this new manner he produced various important works: the charming and intimate ballet *L'Histoire du soldat* (*The Story of a Soldier*); a suite based on melodies of Pergolesi, *Pulcinella;* various concertos; the opera-oratorio *Oedipus Rex;* the ballet *Apollon Musagète,* commissioned by Elizabeth Sprague Coolidge and the first of his works to receive its world *première* in the United States; the *Symphony of Psalms,* commissioned by the Boston Symphony Orchestra for its fiftieth anniversary. *Apollon Musagète* was also presented by Diaghilev's Ballet Russe. With Diaghilev's death in Venice in 1929, Stravinsky's long and rich association with the Ballet Russe came to an end.

Stravinsky visited the United States for the first time in 1925, directing many important American symphonic organizations in programs including his most famous orchestral works. He returned to the United States on several occasions after that, and during those visits he directed world *premières* of several major works. In 1937 he led the first performance of his ballet *Jeu de cartes* (*Card Party*) in New York, and three years later introduced his *Symphony in C major* in Chicago.

With war coming to Europe in 1939, Stravinsky once again made a change of home and country. He married his second wife, Vera Soudeikine, in Bedford, Massachusetts, in 1940, applied for American citizenship in 1941, and soon after that settled in California. He has been highly productive in this country. His major works written here include the *Ode,* for orchestra (written in memory of Natalie, the late wife of Serge Koussevitzky); the *Symphony in Three Movements;* the ballet *Orpheus;* the Mass; the *Cantata on Anonymous Elizabethan Songs;* and, most important of all, the opera *The Rake's Progress,* on a text by W. H. Auden and Chester Kallman. The opera was first seen in Venice in conjunction with the Venice Festival, Stravinsky himself conducting, introduced with all the fanfare of a Hollywood *première.* Tickets were at a premium; the audience included visitors from all parts of the world, many coming to Venice expressly to hear the new work; the theater was elaborately decorated; the limelight of world publicity was focused on the event. It was the first time that an opera by a non-Italian composer had had its *première*—and in the English language. Fortunately the opera justified the effort it cost and the attention it received, as the critics noted without a dissenting voice. After its *première,* the opera was seen without delay at the Opéra Comique in Paris, the Royal Theater in Copenhagen, and major opera houses in Antwerp, Brussels, Cologne, Düsseldorf, Frankfort on the Main, Hamburg, Milan, Monte Carlo, Munich, Münster, Stuttgart, and Zurich. It was given its American *première* by the Metropolitan Opera in New York on February 14, 1953.

With *Canticum sacrum,* for tenor, baritone, chorus and orchestra (1956), Stravinsky veered toward still a new direction in his musical writing. In his indefatigable search for ever greater economy, concentration and abstraction he arrived at a "serial technique," based on the twelve-tone idiom of Anton von Webern rather than Schoenberg. Stravinsky pursued this style further in his ballet, *Agon* (1956), and in *Threni,* on the Lamentations of Jeremiah from the Vulgate, for soloists, chorus and orchestra (1958).

He is a lean, spare man who all his life has been meticulous about his appearance, his way of life, and his working habits. His manuscript, the last word in neatness, with calligraphy that resembles fine print, gives a clue to the man. He is exceptionally precise and methodical—even fussy. His food must follow the accepted recipes rigidly and without the slightest deviation, his highball must always contain exactly the same ratio of Scotch and water. His studio must be neat, or he cannot work well; it is soundproof, for he cannot work out his ideas if he feels someone is listening; and when his door is closed—actually there are two doors to his studio—nobody is allowed admittance. His day is always well ordered, and one day must be like another when he is at his home in Hollywood: breakfast on the outdoor terrace; then a period of work in his studio; lunch; correspondence and attendance to his business affairs; evenings for friends and visitors. There is a precise time for everything each day, even for gymnastics (Stravinsky is ever deeply concerned about his body) and religious services (he is very devout). The year must be planned as carefully as the day, to allow him time for travel and conducting without infringing seriously on his creative work.

He keeps himself aloof from all opinions regarding his works, other than those given him by very close friends whom he admires. He has a quiet contempt for all critics and a controlled hostility toward his public. He feels that they do not know what he is trying to do, while he himself is always completely sure of what he is doing. As he said: "They cannot and will not follow me in the progress of my musical thought. What moves and delights me leaves them indifferent, and what still continues to interest them holds no further attraction for me. For that matter, I believe that there was seldom any real communion of spirit between us. If it happened—and it still happens—that we liked the same things, I very much doubt whether it was for the same reasons."

About his own music he has had this to say: "I live neither in the past nor in the future. I am in the present. I cannot know what tomorrow will bring forth. I can only know what the truth is for me today."

HIS MUSIC

THERE have been several Stravinskys, not just one. The first was the apprentice strongly influenced by his teacher, Rimsky-Korsakov. This was the traditionalist, whose *Symphony in E-flat* had the spirit, if not the very flesh, of the music of the Russian nationalist school.

The second Stravinsky was the *enfant terrible* who evolved under the magnetizing influence of Diaghilev. Beginning with *The Fire-Bird*—and right through *Petrouchka, The Rite of Spring, The Song of the Nightingale,* and *Les Noces*—Stravinsky leaned toward complicated rhythms, dissonance, polytonality, and severe melodies. This was a primitive who delighted in bizarre instrumental colors and orgiastic rhythms and brutal strength and passion. In one respect the second Stravinsky was a logical outgrowth of the first: in his pronounced dependence on Russian lore and backgrounds, in his principal concern to create music of unmistakably Russian character.

A new Stravinsky appeared after World War I. He broke completely with his Russian past (it will be recalled that he applied for French citizenship and intended making France his permanent home) and with his former primitivism and revolutionary tendencies. His goals became clarity, brevity, simplicity, lucidity, economy, and preciseness. He was partial to classical structures and sometimes even utilized materials of the distant past; in short, he had become a neoclassicist. From the exploitation of new rhythms and harmonies, he went on to contrapuntal writing, from the programmatic and the pictorial to the abstract, from iconoclasm to formalism.

He had been an object for bitter controversy and severe denunciation when he first began to revolt. By the time the world caught up with him—and pronounced *Petrouchka* and *The Rite of Spring* masterworks—he was off in an entirely different direction, once again to become controversial and denounced. To this day there are those who insist that the greater Stravinsky is found in those earlier ballet scores he wrote for Diaghilev, while the later Stravinsky represents decadence; and there are others who are equally convinced that the later Stravinsky was the logical, possibly inevitable, evolution from the earlier one, that the later Stravinsky was at the height of his maturity and creative power. However, it is hardly necessary for the concertgoer to make a choice. He will find greatness in the best of the later Stravinsky as there is greatness in the earlier one. In their concentration, purity, and intensity—as well as in their compelling logic—works such as the *Symphony of Psalms, Oedipus Rex, Orpheus,* the Mass, *The Rake's Progress, Agon, Canticum sacrum,* and *Threnl* always reveal the hand of a master.

ANALYTICAL NOTES

Orchestral Music. Stravinsky adapted all of his famous ballet scores into orchestral suites, and it is as orchestral music—rather than as ballets—that these works are continually heard.

The Fire-Bird, his first successful score, was based on an old Russian legend which appears in several different versions in various Russian fairy tales. In preparing the scenario, Fokine drew his material from several different fairy tales. The Fire-Bird is captured by Ivan Czarevitch late one night. When Ivan Czarevitch frees her, the Fire-Bird rewards him with one of her feathers. A castle arises out of the darkness. Thirteen beautiful girls emerge from it and romp around a silver tree with golden fruit. One of these girls presents him with one of the golden fruits, then all thirteen return into the castle. As dawn brings faint illumination, Czarevitch recognizes the castle as the abode of Kastchei, capturer of wayfaring strangers. Boldly, Ivan enters the castle, past horrendous monsters. Kastchei tries to bewitch Ivan, but is helpless because of the feather in the young man's hand. The Fire-Bird now returns and conducts Ivan to a casket in which is sealed Kastchei's fate. It contains an egg, which Ivan smashes. Out of the egg-shell emerges Death and enters the body of Kastchei. With Kastchei's

doom, the castle evaporates and the thirteen beautiful girls are released from their imprisonment. One of them is given to Ivan as a
bride.

Stravinsky arranged three suites from this score, the finest being the
second. It is in six sections. The first, "Introduction," begins with an
ominous theme in the low register of the strings. An atmosphere of
mystery is thus created and is soon heightened by the somber voice of
the woodwinds and by weird harmonics in the violins and cellos. The
introduction blends into the "Dance of the Fire-Bird." The sinuous
movement of the bird is imitated by the strings and the woodwinds;
the luminous orchestration catches the glow of the bird's feathers.
"The Dance of the Princesses" is graceful, the main dance melody
being given by the oboe with harp accompaniment. In the next part
we have demoniac energy: the wild and orgiastic music of the "Dance
of Kastchei." This section begins and ends with a shattering chord in
full orchestra. After a moment's pause there comes the tenderest lyrical
part of the entire suite, the sensitive "Berceuse" sung by the bassoon.
The "Finale" comes without pause, opening with a gentle melody for
horn solo against tremulous strings. The music grows in power until
an ecstatic passage for the strings brings the suite to a jubilant conclusion.

The setting of *Petrouchka*, the scenario for which was planned by
Stravinsky but put into its definitive ballet form by Alexandre Benois,
is a public square in St. Petersburg; the time is about a century ago.
A carnival is taking place, and the public square is alive with movement, noise, color, and activity. The principal attraction is a puppet
show, one of whose main characters is Petrouchka, an uncouth and
ugly victim of persecution. He is in love with the puppet ballerina, but
she is repelled by him and attracted to the handsomely attired Moor.
Petrouchka interrupts a love scene between the two and is unceremoniously ejected. While all this is taking place, the carnival grows
gayer, more alive with activity. There are dances by the Nurses and
by coachmen; there is a performance by a trained bear; a merchant,
accompanied by two gypsies, is throwing money at the crowd. Suddenly the merry proceedings are interrupted by Petrouchka, fleeing
for his life out of the showman's booth, pursued by the Moor, who
catches up with him and kills him. A policeman is called. He quiets the
crowd by informing them that the dead Petrouchka is, after all, only
a puppet.

There are three different suites. The one most usually heard, an abbreviated one, opens with a "Russian Dance," of recognizably folk character; it is for full orchestra, brilliantly orchestrated. A cry in the full orchestra then brings Petrouchka to the scene; he has been kicked into his own room. The agitation of the music tells us of the anger of his assailant and the reaction of the crowd. The ballerina is introduced with a delightful theme for piano solo, later joined by the flute. Petrouchka is in love and is rejected; a loud cadenza in the clarinet tells of the rejection. There is an undercurrent of pity for Petrouchka in a sympathetic theme for horns. We next have a picture of the carnival itself, with all its frenetic gaiety and bustle. The "Dance of the Nurses" is heard in a lively theme, first in the oboes, then in the horns, and after that in the violins. And now the bear and the peasant appear. The bear dances to a tune in the upper register of the clarinet which imitates the reed used by the peasant; the awkard, heavy-footed movements of the bear are humorously described by the tuba. The strings, against trills in the winds, tell us that the merchant and two gypsies have made an appearance, the gypsies dancing to the accordion music of the merchant (oboe against plucked strings). This is followed by the vigorous dance of the coachmen, a Russian melody forcefully shared by trumpets and plucked strings. After this comes the masquerade, the strange disguises of the participants suggested by picaresque themes in the bass. All the masqueraders join in a dance. The music of this dance, presented by flute, piccolo, and bells, to a background of violin trills, brings the suite to a dynamic conclusion.

In *The Rite of Spring* Stravinsky drew a picture of pagan Russia on an immense tonal canvas. Each part describes some ritual to Spring; and the sum total of the different parts is the adoration of Nature by primitive man. The entire work is in two uninterrupted sections, each made up of several different parts. The first section is called "The Fertility of the Earth"; the second, "The Sacrifice."

An atmospheric seventy-five-bar introduction opens with the lonely voice of a solo bassoon in the uppermost register. Other woodwind and brass instruments join in as the mystery of the vernal season is evoked. The introduction leads into the "Ballet of the Adolescents." A vigorous rhythm is enunciated to portray the stamping of feet in a primitive dance. The increasingly febrile rhythms bring on mounting excitement. Four trumpets later intone a solemn chant against a little dance melody in the flutes. The excitement does not subside all this while. A new part arrives, "Spring Rounds," introduced by a theme for unison clarinets and bass clarinets and accompanied by trills in the flutes. The heavily accented dance that follows utilizes the chant of the trumpets heard in the preceding division. The return of the clarinet theme brings back the opening mood before we are confronted with a new ritual, "The Games of the Rival Tribes." This consists of a contest in which two groups enter into competitive gymnastics and battles. The Sage of the tribe then appears to consecrate the soil. The games are set forth in propulsive rhythms and rapidly changing meters. A vigorous theme for four tubas brings on the Sage. An effective pause follows. After the earth has been consecrated by the Sage, there takes place a demoniac dance of the earth.

The second section of *The Rite of Spring* begins with a nostalgic portrait of a pagan night. There is mystery and gloom; the harmonic colors are dark; the thematic germs are of a somber character. Soon we have the dance of the "Mysterious Circle of Adolescents," beginning with a winding and solemn theme in the flute which grows in intensity as the dance is evolved. In the next two brief rituals—"Evocation of the Ancestors" and "Ritual of the Ancestors"—the music becomes ponderous, primeval, at times even barbaric, with heavy chords and savage themes. We come now to the final sacrifice, in which the victim must dance to her death. More and more feverish does the mood grow, as the rhythms become enormously complex and with immense kinesthetic drive, and as the meters change with breath-taking rapidity. A frenzy is reached; with a last devastating outburst from the orchestra the rite is terminated.

The *Card Party* was written not for Diaghilev and the Ballet Russe, but for the American Ballet Theater. It represents a radical departure from the three preceding ballet scores. The procedures are much more simple, and the approach much more impersonal. There is a pronounced tendency toward satire. Most important, the onetime bond between the composer and his Russian background has been broken.

The following programmatic explanation of the ballet scenario appears in the published score: "The characters are the chief cards in a game of poker, disputed between several players on the green cloth of a card table. In the course of each deal the situation is complicated by the endless machinations of the perfidious Joker, who considers himself invincible by virtue of his ability to assume the role of the desired card. During the first deal, one of the players is beaten, but the other two remain with even 'straights' although one of them holds the Joker. In the second deal, the hand that holds the Joker is victorious, thanks to the four Aces who easily win out over four Queens. In the third and last deal, it is a struggle among three 'flushes.' Although at first victorious over one adversary, the Joker, strutting at the head of a sequence of Spades, is beaten by a 'royal flush' in Hearts. This puts an end to his malice and knavery."

The orchestral suite utilizes the entire ballet score without alteration. It consists of three "deals" (instead of movements). Each "deal" is prefaced by an introduction in which appears a marchlike subject for full orchestra representing the shuffling of the deck. There are several subdivisions within each "deal." The first is made up of a *"Pas d'action,"* "Dance of the Joker," and "Little Waltz." In the second we have a "March," "Variations of the Four Queens," "Variation of the Knave of Hearts," and "Coda." The concluding "deal" consists of a "Waltz Minuet" and a "Final Dance."

We have thus far confined ourselves to Stravinsky's music for the ballet. But he has also written many orchestral works designed exclusively for concert use. Among the most significant of these is the *Symphony in Three Movements,* completed in 1945. This is the third of Stravinsky's symphonies, the First Symphony (E-flat major) having been written in his youth, and the Second (C major) in 1940, for the fiftieth anniversary of the Chicago Symphony Orchestra. (Two other Stravinsky works with a symphonic nomenclature are not symphonies in the accepted meaning of that form: the *Symphonies of Wind Instruments* and the *Symphony of Psalms.*)

The first movement of the *Symphony in Three Movements,* which is made up of thematic germs rather than fully developed themes, derives its effect from rapidity of motion and brilliance of sonorities. The appeal is mostly kinesthetic. This is followed by a movement that is more economical in texture and more delicate in feeling. It opens with a graceful classical theme in the strings and proceeds with a lyrical passage for solo harp and flute. The third movement, which erupts without a break, begins with a lofty idea for full orchestra. Three brief sections follow, which have been described as preludes, and they lead to a fugue, the theme of which is heard in trombone and piano.

Among Stravinsky's orchestral works of smaller dimensions, there is the charming *Capriccio,* for piano and orchestra (1929), which, in form, has the freedom and elasticity of a fantasia and is filled with whimsical, satirical, even capricious attitudes. A forceful introduction leads to a representative idea of the first movement, a rhythmic figure in piano and timpani. Various terse thematic statements (some of them dancelike in character) follow; the motor activity is never allowed to slacken. The movement ends with the return of the forceful introduction. The composer designated his second movement as an "Andante rapsodico." The rhapsodic mood is established at the very beginning with a dialogue between piano and woodwinds. But tongue-in-cheek levity is not absent in the succeeding ideas. After a powerful cadenza for the piano, there is a sustained note in the flute to lead into the third movement. In this movement, wit and sophistication are given full freedom of expression, as dance ideas (sometimes even those of jazz) are prominent.

Stravinsky wrote two concertos for chamber orchestra which bring twentieth-century thinking into the seventeenth-century concerto-grosso form. The first of these, in E-flat major (1938), is known as the *Dumbarton Oaks* Concerto. This is because the work is dedicated to the owner of the Dumbarton Oaks estate, in Washington, D. C., on the occasion of the thirtieth anniversary of his marriage. (The same estate was later the scene of an important monetary conference; but Stravinsky's concerto has no relation to that event.) The second (D major), written eight years later, also has an identifying tag, *Basel* Concerto, because it was commissioned by the Basel Chamber Orchestra, in Switzerland, on the occasion of its twentieth anniversary. Both works have the same approach. They are (as Ingolf Dahl said so well of the *Dumbarton Oaks* Concerto) "a portrait of the concerto grosso painted by a modern artist." The classical form, the contrapuntal style (often strictly fugal), and the use of a small group in the orchestra against a larger one remind us of Bach's Brandenburg concertos; but the astringent thematic material and the rhythmic force belong essentially to our own times. Both works are in three movements, and both have slow movements whose elevated thought is presented through sustained and affecting lyricism.

Choral Music. *Oedipus Rex* (1927) has been presented in two different ways: as an oratorio, without scenery and costumes, and as an opera. This carries on a Handelian tradition, for some of Handel's oratories were also given on the stage with full theatrical trappings.

Jean Cocteau prepared the text (in French) from the Sophocles tragedy. But *Oedipus Rex* is always heard in a Latin translation because of the composer's conviction that his artistic effect—classical objectivity and remoteness, a "statuesque plasticity"—can be achieved only if a dead language is used. However, the audience is enlightened on the action by a narrator (dressed in evening clothes whether the performance is in a stage or concert version). He appears at intervals to elucidate the action about to take place, expressing himself (in Stravinsky's explanation) "like a master of ceremonies, presenting the narrative in a passive voice."

This "opera-oratorio" is in two acts, in turn divided into three episodes each. The first act begins with a choral number in which the men of Thebes bewail the plague ravaging the town. It continues with an air of Oedipus, promising help. The second episode begins with Creon's air telling the people of Thebes that according to the Oracle of Delphi the murderer of their former king, Laius, is among them; that no help will be forthcoming for the stricken people until the murderer is found and punished. Oedipus' air promises to track down the culprit. In the third episode, a choral invocation by Athene, Artemis, and Apollo is succeeded by the air of the Blind Tiresias, which discloses that it is a king who is the murderer of King Laius. Oedipus replies with an air condemning Creon and Tiresias for plotting against him. And the first act ends with a rousing chorus by the men of Thebes acclaiming the arrival of Jocasta, widow of Laius, and now wife of Oedipus.

The chorus that ended the first act reappears to introduce the second. Jocasta discloses, in an air, that her former husband was killed outside Thebes, at the crossroads between Daulia and Delphi. The duet of Oedipus and Jocasta then brings the information that some years back Oedipus had killed a stranger at just that juncture. The fifth episode starts with a messenger's air announcing the death of Polybus, king of Corinth, and disclosing that Oedipus was only his adopted son. Two more airs follow. One is by a shepherd, telling how he had found Oedipus, as a child, abandoned on Mount Cithaeron; in the other, Oedipus recognizes the full extent of his unfortunate position. Within an air and chorus of the final episode, the tragic fates of Jocasta and Oedipus are lamented. Jocasta has committed suicide, and Oedipus has pierced out his own eyes. The opera-oratorio ends with a farewell chorus to Oedipus by the men of Thebes.

The *Symphony of Psalms* (1930)—written on a commission from the Boston Symphony Orchestra for its fiftieth anniversary—is a setting of excerpts from the Psalms (text in Vulgate). It is in three parts, played without pause. In the first, a prelude, a sinner prays for divine pity (Psalm 39, "Hear my prayer, O Lord, and give ear unto my cry, Hold not Thy peace at my tears"). The next part is a double fugue, an expression of gratitude for grace received (Psalm 40, "I waited patiently for the Lord, and He inclined unto me, and heard my cry"). The concluding section is a hymn of praise and glory (Psalm 60, "Praise ye the Lord, Praise God in his Sanctuary").

In his musical treatment, Stravinsky relied mainly on counterpoint, with choral and instrumental groups getting equal attention. The style is bleak, austere, and objective—the austerity further intensified by the instrumentation, which dispenses with violins and violas altogether and uses other strings only to fill out the tonal structure.

In *Canticum sacrum* (1956) and *Threni* (1958) the composer passes from neo-classicism to expressionism. These two choral works are in the twelve-tone idiom (*Canticum sacrum* only partially, but *Threni* throughout), reducing musical expression to its barest essentials. Both works were introduced in Venice (*Canticum sacrum* having been written to honor St. Mark, the patron saint of that city); both works have Latin texts from the Vulgate prepared by the composer (that of *Threni* coming specifically from the first, third, and fifth Lamentations of Jeremiah); both works are scored for vocal soloists, chorus, and orchestra (the orchestra in *Canticum sacrum* dispensing with violins and cellos). Stravinsky's transparent and at times dramatic serial technique in his choruses in both compositions finds him at the height of his technical mastery and creative power. In *Threni* he achieves further emotional and dramatic impact through the effective use of song speech.

Peter Ilitch Tchaikovsky

"Tchaikovsky's music is not only one of the cornerstones of Russian musical culture and world music. . . . It is at the same time a creative and technical encyclopedia to which every Russian composer has reference in the course of his own work."

—Dmitri Shostakovich

BORN: Votinsk, Russia, May 7, 1840.

DIED: St. Petersburg, November 6, 1893.

MAJOR WORKS: *Orchestral Music*—Symphony No. 4, in F minor; Symphony No. 5, in E minor; Symphony No. 6, in B minor, "Pathétique"; Concerto No. 1, in B-flat minor, for piano and orchestra; Concerto in D major, for violin and orchestra; Romeo and Juliet, fantasy-overture; Marche slave; Francesca da Rimini, symphonic fantasy; 1812 Overture; Capriccio Italien; Nutcracker Suite. ALSO: Eugene Onegin, Pique Dame, operas; Swan Lake, Sleeping Beauty, ballets; Manfred Symphony; Serenade, for string orchestra; Mozartiana, Suite No. 4 for orchestra; Hamlet, fantasy-overture; String Quartet No. 1, in D major (with the celebrated Andante Cantabile); Trio in A minor; "None but the Lonely Heart," "One Small Word," "He Loves Me Dearly," "A Heavy Tear," "Invocation to Sleep," and other songs; pieces for piano.

HIS LIFE

THE greatest of Russian composers was also the most tragic. He once wrote: "The greater reason I have to be happy, the more discontented do I become. A worm gnaws continually in secret in my heart." And again: "I suffer from torments which cannot be put into words." Throughout his life he was haunted by an inescapable terror. He wept at the slightest provocation. He was always running away, he knew not from what, trying to find peace in new environments. People upset him. "Every new acquaintance," he said, "every fresh contact with strangers has been a source of acute moral suffering." Yet solitude was also torture. Strange fears obsessed him. All his life he was in terror of electrical storms, hiding from them like a child. His dream life, faithfully recorded in his diary, was filled with "cliff-hanging" episodes. When he conducted an orchestra, early in his career, he was in continual dread that his head might slip off his shoulders; while conducting, he would hold up his chin with his left hand. He was sure that some day he would die as his mother had, through cholera; and, eventually, he did.

The root of his troubles was his hypersensitivity, which was outright neurotic—probably an inheritance from a grandfather who had been a victim of epilepsy. He had several nervous breakdowns; once or twice he thought he was going mad; and on one occasion he tried to commit suicide.

But his most terrible cross was fear of his homosexual tendencies. He kept his aberration a secret, dreading that it might be discovered. Only to his brother Modeste (also a homosexual) did he refer to it at all, and then only by speaking of it cryptically as "The." This aberration made him psychopathically shy; it induced continual melancholia; it made him, in his own eyes, a misanthrope. It also tempted him to enter upon a foolish marriage which was a catastrophe from the very first.

That a life so disturbed by emotional upheavals, suffering, and maladjustment could have been productive of so much music, and so much great music, is surely a cause for wonder. The wonder grows when we realize how comparatively late in life Tchaikovsky began concentrating on composition. He did not devote himself completely to music study until he was twenty-two years old. Up to then he was an amateur with little training to speak of, having specialized in the study of law and having for three years filled a post in the Ministry of Justice.

Tchaikovsky's first musical impression came in early childhood when he heard opera airs tinkled on a little mechanical instrument called the "orchestrion." Before long, he tried reproducing these tunes on the piano, and when he was five he was given some lessons. Music excited him. Once, going to bed after hearing a concert, he was found weeping. "The music won't leave my head," he whimpered. "It won't let me go to sleep."

This incident betrays his exceptional sensitivity. His French governess revealed how carefully he had to be handled. "A trifle was able to wound him. He was a 'porcelain' child. It was impossible to punish him, and the least criticism—a single word of rebuke, usually quickly forgotten by other children—upset him alarmingly. . . . Left to himself, he preferred to play the piano, and to read or write poetry."

The law, and not music, was selected as his career. In 1850 his mother conducted him to St. Petersburg and deposited him in a preparatory school. This first separation from his mother (whom he adored) was a wound that never healed. When she left in her carriage, he pursued and caught up with it and tried to hold back the wheels, crying bitterly as he did so. For the next two years at school, until his family came to live in St. Petersburg and he could see his mother regularly, he was intensely unhappy. But in 1854 his mother died of cholera, and his former unhappiness became chronic.

Meanwhile, in 1852, he had entered the School of Jurisprudence. When these studies ended he became a clerk in the Ministry of Justice, a position he held for three years. He was so disinterested and negligent in his work that, some years later, he could not recall what his specific duties had been. He became a fop and a snob, had neither direction nor ambition, and was concerned only with having a good time. Music was the only interest that lifted him out of his shiftless existence. He went to the opera regularly, was profoundly moved by Mozart's *Don Giovanni* and Glinka's *A Life for the Czar*. And, having begun to study the piano again in his last years at law school, he became absorbed with improvisation. He even started composing, completing in 1860 an Italian song which was published.

He began thinking more seriously about music in 1861. In that year he wrote to his sister: "I have begun studying thorough bass and am making good progress. Who knows? Maybe in three years you will be hearing my operas and singing my arias." "With my fairly respectable talent (I hope you don't take that for bragging), it would be silly for me not to try my fortune in the direction of music," he wrote his sister a second time. "I am fearful only of my own lack of character. In the end my laziness will conquer. But if it doesn't, I promise you something will come of me. Fortunately, I still have time."

His teacher, Nicholas Zaremba, became such a source of inspiration that Tchaikovsky overcame his natural tendency toward indolence and worked hard and well. Significantly enough, the onetime fop was now completely negligent of his appearance. In 1862 he enrolled in the newly founded Conservatory, combining his studies under Zaremba (now a member of the Conservatory faculty) with other lessons in harmony, counterpoint, and orchestration. He knew by then that he wanted to become a musician. "Do not for a moment think that I expect to be a great artist," he wrote to his sister. "Whether I become a famous composer or a poor music teacher is a matter of indifference to me. At all events, my conscience will be clear and I shall no longer have the right to complain about my lot."

He gave up his post at the Ministry and devoted himself completely to music study and musical interests. He wrote his first ambitious works. *Characteristic Dances,* for orchestra, was introduced by Johann Strauss II during the summer season in Pavlovsk in 1865. A string quartet and an *Overture in F,* for orchestra, were heard at students' concerts at the Conservatory in 1865 and 1866 respectively. A cantata, *Ode to Joy* (written—as a graduating exercise—to Schiller's words, the same text used by Beethoven in the Ninth Symphony), won a silver medal and inspired his young friend Hermann Laroche, later a famous critic, to say, "You are the greatest musical talent of contemporary Russia, more powerful and original than Balakirev, more creative than Serov, infinitely more cultivated than Rimsky-Korsakov. In you, I see the greatest, or rather the only, hope of our musical future."

Upon being graduated, Tchaikovsky had to face the problem of earning a living. Nicholas Rubinstein—brother of Anton, one of Tchaikovsky's teachers—provided an answer. He had just founded the Moscow Conservatory, and he was in need of teachers who would not tax his meager budget. He offered Tchaikovsky the post of professor of harmony; despite the niggardly salary of fifty rubles a month, Tchaikovsky accepted. He moved into Nicholas Rubinstein's apartment, which he continued to share with him for several months. He gradually became accustomed to his new duties as Conservatory teacher. "Much to my surprise," he wrote to his sister on February 19, 1866, "my course is very successful. My nervousness has completely vanished, and I am gradually acquiring the proper professional demeanor. My hypochondria is also disappearing. But Moscow is still a strange town for me, and it will be a long time before I will be able to think without dread of having to stay here for years, perhaps forever."

He soon started to work on his First Symphony, subtitled "Winter Dreams." Worry, lack of confidence in his ability, and dissatisfaction with what he was writing upset him so greatly that he soon began to suffer from pains in the head and insomnia. He was sure that he would die before he could complete his symphony; he worked feverishly, and frequently through the night, to win his race with death. A nervous breakdown followed. A summer holiday at a country place near St.

Petersburg, however, brought relief, and he was able to finish his symphony the following fall. Anton Rubinstein, to whom Tchaikovsky showed the score, was not greatly impressed with it and refused to conduct its *première* performance. But Nicholas Rubinstein accepted it and played it at one of his Moscow concerts on February 15, 1868. It was a resounding success. "The warm reception of the Symphony," wrote Kashkin, "exceeded all expectations even of Tchaikovsky's friends."

Tchaikovsky's next important work, the opera *The Voivode,* was introduced in Moscow on February 11, 1869, and was so well liked that it was given five more performances. Sixteen days after this *première,* Nicholas Rubinstein conducted the first performance of an orchestral fantasy, *Fatum.* But Tchaikovsky was so dissatisfied with the scores of both his opera and his fantasy that he destroyed them. (Both works were recently restored from the orchestral parts.)

Tchaikovsky completed his first masterwork in 1869. It was the orchestral fantasy-overture *Romeo and Juliet,* written on the advice and encouragement of Balakirev. Its greatness was not at first recognized. When Nicholas Rubinstein introduced it in Moscow on March 16, 1870, it was received apathetically. Tchaikovsky wrote: "My overture had no success at all here, and was wholly ignored. . . . During the whole evening no one spoke to me a word about it." He rewrote the fantasy completely in 1870 and then revised it again in 1881.

In the fall of 1868 Tchaikovsky fell in love with Désirée Artôt, a rather unattractive opera singer who, in the words of Laroche, "conquered hearts by her charm rivaling the greatest beauties." "We are inflamed by very tender sentiments," Tchaikovsky wrote to his father, "and mutual declarations to that effect were exchanged. Naturally, the question of marriage came up. We both desire it very much, and if nothing interferes we will be married in the summer." But there was interference. Désirée suddenly married the Spanish baritone Mariano Padilla. It cannot be said that Tchaikovsky took this rejection to heart. To his brother Modeste, he referred to the denouement of the affair as "amusing" and "ridiculous."

There were several other women in his life. One was Antonina Miliukova, a high-strung and emotionally unbalanced young music student. She wrote him begging for an interview, during which she impulsively fell on her knees and begged tearfully for the privilege of serving him for the rest of her life. "Some mysterious power drew me to the girl," he wrote. "One evening I went to her, told her frankly that I could not love her, but that I would be her faithful and grateful

friend. I described my character in detail, my irritability, the uneven-
ness of my temperament, my misanthropy, and my material condition.
Then I asked her to marry me. The reply was, of course, in the affirma-
tive."

What made him enter upon marriage so precipitately and without
the pretense of being in love? Tchaikovsky himself provides the answer
in a candid letter to his brother Modeste, written on September 22,
1876, even before he had met Antonina: "From this day on I will seriously consider entering matrimony with any woman. I am convinced
that my *inclinations* are the greatest and insuperable barrier to my well-
being, and I must by all means struggle against my nature." And in
another letter to Modeste, three weeks later, he wrote further: "What
a dreadful thought that people close to me may be ashamed of me! In
a word, I am determined by means of marriage or public connection
with a woman to shut the mouths of sundry despicable creatures whose
opinions I despise but who may cause pain to people I love."

He married Antonina on July 18, 1877. The marriage was a night-
mare from the very first day. He confessed that he "was ready to
scream" when they were alone for the first time. The next few weeks
was a period of unrelieved torment. For hours each night Tchaikovsky
roamed the streets of Moscow, trying to summon the courage to return
home to his wife. On one of those nights he tried unsuccessfully to
commit suicide by standing in the icy Moscow River and provoking an
attack of pneumonia. At last he escaped to his brother's house, where
he collapsed. Partially recovered, he spent a year traveling throughout
Europe, fleeing from the memory of his gruesome experience. He
never saw Antonina again, but he was by no means rid of her. For
many years she continued to torment him by calling on his friends and
relatives and trying to arouse them against him, and by badgering him
with excessive demands for money and with letters carrying veiled
threats of blackmail. In 1896 she was confined to an insane asylum,
where she lived the last twenty years of her life.

Even while he was involved in this marriage, Tchaikovsky was
already drawn toward the person who played the most important, and
the most curious, role in his life: the patroness Nadezhda Filaretovna
von Meck. She was an extremely affluent widow who was an intelligent
dilettante and a profound lover of music. She learned about Tchaikovsky's works through Nicholas Rubinstein and became an immediate enthusiast. She wrote to Tchaikovsky expressing her great admiration; he replied with a formal letter of thanks. This was the beginning

of an exchange of correspondence which lasted thirteen years. Letters passed between them almost daily, in which the admiration of the patroness for the composer and the gratitude of the composer for the patroness developed into expressions of passionate, undisguised love.

But in all those thirteen years the two never met. One of the conditions Madame von Meck had originally imposed upon the continuation of their friendship—and her generous subsidies—was that Tchaikovsky make no attempt to meet her personally. She may have been aware that the difference in their stations could never be resolved; or she may have rejected Tchaikovsky because of an excessive devotion to her children. In any event, she kept him at a distance; and Tchaikovsky, always in dread of any demands a woman might make upon his emotional life, was grateful for this arrangement. Sometimes they saw each other for brief moments in a concert hall or in the streets of Moscow. Sometimes, as in Florence, Tchaikovsky would walk under her window at a specified hour each day so that she might catch a glimpse of him. In Florence, where they lived only a short distance from each other, Madame von Meck broke down and invited Tchaikovsky to visit her. But Tchaikovsky replied weakly that one should never meet a guardian angel face to face.

For thirteen years, then, Tchaikovsky had a "precious friend," a "superlatively good, dear friend," to whom he could confide his inmost struggles, torments, and aspirations, from whom he could always get sympathetic understanding and appreciation, who could inspire him in the writing of his most ambitious works, and who was able to relieve him of financial problems. Tchaikovsky's sudden marriage to Antonina was a shock which Madame von Meck did not try to conceal, though she handled the whole affair gracefully. And when the marriage was just as quickly disrupted, she expressed her relief and pleasure by increasing her annual subsidy to Tchaikovsky, so that he could thenceforth be completely independent. And when Tchaikovsky was overwhelmed by his wife's demand for money, Madame von Meck paid a large part of the sum that was asked.

This financial independence enabled Tchaikovsky to give up all his musical activity except composition, to travel throughout Europe freely, and to direct his energies into creative work. It was surely no coincidence that he now wrote some of his finest and most popular works: the opera *Eugene Onegin;* the *Symphony No. 4,* which he often described to Madame von Meck as "our symphony"; the Concerto for Violin and Orchestra; the *Capriccio Italien;* the *Ouverture solennelle,*

1812; numerous songs, including his most famous one, "None But the Lonely Heart."

Edward Lockspeiser reveals the dilemma of Tchaikovsky's life at this time. He was the cultured and frequently sentimental gentleman who worked systematically and well, who traveled extensively, and when home spent many an evening playing cards with his nephews. "He rose between seven and eight, drank tea and read the Bible, then studied English or read serious books and took a short walk. He worked from half-past nine to one o'clock, which was his dinner hour. After dinner, no matter what the weather, he took a solitary two-hour walk . . . and it was during these afternoon walks that he did most of his creative work, jotting down memoranda in innumerable notebooks. . . . When he was not composing on his walks, he would recite aloud—usually in French. At four o'clock he had tea, worked from five to seven; then took another walk, this time with company if any were available, before supper at eight o'clock. After supper he would read or play cards—solitaire, if alone—talk or play the piano until eleven, when he retired."

It would have been difficult for a casual acquaintance to associate this "perfect bourgeois" with the man who had to use all manner of subterfuge and duplicity to conceal his sexual deviation, who made cryptic annotations in his diaries about "Sensation Z," and who fell prey frequently to drunken spells. His character was, in Lockspeiser's words, "a formidable contradiction of genuine passion and hypocritical sham."

Between 1881 and 1888 Tchaikovsky did more traveling than composing; and what he wrote was of no particular importance. For a while he was obsessed with the fear that he had written himself out. "Not the slightest musical idea in my head!" he lamented in a letter to Balakirev. "I am beginning to fear that my muse has flown far, far away." Not until 1888 did he produce another masterwork: the *Symphony No. 5.* When the *première* of the symphony was unsuccessful, he was surer than ever that he was through.

In spite of his meager output and the comparative failure of his new symphony, his fame had been growing all the while. In 1884 he had received the Order of St. Vladimir from the Czar. Four years later an annual government pension was conferred on him for life. An extensive tour of Europe as conductor of his works, begun in 1888, was an immense personal success.

While he was in the Caucasus in 1890 he received shattering news. Madame von Meck wrote saying that, due to financial reverses, she had to terminate her annual subsidy. Tchaikovsky replied expressing sympathy for her misfortune, but pointing out that he was now financially self-sufficient and no longer dependent on her generosity for his livelihood. He expressed the hope that their friendship would continue. His letter went unanswered. He wrote others, increasingly concerned over the future of their friendship. These, too, met silence. After he returned to Moscow, Tchaikovsky learned that Madame von Meck was not in financial difficulty and never had been; that she had concocted the story to end their relationship. It may be that she had grown bored with Tchaikovsky and his letters; or that she had discovered that he was a homosexual and was shocked; or, most probable of all, that her strange relationship with Tchaikovsky had created a great deal of unpleasant gossip, and pressure had been put on her by her brother, children, and intimate friends to bring the friendship to a definite end. This was one of the most crushing disasters of Tchaikovsky's life; he suddenly felt that his supports had given way.

In 1891 Tchaikovsky consented to tour the United States for the first time. He arrived in New York City in the spring, and on May 5 helped celebrate the opening of Carnegie Hall by conducting his own *1812* Overture. Everything about America excited him, particularly the ovations that met him everywhere. He was amazed to find that he had so many admirers here, that his music was so well known. But he was far from happy. His stifling depression persisted. Once or twice he burst into tears. He was painfully homesick. "American customs, American manners, and habits generally are attractive to me," he wrote in his diary, "but I enjoy all this like a person sitting at a table set with marvels of gastronomy, devoid of appetite. Only the prospect of returning to Russia can awaken an appetite within me."

But back in Russia his misery deepened; once again he thought he would go mad. In this mood he wrote his last symphony, the Sixth— the *Symphonie pathétique* (*Pathetic* Symphony), title suggested by Modeste. Its concluding movement, one of the most pessimistic utterances in all music, was Tchaikovsky's last will and testament, his own requiem. But there was also a premonition of death in the first movement. Tchaikovsky quoted in the first trombone a phrase from the Russian requiem service, "And Rest Him with the Saints." This theme is not developed; it has no relation to the rest of the melodic material; and it is covered up so as not to be readily observed. This interpolation can only be regarded as Tchaikovsky's awareness that he was writing his last work.

Tchaikovsky himself conducted the *première* of his *Symphonie pathétique* on October 28, 1893. The symphony was not well received. "There was applause and the composer was recalled," reported Modeste, "but with no more enthusiasm than on previous occasion. There was not the mighty, overpowering impression made by the work when it was conducted by Napravnik, on November 18, 1893, and later, wherever it was played."

One day in November 1893—suffering from painful gastric disturbances—Tchaikovsky drank a glass of unboiled water. With a cholera epidemic then raging in St. Petersburg, this was so reckless an act that some have been led to believe (but without a shred of substantiating evidence) that Tchaikovsky was trying to commit suicide. He was infected. Delirium was followed by suffocation. It was impossible to administer the Communion. In his unconscious state he kept repeating the name of Madame von Meck. Modeste told several friends many years later that, in his delirium, the composer kept muttering the word *"Proklyatayal"* It means "Accursed one," and since the feminine gender was used, the reference undoubtedly was to Madame von Meck.

Then "Peter suddenly opened his eyes," wrote Modeste. "There was an indescribable expression of unclouded consciousness. Passing over the others standing in the room, he looked at the three nearest him, and then toward heaven. There was a certain light for a moment in his eyes, which was soon extinguished, at the same time with his breath."

The funeral was impressive. The procession extended for half a mile. Flowers, wreaths, and expressions of grief came from all parts of Russia. Tchaikovsky's story, however, cannot be said to have ended until three months after the composer's death. On January 13, 1894, Nadezhda von Meck died in Wiesbaden, Germany.

HIS MUSIC

THE history of musical Russia in the late nineteenth century is essentially a tale of two cities—St. Petersburg and Moscow. In the former city, "The Russian Five" were fighting a vigorous war for national music (see Rimsky-Korsakov). Moscow became the seat of composers who did not espouse the national cause, but preferred going their own way; and the leading figure in that camp was Tchaikovsky. For several years the undeclared musical war was waged between St. Petersburg and Moscow, with St. Petersburg recognizing no music as Russian unless it followed the patterns and style established by "The Five."

The accusations hurled by St. Petersburg against Tchaikovsky were: (1) he was too eclectic in style; and (2) he was too prone to submit to and be influenced by Western musical culture. "The Five" did not take seriously Tchaikovsky's excursions into musical nationalism, nor the profound influence that the Russian folk song and dance, the Russian temperament and background, had had on his music. To the nationalists, Tchaikovsky's works represented the Western world and not Russia. Tchaikovsky's music—with its elegance, sophistication, and poise—was in striking contrast to the brutal realism, exotic Orientalism, and demoniac primitivism of "The Russian Five." It was, in truth, a compromise between the West and the East; but "The Five" did not tolerate such compromises.

But what sets Tchaikovsky's music most strongly apart from that of "The Five" is its intense emotionalism and subjectivity. "That which is unfamiliar to the human heart," Tchaikovsky once wrote, "should never be the source of musical inspiration." His music is an emotional autobiography in which he confided his inmost feelings. As James Gibbons Huneker once wrote, he delineated "the human soul in the convulsions of love, hate, joy, and fear." And the human soul that he delineated was his own. The effect on an audience is immediate and profound; there are few who can remain untouched by his expressions of grief and inner torment. Unfortunately, never too critical—and always writing too much and too quickly—he sometimes permits his grief to become hysterical, his tenderness to become cloying, his pessimism to degenerate into self-pity.

We recognize these weaknesses; we recognize the fact that much of what he wrote was not inspired. He himself knew that he often combined genius with poor taste, and for this reason he destroyed much and was dissatisfied with more. If he had been as critical while writing a piece of music as he was when it was completed, he would not only have been capable of sweeping to the heights but also of staying there. As it is, only a few of his works are unblemished masterpieces. But even in other compositions there are pages that exert a spell which is irresistible, pages of music filled with incomparable melody and tenderness that come from the heart and go to the heart.

ANALYTICAL NOTES

Orchestral Music. The *Symphony No. 4,* in F minor, completed in 1878, was written for Madame von Meck, with whom Tchaikovsky had begun what was destined to be a unique epistolary friendship. During this correspondence, while Tchaikovsky was working on and completing his symphony, the composer gave his "precious friend" a programmatic guide to his music.

"The introduction is the kernel, the chief thought of the whole symphony," he wrote. "This is Destiny, the fatal power which prevents an impetus toward happiness from reaching its goal, which jealously watches that peace and comfort be not full and cloudless. . . . This might is overpowering and invincible. There is nothing to do but to resign to futile brooding." (The main subject of the introduction is a forceful fanfare for horns and bassoons in octaves; the trombones soon join in, and after them, the woodwinds.)

The main body of the movement begins immediately with the first theme, a syncopated melody for the first violins and cellos. This melody grows in passion and torment before the second important theme is heard—in the clarinet. Tchaikovsky's interpretation follows: "It is better to turn from the realities and to lull oneself in dreams. Oh joy! What a sweet and tender dream. Some benevolent, radiant human image floats by and beckons to me. The importunate first theme of the allegro is now heard far off and now the soul is wholly enwrapped with dreams. All that is gloomy and cheerless is forgotten. Happiness! Happiness! Happiness! No, they are only dreams, and Fate dispels them. . . . There is no port. Sail this ocean until it absorbs you and swallows you in its depth."

The second movement begins with a sweetly sad melody for oboe and plucked strings. After the cellos repeat this melody with countersubjects in woodwinds, the violins and cellos arrive with a new emotional subject against woodwinds and horn harmonies. A much brighter tune appears midway in clarinets and bassoons, after which earlier material is repeated. Tchaikovsky said of this movement that it shows "another phase of sadness. Here is that melancholy feeling which enwraps one when he sits at night alone in the house, exhausted by work. . . . One regrets the past and there is no desire to begin life anew. There were joyful minutes when young blood was seething and life gave gladness. There were also sad moments and irrevocable losses.

All this is now so far away. And it is all so sad and yet so sweet to muse over the past."

About the third movement, Tchaikovsky said: "There is no determined feeling, no exact impressions. . . . Here are capricious arabesques, elusive images which pass in the imagination when one has tasted a little wine and experiences the first phase of intoxication. The mood is not joyful, but it is not sad." Tchaikovsky also provided a succinct analysis of this music: "There is a new effect. . . . At first the strings play alone and pizzicato throughout. In the trio, the woodwind instruments enter and play alone. At the end all three choirs toss short phrases to each other. I believe that the effect of sounds and colors will be most interesting."

The finale begins with a tempestuous theme in strings and woodwinds. There follows the well-known Russian folk melody, "In the fields there stands a birch tree," given by the woodwinds. After a return of the opening stormy subject, a majestic melody is pronounced by full orchestra. Tchaikovsky's description of this movement is as follows: "If you find no pleasure in yourself, look about you. Go to the people. See how they enjoy themselves. . . . This is a picture of a folk holiday. . . . Blame yourself if you find the world sad and gloomy. There is still happiness, simple native happiness. Rejoice in the happiness of others, and you will be able to live."

Fate speaks even more forcefully in the *Symphony No. 5*, in E minor (1888), than in the introduction to the Fourth Symphony. The "Fate" theme is heard at the beginning of the first movement, in the clarinets, then is worked out in a thirty-seven-measure slow introduction. It also recurs in the other three movements—relentless, inescapable. After the introduction, the principal section of the first movement begins with a gentle theme in clarinets and bassoons. This theme is given excited attention. A highly emotional second theme suddenly appears in the violins, is evolved with great feeling, then dies out. A pizzicato chord in the strings and a brief passage for the woodwinds lead to the third major melody of the movement: a song of great yearning for the violins. The development section elaborates on the two principal themes, while the recapitulation (ushered in with the first theme in the bassoon) restores the material as it appeared in the exposition. The first theme is prominent in the coda.

An introductory passage in the lower strings prefaces the main subject of the second movement. It is a romantic melody for solo horn which a Tin Pan Alley tunesmith appropriated for "Moon Love." A second poignant melody follows in the oboe, after which both themes are given passionate treatment by the strings. A third theme with a Russian folk-song inflection then appears in the solo clarinet, beginning calmly enough, but soon growing in excitement. The full orchestra now exclaims the "Fate" theme, after which the earlier melodies are repeated.

The third movement is, in place of the usual scherzo, a waltz. The principal subject is given by the first violins. Toward the end of the movement, the "Fate" theme returns ominously in clarinets and bassoons. The "Fate" theme also opens the finale. Transposed from minor to major, it is now given proudly, even triumphantly, by the strings. As was the case with the first movement, this "Fate" theme is the basic material of a long, slow introductory section. When it is over, a volcanic theme erupts in the strings to begin the allegro section. The lyrical second theme, first in the woodwinds and after that in the strings, brings some repose. But with another outcry of the "Fate" theme by the brass, the mood once again becomes stormy; the agitation continues with the development of the two new themes of the movement. A climax is reached with a majestic presentation of the "Fate" theme by the strings against triplets in the woodwinds, and after that by two trumpets in unison. The symphony ends with a brief and energetic recollection by the wind instruments of the main theme of the first movement in the major.

While Tchaikovsky was writing his *Symphony No. 6,* in B minor (1893), he had some mysterious program in mind, which, as he said, "will remain an enigma to all." He never revealed what that program was. When the symphony received its first performance—in St. Petersburg on October 28, 1893—it appeared on the program merely as *Symphony No. 6,* in B minor. But when, soon after the *première,* Tchaikovsky was ready to dispatch his manuscript to his publishers, he felt the need for some descriptive title and said so to Modeste. Modeste made one or two unsatisfactory suggestions. "Suddenly," he revealed, "I thought, 'Pathetic.' I went back to the room—I remember it as though it were yesterday—and I said the word to Peter. 'Splendid, Modi, bravo, *Pathetic,'* and he wrote in my presence the title that will remain forever."

Tchaikovsky had had qualms about the merits of the Fifth Symphony, particularly after its unsuccessful performance. But though the *Symphony No. 6* was not received more enthusiastically, he had no doubts. "I consider it the best of all my works to date. . . . I love it as I never loved any of my musical children."

The pathos of the symphony is felt immediately in the first movement, which has been described as a "convulsion of the soul." It begins with a theme filled with foreboding in the solo bassoon. When this theme is taken over by the strings and woodwinds (in a brisker tempo and with a change of key), it loses its ominous character but has acquired greater melancholy. An emotional upheaval follows and is dissipated. A plangent melody is now given by the strings. Grief turns to resignation with a succeeding theme, presented first as a dialogue between flute and bassoon, but the plangent melody is back with richer orchestration and greater intensity of feeling. Suddenly there comes a shattering chord. The first subject is now treated with considerable agitation. It is at this point that a funereal idea is interpolated—a quotation from the Russian requiem service—in the first trombone; Tchaikovsky is believed to speak here about his premonition of death. The agitation continues until a return of the grief-stricken melody restores an atmosphere of utter depression. The grief now becomes almost too intense to be borne. With quiet dignity, a subject in the brass, against a descending scale in plucked strings, brings the pathos to a resolution.

The second movement, while marked "Allegro con grazia," is a scherzo in form. A graceful dance melody is begun by the cellos and carried on by the woodwinds against plucked strings. If there is joy in this music, the joy in evanescent. The trio, with its lugubrious melody set against the beat of timpani, is once again in the tragic vein. The opening scherzo section returns in a different and more outspoken instrumentation.

The third movement is a march in which a single theme is prominent. Before that theme appears, there is an eight-bar introductory passage for strings and woodwinds. The germ of a march theme is heard in the oboe, then in other sections of the orchestra. For a while the introductory material is brought back. The march theme, at last, emerges with full force in the entire orchestra.

There is optimism in the vigor of the third movement; but in the fourth there is only despair. This is a lamentation sometimes described as "suicide music." The movement opens with an outcry of grief. A succession of ideas plunge us ever deeper into the morass of despair; the most important of these is a mournful elegy for the strings begun quietly, but increasing in emotional intensity as the wind instruments join in. The opening outcry is heard again; the mournful elegy is repeated for the last time. The music ebbs away into a deathlike silence: the pain has now become too great to be openly expressed.

The *Concerto No. 1,* in B-flat minor, for piano and orchestra, begins with one of Tchaikovsky's best-loved themes—having been given wide circulation through a motion picture and as a Hit Parade song, "Tonight We Love." This theme is the core of an extended introductory section and is never again referred to in the rest of the movement. The main section concerns itself with two new ideas. The first is a lively, rhythmic melody which Tchaikovsky said he had heard blind Ukrainian beggars sing; the second is lyrical, given first by horns and woodwinds before being discussed by the piano. Both subjects are worked out with dramatic power and with many bravura passages for the piano. The second movement is a succession of melodies in Tchaikovsky's ingratiatingly tender vein. The first appears in the flute; the second is given by the oboe and clarinet, accompanied by the bassoon; the third —a waltz tune that Tchaikovsky transformed from a French melody— is found in violins and cellos. The finale has unmistakable national character. The piano plunges into the vertiginous music of the first theme, which has the rhythmic energy of a Cossack dance. In a more relaxed mood, the violins (accompanied by horns) present a folk song. These ideas are worked out with breadth. In the coda, the first dance melody is given prominent treatment.

The *Concerto in D major,* for violin and orchestra, was written in 1878, three years after the First Piano Concerto. It begins with a declamation for the soloist. The orchestra enters to hint at the first theme, which is soon fully presented by the violin. There is some decorative treatment of this refrain before the expressive second melody arrives, also in the violin; this, too, is subjected to virtuoso elaboration. The beautiful melody of the second movement unfolds in the muted violin after twelve introductory measures in the woodwinds. There is a second effective strain (again in the violin), but the first is recalled for more intensive discussion. Without any interruption, the orchestra enters with nervous accents in a sixteen-measure introduction. The violin is heard in a short cadenza, after which it launches upon an impetuous Russian dance, evolved from the opening orchestral accents. The lyrical second episode, heard in the solo violin, brings repose after this exciting outburst of energy.

The fantasy-overture *Romeo and Juliet* is the most glowing love music Tchaikovsky ever wrote. Balakirev, the founder of "The Russian Five," suggested to Tchaikovsky that he set the Shakespeare drama to music in an orchestral composition and even outlined its structure. Tchaikovsky—still young and an apprentice—followed Balakirev's advice and outline. And he produced his first masterwork—though not before he had subjected his work to two extended revisions.

A solemn chant for the woodwinds, describing Friar Laurence, is heard in the opening measures. A darker atmosphere enters in the strings and becomes ominous with a theme for plucked strings. It is a warning of the storm that soon rages with fury in the orchestra, describing the feud between the Capulets and the Montagues. But soon we hear the wonderful love music of Romeo (in English horn, muted violas, against plucked strings and syncopated horns), which so many have come to know through the popular-song hit "Our Love." Juliet answers Romeo with a tender, undulating melody in muted and divided strings. The woodwinds grow more ardent as they return with Romeo's melody. But the idyl is shattered with the intrusion of the feud music. Above the fever and storm of this music rises Juliet's sinuous song, now in the woodwinds, inspiring the orchestra to erupt into a passionate declaration of Romeo's melody. But as the orchestra becomes agitated, there is a hint of coming tragedy. A rumbling in the kettledrums and a sudden silence tell of the tragic destiny of the lovers. The fantasy ends with a tender epilogue, an expression of grief over the death of Romeo and Juliet.

Marche slave (1876) was written for a concert held for the benefit of Serbian soldiers wounded in the war of liberation against the Turks. It is in three sections. In the first, the strings give the principal march melody after a brief introduction. Derived from an old Serbian folk song, it has a dirgelike character. The trio section quotes two other folk songs together with the Russian national anthem, "God Save the Czar." In the concluding part, the opening march becomes an exultant song of triumph, as a Serbian victory is assured.

Francesca da Rimini, a symphonic fantasy inspired by Dante's *Inferno,* was completed the same year as *Marche slave.* The fantasy begins with torrential music describing that part of the medieval Hell to which the damned are consigned for torture. A brief pause separates this disturbed section from the tender page speaking of the love of Francesca and Paolo; here the principal love theme is heard in the clarinet to the accompaniment of plucked strings. The fantasy ends as it began, with the turbulent music describing Hell and its punishments.

The *1812* Overture was commissioned in 1880, to be played during the consecration of the Temple of Christ the Redeemer in Moscow.

The Temple (completed in 1880) had been built as a memorial to Napoleon's defeat in Russia in 1812; therefore, Tchaikovsky used that historic event as the program for his work. Intending his music for outdoor performance, Tchaikovsky scored it for large orchestra and an expanded percussion section that included actual cannon which were to boom at intervals.

The introductory theme in woodwinds and strings is the Russian hymn "God, Preserve Thy People." In the main body of the overture, the Battle of Borodino is described realistically. In this struggle, the two opposing armies are identified by quotations from their national anthems—*"La Marseillaise"* and "God Save the Czar." After a thunderous climax, the Russian national anthem is sounded jubilantly to proclaim a Russian victory.

Capriccio Italien (1880), which makes use of Italian folk themes, was inspired by a visit to Italy. In the slow introduction, there is a trumpet fanfare based on bugle calls heard by Tchaikovsky at the barracks of the Royal Cuirassiers. Two popular Italian tunes follow: a flowing melody in the strings and a popular tune in the oboes. A change of tempo to allegro brings on march music. A repetition of some of the introductory material leads to a tarantella, with which the fantasy is brought to an exciting conclusion.

The *Casse-Noisette,* or *Nutcracker Suite* (1892), originated as a ballet score. The text came from a story of E. T. A. Hoffmann adapted by Dumas. A girl dreams that the nutcracker she received as a Christmas gift is a handsome prince. He leads the toys to battle against the mice. Then he takes the girl to Jam Mountain, in Arabia, where she is greeted by the Sugarplum Fairy and is entertained with games, dances, and toys.

This is one of the few works which reveal Tchaikovsky in a lighthearted mood—with delight and wonder in a child's fanciful world. It begins with a "Miniature Overture," the instrumentation of which dispenses with the lower string instruments. There are two gay themes, the first heard immediately in the violins and the second coming in the violins as the other strings provide a pizzicato accompaniment. The "March" that follows has a pert march melody in clarinet, horn, and trumpets. The main subject of the trio is a staccato theme divided between woodwinds and strings. In the "Dance of the Sugarplum Fairy" the celesta becomes a member of the symphony orchestra. It is heard in a delicate melody after four introductory measures. Several dances follow. The first is a rhythmically exciting "Trepak." Next comes an exotic "Arab Dance," with a languorous melody played by the clarinet in the low register. A "Chinese Dance" begins with a capricious subject mainly for the flute with the piccolo. In the "Dance of the Flutes" the rhythm is given in the introduction, followed by a gracious dance melody for three flutes, contrasted with another dance idea in the trumpet. The closing piece is the "Waltz of the Flowers." The lilting waltz appears in the horns and is continued in the clarinets. A second subject is given by the strings, and a third by flute and oboe; after each of these, the waltz melody is brought back.

Ralph Vaughan Williams

"In Vaughan Williams we hear the historic speech of the English people. What he gives us, in music, is the language of the breakfast table. It is also the language that Shakespeare wrote."

—*Hubert Foss*

BORN: Down Ampney, England, October 12, 1872.

DIED: London, England, August 26, 1958.

MAJOR WORKS: *Orchestral Music*—Fantasia on a Theme by Thomas Tallis, for double string orchestra; A London Symphony; A Pastoral Symphony; Symphony No. 4, in F minor; Symphony No. 6, in E minor; *Sinfonia Antartica;* Symphony No. 8; Symphony No. 9. ALSO: A Sea Symphony; Symphony No. 5, in D major; Symphony No. 7; The Lark Ascending, for violin and orchestra; Concerto Accademico, for violin and orchestra; Concerto for Piano and Orchestra; Suite for Viola and Orchestra; Concerto for Oboe and Strings; Serenade to Music; Hugh the Drover, Sir John in Love, Riders to the Sea, The Pilgrim's Progress, operas; Job, masque; Mass in G minor; Sancta Civitas, oratorio; On Wenlock Edge, cycle for tenor, string quartet, and piano.

HIS LIFE

UP TO the time he was thirty-two years old, Ralph Vaughan Williams gave no indication of becoming much more than an industrious and efficient church musician. He had been well trained: he had attended the Royal College of Music in London, where his teachers included Stanford and Parry, and after that he had studied with Max Bruch in Berlin. He had also received a comprehensive academic schooling at Charterhouse and Trinity College, Cambridge. After having received his doctorate in music at Cambridge, in 1901, he assumed his first professional post, that of organist at the St. Barnabas Church in London's South Lambeth. For the next three years he accompanied the services, trained the church choir, gave organ recitals, and directed a choral and orchestral society which he had helped organize. His most important achievement up to 1904 was the editing of an English hymnal, the sum total of his creative activity up to that year being the writing of a few hymns and a few minor orchestral pieces. "I wondered if I was wasting my time," he wrote in retrospect many years later. "The years were passing and I was adding nothing to the sum of musical invention. But I know now that two years of close association with some of the best (as well as some of the worst) tunes in the world was a better musical education than any amount of sonatas and fugues."

Then something happened to change his musical life and at the same time to convert him from a humble musician into England's greatest twentieth-century composer. That "something" was contact with English folk music. A few examples of Tudor folk songs happened to come to his notice. He felt as if he had suddenly come upon a new world. His former interest in church music was superseded by a veritable passion for the English folk song. In the crucial year of 1904 he became a member of the Folk-Song Society, which was then devoting itself to the study of and research in the field of English folk music. As a member of this group he made a firsthand study of the native music of Norfolk. Many of the songs uncovered by the Society had been forgotten for generations. Some of them were given a fresh life through tasteful harmonizations and adaptations by Vaughan Williams and were later to be popularized among the concert audiences of the world by famous choral groups. The most notable of these songs are: "The Turtle Dove," "Down in Yon Forest," "We've Been Awhile Awandering," and "The Dark-Eyed Sailor."

Contact with an enthusiasm for the English folk song gave Vaughan Williams the materials he needed to build ambitious new musical works. Between 1905 and 1907 he wrote three Norfolk rhapsodies for orchestra, which drew their content from the songs he had uncovered in that section of England. He also produced a major choral work entitled *Toward the Unknown Region,* which was English in style and feeling even though it was inspired by an American poet, Walt Whitman. But the composer was not satisfied with the results. He had found the materials, but what he lacked was the necessary skill. Impatiently, he discarded what he had written and for a time deserted composition altogether. In 1908 he went to Paris to study with Maurice Ravel for a few months. Although the teacher was younger than his pupil, Vaughan Williams learned much from Ravel. Contact with the music of Ravel and other contemporary composers taught him subtlety of effect, nuance, color, and atmosphere. Most important of all, Vaughan Williams' abstention from creative work brought perspective. He now knew that his primary mistake in the *Norfolk Rhapsodies* had been in making the folk song his final goal instead of merely a point of departure.

In 1909 Vaughan Williams completed his first important piece of music, and one of his most frequently heard compositions, the *Fantasia on a Theme by Thomas Tallis*. Within the next few years he made rapid progress, his most important works including two symphonies, one of which was the famous *London* Symphony.

At the outbreak of World War I, Vaughan Williams was forty-two. Despite his age, he enlisted in the Territorial Royal Army Military Corps. For the first three years of the war he scrubbed floors and served as stretcher-bearer in hospitals in France and Macedonia. He then passed an examination for a commission in the Artillery and saw service on the battlefields of France.

After the war he joined the faculty of the Royal College of Music. He conducted classes in composition at the Royal College, though he was never enthusiastic about teaching. He felt strongly that his classes enabled him to keep in direct contact with the younger men and their thinking; that an older and an established composer was made to question his own standards and aesthetics by the reactions of his students to them.

The onetime humble organist had become one of England's greatest musicians. For six years, 1920–26, he was the conductor of the renowned Bach Choir in London. *Premières* of his new works became events of national significance. Among his most important compositions in the decade following World War I were his *Pastoral* Symphony, the *Concerto Accademico,* for violin and orchestra, *Flos Campi* (a suite for viola, small chorus, and small orchestra), an opera-oratorio, *Shepherds of the Delectable Mountains* (the first ingredient of his opera *The Pilgrim's Progress,* which he completed and introduced several decades later), the oratorio *Sancta Civitas,* and the "masque for dancing," *Job.*

In 1922 he paid a brief visit to the United States, conducting his *Pastoral* Symphony at the Norfolk Music Festival on June 7. He returned to the United States a decade later to deliver at Bryn Mawr College some lectures later published as *National Music;* and in 1954 he lectured at Cornell and Yale universities.

He was a familiar figure to Londoners near the Victoria Embankment in the years after World War I. On his way to and from the Royal

College of Music he used to pass the Embankment every day in the week with meticulous punctuality, his large head lowered in contemplation. His appearance suggested the storybook composer, particularly in his indifference to dress. His coat was usually too large and was generally thrown out of shape by the fact that one of the buttons was attached to the wrong buttonhole. He wore an old bowler hat which showed signs of abuse and age. In his hand was a frayed carpetbag holding his books and papers.

When Elgar died, in 1934, the first position in English music was automatically assumed by Vaughan Williams. In 1935 he received one of the highest awards that can be bestowed on a composer by His Majesty's government: the Order of Merit. The world outside England readily acknowledged him as one of the half dozen or so great creative figures in twentieth-century music. His seventieth birthday was celebrated as a national event in England, in 1942, despite the fact that the country was then in one of the grimmest phases of World War II. Six concerts of his works were broadcast in his honor, while several English composers wrote new works to pay him tribute. Once again all England honored Vaughan Williams on his birthday, on October 12, 1952. Four months after his eightieth birthday, Vaughan Williams married his secretary, Ursula Woods, at the St. Pancras Church in London. He died half a dozen years later, in London, on August 26, 1958.

HIS MUSIC

IN HIS book, *National Music,* Vaughan Williams wrote: "If the roots of your art are firmly planted in your own soil and that soil has anything individual to give you, you may still gain the whole world and not lose your own soul."

The roots of Vaughan Williams' art are in the soil of the English folk song, and the soil has proved fertile. But before he could make his country's folk music an integral element of a vibrant and living art, Vaughan Williams had to arrive at a basic truth: adaptation and quotation were not enough. His first attempts at national music represented nothing more than an attempt to provide a symphonic dress for folk songs. The *Norfolk Rhapsodies* used such airs as "The Captain's Apprentice" and "A Bold Young Sailor Courted Me" (native to King's Lynn, Norfolk) in a kind of orchestral potpourri. This was good editing, good adapting, and good organizing—but Vaughan Williams immediately realized that it was not good art. It was only after his study in Paris and his temporary absence from composition that Vaughan Williams discovered how to make English folk art serve him, instead of him serving English folk art. Thenceforth it was to be a stimulus. Its melodic, rhythmic, and contrapuntal traits would dictate the style of Vaughan Williams' own music. A folk song would serve the function of stirring and arousing his imagination toward the production of entirely new material.

Without question, Vaughan Williams' partiality to modal writing and to counterpoint—and the sobriety and serenity of his style—stems from English folk music. But these elements have been fused with an introspection and at times a mysticism that are Vaughan Williams' own traits. Nor has Vaughan Williams been content to live exclusively in the past. Through the years his style has continually undergone transformation as, aware of what was happening in the musical world around him, he leaned toward greater boldness in his harmonic and rhythmic language and showed greater independence in his use of tonality. Through a graceful fusion of the English musical past with the contemporary musical world—and a further fusion of these with his own individual idiosyncrasies and approaches—Vaughan Williams has realized an art that is highly personal.

ANALYTICAL NOTES

Orchestral Music. The *Fantasia on a Theme by Thomas Tallis,* for double string orchestra, combines two old forms: the fantasia and the concerto grosso. The fantasia form provided Vaughan Williams with a mold in which a germinal idea could grow and change elastically without structural restrictions. The concerto grosso allowed Vaughan Williams to divide his string orchestra into several groups, including a quartet of solo instruments.

Thomas Tallis (c.1505–85) was an English church composer who, in 1567, had written eight tunes on eight church modes for the Archbishop's Metrical Psalter. The third of these tunes was the inspiration for Vaughan Williams; but though the germinal idea is by Tallis, the *Fantasia* as a whole represents only Vaughan Williams. We hear passing suggestions of the Tallis theme in the lower strings after a few subdued chords for the rest of the orchestra. The Tallis melody then appears in the orchestra against tremolo chords in the violins and is repeated by the first violins with some decoration. The theme now becomes the subject of a dialogue between the complete string orchestra and the smaller section; it is then taken up by the quartet. The melody receives varied treatment and imaginative elaboration. It is heard antiphonally; it appears as material for solo instruments; it becomes the core of a contrapuntal network. All the while, the melody expands and changes, acquiring new interest. A tranquil mood is maintained almost to the very end.

The *London* Symphony, completed in 1913 but greatly revised seven years afterward, is a musical picture of the city, though the composer tried at first to disavow any specific program. A program was, however, provided by the English conductor Albert Coates and has been accepted by the composer as functional.

The first movement represents to Coates the following: "London sleeps; the Thames flows serenely through the city; the city awakens; we get glimpses of different parts of the city, its varied character, its humor, its activity." A tranquil passage for muted strings, clarinet, and horns opens the first movement, giving a picture of the sleeping city. Quivering strings suggest the flowing Thames, while brief motives in horns, trumpets, and trombones tell of the awakening city. The main body of the movement is introduced by the forceful entry of the entire orchestra: the city is awake. The fragmentary material in the introductory section is now developed into spacious themes, which are evolved slowly rather than being fully presented at once.

The second movement is "a portrait of the region known as Bloomsbury; a damp and foggy twilight; poverty and tragedy; an old musician outside a 'pub' plays 'Sweet Lavender.'" This movement is an atmospheric tone poem, the mood for which is immediately established with a nostalgic theme for English horn against muted strings. The song "Sweet Lavender" appears in the solo viola; and it is the solo viola (representing the old musician) that speaks the last word in the movement.

In the third movement, Coates has written, "one must imagine oneself sitting late on a Saturday night on one of the benches of the Temple [Victoria] Embankment. The Thames flows serenely by." This is an orchestral nocturne, though in the scherzo form. There is a vivacious dance theme in the clarinets and after that in the violins and woodwinds. A less rhythmic melody later appears in cellos and horns. After a return of the dance melody, a new idea is found in flutes and oboes and is built up with considerable force. Earlier material is repeated. The movement ends with a faint murmur in the strings: the fog is descending over the Thames.

The fourth movement is a "picture of the crueler aspects of the city: the unemployed and the unfortunate. The music ends with chimes of Big Ben on Westminster Tower. The Epilogue presents a picture of London as a whole." After a loud and energetic introductory section, the first important theme—a vigorous march tune—arises in violas, cellos, clarinets, and bassoons. This theme evolves fully and is extensively elaborated upon. After a repetition of the introductory measures, a forceful statement is made by cellos and trombone. After it has died out, the march theme is brought back. The chiming of Big Ben on Westminster Tower is reproduced in the harp. There is a pause, and the Epilogue begins with an undulating figure in strings and flute, followed by the themes of the first-movement introduction.

In writing his third symphony, the *Pastoral* Symphony (1922), Vaughan Williams had no intention of creating a nature portrait or even of conveying tonally his emotional response to the beauties of nature. "Pastoral" refers to the prevailing mood of the entire work: serenity and contemplation. The composer himself pointed out how limited was the range of his dynamics and tempo: "There are few fortissimos and few allegros; the only real quick passage is the coda to the third movement, and that is all pianissimo."

In the first movement, the principal melody is given by the harp, cellos, and double basses. A solo violin, soon joined by oboe, gives reply. For a while, but only for a while, the tranquillity is disturbed by an outburst in the orchestra. But the briefly shattered idyllic atmosphere returns with a delicate melody in the English horn and a diaphanous passage for the strings, and continues to the end of the movement.

An even more profound serenity pervades the second movement. There is a haunting melody for solo horn over divided muted strings. With this melody, a wonderful feeling of repose settles over the music. There is later a fanfare passage for a "natural" trumpet (a bugle), culminating in a cadenza consisting of natural tones suggesting a shepherd's horn in soliloquy. After a brief loud eruption in full orchestra, the repose returns with the gentle voice of the "natural" horn and with chords for divided strings played *ppp*.

The third movement was described by the composer as "a slow dance." Three ideas are important: the first is for trumpets and trombones; the second is for flute accompanied by harp arpeggios, and string tremolos; the third is for trumpet.

In the finale, above a gentle roll of the timpani, there is heard (as if from a distance) a wordless chant for soprano or tenor solo. After the chant has ebbed away, we come to the principal theme of this movement, heard in the woodwinds, harp, and horns. The orchestra recalls the wordless chant before working itself up into a dramatic climax. The main theme is brought back in muted strings. After this, the wordless chant once again rises above the violins and sinks back into silence.

The *Symphony No. 4,* in F minor (1935), was a radical departure from anything Vaughan Williams had written up to that time. In this symphony the composer utilized astringent modernism. Two themes, heard in the opening measures of the first movement, return in various transformations throughout the entire work. The first is a chromatic four-note motive in violins and woodwinds appearing after five introductory measures; the second, by contrast, is a motive with giant intervallic strides shooting upwards which comes a few bars later in woodwinds and plucked strings. The exposition brings up two other important themes—one, a rhapsodic and singable melody for strings; the other, a forceful subject for strings, horns, and woodwinds. But it is the two basic ideas heard at the beginning of the movement that come in for attention in the development section. Only after the development do the two important melodies of the exposition return in a varied form.

The second movement is brought in by the theme from the preceding movement built on wide ascending intervals. This is followed by a new, folklike melody in the violins against pizzicato of cellos and basses. Another important idea in this movement is a theme for solo flute. The movement ends with the first basic motive in muted trombones, followed by a rhapsodic cadenza for solo flute.

The scherzo, which is the third movement, is constructed mainly out of the narrowly chromatic motive of the first movement, though a sailor's-hornpipe subject appears intermittently. The two basic ideas of the first movement are combined with new ideas in the finale. One of these new subjects is a vigorous marching tune, with which the movement opens; a second is a singing passage for horns and woodwinds. The basic motives are now heard in a variety of guises. In the spacious fugue which comes as an epilogue, these motives are contrapuntally interwoven with consummate skill.

The *Symphony No. 6,* in E minor, was begun toward the end of World War II and completed in peacetime, in 1947. It is in four movements, each of the three (in the composer's words) having "its tail attached to the head of its neighbor." The nucleus of the first movement is a noble choralelike melody first heard glowingly in first violins, supported by violas, flutes, and English horn. The syncopated main theme of the second movement is heard at once. After this comes a loud flourish in the brass and in the woodwinds, and a soft one in the strings. There is an important subject for the trumpets which takes its figure from the main theme. A passage for English horns leads into the third movement, a scherzo, which (once again in the composer's description) is "fugal in texture but not in structure." The Epilogue, as Vaughan Williams calls the finale, is the apotheosis of the symphony, one of the most striking pages of music in contemporary symphonic literature. It is played quietly throughout, and the music "drifts about contrapuntally with occasional whiffs of themes" (the composer's words). The English music critic Dyneley Hussey said that this movement is "the quietest piece of music imaginable and has so little apparent movement that it might be described as stillness made audible."

The *Sinfonia Antartica*—Vaughan Williams' Seventh (1952)—was derived from music for a motion picture, *Scott of the Antarctic*. Much of the interest of this score lies in its atmospheric effects: in the landscape picture of the frozen South; in the picturesque description of such antarctic animals as penguins and whales. Besides a large orchestra—including such unorthodox instruments as a vibraphone and a wind machine—this score requires a soprano (singing a wordless chant) and a female chorus.

The *Symphony No. 8*, in D minor (1956), is an unusual work in that the first movement consists of a set of variations on isolated figures rather than a stated theme. Perhaps the high point of this work is the slow movement, scored entirely for strings, as deeply poetic a page as this composer ever produced.

Vaughan Williams intended his *Symphony No. 9*, in E minor (1958), as a personal testament, almost as if he realized that this was his swan song. After the final bar the composer appended the word "niente" (nothing) underscoring the prevailing pessimism and despair of the music from the first movement to the finale. An integrating element in this work is the recurrent use (in various guises) of a poignant theme which first makes its appearance in the first movement.

Giuseppe Verdi

"Verdi was the last great hero of Italian opera, and with him ends the lineage that started with Monteverdi."

—*Paul Henry Láng*

BORN: Le Roncole, Italy, October 10, 1813.

DIED: Milan, January 27, 1901.

MAJOR WORKS: *Operas*—Rigoletto; Il Trovatore; La Traviata; Aida; Otello; Falstaff. *Choral Music*—Requiem Mass. ALSO: Ernani, Luisa Miller, I Vespri Siciliani, Simon Boccanegra, Un Ballo in Maschera, La Forza del Destino, Don Carlos, operas; Quattro Pezzi Sacri; Quartet in E minor.

HIS LIFE

VERDI was of peasant stock, the son of the local innkeeper and grocer. The child gave frequent evidence of his interest in music, though at first he showed no signs of great talent. His parents, however, noticed his instinctive responses to the organ music in the church, the violin playing of a ragged wandering fiddler, and the grinding of hand organs in the streets. They got him an old spinet, and from the first day it became his most precious possession. A story is told of how the child, unable to get the chords he wanted, pummeled the strings of the spinet until some of the hammers broke. A kindly neighbor repaired the instrument and placed a plaque inside reading: "These hammers were repaired by . . . me . . . seeing the good disposition the young Verdi has shown for learning to play this instrument . . ." The spinet, with the plaque in it, is preserved in the Milan Museum.

The local organist was recruited to teach the boy. He made excellent progress. Verdi's father was astute enough to realize that a village such as Le Roncole could never provide the education required by a gifted boy. He sent his son to nearby Busseto to live with a cobbler's family. There, Verdi attracted the interest of Antonio Barezzi, a merchant of groceries and wines, from whom Father Verdi bought much of his stock. Barezzi was a fine amateur musician who played several instruments and was president of the Busseto Philharmonic Society. He offered young Verdi a job and made it possible for him to study with the organist of the Busseto Cathedral and the director of the local Philharmonic Society, Ferdinando Provesi. Verdi made notable strides. One day, when the organist of the Busseto Cathedral failed to appear, Verdi substituted for him and impressed everybody present with his talent for improvisation. He helped Provesi in directing the orchestra and by copying out the instrumental parts. He also did a great deal of composing—mostly tunes and marches played by the town band, as well as some cantatas and smaller vocal pieces. An orchestral overture, written when he was fifteen, was played in one of the Busseto theaters as an introduction to Rossini's *The Barber of Seville*. So deeply were the citizens of Busseto impressed with the boy's ability that they provided a fund to send him to Milan to study at the Conservatory.

Verdi went to Milan in 1832. He was turned down for the Conservatory for three reasons: he was too old, the maximum age for admission being fourteen; his training in harmony and theory had been inadequate; and he had thus far shown too few indications of talent for the rules to be waived in his favor. The Conservatory committee ruled that he was *"privo di talento musicale"*—"lacking in musical talent." Verdi's disappointment was great. He had to study privately with Vincenzo Lavigna, a local opera composer of considerable renown and a splendid musician.

Soon after coming to Milan, Verdi made his public debut—but as the director of a musical performance rather than composer. Attending a rehearsal of Haydn's *The Creation*, Verdi was asked to substitute for the absent music director. He did so well that he was invited to take over the actual performances.

When Ferdinando Provesi died in 1833, Verdi decided to go back to Busseto. For one thing, he hoped to get the Cathedral post vacated by Provesi's death. For another, he was lonesome for the lovely Margherita Barezzi, daughter of his onetime benefactor, with whom he used to play piano duets. He returned to Busseto, but was able to realize only one of his two ambitions. As the Cathedral post was already filled, he had to satisfy himself with an appointment as conductor of the Philharmonic Society. He did succeed, however, in winning Margherita, and married her on May 4, 1836.

He stayed in Busseto on and off for about four years. This period did little to advance his career as composer. He decided, at last, to return to Milan, bringing back with him not only his family (increased by a child) but also the manuscript of his first opera, *Oberto*. Securing a performance for his opera presented heartbreaking obstacles. Verdi persevered, hurdled those obstacles, and saw *Oberto* produced at La Scala on November 17, 1839. It was so successful that it was given several performances, was accepted for publication by Ricordi, and won for its young composer a La Scala contract for three new operas.

For the first of these three projects Verdi decided to try his hand at a comic opera, *Un Giorno di Regno*. While he was deep at work, disaster struck. First he fell ill. Then his son, Icilio, died. Eight months later his wife also died. His comic opera was written during one of the most tragic periods of his life and, as though to provide a fitting ending, was a fiasco when produced at La Scala on September 5, 1840.

For a while Verdi courted the idea of renouncing composition altogether. But the director of La Scala had not lost faith in him. He put a new libretto in Verdi's hands, *Nabucco*. "With this score," wrote Verdi, "my musical career really began. . . . It was a group of carpenters that gave me my first assurance of success. The artists were singing as badly as they knew how and the orchestra seemed bent only on drowning out the noise made by the workmen who were doing some alterations in the building. Presently, the chorus began to sing, as carelessly as before, the *'Va, pensiero,'* but before they had got through half a dozen bars the theater was as still as a church. The men had left off their work one by one and there they were sitting about on the ladders and scaffolding, listening. When the number was finished, they broke out into the noisiest applause I ever heard, crying, *'Bravo, bravo, viva il maestro!'* and pounding on the woodwork with their tools."

Nabucco, introduced at La Scala on March 9, 1842, was a triumph. It made Verdi one of the most popular composers of the day. Food, delicacies, clothing, and toys were named after him. The opera went from one Italian city to the next, gathering new tributes wherever it was heard. For his next opera, Verdi received the highest fee any Italian composer could command at that time.

That opera, *I Lombardi,* involved Verdi in the first of several conflicts with the censor. The Austrian authorities, then politically in control, were bent on keeping Italy in complete subjection. Patriotic Italians were everywhere secretly nursing the dream of freedom, but nowhere more so than in Milan. What Austrian officials objected to in *I Lombardi* was the representation on the stage of a church ritual. But what really disturbed them was the contemporary political significance in some of the numbers. Verdi insisted that he would not allow a change of text. A compromise was finally reached with the substitution of a single religious number for another (with which the censor saved face), and *I Lombardi* was seen at La Scala on February 11, 1843. The audience responded warmly to Verdi's music, but excitedly to the pieces with political overtones. Thenceforth, Verdi was to the Milanese a political as well as a musical hero.

With *Ernani* (written on order for the celebrated Teatro La Fenice in Venice), Verdi had other troubles, besides the censor, to worry about. The principal soprano wanted a bravura aria for the closing scene. The director of the Venetian opera company objected to Verdi's choice of a basso and to his insistence on having the horn played on the stage in one of the scenes. The censor found one of the episodes politically dangerous. Verdi stood his ground on basic issues, though he was ready to make minor compromises. *Ernani* was performed on March 9, 1844, and was a huge success. It was seen in fifteen Italian theaters that year and became the first Verdi opera to be performed in London and New York.

Between 1844 and 1851 Verdi wrote ten operas, most of them successes, some failures. He was now the most successful composer in all Italy, even though his best works were yet to come.

Verdi did not begin his march to greatness until 1851, with the *première* of *Rigoletto*. This opera, introduced at the Teatro La Fenice in Venice on March 11, 1851, marks the beginning of the second period of Verdi's career. He was now to produce, and in rapid successssion, a series of operas which was to make him the best loved and the most widely performed Italian composer of all time. *Rigoletto* was followed by *Il Trovatore*, first heard at the Teatro Apollo in Rome on January 19, 1853. After that came *La Traviata*, introduced at the Teatro La Fenice on March 6, 1853. After this trio of masterworks, Verdi produced *I Vespri Siciliani*, *Simon Boccanegra*, *Un Ballo in Maschera*, *La Forza del Destino*, *Don Carlos* and—greatest of all—*Aida*.

Both *Rigoletto* and *Il Trovatore* were immediately acclaimed. Although the Roman *première* of *Il Trovatore* took place on the same day that the Tiber overflowed, and the audience had to wade through water and mud to get to the theater, the house was crowded and the enthusiasm highly vocal. Both operas began to circle the music world soon after their *premières*. In Venice, three different companies had to play *Il Trovatore* simultaneously to meet the great public demand.

The first performance of *La Traviata,* however, was a different story. Some thought the play immoral. Others did not like to see contemporary costumes in an opera. Still others found it incongruous for a buxom prima donna to play the role of a tubercular heroine. To make matters still worse, the opera suffered from an execrable performance. The *première* was a fiasco, the audience responding with hisses and shouts of disapproval. Not until Verdi revised his opera, had his characters wear costumes from the time of Louis XIII, and saw to it that the production was a worthy one, did the great emotional impact of music and drama strike the audience. "Time will tell," Verdi had written immediately after the unfortunate *première*—and it did. *La Traviata* established itself as one of the most popular operas ever written.

Aida was commissioned by the Khedive of Egypt, who wanted a new work with which to open an opera house in Cairo, built to celebrate the opening of the Suez Canal. The *première* was delayed two years. There were difficulties in the adaptation of the libretto. Then again, due to the Franco-Prussian War, it was impossible to transport the scenery and costumes which had been ordered in Paris.

Finally, on Christmas Eve 1871, *Aida* was presented; the event was of incomparable brilliance. There was the sumptuous new opera house for the occasion, built of gold and ivory as well as stone, with a majestic colonnaded arcade and a foyer constructed of floor-to-ceiling mirrors. No expense was spared in the scenery and costumes; Radames' helmet and shield were made of solid silver, while the throne in the third act had material copied from artwork in the Louvre.

A part of the audience (which had come from all parts of the world for the performance) brought elegance; another part contributed a touch of the exotic with ornate native costumes. The Khedive was there with his entire harem (they occupied three boxes). There were cheers when he made his entrance immediately after the prelude, but after that the Khedive was forgotten and the cheers were directed toward the new opera. There was so much uncontrolled enthusiasm after some of the numbers that the conductor had to turn around to the audience and shout angrily, "That isn't done!"

Verdi did not come for his *première* because all his life he had a horror of such garishly publicized events and because he disliked ocean travel intensely. But he got a full report of everything that happened. And he was not pleased. He said that "the sentiment produced in me is one of disgust and humiliation." He went on to add that *Aida,* as seen in Cairo, "was no longer art, but a trade, a pleasure party, a hunt, anything that can be run after, to which it is desired to give, if not success, at least notoriety."

Verdi was now a rich man as well as a famous one. He had already bought a large farm at Sant' Agata where, for the rest of his life, he would spend his summers. (Winters were lived in a palatial home in Genoa.) He, who had been born a peasant, was only too happy to return to the soil, where he always said he belonged. He often remarked that if he had not been a composer he would have liked to be a farmer. Certainly he was happiest in Sant' Agata, where he would superintend the development of his crops, breed his horses, and personally attend to his gardens. Except for an infrequent game of billiards or cards, he had no social life to speak of. In 1859 he married a second time: Giuseppina Strepponi, a singer who had appeared in *Nabucco* and whom he had known and loved for a long time. To the end of her life, she brought him the companionship he needed and a gentle contentment.

Franz Werfel has vividly recreated Verdi's life at Sant' Agata: "Verdi rises early. Like most Italians, he takes nothing but a cup of unsweetened black coffee. Then he goes out on horseback—in later years he has the carriage hitched up—to inspect the work in fields, barnyards, and at the dairy farms, and to call on some of his tenants. He is the squire, not the maestro. Between nine and ten he comes home. Meanwhile, the mail has arrived. The mail is of course the great daily event at any country house. Signora Giuseppina has sorted the letters, separating the nuisances attendant on a celebrity from the important correspondence. Some time is spent every day in dealing with this. If guests come, they generally arrive about noon. Verdi's equipage usually fetches them from the nearest railway station, Firenzuola-Arda. His circle of friends is small, and grows no larger despite the vast number of connections formed in the course of a long, brilliant life. . . . The main meal comes at about six in the evening. Verdi has the reputation of a lover and connoisseur of good cooking; though he does not compare with Rossini in that respect, he sets a splendid table. He loves the light wine of Italy and heavy Havana cigars, nor does he disdain a game of cards after the evening meal.

"Music seems to cut no great figure in the house. Verdi is not fond of musical discussions. He warns some of his visitors that they will find no scores at his house, and a piano with broken strings."*

For a period he combined his farming interests with political activity. When the first Italian parliament was inaugurated by Cavour, Verdi was elected deputy. He disliked politics and the limelight intensely, but he felt he had to serve his country. In 1874 he was appointed a Senator by the King; but this was an honorary position, requiring no obligations on his part.

For fifteen years after *Aida,* Verdi produced no new operas. The only compositions written in that time were the Requiem (in memory of Manzoni, author of *I Promesi sposi,* who died in 1873), an Ave Maria, and a string quartet. He was tired. The defeat of France in the Franco-Prussian War, and the failure of Italy to enter that war and turn the tide for France, upset him greatly. He was sure that he was written out as an opera composer. He had not failed to remark the rising star of Wagner over the world of music; he was fully conscious of the new horizons Wagner had opened with his music dramas. The traditions that had produced his own great operas, Verdi felt strongly, were now dated. He preferred silence to writing in a vein now obsolete. And so, during those many years, he led his quiet life—tending to his farm at Sant' Agata, introducing innovations (such as the threshing machine and the steam plow) that revolutionized the agricultural life of his community. He made money from his farm, and was prouder of this income than of the great wealth gathered by his operas.

He would probably have kept to his resolve never again to write another opera if Arrigo Boïto (1842–1918)—famous critic, composer, and poet—had not one day brought him a powerful libretto. It was based on Shakespeare's drama *Othello* and it stirred the dying embers of Verdi's creative gift and started the flame again. Reading the libretto, Verdi felt dramatic music surging within him for the first time in many years; he would have no rest till he put it down on paper.

The first performance of *Otello* at La Scala on February 5, 1887—the *première* of a new opera by Italy's greatest composer after so many years of silence—inevitably attracted world-wide interest. Music lovers from all parts of Europe came to hear a new Verdi, a greater and maturer artist more concerned with dramatic effect than with lovable melodies. They thundered their appreciation. One member of that first-night audience, Blanche Tucker Roosevelt, reported: "The ova-

*"A Portrait of Giuseppe Verdi," preface to *Verdi: The Man in His Letters,* edited by Franz Werfel and Paul Stefan. New York: L. B. Fischer, 1942.

tions . . . reached the climax of enthusiasm. Verdi was presented with a silver album filled with autographs and cards of every citizen in Milan. He was called out twenty times, and at the last recalls hats and handkerchiefs were waved, and the house rose in a body. The emotion was something indescribable, and many wept. Verdi's carriage was dragged by the citizens to the hotel. He was toasted and serenaded; and at five in the morning . . . the crowds were still shrieking, 'Viva, Verdi!' "

Old and sick, he was ready to call it a day. But once again Boïto came to him with a libretto that would give Verdi's imagination no peace. The source was, again, Shakespeare—Shakespeare of the comedies; from *The Merry Wives of Windsor* and *Henry IV,* Boïto had carved his own *Falstaff.* Verdi had not written a comic score in half a century. But he was so taken with the libretto that he set to work. And once again he did the incredible, realizing a masterwork, his greatest comedy in music. Heard for the first time at La Scala on February 9, 1893, *Falstaff* duplicated the success of *Otello.*

He was to write one more complete piece of music, the *Quatro Pezzl Sacri,* made up of four religious choral compositions—and he was through. When his wife died in 1897, he lost the will to live. He fled from his beloved Sant' Agata—he would live there alone no longer— and took up residence at the Grand Hotel in Milan. He lingered on for years (as he described it) of "vegetation." "Although the doctors tell me I am not ill, I feel that everything tires me," he wrote to a friend in 1900. "I can no longer read or write. My sight is not good, and my hearing is worse still. And above all, my limbs no longer obey me."

He was dressing one day in his hotel room when a stud fell out of his hands, under the bed. He bent down to look for it and while doing so suffered a paralytic stroke. He struggled against death for six days. During that entire week, hundreds of opera lovers stood outside his hotel apprehensively awaiting word of the master's condition. He finally succumbed before dawn of January 27, 1901.

His death was mourned throughout the length and breadth of Italy. A special session of the Senate was called in Rome to listen to appropriate eulogies, while the schools were closed for the day. In Milan, the civic fathers were hastily gathered shortly after midnight, immediately after Verdi's death, to discuss proper ceremonies. Almost a quarter of a million of Verdi's compatriots lined the streets as his body was conveyed from the hotel to the oratory of the Musicians Home, which he had helped found, where it was buried. This cortege was accompanied by the singing of a chorus from *Nabucco,* led by Toscanini. That same evening Toscanini led a performance of Donizetti's *Elisir d'Amore* at La Scala; when the opera was over he led the *Nabucco* chorus again as a final gesture of farewell.

HIS MUSIC

ALTHOUGH the line of Verdi's development was unfaltering from *Nabucco* to *Falstaff,* there were two different Verdis. One was the genius of Italian lyricism, of *bel canto.* From his sleeves he could shake arias and ensemble numbers that were incomparable for melodic variety. This was the Verdi who produced the famous operas of the middle period and the apprentice works of the first. The other Verdi was the supreme dramatist, whose music was the servant of the play, the music and the play being inextricable parts of an artistic whole. This other Verdi was the creator of the last two masterworks, *Otello* and *Falstaff.*

The first Verdi could hardly have become the Olympian figure in Italian opera that he was if he had been a writer of good tunes and nothing more. The truth is that the best operas of the first period and the works of the middle period continually reveal Verdi's sound theatrical sense. Where his librettos falter and fail (as they often do), the music steps in to fill the gap. He could write not only good melodies but dramatic melodies, which carry the action, give insight into the characters, emphasize and stress the emotion. Within the established conventions of grand opera, he was able to create a forceful and living theater —through the power of his musical genius.

He was twenty-eight when he wrote *Nabucco.* This opera was steeped in the traditions of Rossini and Bellini, but there was a difference. Song, without sacrificing its sovereignty, had to share the spotlight with a new dramatic force. As Franz Werfel noted: "The tingling agility of Rossini, the divinely gentle melancholy of Bellini, the sensually ecstatic melodiousness of Donizetti gradually faded into the shadows of the past. Quite beyond the purely musical values, suddenly something new struck a surprising chord: energy and angry passion. Roughness, '*Ruvidezza,*' the Italians call it. Hidden under this *ruvidezza,* a grinding, an underground rumbling which produced the amazing effect known to Italy under the apt name of *furore.*"

Five years after *Nabucco* came *Macbeth* which, while still being true to operatic traditions, became pulsing human drama. And Verdi continued to adapt the existing traditions of opera to dramatic purposes. "If I am told that my music will fit this version as well as the other," he once said, "I reply that such an argument is utterly beyond me; my music—good or bad as it may be—is written in no casual manner. I invariably try to give it a character of its own." He always felt that great opera had to be great theater as well as great music. No Italian composer was so ruthless a tyrant as he at rehearsals, meticulous about every detail of stagecraft and fastidiously concerned that every dramatic effect be properly exploited. He constantly worked with his librettists over the characterization, a piece of dramatic business, the authenticity of a line of dialogue, even the importance of a single word.

If Verdi did not fail to be dramatic in the operas of his first two periods, which are so notable for their lyricism, he also did not fail to be lyrical in his last two operas, which are most notable for their dramatic values. *Otello* and *Falstaff* are almost Wagnerian in the wonderful unity of music and text. Melodic genius is omnipresent. In such pages as the "Willow Song" and the "Ave Maria" of *Otello* and the "Oberon Song" in *Falstaff*, Verdi is still a lord of wonderful melody, just as he is also the supreme musical dramatist.

ANALYTICAL NOTES

Operas. *Rigoletto*, though Verdi's sixteenth opera, was his first to acquire a permanent place in the operatic repertory. It was also the first of his operas to be filled with the most wonderful lyricism. It contains one of the most popular of all tenor arias, *"La Donna è mobile."* Apparently, Verdi well knew how good this tune was, for he refused to give its music to the leading tenor until the evening of the *première,* fearing that it would get to be known in Venice before being introduced in the opera house. Besides *"La Donna è mobile,"* the opera includes a brilliant coloratura aria, *"Caro nome,"* and one of the most celebrated of all ensemble numbers, the Quartet.

It is these and other similarly wonderful melodies that made *Rigoletto* famous. But this opera is much more than a showcase for Verdi's lyricism. Melody serves the theater. Never before had Verdi succeeded so forcefully in etching character in music. The philandering Duke of Mantua, the hideous Sparafucile, the scheming Rigoletto, the vengeful

Monterone, and the easily deceived Gilda are all sketched vividly in the score. All the sinister overtones of the tragedy vibrate in the music, helping to heighten tensions, to create emotional climaxes.

Rigoletto was based on Victor Hugo's play *Le Roi s'amuse,* which was adapted into a libretto by Francesco Piave. Rigoletto, hunchbacked jester to the Duke of Mantua, keeps his beautiful daughter in hiding in a remote part of the city, lest she become tainted by the corrupt court. The Duke, however, has seen Gilda in a nearby church and is interested in her. Disguised as a student, he courts her and she responds tenderly to his suit. A group of masked courtiers, believing that Gilda is Rigoletto's mistress and eager to harass Rigoletto, whom they hate, abduct her and bring her to the court. That is when Gilda learns that her disguised lover is the Duke. When Rigoletto arrives at court to save his daughter, she confesses to him that she loves the Duke. Rigoletto realizes that he can keep his daughter out of the Duke's hands only by murdering him. He engages an assassin with the picturesque name of Sparafucile (which, literally, means discharger of a gun). But the latter decides to fool Rigoletto by killing the first person he meets, dumping the body into a sack, and giving the sack to Rigoletto as proof that the job was done. The first person met by the assassin is Gilda, disguised as a young man, on her way to a rendezvous with the Duke. Rigoletto is about to dump the sack with the dead body into the river when he hears the Duke singing in the distance a strain from *"La Donna è mobile."* He looks into the sack, discovers to his horror that he was responsible for his own daughter's death, and shrieks out, *"Maledizione!"*

The curtain rises on the *salon* in the ducal palace, where a party is taking place. In this act, the Duke gives expression to his cynical philosophy on love and women in *"Questa o quella."* After this, the guests join in dancing a minuet. The scene changes to a deserted street. Rigoletto speaks of his distaste for being a hireling of the Duke, *"Pari siamo."* The Duke then arrives, disguised as a poor student, and ardently woos Gilda with the love song *"E il sol dell' anima."* When he has gone, Gilda muses about her strange lover in the celebrated coloratura aria *"Caro nome."*

In the second act we are brought back to the *salon* in the ducal palace. Not knowing that Gilda has been abducted and brought here, the Duke laments his inability to find his beloved in *"Parmi veder le lagrime."* But he finds Gilda in the palace, and she is in love with him.

After Rigoletto breaks into the *salon* to demand the return of his daughter, she tells him of her great love for the Duke in *"Tutte le feste."*

Early in the third act, set near the deserted banks of the Mincio river, the Duke once again sings cynically about all womankind. This is the ever popular aria *"La Donna è mobile."* In a nearby inn, the Duke (disguised as a soldier) is flirting with a gypsy girl, observed by a heartbroken Gilda and by a stern Rigoletto. Each of the four characters expresses his own, or her own, feelings in the wonderful Quartet, *"Bella figlia dell' amore."* Later in the act, as Rigoletto carries the sack to the river, he hears from a distance the Duke's cynical song, *"La Donna è mobile."* Opening the sack, he discovers the body of his own daughter, who is dying. A pathetic duet between father and daughter —*"Lassù in cielo"*—is followed by Gilda's death and Rigoletto's terrible grief.

The absurdity to which opera stories sometimes descend is perhaps nowhere more evident than in *Il Trovatore*. The plot is for the most part confused and confusing. Even when one is able to unravel the tortuous strands of the story, the effort is hardly worth while, since so much that takes place taxes the credulity of the spectator. It is, indeed, a cause for wonder that so unreal and stilted a libretto could stimulate a composer's creative processes. Yet by some mysterious power, Verdi was able to produce one of his most jewel-studded scores, as well as one of his most telling characterizations in the gypsy woman, Azucena. The alchemy of genius that can turn brass into gold is surely nowhere at work with greater success than in this opera. It is the score, a veritable treasure house of musical delights, that has kept *Il Trovatore* so popular and vital through the years.

The libretto was prepared by Salvatore Cammarano from a Spanish play by Antonio Garcia Gutiérrez. Twenty-five years before the actual story begins, the father of Count di Luna had had a gypsy woman burned at the stake as a witch; the gypsy's daughter, in reprisal, abducted one of the two sons of the old Count and is believed to have killed him. The other son, the younger Count di Luna, is now a commander of the Spanish army. He has never lost hope that his long-lost brother may still be living. The Count is a rival of Manrico (foster son of Azucena, a gypsy) for Leonora's love. But Leonora loves only Manrico. Disguised as a troubador, Manrico makes love to Leonora and while doing so is confronted by the Count, who engages him in a duel. Some mysterious and inexplicable force keeps Manrico from giving the fatal coup. When Azucena hears this she is enraged, for she demands that Manrico must kill the Count to avenge the death of the gypsy woman who—as Azucena insists—was Manrico's mother. Manrico promises to do so the next time.

Meanwhile, Leonora is about to enter a convent. The Count's men arrive to abduct her, are met and defeated by Manrico's men, while Manrico himself takes Leonora away with him. He is about to marry her when he hears the news that the Count has captured Azucena and is sentencing her to death as a spy. He must rush off to save the gypsy, and in the attempt he is captured, imprisoned, and doomed to death. Leonora makes a bargain with the Count: she will marry him if Manrico is freed. She comes to tell Manrico that he is free. As life with the Count would be intolerable, she poisons herself and falls dead at Manrico's feet. The Count now orders Manrico's immediate death and insists that Azucena watch his death from the prison window. As Manrico is burning, the dying Azucena reveals to the Count that the victim is none other than his long-lost brother.

In the first scene of the first act, the palace of Count di Luna, a captain of the guards reveals the tragic history of the Count's long-lost brother in the gripping narrative *"Abbietta zingara."* With a change of scene to the palace garden, Leonora tells her attendant of her great love for Manrico, *"Tacea la notte placida."* The first scene of the second act —a gypsy haunt at the foot of a mountain in the Biscay—opens with the famous "Anvil Chorus." One of these gypsies is Azucena, who soon recalls how her mother was burned at the stake, *"Stride la vampa."* Later on, in *"Mal reggendo all' aspro,"* Manrico tells her how some strange force kept him from killing the Count in their duel. Meanwhile, at a convent, the Count and his men lie in wait to abduct Leonora; the Count muses on how happiness will soon be his, in the tender aria *"Il balen del suo sorriso."* In the first scene of Act III, the soldiers of Count di Luna come to a military encampment to rescue Leonora from Manrico, singing the rousing and popular "Soldier's Chorus." In the following scene—within the stronghold of Castellor— Manrico speaks his love and devotion to Leonora in *"Ah! si ben mio,"* then expresses his rage and his determination to avenge Azucena's imprisonment in the fiery aria *"Di quella pira."*

Outside the prison in which Manrico and Azucena are held, in the first scene of the final act, Leonora wishes that her love could raise her above the prison walls and into the cell of her beloved, *"D'amor sull' ali rosee."* From the tower comes the poignant (and world-famous) chant of the *"Miserere,"* above which rise the voices of Manrico and Leonora saying farewell to each other. In the concluding scene, within the dungeon, Azucena recalls happier days in the mountains, *"Ai nostri monti,"* before both she and Manrico come to their tragic end.

If a single opera had to be selected as the greatest favorite with the largest number of operagoers, the choice would probably fall on *La Traviata*. The story blends all the elements so effective on the operatic stage: love and sacrifice; vengeance and hate; sentimentality and tragedy. And the score is a veritable cornucopia of operatic gems, one bewitching melody following another in a seemingly endless procession.

The libretto by Francesco Piave was based on the famous play of Alexandre Dumas, *La Dame aux camélias*. The Dumas play, in turn, was based on the true story of a famous Paris courtesan whom Dumas knew personally. In the opera the courtesan is Violetta, who falls in love with and is loved by Alfredo Germont. They go off together to a country house near Paris. Alfredo's father comes there, during his son's absence, to break up the affair, which he insists will spell ruin for his son. To save her beloved from disaster, Violetta is ready to give him up. She leaves a note for Alfredo saying she is leaving him forever.

She returns to her old life and ways. Accidentally she comes across Alfredo who, since he is unaware of the reason for her renunciation, spurns her. Eventually he learns the truth. But it is too late. Violetta, a victim of tuberculosis, is dying. But she lives long enough to hear Alfredo, at her side, repent what has happened and express his undying love.

There is a brief orchestral prelude. A tender strain in the strings is followed by a passionate melody for the violins. The cellos take over this melody with decorative treatment by the violins. The music dies out, and the curtain rises on a *salon* in Violetta's house, where a party is taking place. Alfredo Germont, introduced to Violetta, sings a robust drinking song, *"Libiamo ne' lieti calici,"* in which Violetta and her guests join. After the guests have left for the adjoining ballroom, Violetta and Alfredo speak of their love for each other, *"Un dì felice."* When Alfredo has gone, Violetta reviews his ardent expression of love in the most famous aria of the opera, *"Ah, fors' è lui,"* which is immediately followed by *"Sempre libera,"* her belief that a new life is awaiting her.

The second act finds the lovers in their country house near Paris. Alfredo tells Violetta how he has found true happiness with her, *"De' miei bollenti spirit."* After Violetta has informed the elder Germont that she is ready to renounce Alfredo, "*Ah, dite alla giovine,*" the father consoles his heartbroken son by reminding him of their home in the Provence, "*Di Provenza il mar.*"

In the concluding act, in Violetta's bedroom, she bids farewell to the world in the tragic aria "*Addio del passato.*" Alfredo then pathetically contemplates their return to old haunts and their former happiness, in the duet "*Parigi, O cara.*" But Violetta is dying and soon emits a last cry of anguish.

Aida is the last opera in the richly productive second period of Verdi's career. For pageantry, spectacular effects, big emotional scenes, and elaborate ballets it has no equal among Verdi's operas. Both as play and as music it is always a magnificent "show"—one that has never failed to hypnotize audiences with the glamour of wonderful theater.

The libretto, by Antonio Ghislanzoni, came from a prose sketch of Mariette Bey translated into French by Camille du Locle. Aida is the daughter of the Ethiopian king. Taken slave by the Egyptians, Aida is loved by Radames, captain of the Egyptian guard, while Radames, in turn, is loved by Amneris, daughter of the Egyptian king. Radames must leave the country to fight the invading Ethiopians; before he goes, Amneris discovers that it is Aida, and not herself, with whom Radames is in love. Victorious in the war, Radames returns to be given a rousing hero's welcome. One of his prisoners is the Ethiopian king (Aida's father), whose true identity is not known to the captors. The Ethiopian king prevails upon Aida to get the secret military plans from Radames. This act of treason is uncovered by Amneris. Radames is seized, tried, and found guilty; his sentence is burial alive. But Amneris is ready to save him if Radames will give up Aida and marry her. When the Egyptian captain refuses to do this, he is imprisoned within a tomb. There, after it has been completely sealed, he finds Aida awaiting him, willing to share his fate.

The opera's most famous aria is heard early in the first scene of the first act, which is set in a hall of the palace of the Egyptian king. It is the tenor aria "*Celeste Aida,*" Radames' rhapsody on Aida's beauty. Toward the end of this scene, Aida prays for Radames' victorious return from war in "*Ritorna vincitor.*" In the next scene (the Temple of the Vulcan) we have the first of several colorful ballets. The priestesses perform a ritual dance just before Radames arrives to receive the consecrated veil.

In Amneris' apartment, in the first scene of the second act, her slave girls sing praises of her beloved, Radames, and then execute an exotic dance. This is followed by a scene outside the city walls in which Radames is welcomed back from the war with magnificent ceremonies. These festivities include the famous Grand March and chorus, *"Gloria all' egitto,"* and a picturesque ballet.

In Act III, on the banks of the Nile, Aida sings the famous "Nile Song" (*"O Patria mia"*), recalling her childhood in Ethiopia. Radames' sentence comes in the first scene of Act IV, in the palace of the Egyptian king. The concluding scene, within the Temple of Vulcan, ends with the poignant duet of Radames and Aida as they bid farewell to the world, *"O Terra, addio."*

Aida was written in 1871. For fifteen years after that Verdi wrote no more operas, though he made several attempts to start one. He was experiencing a change of operatic values. The old way of writing— in the grand manner—no longer satisfied him. It took him many years to find the spiritual strength and courage to renounce the old and assume a new style.

The final stimulus was Boïto's magnificent libretto *Otello,* based on Shakespeare's tragedy. This kind of libretto required a score far different from those that Verdi had given his earlier operas. The formal arias and ensemble numbers had to be dispensed with. The music had to be a continuous, indivisible texture, serving the purpose of the play, never independent of it. In putting first importance on the drama, Verdi was probably revealing the influence that Wagner's music dramas had had upon him. *Otello* was also the culmination of his life-long tendency to serve the play.

One should not overestimate the influence of Wagner on *Otello.* While it is, in its way, a music drama, it is an *Italian* music drama. The music is pure Verdi—in its flood of melody, tenderness and beauty, and Italian sunshine. Melody is made more expressive through vivid characterization and subtle psychological suggestions; it is made richer through the introduction of new techniques and more vital harmonies.

Verdi was not quite sure how successfully he had achieved his artistic aim. He insisted on the right to withdraw the opera if rehearsals proved to him that the work was not worthy. But once the opera was rehearsed he had no further doubts.

Although Boïto made some necessary alterations and some interpolations in molding a Shakespearean tragedy into a workable opera libretto, the plot remains basically unchanged. Otello, new Governor of Cyprus, is married to the beautiful Desdemona. His aide, Iago, arouses him to jealousy with veiled suggestions and hints that Desdemona is unfaithful to him and is in love with Otello's lieutenant, Cassio. Otello's jealousy reaches such a point of madness that it becomes impossible for him to give credence to Desdemona's denials. Desdemona's handkerchief, which Iago has stealthily concealed in Cassio's room, provides Otello with all the evidence he needs. He chokes his wife to death, and only then does he discover how he has been betrayed by Iago. He kills himself with a dagger.

In the first act, outside Otello's castle overlooking the harbor, there is a beautiful love duet between Otello and Desdemona—"*Già nella notte densa.*" Iago's famous aria, "*Credo in un Dio crudel*"—a cynical philosophy of a hardened cynic—appears in the second act, which is set in a hall within the castle of Otello. In the third act, within the great hall of the castle, Otello delivers his powerful soliloquy, lamenting the terrible fate that has befallen him in Desdemona's infidelity, "*Dio! mi potevi scagliar.*" The final act, in Desdemona's room, contains Desdemona's two most celebrated arias: the "Willow Song" ("*Salce, Salce*") followed by the majestic "Ave Maria." The opera ends with the dramatic "*Nium mi tema*" (Otello's death).

Falstaff, completed six years after *Otello,* was Verdi's last opera. It is sometimes said that *Falstaff* is Verdi's *Die Meistersinger.* It is also called his *The Marriage of Figaro* and *The Barber of Seville.* One of the greatest of all lyric comedies, *Falstaff* boasts the finest qualities of the three great comic operas that preceded it: its integrated musical texture, a miracle of workmanship, is Wagnerian; its musical characterization is Mozartian; its gaiety and laughter, Rossinian. Not that the grand old man of Italian opera had taken to imitating others! *Falstaff* is Verdi at his best, even though the Verdi who wrote this opera was a different artist from the one who wrote *La Traviata* or *Aida.*

Perhaps one of the abiding wonders of *Falstaff* is Verdi's ability, in his eightieth year, to find the strength and freshness to turn to an entirely new facet of artistic expression. For up to the time of *Falstaff,* Verdi had concerned himself almost exclusively with tragedy: a comic opera written a half century earlier had been a failure.

Unlike the great Verdi operas of the middle period, *Falstaff* has no big arias (except for a love song), no spectacular scenes, no overpowering dramatic climaxes. Everything here is conceived on an intimate scale; everything here depends upon grace and delicacy. In place of *bel canto* we have delicate characterization. We need only study the score to understand the personalities of Falstaff, Ford, and the Mistresses Ford and Page. There is always astuteness in the way the music points up the action of the play. Falstaff's growing self-confidence is high-lighted by a trill that develops in sonority with tremendous effect. Flighty woodwinds imitate the gossip and intrigues of chattering women. The mystery of Windsor Park is recreated in vivid tone paint-ing, with the witching hour of midnight tellingly reproduced in a series of effective chords, while the delicate world of would-be fairies is created bewitchingly in the woodwinds.

Verdi, of course, had a wonderful libretto to work with. He knew it and was grateful. The libretto, by Boïto, was adapted from two Shake-speare comedies: *The Merry Wives of Windsor* and *Henry IV*. Falstaff, in sorry financial condition, aspires to rehabilitate his fortunes by enter-ing into a liaison with either of two respectable and affluent ladies: Mistress Ford or Mistress Page. To each he writes identical love letters. The women decide to play a game with the fat old man; they arrange a rendezvous. Falstaff leaves happily for the house of Mistress Ford, but the approaching voice of Ford sends him hiding behind a screen. When Ford goes searching through the house, Falstaff is con-cealed by the ladies in a laundry basket and dumped unceremoniously out of the window into the river below. Another rendezvous is arranged for midnight in Windsor Park, where the women and their friends have planned to taunt and harass him. As he makes love to Mistress Ford, strange sounds make him fear that supernatural powers have been let loose. Disguised as fairies, the conspirators emerge from their hiding place to give Falstaff a resounding beating. Falstaff has met his due and is repentant. And all those involved in these merry proceedings comment, in a concluding refrain, that, after all, the whole world is nothing but a stage.

Individual arias and ensemble numbers do not stand out so promi-nently in *Falstaff* as in other Verdi operas, since the strength of *Falstaff* is the oneness of its musical texture. But certain passages deserve to be singled out: Ford's famous soliloquy in Act II, in which he condemns womankind for infidelity, *"E sogno, O relata"*; the charming serenade of Fenton in Act III, Scene 2, *"Dal labbro il canto"*; and the concluding vocal fugue, *"Tutto nel mondo e burla."*

Choral Music. The Requiem Mass is the only Verdi work outside the field of opera that is widely performed. When first heard—at the San Marco Church in Milan on May 22, 1874—it was so successful that it was immediately heard throughout Italy, frequently in unauthorized performances. In Bologna it was given by four pianos, while in Ferrara the local military band was used. In 1875 Verdi himself took the work on an extensive tour of Europe. In Vienna, despite the heat and excessive admission prices, it had to be given four times.

The Requiem is deeply moving and personal music in which Verdi sublimated his grief at the death of his beloved friend, the novelist Alessandro Manzoni. It begins in an exalted vein. After a few introductory measures for muted cellos, the opening *"Requiem aeterna"* is sung gently by the chorus. This tranquil plea for eternal rest is repeated after the basses forcefully lead the way into a fugue, and once again after the succeeding *"Kyrie."* In the *"Dies irae"* the chorus enters at once with a surge of power. The *"Tuba mirum"* part of this section is dramatic. It begins with a fanfare for trumpets, first quietly, but growing in volume and power until a tremendous climax is reached; at the crest of this climax, the bass chorus enters to announce the arrival of Judgment Day. Other outstanding parts of the *"Dies Irae"* are the beautiful trio, *"Quid sum miser,"* the equally poignant duet, *"Recordare,"* and two impressive solos, the first for tenor (*"Ingemisco"*) and the other for bass (*"Confutatis"*). There is operatic writing in the section that follows, *"Domine Jesu,"* but a sacred style is resumed in the *"Sanctus,"* which is a tremendous eight-part fugue for double choir, introduced by a threefold flourish of the trumpet. The *"Benedictus"* in this section is charged with profound emotional feeling, as the writing once again assumes the operatic manner. The *"Agnus Dei,"* which follows the *"Benedictus,"* begins with a duet for soprano and mezzo-soprano unaccompanied; after this theme has been repeated—first by chorus and orchestra in unison and then by the soloists—the chorus provides the remaining portion of this beautiful melody. The *"Lux aeterna,"* a trio for mezzo-soprano, tenor, and bass, leads directly into the concluding section of the work, *"Libera me."* Here quotations from the opening *"Requiem aeterna"* and *"Kyrie"* parts are heard. The composition closes with a monumental fugue.

Heitor Villa-Lobos

"He summarizes the culture of his country, for, more than any other musical representative of Brazil, he seems to be actuated by the interior flame of his race."

—*Irving Schwerké*

BORN: Rio de Janeiro, March 5, 1887.
DIED: Rio de Janeiro, November 17, 1959.
MAJOR WORKS: *Orchestral Music*—Bachiana Brasileira No. 2; Bachiana Brasileira No. 5, for soprano and eight cellos; Chôros No. 6; Chôros No. 10, for orchestra and mixed chorus; Symphony No. 11. ALSO: 11 other symphonies; Magdalena, play with music; Mandu Carara, symphonic poem or ballet, for two pianos, percussion, large chorus, and children's chorus; Chôros No. 8, for two pianos and orchestra; Chôros Nos. 9 and 12, for orchestra; Chôros Nos. 11 and 13, for piano and orchestra; Chôros No. 14 for chorus, band, and orchestra; Amazonas; Concerto for Violin and Orchestra; Rudepoêma, for piano and orchestra (also for piano solo); Concerto for Piano and Orchestra; Symphony No. 7, "Montanhas do Brasil"; Madona, symphonic poem; Bachianas Brasileiras Nos. 1, 3, 4, 6, 7, 8, 9; Chôros Nos. 1, 2, 3, 4, 7, for various chamber-music combinations; Nonetto; 15 string quartets; 3 piano trios; Cecilio Brasileiro, Alma Brasileira (Chôros No. 5), Prole do Bébé, for piano; songs; 2 cello concertos; harp concerto.

HIS LIFE

SURELY any similarity between Villa-Lobos' career and that of any other important serious composer is purely coincidental. From the beginning, he followed a course uniquely his. He never received formal training, preferring to pick up his information in a haphazard sort of way. He learned to play the violin by holding it in a vertical position, as one does a cello. And he was inspired to call his first piece of music (for guitar) *Pancake,* because its melody had a certain pancake roundness.

When he was six years old he received some lessons on the cello and piano from his father, an amateur musician. Later he made a brief but futile attempt to subject himself to disciplined study at a conservatory; then he tried to take lessons in composition. But he hated anything that smelled of the classroom or bore a resemblance to scholasticism. By trial and error he learned to play the piano, and after that some of the wind instruments. He derived his greatest stimulation not from the classics, but from popular Brazilian music. With this kind of music, and with its performers and composers, he was completely at home. When he started writing music, it was in a popular vein. If the serious musicians of Brazil looked somewhat askance at such unorthodoxy, they were to be completely nonplused by his later creative practices: for it is not unusual to find Villa-Lobos writing a piece of music about the New York skyline or a mountain range in Brazil by tracing its outline on a piece of graph paper and then transferring the undulations into the rise and ebb of a melodic line.

He was eleven years old when his father died, from which time his life forsook normal patterns. He stopped going to school altogether and earned his living by playing popular music in theater and restaurant orchestras. His free time was usually spent in haunts which specialized in the popular songs and dances of Brazil.

To fill in the yawning gaps in his musical knowledge, he tried attending the National Institute of Music in Rio de Janeiro. He left it precipitately and continued to go his own way. A much more vital and living conservatory for him was the folk music of Brazil. He was drawn to national and popular idioms, and his earliest works included many pieces in this vein, such as the *Canticos Sertanejos,* a suite for orchestra based on Brazilian country airs, written in 1909.

In 1910 Villa-Lobos decided to make his way as best he could to the United States. En route he was marooned in Barbados. There he listened fascinated to native Negro chants, an experience that led him to wrote *Three African Dances,* for orchestra, based on the melodies and rhythms and utilizing some of the native instruments he confronted in Barbados.

He did not reach the United States at this time. Instead, in 1912, he went on the first of several expeditions to the interior of Brazil for the purpose of acquainting himself still further with the music of different regions and to witness local rites and ceremonials. This was a definite turning point. "For a temperament like Villa-Lobos," wrote his compatriot Burle Marx, "inclined to the strange, fantastic, and exotic, such direct contact with a primitive culture would lead naturally to a new path and a new goal. . . . Villa-Lobos not only recorded, learned, and absorbed, but he merged what he found with that which he recognized as his own. The result was a fusion of all the elements in his nature."

He now wrote abundantly. Continually deriving his inspiration and materials from either native or popular sources, he produced one work after another with incredible facility. Within the formal structures of the string quartet and the concerto, he utilized unorthodox styles; more frequently he adopted unusual forms and instrumentations. In 1915 there took place in Rio de Janeiro the first concert devoted entirely to his works. But most musicians in Brazil—steeped in and subservient to European traditions—either ignored him completely or regarded him as a musical savage.

Villa-Lobos was first discovered for the outside world by the piano virtuoso Artur Rubinstein. This happened in 1919, while Rubinstein was on tour in South America. Rubinstein attended a motion-picture show in Rio de Janeiro where an unusual piece of music was played. He was attracted to its exotic melody and to its primitive colors and force. Discovering that it had been written by a local composer named Villa-Lobos, he sought out the composer to tell him how much he liked what he had heard. A few days later Villa-Lobos came to call on Rubinstein at his hotel, bringing with him a small orchestra. In Rubinstein's hotel room, Villa-Lobos conducted a concert of his own works, all of which made a deep impression on the pianist. He proceeded at once to use his influence in Brazilian government circles to get a government stipend for the young composer. (Several years later Villa-Lobos wrote a piano piece for Rubinstein called *Rudepoêma*. What he wanted to accomplish in this piece, he said, was to write with such technical complexity that only Rubinstein would be able to play it. Some have seen in this work a personal portrait of Rubinstein.)

The government stipend enabled Villa-Lobos to go to Europe in 1923 and spend three years in Paris. The purpose of the visit was to study French musical culture. But French sophistication was not for him. He renounced it, preferring to remain himself: a Brazilian primitive. "I listened attentively," he said, "but never allowed myself to be influenced by any of the novelties I heard. I claim to be all myself, and I conceive my music in complete independence and isolation." The Brazilian who had come to absorb French musical ideas began, instead, to propagandize his own thinking to the French. In 1927 there took place in Paris a Villa-Lobos festival. "Did you think I came here to absorb your ideas?" he asked a French interviewer. "I came here to show you what I've done. If you don't like what I do, I'm going away."

He had returned to Brazil for a brief visit in 1926, but between 1927 and 1930 he once again lived in Paris, spreading the gospel of his own music to the French. When he once again returned to his native land, he was made Brazil's Director of Musical Education. His approach to education was as novel and as unorthodox and as personal as his approach to composition. He evolved a new method by which teachers could instruct children in sight singing not through written notes, but through the position of fingers indicating the degree of the scale. He banded children into Gargantuan choruses and had them sing everything from Handel to popular songs; he allowed them as they sang to give vent to their exuberance through stamping, hissing, whistling, shouting, clapping, and swaying. He wrote special works for such performances, some of them vocalizations on a single vowel or consonant. He led them not with a baton, but with flags. He aroused the Brazilian child's consciousness for music, "the world's greatest achievement in the field of practical music pedagogy," said the Uruguayan musicologist Francisco Curt Lange.

By the time Villa-Lobos paid his first visit to the United States—in the winter of 1944–45—he was Brazil's most influential musician and its greatest composer. He was, consequently, welcomed with proper ceremony. The League of Composers set aside a "Villa-Lobos Week." The major orchestras had him give guest performances in programs of his works. Koussevitzky commissioned him, through the Koussevitzky Foundation, to write a new work: *Madona, Poema sinfonico,* completed the same year.

He appeared to his American hosts as a man of irrepressible energy. One interviewer said that conversing with him "is rather like driving without brakes; one doesn't know exactly where one is going to land, but there is never a dull moment." Nicholas Slonimsky, who visited him in South America, described how he could carry on for hours—talking, playing, conducting, and entertaining—without the least visible sign of fatigue.

Villa-Lobos wrote so many works—almost fifteen hundred—that he himself forgot many of them. He allowed his manuscripts to pile up carelessly in his office in Rio de Janeiro. Manuscripts vanished—probably lifted as souvenirs by admiring visitors. He appeared uninterested in their loss, even when he had no other copy. He was just as indifferent to whether his music got published and—if published—whether it stayed in print and reached the stores. Slonimsky once inquired why he did not make an effort to see his piano pieces were made available in large American music stores since the demand would be great. He just shrugged his shoulders nonchalantly. "I don't want to. I'm afraid of being the best composer in the world."

His hobby was to make elaborate charts (one of them detailed Brazil's position in the world of music) and in his composition he used graph paper almost as often as music paper. "My processes of composition are determined by cool reasoning," he said. "Everything is calculated, constructed." To prove his point, he wrote an "enigma canon, with large squares in place of notes," signifying, so he explained, "the immoderate ambitions of aggressor nations."

Towards the end of his life, Villa-Lobos divided the year between Rio de Janeiro and New York. Though seriously ill, he remained prolific, completing one work after another. He died at his home in Rio de Janeiro on November 17, 1959, a victim of uremia.

HIS MUSIC

ONCE asked by an interviewer, "What is folklore?" Villa-Lobos responded: "I am folklore." Like other nationalist composers, Villa-Lobos made extensive use of folk and popular songs. But his own melodies and rhythms are also unmistakably national. The qualities that distinguish Brazilian music give Villa-Lobos' compositions their personality: the vivid harmonization and instrumentation; the tendency toward improvisation; the kinetic rhythms and syncopation. Brazilian music can be sentimental and gently tender as well as dynamic and primitive, and so is Villa-Lobos' music. Brazilian music makes use of native percussion instruments, and so does Villa-Lobos.

His most famous works are found in two forms of his own creation: the *"Bachiana Brasileira"* and the *"Chôros."* The first is a suite in which Bach's contrapuntal style is combined with basic elements of Brazilian folk music. The *"Chôros"* represents a street serenade, which emphasizes rhythm and popular melodies and synthesizes the modalities of Brazilian, Indian, and popular music. It has varied instrumentation. Some of these works are for solo instruments (for guitar, for example, or for piano); some are for full orchestra; some are for chorus; some are for various chamber-music combinations; some are actually piano concertos.

ANALYTICAL NOTES

Orchestral Music. The *Bachiana Brasileira No. 2*, is for full orchestra, which includes an extended percussion section embracing four native Brazilian instruments. It is in four movements, each with two titles, one suggesting Bach, the other Brazil. The first is Prelude (or "Song of the Hoodlum"), in which a slow and melancholy melody for baritone saxophone is the principal idea. This is followed by Aria (or "Song of Our Country"), emphasizing a cello solo of great expressive beauty. The third part, Danza (or "Woodland Memory"), begins with a solo for trombone and continues with a contrasting scherzando section. The concluding movement, Toccata, is subtitled "The Little Train to Caipira." It reproduces rhythmically the progress of a little train as it puffs along to its destination and comes to a halt; the body of the movement is a popular South American tune for the strings.

The most famous work in this form is the *Bachiana Brasileira No. 5*. It is in two movements—Aria and Danza. The second movement was written five years after the first, but it is the first movement that is heard most often. The Aria is scored for soprano and eight cellos and is in three-part-song form. The first and third parts are made up of a wordless chant on the syllable "Ah"—a beautiful mobile melody supported by a solo cello to an accompaniment of plucked strings in the other cellos. The middle section is in a more virile character and has the unmistakable identity of a Brazilian folk song. This portion has a Portuguese text, which begins with the following lines:

> Afternoon . . . pink and gold;
> Dusk falls,
> Tingeing the surface of the sea. . . .
> Without knowing why people sadden,
> Without wanting, eyes, begin to weep. . . .

Villa-Lobos has provided the following description of his *Chôros:* "I have no fixed formulas for the use of themes. I use them for development or atmosphere, as I feel the need. I never repeat themes purely for the pleasure of repetition or to create 'cyclic' music. I bring a theme back only as its return grows out of necessity. I do not use ready-made folk songs and dances. My themes *suggest* folk themes, that is they have the *aspect* of folk themes."

The *Chôros No. 6* is for large orchestra, including native percussion instruments, a guitar, and a "bombardine" (the last is a brass instrument resembling a tuba). It is, for the most part, in a melancholy vein, beginning with an elegiac melody introduced by the flute. Later the themes suggest the little dance tunes and popular melodies sung and played by itinerant musicians in the streets of Brazil, and are developed with great contrapuntal skill. The *Chôros No. 10* has greater emotional intensity and rhythmic force. It is for a large orchestra and mixed chorus, as well as a variety of native percussion instruments, the chorus being used for a savage Brazilian popular song named *"Rasga o Coração."* Villa-Lobos explained that this work represents "the reaction of a civilized man to stark nature; his contemplation of the valleys of the Amazon, and the land of Mato Grosso and Para. The vastness and majesty of the landscape enrapture and captivate him. The sky, the waters, the woods, the birds fascinate him. But little by little humanity asserts itself: there are living people in this land, even though they are savages. Their music is full of nostalgia and of love; their dances are full of rhythm. The Brazilian song *'Rasga o Coração'* is heard, and the Brazilian heart beats in unison with the Brazilian earth."

Villa-Lobos wrote twelve symphonies, the first *(Imprevisto)* in 1920, and the twelfth in 1958. One of the most significant is the *Symphony No. 11* (1955) commissioned by the Koussevitzky Foundation for the seventy-fifth anniversary of the Boston Symphony, which presented its world *première* in 1956. The first movement has a stately introduction for full orchestra. In the main section that follows, the two principal themes appear respectively in the strings, and in the horns and trumpets accompanied by ostinato figures in strings and harp. There are two sections in the Largo that follows. In the first, a main thought is found in the flutes, before it is repeated by full orchestra; in the second, a figure first heard in the bass clarinet passes on through the various woodwinds. In the third-movement scherzo, the main material is built from successive woodwind solo passages. The finale is strong fibered and sharply accented music, bringing the symphony to an exultant conclusion.

Richard Wagner

"In the whole range of opera . . . will be found no greater name than that of Wagner. He has clothed it with a new life, he has taught it to deliver a new message, and the echoes of his voice will last, not only in his own work but in the days to come."

—*W. H. Hadow*

BORN: Leipzig, May 22, 1813.

DIED: Venice, February 13, 1883.

MAJOR WORKS: *Operas*—Tannhäuser; Lohengrin; Tristan und Isolde; Die Meistersinger; The Ring of the Nibelungs (The Rhinegold, The Valkyrie, Siegfried, and The Twilight of the Gods); Parsifal. *Orchestral Music*—Siegfried Idyl; Overture to the Flying Dutchman. ALSO: Rienzi, The Flying Dutchman, operas; A Faust Overture, for orchestra; Five Wesendonck Songs (including *"Träume"*), for voice and orchestra.

HIS LIFE

WHEN Wagner was twenty-two years old, he purchased a large notebook in which to jot down every detail of his life for later use in the writing of his autobiography. He was then the conductor of a decrepit small-town opera house and the composer of two unproduced operas. But already he had the feeling that he had a rendezvous with destiny, that he would become an immortal. He lived to write that autobiography. He lived to accept as a basic truth—and to promulgate that truth to anyone who would listen—that he was the greatest musician who ever lived and one of the greatest dramatists, poets, and intellects of his generation.

The egocentricity of his later years, which made it impossible for him to be concerned with anybody but himself and led him to use everybody and every situation exclusively for his own advantage, revealed itself early. It was an objectionable trait; but we must be grateful for it. Without that abnormal vanity and self-glorification, he would never have dared to conceive a musical structure unparalled for immensity of design and vastness of scope; or conceiving it, he would never have found the strength to bring it into existence; or bringing it to life, he would never have had the selling power to interest a skeptical world in it.

Several other traits of the mature Wagner were evident early: notably, his ruthlessness, his extraordinary selfishness, his driving perseverance, his contempt for existing mores. Only his titanic genius was late in revealing itself. He was no musical prodigy. Indeed, few of the world's great composers took so long to begin studying music, few so long to demonstrate the full extent of their creative powers.

His father, Karl Friedrich Wagner (if he *was* his father), was a police official in Leipzig; his mother, Johanna, the daughter of a baker. Neither one was musical. The question of Wagner's paternity deserves elaboration. The evidence gathered within the past half century has strengthened the case of those who believe that it was not the police official, but the actor Ludwig Geyer, who was Richard's father. Geyer was a close friend of the family and was obviously attached to Johanna. When Karl Friedrich died on November 2, 1813 (a half year after Richard's birth), Geyer took complete charge of the widow, her family, and her tangled affairs. They were married the following year, six months before a daughter, Cäcilie, was born to them. Wagner's resemblance to Geyer, their mutual attachment and devotion, and the fact that it was Geyer's picture (and not Karl Friedrich's) that hung in Wagner's home in later years are additional items pointing to the Geyer paternity.

Two documents uncovered by Ernest Newman in his monumental biography of Wagner further substantiate this case. One proved that Johanna and her infant son, Richard, traveled from Leipzig to visit Ludwig Geyer while Karl Friedrich was still alive. To get to Teiplitz, she had to pass through Napoleon's army. Obviously so arduous a trip, with an infant, would not have been undertaken had there not been an all-important tie between Johanna and Geyer. The second document was a letter written by Wagner to his stepsister, Cäcilie, in which he speaks of "our father Geyer" and tenderly describes his sacrifices, which Wagner interpreted as an atonement "for a guilt." To Newman, these two documents were further proof that "the gallant opponents of the theory of Geyer's paternity have been defending a lost cause."

The mystery of Wagner's legitimate or illegitimate birth would hardly have engaged the fascinated interest of the world for so long a time if the report had not gained credence that Geyer was a Jew. Obviously, to prove Wagner the son of a Jew—he who was so passionate an anti-Semite and who, in 1933, was glorified by the Nazis—was a startling paradox. There is, however, no reason to believe that Geyer was a Jew or that there was Jewish blood in any of his ancestors.

Geyer's influence on Wagner was profound. Besides being an actor, Geyer was a lover of great literature, a writer, and a portrait painter. He brought into his household a love of culture. In such a stimulating atmosphere Richard Wagner spent the formative years of his childhood. Geyer died when Richard was only eight years old, but by then his step-father had planted the seeds of culture in the boy and they were bearing fruit.

Literature, rather than music, was Wagner's first love. As a boy he was so taken with the Homeric epics that he studied Greek in order to read them in the original. Not much later his interest in Shakespeare induced him to study English. He was only eleven when he wrote a lurid poetic drama entitled *Leubald,* inspired by Shakespeare and the Greeks, in which forty-two characters died within the first four acts and some of them reappeared as ghosts in the fifth. He came to the study of music only after an intensive preoccupation with academic and classical subjects. As a matter of fact, his first lessons at the piano proved highly distasteful to him.

Wagner's latent love for music was first aroused by a performance of Weber's *Der Freischütz*. But not until he heard the Beethoven symphonies at the Gewandhaus in Leipzig, and soon after that a performance of *Fidelio,* did music become an obsession. All school work was now neglected; he no longer found pleasure in reading. Inspired by Beethoven, Wagner struggled through a book on musical theory (which he borrowed from Friedrich Wieck, father of Clara Schumann), acquiring for the first time a few tools of composition.

His mother did not object to a musical career. But she insisted that he first continue with his academic education, even though (now that music was a dominating influence) he had become so indifferent to school that at one time he was a truant for a six-month period. He entered, and was expelled from, the Thomasschule at Leipzig. At the University of Leipzig he was more concerned with the rowdy extra-curricular activities of the students—gambling, dueling, drinking, and loving—than with his courses. But the dissolute young man became deadly serious when it came to music. In order to penetrate still more deeply into Beethoven's music, he made piano arrangements of the Fifth and Ninth Symphonies and after that of the *Missa Solemnis.* He also did some composing, completing two orchestral overtures. One of these was Wagner's first work to be performed, the event taking place in Leipzig in 1829 under Heinrich Dorn. Some deep and unexplained compulsion made him write his score in three different inks and use eccentric percussive effects. As if to warn of still greater storms to come, the overture was received with either anger or derision; mercifully for the composer, it had been presented anonymously.

His first period of formal music study—six months of theory with Theodor Weinlig, the cantor of the Thomasschule, in 1831—further stimulated Wagner. His most important work was a symphony, which was liked when it was performed in both Leipzig and Prague in 1833. He had also begun trying to write an opera. He started writing music for his own bloodcurdling text, *Die Hochzeit,* and abandoned it. His second attempt, the no less bloodcurdling *Die Feen,* was completed. (It was destined not to be performed until five years after the composer's death.) *Die Feen* was followed by a second opera, *Das Liebesverbot* (based on Shakespeare's *Measure for Measure*).

But the young composer had the faculty of getting into trouble. Gambling reverses put him heavily in debt; the creditors hounded him ceaselessly. He had become involved in troublesome love affairs. His own mother was ready to wash her hands of her irresponsible son. Partially to seek escape in a change of scene—partially because he had come upon a pretty face in Magdeburg that attracted him—he accepted an offer to become conductor of the Magdeburg Opera, a small-town theater with poor facilities and continually on the brink of bankruptcy. It was with this company that Wagner had his debut as conductor in Mozart's *Don Giovanni*. But the job was a thankless one. Wagner stuck to it because he was in tireless pursuit of attractive Minna Planer, an actress. It took him two years to overcome her apathy toward him, but he was indefatigable and in the end he was victorious. They were married on November 24, 1836. Almost from the moment the marriage was sealed, Wagner regretted the act. She *was* pretty, but she was also of bourgeois mentality and tastes. Once she was his, he was bored with her.

On March 29, 1836, the Magdeburg Opera introduced Wagner's *Das Liebesverbot*. The performance was such a fiasco that the house was empty when the opera was repeated. A failure of such proportions was fatal to an opera company that was usually tottering on the brink of disaster. The company was dissolved, leaving Wagner overwhelmed by his debts without the means of earning a living. Another conductorial post materialized in Königsberg, but this theater also dissolved, almost as soon as Wagner had assumed the position. Still another job was made available—this time in Riga, Russia. He stayed there for two years, unhappy with some of the operas he had to conduct and continually in conflict with the director of the opera house and with the growing army of his creditors. One day he came to the opera house only to discover that he had been dismissed and replaced. With his passport confiscated by creditors, he had to flee from Russia by a smuggler's route. He and his wife boarded the merchant vessel *Thetis* at Pillau, a Baltic harbor, their ultimate destination being Paris. In his baggage was the manuscript of a new, but as yet unfinished, opera, *Rienzi*, with which he expected to storm musical Paris. He was convinced that he had left behind him forever the cares and woes that had so long besieged him. He was sure that he was a man of genius. And as he bore letters of introduction to Giacomo Meyerbeer (then the most famous opera composer in Paris), he was confident of his future.

The Wagners stayed in Paris from 1839 to 1842. The swollen hopes with which he had arrived were soon punctured. Everywhere Wagner was greeted politely, and just as politely rejected. Promises made were not kept. Those that were kept yielded nothing: the Théâtre de la Renaissance, which had accepted *Das Liebesverbot,* went into liquidation before the opera could be played. The poverty now experienced by the Wagners made their former hard life appear affluent by comparison. Several times they were on the verge of starvation, and on two occasions he was imprisoned for debts. They had to take in boarders, and each dawn Minna was reduced to cleaning the boarders' shoes. Wagner was forced to accept hack work.

He was humiliated as a man and—worse still—rejected as a composer. But serious composition continued. *Rienzi* was completed in 1840. One year later he finished *Der fliegende Holländer* (*The Flying Dutchman*). Once he completed a poetic text and started to set it to music, his doubts vanished and his defeats turned to victory. He was conscious of rapidly growing creative power. "I began with the 'Sailor's Chorus' and the 'Spinning Song,' " he wrote concerning his first efforts with *The Flying Dutchman.* "Everything went easily, fluently. I actually shouted for joy, as I felt through my whole being that I was still an artist."

Rienzi was accepted by the Dresden Opera. With borrowed funds, Wagner left Paris to attend the *première*, which took place on October 20, 1842. This impressive spectacle for eye and ear, written in the favored Meyerbeer style—and presented in regal fashion—took the audience by storm. Wagner himself was taken aback by the ovation that thundered at him when the opera was over. *Rienzi* was one of the most popular offerings of the Dresden Opera that year, and for the first time Wagner's name was made known throughout Germany.

Such a huge success had two important developments. First, the Dresden Opera accepted *The Flying Dutchman,* presenting it under Wagner's direction on January 2, 1843. As this opera was no longer a distillation of Meyerbeer, but a tentative effort at a new direction, it was a complete failure and was seen only four times. The second development came immediately after this failure. In February 1843 Wagner was given an appointment as Kapellmeister of the Dresden Opera at a comfortable salary.

For the next six years he gave himself unsparingly to his post, doing everything in his power to rehabilitate the opera company and to give vital performances of the German operas. After the misery of Paris, this was both recognition and affluence. But Wagner was not a happy man. The high standards he tried to establish were not always realizable; an extensive program he had evolved for revolutionizing opera performances and repertory had been flatly turned down. There were other worries. His creditors, from different parts of Europe, were descending on him like the locusts. He could not possibly pay them. What is more, he was continuing to collect fresh debts, as he lived far beyond his means.

During this Dresden period Wagner completed two new operas. *Tannhäuser,* introduced in Dresden on October 19, 1845, was at first a failure. Some said that Wagner was pornographic; others condemned his music as being unsingable and unplayable. Even a sympathetic admirer such as the singer Schröder-Devrient, who created the role of Venus, could say to him, "You are a genius, but your music is so eccentric it is impossible to sing it." But with succeeding performances, and with new scenery and costumes, *Tannhäuser* began to appeal to audiences, who started to speak of it in glowing terms. While the critics remained hostile, it developed into a sizable success.

Lohengrin was completed three years after *Tannhäuser.* It was turned down by the Dresden Opera and was not heard until 1850, in Weimar. Wagner could not attend that *première,* nor was he able to hear a performance of this opera for eleven years. For, by 1850 he had become a political exile.

Wagner knew that with *Lohengrin* he had written the greatest German opera up to that time and one of the greatest operas of all time; he also knew that he was only beginning. Convinced of his genius, he felt a grievance against a society that could not recognize his true worth. One way to fight back was to be a revolutionary. The year of 1848 infected all of Europe with the spirit of revolution; it had penetrated into Saxony early in 1849. Wagner eagerly joined up with the revolutionary elements in Saxony. He wrote feverish propaganda pieces for the radical press, delivered a political speech, and was sympathetic to the rioters in Dresden. The revolution was stillborn. Wagner narrowly escaped arrest by fleeing (on a passport supplied by Franz Liszt) first to Weimar and then to Paris.

For the next thirteen years Wagner had to live in exile. For this reason he could not attend the *première* of *Lohengrin,* which Liszt (with remarkable courage in view of Wagner's disgrace) directed in Weimar on August 28, 1850. *Lohengrin,* like *Tannhäuser,* was first met apathetically (for one thing, it was too long; for another, too new in style). But also like *Tannhäuser,* it was destined to grow on audiences. Within the next decade it became the first of Wagner's operas to become both famous and popular. It was heard in opera houses throughout the length and breadth of Germany, and it was acclaimed. Wagner lamented at one time that he was just about the only German who had not seen a performance of *Lohengrin!*

He set up house in Zurich. During this period Wagner was beginning to formulate his new ideas about opera, ideas which rejected the old and formal traditions once and for all and which made possible the emergence of a new art form synthesizing all the arts. He was husbanding his strength for what he knew would be a Herculean effort. And like Hercules, he first had to clean the Augean stables. He wrote numerous articles and pamphlets attacking the obsolete techniques and the shibboleths of Italian opera, at the same time formulating his own theories of the music drama. He began evolving a Gargantuan musical project in which his ideas could be fully realized: a monumental cycle of four music dramas, *Der Ring des Nibelungen* (*The Ring of the Nibelungs*), the writing of which would absorb his energy and efforts for a quarter of a century. He had originally planned only a single music drama based on the Nibelung legend, *Siegfried's Death.* But no single opera could be the medium for his ever expanding dreams. As he wrote, "I found it necessary to indicate a vast number of antecedent facts so as to put the main incidents in the proper light. But I could only *narrate* these subordinate matters—whereas I felt it imperative that they should be embodied in the action. Thus I came to write *Siegfried*. But here again the same difficulty troubled me. Finally I wrote *Die Walküre* (*The Valkyrie*) and *Das Rheingold* (*The Rhinegold*) and thus contrived to incorporate all that was needful to make the action tell its own tale." He completed the text of this immense poetical drama by 1852 and soon after that published it privately.

While he was wrestling with his vast schemes and bursting at the seams with his ideas, matters were coming to a head in his "melancholy home." His marriage to Minna had not been happy; it was marked by continual eruptions of storms and stresses. A limited intelligence made her completely incapable of keeping pace with the growth of her husband. She could not understand why he continually spoke of writing a new kind of opera that was so obviously unmarketable. She regarded it as sheer eccentricity that he should diverge from the style of *Rienzi*—with which he had won public acclaim and with which he could be expected to hold it—to the extravagances of the *Ring* about which he spoke so much, which could not possibly gain a performance, let alone popular success. She did not know what he was talking about half the time, and occasionally thought that he was raving. Besides, she knew he had begun to find love elsewhere. There was the twenty-one-year-old English girl, Jessie Laussot, wife of a wine merchant. When Wagner visited Paris in 1850, he stayed at the Laussot home and did not hesitate to make love to his hostess. He urged her to elope with him, and for a while she listened to him sympathetically; she even tried to get her husband to endow Wagner for life. But eventually she saw him in the true light, or rather was shown the true light by her patient husband, and renounced him. "The woman who was to have brought me salvation has proved herself a child," he moaned. "Forgive me if I can only regard her as pitiable."

After Jennie there was Mathilde Wesendonck, twenty-eight-year-old wife of a wealthy silk merchant. Her husband, Otto, had grown so interested in Wagner that in 1853 he subsidized several Wagner concerts in Zurich, all the proceeds of which went to the composer. Four years later he provided the Wagners with a charming home, the "Asyl," near his own villa. If Wagner was grateful for these and other benefactions, he did not reveal it. He accepted the gifts as if they were due him and proceeded to win Otto's wife away from him. There was no attempt at secrecy about the affair; both Otto and Minna were fully aware of it. Eventually there was an explosion which shook all four of them. Wagner went off to Paris with Minna (funds were provided by Otto Wesendonck), to forget Mathilde and try to mend his sadly mutilated marriage as best he could. His passion for Mathilde was sublimated in the music of *Tristan und Isolde,* which he was now completing. It is often said that *Tristan* was inspired by his love for Mathilde. But Ernest Newman conjectures that the reverse might just as easily have been the case: Wagner fell in love with Mathilde at this time because he was working on *Tristan.*

The pattern of his personality was now set. It is not pleasant to trace it. He could no longer be true to anyone or anything (except his art). He was a liar, a cheat, and a hypocrite, without the slightest regard for ethics, morality, or personal honor. He borrowed money with no intention of repaying it, and he did not hesitate to use the borrowed funds for extravagances—for he always lived beyond his means, usually in regal style. "The world owes me what I need," he said proudly. He made love to women without thought of possible consequences or hurts. He could be as callous to the pain of others as he was neurotically preoccupied with his own. And he was as filled with hate for everyone around him as he was filled with love for himself. He could grow furious at a word of criticism and regarded any disagreement (even on trivial matters) as a personal insult. People were there to be used; he used them unscrupulously. He would accept as friends only those who were ready to take him at his own evaluation and those who could be of service. All others he regarded contemptuously.

He was an objectionable man in every way—except one: his attitude toward his art. Here, at any rate, was the one religion which he could worship with honesty and humility, here was the one truth to which he could remain unswervingly faithful. He doubted if the *Ring* cycle, to which he was giving so much of himself for so many years, would ever be performed in his time, because of the vastness of the scheme, the prodigious demands it made upon singers, musicians, and the stage, and finally the fabulous expense it would involve. But the belief that the supreme artistic effort of his life would not be performed did not deter him from bringing it into existence. Meanwhile he would write music dramas whose scope was more modest—*Tristan und Isolde* and *Die Meistersinger* (*The Mastersingers*). But though more modest in scope than the *Ring,* these two works were no less exacting in their fulfillment of the aesthetics of the new music drama he was conceiving;

for where his art was concerned, he was incapable of opportunism or compromise.

He met one major defeat after another—one greater than the other —without faltering in his belief in himself and in what he was doing, without a moment's temptation to seek out an easier path. A projected performance of *Tristan und Isolde* in Vienna in 1861 was abandoned after fifty-seven rehearsals. His adversaries, who were legion, said that his operas were incapable of being performed. "I have never in my life experienced such a persistent run of adversity. . . . It is the same with me here as everywhere else. The jealousy of the profession is extraordinary, and they do their best to choke me off." The Paris *première* of *Tannhäuser* in 1861 was a fiasco, a riot having been instigated by the snobbish and fashionable Jockey Club, which was antagonistic toward the composer. As for the two completed operas of the *Ring* cycle, there was not even the hope of a performance, successful or otherwise. Yet—dark as the hour was—he could find the inner strength to plan and sketch a new music drama, his first and only attempt at comedy, *Die Meistersinger*. Once he began working, nothing mattered. "I felt once more the master of my Fate."

There was a dramatic and unexpected turn for the better—at a time when his fortunes had plunged to their lowest depths. In 1862 Wagner had at long last been officially pardoned for his radical activities of 1848 and permitted to return to Saxony. Two years later, in 1864, the new young King of Bavaria, Ludwig II, sent word to Wagner of his great admiration for him and of his readiness to be a patron. A strong bond of friendship developed between the two; the King, on his part, gave Wagner the idolization he required. With regal munificence, the King paid Wagner's debts, subsidized him so that he could live in opulent style, and most important of all offered to finance the production of all of Wagner's thus far unperformed works. The first such production was the *première* of *Tristan und Isolde,* which took place in Munich on June 10, 1865. *Die Meistersinger* followed three years after that. And in 1869 and 1870, respectively, the first two dramas of the *Ring* cycle—*The Rhinegold* and *The Valkyrie*—were finally seen.

Wagner's enemies in Munich were numerous and powerful. A music group disapproved of the kind of music he was writing and resented that he, above all others, should have been chosen as the King's favorite. A political group was outspoken in its opposition to the King's extravagance in subsidizing Wagner and his dramas; it hinted that Wagner was using his influence to affect royal decisions in politics. The critics were also hostile—hostile to Wagner's theories and to the pretentious way in which he put them into practice. All these forces were eager to find some vulnerable spot on which to center a vicious attack; and it did not take them long to find it.

In 1862 Wagner and Minna had separated for good, four years before her death. But even before 1862 Wagner was involved in the greatest romance of his life: with Cosima, daughter of Franz Liszt and the wife of Wagner's intimate friend Hans von Bülow. Von Bülow, a pianist and conductor of international repute, was one of Wagner's most passionate admirers. But Wagner was drawn to Cosima, a woman of strong will, expansive intellect, and a profound sympathy for his art. One day, while driving with Cosima in Berlin, they "gazed silently in each other's eyes. . . . With tears and sobs we sealed our vow to belong to each other." They became lovers. When Wagner settled in Munich, he saw to it that Hans von Bülow was appointed court pianist to King Ludwig. There was no effort on the part of either Cosima or Wagner to conceal what was happening. A child was born to them in April 1865 whom—with incomparable brazenness—they named Isolde. The poor and unhappy Von Bülow tried to make the best of a miserable situation. He closed his eyes to the affair as best he could, remained unwavering in his allegiance to Wagner, and accepted Isolde as his own child.

Wagner's enemies made the most of this ugly situation, particularly after a second daughter was born to Cosima and Wagner. Munich became intolerable for the lovers. They fled to Switzerland to set up home with their children at the Villa Triebschen near Lake Lucerne. "If it had been anyone else but Wagner," Von Bülow said bitterly, "I would have shot him." As it was, he nursed his broken heart—and continued working devotedly for Wagner's music. Cosima's father, Franz Liszt, was also horrified. For many years he would have nothing to do with Wagner personally; but, like von Bülow, he remained a faithful propagandist for Wagner's art.

Emotional stability had finally entered Wagner's life. In Cosima he had found the woman for whom he had been seeking so restlessly all his life. To the last years of Wagner's life, they remained devoted to each other, Cosima providing him with the understanding and adulation he needed. A third child, the son Siegfried, was born to them on June 6, 1869, and a year after that Cosima and Wagner were legally married. Wagner could return to composition with a peace of mind he had never known. After twelve years, he went back to the writing of his *Ring* cycle, devoting himself to *Siegfried,* which he finally completed in 1871. He also wrote one of his most eloquent pieces of music, as a touching birthday gift for Cosima—the *Siegfried Idyl*—and had it performed for her as a surprise by a small ensemble outside her bedroom.

The last music drama of the mighty *Ring* cycle, *Götterdämmerung (The Twilight of the Gods)*, was completed in 1874, and with it was completed one of the most ambitious artistic projects ever conceived by man. With one dream finally brought to life, Wagner hurled his demoniac energy and indomitable perseverance into the realization of another: the building of a special festival theater where his *Ring* could be produced in accordance with his own ideas of staging and performance. He found some patrons willing to provide part of the subsidy. He conducted concerts of his music to raise more funds. He sponsored Wagner societies formed in Europe and America to make further contributions. A site was selected in the little Bavarian town of Bayreuth. On several occasions it seemed that the venture would collapse under the crushing weight of its own immensity. But Wagner was relentless, stubbornly overcoming one obstacle after another. At last the theater was built to Wagner's specifications, and a few miles away from it was Villa Wahnfried, Wagner's home for the rest of his life, in whose garden he was buried. The theater was opened on the evening of August 13, 1876, with the first complete performance of the *Ring* cycle—*Siegfried* and *The Twilight of the Gods* receiving their world *premières*. The event attracted world attention. Great musicians from all parts of Europe had come: Tchaikovsky, Saint-Saëns, Gounod, Grieg, Liszt, and many others. The hotels were overtaxed and so were the restaurants; they charged exorbitant rates. Tickets for each performance were at a premium. Correspondents from leading newspapers—including some from New York—were on hand to report the event.

Not everybody liked what they heard; much of it was too new and too startling. But this, the first of the Wagnerian festivals at Bayreuth, was regarded with considerable respect. Tchaikovsky put it this way: "The Bayreuth festival is a lesson for those obdurate persecutors of art who have a proud contempt for it and feel that civilized people should not deal in anything but matters which bring them a direct practical benefit. . . . From the point of view of artistic ideals, it is destined one way or another to have an enormous historic significance. Whether Wagner is right in pursuing his idea to the limit, or whether he stepped over the boundary of aesthetic conventions which can guarantee the durability of a work of art; whether musical art will progress further on the road started by Wagner, or whether the *Ring* is to be the point from which a reaction will set in, remains to be seen. But in any case what happened in Bayreuth will be well remembered by our grand-children and our great-grandchildren."

Wagner was to write one more music drama, the consecrational play *Parsifal*. Helping prepare the *première,* which took place on July 26, 1882, greatly taxed him. He had long suffered from eczema; his skin was so sensitive that he could bear only silk underclothes and fur-lined outer garments. He was now also afflicted with a heart condition. After the performance of *Parsifal,* Wagner went to Venice with Cosima and their children to enjoy a vacation in the fifteenth-century palace Vendramini-Calergi. Liszt, now reconciled with his son-in-law, was also there for a short period. While in Venice, Wagner conducted a private performance of his youthful symphony as a birthday gift to his wife, on December 24, 1882. It was his last musical act. He died six weeks later, suddenly, the victim of a heart attack. Cosima was with him at the end.

His body was brought back to Bayreuth where—to the music of "Siegfried's Death"—it was buried in the garden and where it lies to the present day. Since then, pilgrims from all parts of the world have come to the grave as to a shrine. But the shrine Wagner would have preferred by far is his theater, which since his death has been the scene of the world-famous Wagner Festival, supervised first by Cosima and —after her death—by Wagner's children and grandchildren.

HIS MUSIC

SINGLEHANDED, Wagner changed the destiny of opera. He established his own laws of aesthetics, created his own structures, and evolved his own style, producing an art that was as unique for its vastness of con-cept and iconoclastic approach as for its nobility and grandeur. At last he brought German opera to the goal toward which it had been head-ing since the days of Gluck. Wagner's ideal was a synthesis of the arts into a superart, the perfect marriage of music, poetry, drama, scenery, and acting. This was only an extension of the historic German effort to make music and play a single, indivisible entity. But in com-parison to what Wagner accomplished, all previous efforts in this direction—even those by Gluck and Weber—were at best tentative. Wagner freed opera of its many stultifying conventions. In their place he set up conventions of his own, which to some music lovers appear as stultifying as those he replaced. But whatever diversity of opinion on the subject may exist, there is no doubt that Wagner brought about a unification of text, drama, and music of which Gluck had dreamed.

To fulfill his ideal of a synthesis of the arts, Wagner had to write his own poetic texts so that a more intimate relationship might exist between melody and poetry, music and action. He had to project his individual ideas about scenic design and stage direction. Most important of all, he had to invent new musical devices. The most significant of these was the *leitmotif,* or leading motive (Wagner himself referred to it as *grundthema,* or basic theme): a melodic fragment which identifies a particular character, situation, object, or emotion. Hundreds of these motives are the threads of his musical texture, woven by him with wondrous polyphonic skill and built up with overwhelming theatrical effect. He also had to break, once and for all, with the arbitrary distinction so long existing between recitative and melody. He created a continuous flow of melody—now sensuously lyrical, now approximating actual speech—unobstructed by cadences and always deriving its personality and character from the demands of the drama. Finally, to achieve the musical expressiveness called for in his "synthesis of the arts," he had to give to the orchestra a symphonic importance it had never known in the opera house; he had to extend the technique of singing so radically that for many years his music overtaxed the capabilities of even experienced artists; and he had to enrich the vocabulary of harmony, orchestration, and thematic development far beyond the point that had been reached up to his time.

His ideal was not completely realized in his music dramas. The basic flaw in his artistic make-up was that he was a far greater musician than poet, dramatist, philosopher, or stage director. In spite of his every effort, the music is the dominating element in his unity of the arts, rather than an equal partner. But he happened to be one of the greatest musicians who ever lived. His genius made it possible for the music, when other elements failed him, to rise to the demands of his over-all concept and fill the breach. The poetry may at times be obscure and mystical; the dramatic action, static; the staging, awkward. But musical inspiration rarely failed him. At every climactic moment, it was there to flood the drama with wonder and beauty, with awe and towering majesty, with incandescence and a shattering emotional impact.

He called his music the "Art of the Future." The phrase became the battle cry of the *avant-garde* in music for half a century, and under its banner fierce struggles were waged. It was, indeed, the art of the future. Wagner's revolution affected every composer who followed him. But it is also the apotheosis of the art of the past. Wagner was the last of the Romantics, bringing romanticism to its final flowering. To remain a Romantic after Wagner was to imitate him, and many did that helplessly if hopefully. Those who wanted to retain their individuality had to rebel against him. Many tendencies of twentieth-century music, from impressionism to expressionism, represent just such attempts to escape from the spell of Wagnerism.

ANALYTICAL NOTES

Operas. *Tannhäuser* (1843-45) is the first of Wagner's operas to acquire permanence in the repertory. Its predecessor by three years, *The Flying Dutchman,* is heard only in infrequent revivals. In *Tannhäuser,* Wagner is still faithful to the conventional patterns of opera, consisting as this work does of more or less formal arias, ensemble numbers, choruses, ceremonial scenes, and a ballet. But in its emphasis on the drama, and in its concern over characterization and atmosphere, *Tannhäuser* was an important step in the development of Wagner as a musical dramatist. It contains the first suggestion of "song-speech" (later to become the spine of the music drama), as in the stirring narrative in which Tannhäuser tells of his journey to Rome.

Tannhäuser was a German minnesinger who lived in the thirteenth century. His story came to Wagner by way of a poem of Tieck and a story of E. T. A. Hoffmann. An actual visit to the Thuringian Valley, with the castle Wartburg rising majestically over it, further stimulated the composer.

Wagner intended his adaptation of the Tannhäuser legend to be symbolic of the conflict in man between the spiritual and the sensual. Spiritual love is symbolized by Elisabeth, carnal love by Venus. Tannhäuser renounces Venus for Elisabeth, only to lose her when, in a song contest for her hand, he can sing only of carnal love. Seeking forgiveness from the Pope, he is told that it can come only when the staff in the Pope's hand sprouts leaves. He comes back from his pilgrimage broken in health and spirit, to die at the side of Elisabeth's bier. Only then does the news come that the Pope's staff has sprouted leaves.

The famous overture uses important material from the opera. It begins with the solemn pilgrim's chant, in clarinets, bassoons, and horns, which grows into a stately religious theme for strings symbolizing Tannhäuser's repentance. A crescendo brings on a forceful return of the pilgrim's chant in trombones against broken triplets in the violins, and a restatement of the repentance melody. The pilgrim theme returns in its original instrumentation and dies out. There now emerges the shimmering, voluptuous music of the Venusberg. A peak of excitement and sensuality is reached when we hear Tannhäuser's exultant song of love erupting in the strings. The revels continue, above which rises the seductive song of Venus in the clarinet against quivering strings. More revels follow, and after that Tannhäuser's ecstatic song. When heard in the concert hall, the overture ends with a return of the pilgrim's chant. But in the opera house, the curtain rises on the first act, the Venusberg scene, immediately after Tannhäuser's song in the violins.

We now see and hear the bacchanal that Wagner wrote for the Paris *première*. The music begins passionately, with trills in the violins, crashing of cymbals, and cries in piccolos and oboes. More and more sensual does the music become as the bacchanal becomes a veritable orgy; rhythm, harmony, and instrumentation—rather than melody— convey the intensity of the passion. But the madness dies down and weariness sets in. The music subsides into languor and calm, as from a distance there comes the faint song of sirens. The ecstasy over, passions spent, the music dies out peacefully. Tannhäuser and Venus are left alone—Venus reclining on a couch, the minnesinger beside her. He sings an ecstatic hymn to Venus and to love, *"Dir töne Lob."* But he is weary of sensual love and he is eager to return to earth. When he utters the name of the Virgin Mary, Venus shrieks with horror and escapes, as darkness descends on Venusberg. The scene changes to a valley near the Wartburg Castle, where Tannhäuser finds himself. A shepherd is singing a pastoral tune. Suddenly from the distance there comes the chant of pilgrims on their way to Rome. There is such peace and beauty in the scene that Tannhäuser cannot resist the temptation to fall on his knees and pray. The sound of hunting horns interrupts him. His fellow minstrel-knights arrive and urge him to return with them to the Wartburg—and to Elisabeth.

The second act, within the Wartburg, begins with Elisabeth's exultant apostrophe, *"Dich, teure Halle."* She is overjoyed to see Tannhäuser, delighted that he will engage in the song contest. A fanfare in the trumpets, alternating with a forceful figure in the strings, brings on the stately march music with which the guests file into the hall. They, too, raise their voices in praise of the Wartburg. The Landgraf then announces the terms of the contest and the prize. Wolfram, the first candidate, sings to the purity of love in *"Blick ich umher,"* while Tannhäuser, recalling his song to Venus, can speak only of carnal joys. The assemblage is thrown into confusion; the knights rush at Tannhäuser with drawn swords. Only Elisabeth's poignant pleas save him. But Tannhäuser must seek pardon from the Pope. From the distance the pilgrims en route to Rome are heard chanting their religious song. Tannhäuser rushes out of the Wartburg to join them.

The orchestral prelude to Act III is a somber tone picture in which Tannhäuser's penitence and suffering are described, but it concludes in pastoral serenity with Tannhäuser's salvation. We are back in the Valley of the Wartburg when the curtain rises. Elisabeth is on bended knees before the shrine of the Virgin. Pilgrims return from Rome singing their chant, but Tannhäuser is not with them. Ecstatically, Elisabeth falls on her knees again and sings her celebrated prayer to the Virgin, *"Allmächt'ge Jungfrau."* From a discreet distance, Wolfram watches her and sees her leave. Sadly he strums on his harp and—as a star shines brightly in the sky—sings the ever popular ode to the evening star, *"O Du mein holder Abendstern."* No sooner has he finished his song than Tannhäuser appears, ill, haggard, and unkempt. He tells Wolfram of his futile pilgrimage to Rome, "Rome Narrative," of how the Pope had decreed that forgiveness would come only when the staff in his hand began to sprout leaves. Seductive voices now recall to him the delights of Venusberg. He is ready to return, but the name of Elisabeth brings him to his senses. A funeral procession enters, carrying the bier of Elisabeth. Tannhäuser falls beside it, dead. A chorus of pilgrims arrive to tell of a miracle: the staff of the Pope has sprouted leaves. Tannhäuser has found redemption.

Lohengrin (1846–48) represents the end of one epoch in Wagner's career. With his works up to and including *Lohengrin* he had paid his debt to the past; after *Lohengrin* he would become a prophet of the future.

Although *Lohengrin,* more or less, represents the operatic past, it opened up a new world for the form of opera. Within the old, accepted formulas Wagner had succeeded in creating new artistic concepts. He was not yet to make elaborate use of the *leitmotif,* but the *leitmotif* technique is definitely suggested throughout the score. The supreme importance of the orchestra within the operatic framework had not yet been established. And still, what extraordinary richness and imagination and variety of color he brought to it in this opera. He had not yet developed his immensely expressive melodic line, and he was still faithful to formal arias, duets, and choral numbers. On the other hand, these formal passages rise inevitably and naturally out of the musical texture.

Most important, in *Lohengrin* Wagner reveals himself to be a skillful dramatist whose demands on music and on text are equally exacting. In the coherence and unanimity of its mood—even, at times, at the price of montony—*Lohengrin* is a warning of things to come. As Liszt put it: "With *Lohengrin* the old world of opera comes to an end."

Wagner derived the Lohengrin legend from two sources. One was a thirteenth-century poem by the minnesinger Wolfram von Eschenbach (who appears as a character in *Tannhäuser*). The other was *The Knight of the Swan,* a volume of poems by Conrad von Würzburg published in 1816. But the central theme of *Lohengrin* appears also in *The Flying Dutchman:* man's eternal search for a woman who trusts him implicitly and who will forever be faithful to him. For Lohengrin is the mysterious champion of Elsa von Brabant, who has been unjustly accused of murder. All he asks is that Elsa make no attempt to uncover his identity. He defeats Telramund, Elsa's accuser, and then marries Elsa. But overpowering curiosity leads her to break her promise: she must learn who he is. Lohengrin then reveals that he is the son of Parsifal, and a knight of the Holy Grail. But having revealed his identity, he must leave her forever.

The prelude to Act I is one of Wagner's serenest and most spiritual pages; only in *Parsifal* was he to write music such as this. There is a single theme, the Holy Grail motive, first heard pianissimo in the violins, then passing to different sections of the orchestra as a slow crescendo is evolved. At the height of this crescendo, the motive is magnificently promulgated by trumpets and trombones. And now a gradual decrescendo takes place, fading out pianissimo in violins (in the upper register) and flutes. Wagner explained that this prelude was intended to give an ethereal portrait of a vision in the sky with angels bearing the Grail. Its brilliant glory touches a kneeling worshiper, after which the vision vanishes.

In the first act, on the banks of the Scheldt River near Antwerp, Elsa is unjustly accused by Telramund of having murdered her brother. King Henry announces that a duel must decide Elsa's innocence or guilt—a duel between Telramund and Elsa's champion. In her beautiful aria, known as "Elsa's Dream" (*"Einsam in trüben Tagen"*), she reveals that such a champion appeared in her dreams, and she begs for him to make an appearance. He is Lohengrin, and he arrives in a boat drawn by a swan, whom he bids a touching farewell, *"Nun sei bedankt."* He reveals that he is ready to fight for Elsa, but only if she promises that she will never attempt to uncover his identity. Elsa promises. Lohengrin defeats Telramund and then begs for Elsa's hand in marriage.

The second act takes place in a fortress in Antwerp. Elsa sings of her ecstatic happiness, *"Euch Lüften, die mein Klagen."* Fanfares from trumpets announce the approach of dawn—and Elsa's wedding day. Telramund's wife, Ortrud, fills Elsa with doubts about Lohengrin by suggesting that he is a magician, while Telramund insists that he was defeated by foul means. They insist that there is only one way in which Elsa can find peace of mind and be sure of her future husband: by compelling him to reveal who he is. But Elsa remains faithful to Lohengrin and her promise.

The orchestral prelude to Act III is descriptive of the joy of Elsa and Lohengrin on the evening of their wedding. It begins with a jubilant theme in full orchestra in which the festive atmosphere of the wedding is set forth. There is a second vigorous theme, for cellos, horns, and bassoons in unison, followed by a brief marchlike idea for the winds. Both main themes return, and after the second theme has become quietly subdued, the curtain rises on the bridal chamber. The wedding procession enters to the strains of the world-famous Wedding March, and the guests raise their voices in the "Bridal Chorus." When the guests have departed, Elsa and Lohengrin speak rapturously of their love for each other. But Elsa's rapture is not undiluted, for she is beginning to be disturbed by doubts of Lohengrin's background and origin. She begs, laments, then demands to know who he is. Suddenly, Telramund bursts into the room, attacks Lohengrin, and is killed. Sadly, Lohengrin remarks that happiness for him and Elsa has vanished and that he can never tell Elsa what she wants to know.

The scene changes to the banks of the Scheldt River. Lohengrin can now reveal that he is a knight of the Holy Grail who can perform good deeds just as long at he remains unidentified. He must now take his leave forever. He bids Elsa farewell tenderly, mourning the fate that is separating them. His swan returns to take him away. It is then that Ortrud reveals that the swan is Elsa's brother, transformed by Ortrud's witchcraft; if Elsa had not forced Lohengrin to reveal himself, she would not only have had Lohengrin as a husband but the spell that kept her brother a swan would have been permanently broken. Lohengrin unclasps the chain on the swan's neck, whereupon the swan disappears and Elsa's brother reappears in human form. Lohengrin takes his leave, his boat now being drawn by a dove. And Elsa, heart-broken, dies in her brother's arms.

In *Tristan und Isolde* (1857–59), Wagner is most successful in inte-grating drama and music into a single artistic entity. No other Wagner music drama has such consistency of emotion and atmosphere. No-where else has he made use of so elementary a plot, freed of any con-fusing symbolism and of his usual tendency toward dull repetition and windy explanations to unravel the plot. With remarkable single-ness of purpose, and with inexorable logic, *Tristan* progresses from the opening bar of the prelude to the closing chord of the *"Liebestod"* without deviating from its tempestuous love story. It remains one of the most moving, one of the most passionate interpretations of physi-cal love in music, a love that first exalts and then destroys its pro-tagonists.

It is based on a legend retold many times by poets and storytellers. Tristan is sent to Ireland to bring back Isolde, daughter of the Irish King, as a bride for his uncle, King Mark of Cornwall. But a love potion is the undoing of Tristan and Isolde, and they fall in love with each other. Back in Cornwall, where Isolde is married to King Mark, the two lovers are consumed by desire for each other. They are dis-covered one night in the garden, and Tristan is wounded by one of the King's men. Tristan's trusted friend, Kurwenal, takes him to his castle in Brittany, where he is later followed by Isolde. He dies in her arms, and she follows him to death.

The prelude follows the dynamics pattern of the *Lohengrin* prelude. There is a long sustained crescendo erupting into a climax, followed by a long and sustained decrescendo that dies out into a whisper. The prelude begins with a slow phrase in the cellos (motive of "longing"), followed and joined by another phrase in the oboes ("desire"). These ideas are repeated twice more, after which there is an exchange of yearning cries between strings and woodwinds. The orchestra erupts with a loud chord. The principal melody is now heard: an ecstatic song for the cellos symbolizing Tristan's love glance. The music becomes more intense and restless as this material is worked out with marvelous polyphonic skill. The prelude ends with a return of the "longing" and "desire" motives, and the phrase is allowed to die out.

The curtain rises at once on the first act, the deck of a ship. An unaccompanied sailor's song is heard from the masthead. Within the ship, Isolde is fretting because Cornwall will soon be reached and Tristan has as yet taken no notice of her. She orders her servant, Brangäne, to prepare a death potion with which she plans to destroy both herself and Tristan. But, without Isolde's knowledge, Brangäne substitutes a love potion. When Tristan and Isolde drink it in a toast, they become overcome with passion. They rush to each other's arms as shouts from the deck announce the arrival at Cornwall.

The next act takes place in Isolde's garden in Cornwall. Distant hunting horns tell us that King Mark has gone on a hunt. Isolde signals her beloved, Tristan, to come—waving her scarf in the air at his approach. From the tower, Brangäne sings words of warning, as the lovers embrace passionately. They surrender to their love with one of the most rapturous pages of love music ever conceived: the *"Liebesnacht"* music, beginning with the passionate duet *"O sink hernieder, Nacht der Liebe."* Once again Brangäne sounds her warning, *"Habet acht,"* but the lovers no longer hear her. Suddenly the love idyl is shattered. King Mark and his men burst upon the scene. In place of anger, King Mark gives expression to his terrible hurt in being betrayed by his own nephew. One of the King's men, Melot, rushes to Tristan with drawn sword and wounds him.

The prelude to Act III is a gloomy tone picture of the garden in Brittany, on a bleak cliff overlooking the sea; it touches on Tristan's suffering. As the curtain rises on this desolate scene, we hear a shepherd piping an elegiac melody. Kurwenal is tending the wounded Tristan. When Kurwenal tells him that Isolde has been sent for, Tristan grows delirious with excitement and believes he sees a ship approaching. Isolde comes at last; the lovers are reunited; and Tristan dies in her arms. King Mark also arrives; having heard of the love potion, he has come to forgive Tristan and Isolde. But Kurwenal believes the King and his men have come to fight, and he attacks them with his own followers. In this fray, both Melot and Kurwenal are killed. Isolde is oblivious to everything, even to Mark's terrible grief at Tristan's death. With Tristan in her arms, she sings the *"Liebestod"* ("Love Death"), her last message of love and her search for release in death. It begins calmly and sadly with the words *"Mild und leise wie er lächelt"*—we heard this music in the love scene of the second act. The funereal voice of a clarinet joins that of Isolde in her poignant song. But with the words *"Heller schallend, mich umwallend"* the emotions grow increasing turbulent and ecstatic, to a point of delirium; then the emotions subside and it is over. The violins provide a gentle, tender valedictory to Isolde's song of love and death, and Isolde joins her beloved.

In writing *Die Meistersinger* (1862–67), his only comedy, Wagner produced his most human and lovable opera. It is a far different Wagner we confront here from the one in *Tristan*. The main point of difference is that here, in place of violent and neurotic emotions and turbulence of mood, we have serenity and gentleness. A character such as Hans Sachs—a three-dimensional portrait of a benign, tolerant, wise, and proud cobbler-philosopher—is unique in the Wagnerian gallery. This is a man ruled not by raging feelings, but by quiet reason. This three-dimensional portrait is found not only on the stage, but within the texture of the music—in such unforgettable pages as the monologue *"Wahn, Wahn"* and the beautiful and tranquil prelude to Act III. But the character of Sachs is not all that sets *Die Meistersinger* apart from the other music dramas. The healthy love affair of Walther and Eva inspires the composer to produce music of sweetness, rather than of surging passion. Even the ridicule heaped upon the villain lacks violence and malice, but is full of gentle mockery!

Before putting his opera down on paper, Wagner made an intensive research into the subjects of Nuremberg (the scene of the opera) and the mastersingers. The fruits of this research are found both in the authenticity of the drama and in the quality of the music. Wagner drew from old German music that which served him; the opera is filled with memories of old German chorales, lute songs, part songs, fugues, and street ditties. He even borrowed two of his musical motives from old "prize master-tones," which he found in a book printed in Nuremburg in the seventeenth century. The interpolation of such materials suggests the operatic, rather than the musical-dramatic, treatment. And the truth of the matter is that *Die Meistersinger* is more of an opera than a music drama. Wagner uses full-fledged arias (the "Prize Song," for example), ensemble numbers (the Quintet), choral pages (the street scene in Act II), processions (the entrance of the mastersingers in Act III), and even dances ("The Dance of the Apprentices"). So wonderfully are these elements of grand opera assimilated within the artistic whole that dramatic truth is never sacrificed.

As with *Tannhäuser,* the focal point of *Die Meistersinger* is a song contest, the winner of which gains the hand of the heroine. The knight

Walther von Stolzing, who is eager to win Eva, enters the contest. He is aided and abetted by the philosophical cobbler Sachs, to whom Walther sings a song of heavenly beauty that came to him in a dream. His antagonist, Beckmesser—he who follows all the rules—proves ridiculous, while Walther's song, even though it fails to follow accepted laws, wins the coveted prize.

It is not difficult to guess the moral Wagner had in mind in writing such a text. Wagner is Walther von Stolzing, who can produce musical beauty in defiance of accepted traditions and rules. He is assured of victory over the Beckmessers of the world, ever enslaved to textbook precepts, incapable of arriving at originality and greatness through their allegiance to tradition. Beckmesser was actually intended by Wagner as a portrait of his hated Viennese critic, Eduard Hanslick, who had been attacking him with such undiminished fury. Originally, Wagner had intended calling his villainous character Hans Lick.

The prelude to *Die Meistersinger* is one of the glories not only of Wagnerian music, but of all symphonic literature. There are five major themes, all drawn from the opera. It opens with an august and stately march in full chords; this is the theme of the mastersingers. This is followed by a gentle subject for woodwinds representing "Waking Love." Another march theme in the brass, brisker than the first, stands for the "Banner of the Mastersingers." We now hear the famous "Prize Song" in the violins, and this grows into an impassioned idea for the strings connoting "Love's Ardor." In the development these themes are varied and often combined with breath-taking polyphonic virtuosity. The prelude is built into an overpowering climax and comes to a stunning conclusion with the mastersinger theme sounding resplendently in the full orchestra.

With the last chord of the prelude, the curtain rises on the church of St. Catherine in Nuremberg. A chorale is being sung as the services come to an end. Walther, a stranger in Nuremberg, and Eva exchange sympathetic glances as the congregation files out. Walther learns that he can win Eva in a song contest of the mastersingers, and Eva urges the apprentice David to prepare Walther. But David confuses rather than enlightens Walther. The mastersingers come upon the scene. Pogner addresses them and announces the terms of the contest in *"Das schöne Fest."* Walther applies for admission into the guild and asks for a trial. To the interrogation of the mastersingers, Walther explains where he acquired the art of song, *"Am stillen Herd."* His improvised song, *"Fanget an,"* violates so many rules (as Beckmesser gleefully notes on his slate) that he is interrupted and rejected. Sachs has found a touch of genius in his unorthodox song and tries to speak for Walther, but Beckmesser rallies the men to his point of view. The mastersingers then take their leave, singing praises to their guild, *"Glück auf zum Meistersingern."*

In the next act we are in a Nuremberg street. It is evening, and the apprentices are putting up their shutters. Sachs is still outside working. His thoughts wander; he cannot forget the beauty of Walther's song; he muses in *"Wie duftet doch der Flieder."* In the secret depths of his heart he, too, is in love with Eva, but he recognizes the futility of his love. Eva appears; she is coy and flirtatious with the cobbler, *"Gut'n Abend, Meister!"* Before long, Sachs realizes that she is in love with Walther. He soon becomes a silent witness to their exchange of tender sentiments and their plans to elope. They are interrupted by the arrival of Beckmesser and seek cover. Beckmesser has come to serenade Eva with the ludicrous song he has prepared for the contest. Poor Beckmesser!—hardly has he sung a phrase when he is interrupted by the loud hammering of Sachs's cobbling and by his lusty cobbling song, *"Jerum! Jerum!"* The singing and the hammering arouse the neighborhood. One of those aroused is David who, seeing his beloved Magdalena in one of the windows and Beckmesser below, jumps to conclusions and administers a sound thrashing to the serenader. In the ensuing confusion Walther and Eva try to make their escape, but they are stopped by the solicitous Sachs. Suddenly the confusion in the street is resolved into order. All is quiet and peace again. A watchman strolls through the streets and announces the hour through the stillness of the night.

The prelude to Act III is a portrait of Hans Sachs. It begins with a majestic theme for cellos, which will soon reappear in his monologue *"Wahn, Wahn."* After a fugato treatment of the second part of this theme there appears an impressive chorale for brasses and trombones, with which Sachs is greeted by the people in the closing scene. Toward the end of this prelude we hear a brief recollection of the "Prize Song." The prelude ends with the opening melody, proclaimed first by the entire orchestra and then tenderly by the strings.

The first scene of the concluding act is in Hans Sachs's workshop. David sings to Sachs a chorale of the festival day, *"Am Jordan Sankt Johannes stand."* Midway in his song David realizes that this festival day is also the name day of Sachs; he showers the cobbler with felicitations, flowers, and cakes. When he leaves, Sachs reflects on the state of the world, with its loves and hates, in *"Wahn, Wahn."* When he has completed his revery, Walther enters. After a brief dialogue, *"Grüss' Gott, mein Junker,"* he tells Sachs of the wonderful melody that came to him in a dream. It is the popular "Prize Song," which is now being sung for the first time. Sachs writes down the song, and both men leave. Beckmesser arrives, sees the song, and regards it as evidence that Sachs is planning to enter the contest. But Sachs return and convinces Beckmesser that this is not the case, even going so far as to offer the song to Beckmesser as a gift. Satisfied, Beckmesser takes his leave. Eva now appears, beautifully attired in her festive dress. She is a vision of beauty. When Walther sees her, he is so enraptured that he bursts into one of the stanzas of his "Prize Song." This song has its effect on Eva, who falls into Sachs's arm and tearfully confesses to the cobbler the immensity of her love for Walther, *"O Sachs, mein Freund."* (In the orchestra there is an intriguing quotation from *Tristan and Isolde!*) With the arrival of David and Magdalena, Sachs decides that the birth of a new song requires christening and that he and Eva shall be the godparents, with Magdalena and David as witnesses. The scene ends with the magnificent Quintet, in which each gives expression to his or her inmost feelings, *"Selig wie die Sonne."*

It is the day of the contest, and the scene changes to a field on the shore of the Pegnitz River. A brilliant procession of the different guilds takes place, followed by the entrance of the mastersingers. Hans Sachs is greeted with a rousing chorale, *"Wach' auf!"*—to which Sachs responds with dignity and deep feeling, *"Euch macht ihr's leicht."* Beckmesser is the first called to sing; he makes a complete mess of his effort and then accuses Sachs of having been the author of this monstrosity; for Beckmesser, in trying to steal the "Prize Song," has distorted it completely. Proudly, Sachs justifies himself by calling Walther to sing the same song. The "Prize Song" is now heard in all its beauty. Walther is, of course, the victor. Eva places a wreath on his head, and they both get Pogner's blessings. Pogner tries to place around Walther's neck the chain of the mastersingers, which Walther spurns, remembering that he was once rejected by them. But Sachs kindly advises him to spurn neither the honor nor the wisdom and counsel of the masters who keep alive the finest traditions of German art. The sagacity of Sachs's exhortation is rousingly acclaimed by the people, who enter into a spirited tribute to the wise cobbler, *"Heil Sachs!"*

The Ring of the Nibelungs is one of the most monumental structures in all art. It took Wagner a quarter of a century to complete it. It requires four evenings for a complete performance, and the last of these operas consumes five hours. Individually and collectively, the four operas of this cycle tax fully the musical, dramatic, and stage resources of even the best-equipped opera house.

The *Ring* represents the apex of Wagner's artistic achievement. He poured into it the full tide of his musical genius. To it he gave the best of his dramatic and poetic powers, regarding it as the complete realization of his aesthetic and musical theories. The writing of works even as formidable as *Tristan und Isolde* and *Die Meistersinger* was for him a relaxation from the Gargantuan task of the *Ring*. He went to *Tristan* and *Die Meistersinger* to renew his strength and nurture his spirit before returning to the prodigious job of completing his cycle, which so sapped his energies.

He did not think he would live to see the *Ring* performed. He knew that a special theater would have to be built before it could be properly presented. Nevertheless, he had to bring his vision to life, consoled by the fugitive thought (as he wrote in the preface to the entire poem, published in 1853) that some day, somewhere, there would arise a wealthy and idealistic prince sufficiently interested in this work of art to create a theater for it. That such a prince did appear, and in Wagner's lifetime, can be considered a miracle.

The *Ring* is not the complete fulfillment of the ideal to synthesize the arts that Wagner regarded it. The drama is serviceable, but little more than that. Too often the action is static; too often the long monologues are repetitious to the point of boredom. The poetry is adequate, and that is about all. But there can be no question about the greatness and majesty of the music. It is the music that transforms what might otherwise be mediocrity into magic, providing the eloquence and dramatic impact not found in either the poetry or the stage action. It is in the music that we are confronted with overpowering conflicts, tenderness, grandeur, heroism, passion—these, and a tragedy that stirs us to the depths of our beings.

In the *Ring,* even more than in his other music dramas, Wagner is the symphonist *in excelsis*. The orchestra is the principal protagonist (the voices are treated as instrumental parts) and is handled with a variety and wizardry that is continually a source of wonder. It is in the often astute, often superlatively agile handling and development of his thematic material within the orchestra that the most stirring effects are evolved. Each of the great climaxes of the *Ring*—the closing scenes of *The Rhinegold* and *The Valkyrie,* the concluding love music of

Siegfried, and the death music and final pages of *The Twilight of the Gods*—is evolved out of material used in these operas time and again. And yet Wagner never fails to sculpture this familiar material into new designs of incredible beauty and overpowering effect.

Although the *Ring* comprises four operas, it is called a "trilogy" because the first of these—*The Rhinegold*—was designated by Wagner as a prologue to the other three works. It is in four scenes played without interruption.

The prelude to *The Rhinegold* is built out of a single chord. From this chord there evolves a slow, long phrase heard in bassoons and horns. This phrase gathers momentum, and before long we have the flow and surge and swell of the Rhine River. The curtain then rises on the first scene: the river. The Rhine maidens, guarding the precious Rhinegold, are swimming and singing. Alberich, the Nibelung, realizes that he who gets the Rhinegold and fashions it into a ring can rule the world. He seizes the gold from the maidens. Darkness descends on the river, as if in premonition of inescapable doom.

The scene changes to the mountain tops of Valhalla, where two giants are building a palace for the god Wotan and his wife, Fricka. Their price is: Freia, goddess of love. But with the palace completed, Wotan regrets the bargain and offers instead the treasures of the Nibelung, which the giants are willing to accept.

Wotan descends to Nibelheim, the home of the Nibelungs. Through guile and artifice he manages to get the precious hoard from Alberich. Alberich hurls a mighty curse at anybody who possesses them.

Back in Valhalla, Wotan is ready to turn the treasures over to the giants. Suddenly Erda arises out of the earth and gives an awesome warning to Wotan not to relinquish the ring, which Alberich has fashioned from the Rhinegold, *"Weiche, Wotan, Weiche!"* But Wotan must stick to his word and deliver the ring. It does not take long for the ring to work its havoc: to gain possession of it, the giant Fafner kills his brother Fasolt. But now the gods are ready to enter their new abode. The majestic music of the "Entrance of the Gods into Valhalla" (the basic materials of which include the Rhinegold motif, heard in the prelude, and a regal theme for horns representing Valhalla) is heard, and the gods pass over a bridge toward the palace, shining resplendently in the sun.

Between the action of *The Rhinegold* and that of the second drama, *The Valkyrie,* the giant Fafner has transformed himself into a dragon to guard the all-powerful and much-coveted ring. Wotan realizes that only a hero can recapture it. He comes down to earth as a human to create such a hero. His offspring are the Wälsung twins—Siegmund and Sieglinde. The twins are separated in childhood when the house of their mother is burned to the ground. It is at this point that *The Valkyrie* resumes the story.

The brief prelude gives a tonal picture of a raging storm. When the storm relents, the curtain rises on the interior of Hunding's house. Siegmund comes in out of the storm seeking shelter and a drink, and he is ministered to by Sieglinde, wife of Hunding. Siegmund and Sieglinde, of course, do not know that they are brother and sister. Sieglinde tells him of her forced marriage to Hunding. She also reveals that a stranger had come to their house and implanted a sword in a tree, to belong to anyone who can remove it. Siegmund, at this point, recalls that his father had promised him a weapon as protection. Before long the two realize that they are in love. The door swings open to reveal a beautiful spring night outside, the moon flooding its light across the threshold. The beauty of the night and Siegmund's ardor bring forth from him a rapturous song, *"Winterstürme wichen dem Wonnemond"* (Siegmund's "Spring Song"). No less ardently does Sieglinde reply with her own expression of love, *"Du bist der Lenz."* Discovering that Siegmund is a Wälsung, Sieglinde realizes their true relationship, but the discovery can no longer affect their love. Sieglinde urges Siegmund to remove the sword from the tree. When he does so, they escape from Hunding's house.

A second brief orchestral prelude pictures the feverish flight of the lovers. The second act is set in a wild and rocky pass. The Valkyrie Brünnhilde, the favorite daughter of Wotan, is in battle dress, sending out her battle cry—"Ho-yo-to-ho"—to the other Valkyries. Fricka, wife of Wotan, enters angrily. She is disturbed over the flight of Siegmund and Sieglinde and the hurt they have brought to Hunding's house, and demands that they be punished. To this Wotan agrees reluctantly. Brünnhilde is loath to bring harm to the young lovers, but Wotan is adamant and insists that his wish be carried out. When the gods have left, the two Wälsungs appear, exhausted by their flight from the vengeful Hunding. Brünnhilde is so moved by the pathetic plight of the Wälsungs and their great love for each other that—in spite of herself—she defies her father's orders and tries to protect them, as Siegmund goes forth to battle the approaching Hunding. But Wotan intervenes, and by plunging his sword between the protagonists he enables Hunding to administer the death blow. Enraged at Brünnhilde's disobedience, Wotan vows vengeance on his beloved daughter.

The third act, the summit of a rocky mountain, begins with the celebrated "Ride of the Valkyries," one of the most realistic and exciting translations of motion into music. This piece of music accompanies the aerial flight of the Valkyries on their steeds to their retreat. But Brünnhilde is not with them; she has taken Sieglinde under her protection, knowing as she does that Sieglinde is to become the mother of Siegmund's child. With the aid of her sisters, she has Sieglinde secreted in the forests where the dragon guards the ring; she gives Sieglinde the shattered blade of the sword Siegmund had withdrawn from the tree. A hero will reforge that sword, Brünnhilde tells Sieglinde, and that hero's name will be Siegfried. A furious Wotan bursts upon the scene, demanding Brünnhilde's presence. She has defied him and must be punished: she is to be banished from Valhalla forever, no longer to be a Valkyrie. At this sentence, the other Valkyries flee in terror. Pathetically, Brünnhilde pleads with Wotan to forgive her, *"War es so schmählich?"* But, though his heart is broken, Wotan must go through with the punishment. He makes only one concession: Brünnhilde will be put into a deep sleep and protected by a circle of flame until a hero comes through the fires to awaken her. Tenderly, Wotan embraces his beloved daughter and bids her a poignant farewell, *"Leb' wohl, du kühnes, herrliches Kind."* He kisses her on the eyelids and carries her to a grass mound, where he gently puts her down and covers her with her shield. He then calls on Loge, the God of Fire, to create the circle of fire. "The Magic Fire Music" *"Feuerzauber"* graphically recreates the flicker and dance of the flames as they pierce through the ground. He who fears my spear, Wotan announces, shall never cross these flames. He takes a last lingering look at his daughter and departs sorrowfully.

The third drama, *Siegfried,* opens in the forest cave of the dwarf Mime. Mime has raised Sieglinde's son, Siegfried, hoping that he may some day forge his father's broken sword, Nothung, and use it to slay the dragon, Fafner, and capture the ring. Mime himself has failed in his every effort to forge the broken pieces together. Siegfried enters, leading a bear by a rope, with which he frightens the poor dwarf. His delight in torturing Mime is succeeded by petulance and ill temper. What disturbs Siegfried is his desire to know his origins, and he forces the truth from Mime. Learning that the broken sword belonged to his

father, he orders Mime to mend it and leaves for the forest. As Mime
makes another hopeless effort to forge the sword, Wotan enters disguised as the Wanderer. He offers to answer any three questions put to
him by Mime, willing to pay with his life if he fails. Wotan answers all
three questions—about the Nibelungs, Fafner, and Wotan—and then
insists that Mime subject himself to similar conditions. Mime answers
two of these questions, which are concerned with the birth of Siegfried
and the sword, but is unable to tell Wotan who will forge the sword.
Generously, Wotan forfeits his right to claim Mime's life. When Wotan
has gone, Siegfried returns. Enraged that Mime has failed to mend the
broken sword, he goes to the anvil and does it himself, singing the
"Forging Song" (*"Nothung, Nothung"*) as he works. With one sweep
of his sword, Siegfried smashes the anvil in two. Mime realizes that
Siegfried will gain possession of the ring, and he makes plans to poison
the hero once the prize falls into his hands.

A brief prelude sets an ominous mood for the second act, which takes
place in a forest by Fafner's cave. Wotan urges Alberich to call on
Fafner, the dragon, to give up the ring, which Fafner refuses to do.
When Alberich and Wotan have gone, Siegfried and Mime arrive.
Siegfried lies under a tree and begins to muse about his past and listens
to the song of the birds. This page, known as the "Forest Murmurs," is
an exquisite pastoral tone poem. He imitates the call of the birds with
his horn and thus awakens the slumbering dragon. Fearlessly he attacks
Fafner and kills him. Accidently he puts his finger, still wet with the
dragon's blood, to his mouth and is thus magically endowed with the
power of understanding the language of birds. A bird reveals to him
that the dead dragon's cave contains a treasure trove, including the ring,
which can bring him unlimited power. After Siegfried has acquired the
hoard, the bird tells him of Mime's deceit and of the dwarf's intention
of poisonging him. Siegfried kills him mercilessly. Finally the forest
bird tells Siegfried that a bride is awaiting him and offers to lead him
to her. Siegfried follows the bird eagerly.

The third act is in two scenes. In the first, a wild region, Wotan,
still disguised as the Wanderer, calls to Erda for counsel. She rises out
of the bowels of the earth, but is unable to help him. He then confronts
Siegfried, learns from him of the death of Fafner and the forging of the
sword. When Wotan tries to stand in his way, Siegfried smashes
Wotan's spear with his sword and proceeds in quest of his bride. The
scene changes to the Valkyr rock, where Brünnhilde lies sleeping surrounded by flame. Siegfried penetrates the ring of fire, awakens her

with a kiss, and claims her as his bride. They express their love for each other in an ecstatic duet, *"Heil dir, Sonne!"*

The Twilight of the Gods begins with a prologue. Three Norns (Nordic goddesses presiding over human destinies) are spinning the golden rope of Fate. When it snaps in their hands, they realize that the final doom is at hand. Dawn breaks, lighting up the rocky heights which Brünnhilde and Siegfried have made their home. Siegfried must be off for exploits, but before he goes he gives his bride the fatal ring as a token of his love. There is a recollection of the love duet of the closing scene of *Siegfried* as they bid each other a tender farewell. Siegfried leaps on Brünnhilde's horse and rides off, the call of his horn soon being heard from a distance. It is at this point that we hear the famous orchestral excerpt "Siegfried's Rhine Journey," in which the principal melodic subjects include a strong theme for strings and clarinets known as the "Decision to Love" motive, Siegfried's famous horn call, and the motives of the Rhine and the Rhinegold. With the last strains of the "Rhine Journey" the curtain rises on the first act, the Hall on the Rhine, the home of Gunther and his sister, Gutrune. Their half brother, Hagen, is desirous of owning the ring and comes to the realization that he might obtain it if he could succeed in getting Siegfried married to Gutrune and Brünnhilde to Gunther. After Siegfried has arrived at the Hall, Hagen has Gutrune give him a magic potion which will bring about a loss of memory. Siegfried now falls in love with Gutrune, and when he learns that Gunther is seeking Brünnhilde as his wife, offers to accompany him in this quest.

A change of scene recalls the Valkyr rock. Waltraute, a Valkyrie, comes to beg Brünnhilde to return the ring to the Rhine, but as it is a symbol of Siegfried's love, she refuses to do so. The sound of Siegfried's horn announces his return. But he has come disguised as Gunther, and claims her as his bride. When Brünnhilde resists, he seizes her, snatches the ring from her finger, and carries her off.

The real Gunther brings Brünnhilde back to the Hall and is hailed by his vassals in the opening of the second act. When Brünnhilde meets Siegfried, who does not recognize her and makes violent protests when she points him out as her husband, she is convinced that he has betrayed her and vows vengeance. She gains an ally in Hagen, suggests a hunting trip for Siegfried, and reveals to Hagen a vulnerable part of his body where he can be killed. When the wedding procession of Siegfried and Gutrune arrives, Hagen prevails upon Brünnhilde to join it with Gunther.

The third act takes place in a wooded valley on the banks of the river. The Rhine maidens, swimming in the waters, wait for the approaching Siegfried. They tell him of the evil of the ring, urge him to return it to the Rhine. But Siegfried is deaf to their warnings, and they swim away with apprehension. The sound of hunting horns betrays the approach of Hagen and his men. Hagen gives Siegfried a new potion which, this time, restores his memory. Suddenly, Siegfried recalls Brünnhilde and his great love for her. Two ravens fly over his head. As Siegfried watches them, Hagen plunges his spear into the hero's back. The blow is fatal. Dying, Siegfried addresses his last words to his beloved Brünnhilde, *"Brünnhilde, heilige Braut!"* His dead body is lifted by the vassals, and, to the accompaniment of the majestic and moving "Siegfried's Death Music," it is carried back to Gunther's Hall. The "Death Music" begins with roll of the kettledrums, a wail in the strings, and shattering chords in the orchestra. Principal motives from the four operas review for us the career of the hero, always dominated by the opening Death theme. The motif of "Siegfried the Hero" is heard in a minor key as the second scene brings us back to Gunther's Hall. There, Brünnhilde, who has learned the truth, commands the vassals to build a funeral pyre, into which Siegfried's body is brought. Savagely, Brünnhilde throws into the leaping flames the cursed ring, which she had removed from Siegfried's finger. The celebrated "Immolation Scene" begins at this point. Summoning her horse, Brünnhilde sings a magnificent farewell, *"Starke Scheite schichtet mir dort."* Then, mounting her horse, Brünnhilde rides into the flames to her death. The Rhine rises; at its crest are the Rhine maidens, who carry Hagen to his death when he leaps into the river to regain the ring. Valhalla crumbles. The twilight of the gods has come.

Parsifal (1877–82) was Wagner's last music drama. Having glorified sensual and physical love in *Tristan and Isolde,* he now turned to spiritual love. The idea of writing a religious music drama—possibly based on the life of Christ—had haunted him for a long time. But not until the closing years of his life—and almost as if conceding that he was ready to reject the pleasures of the body for those of the soul—did he realize this ambition. He went for his text to a medieval legend found in the poems of the German minnesinger Wolfram von Eschenbach. His theme was centered around the legend of the Holy Grail, the cup from which Christ drank at the Last Supper and which afterward was reputed to hold drops of his blood following his crucifixion.

Wagner put *Parsifal* in a special category, calling it not an opera or a music drama, but a "stage-consecrating festival play." As a religious drama, *Parsifal* is a devout and spiritual work. But, in the last analysis, it must stand or fall as a work of art. On this point there has been considerable difference of opinion. There are some who regard *Parsifal* as the apotheosis of Wagner's art, as the last will and testament of a great musical dramatist. Others, while respecting many of its sublime pages, are inclined to consider it among his weaker works. Both sides have potent arguments to prove their points. Those who consider *Parsifal* weak single out its many faults: the interminable and boring monologues (particularly those by Gurnemanz); the lack of action; the artificiality of having such leading characters as Parsifal or Kundry on the stage without doing or saying anything; the incongruities and inconsistencies in the plot; the lifelessness of the characters. And yet the opposing faction also has powerful arguments. There is a radiant spirituality in *Parsifal* which puts it in a class by itself. If the text has weaknesses, the music has wonderful compensations. The characters may lack humanity on the stage, but not in the score; it is in the music that we understand and sympathize with the terrible suffering of Amfortas, the purity of Parsifal, the blending of good and evil in Kundry. What may be static on the stage, moves with inexorable logic in the music, which is rarely boring and usually on the highest plane of inspiration.

The prelude begins with the motive of the "Last Supper" in strings and woodwinds. This motive is repeated with changed instrumentation and an accompaniment of arpeggios. After a slight pause the motive appears in a minor key, and after another pause there comes the solemn theme of the Grail, which is a version of the "Dresden Amen." When the Grail theme dies out, the "Faith" motive is sounded loud and triumphant in horns and trombones, to be followed by a repetition of the Grail theme in the strings. The opening "Last Supper" melody returns after a passage for drums and tremolos for strings. This is followed by the "Lance" motive, which is derived from four notes of the "Last Supper" subject. There is a working out of some of this material, after which the "Last Supper" motive leads into the opening scene of the music drama.

The action preceding the drama concerns the Knights of the Holy Grail who, on Montsalvat, guard two holy relics: the spear with which Christ was pierced and the cup from which he drank at the Last Supper and which now contains the blood he shed at the Cross. Since

Klingsor was denied admission to this holy order, he aspires to get the holy cup through sorcery; he has a garden of beautiful women who tempt and ruin knights. Through his magic, Klingsor has wounded Amfortas, ruler of the knights, with the holy spear. Only if this holy spear is regained from Klingsor and if the wound of Amfortas is touched with it by one who is pure of heart, can the knight be cured.

It is at this point that the first act begins, in a forest near Montsalvat. Parsifal comes into this wood and is caught by the knights for killing a swan. In answering their questions, Parsifal reveals himself to be a "guileless fool." Gurnemanz, one of the knights, is tempted to believe that perhaps this boy is the one destined to regain the spear and cure Amfortas. Gurnemanz leads the boy to the hall of the Grail as solemn "Transformation Music," with pealing bells, marks a change of scene. The knights fill the hall and go through their religious ceremony. Parsifal watches the proceedings, incapable of understanding their meaning.

At Klingsor's castle, in the first scene of the second act, the magician calls on Kundry to tempt Parsifal. At first Kundry resists wildly, but she is under Klingsor's spell and must do his bidding. The scene changes suddenly and becomes the magic garden of Klingsor, to which Parsifal comes. The garden is filled with beautiful women, and among them is Kundry transformed into a woman of great beauty. She tries to seduce Parsifal; when he resists her, she calls to Klingsor for assistance. Klingsor hurls at Parsifal the magic spear, which remains suspended in mid-air. Parsifal seizes it and makes the sign of the Cross. Klingsor's castle and garden both disintegrate into ruin.

It is now Good Friday; Parsifal has arrived at a hermit's home in the domain of the Grail, the first scene of the third act. He tells Gurnemanz of his experiences and asks to be led to Amfortas. Kundry washes his feet and dries them with her hair, and Gurnemanz baptizes him with holy water. Now consecrated as King of the Grail, Parsifal, in turn, baptizes Kundry. The meadow suddenly becomes bathed with peace and beauty. Gurnemanz explains to Parsifal that it is the Good Friday spell. The wondrous music of the "Good Friday Spell," with its tenderness and spirituality, is now heard; the core is a song of incomparable sweetness and gentleness for the oboe. With tolling bells, the scene changes to the Hall of the Grail, to which Parsifal is conducted by Gurnemanz. There, during the ceremonial of the Knights of the Holy Grail, Parsifal heals Amfortas by touching his wound with the holy spear.

Orchestral Music. Most of Wagner's music regularly heard in symphony concerts is extracted from his music dramas. The *Siegfried Idyl,* which Wagner wrote in 1870 as a birthday gift to his wife, is not a part of any opera, though it has an intimate relationship to *Siegfried.* All the themes, except one, appear in that opera, the exception being the cradle folk song, *"Schlaf, mein kind, schlaf' ein."* The treatment of all this material, however, is new; the work as a whole is an exquisitely tender lullaby, one of the most poignant in orchestral literature. It begins with a theme for strings taken from Brünnhilde's awakening. This is followed by a delicate motive for the flute suggesting Brünnhilde's slumber. Then we hear material from the love music with which *Siegfried* ends, and after that recollections of Siegfried's horn call, the song of the bird, and Siegfried's melody *"Ein herrlich Gewassertragt wogt vor mir."*

The overture to *The Flying Dutchman* begins with the vigorous "Flying Dutchman" motive in horns and bassoons against tremolos in strings. A stormy chromatic passage follows. When it has subsided, we hear a passage from the beautiful ballad of Senta, given by the wind instruments. Another stormy section arrives in the strings, with which the Senta melody is interwoven. After this comes the second principal theme of the overture, the "Sailors' Chorus" of the third act, heard in the winds. Development of earlier ideas follows, and a climax is reached with a loud presentation of the Senta melody by full orchestra.

William Walton

"There is nothing haphazard about his composing, no dashing off of a little piece in a moment of heated genius. Both life itself and the composing of music are too closely real to this finely wrought mind for such nonsense."

—*Hubert J. Foss*

BORN: Oldham, Lancashire, England, March 29, 1902.
MAJOR WORKS: *Orchestral Music*—Symphony, Concerto for Violin and Orchestra; Portsmouth Point, overture; Scapino, A Comedy Overture. *Opera*—Troilus and Cressida. ALSO: The Quest, The Wise Virgins, ballets; Belshazzar's Feast, cantata; Façade, two orchestral suites; Sinfonia Concertante, for piano and orchestra; Concerto for Viola and Orchestra; 2 string quartets; Sonata for Violin and Piano; Concerto for Cello and Orchestra; Johannesburg Festival Overture; Partita, for orchestra; Second Symphony.

HIS LIFE

BOTH parents of Sir William Walton were singing teachers. His father, in addition, was the choirmaster of the local church. William was an intensely musical child. He could sing complete airs of Handel before he could speak. He was only five when he joined his father's choir as a regular member, and soon after that he started taking lessons on the violin. In his tenth year he won a scholarship for the Choir School of Christ Church. In his first years at Oxford he heard a symphony orchestra for the first time, an experience which affected him profoundly and inspired him to try his hand at composition.

When he was sixteen he received his baccalaureate in music, being one of the youngest Oxford students to get that degree. He now entered Christ Church College, Oxford. Music so dominated his life that he was incapable of applying himself to any other subject. He failed in all classes but those in music, and when he was twenty he was formally expelled from Oxford. Possibly in some measure of retribution, Christ Church made him, many years later, an Honorary Fellow.

While at Oxford he met and was befriended by several important musicians, who gave him direction in his efforts to learn theory and composition autodidactically. They included Sir Hugh Allen, professor of music at Oxford, the conductor Ernest Ansermet, and the composer and pianist Ferruccio Busoni.

At Oxford, Walton met another group of people who were of decisive importance in his early development as a composer: the Sitwell family, Edith, Osbert, and Sacheverell. They were people of station, wealth, and immense culture. When he left Oxford, Walton went to live with them in London. Guided and stimulated by their advice, he wrote his first ambitious work, a string quartet which was introduced at the International Society for Contemporary Music Festival at Salzburg in 1923. One year after this, Walton's Quartet for Piano and Strings was published under the auspices of the Carnegie Trust Fund.

Performed and published, Walton could now regard himself as a professional composer. He was, of course, still unknown except to a small circle of friends and admirers. Fame came sooner than even he had dared to hope. It came in 1926, with the provocative and unorthodox *Façade,* a setting for narrator and seven instruments of twenty-one abstractionist poems by Edith Sitwell. This was first heard on April 27, 1926, at the Chenil Gallery in an unusual performance. Edith Sitwell, unseen by the audience, recited the poems through a megaphone-shaped mouth that was painted on the curtain. The instrumentalists who provided the musical background for these unusual poems were also hidden from view. The unique character of this entertainment—together with the music's wit, satire, impudent parody and tongue-in-cheek quotations—attracted a great deal of attention and made Walton's name known for the first time to a wide audience.

In the decade of 1929–39 Walton produced some of his most important works, beginning with the Concerto for Viola and Orchestra and continuing with the cantata *Belshazzar's Feast,* the Symphony, and the Concerto for Violin and Orchestra. The Viola Concerto and *Belshazzar's Feast* were introduced in 1929 and 1931, respectively, with immense success, the former performed in London by Paul Hindemith and the latter presented at the Leeds Festival. No English choral work since Elgar's *The Dream of Gerontius* had received such instantaneous acclaim as *Belshazzar's Feast.* It was due largely to this work that Walton became a major figure in English music, and there were many who placed him second only to Vaughan Williams. There was so much interest in Walton and his latest works that the Symphony did not wait for completion to be heard. Three movements were heard at a concert of the London Symphony Orchestra, under Sir Hamilton Harty, on December 3, 1934—before the final movement was written. That finale was completed the following summer, and on November 6, 1935, the Symphony received its second *première*—this time in its entirety—at a concert of the BBC Symphony under Harty.

A few months before the outbreak of World War II, Walton visited the United States. He brought with him his recently completed Concerto for Violin and Orchestra, which had been commissioned by Jascha Heifetz. He planned to return to the United States for a second visit that same year, to attend the *première* of this concerto in Cleveland on December 7, 1939—but by then war had broken out in Europe. He enlisted in the British Army and was assigned to the Ambulance Corps in London. While in uniform, he wrote a comedy overture, *Scapino,* for the Chicago Symphony Orchestra to commemorate its fiftieth anniversary, the ballets *The Quest* and *The Wise Virgins,* and several important scores for motion pictures, including those for *Major Barbara, Henry V,* and *Hamlet.* He was also required by the Ministry of Labor and National Service to write music for films issued by the Ministry of Information and the War Office, among them *Next of Kin* and *Spitfire.*

Since the end of World War II, Walton (who has never been prolific) has written only a few works: among these are a string quartet in 1947; the Sonata for Violin and Piano, written in 1949 for Yehudi Menuhin and Louis Kentner; Two Pieces for Violin and Piano, completed in 1951 and dedicated to Sir Laurence Olivier and Vivien Leigh; a cello concerto written in 1957 for and introduced by Gregor Piatigorsky; and several shorter works for orchestra. But the most important work to engage him during this period was the opera, *Troilus and Cressida,* introduced in London on December 3, 1954, and in the United States, in San Francisco, on October 7, 1955.

His personal life underwent a major transformation in those postwar years. For one thing, in 1949 he was married to Susana Gil Passo in Buenos Aires. For another, he achieved complete financial independence not only through his now profitable profession, but also by virtue of a legacy bequeathed him by an intimate friend. Marriage and financial independence were followed, in 1951, by more or less formal recognition of his pre-eminent position in music when his government bestowed knighthood upon him.

HIS MUSIC

WALTON's interest in jazz, out of which developed such infectious early works as *Façade* and the overture *Portsmouth Point,* may be regarded as the wild oats of a young composer. These wild oats brought to him the curiosity and attention of the world of music. But it was the more sober, the more aristocratic, and the more complex music of his maturity that made him keep the admiration of his public. Rhythmic peculiarities of jazz still appear in the Viola Concerto and *Belshazzar's Feast,* together with strong indications of his later style. But with the Symphony, Walton shook himself free of jazz influences completely; and from that time on, his mature style was crystallized.

His style has changed with different works. Sometimes it is dramatic and sometimes epic. Occasionally it exploits modern terminology and becomes objective, while at other times it adopts a more romantic and traditional approach. But the common denominators of that style are easily detected: the spacious arch of the melodies; the detail work of his harmonies and counterpoint; the complex fabric of his rhythms; and, above everything else, his consistently aristocratic workmanship.

ANALYTICAL NOTES

Orchestral Music. Walton's Symphony is in a complex idiom. Three of the four movements are constructed of epigrammatic and often acrid thematic ideas. The first movement consists of a succession of such themes, the composer making no effort to submit to the sonata form by indulging in extensive development or recapitulation. The main themes (there are three) are presented one after another, as if on parade. The core of the entire movement is found in these opening measures. The scherzo, marked in the score "with malice," follows traditional lines both of form and (in its pervading attitude of gentle mockery) content. The slow movement is the only one in which Walton permits his lyricism to soar. It begins with an idyllic melody for the flute which forthwith establishes a mood of contemplation and melancholy. Other melodies follow, including a highly expressive subject for solo clarinet. The finale is made up of four sections. The first is in a heroic vein. This is followed by an energetic section built out of crisp, brittle phrases. The third section contains fugal writing, while the concluding portion returns to the style and ideas of the opening.

The Concerto for Violin and Orchestra begins poetically with a wavelike passage for the clarinet. The solo violin enters accompanied by contrapuntal figures in the cellos and bassoon filling in the rhythmic gaps in the solo. The subdued feeling is sustained for a while; when it has passed, the music grows restless, passionate, even violent. The solo instrument engages in electrifying virtuoso passages culminating in a cadenza. In the second theme, sobriety once again replaces agitation, as the violin sings a contemplative song against a rhythm in pizzicato strings and a gentle rolling figure in the woodwinds.

The concerto has no slow movement. The second movement is full of capricious and whimsical moods, with emphasis on two Neapolitan dance themes, both for the solo instrument. The whimsical element is still pronounced in the concluding movement, though there is an occasional change of mood. The finale begins with a grim, rhythmic theme in the lower strings and bassoons. But when the violin accepts the theme and discusses it with the orchestra, it becomes alive and vital. After a retard and some preparation, the violin embarks on a meditative subject. The opening idea returns, following which the violin yields to an ecstatic melodic outburst. There is soon another vigorous section, but the ecstatic feeling is brought back and intensified. After the violin has engaged in a dramatic recitative, the grim material of the opening is brought back and the movement progresses to a powerful conclusion.

Portsmouth Point, a work of Walton's youth, is a breezy little overture inspired by a print of Thomas Rowlandson. The print depicts a naval arsenal (Portsmouth Point) opposite the Isle of Wight. "It was," wrote Charles G. Harper in *The Portsmouth Road: The Sailor's Highway,* "a collection of taverns giving upon the harbor . . . whence departed a continuous stream of officers and men of the navy. It was a place throbbing with life and excitement—the sailors going out and returning home; the leave-takings, the greetings, the boozing and the fighting all shown in Rowlandson's drawings as on a stage, while the tall ships form an appropriate background like the backcloth of a theatrical scene."

The overture begins robustly with a nervously syncopated theme for full orchestra which leads at once into a strongly rhythmed dance in the strings. After that come a procession of gaily orchestrated eighteenth-century nautical melodies and muscular sailor dances. The breathless pace is maintained with rapid changes of time signature and strong syncopation, while the excitement is kept on a high pitch with recurrent dissonance.

Scapino, A Comedy Overture, was written fifteen years after *Portsmouth Point.* The two works have much in common. Both owe their origin to pictures, *Scapino* having its source in two seventeenth-century etchings of Jacques Callot. And both are vivacious, forceful, and highly pleasing pieces of music. Scapino was a character in the old Italian *commedia dell' arte.* He appears at once in Walton's overture—with all his arrogance and bluster—in the opening vigorous section. A more lyrical passage follows, first in horns and violas, then in the violins. After that a whimsical, quasi-sentimental episode is found in the cellos against violins imitating the strumming of a guitar through plucked strings. The overture closes with the opening material presented playfully.

Opera. *Troilus and Cressida* (1954) is Walton's first opera. Completed in his fifty-seventh year, it is a work that finds him at the height of his technical mastery and artistic maturity. The text, by Christopher Hassall, was based on the well-known Greek legend of the tragic love of Troilus and Cressida, and their final doom, as adapted by Chaucer. Without neglecting the dramatic values of his text, Walton brings to his writing a seemingly inexhaustible flow of expressive lyricism which is particularly eloquent in the second-act love scene. A skillful use of the leitmotiv technique, and an ingenuity in having arias and ensemble numbers evolve naturally from the musical texture, give the opera a remarkable cohesion.

Karl Maria von Weber

"The most German of German composers."
—*Wagner*

BORN: Eutin, Oldenburg, November 18, 1786.
DIED: London, June 5, 1826.
MAJOR WORKS: *Orchestral Music*—overtures to Der Freischütz,
Euryanthe, Oberon; Invitation to the Dance (orchestrated by Hector
Berlioz). ALSO: Der Freischütz, Euryanthe, Oberon, operas; 2 sym-
phonies; Konzertstück, for piano and orchestra; 2 concertos for piano
and orchestra; 2 concertos for clarinet and orchestra; Concerto for
Bassoon and Orchestra; Concertino for Clarinet and Orchestra; can-
tatas; Masses; ballads; romances; songs; 4 sonatas for piano; valses,
ecossaises, fughetti, variations, for piano.

HIS LIFE

WEBER's father, like the fathers of Mozart and Beethoven, had
set his heart on bringing a musical genius into the world.
(His most important association with musical greatness,
before his own son became famous, was through marriage: his niece
was the wife of Mozart.) He himself had been a talented violinist and
composer. A shiftless and irresponsible nature led him to inevitable
ruin. He wasted his musical talent. He lost a reputable position as
councilor and district judge with the Elector of Cologne. He completely squandered his wife's fortune and destroyed both her health
and spirit.

Delusions of grandeur first made him appropriate a title of nobility
to which he had no legal right. Then he sought a passport to affluence

and high station through one of his sons. Both sons of the first marriage failed to fulfill his deep-rooted musical ambitions. But Herr von Weber, while temporarily frustrated, was not altogether discouraged. After the death of his first wife he married a young girl. Their first child was Karl Maria.

Karl Maria was born sickly, having inherited a delicate constitution from his mother. A congenital disease of the hip made it impossible for him to walk until he was four years old, and after that he had a perceptible limp. Besides his physical disability, weakness, and a finely wrought nervous system to upset Father Weber's soaring ambitions for the boy, there was the additional fact that at first Karl did not reveal any noticeable talent for music. But Von Weber was a man of dogged perseverance. He kept his son working at the piano and at his singing lessons even though Karl's half brother stoutly insisted that the boy would grow into almost anything *but* a musician.

While Karl was still a child, his father earned his living by traveling from one small town to the next, playing the violin in theater orchestras and on other occasions serving as an impresario for small-town opera houses. Despite the boy's poor health, he was compelled to pursue this nomadic kind of existence and spend much of his time in theaters. The effect of such a life on Karl Maria's health was, of course, bad; but he was given a behind-the-scenes education in the theater and the opera which was to serve him well. His musical studies continued all the while, though intermittently. When he was nine he studied piano and figured bass. At eleven he spent six months in Salzburg as a pupil of Michael Haydn, younger brother of the great Joseph. It was at this time that he wrote his first real composition, *Six Fughetti,* for the piano, published in 1798. Further study took place in Munich. There the Webers met Aloys Senefelder, the inventor of lithography. Karl Maria interested himself in this process and actually engraved his second opus, *Six Variations on an Original Theme.* The thought of becoming a professional lithographer intrigued him, and there was a brief period when he entered into the business with his father.

While studying in Munich, Weber completed his first opera, *Die Macht der Liebe und des Weins.* Soon after this, on November 23, 1800, his second opera—*Das Waldmädchen*—was publicly performed in Freiberg (near Dresden) and was a failure. It was, however, also produced in several other cities including St. Petersburg. A third opera, *Peter Schmoll und seine Nachbarn,* was also a failure when seen in Augsburg.

These failures convinced both father and son that more study was required. In the fall of 1803 Karl Maria settled in Vienna to study with one of the most distinguished theorists and contrapuntists of the day, Abbé Vogler. Two years of intensive study under Vogler prepared Weber for his first musical post (procured through the Abbé's influence), that of conductor at the Breslau Opera. It was not a happy experience. The management resented the mounting expenses incurred by his continued innovations. The singers and orchestra men objected violently to working under an eighteen-year-old director. Weber was continually confronted by interference, opposition, and malice. There were other problems, too. Being the son of his father, he indulged in dissipation and escapades that often shocked the good citizens of Breslau and, worse still, involved him in debts from which he was unable to extricate himself. An accident provided the final touch to this unhappy picture. One day he mistook nitric acid (which he and his father used in their lithographic work) for wine. It made him violently ill, ruined his singing voice, and permanently injured his vocal cords.

He had had enough of Breslau, and vice versa. There were few regrets on either side when Weber and the Breslau Opera parted company in 1806. For a brief period he conducted an orchestra for Duke Eugen Friedrich of Württemberg at his palace in Karlsruhe. When financial reverses compelled the Duke to give up his musical establishment, Weber went on to Stuttgart (on the Duke's personal recommendation) to become secretary to Duke Ludwig, brother of Eugen. The job was suddenly lost two years later when some ducal funds, entrusted to Weber, disappeared. It is believed that Weber's father was the culprit and that Weber shielded him and assumed the blame. However, since Weber had by no means surrendered his dissolute ways or his capacity for running up huge debts, it is also possible that he was guilty. In any event, the police invaded the opera house in which Weber's opera *Silvana* was being rehearsed, seized the composer, and dumped him in jail for sixteen days. He was released only on the condition that he leave Stuttgart for good; to see that he did so without delay, the police escorted father and son across the border.

Weber now took inventory of himself and did not like what he found. He had only to look at the pathetic figure of his own father to realize which way he was heading. This self-analysis had a sobering effect. He went first to Mannheim; after that he traveled to Darmstadt to renew association with his old teacher, Abbé Vogler, and to work hard on composition. One of the first things he completed was a comic opera *Abu Hassan,* a success when introduced in Munich in 1811. He did a great deal of traveling, a great deal of concert work as pianist, and a great deal of planning. Ideas germinating in his mind at this time were, in later years, to flower into masterworks.

For three years, beginning with 1813, Weber directed the Prague Opera. In Mozart's time it had been one of the foremost musical theaters in Europe, the birthplace of *Don Giovanni.* But since then it had come upon evil days. To Weber fell the Gargantuan task of re-organizing the opera house from the ground up. It was an all-consuming job that left little time for composition, but it proved Weber to be one of the greatest operatic impresarios of his day.

As it turned out, his studies in Prague were merely a rehearsal for a much more important post. Late in 1816 Weber was appointed direc-tor of German opera in Dresden. He gave his first performance on January 30, 1817—with a French opera instead of a German one, Méhul's *Joseph*—and realized such an instantaneous success that he was soon given equal status with the powerful director of the Italian opera; before the end of the year his position was confirmed for life. Stability had finally come to Weber. In November he was married to the singer Caroline Brandt.

His work in Dresden, which focused his interest and energies on German opera, aroused in him the ambition to write a national folk opera. He happened to come upon a story in a volume of ghost tales edited by Apel and Laun. One of them answered his need for a text. He referred it to the German writer Friedrich Kind, who set to work at once preparing the libretto of *Der Freischütz.* But the writing of the score went slowly, engaging Weber for almost three years.

As Dresden was more interested in him as an impresario than as composer, he had to look to Berlin for the first performance of his new opera. Berlin was by no means the happiest possible place for the *première* of a German folk opera. The Italians were then in vogue. Gasparo Spontini (1774–1851), who had just achieved a major triumph with *Olympie,* was king. It hardly seemed likely that Berlin would respond favorably to a new opera which was a complete negation of everything for which the Italians in general, and Spontini in particular, stood.

But the *première* of *Der Freischütz* on June 18, 1821—Weber's wife was cast in the role of Agathe—was a major triumph. "The curtain fell," Weber's son wrote in his biography of his father, "but not a soul left the house. Thunders of applause and thousands of voices summoned the composer before his enraptured audience. At last he appeared. . . . Amid the deafening shouting, flowers and verses were flung from all directions. The success of *Der Freischütz* had been immense—unparalleled." There could be no question but that the gods of Italian opera had been thrown into a shade that night. Early the next morning the German Romanticist, E. T. A. Hoffmann, placed a laurel wreath on Weber—a sentimental gesture to point up the emergence of a new Romantic in German music.

Der Freischütz was given fifty performances in Berlin in the next year and a half. In 1822 it was brought to Dresden, where its Berlin triumph was repeated. In the same year it was also produced in Vienna, where the Italian faction (whose god, Rossini, was in the city) was temporarily silenced. Rossini, who attended the Vienna *première,* said that the opera gave him the colic, and his most ardent admirers echoed his displeasure. But young Vienna went wild, hailing the triumph of German opera.

Domenico Barbaja, the Viennese impresario who was responsible for bringing *Der Freischütz* to Vienna, had also commissioned Weber to write a new opera for his theater. That new work was *Euryanthe,* seen on October 25, 1823, before a brilliant audience that included the Emperor himself. Although the libretto of Wilhelmine von Chézy was clumsy and at times incredible, the genius of Weber's music found strong support. Once again, young Vienna responded to Weber's dream world with fervor and rallied around the standard-bearer of the new imagination. They found in this music the affirmation of the German soul.

The success of *Der Freischütz* in London, where it was seen simultaneously in three different theaters, brought Weber a commission from that city. Covent Garden wanted a new opera in English and stood ready to pay munificently for it. Weber's physician insisted that he turn down the offer. Tuberculosis had completely undermined the composer's delicate health. Complete quiet and rest in a warm climate were prescribed to avoid fatal consequences. But the earnings from the London commission would be all that Weber could leave his family, and he had a strong presentiment that in any event death was not far off. He accepted the offer, devoted himself immediately to learning the English language, and—after the libretto of *Oberon* had arrived from London—plunged into the task of writing his music. When he set off for London to complete his score and to supervise the rehearsals, his wife (who was left behind because she was expecting a second child) remarked sadly, "I have just heard his coffin lid shut!"

The premiere of *Oberon,* on April 12, 1826, was (in Weber's own report) "the greatest success of my life. The emotion produced by such a triumph is more than I can describe. To God alone belongs the glory. When I entered the orchestra, the house, crammed to the roof, burst into a frenzy of applause. Hats and handkerchiefs were waved in the air. The overture had to be executed twice, as had also several pieces in the opera itself. At the end of the representation, I was called on the stage by the enthusiastic acclamations of the public; an honor which no composer had ever before obtained in England."

It was the crowning triumph of his life, and the last one. After *Oberon,* Weber gave a few concerts, made several appearances in fashionable *salons,* and was an honored guest at the houses of royalty. But the strain told. His health disintegrated alarmingly. He was making preparations to return home, but inwardly he knew that he would never make it. Early one morning he was found dead in bed. He was buried in Moorfields Chapel in London. Eighteen years later his body was exhumed, transferred to Dresden, and buried a second time in the family vault. Richard Wagner wrote special music for this occasion and delivered the eulogy.

HIS MUSIC

WEBER is a composer who is more often spoken about than heard from. It is axiomatic for the historian and the musicologist to speak reverently of his three greatest operas—*Der Freischütz, Euryanthe,* and *Oberon.* Yet it is extremely doubtful if one music lover in a thousand has seen a complete performance of any one of these works. Their wonderful overtures are, of course, heard and known, together with an occasional aria such as Agathe's prayer, *"Leise, Leise,"* from *Der Freischütz* or "Ocean, Thou Mighty Monster" from *Oberon.* But beyond this, these three Weber operas are a completely unexplored world for many and an unfamiliar world to most others. This neglect is particularly regrettable in the case of *Der Freischütz,* which is a much greater opera and has far more vibrant contemporary interest than its absence from the opera stage would suggest. Among Weber's other works—and he was productive in all branches of composition—all we get to hear is the *Invitation to the Dance* (and that in an orchestral adaptation by somebody else) and (but not too frequently) the *Konzertstück,* for piano and orchestra.

The sorry truth is that most of Weber's works deserve the obscurity into which they have fallen. Occasional revivals of a forgotten Weber symphony, concerto, or sonata have restored to us music that is pleasing to hear but which contributes nothing whatsoever to his stature.

But his historical importance can never be disputed. He was the founder of German Romantic opera, filling his scores with echoes and recollections of German folk song and dance, and seeking out texts that used German backgrounds and landscapes. A German opera—as opposed to the Italian—became an established institution with *Der Freischütz.* Thus Weber was to prepare the ground for Wagner. He was one of the first to make use of the *leitmotiv* (leading motive), a technique which became one of Wagner's basic tools (see Wagner). He integrated the recitative into the operatic texture as no one before him had succeeded in doing, and he used the orchestra with symphonic breadth and an understanding of its role to project atmosphere and heighten dramatic effect. Finally (though hampered by poor librettos) he always aimed at a unity of the arts. Wagner fully recognized his debt to Weber; and so does history. Weber was the most important of Wagner's predecessors, a milestone in the evolution of the music drama.

ANALYTICAL NOTES

Orchestral Music. The overture to *Der Freischütz* begins with a slow introduction. The heart of this introduction is a solemn, religious-sounding melody for four horns accompanied by strings; this melody is heard after nine prefatory measures. A nervous, swiftly moving theme marks the entrance of the principal section of the overture. The music becomes excited, assumes a sinister character. But a change of mood comes with a passage for clarinet over tremolo strings. This is immediately followed by a beautiful melody for first violins representing Agathe. All the material of the principal section is now worked out freely. Two loud chords for full orchestra, separated by a sweeping figure for strings, bring on the coda, in which the Agathe melody is exultantly presented.

The opening to the *Euryanthe* Overture is an eight-measure impetuous outburst. The wind instruments then present the first principal theme, which is worked out forcefully by the orchestra. There is a resounding chord in full orchestra, some drum beats, and a passage for the cello—this is the transitional material to the second important theme: a soaring song for the first violins. After a change of pace, with the return of the impetuous opening, there is a moment of silence. The most wonderful page of the overture is now heard—a spiritual largo for muted violins. It is a page such as this which must have given Wagner the vision of a new world, for it is not difficult to find a kinship between this music and the prelude to *Lohengrin*. The largo dies out. A transitional fugal section, with the subject first given by the basses, is followed by a return of the first and second themes, given full presentation and elaboration.

With the overture to *Oberon* we are thrust into the magic fairy world which Mendelssohn also penetrated in his overture to *A Midsummer Night's Dream* (written in the same year as *Oberon*). A slow, sustained horn call of three ascending notes of the scale, answered by muted strings and after that set against descending figures in flutes and clarinets, evokes at once a sylvan scene. The serenity continues with a beautiful passage for the cellos, but is shattered by a loud chord in the orchestra. The principal section now begins. The first theme is turbulent. A return of the opening horn call introduces the second main theme, an idyllic melody for solo clarinet, repeated by strings. This leads directly into a portion of the great aria "Ocean, Thou Mighty Monster." First and second themes are now developed in a free fantasia section which includes a fugal passage. The overture ends with a rousing presentation of the quotation from the "Ocean, Thou Mighty Monster" aria.

The *Invitation to the Dance* was written by Weber in 1819 as a "rondo brilliant" for the piano. It established a form in which the later waltz-kings of Vienna—Joseph Lanner (1801-43) and the two Johann Strausses (1804-49; 1825-99)—were to write their most famous works. It integrated several different waltz melodies into a single, uninterrupted piece of music prefaced by an introduction and concluded by a coda.

This work is best known to us in the orchestral adaptation which Hector Berlioz made in 1841 for a performance of *Der Freischütz,* to serve as background for an interpolated ballet. This Berlioz adaptation begins with a slow introduction in which the cello enters into a dialogue with the woodwinds. The cello speaks in a tender phrase and receives a tender response. The colloquy grows more ardent. The young man is asking a young lady for the dance, presses his request, and is accepted. The first dance now erupts vigorously in full orchestra. The second dance is a gentle waltz in the strings. Other dance tunes follow, some robust, some graceful and haunting; strains of earlier dances are ingeniously recalled. The dancing is brought to a vertiginous conclusion. The slow opening dialogue is recalled. The gentleman and lady exchange words of gratitude for the dance.

Hugo Wolf

"To think of his songs one by one is to see defiling before the eye a veritable pageant of humanity in epitome, a long procession of forms of the utmost variety, all drawn to the very life."
—*Ernest Newman*

BORN: Windischgraz, Austria, March 13, 1860.

DIED: Vienna, February 22, 1903.

MAJOR WORKS: *Vocal Music*—Spanisches Liederbuch, Italienisches Liederbuch, Mörike Lieder, Eichendorff Lieder, Goethe Lieder, Alte Weisen (Keller), and other songs and cycles. ALSO: Der Corregidor, opera; Penthesilea, tone poem for orchestra; Italian Serenade, for chamber orchestra (also for string quartet).

HIS LIFE

THERE was no period in Hugo Wolf's life when he did not have some cross to bear. First there was his father's opposition to a musical career, and after that the discipline of formal study for which an unbridled temper and fiery independence made him completely unfit. Later there came abject poverty, the violent even cruel hatred of his enemies, and the failure of his music to get a sympathetic hearing.

Others, stronger than he, would have been crushed by these unceasing struggles. But—together with his nervousness, a sensitivity that approached morbidity, and an explosive temper—he had an inward strength that for a long time carried him through defeat and frustration (though at times he seemed to have reached the breaking point). When in possession of his creative powers he was invincible. But the incessant hammer blows of adversity and struggle ultimately destroyed him—ironically, at a time when his genius was being recognized for the first time.

Hugo's musical talent was early recognized by his father, who was his first teacher. But the father insisted that music was an avocation, not a profession, and that Hugo should prepare himself for some honorable trade. The boy entered the elementary school in his native town and in his tenth year passed on to the high school in Graz. He was hopeless in all studies but music. He was expelled from three different schools and described as "defiant, proud, and stubborn."

With half a heart, Wolf's father had to consent to music study, since the boy was apparently unsuited for anything else. An aunt stood ready to provide Hugo with board and lodging in Vienna. He entered the Vienna Conservatory in 1875. But even there he did not get along any too well. He refused to be enslaved to routine; he engaged in hotheaded controversies with his teachers; he neglected his lessons; he was sullen and unruly. When he was finally thrown out of the Conservatory, it was not for any of these reasons but because he was the innocent victim of a malicious hoax: somebody had sent a threatening letter to the director with Hugo Wolf's name on it.

That was the end of all formal schooling for Wolf. From then on, whatever he learned, he had to learn by himself—by memorizing textbooks; by studying musical scores. Too poor to own a piano, he would study piano literature by reading works as if they were novels. As his aunt's house would no longer hold him, he had to seek shelter elsewhere. Without home and funds, he was dependent on the kindness of friends. They provided him with food and lodging. He accepted these with reluctance at times, for he was proud and wilful, and with indifference at other times, for his mind was elsewhere. He was always studying music. "Restlessly, I am driven to improve my weak talents, to extend my horizon, to endow my thoughts, my actions, my feelings with as ripe an expression as possible," he wrote. When he was not studying music he was reading hungrily—mostly German poets of romantic and morbid inspiration.

He was small, of mean build, thin and undernourished. His eyes looked out starkly. He seemed always on the brink of hysteria. He was wild and excitable in gesture and expression, his heart always pounding—either in admiration or hatred. The small body was an inexhaustible storehouse of energy, or fiercely burning hysterical energy. When he went through a Beethoven sonata or read a favorite poet "his hands trembled . . . his eyes lit up, and he appeared transfigured, as if at the sight of higher, brighter regions, the gates of which had suddenly sprung open. He gasped for air."

He was, most of the time, penniless. Frequently he had to live on a single meal a day, and just as frequently that meal consisted of little more than a bowl of soup or a few slices of bread. He had to borrow money for stamps before he could write home. He had a small income from teaching, but through his fierce temper and his insults he would lose his pupils as quickly as he got them. But when he had in his hand a book of poems or a beloved symphony, which he would take with him to the Prater for companionship, he was unassailable.

He was passionate in all things, even in the way he worshiped his musical gods. He regarded Gluck, Mozart, and Wagner as a divine trinity, "which Holy Three become One in Beethoven." But for Wagner he reserved his greatest adoration; and Wagner was the composer who had the greatest influence over him.

It was during his first year at the Conservatory that Wolf heard Wagner's music for the first time. High up in the gallery of the Court Opera, he heard a performance of *Tannhäuser*. He shouted himself hoarse. "I find no words for it . . . and will only tell you that I am an idiot. . . . The music of this great master has taken me out of myself." As Wagner was then in Vienna, he sought him out at the Imperial Hotel (where Wagner was living), spending hours outside the entrance with the hope of catching a glimpse of the great man. The hotel manager observed this indefatigable vigil, questioned Wolf, and promised to help him meet Wagner. When this meeting was finally arranged, Wolf showed Wagner a song he had recently written (*"Auf dem See"*), begging for criticism. But the master was patronizing toward the fifteen-year-old boy. "My dear boy," he said, "I cannot give you an opinion of your compositions. I have too little time . . . When I was your age and composing music no one could possibly foretell if I should ever do anything great or important. When you are older and have composed larger works, and if I chance to return to Vienna, you must show me what you have done. But it is of little use now. It is far too soon to give you any opinion."

Wolf never met Wagner again, but his idolatry continued. He made pilgrimages to Bayreuth. After the *première* of *Parsifal* he was found on a bench in the street, his head buried in his hands. A friend said "he seemed completely removed from the world and shaken to the very depths." Wagner's death, in 1883, overwhelmed him. When he heard the news "he went to the piano and played the Funeral Music from the

Götterdämmerung. Then he shut down the piano, and went—silently as he came. In the evening he reappeared in a subdued and deeply sorrowful mood: 'I have wept like a child.'" Later he told the conductor Felix Mottl that he often saw Wagner in his dreams and spoke to him. "How strange! Even today, I can scarcely believe that the man who changed us lumps of clay into human beings is dead. . . ."

In 1881 Wolf was given a post as assistant conductor to Karl Muck in Salzburg. He arrived there with a bundle of clothes under one arm and a bust of Wagner under the other. His hopes were high. He had found, at last, relief from poverty, and he was assuming his first musical post. But he lasted only a few months. His honest dread of mediocrity and his intemperate rages involved him in continual quarrels until he could stand it no longer. He went back to Vienna. One friend gave him a room in a garret and others tried to provide him with food, though he continually refused their generosity because his fierce pride would not allow him to be the object of charity.

In 1884 he became the music critic of the *Salonblatt.* This time he kept his job for three years. The critic, like the man, was honest, intransigent, devastating in his attacks, and rhapsodic in his praise. He fought a courageous battle for Wagner and Bruckner. With even greater courage he annihilated those musical gods of Vienna for whom he had no sympathy. He made some friends, but many enemies, and the latter were bent on destroying him. The two leading string quartets —the Rosé and the Hellmesberger—contemptuously turned down his *Quartet in D minor.* Hans Richter, the conductor of the Vienna Philharmonic, accepted his tone poem *Penthesilea,* but only to humiliate him. At the rehearsal, on October 15, 1886, Richter allowed his men to go through the music as lackadaisically as they wished. When the farce was over, he remarked acidly, "Gentlemen, I would not have had this piece performed to the end, were it not that I wanted to see the man who dared to write *that* way about our master, Brahms."

But there was also some encouragement. A small publishing house, subsidized by one of Wolf's friends, issued two volumes of his songs in 1888. This humble appearance of a handful of songs was a stimulus to open a miraculous period of creativeness. Suddenly, with a force which he himself did not understand but could merely wonder at, he found his full-blown strength. He was living at a friend's villa when the great force of his genius found utterance—for the first time. Excitement seized him. The poems he read came to life—those of Eduard Mörike, a kindred spirit, since he was a romantic poet of extreme sensitiveness who explored the innermost recesses of the human soul and dwelt on irremediable suffering. In a few months Wolf had set forty-three lyrics to music, selecting texts which, as he wrote, "would shatter the nervous system of a marble statue." He gazed at his work in astonishment. "Am I one who has been called—am I of the elect?" He could not believe his eyes. At the end of the year he brought the number to fifty-three. "All my songs have in truth been composed under strong convulsions. I have often wept while composing them." Then he turned to Eichendorff's poems, completing twenty songs. Day after day there were new poems, new thoughts, new ideas. In 1888 he set fifty of Goethe's compositions to music in three and a half months.

The following year the poetic raptus continued. He discovered Spanish poems translated into German by Geibel and Heyse, and Italian poems translated by Heyse, and set them to music. He was sure of himself, sure of his powers. "I have just written a new song, a song for the gods," he wrote a friend one day. "Quite divine! Wonderful!" The following day he wrote: "I take back what I said . . . for what I wrote this morning is a million times better still." And once again: "I work at a thousand horsepower. What I write now, I write for the future. They are masterpieces. There has been nothing like it since Schubert and Schumann."

A few sympathetic friends agreed with Wolf—such men as the singer Ferdinand Jäger, the conductors Franz Schalk and Ferdinand Loewe, and Josef Schalk, head of the Wagner Society—and they tried to rescue him from his obscurity. But the forces against Wolf were too strong to be overcome. When Josef Schalk gave a concert devoted entirely to the music of Beethoven and Wolf, he aroused so much antagonism in Vienna that the Wagner Society, which sponsored the concert, was almost wrecked. When Jäger, accompanied by the composer, sang some of Wolf's songs, he was criticized by the press.

Meanwhile the fountain poured forth ever fresh streams of song until 1891. Suddenly, inexplicably—after four years of uninterrupted creative wonder—there was silence. "What a fearful lot for an artist not to have anything new to say," Wolf moaned. "It were a thousand times better to be dead and buried." Again and again he tried to write a new song, only to find the onetime imagination parched. In May 1891 he wrote to a friend: "I have given up the idea of composing. Heavens knows how things will finish. Pray for my poor soul!"

By the end of the year his creative strength had returned and he was once again producing masterpieces with his old assurance, including fifteen more of the Italian songs. But another agonizing period of sterility followed between the years of 1892 and 1894, and once again he was plunged in despair. "If you can give me back my inspiration, wake the familiar spirit asleep within me, I will call you a god and raise altars to your name," he wrote a friend in June 1894. The sleeping spirit was awakened a second time in 1895. He now completed his first opera, *Der Corregidor* (the same text that some years later Manuel de Falla would use for his ballet *The Three-Cornered Hat*). He also wrote a second volume of Italian songs and was hard at work on a second opera, *Manuel Venegas*.

There were now encouraging signs of recognition. His works were heard sympathetically in Berlin, Cologne, and Stuttgart, while in 1895 a Hugo Wolf Society was organized in Berlin to propagandize his music. Even in Vienna there were fortunate developments. Two choral pieces, heard in 1894, drew grudging words of praise from one of his most violent antagonists, the critic Eduard Hanslick. A concert of his works, in February 1897, was an immense success, and two months later a second Hugo Wolf Society was launched by his Viennese friends.

Victories were not to be won without further taste of defeat. *Der Corregidor* was a failure when introduced in Mannheim in 1896 and was suddenly turned down by the Vienna Opera after it had encouraged him to believe that it would be performed. This last disappointment upset him greatly. He began to be troubled by sleepless nights and horrifying nightmares. One night he was found wandering aimlessly through the streets of Vienna, and on another occasion a friend found him at home looking wild and speaking incoherently. He succumbed to delusions. He told his friends that he was the director of the Vienna Opera and he raved angrily against his incompetent "subordinates." Once, while playing a part of *Die Meistersinger,* his memory gave way completely. For the first time he became violent and hysterical.

He was confined to a sanitarium, where he stayed a year and profited from the quiet and rest. He was released as cured. After a holiday in Italy he returned to Vienna fresh of body and spirit, ready to reassume the task of writing the opera *Manuel Venegas*. But early one morning he tried committing suicide in the Traunsee. After that he asked to be confined to an institution. He lived the last years of his life in heartbreaking solitude in the Lower Austrian Mental Hospital, his mind growing increasingly confused, his body more and more paralyzed. He had the delusion that he was somebody else and would cry out: "If only I were Hugo Wolf!" Eventually he lost complete control of both mind and body. In the world outside, his fame was growing. But the little man with the pale, thin face and blazing eyes was past understanding.

He died on February 22, 1903. The funeral ceremonies were but another instance of belated tribute. The greatest musicians of Vienna were there to pay him homage; there were delegations from the Opera and the Conservatory, from both of which he had received his deepest wounds. A chorale by Bruckner accompanied the body to its grave. Soon after his death the city of Vienna provided the funds for an honorary tomb.

HIS MUSIC

HUGO WOLF was a genius only in the art-song form. He could bring wonderful lyrics to the opera, but was incapable of giving a work continuity, movement, or design. *Der Corregidor*—which is occasionally revived in Europe and is available in a recording—is a beautiful series of lovely, gemlike fragments; but it is not an opera. Of his instrumental works, only the charming *Italian Serenade* (originally for chamber orchestra, but more often heard for string quartet) is performed; but this work, while consistently pleasant, makes no pretense at greatness. It was in the art song, the *lied,* that he was one of music's most potent creative forces.

In one sense he was the Wagner of the *lied*—who utilized Wagnerian chromaticism in his writing and who created vibrant dramas, even though in miniature. In another sense he was the Chopin of the *lied* —the only composer to achieve greatness exclusively in the song, just as Chopin was the only immortal in the smaller piano forms. His world, like that of Chopin rather than of Wagner, was circumscribed. But it was *his* world; and his imperial position in it has not yet been threatened.

ANALYTICAL NOTES

Vocal Music. Hugo Wolf wrote over 250 songs for voice and piano, many of them gathered into song cycles. The song of Hugo Wolf is the culmination of a tendency that began with Schubert and continued with Schumann and Brahms: to make poem and melody an inextricable unity. But with no composer did music serve the text so completely and so unselfishly as with Wolf. Inspired by Wagner, Wolf set out in each of his songs to create a drama. The drama and the poetic expression were his primary concerns, not the melody. Consequently he resorted to expressive declamation which sometimes approximated actual speech and which concentrated on the dramatic content of the poem. He gave a new importance to the piano accompaniment, making it the equal partner of the voice in the interpretation of the poem. And to seek out the ultimate possibilities of music in giving expression to nonmusical ideas, he embarked on startling harmonic progressions, unorthodox intervals, and daring modulations that anticipated the iconoclasm of the twentieth century. What he aspired to—and what he realized—was such a singleness of artistic concept in music and text that the "melody" could not be understood or appreciated without the words. Every musical accent must conform to the verbal accent; every musical detail must be influenced by the word, or the image evoked by the word.

Ernest Newman has summed up the three problems that faced Wolf in setting a poem to music: unifying the song with the piano part; making the piano accompaniment follow all the subtle moods of the poem; catching these moods in the vocal part while leaving "the words complete freedom to strike into the tissue, not according to a conventional melodic or rhythmic sense, but according to their natural sense and the double part they have to play in the expression of the poetic idea and in the formation of the total musical matter."

In setting a poem to music, Wolf had an incomparable ability to penetrate in every case to the essence of his text. He always seemed able to find the musical *mot juste* for every thought and feeling. His ability at musical characterization is Wagnerian in its definitiveness. Newman pointed out: "No two characters are the same; each bears about him all the distinguishing songs of his native land, breathes his own atmosphere, wears his own dress, thinks with his own brain. A religious song in the *Spanisches Liederbuch* is as different from one in the Mörike volume as Spain is from Swabia, as Southern Catholicism is from Northern Protestantism. The passion of the women in the Spanish or Italian songs is another thing than the passion of those in the Mörike or Goethe songs. When Wolf, again, plays humorously with life it is in a style and an idiom that vary with each character he represents. . . . *Truer* music, in the full sense of the word, there has never been. Wolf practically never repeats himself in the songs; every character is drawn from the living model."

His greatest and most famous songs are found in his various cycles: *"Anakreons Grab," "Frühling übers Jahr,"* and the three *"Harfenspieler"* songs from the Goethe set; *"Auch kleine Dinge"* and *"Du denkst mit einem Fädchen"* from the Italian book; *"In dem Schatten meiner Locken"* and *"Herz, verzage nicht geschwind"* from the Spanish book; *"Auf einer Wanderung," "Fussreise," "Der Gärtner," "Storchenbotschaft," "Der Feurreiter,"* and *"Verborgenheit"* from the Mörike group; and, in the Eichendorff volume, *"Heimweh," "Das Ständchen," "Erwartung,"* and *"Verschwiegene Liebe."*

Part Three

A BRIEF HISTORY OF MUSIC
SINCE BACH

A BRIEF HISTORY OF MUSIC
SINCE BACH

The following historical survey of music from Johann Sebastian Bach to the present time is intended to provide the layman with a bird's-eye view of how music developed, changed, and grew through the years. If used in conjunction with the essays on the individual composers in this book, the survey will provide an informative and complete history. All the major trends and epochs are explained and discussed. Musical forms mentioned in this history —concerto, symphony, symphonic poem, and so forth—are explained in Section V of the Appendix; all other musical terms are defined in Section VI.

The Baroque period in music was brought to a culmination with Johann Sebastian Bach (1685-1750) and George Frideric Handel (1685-1759). These two giant figures represent the greatest flowering of polyphony and the mighty conclusion of the era of grand polyphony. Thenceforth, composers would emphasize secular rather than liturgical music and homophonic instrumental works rather than contrapuntal choral music.

THE CLASSICAL PERIOD

The age spanning the death of Bach and the first decade of the nineteenth century is the age of *classicism*. The prevailing style was Rococo: delicate, refined, and with aristocratic polish.

During this period composers concerned themselves with correctness of form, clarity of writing, precision, and emotional restraint. Order and reason governed their thinking. Instrumental music achieved new significance, and the newer forms of *sonata, symphony, concerto,* and *string quartet* became prominent. Polyphony was not completely abandoned; after Bach and

Handel composers still wrote in the contrapuntal style and within large church forms. But they concentrated on homophony.

The leading composers of this period were Joseph Haydn (1732–1809) and Wolfgang Amadeus Mozart (1756–91). This period was brought to its apogee with Ludwig van Beethoven (1770–1827).

The word "symphony" was derived from "sinfonia," originally used for any piece of music for a group of instruments. The term symphony, as distinguished from sinfonia, occurs with some of the early seventeenth century Italian composers, notably Giovanni Battista Sammartini (1698–1775); but Sammartini's works in this form are symphonies in name only.

The form, as we know it today, first becomes recognizable with a group of composers known as the "Mannheim School," after the city of Mannheim (Germany), where they lived and worked. The most important of these composers was Johann Wenzel Anton Stamitz (1717–57), who may be regarded as the father of the symphony. As the concertmaster and conductor of the Mannheim Orchestra, he helped establish the modern symphony orchestra both as to organization and technique. As the composer of some fifty symphonies, he helped evolve the symphonic form. The form and symphonic style of Stamitz were inherited by Joseph Haydn, who enlarged the structure, developed the orchestration, and crystallized the so-called *sonata form* (thenceforth the spine of the classical symphony, sonata, and string quartet). Further significant growth took place with Mozart and Beethoven.

The *sonata* is hardly recognizable as such with the masters Kuhnau and Domenico Scarlatti. It was one of Bach's sons, Karl Philipp Emanuel Bach (1714–88) who helped create the piano sonata. He published his first piano sonatas in 1742 and issued his famous *Württemberg* Sonatas two years after that. His most important sonatas are found in a volume published in 1781, entitled *For Connoisseurs and Amateurs.* Not only did Bach stabilize the form of the piano sonata, but he also evolved a refined and sensitive style known as the *galant,* found in the piano music of Haydn and Mozart. Haydn studied the sonatas of Karl Philipp Emanuel Bach and used them as a model when he wrote his own works in that form; Mozart, too, expressed his indebtedness to Bach. The piano sonata, like the symphony, grew and was fructified with Haydn, Mozart, and Beethoven.

Johann Sebastian Bach had written solo sonatas for unaccompanied violin or cello, and sonatas for violin and piano and cello and piano. But Mozart gave us the first violin sonata as we recognize the form today; and Beethoven developed it to prodigious proportions.

There were *string quartets* before Haydn's day. The early Italians—Alessandro Scarlatti and Sammartini, for example—produced music for four stringed instruments. But Haydn was the first composer to recognize fully the artistic potentialities of the string quartet and to realize these potentialities. The formulation of a definite chamber-music style, the arrival at individuality for the four instruments (two violins, viola, and cello), and the establishment of a serviceable form for string-quartet music is found in the quartets written by Haydn in 1772 (Op. 20). Later Haydn quartets and the quartets of Mozart and Beethoven represent a formidable extension of the form and an enrichment of poetic content.

At the same time other chamber-music combinations were evolved: trios; and quartets and quintets for various combinations of instruments.

The first concertos for violin and orchestra had been produced by such early Italian masters as Vivaldi (c.1678–1741) and Giuseppe Tartini (1692–1770). Johann Sebastian Bach wrote the first concerto for piano and orchestra, as well as concertos for various other solo instruments and orchestra. The development of the classical concerto parallels that of the symphony and the sonata, from Karl Philipp Emanuel Bach through Haydn, Mozart, and Beethoven.

Composers of the classical period still produced works in the older polyphonic style and within the older church forms, as demonstrated in such oratorios as *The Creation* and *The Seasons* by Haydn, the Masses of Haydn and Mozart, Mozart's Requiem, and Beethoven's *Missa Solemnis*.

In opera, the classical period saw the first successful break with Italian traditions. This took place in Vienna with Christoph Willibald Gluck (1714–87), Mozart, and Beethoven, and in France with Jean Philippe Rameau (1683–1764). The new tendencies emphasized the importance of the drama; sought a closer relationship between music and play; extended the expressiveness of the orchestra; reached for musical characterization; and avoided the meretriciousness and artificiality of Italian-made librettos and the ornateness of the Italian aria. Simplicity, feeling, and dramatic truth were emphasized.

THE ROMANTIC PERIOD

The climax of the classical period came with Beethoven. He was also the transition to the Romantic period, incorporating as he did (in his later works) many of the salient features of Romanticism.

The Romantic spirit pervaded the literature, thought, art, and music of the nineteenth century. It emphasized the importance of the individual, glorified the creative ego, and encouraged subjectivity of expression. Emotion, feeling, and sentiment were given greater importance than traditional rules of procedure.

In music, Romanticism realized an enlargement of the symphonic structure with a greater flexibility in the use of form. Thematic development arrived at greater freedom. New colors were introduced in orchestration as the

science of instrumentation was extended. The role of melody was emphasized, and harmonic language was enriched. Rhythm acquired increased
variety.

Many new forms came into being; several older ones acquired a new
significance. Smaller forms for the piano were employed with increasing
artistic effect, first by Franz Schubert (1797–1828), who popularized such
forms as the *intermezzo* and the *Moment musical* in piano literature. Robert
Schumann (1810–56) evolved a new form for piano music by combining
smaller pieces into a single work integrated by a central poetic idea, and
Felix Mendelssohn (1809–47) created a new genre with the *Song Without
Words*. The crowning genius of the smaller forms for the piano was Frederic
Chopin (1810–49). This field was further cultivated successfully by Johannes
Brahms (1833–97) and Franz Liszt (1811–86).

During the Romantic period the *lied* (or *art song*) fulfilled its destiny.
Songs had been written by Haydn, Mozart, and Beethoven; and the first
song cycle was created by Beethoven (*An die ferne Geliebte*). But Schubert
was the first to recognize the song as a miniature drama in which words and
music share responsibility; and it was Franz Schubert who became the first,
and one of the greatest, of all *lieder* composers. Having brought new artistic
significance to this form, Schubert gave direction to all the composers of the
lied who followed him, the most influential being Robert Schumann, Robert
Franz (1815–92), Johannes Brahms, Hugo Wolf (1860–1903), and Richard
Strauss (1864–1949). The French art song was developed by Gabriel Fauré
(1845–1924).

Among the newer orchestral forms to engage the Romantic composer
were the *concert overture, symphonic variations,* and the *symphonic poem*
(or *tone poem*).

Beethoven had written orchestral overtures which had no association with
operas. Concert overtures were subsequently written by Schubert, Mendelssohn, Schumann, and Brahms. The variation form is found in symphonic
music of the classical period; but it was during the Romantic era that individual works for orchestra were devoted exclusively to the variation form,
as was the case with Brahms's *Variations on a Theme by Haydn* and the
Symphonic Variations of César Franck (1822–90). The symphonic poem
was created by Franz Liszt as a natural result of the influence that the Wagnerian music drama and Wagnerian principles had had upon him. The most
vital and original composer of symphonic poems was Richard Strauss.

During the Romantic period a new concept of the symphonic form came
into being, calling for an enlarged structure and a greater independence in
following the rules of form. The introduction of new instruments into the
symphony orchestra greatly enriched the orchestral palette. The first of the
Romantic spirits in symphonic music after Beethoven was Hector Berlioz

(1803–69). The most prominent figures in the French Romantic movement after Berlioz—authors of the best French symphonies, other orchestral works, chamber music, piano music, and so forth—were César Franck, Ernest Chausson (1855–99), and Vincent d'Indy (1851–1931). In Germany, the Romantic symphony, concerto, string quartet and sonata were developed by Schubert, Schumann, Mendelssohn, and Brahms. The Romantic symphony acquired unprecedented structural dimensions and aimed for increased articulateness with Gustav Mahler (1860–1911) and Anton Bruckner (1824–96). The Germanic traditions of symphonic music were carried on in Norway by Edvard Grieg (1843–1907) and in Bohemia by Antonín Dvořák (1841–1904).

In opera, the art of *bel canto* and the well-established traditions of Italian opera were glorified in the works of Gaetano Donizetti (1797–1848). Giuseppe Verdi (1813–1901) represents the apotheosis of the Italian opera. Another vein of Italian opera was tapped: that of *opera buffa*. The Italian opera buffa emerged in the eighteenth century with *La Serva Padrona* of Giovanni Pergolesi (1710–36), and its first genius was Gioacchino Rossini (1792–1868).

Opera, of course, also flourished outside of Italy. The French tradition, crystallized by Lully and Rameau, was carried on by Giacomo Meyerbeer (1791–1864) and found its most significant protagonists in Georges Bizet (1838–75), Charles Gounod (1818–93), and Jules Massenet (1842–1912). The French version of the opera buffa—*opéra comique*—came into being with François Boïeldieu (1775–1834) and Daniel-François Esprit Auber (1782–1871) and reached its zenith with Jacques Offenbach (1819–80).

The German Romantic opera had its source in a work such as Mozart's *The Magic Flute*. But it did not come to full flower until Karl Maria von Weber (1786–1826). The concept of a German opera as opposed to the Italian—its music and text stimulated by Germanic backgrounds and traditions—was first arrived at by Weber. And it was realized completely by Richard Wagner (1813–83), with whom the center of the opera world shifted from Italy to Germany. The aesthetics of the Wagnerian music drama and the Wagnerian style formed a tidal wave which swept over the music world in the closing decades of the nineteenth century.

During the Romantic period, *nationalism* became a vital influence in music. The first nationalist school arose in Russia with a group of composers now identified as "The Russian Five" or "The Mighty Five": Mily Balakirev (1837–1910), Alexander Borodin (1833–87), César Cui (1835–1918), Modest Mussorgsky (1839–81) and Nicolas Rimsky-Korsakov (1844–1908). The aim of this school was to free Russian music for subservience to German and French influence through the creation of a basically Russian art. These composers sought to write music derived from the styles of Russian folk songs and dances and church music, to interpret in it the people and the country, and to be inspired by Russian history, culture, and backgrounds. Other and later national schools of the Romantic period included: the Norwegian, with Edvard Grieg (1843–1907); the Bohemian, with Bedřich Smetana (1824–84); and the Spanish, with Isaac Albéniz (1860–1909).

THE "MODERN" PERIOD

The so-called *modern* period in music can be said to span the closing decade of the nineteenth century and the present time.

It brought about sharply changing values: new styles, techniques, principles, tendencies, and concepts. A wave of reaction against German Romanticism and Wagnerism swept through the world of music. Experimentation became a major trend. But experimentation was only a single facet of the contemporary musical scene. A reaction against the more radical tendencies of the times brought about, in some composers, a reversion to older forms and styles; in other composers this reaction expressed itself in a preference for popular and folk idioms.

Among the most important new trends and movements are:

Impressionism, realized by Claude Debussy (1862–1918) and affecting the style of many other composers, including Maurice Ravel (1875–1937) and Frederick Delius (1862–1934).

Expressionism, which produced such new techniques as atonality and the twelve-tone row and whose prophets were Arnold Schoenberg (1874–1951) and Alban Berg (1885–1935).

Dynamism, or *Neoprimitivism,* which emphasized the use of primitive rhythms and a savage and elemental power as found in the earlier works of Igor Stravinsky (1882–   ).

Neoclassicism, or the return to the forms and styles of the sixteenth, seventeenth, and early eighteenth centuries, but frequently without altogether abandoning the harmonic and tonal apparatus of the contemporary school. In the vanguard of this movement were Paul Hindemith (1895–   ) and the later Stravinsky.

Neo-Romanticism, an extension of the German Romantic movement and expressed in the works of Ernst von Dohnányi (1877–   ), Richard Strauss, and Gustav Mahler.

Jazz, or the infiltration of jazz techniques and style within the serious forms of music as manifested in the works of George Gershwin (1898–1937) and the earlier works of Aaron Copland (1900–   ).

Modern music also developed many new techinques. Among these are the following:

Whole-Tone Scale—*see* Debussy

Verismo—*see* Mascagni and Puccini

Atonality—*see* Schoenberg
Polytonality—*see* Milhaud
The Twelve-Tone Row, or Technique—*see* Schoenberg and Berg
Linear Counterpoint—*see* Hindemith
Mystery Chord—*see* Scriabin

Part Four

ONE HUNDRED BASIC WORKS
FOR THE RECORD LIBRARY
(with recommended recordings)

BASIC WORKS FOR THE
RECORD LIBRARY

The following list has been compiled to embrace not only the representative works of the foremost composers from Bach to Gershwin, but also the major styles and periods in music history. Novitiates will find this list useful as a systematic guide for acquainting themselves with the staples in the musical repertory. It will be even more useful to all those planning to start, or to add to, a library of recorded music.

Each of the works listed below is in its entirety. Where there are two or more recordings of a single work, the one most outstanding either for performance or for quality of reproduction, or for both, has been selected. For stereophonic recordings of compositions listed below consult your record dealer.

CHAMBER MUSIC

BEETHOVEN:

String Quartet in B-flat major, Op. 18, No. 6. Columbia ML-5395. Budapest String Quartet.

String Quartet in E minor, Op. 59, No. 2. Columbia ML-4580. Budapest String Quartet.

String Quartet in C-sharp minor, Op. 131. Columbia ML-4585. Budapest String Quartet.

Sonata in A major, for violin and piano, "Kreutzer." Columbia ML-5453. Francescatti and Casadesus.

BRAHMS:

Quartet in G minor, for piano and strings. Victor LM-2473. Babin and Festival Quartet.

Quintet in F minor, for piano and strings. Columbia ML-4336. Curzon and Budapest String Quartet.

FRANCK:

Sonata in A major, for violin and piano. Columbia ML-4178. Francescatti and Casadesus.

HAYDN:

String Quartets, Op. 76. Columbia SL-203. Budapest String Quartet.

MOZART:

String Quartet in B-flat major, K. 458, "Hunt." Columbia ML-4727. Budapest String Quartet.

String Quartet in C major, K. 465, "Dissonant." Columbia ML-4728. Budapest String Quartet.

Quintet in A major, for clarinet and strings, K. 581. Decca 9600. Kell and the Fine Arts String Quartet.

SCHUBERT:

String Quartet in A minor, Op. 29. Columbia ML-4831. Budapest String Quartet.

Quintet in A major, for piano and strings, "The Trout." Columbia ML-4317. Horszowski and Budapest String Quartet.

SCHUMANN:

Quintet in E-flat major, for piano and strings. Columbia ML-4426. Curzon and Budapest String Quartet.

CHORAL MUSIC

BACH:

The Passion According to St. Matthew. Westminster XWN-4402. Orchestra, soloists and chorus under Scherchen.

Mass in B minor. Westminster XWN-3305. Vienna State Opera Orchestra, soloists and chorus under Scherchen.

BEETHOVEN:

Missa Solemnis. Victor LM-6013. NBC Symphony, soloists and chorus under Toscanini.

HANDEL:

Messiah. Victor LD-6409. Royal Philharmonic Orchestra, soloists and chorus under Beecham.

MENDELSSOHN:

Elijah. London A-4315. London Philharmonic Orchestra, soloists and chorus under Krips.

VERDI:

Requiem Mass. Victor LM-6018. NBC Symphony, soloists and chorus under Toscanini.

OPERAS

BIZET:

Carmen. Capitol GCR-7207. Orchestra of Radiodiffusion française, soloists and chorus under Beecham.

LEONCAVALLO:

Pagliacci. Angel 3618 B/L. La Scala Opera under von Matacic.

MASCAGNI:

Cavalleria Rusticana. Angel 3528 C. La Scala Opera under Serafin.

MOZART:

Don Giovanni. Victor LM-6410. Vienna Philharmonic, soloists and chorus under Leinsdorf.

PUCCINI:

La Bohème. Victor LM-6006. NBC Symphony, soloists and chorus under Toscanini.

ROSSINI:

The Barber of Seville. Angel 3559 C. Philharmonia Orchestra, soloists and chorus under Galliera.

STRAUSS:

Der Rosenkavalier (excerpts). Angel GRB-4001. Vienna Philharmonic Orchestra, soloists and chorus under Heger.

VERDI

Aïda. Victor LM-6132. NBC Symphony, soloists and chorus under Toscanini.

La Traviata. Victor LM-6003. NBC Symphony, soloists and chorus under Toscanini.

WAGNER:

Die Meistersinger. London A-4601. Vienna State Opera under Knappertsbusch.

Tristan and Isolde. London A-4506. Vienna Philharmonic, soloists and chorus under Solti.

The Valkyrie. Electrola 90100/4. Vienna Philharmonic, soloists and chorus under Furtwängler.

ORCHESTRAL MUSIC

CONCERTOS (for orchestra)

BACH:

Brandenburg Concertos, Nos. 1–6. Deutsche Grammophon ARC-3156/7. Lucerne Festival Strings under Baumgartner.

BARTÓK:

Concerto for Orchestra. Columbia ML-5471. New York Philharmonic under Bernstein.

CONCERTOS (for solo instruments and orchestra)

BEETHOVEN:

Concerto No. 5 in E-flat major, for piano and orchestra, "Emperor." Victor LM-2562. Cliburn and Chicago Symphony under Reiner.

Concerto in D Major, for violin and orchestra. Capitol G-7229. Menuhin and Vienna Philharmonic under Silvestri.

BRAHMS:

Concerto No. 2 in B-flat major, for piano and orchestra. Victor LM-2466. Richter and Chicago Symphony under Leinsdorf.

Concerto in D major, for violin and orchestra. Columbia ML-5486. Stern and Philadelphia Orchestra under Ormandy.

CHOPIN:

Concerto No. 1 in E minor, for piano and orchestra. Victor LM-1810. Rubinstein and Los Angeles Philharmonic under Wallenstein.

GRIEG:

Concerto in A minor, for piano and orchestra. London CM-9029. Curzon and London Philharmonic under Boult.

MENDELSSOHN:

Concerto in E minor, for violin and orchestra. Columbia ML-5085. Oistrakh and Philadelphia Orchestra under Ormandy.

RACHMANINOFF:

Concerto No. 2 in C minor, for piano and orchestra. London CM-9154. Curzon and London Philharmonic under Boult.

SCHUMANN:

Concerto in A minor, for piano and orchestra. Victor LM-2455. Cliburn and Chicago Symphony under Reiner.

TCHAIKOVSKY:

Concerto No. 1 in B-flat minor, for piano and orchestra. Victor LM-2252. Cliburn and symphony orchestra under Kondrashin.

SYMPHONIES

BEETHOVEN:

Symphony No. 3 in E-flat major, "Eroica." Victor LM-2387. NBC Symphony under Toscanini.

Symphony No. 5 in C minor. Victor LM-1757. NBC Symphony under Toscanini.

Symphony No. 9 in D minor, "Choral." Victor LM-6009. NBC Symphony, soloists and chorus under Toscanini.

BRAHMS:

Symphony No. 1 in C minor. Columbia ML-5602. New York Philharmonic under Bernstein.

DVOŘÁK:

Symphony No. 5 in E minor, "From the New World." Columbia ML-5115. Philadelphia Orchestra under Ormandy.

FRANCK:

Symphony in D minor. Victor LM-2131. Boston Symphony under Munch.

HAYDN:

Symphony No. 88 in G major. London CM-9130. Vienna Philharmonic under Münchinger.

Symphony No. 101 in D major, "Clock." Victor LM-2394. Vienna Philharmonic under Monteux.

HINDEMITH:

Mathis der Maler. Capitol P-8364. Pittsburgh Symphony under Steinberg.

MENDELSSOHN:

Symphony No. 4 in A major, "Italian." Columbia ML-4498. Cleveland Orchestra under Szell.

MOZART:

Symphony No. 40 in G minor, K. 550. Columbia ML-4693. New York Philharmonic under Walter.

Symphony No. 41 in C major, K. 551, "Jupiter." Columbia ML-5655. Columbia Symphony under Walter.

PROKOFIEV:

Classical Symphony in D Major. London CM-9077. Paris Conservatoire Orchestra under Ansermet.

SCHUBERT:

Symphony No. 8 in B minor, "Unfinished." Columbia ML-5618. New York Philharmonic under Walter.

Symphony No. 9 in C major. Victor LM-2344. Boston Symphony under Munch.

SCHUMANN:

Symphony No. 3 in E-flat major, "Rhenish." Epic LC-3774. Cleveland Orchestra under Szell.

SHOSTAKOVICH:

Symphony No. 1 in F major. Westminster 18293. National Symphony under Mitchell.

SIBELIUS:

Symphony No. 2 in D major. Columbia ML-5207. Philadelphia Orchestra under Ormandy.

TCHAIKOVSKY:

Symphony No. 4 in F minor. Victor LM-2369. Boston Symphony under Monteux.

Symphony No. 6 in B minor, "Pathétique." Columbia ML-5235. New York Philharmonic under Mitropoulos.

MISCELLANEOUS WORKS FOR ORCHESTRA

BEETHOVEN:

Leonore Overture No. 3. Columbia ML-5623. New York Philharmonic under Bernstein.

DEBUSSY:

The Afternoon of a Faun. London CM-9228. Suisse Romande Orchestra under Ansermet.

DUKAS:

The Sorcerer's Apprentice. London CM-9119. Paris Conservatoire Orchestra under Ansermet.

ENESCO:

Rumanian Rhapsody No. 1 in A major. Columbia ML-5242. Philadelphia Orchestra under Ormandy.

FALLA:

El Amor Brujo. Columbia ML-5479. Philadelphia Orchestra under Stokowski.

GERSHWIN:

Rhapsody in Blue. Columbia ML-5413. Bernstein and New York Philharmonic under Bernstein.

LISZT:

Les Préludes. Angel 35613. Philharmonia Orchestra under von Karajan.

MENDELSSOHN:

A Midsummer Night's Dream. Angel 35146. Philharmonia Orchestra, soloists and chorus under Kletzki.

MUSSORGSKY:

Pictures at an Exhibition (orchestrated by Ravel). Columbia ML-5401. New York Philharmonic under Bernstein.

PROKOFIEV:

Peter and the Wolf. Columbia ML-5183. Ritchard and Philadelphia Orchestra under Ormandy.

RAVEL:

Bolero. Victor LM-1984. Boston Symphony under Munch.

RIMSKY-KORSAKOV:

Scheherazade. Victor LM-2008. London Symphony under Monteux.

SIBELIUS:

Finlandia. Angel 35002. Philharmonia Orchestra under von Karajan.

STRAUSS:

Till Eulenspiegel's Merry Pranks. Victor LM-2077. Vienna Philharmonic under Reiner.

STRAVINSKY:

Petrouchka. Victor LM-2376. Boston Symphony under Monteux.

TCHAIKOVSKY:

Nutcracker Suite, Op. 71A. Columbia ML-4729. Philadelphia Orchestra under Ormandy.

Romeo and Juliet. Victor LM-2043. Boston Symphony under Munch.

VAUGHAN WILLIAMS:

Fantasia on a Theme by Tallis. Columbia ML-5285. New York Philharmonic under Mitropoulos.

WEBER:

Overture to Der Freischütz. Victor LM-6026. NBC Symphony under Toscanini.

MUSIC FOR SOLO INSTRUMENTS

Organ Music

BACH:

Organ Works. Deutsche Grammophon ARC-3013/30. Walcha.

Piano Music

BACH:

The Well-Tempered Clavier, Books I and II. Victor LM-6801. Landowska.

BEETHOVEN:

Sonata in C-sharp minor, Op. 27, No. 2, "Moonlight." Columbia ML-5164. Serkin.

Sonata in F minor, Op. 57, "Appassionata." Columbia ML-5164. Serkin.

CHOPIN:

Selected Piano Pieces. Victor LM-1137, 1707. Horowitz.

Sonata No. 2 in B-flat minor, Victor LM-1235. Horowitz.

DEBUSSY:
Preludes, Books I and II. Angel 35066, 35249. Gieseking.
SCHUMANN:
Études symphoniques. Columbia ML-5642. Casadesus.
SCRIABIN:
Sonata No. 3 in F-sharp minor, Op. 23. Victor LM-2005. Horowitz.
(See also ORCHESTRAL MUSIC—Concertos.)

Violin Music

BACH:
Partita No. 2 in D minor, for solo violin (including the famous Chaconne). Victor LM-1976. Heifetz.
PAGANINI:
Caprices, Op. 1. Columbia ML-4219. Francescatti.
(See also CHAMBER MUSIC—Beethoven "Kreutzer" Sonata; Franck Sonata in A major. See also ORCHESTRAL MUSIC—Concertos.)

Vocal Music

SCHUBERT:
Selected Songs, 3 volumes, Angel 35624, 35656, 35699. Fischer-Dieskau.
SCHUMANN:
Dichterliebe. Columbia ML-4788. Lehmann.
WOLF:
Italienisches Liederbuch. Deutsche Grammophon 18568/9. Seefried and Fischer-Dieskau.

Part Five

THE ANATOMY OF THE SYMPHONY ORCHESTRA

THE ANATOMY OF THE SYMPHONY
ORCHESTRA

The symphony orchestra is the most complex of the "instruments" for which composers write music. It is an organism made up of many different parts: several entities functioning as a single entity. To understand the orchestra, it is essential to reduce it to its component parts and to analyze each of these parts.

The modern symphony orchestra can be divided into four groups: the strings, woodwinds, brass, and percussion.

THE STRINGS

The string section is the largest in size and the most important in function. More than half of every symphony orchestra is made up of strings. No other group equals them for range, variety of dynamics, or appealing tone quality, and a composer usually assigns his most expressive passages to them.

There are four units to the string section: violins, violas, cellos, and doublebasses.

The violin is the most lyrical instrument in the orchestra. Violins are divided into "firsts" and "seconds." The viola (which, like the violin, is played under the chin and supported by the shoulder) is larger; its strings are thicker, its tone is mellower, and its pitch is one fifth lower. The cello is so much larger than the viola that it is played in a vertical position, resting on the ground and supported by the knees. In pitch, it is an octave lower than the violin. The doublebass, which is an octave lower than the cello, is almost twice as large. Its deep voice makes it difficult to sustain a lyrical passage, and its basic use is to emphasize the rhythm or fill in the harmony.

At the head of each of the string units is a first-desk man. (The first-desk man of the first violins is called the concertmaster.) The first-desk man helps the players in his unit to solve various technical problems that may arise in the music; he also takes over the performance of any solo music for his instrument designated in the score.

There is still one more string instrument found in symphonic music of the post-classical era: the harp.

A great symphony orchestra such as the Boston Symphony has seventeen first violins, sixteen second violins, twelve violas, ten cellos, ten doublebasses, and two harps.

THE WOODWINDS

As the name implies, the woodwinds are wind instruments generally constructed out of wood. Once again we have four units: flutes, oboes, clarinets, and bassoons.

The flute and the piccolo, its high-pitched associate, provide the highest registers in the woodwinds. The flute and piccolo differ from all other woodwinds in that they have a mouth hole through which breath is blown to produce a tone; all other woodwind instruments use a reed (or double reed) in the mouth; this reed quivers slightly when blown upon, setting into motion an air column. The dulcet, silvery tone of the flute is familiar. The piccolo, which means "little flute," is half in size and an octave higher in range.

The oboe has a lower register than the flute, and its tone is more poignant, more bittersweet. It has a conical tube, and a double reed in its mouthpiece. The English horn (which, strange to report, is neither English nor a horn!) is a member of the oboe family: the tenor voice.

Custom dictates that when an orchestra tunes up before a concert it is the oboe that provides the pitch. This is because the oboe cannot adjust its pitch. It is also probable that this practice goes back to the time when the oboe was placed in the center of the orchestra.

The clarinet has a cylindrical, instead of conical, tube and uses a single reed instead of a double one. The tone is more masculine than that of the oboe, and its range is wider. There are several varieties of clarinets. The one used most often is the B-flat clarinet, but the A clarinet and the bass clarinet are also familiar. The tonality of a composition determines whether it is more practical to use a B-flat or an A clarinet: compositions with sharps call for the A clarinet, while those with flats require the one in B-flat.

The bassoon and the doublebassoon (or contrabassoon) are the lowest-pitched instruments in the woodwind section. The bassoon has a double tube and a double reed. Its tone has a ponderous quality which makes it particularly suited for humorous passages.

The Boston Symphony has three flutes and one piccolo, three oboes and an English horn, three clarinets and a bass clarinet, and three bassoons and a doublebassoon.

THE BRASSES

The brasses are the muscle and the sinew of the symphony orchestra. They contribute the most brilliant sonorities and they resound the loudest. The trumpet, which is operated through three pistons, has the highest range in the brass. Its voice is brilliant and sharply metallic.

Next in register come the French horns. The French horn has tubes coiled in circles. From one end expands a wide open bell and from the other a funnel-shaped mouth. The tone of the French horn has a gentle, romantic quality.

The trombone is manipulated by means of a slide. Its tone has greater solemnity than that of the trumpet. There are tenor and bass trombones.

The lowest voice in the brass section is that of the tuba, which is used as a bass for the trombones. The tuba has a coiled tube with a deep funnel mouthpiece.

In the Boston Symphony there are five trumpets, seven horns, four trombones, and a single tuba.

THE PERCUSSION

The percussion section is used to emphasize rhythm and to assist in building dramatic climaxes.

The kettledrums (or timpani) are the most important percussion instruments. They consist of two drums (representing the tonic and the dominant), the pitch of each being adjusted by tightening or loosening the screws on the drum. The kettledrums are struck with two long drumsticks made of flexible cane and with heads covered with felt.

The percussion section also includes the following instruments:

The cymbals, two metallic plates struck together and allowed to vibrate; it is possible to produce an effective cymbal roll by striking one of the plates with a kettledrum stick.

The triangle, a steel rod bent into triangular form and struck with a small metal rod; its tone has a delicate tinkling quality.

The celesta, which is shaped somewhat like a harmonium. It has a keyboard which strikes hammers on steel plates. The tone is highly sensitive and ethereal.

The xylophone, a series of horizontal bars of wood struck by two hammers.

The glockenspiel, which resembles the xylophone, except that the bars are made of steel instead of wood.

The bass drum.

Tubular chimes, long tubes of steel struck with a hammer.

Sometimes musical works call for other percussion instruments, exotic in origin, to provide authentic local color: the Tam-Tam (China), castanets (Spain), and tambourine (Spain) are notable examples.

Many modern scores call for a piano. The piano is regarded as a percussion instrument.

The Boston Symphony has two timpanists. There are two additional percussion players, who are adept at many of the other percussion instruments and who are able to perform on any percussion instrument required in the score. There is also a staff pianist.

The usual position of the different groups of the orchestra on the platform is as follows: the first violins are grouped at the left hand of the conductor, and the second violins at his right; violas and cellos are behind the violins, and the doublebasses are lined up in the rear of the orchestra; the woodwinds are usually in two rows behind the violas and cellos, and directly behind the woodwinds are the brasses; the percussion instruments are assembled behind the brasses.

Sometimes there is a slight variation to this seating arrangement. In the Boston Symphony, the violas are at the right hand of the conductor, with the cellos behind them. In the Philadelphia Orchestra the arrangement is as follows: all the violins (first and second) are in a single group at the conductor's left; cellos and violas are at his right; harps and celesta are behind the cellos and violas; flutes and oboes are placed in front of the conductor, while the clarinets and bassoons are behind them; after these woodwinds come the French horns and tuba, and after them the trumpets and trombones; the piano and other percussion instruments are in the left corner and in the rear center, while the doublebasses are lined up in a diagonal row reaching from the rear center.

Part Six

A DICTIONARY OF MUSICAL FORMS

A DICTIONARY OF MUSICAL FORMS

Throughout this volume mention is made of the various forms of music—such as the symphony or concerto, or minuet or scherzo, and so forth—particularly in the Analytical Sections. A knowledge of musical structure is basic to an understanding of the music itself. The principal forms in music are explained in this dictionary and should be consulted whenever these forms are confronted in the text.

ALLEMANDE: A German peasant dance generally cast in quadruple rhythm and with a flowing decorated melody. It is the first movement in the classical suite.

ARABESQUE (or ARABESK): A form of piano music conceived by Robert Schumann. It has a highly decorative melodic line, resembles the rondo in form, and usually ends in a poetic epilogue.

ARIA: A song, a melodic composition in an opera or oratoria.

AUBADE: A morning serenade, morning music (the equivalent in Spanish is alborada). Rimsky-Korsakov's *Capriccio espagnol* opens with an alborada, and Lalo included an aubade (*"Vainement, ma bien aimée"*) in his opera *Le Roi d'Ys*.

BAGATELLE: Literally a "trifle." A short instrumental composition, often in song form. Beethoven wrote several bagatelles for the piano.

BALLADE: An instrumental composition that seems to tell a story even though it may not have a definite program. In form, it has the character of an improvisation. Chopin was one of the first masters to write ballades for the piano.

BARCAROLLE: A boat song believed to have originated with the gondoliers in Venice. The best known of all barcarolles is the one in Offenbach's *The Tales of Hoffman*. Chopin wrote a barcarolle for the piano, in F-sharp major, which rhythmically simulates the swaying of a boat.

BERCEUSE: A cradle song, the melody having the gentle character of a lullaby. Benjamin Godard's berceuse, from his nowforgotten opera *Jocelyn,* is famous. Chopin wrote a berceuse for the piano, in D-flat major.

BOLERO: A lively Spanish dance in triple rhythm. Ravel's *Boléro* is particularly celebrated.

BOURREE: A lively old dance of French or Spanish origin, usually in 2/4 or 4/4 time. It was one of the movements of the classical suite or partita.

CANON: A composition in strict imitation—the melody given by one voice is repeated by a second, third, or fourth voice at spaced intervals, each voice continuing with its melody as the other voices enter. Canonic writing is the basis of the fugue.

CANTATA: An extended work for solo voice or voices and chorus, frequently with orchestral accompaniment. It is narrative in style. There are secular and church cantatas, with notable examples in both categories among the works of Johann Sebastian Bach: works such as *Wachet auf!* and *Christ lag in Todesbanden* are church cantatas; the *Coffee* Cantata and the *Wedding* Cantata are secular.

CANZONA (or CANZONE): An instrumental piece written in contrapuntal style usually in two or three parts (sixteenth century).

CAPRICE: A short piece of instrumental music, often in quick tempo, which produces surprises or whimsical effects of rhythm, melody, modulation, or form. The most famous caprices are the twenty-four that Paganini wrote for unaccompanied violin.

CAPRICCIO: A small caprice. Brahms wrote seven capriccios for the piano. It is also a form of orchestral music, as in Tchaikovsky's *Capriccio italien* and Rimsky-Korsakov's *Capriccio espagnol.*

CHACONNE: Like the passacaglia, the chaconne is an old sedate dance probably of Spanish origin; and like the passacaglia, its principal characteristic is that a theme heard in the bass is repeated throughout the work. The chaconne was one of the movements of the classical suite or partita. The most celebrated chaconne is that of Johann Sebastian Bach—the closing movement of his *Partita No. 2,* in D minor, for unaccompanied violin.

CHORALE: A hymn for chorus in early German Protestant services.

CHORALE-PRELUDE: A composition for organ based upon a chorale melody.

CONCERTANTE: A piece of music in which two principal parts are presented alternately; also a concerto for two or more instruments and orchestra.

CONCERTINO: A small concerto.

CONCERTO: An extended work, evolved from the concerto grosso, for a single instrument—or two, three, or four instruments—and orchestra. The form and style as we know them today were established by Mozart and developed by Beethoven. The concerto is generally in three movements. The first is more or less in sonata form. The second is lyrical, sometimes in the form of a theme and variations, sometimes in the song form. The third movement is a lively section, frequently in rondo form. The concerto emphasizes the individuality and importance of the solo instrument and exploits the virtuosity of the performing artist with florid, technical passages. It is customary to include a cadenza toward the close of the first movement to highlight further the technical adroitness of the soloist (the other two movements sometimes have brief cadenzas too). Originally these cadenzas were improvised by the performing artist. Subsequently they were written into the concerto, at times by the composer or by the performer, but most often by some other composer. Cadenzas to the Beethoven Violin Concerto, for example, have been written by Joseph Joachim and Fritz Kreisler, among others. Joachim also wrote frequently performed cadenzas for the violin concertos of Brahms and Mendelssohn.

CONCERTO GROSSO: The predecessor of the concerto. A form developed in the sixteenth and seventeenth centuries, consisting of several movements in which a group of solo instruments was set against the rest of the orchestra, sometimes antiphonally, sometimes in unison. Arcangelo Corelli was the first to establish the concerto-grosso form, which was further developed and extended by Vivaldi, Handel, and Bach.

CONDUCTUS: An extended piece of polyphonic music created in the twelfth century. It is in two, three, or four parts, each part consisting of a fluid melody; but the words are sung only by the tenor voice.

COURANTE: An old dance usually in 3/2 or 3/4 time. It was a movement in the classical suite.

CYCLIC FORM: A technique devised by César Franck. The building up of fully developed themes out of melodic germs, these germs known as "generative phrases." In later movements of a work, thematic material of earlier movements is repeated to provide structural unity.

DA CAPO ARIA: An aria in three-part form, in which the third part is a repetition of the first. This aria form was introduced by Alessandro Scarlatti.

DISCANT: A florid, unmeasured improvisation used in early polyphonic music as a background for a Gregorian melody in the Organum.

DIVERTIMENTO: An instrumental form popular in the second half of the eighteenth century. It was actually a suite in more than four movements, light in style, written for various combinations of instruments. Haydn and Mozart often used this term interchangeably with "Serenade," making little distinction between the two.

ECOSSAISE: A lively dance in either 2/4 or 3/4 time, reputed to be of Scottish origin and to have been introduced into France at the close of the eighteenth century. Beethoven, Chopin, and Schubert wrote écossaises for the piano, but these have little Scottish identity.

ETUDE: Essentially a musical exercise in which a particular technical problem is posed for an instrumentalist. Thus, etudes are the meat and potatoes of the diet of every young instrumentalist. Pianists have been fed on the etudes of Czerny, Cramer, and Clementi; violinists on those by Rode and Kreutzer. Chopin wrote twenty-four etudes which treat technical problems but which are also genuine works of art. The musical significance of these pieces brought them the designation of "concert etude," to distinguish them from exclusively pedagogical pieces. Concert etudes were also written by Liszt, Scriabin, and Debussy, among others.

FANDANGO: A popular and lively Spanish dance in triple time, accompanied by castanets and interrupted by songs.

FANTASIA: An Italian word meaning "whim" or "fancy." This is a flexible form allowing the composer freedom of expression and often giving the impression of an improvisation. Bach sometimes used the fantasia to preface a fugue; in his hands the form was a logical and well-ordered piece often grandoise in architecture, as in the *Fantasia and Fugue in G minor*. Notable fantasia for the piano were written by Mozart, Schubert, and Schumann, while in the field of orchestral music Vaughan Williams' *Fantasia on a Theme of Thomas Tallis* is an example.

FARANDOLE: A lively dance in 6/8 time originating in the Basque and Provence regions of France. Bizet wrote a farandole in his *L'Arlésienne Suite No. 2.*

FOLIA: A dance of Spanish or Portuguese origin in 3/4 time. One of these dance melodies achieved great vogue in the seventeenth century and was used by composers of that period for variation treatment. A famous example is Corelli's *La Folia.*

FORLANA (or FORLANE): An old Italian dance in 6/4 or 6/8 time. It was one of the movements of the classical suite. A twentieth-century use of this form is found in Ravel's *Le Tombeau de Couperin.*

FRENCH OVERTURE: One of the earliest forms of operatic overtures, created in the seventeenth century by Lully. It began with a slow movement ending in a quick fugal section. This was followed by a short dance movement, frequently the minuet.

FUGATO: A passage in an instrumental or vocal work in fugal style, but without conformance to the strict form of the fugue.

FUGHETTA: A little fugue.

FUGUE: The most complicated of the contrapuntal forms. It is usually in three-part form: exposition, development, and recapitulation. Fugues are usually written in three, four, and very occasionally in five, voices (parts), the voices being treated in imitation. The subject of the fugue is presented at once; it is followed by an answer, the answer being the subject repeated a fifth higher or a fourth below. A countersubject is introduced contrapuntally with the answer. The subject reappears in the third voice, after which the fourth voice appears with the answer while the third voice proceeds with the countersubject. This is the procedure for a four-voice fugue within the exposition. In the development that follows, treatment may be given to a new subject or to a motive from the original subject. A modulation brings on a return of the original subject in the four voices in imitation. The recapitulation frequently begins with a stretto—the original subject presented in telescoped version—and ends in a coda.

GAVOTTE: An old French dance in 4/4 time beginning on the third beat. A popular gavotte was written by François Gossec. Thomas' opera *Mignon* has a gavotte and so does the *Classical* Symphony of Prokofiev.

GIGUE: An old English dance usually in 6/8 time from which the English jig was derived. It is the concluding movement of the classical suite.

HABANERA: A slow dance in 2/4 time originating in Havana and achieving popularity in Spain. One of the most famous of all habaneras is found in Bizet's opera *Carmen;* but this melody was not original with Bizet, who appropriated it from a song by Yradier. The third movement of Ravel's *Rapsodie espagnole,* for orchestra, is a habanera, and Camille Saint-Saëns wrote a popular habanera (havanaise) for violin.

HUMORESQUE (or HUMORESKE): A short, lively, and pleasant composition. The most celebrated of all humoresques is one by Dvořák: the seventh in a set published as Op. 101. Schumann wrote a humoreske that is more spacious in form and resembles a suite. Grieg also wrote humoresques.

IMPROMPTU: A short instrumental piece that gives the feeling of spontaneity or improvisation. Schubert popularized this form with eight impromptus for the piano; they have the character of extended songs. Chopin wrote three impromptus for the piano.

INTERMEZZO: A short orchestral interlude performed between the acts of an opera or play, frequently with the curtain raised, to denote passage of time. (This term is the same as interlude and entr'acte.) The most famous examples of intermezzos are those by Mascagni, in *Cavalleria Rusticana,* and Granados, in *Goyescas.* Less frequently, an intermezzo is used as a slow transition movement between two major movements of a symphony, sonata, or quartet, as in Beethoven's *Waldstein* Sonata, for piano, and Brahms's *G minor Piano Quartet.* Several important composers have written small piano pieces termed intermezzi. Robert Schumann was among the first, producing six, which are extended songs for the piano. The most famous piano intermezzi are by Brahms.

INVENTION: A form developed by Johann Sebastian Bach as a short contrapuntal piece in two or three parts (or voices) for keyboard instruments.

ITALIAN OVERTURE: One of the earliest forms of operatic overture, created toward the end of the seventeenth century by Alessandro Scarlatti. It consists of three movements, in which two fast sections flank a slow one.

JOTA: A fast Spanish dance in 3/4 time accompanied by castanets and singing. Manuel de Falla included a jota in his *The Three-Cornered Hat.*

LIED: Song, which acquired in Germany a special connotation: namely, an art song in which words and music are a single artistic entity, the song becoming something of a miniature drama. The first great composer of the *lied* was Franz Schubert.

LOURÉ: An old dance in 6/4 time, slow and strongly accented. It was one of the movements of the classical suite.

MADRIGAL: The secular counterpart of the motet. An early form of music for several voices (generally unaccompanied) to a pastoral or amorous text. A characteristic example is Thomas Morley's "Now is the Month of Maying."

MAGNIFICAT: A contrapuntal setting of the Latin hymn of Virgin Mary in the Gospel of St. Luke, a part of the Vesper services of the Roman Catholic Church. Notable settings were made by Palestrina, Johann Sebastian, and Karl Philipp Emanuel Bach.

MALAGUEÑA: A Spanish dance originating in Málaga, in Andalusia. The melody usually has the character of an improvisation, while the harmony is formal. Pablo de Sarasate's *Malagueña* (Op. 21, No. 1) is a staple in the violin repertory. A very popular malagueña for the piano was written by the contemporary Cuban composer Ernesto Lecuona; it is a movement from his *Suite Andalucia.*

MARCH: A musical composition designed for use in marching. It is most usually in 4/4 time (though sometimes in 2/4 or 6/8 time) and is generally in three sections, the second section being a trio of lyrical character, and the third a repetition of the first. The American bandmaster John Philip Sousa won the sobriquet of "march king" by virtue of his numerous works in that form, the most famous being *The Stars and Stripes Forever.* Beethoven interpolated a funeral march in his *Eroica* Symphony, while the funeral march in Chopin's *Sonata No. 2,* for piano, is undoubtedly the most famous one ever written. The two most celebrated wedding marches are found in a suite and an opera: in Mendelssohn's *A Midsummer Night's Dream* Suite and Wagner's *Lohengrin.*

MASS (or MISSA): The principal ritual of the Roman Catholic Church. An elaborate polyphonic work, originally for unaccompanied chorus (as, for example, Palestrina's *Missa Papae Marcelli*), but subsequently for solo voices and orchestra as well as chorus. It is usually made up of the following sections: *"Kyrie," "Gloria," "Credo," "Sanctus," "Benedictus,"* and *"Agnus Dei."* Bach's *Mass in B minor* is the crowning work in this form. Haydn wrote fourteen Masses for the church. Mozart also wrote splendid Masses, including the *Coronation* Mass and the *Great Mass in C.* Many Romantic and modern composers have produced works in this form.

MAZURKA: A national dance of Poland believed to have originated in the sixteenth century. It is in triple time, usually in two or four sections (each section of eight bars) and with accent usually on the second or third beat. Dancers of the mazurka were allowed to improvise steps, and for this reason the musical form is comparatively elastic. Chopin brought the mazurka into the concert hall with his fifty-one works in that form for the piano. The twentieth century nationalist composer Karol Szymanowski, also wrote effective mazurkas for the piano.

MINUET: A stately dance first popular in France at the court of Louis XIV, subsequently in vogue throughout Europe. The minuet became a form favored by most composers of the classical period. Suites by Handel and Bach have minuet movements and so do the symphonies of Haydn and Mozart. Beethoven had a minuet in his First Symphony, but abandoned it for the scherzo in all his later symphonies except the Fourth and Eighth. The minuet is in three-part form, the middle being a trio, and the first and third parts being identical. The most celebrated minuets in musical literature are by Boccherini, Beethoven (*Minuet in G*), Mozart (from *Don Giovanni*), Verdi (from *Rigoletto*), and Paderewski (*Menuet à l'antique*).

MOTET: The liturgical counterpart of the madrigal. A contrapuntal form of religious music originally for unaccompanied voices. The form reached advanced stages of development with Palestrina, who wrote over 250 motets, and Johann Sebastian Bach.

MUSIC DRAMA: A new concept of opera fully developed by Richard Wagner in which the old formal techniques and traditions of the Italian school were abandoned for a new style in which music, drama, poetry, scenery, and staging are partners in a unified artistic project.

NOCTURNE: A dreamy piece of music suggesting the night. There are orchestral nocturnes (notturno) in early classical music—notably by

Haydn—at which time the term was used interchangeably with divertimento and serenade. But the form is most usually associated with romantic piano literature. The first piano nocturnes were written by John Field, but it was with Chopin that the form achieved universal significance. The Chopin nocturne is a poetic, sentimental, and romantic piece of music usually in three sections, the third section repeating the first; the melody is long and graceful, subjected to decoration. Debussy wrote a set of three orchestral pieces collectively entitled *Nocturnes*.

NOVELETTE: A term originated by Robert Schumann for a short and romantic piece for the piano, free in form and elastic in development of material.

OPERA: An extended dramatic work designed for stage production in which all the resources of the musical art are incorporated. It was created during the Renaissance in Florence, Italy, by a group of dilettantes known as the *"camerata,"* which set out to restore the classic Greek drama. At that time it was called *"dramma per musica,"* ("drama through music"). The word "opera" first was used by Pietro Francesco Cavalli in the seventeenth century.

OPERA BUFFA: An Italian comic opera, a form first crystallized early in the eighteenth century with Pergolesi's *La Serva Padrona* and which achieved artistic significance with Rossini.

OPÉRA COMIQUE: A French comic opera with spoken dialogue. Its first important composers were Auber, Boieldieu, Adam, and Offenbach.

OPERETTA: A light opera; it differs from the opera buffa and the opéra comique in that greater emphasis is placed on the farcical play and dialogue than on the music, which consists for the most part of interpolated songs and dances.

ORATORIO: An extended work for soloists, chorus, and orchestra on a dramatized Biblical text; it is presented without scenery or costumes. It derived its name from the oratory of San Girolamo della Carità, where Filippo Neri, in the middle of the sixteenth century, encouraged composers to write music to Biblical subjects. The oratorio was further developed by Carissimi and reached its zenith with Handel.

ORGANUM: The first of the polyphonic forms. A Gregorian melody or plain song in long notes given by two voices moving in intervals of fourths or fifths. In or about the twelfth century a florid, unmeasured improvisation, known as discant, became the second voice, while the first voice remained a Gregorian chant.

OVERTURE: An orchestral introduction to an opera, play, or oratorio; sometimes designated as a prelude. Early forms included the Italian Overture and the French Overture. Concert overtures, as distinguished from opera or oratorio overtures, first came into prominence with Beethoven and were written by many of the Romantic composers.

PART SONG: A song in the contrapuntal style for three or more voices.

PARTITA: A suite of dances. The term was used interchangeably with suite by Johann Sebastian Bach.

PASSACAGLIA: Believed to be an old slow Spanish dance, similar to the chaconne. Its chief musical characteristic is a phrase played in the bass and repeated throughout the entire piece. The passacaglia becomes a kind of theme-and-variations composition, with the principal theme stated by and recurring in the bass (in triple time). Johann Sebastian Bach's *Passacaglia in C minor,* for organ, is an example.

PASSEPIED: A lively old French dance in either 3/4 or 3/8 time, resembling a quick minuet. It was one of the movements of the classical suite.

PASSION: A musical setting, similar to an oratorio, of the Passion of Christ according to the Gospels, intended for performance during Holy Week. The two Passions that are probably the greatest in musical literature are both by Johann Sebastian Bach: the *Passion According to St. John* and the *Passion According to St. Matthew.*

PAVANE: A stately dance in 4/4 time, usually in three sections. Ravel's *Pavane pour une Infante défunte* is famous.

PERPETUAL MOTION: A virtuoso piece in fast tempo in which the notes are generally given equal value and which proceeds without pause until the end, giving the suggestion of undisturbed motion. Brilliant perpetual motions for the violin were written by Paganini and Nováček; Johann Strauss II wrote a delightful orchestral number in this vein.

PLAIN SONG: An old form of church song, sung in unison, with all notes of equal value.

POLKA: A quick dance of Bohemian origin in duple time, generally with accent on the second beat. There is a polka in Smetana's *The Bartered Bride.* The waltz king, Johann Strauss II, wrote many popular polkas, one of the best known of which is the *Pizzicato Polka.*

POLONAISE: A national Polish dance believed to have originated in the sixteenth century. It is in triple time, somewhat slower than the waltz, and usually in two or three parts; it is characterized by marked syncopation and accentuation on the half beats. The polonaise was one of the movements of the classical suite. Handel, Mozart, Beethoven, Weber, and Schubert all wrote polonaises; the most celebrated use of the form in serious music was made by Chopin, who wrote ten polonaises for the piano, the *Military* Polonaise being particularly famous. There is a polonaise in Tchaikovsky's opera *Eugene Onegin* and one in Thomas' opera *Mignon.*

PRELUDE: A piece of music usually serving as a preface to another piece of music, or to an act of an opera or a play. It is most often used in opera as a substitute for the traditional overture, to set the mood for the section to follow—as in the preludes to each of the acts in Debussy's *Pelléas et Mélisande* and the preludes to the four dramas of Wagner's *Ring* cycle. Bach's *Well-Tempered Clavier* contains forty-eight preludes and fugues, each prelude serving as a preliminary to the fugue. Once again, in piano literature the prelude is a brief piece, almost extemporaneous in character, which stands independently but gives the feeling that something is to follow. It is a piece of music which paints a picture or describes a fleeting emotion. Chopin's twenty-five preludes for the piano established the form in Romantic music. Later composers also wrote successfully in this form, notably Debussy, Scriabin, and Rachmaninoff.

QUINTET: A composition for five voices or instruments. A piano quintet is written for piano and string quartet. A string quintet is usually written for a string quartet with an additional viola. Piano and string quintets are similar in form to string quartets.

REQUIEM: A Mass for the dead which uses the text of the Mass, with the omission of the *"Gloria"* and *"Credo"* sections and the interpolation of the *"Dies Irae"* and several other parts. Among the greatest Requiems in music are those by Mozart, Berlioz, Fauré, Brahms, and Verdi.

RHAPSODY: A Bohemian composer, Tomaschek, used this term for the first time in music when he wrote six rhapsodies for the piano. But it did not come into general usage until Liszt wrote the *Hungarian* Rhapsodies. With some composers, the rhapsody is a poetic utterance of epic character: for example, Brahms in his three piano rhapsodies and in the *Alto* Rhapsody. A more popular meaning of the term is an orchestral fantasia, gay in mood, often with sharply contrasted feelings, and utilizing popular or folk melodies. In this category we find Enesco's *Rumanian* Rhapsodies, Chabrier's *España,* Dvořák's *Slavonic* Rhapsodies, Ravel's *Spanish* Rhapsody, and Gershwin's *Rhapsody in Blue.*

RICERCARE: An early instrumental piece in the contrapuntal style in which several motives are developed in imitation.

ROMANZA (or ROMANCE): A romantic song or an instrumental piece in the style of a romantic song.

RONDO: A form of instrumental music derived from the old round dance. It calls for the repetition of the principal subject several times. The appearance of different subjects and the reappearance of the main one can be designated as follows: A-B-A-C-A; or A-B-A-C-A-D-A; or A-B-A-C-A-B-A; and so forth. The rondo form is frequently found in the last movements of sonatas and concertos.

ROUND: A canon.

SALTARELLO: A quick Italian dance, with skips and lively jumps, in 3/4 or 6/8 time. The principal theme of the last movement of Mendelssohn's *Italian* Symphony and the main theme of Berlioz' *Roman Carnival* Overture are saltarellos.

SARABANDE: An old stately dance, probably of Spanish origin, in triple rhythm, its phrase usually beginning on the first beat. It is a movement of the classical suite.

SCHERZO: The third movement of many symphonies and sonatas after Beethoven, replacing the minuet. Like the minuet, the scherzo is in 3/4 time and has three sections, the second being a trio and the third repeating the first. In the scherzo, the trio part is usually more extended than it is in the minuet.

SEGUIDILLA: A slow Spanish dance in 3/4 time accompanied by castanets. There is a familiar seguidilla in Bizet's opera *Carmen*.

SERENADE: Evening music. In vocal music, it is a love song sung beneath a lady's window. Schubert's "Serenade" is a familiar example. In instrumental music, the term was used in the eighteenth century—interchangeably with divertimento and nocturne—for a suite of several movements, lighter in style than the classical suite. Mozart's *Eine kleine Nachtmusik* represents such a serenade.

SICILIANO (or SICILIANA): Originally a slow dance with six or twelve beats in a measure said to be of Sicilian origin. It was one of the movements of the classical suite. A siciliana is also a vocal aria of slow tempo simulating a Sicilian folk song, as in the aria "O Lola" in Mascagni's *Cavalleria Rusticana*.

SINFONIA: In early instrumental music any composition for instruments; the earliest form of opera overture and entr'acte.

SONATA: An extended instrumental work in three or four movements, either for solo piano or for an instrument and piano. The first movement is usually in the sonata form; the second is lyrical and slow, generally in song form; the finale is either a rondo, a theme and variation, or in sonata form. When a sonata has four movements, a minuet or scherzo is interpolated between the second movement and the finale.

SONATA DA CAMERA: Literally, a chamber sonata. An instrumental form developed in the seventeenth century which consisted of a group of dances and which was to develop into the later suite.

SONATA DA CHIESA: Literally, a church sonata. An instrumental form developed in the seventeenth century which consisted of a slow, broad introduction followed by a fugato, and a short largo also followed by a fugato. This was the forerunner of the later sonata.

SONATA FORM: A form developed in the eighteenth century for the first movement of the sonata and generally found in the first movements of the symphony, concerto, sonata, and string quartet. It is in three distinct sections consisting of an exposition, in which the principal themes are stated, a development, in which they are varied and enlarged, and a recapitulation, in which they are repeated as they appeared in the exposition. There are two principal themes in the exposition, the first in the key of the tonic and the second (of contrasting nature) in a complementary key, usually the dominant or the relative major or minor.

SONATINA: A short, simple sonata, without any elaborate development sections and usually in three brief movements.

SONG: A melodic setting, usually for a single voice, of a poetic text.

SONG CYCLE: A group of songs related to each other in mood or thought and which can be sung consecutively. This form was first created by Beethoven in *An die ferne Geliebte*.

SONG FORM: A structure consisting of either two or three parts. The two-part-song form is made up of a melody and a contrasting second melody. In the three-part-song form, the opening melody is repeated after the contrasting subject. (The two-part-song form is designated as A-B, while the three-part form is A-B-A.) In the classic song, the same two- or three-part melody section is repeated for each stanza. During the Romantic period a style was developed called *Durchkomponieren* (through-composition), in which the melody is continually subjected to variation and change to interpret the text with greater realism. One of the first great songs in this new style was Schubert's *"Gretchen am Spinnrade."*

SONG WITHOUT WORDS: A term introduced by Mendelssohn for a short instrumental composition which has the character of a song with accompaniment.

SPIRITUAL: A religious song of the Negro originating during his period of slavery in America.

STABAT MATER: After 1727, a part of the liturgy of the Roman Catholic Church for the Friday of Passion Week and the third Sunday in September. Some of the earliest musical settings of this text were by Josquin des Prés, in the fifteenth century, and Palestrina, in the sixteenth. Pergolesi, Haydn, Rossini, Dvořák, and Verdi wrote Stabat Maters.

STRING QUARTET: An extended work, usually in four movements, for two violins, viola, and cello. The forms used in the four movements are basically those found in the symphony or sonata.

STYRIENNE: A slow air in 2/4 time, frequently in the minor. There is a Styrienne in Thomas' opera *Mignon*.

SUITE: In the sixteenth, seventeenth and eighteenth centuries the suite was a grouping of old dance forms, such as the allemande, sarabande, gigue, minuet, gavotte, bourrée, louré, passepied, polonaise, chaconne, passacaglia, and so forth (same as partita). In the more contemporary meaning of the term, a suite is a group of instrumental pieces with a unifying subject or program, as in Rimsky-Korsakov's *Scheherazade* or Tchaikovsky's *Nutcracker* Suite or Grieg's *Peer Gynt* Suites.

SYMPHONIC POEM: A term originated by Franz Liszt for a one-movement orchestral work, elastic in form, interpreting a program or story. Liszt's *Les Préludes* and Richard Strauss's *Don Juan* and *Till Eulenspiegel* are examples.

SYMPHONY: An extended work for large orchestra in several movements, most usually four. It is actually a "sonata" for orchestra. The first movement is generally in sonata form. The second is slow and lyrical, sometimes in song form, sometimes a theme and variations. In the classic symphony of Haydn and Mozart, the third movement is invariably a minuet, but Beethoven made it a practice to replace the minuet with a scherzo, and most composers after Beethoven have followed him. The finale is generally in rondo, variation, or sonata form.

TARANTELLA: A Neapolitan dance in very fast tempo, almost like a perpetual motion, usually in 3/8 or 6/8 time. Many composers wrote whirling, exciting pieces of music called tarantellas, as, for example, Chopin, Liszt, Mendelssohn, Rossini, and Wieniawski.

THEME AND VARIATIONS: A form in which the theme is given at the beginning and is then subjected to a series of variations in which either the melody, the rhythm, or the harmony is altered. For a long time the theme-and-variations form was utilized within a larger mold, such as the sonata, symphony, or quartet. But the Romantic-period composers began using the theme and variations as an independent form, as in Mendelssohn's *Variations serieuses* and Brahms's *Variations on a Theme by Haydn*.

TOCCATA: A display piece intended to exhibit the virtuosity of a performer. The form was developed early in the seventeenth century by the early organ composers, but it arrived at its ultimate evolution with Johann Sebastian Bach. Later composers sometimes used the toccata as a means for bravura writing, as in Schumann's *Toccata*, for the piano.

TOMBEAU: A dramatic elegy, as in Ravel's *Le Tombeau de Couperin*.

TRIO: Most common usage is for a vocal or instrumental composition requiring three performers. The piano trio is made up of piano, violin, and cello; a string trio consists of either a violin, viola, and cello or two violins and cello. The trio is also the middle section of a minuet or scherzo, so called because it is the middle part of three. The trio of the scherzo is usually more extended than that of the minuet.

VARIATIONS: *See above,* Theme and Variations.

VOLUNTARY: An introductory or concluding, and usually extemporaneous, piece for the organ.

WALTZ: A dance in 3/4 time, of Austrian peasant origin, originally slow and sluggish; when taken up by the Viennese nobility it acquired grace and a faster movement. The waltz came into vogue in Vienna in the eighteenth century. Haydn, Schubert, Hummel, and Weber all wrote waltzes that are light and infectious, many of them for the piano. As a form of popular music, the Viennese waltz was developed by Joseph Lanner and the first Johann Strauss, the first of the Viennese waltz kings, and reached its apotheosis with the great Johann Strauss II. But the waltz was also used for serious music. Chopin wrote fourteen waltzes and Brahms wrote sixteen, all of which are staples in the piano repertory. Brahms also wrote a set of vocal waltzes, for vocal quartet and two pianos: the *Liebeslieder* Waltzes. Ravel glorified the waltz in the *Valses nobles et sentimentales,* for piano, and *La Valse,* for orchestra. The waltz also penetrated opera: in Gounod's *Roméo et Juliette,* Tchaikovsky's *Eugene Onegin,* Puccini's *La Bohème,* and Richard Strauss's *Der Rosenkavalier.*

Part Seven

A GLOSSARY OF MUSICAL TERMS

A GLOSSARY OF MUSICAL TERMS

The musical art has its own vocabulary, and it is imperative for the intelligent music lover to become familiar with it. This glossary includes basic musical terms, indispensable to a mature understanding of music. (Musical Forms are listed and analyzed in the preceding section. Instruments of the orchestra are explained in Section IV.)

ABSOLUTE MUSIC: Music that is not dependent on a program or dramatic text; pure music (opposite of program music).

A CAPPELLA: Unaccompanied vocal music.

ACCELERANDO: Increase in velocity.

ACCENT: Emphasis on a tone or chord.

ACCIDENTAL: Sharp, flat, or natural that is not within the key signature.

ACOUSTICS: The science of sound.

ADAGIO: Very slow (slower than andante).

AD LIBITUM: At the discretion of the performer as to tempo, expression, and so forth; an instrumental part that may be omitted.

AEOLIAN MODE: One of the Gregorian modes, corresponding to the scale from "A" to "A" on the white keys of the piano.

AFFETTUOSO: With tender expression.

AGITATO: Hurried, agitated.

ALLEGRETTO: Quickly (slower than allegro).

ALLEGRO: Quick and lively.

ALTO: Lower range of woman's voice.

ANDANTE: Moderately slow.

ANIMATO: Animated.

ANTIPHONY: Alternate singing of lines by two choirs, one choir answering the other.

APPASSIONATA: Passionately.

APPOGGIATURA: An ornament.

ARCO: Bow. When the term appears after a pizzicato passage, it implies that the bow is now to be used.

ARPEGGIO: An ascending or descending series of tones of a chord, one tone played after another.

ASSAI: Very.

ATONALITY: Absence of a key center or tonic, music without a definite tonality.

AUGMENTATION: Repetition of a thematic subject while lengthening the value of each note (opposite of diminution).

AUGMENTED: In intervals, those that are a semitone greater than major intervals. In chords, those made up of augmented intervals.

AUTHENTIC CADENCE: A dominant chord followed by the tonic.

BAR: A vertical line separating measure; also the measure itself.

BAROQUE STYLE: A style utilizing elaborate structures, grand effects, and highly ornamented details, in vogue in the sixteenth and seventeenth centuries.

BARITONE: A lower range in male voice; between bass and tenor.

BASS: Lowest range of male voice; also shortened form for doublebass.

BASSO OSTINATO: A recurrent thematic figure in the bass.

BATON: A stick used by the orchestra conductor to beat time.

BATTERY: A group of percussion instruments.

BEAT: A pulsation, a part of a measure.

BEL CANTO: Beautiful song, generally used in connection with the Italian opera aria.

BINARY FORM: A movement with two main sections.

BITONALITY: The use of two different keys at the same time.

BRAVURA: With dash, display.

BRIO: Vigorously, with spirit.

BUFFA: Comic (*opera buffa:* comic Opera).

CADENCE: A chord or melodic progression terminating in a phrase or section of a composition.

CADENZA: A florid, improvised passage to exhibit the virtuosity of a performer, usually found in concertos. (*See* Concerto in Section V.)

CALANDO: Diminishing, retarding.

CAMERA: Chamber (*sonata da camera:* chamber sonata. *See* Section V).

CANTABILE: Singing style.

CANTILENA: Melody, air.

CASTRATO: A eunuch with an artificial female voice.

CHAMBER MUSIC: Music written for small combinations of instruments and intended for performance in an intimate auditorium.

CHIESA: Church (*sonata da chiesa:* church sonata. *See* Section V).

CHORD: A combination of three or more tones simultaneously.

CHORUS: A group of singers.

CHROMATIC: A scale proceeding by semitones; also tones foreign in a key.

CLASSICAL PERIOD: A period in music spanning roughly the death of Bach (1750) and the first decade of the nineteenth century. During this period composers leaned toward correctness of form, clarity of writing, emotional restraint, order, and precision.

CLAVIER: Keyboard. Early designation of a keyboard instrument other than organ, such as the clavichord, predecessor of the piano.

CODA: A concluding section in an instrumental composition, or in part of a composition.

CODETTA: A brief coda.

COLORATURA: Rapid ornamental vocal passages in an opera.

COMODO: Leisurely.

CONSONANCE: A combination of tones that is pleasing and restful (opposite of dissonance).

CONTRAPUNTAL: Relating to counterpoint.

COUNTERPOINT: The simultaneous combination of two or more melodies.

CRESCENDO: Gradually increasing sonority.

DA CAPO: From the beginning. Indication that the first part of a composition is to be repeated.

DECISO: Boldly, decisively.

DECLAMATION: Singing in a declamatory style.

DECRESCENDO: Diminishing in sonority (same as diminuendo).

DELIBERATO: Deliberately.

DEMISEMIQUAVER: A thirty-second note.

DEVELOPMENT: The working out of thematic material.

DIAPASON: An octave.

DIATONIC: A scale consisting of the tones of any key without foreign sharps, flats, or naturals.

DIMINISHED: In intervals, those that are a semitone smaller than minor intervals. In chords, those made up of diminished intervals.

DIMINUENDO: Diminishing in sonority (same as decrescendo).

DIMINUTION: The repetition of a theme while shortening the duration of each note (opposite of augmentation).

DISCORD: An unharmonious combination of tones.

DISSONANCE: Tones or combinations that give the feeling of unrest and require resolution in some other tone or chord.

DIVISI: Divided.

DOLCE: Sweetly.

DOLOROSO: Sadly.

DOMINANT: Fifth tone of a scale.

DORIAN MODE: A medieval scale corresponding to the scale from "D" to "D" on the white keys of the piano.

DOUBLE STOP: Bowing on two strings simultaneously.

DRONE BASS: A pedal point suggesting the sound of a bagpipe.

DUET: A composition of two voices or instruments.

DURCHKOMPONIEREN: Through-composition (*see* Song Form, Section V).

DYNAMICS: Contrasts between, and progressions from, loud and soft.

EMBELLISHMENT: Melodic decoration (trill, grace note).

ENCORE: French for "again." A request by English audiences for repetition of a composition. (French use *"bis."*)

ENHARMONIC: Different in name or notation, but not in sound (as "C-sharp" and "B-flat").

ENSEMBLE: A combination of voices or instruments.

ESPRESSIONE: Expression.

EXPOSITION: The subject matter in the sonata form (*see* Section V), also in the fugue (*see* Section V).

EXPRESSIONISM: A style seeking the essence of a subject through abstraction, as in atonality. (Opposite of impressionism.)

EXTEMPORE: Extemporaneous.

FANFARE: A flourish of trumpets.

FERMATA: ⌢ This symbol denotes a long pause.

FEROCE: Fiercely.

FERVENTE: Fervently.

FIFTH: The fifth note of a scale; an interval spanning five tones, including the first and fifth ("C" to "G").

FIGURATION: An ornamental passage in the variation of a theme.

FIGURATO: Florid, free.

FIGURED BASS: Numerals placed before a bass melody to indicate harmony (also through bass).

FINALE: The concluding movement of a symphony, sonata, concerto, and so forth; also the closing part of an act in opera.

FINE: The end.

FIORITURA: Florid ornament.

FLAT: ♭ This symbol lowers a note by a semitone.

FLAUTANDO: Drawing bow gently across strings near bridge.

FORM: Structure of a musical composition (*see* Section V).

FORTE: Loud.

FORTISSIMO: Very loud.

FORZA: Force, power.

FOURTH: Fourth tone of a scale. An interval spanning four tones including the first and fourth ("C" to "F").

FUNDAMENTAL: The root of a chord.

FUOCO: With energy, fire.

FUGAL (or FUGATO): In the style of a fugue (*see* Section V).

GALANT: A style of writing for the harpsichord, developed in the eighteenth century by Karl Philipp Emanuel Bach, Haydn, and Mozart, that was refined, graceful, and polished.

GEBRAUCHSMUSIK: Functional music, first applied to the functional pieces of Paul Hindemith.

GIOCOSO: Cheerfully.

GIOVIALE: Jovial.

GIUSTO: Precise.

GLISSANDO: A scale produced rapidly by sliding the finger across the keys of a piano or on a string of the violin.

GOTHIC PERIOD: The first important period in musical history, in the thirteenth and fourteenth centuries, which emphasized contrapuntal music for the church.

GRACE NOTE: An ornament written in small notation.

GRANDEZZA: Grandeur.

GRAVE: Slow, grave.

GROUND BASS: A bass subject repeated throughout a piece.

HARMONIC: A flutelike sound produced on a string instrument by placing the finger lightly on the string instead of pressing it.

HARMONY: The science of chord combinations and chord progressions.

HARPSICHORD: The precursor of the modern piano. It differs from the piano in that the strings are plucked by quills instead of being struck by hammers. It has a more delicate tone.

HEMIDEMISEMIQUAVER: A sixty-fourth note.

HOMOPHONY: A style emphasizing the single melody and its harmony, as opposed to polyphony.

IDÉE FIXE: A recurring theme. The term was coined by Berlioz in *Symphonie fantastique*.

IMITATION: Repetition of a motive or phrase in other voices, usually lower or higher.

IMPRESARIO: Manager of an opera company.

IMPRESSIONISM: A term appropriated from nineteenth-century painting. A style seeking the expression not of a subject or an idea, but of the feelings and impressions which that subject or idea arouses. Impressionism sought subtle suggestions, delicate effects, and nebulous colors. Its most famous exponent was Claude Debussy.

IMPROVISE: To sing or play without preconceived plan.

INSTRUMENTATION: The science of combining instruments in instrumental music.

INTERVAL: The distance in pitch between two notes.

INTONATION: Trueness of pitch.

INVERSION: Turning two tones of an interval upside down; also, changing the position of the tones of a chord so that the bass becomes a note other than the root.

IONIAN MODE: One of the Gregorian modes, similar to the C major scale.

IRONICO: Ironically.

ISTESSO TEMPO L': The same speed.

KEY: A scale or series of tones whose center, or point of rest, is the tonic from which the key derives its name.

KEYBOARD: The series of black and white keys on a piano or organ.

KEYBOARD INSTRUMENT: Any instrument that is manipulated by a keyboard: piano, harpsichord, organ.

KEYNOTE (or KEYTONE): Tonic.

LAMENTOSO: Mournfully.

LANGSAM: Broadly, nobly.

LARGANDO: Broadening.

LARGHETTO: Slow, but not so slow as largo.

LARGHEZZA: Slowness.

LARGO: Very slow, broad, and spacious (slower than lento).

LEBHAFT: Lively.

LEGATO: Smooth and connected (opposed to staccato).

LEGATURA: A slur.

LEGER: Light, nimble.

LEGGIADRO: Gracefully.

LEGGIERAMENTE: Lightly.

LEGNO: Wood. An indication in string music for the performer to use the back of his bow on the strings.

LEISE: Softly, gentle.

LEITMOTIF (or LEADING MOTIVE): A phrase or theme used recurrently in an opera to identify a character, mood, feeling, situation, and so forth. This technique was brought to its highest development by Wagner in his music dramas.

LENT: Slow.

LENTANDO: Retarding.

LENTO: Slow, somewhere between andante and largo.

LESTO: Lively.

LIBRETTO: Text of an opera or oratorio.

LINEAR COUNTERPOINT: Contrapuntal music in which the voices move independently of harmonic relationships. A modern technique found in Hindemith, among others.

LIRICO: Lyric.

LYDIAN MODE: One of the Gregorian modes, corresponding to the scale from "F" to "F" on the white keys of the piano.

MAESTOSO: Majestically.

MAJOR INTERVAL: An interval that is a semitone larger than the minor and a semitone smaller than augmented.

MAJOR SCALE: A scale that has half steps between the third and fourth and the seventh and eighth degrees.

MALICONIA: Melancholy.

MANUAL: Keyboard of an organ.

MARCANDO (or MARCATO): Accented.

MASSIG: Moderato.

MEASURE: A bar.

MEDIANT: Third note of the scale.

MENO: Less.

METER: The measuring of music according to recurrent series of pulses.

METRONOME: An instrument, operated by clockwork, that announces the number of beats in a minute.

MEZZO: Medium, half.

MEZZO-SOPRANO: A voice lower than soprano but higher than contralto.

MINOR INTERVAL: A major interval reduced chromatically by a semitone, and an interval a semitone larger than diminished.

MINOR SCALE: A scale that has half steps between the second and third and fifth and sixth degrees.

MIXOLYDIAN MODE: One of the Gregorian Modes corresponding to the scale from "G" to "G" on the white keys of the piano.

MODE: A species of scale, such as major or minor.

MODERATO: Moderate in time.

MODULATION: Change of key or tonality.

MOLL: Minor.

MOLTO: Very.

MONODY: Homophony.

MORDENT: An ornament.

MOSSO: Rapid.

MOTIVE: A brief melodic subject.

MOTO: Motion.

MOVEMENT: A major part of a composition, with a completeness of its own.

MUSICOLOGY: Scientific study of musical history, knowledge, and so forth.

MUTE: A device to muffle the tone of an instrument.

MYSTERY: A metaphysical concept of Scriabin embracing all the arts as well as the entire history of mankind.

MYSTERY CHORD: A chord evolved by Scriabin derived from the upper harmonics which are inaudible to ordinary musicians but are closer to the idea of subtler overtones. The chord is: "C, F-sharp, B-flat, E, A, D."

NATIONALISM: Reflection in music of the rise of nationalism in Europe. The attempt of composers to express nationalistic feeling in music by giving voice to the backgrounds, history, and culture of their countries in music exploiting folk idioms. The most important of the national schools was "The Russian Five."

NATURAL: ♮ This symbol nullifies a sharp or flat.

NEO-BAROQUE: Reversion to the contrapuntal style of the sixteenth and seventeenth centuries.

NEOCLASSICISM: Reversion to old classical forms and styles.

NEOPRIMITIVISM: The transfer of the dynamic and elemental forces of primitive music into sophisticated forms.

NEO-ROMANTICISM: Reversion to the romantic ideals of the middle nineteenth century and a preference for music with philosophic or metaphysical implications.

NOTATION: The representation of music by symbols.

NOTE: A symbol representing a musical tone.

OBBLIGATO: An accompanying solo passage for instrument or voice.

OCTAVE: A consecutive series of eight diatonic notes.

OPUS: A work, composition; commonly used to denote the number of a published work.

ORCHESTRATION: The science of combining various instruments of the orchestra.

ORGAN POINT: Pedal point; a persistent bass tone against moving voices.

ORNAMENT: An embellishment (for example, a grace note).

OSTINATO: A ground bass.

PARLANDO: In recitative style.

PEDAL POINT: Organ Point.

PENTATONIC SCALE: A five-tone scale generally found in Oriental music.

PERCUSSION: The family of instruments which are played by being struck.

PEU: Little.

PHRYGIAN MODE: One of the Gregorian modes, corresponding to the scale from "E" to "E" on the white keys of the piano.

PIACERE, A: At pleasure.

PIACEVOLE: Agreeable, a style free of exaggerated expression.

PIANGENDO: A style in vocal music signifying weeping.

PIANGEVOLE: Mournful.

PIANISSIMO: Very soft.

PIANO: Soft.

PIANTO: Plaint.

PITCH: Relation, in sound, of one tone to another.

PIZZICATO: Strings plucked, instead of bowed.

PLACIDO: Placidly.

POCO: Little.

POLYPHONY: Simultaneous use of different melodies (same as counterpoint).

POLYRHYTHM (or POLYMETER): Simultaneous use of different rhythms.

POLYTONALITY: Simultaneous use of several keys.

PONDEROSO: Heavily.

PONTICELLO: Bridge of a string instrument.

PORTAMENTO: Gliding in a continuous sound through the gradations of tone in an interval.

POTPOURRI: Medley.

PRESTO: Very fast, faster than allegro.

PRIMO: First.

PROGRAM MUSIC: Music that tells a story or describes a specific situation or mood; music that has a literary description; frequently, music that imitates extramusical sounds to achieve realistic effects (opposite of absolute music).

PROGRESSION: The advance of a melody from one tone to another; the movement of one harmony to the next.

QUARTER NOTE: Half of a half note.

QUARTER REST: A rest of a quarter-note's duration.

QUARTER TONE: An interval that is half of a semitone.

QUASI: Almost.

QUAVER: An eighth note.

RALLENTANDO: Becoming slower.

RANGE: Compass between lowest and highest notes of a melody or voice.

RASEND: Raging.

RAUCO: Harsh.

RECAPITULATION: Restatement of the exposition section in the sonata form and the fugue (*see* Section V).

RECITAL: A concert performance by a single artist.

RECITANDO: In recitative style.

RECITATIVE: Declamation, generally for voice. In traditional opera, the recitative is sometimes accompanied by occasional chords (*recitativo secco*) or by the orchestra (*recitativo stromentato*).

REPRISE: A repeat.

RESOLUTION: The passing of dissonance into consonance.

REST: A period of silence in which the tempo is maintained.

RHYTHM: Pattern of accented and unaccented, long and short, sounds.

RIPIENO: A term used in the concerto grosso (*see* Section V) to denote the accompanying instruments which fill in the harmony for the solo group.

RIPOSO: Restfully.

RISOLUTAMENTE: Resolutely.

RISPOSTA: "Answer" in a fugue (*see* Section V).

RITARDANDO: Gradual retarding of tempo.

RITENUTO: Immediate retarding of tempo.

RITMO: Rhythm.

RITORNELLO: A term used in seventeenth- and eighteenth-century opera and church music to denote an instrumental prelude, interlude, or post-lude.

ROCOCO STYLE: A style prevailing during the classical period (last half of the eighteenth century) which was refined and delicate.

ROMANTIC PERIOD: A period in music spanning the nineteenth century. During this period there was an enlargement of the symphonic structure, greater flexibility of form, greater freedom in thematic development, amplification of the science of orchestration, emphasis on melody, and enrichment of harmony and rhythm. Emotion, feeling, and sentiment were given greater importance than rules of procedure.

ROOT: The tone on which a chord is built.

ROTONDO: Full.

RUBATO TEMPO: Stolen time; varying the given tempo indication by expropriating some of the time of the long notes to short ones without destroying the rhythm.

SALTANDO: Proceeding by skips.

SANFT: Soft

SCALE: The orderly succession of notes, such as the diatonic and chromatic scales.

SCHERZANDO: Playfully.
SCHMACHTEND: Languishing.
SCHNELL: Fast.
SCORDATO: Out of tune.
SCORDATURA: Unusual tuning of an instrument for special effects.
SCORE: The parts in a musical composition for the various performers.
SCORING: Writing out the various parts of a composition.
SCORRENDO: Sliding.
SECULAR MUSIC: Music that is not for the church.
SEMIQUAVER: A sixteenth note.
SEMITONE: Half tone.
SEMPLICE: Simple.
SEMPRE: Always.
SENSIBILE: Expressive.
SENZA: Without.
SEQUENCE: Frequent repetition of a musical pattern in melody or harmony.
SEVENTH CHORDS: Chords consisting of four tones containing, in root position, the interval of a seventh.
SFOGATO: Lightly executed.
SFORZANDO: To be played with sudden force.
SHAKE: Trill.
SHARP: ♯ This symbol raises a note by a half tone.
SIGNATURE: The symbols found at the beginning of a composition indicating key and time.
SLARGANDO: Gradually becoming slower.
SLENTANDO: Becoming slower.
SLUR: ⌒ This arched symbol above or below two notes indicates they are to be played legato or rendered as a single syllable.
SMORZANDO: Dying away.
SOGNANDO: Dreamy.
SOLENNE: Solemn.
SOLFEGE: Exercise for the voice on a single syllable, ear-training and training in sight-reading.
SOLMISATION: Method of singing scales and intervals.
SOLO: A passage or composition for a single voice or instrument.
SONABILE: Sonorous.
SONORITY: Richness of sound.
SOPRANO: Highest range of human voice.
SORDINO: A mute.
SORDO: Muffled.
SOSTENUTO: Sustained, retarded.

SOTTO: Below.

SOTTO VOCE: Undertone.

SOURDEMENT: In a subdued manner.

SPIANATO: Calm.

SPICCATO: A kind of staccato bowing in quick passages in music for strings.

STACCATO: Short, crisp notes.

STAFF: Five parallel, horizontal lines in which notes are placed.

STRETTA: Concluding passage, finale of opera, given in quicker tempo to increase effect.

STRETTO: Quickening of theme in fugue (*see* Section V) by having the subject and answer compressed until they overlap each other.

STRINGENDO: Accelerating.

SUBDOMINANT: Fourth degree of the scale.

SUBITO (or SUBITAMENTE): Suddenly.

SUBJECT: A theme to be developed in a fugue (*see* Section V); a theme.

SUBMEDIANT: Sixth degree of the scale.

SUL: On.

SUSPENSION: A harmonic clash created by holding a note, or notes, from one chord while the others move to a succeeding chord.

SWELL: Gradual increase of sound.

SYNCOPATION: Shifting the accent to a normally weak beat and holding it over to the strong one.

TANTO: So much.

TEDESCO: German; *alla tedesca,* in the German style.

TEMPERAMENT, EQUAL: Method of tuning which distributes the acoustic differences in the various tones equally among the twelve tones of the scale, making possible the evolution of the major and minor scales.

TEMPO: Time.

TENEBROSO: Darkly.

TENENDO: Sustaining (as in a melody).

TENERO: Tender.

TENOR: Highest range of the male voice.

TENUTO: Held.

TESSITURA: Average pitch of a song, phrase, or voice.

THEME: The melodic subject of a composition.

THOROUGH BASS: Figured Bass.

TIMBRE: Quality of tone.

TIME: Tempo, rate of speed.

TONAL: Relating to tone, key, mode.

TONALITY: Suggestion of a definite key.

TONE: A musical sound.

TONE CLUSTERS: Harmonic combinations created through extensive use of simultaneous seconds, produced on the piano keyboard by use of fist, forearm, palm of the hand. A composer who achieved prominence through this technique is Henry Cowell.

TONIC: First note of a scale.

TONIC CHORD: Chord based on the first note of a scale.

TRANSCRIPTION: Rewriting a composition for a different instrument or instruments.

TRANSPOSITION: Changing pitch of composition to a different key.

TREBLE: Highest register.

TREMOLO: Rapid reiteration of a single note, the pitch remaining steady, on a string instrument.

TRIAD: A chord in three tones.

TRILL: A quivering sound produced by rapid alternation between one note and an auxiliary note, a major or minor second.

TRIPLET: A group of three equal notes.

TRITONE: An augmented fourth.

TROPPO: Too much.

TUNING: Adjustment of instrument to correct pitch.

TURCO: Turkish; alla turca, in the Turkish style.

TUTTI: The entire orchestra, used in connection with the entrance of the orchestra after solo passages.

TWELVE-TONE SYSTEM (or TECHNIQUE): Construction of a musical composition out of an established row of twelve tones, the tones established according to a definite plan. Schoenberg was one of the first important composers to make extensive use of this technique.

UNISON: Identity of pitch.

UPBEAT: Raising of the hand of the baton for an unaccented part of measure; an unaccented beat, usually the last of the measure, which precedes the opening bar.

VELOCE: Swift.

VERISMO: Realism, or naturalism, in opera as realized by Mascagni, Leoncavallo, and Puccini.

VIBRATION: Oscillation of a string or sounding board.

VIBRATO: Vibrating, a strongly tremulous note.

VIF: Quick, brisk.

VIGOROSO: Boldly.

VIRTUOSITY: Brilliant display of technique.

VIVACE: Lively, faster than allegro.

VIVACISSIMO: Very fast.

VIVENTE: Animated.
VIVO: Animated.
VOCALISE: Exercise for voice (similar to solfege).
VOCALIZATION: Exercise of the voice.
VORSPIEL: Prelude (to an opera).

A SELECT BIBLIOGRAPHY[1]

I. DICTIONARIES AND ENCYCLOPEDIAS

APEL, WILLI. Harvard Dictionary of Music. Cambridge: Harvard University Press. 1944.

BAKER, THEODORE. Biographical Dictionary of Musicians. Fifth edition completely revised by Nicolas Slonimsky. New York: G. Schirmer. 1958.

COOPER, MARTIN. The concise Encyclopedia of Music and Musicians. New York: Hawthorn Books. 1958.

GROVE, GEORGE, and BLOM, ERIC. Grove's Dictionary of Music and Musicians. Nine volumes. Fifth revised edition. New York: St. Martin's Press. 1954.

HUGHES, RUPERT, and TAYLOR, D., with KERR, R. Music Lover's Encyclopedia. Revised edition. Garden City: Garden City Publishing Co. 1947.

SCHOLES, PERCY A. The Oxford Companion to Music. Ninth revised edition. London: Oxford University Press. 1956.

THOMPSON, OSCAR. The International Cyclopedia of Music and Musicians. Fifth revised edition. New York: Dodd, Mead & Co. 1949.

II. PROGRAM NOTES AND OPERA PLOTS

BAGAR, ROBERT, and BIANCOLLI, LOUIS. The Concert Companion. New York: Whittlesey House. 1947.

BAGAR, ROBERT, and BIANCOLLI, LOUIS. The Victor Book of Operas. New York: Simon and Schuster. 1949.

[1] Some of these books may be out of print, but because they are standard works and may be found in libraries they have been included.

BIANCOLLI, LOUIS (editor). The Analytical Concert Guide. Garden City: Doubleday & Co. 1951.

BIANCOLLI, LOUIS (editor). The Opera Reader. New York: McGraw-Hill Book Co. 1953.

CROSS, MILTON. Complete Stories of Great Operas. Revised edition. Garden City: Doubleday & Co. 1953.

EWEN, DAVID. Encyclopedia of the Opera. New York: Hill and Wang. 1955.

EWEN, DAVID. Music for the Millions. New York: Arco Publishing Co. 1944. (Republished as Ewen's Musical Masterworks. New York: Arco Publishing Co. 1958.)

GILMAN, LAWRENCE. Wagner's Operas. New York: Rinehart & Co. 1937.

HALE, PHILIP. Great Concert Music. Garden City: Garden City Publishing Co. 1939.

NEWMAN, ERNEST. Stories of Great Operas. Garden City: Garden City Publishing Co. 1951.

NEWMAN, ERNEST. More Stories of Famous Operas. New York: Alfred A. Knopf. 1943.

NEWMAN, ERNEST. The Wagner Operas. New York: Alfred A. Knopf. 1949.

NEWMARCH, ROSA. The Concertgoers Library of Descriptive Notes. Six volumes. London: Oxford University Press. 1928–48.

O'CONNELL, CHARLES. Victor Book of Overtures and Tone Poems. New York: Simon and Schuster. 1950.

O'CONNELL, CHARLES. Victor Book of Symphonies. New York: Simon and Schuster. 1948.

SIMON, HENRY W. The Festival of Opera. Garden City: Hanover House. 1957.

TOVEY, DONALD FRANCIS. Essays in Musical Analysis. Six volumes. London: Oxford University Press. 1935–39.

VEINUS, ABRAHAM. Victor Book of Concertos. New York: Simon and Schuster. 1948.

III. MUSIC APPRECIATION

BERNSTEIN, MARTIN. An Introduction to Music. New York: Prentice-Hall. 1951.

BOYDEN, DAVID D. An Introduction to Music. New York: Alfred A. Knopf. 1957.

COPLAND, AARON. What to Listen for in Music. New York: Whittlesey House. 1939.

ERSKINE, JOHN (editor). A Musical Companion. New York: Alfred A. Knopf. 1935.

FINNEY, THEODORE M. Hearing Music. New York: Harcourt, Brace & Co. 1941.

KOLODIN, IRVING (editor). The Composer as Listener. New York: Horizon Press. 1958.

MAREK, GEORGE R. The Good Housekeeping Guide to Musical Enjoyment. New York: Rinehart & Co. 1949.

MAREK, GEORGE R. The World Treasury of Grand Opera. New York: Harper and Bros. 1957.

McKINNEY, HOWARD D., and ANDERSON, W. R. Discovering Music. New York: American Book Co. 1949.

MOORE, DOUGLAS. Listening to Music. Revised edition. New York: W. W. Norton & Co. 1937.

MORGENSTERN, SAM (editor). Composers on Music. New York: Pantheon Books. 1956.

SAMAROFF-STOKOWSKI, OLGA. The Listener's Music Book. Revised edition. New York: W. W. Norton & Co. 1947.

SCHOLES, PERCY A. The Listener's Guide to Music. London: Oxford University Press. 1947.

STRINGHAM, EDWIN J. Listening to Music Creatively. Revised edition. New York: Prentice-Hall. 1947.

WELCH, ROY DICKINSON. The Appreciation of Music. Revised edition. New York: Harper and Bros. 1945.

IV. HISTORIES OF MUSIC (General)

EINSTEIN, ALFRED. A Short History of Music. Third revised edition. New York: Alfred A. Knopf. 1947.

GRAY, CECIL. The History of Music. Second revised edition. New York: Alfred A. Knopf. 1948.

GROUT, DONALD JAY. A History of Western Music. New York: W. W. Norton & Co. 1960.

LÁNG, PAUL HENRY. Music in Western Civilization. New York: W. W. Norton & Co. 1941.

LÁNG, PAUL HENRY (editor). Norton History of Music. Six volumes. New York: W. W. Norton & Co.

  1. SACHS, C. The Rise of Music in the Ancient World. 1943.

  2. REESE, G. Music in the Middle Ages. 1940.

3. REESE, G. Music in the Renaissance. 1954.

4. BUKOFZER, M. F. Music in the Baroque Era. 1947.

5. LÁNG, PAUL H. Music in the Classic Era. In preparation.

6. EINSTEIN, A. Music in the Romantic Era. 1947.

LEICHTENTRITT, HUGO. Music, History, and Ideas. Cambridge: Harvard University Press. 1938.

(OXFORD HISTORY OF MUSIC. Seven volumes. London: Oxford University Press.)

1. WOOLDRIDGE, H. E. Polyphonic Period I. Second revised edition. 1929.

2. WOOLDRIDGE, H. E. Polyphonic Period II. Second revised edition. 1929.

3. PARRY, C. H. The Music of the Seventeenth Century. Second revised edition by E. J. Dent. 1938.

4. FULLER-MAITLAND, J. A. The Age of Bach and Handel. Second revised edition. 1931.

4. HADOW, W. H. The Viennese Period. Second revised edition. 1931.

6. DANNREUTHER, E. The Romantic Period. Second revised edition. 1932.

7. COLLES, H. C. Symphony and Drama. 1934.

PRUNIÈRES, HENRY. A New History of Music. New York: The Macmillan Co. 1943.

SACHS, C. Our Musical Heritage. New York: Prentice-Hall. 1948.

STRUNK, OLIVER (editor). Source Readings in Music History. New York: W. W. Norton & Co. 1950.

V. MODERN MUSIC

ABRAHAM, GERALD. This Modern Music. New York: W. W. Norton & Co. 1952.

BACHARACH, ALFRED LOUIS (editor). The Twentieth Century. London: Pelican Books. 1957.

BAUER, MARION. Twentieth Century Music. Second revised edition. New York: G. P. Putnam's Sons. 1947.

COPLAND, AARON. Our New Music. New York: Whittlesey House. 1941.

DEMUTH, NORMAN. Musical Trends in the Twentieth Century. London: Rockliff Publishing Corp. 1952.

EWEN, DAVID. American Composers Today. New York: The H. W. Wilson Co. 1949.

EWEN, DAVID. The Complete Book of Twentieth Century Music. New York: Prentice-Hall. 1952.

EWEN, DAVID. European Composers Today. New York: The H. W. Wilson Co. 1953.

EWEN, DAVID (editor). The New Book of Modern Composers. New York: Alfred A. Knopf. 1961.

GRAF, MAX. Modern Music. New York: Philosophical Library. 1946.

HARTOG, HOWARD (editor). European Music in the Twentieth Century. New York: Frederick A. Praeger. 1957.

HOWARD, J. T., and LYONS, JAMES. Modern Music. New York: Mentor Books. 1958.

SALAZAR, A. Music in Our Time. New York: W. W. Norton & Co. 1946.

SLONIMSKY, NICOLAS. Music Since 1900. Third revised and enlarged edition. New York: Coleman-Ross Co. 1949.

VI. HISTORIES OF SPECIAL PERIODS, SCHOOLS, BRANCHES, TRENDS, Etc.

ABRAHAM, GERALD. A Hundred Years of Music History. Second edition. New York: The Macmillan Co. 1949.

ABRAHAM, GERALD, and CALVOCORESSI, M. D. Masters of Russian Music. New York: Alfred A. Knopf. 1936.

BEKKER, PAUL. The Changing Opera. New York: W. W. Norton & Co. 1935.

BLOM, ERIC. Music in England. Baltimore: Penquin Books. 1947.

BROCKWAY, WALLACE, and WEINSTOCK, HERBERT. The Opera. New York: Simon and Schuster. 1941.

CHASE, GILBERT. The Music of Spain. New York: W. W. Norton & Co. 1941.

COOPER, MARTIN. French Music: From the Death of Berlioz to the Death of Fauré. London: Oxford University Press. 1951.

EWEN, DAVID, and EWEN, FREDERIC. Musical Vienna. New York: Whittlesey House. 1939.

EWEN, DAVID. Pioneers in Music. New York: Thomas Y. Crowell Co. 1940.

GROUT, DONALD J. A Short History of Opera. Two volumes. New York: Columbia University Press. 1947.

HANSLICK, EDUARD. Vienna's Golden Years of Music: 1850–1900. New York: Simon and Schuster. 1950.

HILL, RALPH (editor). The Concerto. Baltimore: Penquin Books. 1952.

HILL, RALPH (editor). The Symphony. Baltimore: Penquin Books. 1949.

HOWARD, JOHN TASKER. Our American Music. Third revised edition. New York: Thomas Y. Crowell Co. 1946.

HUTCHESON, ERNEST. The Literature of the Piano. New York: Alfred A. Knopf. 1948.

LANDOWSKA, WANDA. The Music of the Past. New York: Alfred A. Knopf. 1924.

LEONARD, RICHARD ANTHONY. A History of Russian Music. New York: The Macmillan Co. 1957.

MAREK, GEORGE R. A Front Seat at the Opera. New York: Allen, Towne & Heath. 1948.

NEWMAN, WILLIAM S. The Sonata in the Baroque Era. Chapel Hill: University of North Carolina Press. 1959.

NEWMARCH, ROSA. The Music of Czechoslovakia. London: Oxford University Press. 1943.

PELTZ, MARY ELLIS (editor). Opera Lover's Companion. New York: Prentice-Hall. 1948.

ROBERTSON, ALEC (editor). Chamber Music. Baltimore: Penquin Books. 1957.

ROLLAND, ROMAIN. A Musical Tour Through the Land of the Past. London: Kegan Paul, Trench, Trubner & Co. 1922.

SCHUMANN, ELISABETH. The German Song. New York: Chanticleer Press. 1948.

SEROFF, VICTOR. The Mighty Five. New York: Allen, Towne & Heath. 1948.

SLONIMSKY, NICOLAS. Music of Latin America. New York: Thomas Y. Crowell Co. 1945.

SMITH, LEO. Music of the Seventeenth and Eighteenth Centuries. London: J. M. Dent & Sons. 1931.

ULRICH, HOMER. Chamber Music. New York: Columbia University Press. 1948.

VEINUS, ABRAHAM. The Concerto. Garden City: Doubleday & Co. 1944.

WALKER, ERNEST. A Short History of Music in England. London: Oxford University Press. 1924.

YOUNG, PERCY M. The Concerto. New York: British Book Center. 1958.

YOUNG, PERCY M. The Symphony. New York: British Book Center. 1958.

VII. COLLECTIVE BIOGRAPHIES

BACHARACH, ALFRED L. (editor). The Music Masters. Four volumes. Baltimore: Penquin Books. 1942–57.

BLOM, ERIC. Some Great Composers. London: Oxford University Press. 1944.

BLOM, ERIC. Stepchildren of Music. London: G. T. Foulis & Co. 1939.

BROCKWAY, WALLACE, and WEINSTOCK, HERBERT. Men of Music. Second revised edition. New York: Simon and Schuster. 1950.

EWEN, DAVID. Composers of Yesterday. New York: The H. W. Wilson Co. 1937.

EWEN, DAVID (editor). From Bach to Stravinsky. New York: W. W. Norton & Co. 1933.

FOSS, HUBERT. The Heritage of Music. Two volumes. London: Oxford University Press. 1927–34.

HORTON, JOHN. Some Nineteenth Century Composers. London: Oxford University Press. 1950.

LEONARD, RICHARD ANTHONY. The Stream of Music. New York: Doubleday & Co. 1943.

MASON, DANIEL GREGORY. Beethoven and his Forerunners. Revised edition. New York: The Macmillan Co. 1940.

MASON, DANIEL GREGORY. The Romantic Composers. New York: The Macmillan Co. 1930.

NETTL, PAUL. Forgotten Musicians. New York: Philosophical Library. 1951.

ROLLAND, ROMAIN. Musicians of To-day. New York: Henry Holt & Co. 1914.

ROLLAND, ROMAIN. Some Musicians of Former Days. New York: Henry Holt & Co. 1915.

ZOFF, OTTO (editor). Great Composers Through the Eyes of Their Contemporaries. New York: E. P. Dutton & Co. 1951.

VIII. INDIVIDUAL BIOGRAPHIES

J. S. BACH

DAVID, HANS T., and MENDEL, A. The Bach Reader. New York: W. W. Norton & Co. 1945.

PIRRO, ANDRÉ. J. S. Bach. New York: Crown. 1957.

SCHWEITZER, ALBERT. J. S. Bach. Two volumes. New York: The Macmillan Co. 1950.

TERRY, CHARLES S. Bach: A Biography. Second revised edition. New York: Oxford University Press. 1949.

BARBER

BRODER, NATHAN. Samuel Barber. New York: G. Schirmer. 1954.

BARTÓK

FASSETT, AGATHA. The Naked Face of Genius. Boston: Houghton Mifflin Co. 1958.

HARASZTI, EMIL. Béla Bartók: His Life and Works. Paris: Oiseau Lyre. 1938.

STEVENS, HALSEY. Bartók. New York: Oxford University Press. 1953.

BEETHOVEN

ROLLAND, ROMAIN. Beethoven the Creator. New York: Harper & Bros. 1929.

SCHAUFFLER, R. H. Beethoven: The Man Who Freed Music. New York: Tudor Publishing Co. 1947.

SULLIVAN, J. W. N. Beethoven: His Spiritual Development. New York: Alfred A. Knopf. 1947.

THAYER, A. W. The Life of Ludwig van Beethoven. Three volumes. New York: The Beethoven Association. 1921.

TURNER, W. J. Beethoven: The Search for Reality. London: J. M. Dent & Sons. 1927.

BERG

REDLICH, HANS F. Alban Berg: The Man and His Music. London: John Calder. 1957.

REICH, WILLI. Alban Berg. London: Dobson Books. 1954.

BERLIOZ

BARZUN, JACQUES. Berlioz and the Romantic Century. Two volumes. New York: Little Brown & Co. 1950.

NEWMAN, ERNEST (editor). Memoirs of Hector Berlioz. New York: Alfred A. Knopf. 1948.

BIZET

COOPER, MARTIN. Georges Bizet. London: Oxford University Press. 1938.

CURTISS, MINA. Bizet and His World. New York: Alfred A. Knopf. 1958.

DEAN, WINTON. Bizet. London: J. M. Dent & Sons. 1948.

BORODIN

ABRAHAM, GERALD. Borodin: The Composer and His Music. London: William Reeves. 1927.

BRAHMS

GEIRINGER, KARL. Brahms: His Life and Work. Second revised edition. New York: Oxford University Press. 1947.

MAY, FLORENCE. The Life of Brahms. Two volumes. Revised edition. London: William Reeves. 1948.

NIEMANN, WALTER. Brahms. New York: Alfred A. Knopf. 1947.

SCHAUFFLER, R. H. The Unknown Brahms. New York: Dodd, Mead & Co. 1933.

SPECHT, RICHARD. Brahms. New York: E. P. Dutton & Co. 1930.

BRITTEN

MITCHELL, DONALD and KELLER, HANS (editors). Benjamin Britten. New York: Philosophical Library. 1952.

WHITE, ERIC WALTER. Benjamin Britten: A Sketch of His Life and Work. Revised edition. London: Boosey & Hawkes. 1954.

BRUCKNER

REDLICH, HANS F. Bruckner and Mahler. New York: Farrar, Straus & Cudahy. 1955.

WOLFF, WERNER. Anton Bruckner: Rustic Genius. New York: E. P. Dutton & Co. 1942.

CHOPIN

LISZT, FRANZ. Frédéric Chopin. London: William Reeves. 1913.

MAINE, BASIL. Chopin. New York: A. A. Wyn. 1949.

MIZWA, STEPHEN P. (editor). Frédéric Chopin. New York: The Macmillan Co. 1949.

WEINSTOCK, HERBERT. Chopin: The Man and His Music. New York: Alfred A. Knopf. 1949.

WIERZYNSKI, CASIMIR. The Life and Death of Chopin. New York: Simon and Schuster. 1949.

COPLAND

COPLAND, AARON. Copland on Music. Garden City: Doubleday & Co. 1960.

SMITH, JULIA. Aaron Copland, His Work and Contribution to American Music. New York: E. P. Dutton & Co. 1955.

DEBUSSY

LOCKSPEISER, EDWARD. Debussy. New York: Pellegrini & Cudahy. 1949.

MYERS, ROLLO H. Debussy. New York: A. A. Wyn. 1949.

SEROFF, VICTOR. Debussy: Musician of France. New York: G. P. Putnam's Sons. 1956.

THOMPSON, OSCAR. Debussy. New York: Dodd, Mead & Co. 1937.

DELIUS

FENBY, ERIC. Delius as I Knew Him. London: Quality Press. 1948.

HUTCHINGS, ARTHUR. Delius: A Critical Biography. New York: The Macmillan Co. 1948.

DVORÁK

ROBERTSON, ALEC. Dvorák. New York: Pellegrini & Cudahy, 1949.

STEFAN, PAUL. Anton Dvorák. New York: Greystone Press. 1941.

ELGAR

CHAMBERS, GEORGE B. Elgar: Centenary Sketches. London: Novello & Co. 1957.

REED, W. H. Elgar. New York: Pellegrini & Cudahy. 1949.

FALLA

PAHISSA, JAIME. Manuel de Falla: His Life and Works. London: Museum Press. 1954.

TREND, J. B. Manuel de Falla and Spanish Music. Revised edition. New York: Alfred A. Knopf. 1934.

FAURÉ

KOECHLIN, CHARLES. Gabriel Fauré. Second revised edition. London: Dobson Books. 1946.

SUCKLING, NORMAN. Fauré. New York: Pellegrini & Cudahy. 1951.

FRANCK

DEMUTH, NORMAN. César Franck. New York: Philosophical Library. 1949.

D'INDY, VINCENT. César Franck. New York: Dodd, Mead & Co. 1931.

GERSHWIN

EWEN, DAVID. A Journey to Greatness: The Life and Music of George Gershwin. New York: Henry Holt & Co. 1956.

JABLONSKI, EDWARD and STEWART, LAWRENCE D. The Gershwin Years. Garden City: Doubleday & Co. 1958.

GLUCK

COOPER, MARTIN. Gluck. London: Oxford University Press. 1935.

GRIEG

ABRAHAM, GERALD (editor). Grieg: A Symposium. Norman: University of Oklahoma Press. 1950.

JOHANSEN, D. M. Edvard Grieg. New York: Tudor Publishing Co. 1945.

HANDEL

DENT, EDWARD J. Handel. New York: A. A. Wyn. 1949.

FLOWER, NEWMAN. George Frideric Handel: His Personality and His Times. Revised edition. New York: Charles Scribner's Sons. 1948.

ROLLAND, ROMAIN. Handel. New York: Henry Holt & Co. 1916.

WEINSTOCK, HERBERT. Handel. Revised edition. New York: Alfred A. Knopf. 1959.

HAYDN

GEIRINGER, KARL. Haydn: A Creative Life in Music. New York: W. W. Norton & Co. 1946.

HUGHES, R. Haydn. New York: Pellegrini & Cudahy. 1950.

JACOB, H. E. Haydn: His Art, Times, and Glory. New York: Rinehart & Co. 1950.

D'INDY

DEMUTH, NORMAN. Vincent d'Indy. London: Rockliff Publishing Corp. 1951.

LISZT

HILL, RALPH. Liszt. New York: A. A. Wyn. 1950.

NEWMAN, ERNEST. The Man Liszt. New York: Charles Scribner's Sons. 1914.

SITWELL, SACHEVERELL. Franz Liszt. New York: Houghton Mifflin Co. 1934.

MAHLER

MAHLER, ALMA MARIA SCHINDLER. Gustav Mahler: Memories and Letters. New York: The Viking Press. 1946.

WALTER, BRUNO. Gustav Mahler. Revised edition. New York: Alfred A. Knopf. 1958.

MENDELSSOHN

RADCLIFFE, PHILIP. Mendelssohn. London: J. M. Dent & Sons. 1954.

MILHAUD

MILHAUD, DARIUS. Notes without Music. New York: Alfred A. Knopf. 1953.

MOZART

BLOM, ERIC. Mozart. New York: Pellegrini & Cudahy. 1949.

BURK, JOHN N. Mozart and His Music. New York: Random House. 1959.

EINSTEIN, ALFRED. Mozart: His Character, His Work. New York: Oxford University Press. 1945.

TURNER, W. J. Mozart: The Man and His Works. New York: Alfred A. Knopf. 1938.

MUSSORGSKY

CALVOCORESSI, M. D. Mussorgsky. London: J. M. Dent & Sons. 1946.

LEYDA, J., and BERTENSSON, S. (editors). The Mussorgsky Reader. New York: W. W. Norton & Co. 1947.

RIESEMANN, OSKAR VON. Mussorgsky. New York: Alfred A. Knopf. 1935.

OFFENBACH

KRACAUER, S. Orpheus in Paris. New York: Alfred A. Knopf. 1938.

PAGANINI

Courcy, G. I. C. de. Paganini, the Genoese. Norman: University of Oklahoma Press. 1957.

Day, Lillian. Paganini of Genoa. New York: Macaulay Co. 1929.

PROKOFIEV

Nestyev, Israel V. Sergei Prokofiev: His Musical Life. Stanford: Stanford University Press. 1960.

PUCCINI

Carner, Mosco. Puccini: A Critical Biography. New York: Alfred A. Knopf. 1959.

Marek, George R. Puccini: A Biography. New York: Simon and Schuster. 1951.

RACHMANINOFF

Bertensson, S., and Leyda, J. Sergei Rachmaninoff: His Life and Music. New York: Philosophical Library. 1956.

Culshaw, John. Rachmaninoff: The Man and His Music. New York: Oxford University Press. 1950.

Seroff, Victor I. Rachmaninoff. New York: Simon and Schuster. 1950.

RAVEL

Demuth, Norman. Ravel. London: J. M. Dent & Sons. 1947.

Manuel, Roland. Maurice Ravel. London: Dobson Books. 1947.

Seroff, Victor I. Ravel. New York: Henry Holt & Co. 1953.

RIMSKY-KORSAKOV

Rimsky-Korsakov, N. My Musical Life. Third revised edition. New York: Alfred A. Knopf. 1942.

ROSSINI

Toye, Francis. Rossini: A Study in Tragi-Comedy. New York: Alfred A. Knopf. 1947.

SAINT-SAËNS

Harvey, Arthur. Saint-Saëns. New York: Dodd, Mead & Co. 1922.

SCHOENBERG

Leibowitz, René. Schoenberg and His School. New York: Philosophical Library. 1949.

Stuckenschmidt, H. H. Schoenberg. New York: Grove Press. 1959.

SCHUBERT

Brown, Maurice J. E. Schubert. New York: St. Martin's Press. 1958.

Deutsch, Otto Erich. The Schubert Reader. New York: W. W. Norton & Co. 1947.

DEUTSCH, OTTO ERICH. Schubert: Memoirs by His Friends. London: A. & C. Black. 1958.

EINSTEIN, ALFRED. Schubert: A Musical Portrait. New York: Oxford University Press. 1951.

FLOWER, NEWMAN. Schubert: The Man and His Circle. Revised edition. London: Cassell & Co. 1949.

SCHAUFFLER, ROBERT HAVEN. Franz Schubert: The Ariel of Music. New York: G. P. Putnam's Sons. 1949.

SCHUMANN

ABRAHAM, GERALD (editor). Schumann: A Symposium. New York: Oxford University Press. 1952.

NIECKS, FREDERICK. Schumann. New York: E. P. Dutton & Co. 1925.

SCHAUFFLER, ROBERT HAVEN. Florestan: The Life and Work of Robert Schumann. New York: Henry Holt & Co. 1946.

SCRIABIN

HULL, A. E. Scriabin. New York: E. P. Dutton & Co. 1916.

SWAN, A. J. Scriabin. London: John Lane. 1923.

SHOSTAKOVICH

MARTYNOV, IVAN. Shostakovich: The Man and His Work. New York: Philosophical Library. 1947.

SEROFF, VICTOR I. Dmitri Shostakovich: The Life and Background of a Soviet Composer. New York: Alfred A. Knopf. 1947.

SIBELIUS

ABRAHAM, GERALD. The Music of Sibelius. New York: W. W. Norton & Co. 1947.

EKMAN, KARL. Jean Sibelius. New York: Tudor Publishing Co. 1945.

GRAY, CECIL. Sibelius. Revised edition. London: Oxford University Press. 1945.

JOHNSON, HAROLD E. Jean Sibelius. New York: Alfred A. Knopf. 1959.

RINGBOM, ERIC. Sibelius. Norman: University of Oklahoma Press. 1954.

WESTERLUND, CY. The Works of Sibelius. Helsingfors: Westerlund Publishers. 1955.

STRAVINSKY

CORLE, EDWIN (editor). Stravinsky. New York: Duell, Sloan & Pearce. 1949.

ONNEN, FRANK. Stravinsky. New York: The Macmillan Co. 1950.

STRAVINSKY, IGOR. Stravinsky: An Autobiography. New York: Simon and Schuster. 1936.

TANSMAN, ALEXANDRE. Igor Stravinsky: The Man and His Music. New York: G. P. Putnam's Sons. 1949.

WHITE, ERIC WALTER. Stravinsky: A Critical Survey. New York: Philosophical Library. 1948.

TCHAIKOVSKY

ABRAHAM, GERALD. Tchaikovsky. New York: A. A. Wyn. 1949.

BOWEN, CATHERINE D., and MECK, B. VON. Beloved Friend. New York: Dover Publications. 1946.

EVANS, EDWIN. Tchaikovsky. New York: Pellegrini & Cudahy. 1949.

LAKOND, WLADIMIR. The Diaries of Tchaikovsky. New York: W. W. Norton & Co. 1945.

WEINSTOCK, HERBERT. Tchaikovsky. New York: Alfred A. Knopf. 1946.

VAUGHAN WILLIAMS

FOSS, HUBERT J. Ralph Vaughan Williams: A Study. London: Oxford University Press. 1950.

PAKENHAM, SIMONA. Ralph Vaughan Williams. New York: Saint Martin's Press. 1957.

YOUNG, PERCY M. Vaughan Williams. London: Dobson Books. 1953.

VERDI

BONAVIA, FERRUCCIO. Verdi. London: Dobson Books. 1947.

SHEAN, VINCENT. Orpheus at Eighty. New York: Random House. 1958.

TOYE, FRANCIS. Giuseppe Verdi: His Life and Works. New York: Alfred A. Knopf. 1946.

WERFEL, FRANZ, and STEFAN, PAUL. Verdi: The Man in His Letters. New York: A. A. Wyn. 1948.

WAGNER

NEWMAN, ERNEST. The Life of Richard Wagner. Four volumes. New York: Alfred A. Knopf. 1933–46.

TURNER, W. J. Wagner. New York: A. A. Wyn. 1948.

WALTON

HOWES, FRANK. The Music of William Walton. New York: Oxford University Press. 1943.

WEBER

POURTALÈS, GUY DE. Weber. New York: Harper & Bros. 1932.

STEBBINS, R. and L. Enchanted Wanderer. New York: G. P. Putnam's Sons. 1940.

WOLF

WALKER, FRANK. Hugo Wolf. New York: Alfred A. Knopf. 1952.

Index

Abdelazar (Purcell), 148
Abduction from the Seraglio, The (Mozart), 519, 520, 525, 543
Abraham, Gerald, 116
"Abscheulicher! wo eilst du hin!" (Beethoven), 72, 73
Abu Hassan (Weber), 891
Academic Festival Overture (Brahms), 129–30
A cappella, 3
Acis and Galatea (Handel), 332
Adagio for Strings (Barber), 34, 36
Adam, Adolphe, 425
Addison, Joseph, 331
"Adelaide" (Beethoven), 50, 695
"Adieu, Sweet Amaryllis" (Wilbye), 5
Adler, Guido, 451, 669
Africana, L' (Meyerbeer), 501, 503–4
Afternoon of a Faun, The (Debussy), 191, 196, 197–98
Agee, James, 35
Age of Gold, The (Shostakovich), 728
Age of Steel, The (Prokofiev), 573
Aglavine et Selysette (Honegger), 398
"Agnus Dei" (Bach), 25
"Agnus Dei" (Beethoven), 74, 75
Agon (Stravinsky), 776, 783, 785
Agrippina (Handel), 331
Ahna, Pauline de, 764
"Ah, vous dirai-je, maman," 218
Aida (Verdi), 587, 824, 825, 835–36
Air for the G string (Bach), 26

Airs from Moravia (Dvořák), 233
Ala and Lolly (Prokofiev), 576
Alamanzor (Heine), 190
Alarcón, Pedro Antonio de, 265
Albéniz, Isaac, 41, 257, 258
Albert Herring (Britten), 143, 144, 146
Alborada del gracioso (Ravel), 615, 616
Albrechtsberger, Johann Georg, 49
Album für die Jugend (Schumann), 708
Alceste (Gluck), 299, 303, 304, 305
Aldrich, Richard, 215
Aleko (Rachmaninoff), 600
Alexander Nevsky (Prokofiev), 578, 584–85
Alexander II, 115
Alexander's Feast (Handel), 328
Alfano, Franco, 593
Alfonso und Estrella (Schubert), 682
Alfred (Dvořák), 233
Alheim, Pierre d', 544
*Allegri, Gregorio, 373, 516
Allegro Barbaro (Bartók), 42
Allen, Maud, 103
Allen, Sir Hugh, 883
"Allerseelen" (Strauss), 761, 774
Almaviva (Rossini), 642
Almira (Handel), 330
Also sprach Zarathustra (Strauss), 761, 762, 768
Alto Rhapsody (Brahms), 134

Altschuler, Modest, 354, 722
Amahl and the Night Visitors (Menotti), 493–94, 497
Amaryllis (Ghys), 611
Amelia Goes to the Ball (Menotti), 491, 492, 495–96
America (Bloch), 103, 104
American in Paris, An (Gershwin), 290, 293–94
American Quartet (Dvořák), 237, 241
Amico Fritz, L' (Mascagni), 461
"Am Meer" (Schubert), 697
Amor Brujo, El (Falla), 260, 262–64
"Am See" (Schubert), 679
"Anakreons Grab" (Wolf), 905
Andersen, Hans Christian, 317
An die ferne Geliebte (Beethoven), 695
"An die Musik" (Schubert), 696
Andrews, Edward D., 184
"An meinem Herzen" (Schumann), 713
Ana Bolena (Donizetti), 220–21
Années de pèlerinage (Liszt), 446
Ansermet, Ernest, 781, 883
Antar Symphony (Rimsky-Korsakov), 631
Antigone (Honegger), 400
Antiphony, 4
Apaches, Société des, 612
Apollon Musagète (Stravinsky), 782
Appalachian Spring (Copland), 182, 183, 184
Appassionata Sonata (Beethoven), 51, 55, 68
Apprenti sorcier, L' (Dukas), 227, 228–29, 259
Après-midi d'un faune, L' (Debussy), 191, 196, 197–98
"Après un rêvu" (Fauré), 272
Apthorp, William Forster, 66
Arcadelt, Jacob, 4
Arensky, Anton, 633

Ariane et Barbe-bleue (Dukas), 227, 228, 259
Arlésienne, L' (Bizet), 95, 97, 99–100
Armida (Dvořák), 236
Arnold, Matthew, 35
Arrgelito, El (Yradier), 98
Ars Antiqua, 4
Ars Nova, 4
Artaserse (Gluck), 298
Art of the Fugue, The (Bach), 16, 20, 22
Artôt, Désirée, 797
Asafiev, Boris, 411
Astarto (Bononcini), 333
Atalanta (Handel), 339
Atlantida, La (Verdaguer), 261
Auber, Daniel François, 500
Aubert, Louis, 268
"Au Bord d'une source" (Liszt), 446
"Auch kleine Dinge" (Wolf), 905
"Au cimetière" (Fauré), 272
Auden, W. H., 141, 149, 782
"Auf dem See" (Wolf), 899
"Auf dem Wasser zu singen" (Schubert), 696
"Auf einer Wanderung" (Wolf), 905
Auric, Georges, 398, 399, 405
"Aus alten Märchen winkt es" (Schumann), 713
Aus Italien (Strauss), 761
Ave Maria (Bruckner), 152
"Ave Maria" (Gounod), 311
"Ave Maria" (Schubert), 696
Ave Verum (Mozart), 524, 525, 539

Baal Shem Suite (Bloch), 103, 107–8
Bach, Anna Magdalena Wülcken, 19, 21
Bach, Johann Christian, 21, 515
Bach, Johann Christoph, 17
Bach, Johann Sebastian, 3, 4, 9, 10, 11, 12, 15–31, 124, 276, 330, 337, 338, 340, 447, 471, 476, 477

Bach, Karl Philipp Emanuel, 16–17, 20, 21, 373

Bach, Maria Barbara, 18, 19, 21

Bach, Wilhelm Friedemann, 17

"*Baches Wiegenlied, Des*" (Schubert), 697

Bach Gesellschaft, 15, 22

Bachiana Brasileira (Villa-Lobos), 844, 845

Balakirev, Mily, 109, 111, 114, 545, 547, 627, 628, 630, 632, 797, 808

Ballo in Maschera, Un (Verdi), 824

Barbaja, Domenico, 642, 892

Barbe-Bleue (Offenbach), 562

Barber, Samuel, 32–36, 494

Barber of Bagdad, The (Cornelius), 440

Barber of Seville, The (Rossini), 223, 642–43, 646, 647–49, 661

Barbier, Jules, 312, 563

Barbier de Séville, Le (Beaumarchais), 642, 648

Barbirolli, John, 142

"Barcarolle" (Offenbach), 564

Bardac, Emma, 194

Barere, Simon, 726

Barezzi, Margherita, 822, 823

Barjanska, Catherine, 105

Barnfield, Richard, 149

Baroque period, 5–6

Bartered Bride, The (Smetana), 232, 751, 752, 754–55

Bartl, Marie, 154

Bartók, Béla, 37–44, 416, 417, 418, 667

Bartók, Peter, 40

Basel Concerto (Stravinsky), 790

Bastien und Bastienne (Mozart), 515

Ba-ta-clan (Offenbach), 558

Baudelaire, Charles, 268, 272

Baumann, Pierre, 422, 425

Bazzini, Antonio, 587

Bear Dance (Bartók), 42

Béatitudes, Les (Franck), 273, 274, 277, 279

Beaumarchais, Pierre de, 521, 642, 648

Beaumont, Francis, 149

Becker, Albert, 740

Beecham, Sir Thomas, 210, 211, 212

Beethoven, Johann van, 46–48

Beethoven, Karl van, 53

Beethoven, Ludwig van, 16, 45–75, 83, 88, 117, 121, 122, 126, 130, 134, 171, 235, 248, 258, 270, 275, 282, 327, 370, 372, 393, 394, 434, 643, 646, 683, 695

Before the Dawn (Hanson), 348

Beggar's Opera, The (Pepusch), 332, 334

"*Beiden Grenadiere, Die*" (Schumann), 713

Bekker, Paul, 55, 297

Belasco, David, 592, 596

Belfagor (Respighi), 623

Belle Hélène, La (Offenbach), 562

Bellini, Vincenzo, 222

Belshazzar (Handel), 337

Belshazzar's Feast (Walton), 883, 885

Benedict, Julius, 474

"*Benedictus*" (Bach), 25

"*Benedictus*" (Beethoven), 74, 75

Benjamin, Arthur, 141

Benois, Alexandre, 786

Benoist, François, 94, 654

Benvenuto Cellini (Berlioz), 92

Berg, Alban, 76–81, 667, 668

Berger, Arthur V., 179

Berger, Ludwig, 472

Bergsma, William, 349

Bériot, Charles de, 611

Berlin, Irving, 34, 288

Berlioz, Hector, 62, 82–93, 309, 312, 436, 439, 500, 565, 895

Bernstein, Leonard, 143

Bethge, Hans, 459

"*Betrachte, meine Seel'* " (Bach), 24

Bey, Mariette, 835

Billy Budd (Britten), 140, 143–44, 146–47

Billy the Kid (Copland), 182, 183

Bird Quartet (Haydn), 381–82

Birds, The (Respighi), 625

Bizet, Georges, 94–100, 311

Black Key Etude (Chopin), 176

Blake, William, 149

Blau, Edouard, 427

Blessed Damozel, The (Rossetti), 190

Bloch, Ernest, 101–8

Blue Danube, The (Strauss), 176

Blue Monday (Gershwin), 289, 294

"Boating" (Bartók), 44

Böcklin, Arnold, 607

Bodanzky, Artur, 103

Boeuf sur le toit, Le (Milhaud), 506, 508

Bogatyrs, The (Borodin), 112

"*Bogatyrskava*" Symphony (Borodin), 116

Bohème, La (Puccini), 430, 589, 593–94

Boïto, Arrigo, 312, 588, 827, 828, 836, 838

Boléro (Ravel), 613, 618, 619

Bolivar (Milhaud), 506, 507, 508

Bolt, The (Shostakovich), 728

Bononcini, Giovanni Battista, 333, 334

Boris Godunov (Mussorgsky) 70, 549, 551, 552–55, 633

Borodin, Alexander, 109–16, 545, 547, 628, 632, 633

Borodin, Porfiri, 110

Boulanger, Nadia, 180, 181, 354, 401

Brahms, Johannes, 38, 39, 117–39, 154, 156, 215, 216, 217, 233–34, 246, 252, 253, 282, 354, 419, 450, 701

Brandenburg concertos (Bach), 10, 22, 26–27

Brandenburgers in Bohemia, The (Smetana), 751

Brandt, Caroline, 891

Brebis égarée, La (Milhaud), 506, 507

Brentano, Bettina, 51

Breuning, Stephan von, 52

Bréville, Pierre de, 160

Bride of Lammermoor, The (Scott), 224

Bridge, Frank, 141, 147

Brief Encounter, 604

Brigg Fair (Delius), 209, 213

Britten, Benjamin, 140–49

Broca, Enrique, 258

Broder, Nathan, 32

Bruch, Max, 623, 812

Bruckner, Anton, 150–59

Brunswick, Therese von, 51

Büchner, Georg, 78

Bull, Ole, 314, 316

Bülow, Hans von, 125, 130, 137, 234, 314, 760, 857

Burk, John W., 71

Burleigh, Harry T., 235

Busoni, Ferruccio, 670, 740, 883

Butterfly Etude (Chopin), 176

Buxtehude, Dietrich, 9, 17–18, 30, 330

"Buzzing" (Bartók), 44

Byrd, William, 5

Byrom, John, 334

Byron, George Gordon, 443

Caccini, Giulio, 6, 7, 304

"*Cäcilie*" (Strauss), 761, 775

Callot, Jacques, 887

Calm Sea and Prosperous Voyage (Mendelssohn), 248

Calvocoressi, M. D., 464

Calzabigi, Ranieri de', 298, 304

Cambiale di matrimonio, La (Rossini), 641, 647

Camerata, 6, 8

Cammarano, Salvatore, 832

Campana sommersa, La (Respighi), 624

Campanella, La (Liszt), 446

Campanella, La (Paganini), 570

Campanini, Italo, 577, 591

Campra, André, 509

Cantata, 8–9

Cantata on Anonymous Elizabethan Songs (Stravinsky), 782

Canticos Sertanejos (Villa-Lobos), 841

Canticum Sacrum (Stravinsky), 776, 783, 785, 792

Canzona, 10

Capriccio (Stravinsky), 789–90

Capriccio brilliant (Mendelssohn), 478

Capriccio espagnol (Rimsky-Korsakov), 634, 635, 637

Capriccio Italien (Tchaikovsky), 799, 810

Caprice, 570–71

Caractacus (Elgar), 246

Cardillac (Hindemith), 387, 390

Card Party (Stravinsky), 782, 788–89

Carissimi, Giacomo, 8–9

Carmagnole, La (Paganini), 566

Carmen (Bizet), 95–96, 97–99

Carnaval (Schumann), 701, 706–7

Carnival (Dvořák), 237

Carnival of Animals, The (Saint-Saëns), 660

Carré, Albert, 192

Carré, Michel, 312, 563

Carvalho, Léon, 95

Casals, Pablo, 252

Casella, Alfredo, 352

Casse-Noisette (Tchaikovsky), 810–11

Catarina Cornaro (Donizetti), 221

"Cathédrale engloutie, La" (Debussy), 202–3

Cavalieri, Emilio del, 8

Cavalier of the Rose, The (Strauss), 765, 773–74

Cavalleria Rusticana (Mascagni), 429, 431, 460, 461, 462–63, 588

Cavalli, Pietro Francesco, 7

Cave of the Heart (Barber), 34

Cazalis, Henri, 659

Cembalo, 27, 28

Cenerentola, La (Rossini), 642, 646

Ceremony of Carols, A (Britten), 144

Cermáková, Anna, 233

Chaconne, 10, 31

"Chaconne" for unaccompanied violin (Bach), 30

Chaliapin, Feodor, 467, 614

Chamisso, Adelbert von, 713

"Chanson d'amour" (Fauré), 272

Chansons de Bilitis (Debussy), 191

Chant de Libération (Honegger), 400

Chant du rossignol, Le (Stravinsky), 781, 784

Characteristic Dances (Tchaikovsky), 796

Charpentier, Gustave, 259, 462, 466, 467

Chase, Gilbert, 257

"Chasse, La" (Paganini), 571

Chatterton (Leoncavallo) 428, 430

Chausson, Ernest, 160–63, 277, 279

Cherubini, Luigi, 167, 275, 435, 475, 500, 502, 559

Chezy, Wilhelmine von, 892

Child and the Magic Spirits, The (Ravel), 613, 615

Children's Corner (Debussy), 204

Chineische Flöte, Die (Bethge), 459

Choice of Hercules (Handel), 337

Chopin, Frédéric, 111, 164–78, 188, 202, 436, 446, 701, 721

Chopiniana (Stravinsky), 778

Chorale, 9, 23

Chorale-prelude, 10, 31

"Chorale St. Antoni" (Haydn), 125

Chôros (Villa-Lobos), 844, 845–46

Chotzinoff, Samuel, 284

Chout (Prokofiev), 577

Christ lag in Todesbanden (Bach), 25–26

Christ Lay in the Bonds of Death (Bach), 25–26

Christmas Eve (Rimsky-Korsakov), 634

Chromatic Fantasy and Fugue (Bach), 30

Church Windows (Respighi), 624, 625

Cid, Le (Massenet), 466

Cinderella (Prokofiev), 578

"Clair de lune" (Debussy), 189, 203

"Clair de lune" (Fauré), 272

Clare, John, 149

Classical Symphony (Prokofiev), 577, 579, 580–81

Claudel, Paul, 506, 508

Clavichord, 27, 28

Clavier, 11

Clementi, Muzio, 498, 519

Cleopatra (Mattheson), 330

Clock Symphony (Haydn), 377–78

"Clouds" (Debussy), 198

Clovis et Clothilde (Bizet), 94

Cobbett, W. W., 71

Cocteau, Jean, 506, 508, 790

Colbran, Isabella, 642, 643

Collin, Heinrich von, 64

"Collines d'Anacapri, Les" (Debussy), 202

Colonne, Edouard, 161, 274

Combattimento di Tancredi, Il (Monteverdi), 6

Commando March (Barber), 34

Comte Ory, Le (Rossini), 646

Concerto, piano, 27

Concerto for Orchestra (Bartók), 41, 42–43

Concerto grosso, 10, 26, 27, 28

Concerto symphonique (Bloch), 103

Conductus, 3–4

Connaissance de l'est (Milhaud), 506

"Consider, My Soul" (Bach), 24

Consul, The (Menotti), 492–93, 494, 496–97

Coolidge, Elizabeth Sprague, 184, 388, 782

Copland, Aaron, 141, 179–86, 289

Coq d'or, Le (Rimsky-Korsakov), 634, 635

Corelli, Arcangelo, 10–11, 331, 344, 622

Coriolanus Overture (Beethoven), 64

Corneille, Pierre, 221

Cornelius, Peter, 440

Corregidor, Der (Wolf), 265, 902

Cosa rara, Una (Martin), 521

Cossel, Otto, 118

Costa, Giacomo, 566

Counterpoint, 21, 372

Couperin-le-Grand, François, 11, 29, 270, 620

Coward, Noel, 604

Cowell, Henry, 357

Crabbe, George, 145

Cramer, J. B., 176

Cranz, August, 68

Creation, The (Haydn), 371, 374

"Credo" (Bach), 25

"Credo" (Beethoven), 74, 75

Crozier, Eric, 146, 147

"Crucifixus" (Bach), 25

Cuban Overture (Gershwin), 290

Cui, César, 111, 547, 628

Cuzzoni, Francesca, 334

"Cyclical form," 162, 279

Czar Saltan (Rimsky-Korsakov), 634

Czar's Bride, The (Rimsky-Korsakov), 634

Czerny, Karl, 176, 434

Da capo aria, 7

Dafne (Peri), 6

Dafne (Schütz), 7–8

D'Alheim, Pierre, 544

Dalibor (Smetana), 751

Dallapiccola, Luigi, 667

Dame aux camélias, La (Dumas), 834

Damnation of Faust, The (Berlioz), 85, 87, 92–93, 312, 660

Damrosch, Walter, 93, 181, 293, 602

"Dance of the Seven Veils" (Strauss), 772

"Dance of the Sylphs" (Berlioz), 92

Dance Symphony (Copland), 181, 182

Dances from Galánta (Kodály), 418, 420–21

Dances of Marosszék (Kodály), 418

Danse macabre (Saint-Saëns) 659–60, 661

Dante Symphony (Liszt), 441

Daphnis et Chloé (Ravel), 613, 615, 616–18

Da Ponte, Lorenzo, 521, 522, 525, 527

Dargomyzhsky, Alexander, 547

Daudet, Alphonse, 95, 99

David, Félicien, 560

David, Ferdinand, 479

David and Jonathan (Carissimi), 8

David Rizzio (Massenet), 465

Davidsbündler, 701

Death and the Maiden Quartet (Schubert), 688, 692

Death and Transfiguration (Strauss), 761, 766–67, 771

Death of Pierrot, The (Menotti), 490

Deborah (Handel), 335

Debussy, Claude, 187–205, 212, 227, 228, 253, 259, 262, 270, 274, 277, 291, 467, 612, 781

De Falla, Manuel. *See* Falla, Manuel de

De Gorgorza, Emilio, 33

Dehmel, Richard, 673

Delacroix, Eugène, 82

Delage, Maurice, 612

Delibes, Léo, 187, 246, 278

Delius, Frederick, 206–14

Delsarte, François, 94

Demoiselle élue, La (Debussy), 190

Denzler, Robert, 78

Des Prés, Josquin, 4

Dessicated Embryos (Satie), 196

Destruction of Sennacherib, The (Mussorgsky), 549

Dettingen Te Deum (Handel), 337

Deux aveugles, Les (Offenbach), 560

Devil's Wall, The (Smetana), 752

Devrient, Eduard, 477

Diabelli, Antonio, 435

Diaghilev, Serge, 261, 265, 395, 576, 577, 613, 778, 779, 780, 782, 784, 785

Diamond, David, 348–49

Dichterliebe (Schumann), 713

Dickinson, Emily, 35

Dido and Aeneas (Purcell), 8, 243

Dieren, Bernard van, 206

Dietrich, Albert, 133, 134

Dillon, Fanny Charles, 354

D'Indy, Vincent. *See* Indy, Vincent d'

Dinorah (Meyerbeer), 501

Dissonant Quartet (Mozart), 525, 540

Dit des jeux du monde, Le (Honegger), 398

Dittersdorf, Karl von, 520

Divine Poem (Scriabin), 714, 715, 719, 722

Djamileh (Bizet), 95

Djinns, Les (Franck), 274

Docteur Miracle (Bizet), 94

Doctor Faustus (Mann), 665

"Doctor Gradus ad Parnassum" (Debussy), 204

Dohnányi, Ernst von, 215–18

"*Dona nobis pacem*" (Bach), 25

"*Dona nobis pacem*" (Beethoven), 75

Don Carlos (Verdi), 824

Don Giovanni (Mozart), 379, 522, 525, 527–29, 532, 646

Donizetti, Gaetano, 219–25

Don Juan (Gluck), 299

Don Juan (Strauss), 761, 765–66, 771

Don Pasquale (Donizetti), 221 223–24

Don Procopio (Bizet), 95

Don Quichotte (Massenet), 467

Don Quichotte à Dulcinée (Ravel), 614

Don Quixote (Strauss), 761, 768–70, 771

Don Sanche (Liszt), 435

"Doppelgänger, Der" (Schubert), 697

Doppler, Franz, 445

Dorati, Antal, 393

Dorn, Heinrich, 700, 850

"Double Concerto" (Bach), 28

"Double Concerto" (Brahms), 132–33

Dover Beach (Barber), 35

Downes, Olin, 105, 489

Dramma per musica, 6–7, 9

Dream of Gerontius, The (Elgar), 243, 245–46, 883

"Dresden Amen," 484, 879

Dreyfus, Max, 288

"Driving Boy" (Britten), 149

Drum Roll Symphony (Haydn), 378

Dubois, Théodore, 610

"Du denkst mit einem Fädchen" (Wolf), 905

Dufay, Guillaume, 4

Dukas, Paul, 226–29, 259, 404, 506

Dumas, Alexandre, 834

Dumbarton Oaks Concerto (Stravinsky), 790

Dumky Trio (Dvořák), 237, 241–42

Duncan, Ronald, 146

Duparc, Marie Eugène Henri Fouques, 277

Duple time, 4

Dupont, Gabrielle, 190

Durand, Emile, 188

Durazzo, Count Giacomo, 298

Durey, Louis, 399

Dustmann, Luise, 120

Dvořák, Antonin, 230–42, 286, 749, 753

Eastman, George, 348

Edgar (Puccini), 588

Egmont (Beethoven), 64

Eichendorff, Joseph von, 901

1812 Overture (Tchaikovsky), 799–800, 801, 809–10

Einstein, Alfred, 385

Eisenstein, Serge, 584

"Elégie" (Massenet), 465

Elektra (Strauss), 762, 772–73

Elgar, Sir Edward, 243–50

Elijah (Mendelssohn), 246, 479, 480, 481, 486–87

Elisabetta (Rossini), 642, 647

Elisir d'Amore, L' (Donizetti), 221

Elsner, Joseph, 164, 166, 167, 171

Emperor Concerto (Beethoven), 52, 66–67

Emperor Quartet (Haydn), 382

Enesco, Georges, 41, 251–56

Enfant et les sortilèges, L' (Ravel), 613, 615

Enfant prodigue, L' (Debussy), 189

"English Bach," 21

English suites (Bach), 19, 29

Enigma Variations (Elgar), 243, 245, 247–49

Enrico di Borgogna (Donizetti), 220

En Saga (Sibelius), 740, 743, 747

Ensign Polka (Mussorgsky), 546

"En sourdine" (Debussy), 189

Entführung aus dem Serail, Die (Mozart), 519, 520, 525, 543

Eolides, Les (Franck), 273

Epstein, Julius, 121, 450

Equal temperament, 29–30

"Er, der Herrlichste von allen" (Schumann), 713

Erdödy, Countess, 52

Erkel, László, 39

"Erlkönig" (Schubert), 678, 679, 681, 692, 696

Ernani (Verdi), 824

Ernesti, Johann August, 20

Eroica Symphony (Beethoven), 51, 55, 56–57, 60, 126

"Errinerung" (Brahms), 139

"Erwartung" (Wolf), 905

Erynnies, Les (Massenet), 465

Eschenbach, Wolfram von, 864, 878

"Es ist vollbracht" (Bach), 24

Essay for Orchestra, Nos. 1 and 2 (Barber), 34, 35, 36

Estampes (Debussy), 203

Estelle et Namorin (Berlioz), 83

Esther (Handel), 335, 339

Etoile du nord, L' (Meyerbeer), 501

Etudes symphoniques (Schumann), 701, 705–6

"Et Vitam Venturi" (Beethoven), 75

Eugene Onegin (Tchaikovsky), 799

Euridice (Caccini), 304

Euridice (Peri), 304

Euryanthe (Weber), 501, 892, 893, 894–95

"Eusebius" (Schumann), 706, 707

Eve (Massenet), 465

Expressionism, 861

Ezio (Handel), 334

Façade (Walton), 883, 885

"Fair as Fair" (Britten), 149

Falla, Manuel de, 41, 200, 203, 257–66, 612, 902

Fall of Berlin (Shostakovich), 731

Falstaff (Verdi), 828, 829, 830, 837–38

Fanfare for the Common Man (Copland), 185

Fantaisie-Impromptu (Chopin), 178

Fantaisie pastorale (Enesco), 252

Fantasia, 10, 31

Fantasia and Fugue in G minor (Bach), 31

Fantasia on a Theme by Thomas Tallis (Vaughan Williams), 814, 816–17

Fantasie in C major (Schumann), 707–8

Fantasiestücke (Schumann), 707

Fantasy Quartet (Britten), 141

Farewell Symphony (Haydn), 373, 375

Farwell, Arthur, 353–54, 598

Fatum (Tchaikovsky), 797

Faune et la bergère, Le (Stravinsky), 778

Fauré, Gabriel, 252, 259, 267–72, 611, 612

Faust (Gounod), 309–10, 311–13

Faust Overture, A (Wagner), 312

Faust Symphony (Liszt), 312, 441

Favorita, La (Donizetti), 221, 222

Feast During the Plague, The (Prokofiev), 575

Feen, Die (Wagner), 850

Feldlager in Schlesien, Ein (Meyerbeer), 501

Fenby, Eric, 210, 212

Fernand (Gounod), 308

Fervaal (D'Indy), 407

"Festivals" (Debussy), 198

Fête-Dieu à Seville (Albéniz), 258

"Fêtes" (Debussy), 198

Feuersnot (Strauss), 762

"Feuerzauber" (Wagner), 875

"Feurreiter, Der" (Wolf), 905

Fidelio (Beethoven), 63, 64, 72–73

Field, John, 175

Fiesque (Lalo), 423

"Fille aux cheveux de lin, La" (Debussy), 202

Fille du régiment, La (Donizetti), 221

Fils prodigue, Le (Prokofiev), 578

Fingal's Cave Overture (Mendelssohn), 477, 478, 486

Finlandia (Sibelius), 740, 747–48

Finta giardiniera, La (Mozart), 517

Finta semplice, La (Mozart), 515

Fire-Bird, The (Stravinsky), 779, 784, 785–86

Fireworks (Stravinsky), 778

Fireworks Music (Handel), 337, 338

Fischer, Adolphe, 427

Fisher, William Arms, 238

"Five, The Russian," 547, 612, 627–28, 802–3

Five Orchestral Songs (Berg), 77

Flabby Preludes for a Dog (Satie), 196

Flaubert, Gustave, 268

Fleg, Edmond, 102

Flemish school, 4, 9

Fletcher, John, 149

Fleurville, Madame Mauté de, 188

Fliegende Holländer, Der (Wagner), 851, 852, 861, 864, 881

Flonzaley Quartet, 103

"*Florestan*" (Schumann), 706, 707

Florida (Delius), 208

Floridante (Handel), 333, 339

Flos Campi (Vaughan Williams), 814

Flying Dutchman, The (Wagner), 851, 852, 861, 864, 881

Fokine, Michel, 779, 785

Folk-Song Symphony (Harris), 359

"*Forelle, Die*" (Schubert), 696

Forelle Quintet (Schubert), 688, 693

"Forest Murmurs" (Wagner), 876

"Forging Song" (Wagner), 876

Forlane, 620–21

Forster, E. M., 147

Förstner, Karl, 215

Forza del Destino, La (Verdi), 824

Foss, Hubert J., 812, 882

Foster, Stephen, 285

Fountains of Rome (Respighi), 623, 625–26

Four Temperaments (Hindemith), 388

France, Anatole, 469

Francesca da Rimini (Tchaikovsky), 809

Francescatti, Zino, 570

Franchetti, Alberto, 589

Franck, César, 161, 162, 271, 273–83, 356, 405, 406

Frandin, Lison, 429

Frankh, Johann Matthias, 364, 368

Frauenliebe und Leben (Schumann), 713

Frederick the Great, 20

Freischütz, Der (Weber), 474, 891–92, 893, 894

Fremstad, Olive, 453

French overture, 8

French suites (Bach), 19, 29

Frescobaldi, Girolamo, 10, 30

Fricken, Ernestine von, 706, 707

Frische Klavier Früchte (Kuhnau), 11

Friskin, James, 348

From the Bohemian Forest (Dvořák), 237

From the New World (Dvořák), 235–36, 237, 238–39

"*Frühlingstraum*" (Schubert), 697

"*Frühling übers Jahr*" (Wolf), 905

Fuchs, Robert, 740

Fuchslied, 130

Fugue, 10, 31

"*Funérailles*" (Liszt), 446–47

Funeral March for the Victims of the Revolution (Shostakovich), 726

Furtwängler, Wilhelm, 391

"*Fussreise*" (Wolf), 905

Gabrieli, Giovanni, 4, 9, 10

Gade, Niels, 317, 318

Gallot, Jacques de, 625

Galluzo, Elois, 258

Gammerano, Salvatore, 223

Garbousova, Raya, 34

García, Manuel, 646

Garcin, Jules, 277

Garden, Mary, 192, 578

"*Gärtner, Der*" (Wolf), 905

Gaspard de la nuit (Ravel), 612–13

"Gathering Mushrooms" (Mussorgsky), 557

Gatti, Guido M., 105

Gaudeamus Igitur, 129, 130

Gauthier, Eva, 289
Gautier, Théophile, 82, 259, 272
Gavotte, 581
Gayane (Khatchaturian), 412, 414–15
Gazza ladra, La (Rossini), 651
Gebrauchsmusik, 388
Gédalge, André, 252, 398, 466, 506, 611
Geiringer, Karl, 134
"Geistliches Wiegenlied" (Brahms), 139
German Requiem, A (Brahms), 121, 133–34
Gershwin, George, 284–96
"Gestillte Sehnsucht" (Brahms), 139
Gesualdo, Carlo, 5
Gevaert, François Auguste, 379
Geyer, Ludwig, 848, 849
Ghedeanishvili, Prince Luke, 109
Ghislanzoni, Antonio, 835
Ghys, Henri, 611
Gianni Schicchi (Puccini), 592
Giant, The (Prokofiev), 575
Giant Symphony (Mahler), 458
Gibbons, Orlando, 5
"Gigues" (Debussy), 200
Gilman, Lawrence, 251, 758
Gioconda, La (Ponchielli), 587
Giorno di Regno, Un (Verdi), 823
Girl of the Golden West, The (Puccini), 592
Gladkowska, Constantia, 166, 174
Glazunov, Alexander, 112, 576, 600, 633, 634
Glinka, Michael, 547, 627–28, 629, 777, 795
Gli scherzi Quartets (Haydn), 381–82
"Gloria" (Bach), 25
"Gloria in Excelsis" (Beethoven), 74–75
Gloriana (Britten), 144
Gluck, Christoph Willibald, 83, 276, 297–306, 338, 366, 515, 522, 859, 860

"Goat, The" (Mussorgsky), 557
God and Nature (Meyerbeer), 499
Goethe, Johann Wolfgang von, 51, 54, 64, 134, 228, 310, 443, 474, 514, 695, 696, 901
Goetschius, Percy, 348
Gogorza, Emilio de, 33
"Goin' Home" (Fisher-Dvořák), 238
Goldberg, Johann Gottlieb, 30
Goldberg Variations (Bach), 30
Golden Cockerel, The (Rimsky-Korsakov), 634, 635
Goldmark, Karl, 740
Goldmark, Rubin, 180, 287, 288
"Golliwogg's Cake Walk" (Debussy), 204
"Good Friday Spell" (Wagner), 880
Gothic period, 3
Götterdämmerung (Wagner), 858, 873, 877–78
Gould, Morton, 289
Gounod, Charles, 87, 97, 268, 278, 307–13, 654
Gradus ad Parnassum (Clementi), 498
Graham, Martha, 34, 184
Grainger, Percy, 213, 321
Grande valse brillante (Chopin), 177
Grand'tante, La (Massenet), 465
"Gratias Agimus" (Beethoven), 75
Gray, Cecil, 219, 433, 738
Great Friendship (Mauradeli), 573
Green, William Hatton, 32
Greis, Der (Haydn), 371
"Gretchen am Spinnrade" (Schubert), 678, 679, 695
"Grief and Pain" (Bach), 24
Grieg, Edvard, 208, 314–26
Grofé, Ferde, 289, 293
Grohg (Copland), 180
Grosse Fugue (Beethoven), 71
Grove, Sir George, 53
Grünewald, Matthias, 391, 392
Guarnieri, Antonio, 623

Guicciardi, Countess Giulietta, 51, 71
Guiraud, Ernest, 95, 99, 189
Guntram (Strauss), 761, 771
Gurre-Lieder (Schoenberg), 665, 668, 669
"Gute Nacht" (Schubert), 697
Gutiérrez, Antonio Garcia, 832
Guzla de l'Emir, La (Bizet), 95
Gymnopédies (Satie), 611

Habanera, 98
Habeneck, François, 86
Hadow, W. H., 117, 847
Haffner Serenade (Mozart), 517
Haffner Symphony (Mozart), 520, 531
"Hagars Klage" (Schubert), 677
Hagerup, Nina, 317
Hail California (Saint-Saëns), 657
Hakon Jarl (Smetana), 751
Hale, Philip, 42, 698
Halévy, Geneviève, 95
Halévy, Jacques, 94, 95, 308, 500, 559, 654
Halévy, Ludovic, 96
Hambitzer, Charles, 285, 286, 287
Hammerklavier Sonata (Beethoven), 52, 68–69
Handel, George Frideric, 9, 10, 20, 53, 137, 246, 298, 327–46, 383
Hanslick, Eduard, 869, 902
Hanson, Howard, 347–51, 354
Haraszti, Emil, 37
"Harfenspieler" songs (Wolf), 905
"Hark, hark, the Lark" (Schubert), 696
Harmonie der Welt, Die (Hindemith), 385, 396
Harmonies poétiques et religieuses (Liszt), 446–47
Harmonious Blacksmith, The (Handel), 333, 338, 346
Harold in Italy (Berlioz), 87
Harpsichord, 27, 28

Harris, Roy, 352–61
Harte, Bret, 592
Hartmann, Victor, 550, 555
Harty, Sir Hamilton, 884
Háry János (Kodály), 418, 419–20
Harzreise im Winter (Goethe), 134
Hasidism, 107
Haydn, Joseph, 21, 48, 49, 54, 56, 67, 69, 74, 88, 125, 258, 362–84, 520, 521, 646
Haydn, Michael, 889
Haydn Quartets (Mozart), 525, 539–41
Heart and Spirit (Bach), 26
Hebrides Overture (Mendelssohn), 477, 478, 486
Heifetz, Jascha, 284, 884
Heiligenstadt Testament (Beethoven), 50–51
"Heimweh" (Wolf), 905
Heine, Heinrich, 82, 190, 697, 713
Heirs of the White Mountain, The (Dvořák), 233
Heldenleben, Ein (Strauss), 761, 762, 770–71
Helfert, Vladimir, 749
Hellmesberger, Joseph, 121, 134, 252
Helvetia (Bloch), 104
Henrici, Christian Friedrich, 24
Herbeck, Johann, 151, 685
Hercules (Handel), 337
Herke, Anton, 546
Herodiade (Hindemith), 388
Hérodiade (Massenet), 465
"Hero Quartet" (Beethoven), 55, 69–70, 539
Hero's Life, A (Strauss), 761, 762, 770–71
Herrick, Robert, 149
Hertz, Alfred, 353
Hervey, Arthur, 307
"Herz, verzage nicht geschwind" (Wolf), 905
Herz und Mund (Bach), 26

Heure espagnole, L' (Ravel), 612, 615

Heyward, DuBose, 294

Hiller, Ferdinand, 167

Hindemith, Paul, 385–96, 763, 883

Histoire du soldat, L' (Stravinsky), 782

Histoires naturelles (Ravel), 610, 615

Hiver (Bloch), 102

Hoary Old Man, The (Haydn), 371

Hochstein, David, 138

Hochzeit des Camacho, Die (Mendelssohn), 476

Hoffmann, E. T. A., 563, 810, 861, 892

Hofmannsthal, Hugo von, 772, 773

Holberg Suite (Grieg), 322, 325–26

Holzer, Michael, 676

Homer, Louise, 32

Homme et son désir, L' (Milhaud), 506

Homophony, 6, 21, 372

Honegger, Arthur, 397–403, 405

"*Hopak*" (Mussorgsky), 549

Horace Victorieux (Honegger), 399, 400

Horizon chimérique, L' (Fauré), 272

Horowitz, Vladimir, 34, 555

Housman, A. E., 35

Housman, Laurence, 250

Howard, John Tasker, 347

Hugo, Victor, 82, 272, 443, 486, 831

Huguenots, Les (Meyerbeer), 500

Hummel, Johann Nepomuk, 52, 74, 275, 499

Humoresque (Dvořák), 236, 286

Humoresques (Grieg), 317

"Hungarian March" (Berlioz), 92–93

Hungarian Rhapsodies (Liszt), 441, 444, 445–46

Hunt Quartet (Mozart), 540

Hurst, Fannie, 236

Hutcheson, Ernest, 137

Hüttenbrenner, Anselm, 680, 685

Huxley, Aldous, 70

Hymn for the Pioneers (Hanson), 347

Hymn of Labor (Mascagni), 461

Hymn to Liberty (Shostakovich), 726

"*Ibéria*" (Debussy), 199–201, 262

Ibsen, Henrik, 76, 318, 319–20, 324

"*Ich grolle nicht*" (Schumann), 713

"*Ich kann's nicht fassen*" (Schumann), 713

"*Ich steh' mit einem Fuss im Grabe*" (Bach), 26

Idomeneo (Mozart), 518, 524

Illica, Luigi, 589

"I Love You" (Grieg), 317

Images (Debussy), 199–201, 262

Images for piano (Debussy), 203

"I'm Always Chasing Rainbows," 178

"*Immer leiser wird mein Schlummer*" (Brahms), 132, 139

"Immolation Scene" (Wagner), 878

Impervio, Pastora, 262–63

Impressionism, 162, 195–96, 861

"*Im Rhein, im heiligen Strome*" (Schumann), 713

"*Im wunderschönen Monat Mai*" (Schumann), 713

In a Summer Garden (Delius), 209, 213–14

In Autumn (Grieg), 318

Incoronazione di Poppea, L' (Monteverdi), 6

"In Deepest Grief We Sit Here Weeping" (Bach), 24

"*In dem Schatten meiner Locken*" (Wolf), 905

"*In des Lebens Frühlingstagen*" (Beethoven), 64, 173

Indy, Vincent d', 96, 193, 275, 276, 277, 279, 398, 404–10

"*In Excelsis Deo*" (Beethoven), 75

In Nature's Realm (Dvořák), 237

Intimate Voices Symphony (Sibelius), 741, 745–46

Invisible City of Kitezh, The (Rimsky-Korsakov), 634

Invitation to the Dance (Weber), 893, 895–96

Iphigénie en Aulide (Gluck), 276, 300, 305

Iphigénie en Tauride (Gluck), 83, 301

Ippolitov-Ivanov, Michael, 633

Ireland, John, 141

Iris (Mascagni), 461

Irmelin (Delius), 208

Island God, The (Menotti), 492

Isle of the Dead, The (Rachmaninoff), 602, 607–8

Israel in Egypt (Handel), 335, 338, 339, 343

Israel Symphony (Bloch), 103

I Stand With One Foot in the Grave (Bach), 26

Istar Variations (D'Indy), 407, 409–10

Italiana in Algeri, L' (Rossini), 642, 646, 650

Italian overture, 7

Italian Serenade (Wolf), 903

Italian Symphony (Mendelssohn), 478, 482–84

Iturbi, José, 284

Jacobin, The (Dvořák), 231

Jacobsen, Jens Peter, 668

Jadassohn, Salomon, 208

Jäger, Ferdinand, 901

Jammes, Francis, 508

Janssen, Werner, 33

Jaques-Dalcroze, Emile, 101

"Jardins sous la pluie" (Debussy), 203

Järnefelt, Aino, 740

Jean-Aubry, G., 226

Jean Hunyade (D'Indy), 407

Jeanrenaud, Cecile, 478

Jennens, Charles, 341

Jephtha (Carissimi), 8

Jephtha (Handel), 337, 344

Jephtha's Vow (Meyerbeer), 499

"Jesus, Joy of Man's Desiring" (Bach), 26

"Jesus Christ, the Son of God" (Bach), 25–26

Jeu de cartes (Stravinsky), 782, 788–89

Jeunesse de Figaro, La (Leoncavallo), 430

Jeux d'eau (Ravel), 610, 612, 620

"Jeux d'eaux à la Villa d'Este, Les" (Liszt), 446

"Jimbo's Lullaby" (Debussy), 204

Joachim, Joseph, 119, 121, 130, 234, 239

Job (Carissimi), 8

Job (Vaughan Williams), 814

Johannesburg Overture (Walton), 882

Joke Quartet (Haydn), 381

Jolie Fille de Perth, La (Bizet), 95

Joseph (Méhul), 891

Joshua (Handel), 337, 344

Josquin des Prés, 4

Jour d'été à la montagne (D'Indy), 407

Joyce, James, 35

Judas Maccabaeus (Handel), 337, 339, 344

Judith (Honegger), 400

Juive, La (Halévy), 500

Junge Magd, Die (Hindemith), 387

Jupiter Symphony (Mozart), 533–34

Kajanus, Robert, 740, 741

Kamarinskaya (Glinka), 628

Kammermusik (Hindemith), 387, 390

Karelia Suite (Sibelius), 740

Keiser, Reinhard, 329, 330

Keller, Anna Maria, 367

Kentner, Louis, 884

Khatchaturian, Aram, 411–15, 573

Khovantschina (Mussorgsky), 550, 556–57

Khrennikov, Tikhon, 574

Kilenyi, Edward, 287

Kind, Friedrich, 891
Kinderscenen (Schumann), 708
Kindertotenlieder (Mahler), 452
King and the Collier, The (Dvořák), 233
King David (Honegger), 399, 400
Kiss, The (Smetana), 752
Kjerulf, Halfdan, 318
Kleineke, Avdotya, 109
Kleine Nachtmusik, Eine (Mozart), 534
Klemperer, Otto, 454
Knaben Wunderhorn, Des (Mahler), 457
Knight of the Swan, The (Würzburg), 864
Knorr, Ivan, 101
Knoxville: Summer of 1915 (Barber), 34, 35
Koanga (Delius), 208
Köchel, Ludwig von, 531
Kodály, Zoltán, 38, 416–21
Koechlin, Charles, 268, 271
Koessler, Hans, 39, 215, 416
Kolař, Katharina Ottilie, 750
Konzertmusik, Op. 50 (Hindemith), 386, 394–95
Konzertstück (Weber), 894
Kossuth (Bartók), 39
Koussevitzky, Serge, 34, 40, 142, 143, 181, 185, 350, 355, 356, 555, 624, 674, 720, 721, 725, 730, 782, 843
Kraft, Anton, 378
Krassner, Louis, 78
Krehbiel, Henry E., 235, 247
Kreisler, Fritz, 236, 266, 570, 691
Křenek, Ernst, 289, 667
Kreutzer Sonata (Beethoven), 51, 71
Kreutzer Sonata, The (Tolstoy), 71
Krzyzanowska, Justina, 165
Kuhnau, Johann, 11, 12, 19
Kullervo (Sibelius), 739

"Kyrie" (Bach), 25
"Kyrie eleison" (Beethoven), 74

Lablache, Luigi, 221
Lady Macbeth of Mzensk (Shostakovich), 728–29
Lalo, Edouard, 202, 422–27
Lalo, Pierre, 610
Lamartine, Alphonse Marie de, 442
Lambert, Constant, 289
Landesvater, Der, 130
Landowska, Wanda, 261
Lang, Josephine, 154
Láng, Paul Henry, 56, 821
Lanner, Joseph, 895
Largo Quartet (Haydn), 382
Lasso, Orlando de, 4
"Laudamus te" (Bach), 25
Lauska, Franz Ignaz, 498
Laussot, Jessie, 854
Lavigna, Vincenzo, 822
Lavignac, Albert, 189, 406
Lawrence, Robert, 428
Leblanc, Georgette, 192
Legend (Delius), 208
Leichtentritt, Hugo, 471
"Leiermann, Der" (Schubert), 697
Leitmotif, 89, 97, 860, 894
Lemaire, Ferdinand, 663
Lenau, Nicholas, 444, 765
Leningrad Symphony (Shostakovich), 729–30, 735–36
Leoncavallo, Ruggiero, 428–32, 460, 462, 589
Leoninus, 3
Leonore (Bouilly), 72
Leonore Overture No. 1 (Beethoven), 63
Leonore Overture No. 2 (Beethoven), 63
Leonore Overture No. 3 (Beethoven), 63–64, 73
Leonova, Daria, 550

Leschetizky, Theodor, 32

Lesueur, Jean François, 83, 84, 308

Let's Make an Opera (Britten), 144, 146, 148

Levander, Gustav, 739

Levant, Oscar, 291

Levi, Hermann, 155, 759

Liadov, Anatol, 576, 633, 634, 778–79

Libussa (Smetana), 751

Lichnowsky, Prince, 49

Liebe der Danae, Die (Strauss), 763, 765

"*Liebesbotschaft*" (Schubert), 697

Liebeslieder waltzes (Brahms), 134

Liebestraum (Liszt), 441, 446

Liebesverbot, Das (Wagner), 850, 851

Lied von der Erde, Das (Mahler), 454, 458–59

Liehmann, Antonín, 231

Lieutenant Kije (Prokofiev), 578, 584

Life for the Czar, A (Glinka), 547, 627–28, 629, 777, 795

Limpid Stream, The (Shostakovich), 729

Lind, Jenny, 318

Linda di Chamounix (Donizetti), 221

"*Lindenbaum, Der*" (Schubert), 697

Linz Symphony (Mozart), 531

Liszt, Franz, 38, 42, 85, 88, 119, 123, 124, 164, 167, 202, 234, 268, 276, 312, 319, 433–47, 465, 559, 656, 659, 853, 857

Li-Tai-Po, 459

Little Clavier Book of Anna Magdalena Bach (Bach), 19

"Little Shepherd, The" (Debussy), 204

Lobkowitz, Prince, 49, 52

Locle, Camille du, 835

Loewe, Ferdinand, 901

Lohengrin (Wagner), 439, 440, 852–53, 863–66

Lombardi, I (Verdi), 823–24

London, Jack, 285

"London" symphonies (Haydn), 374, 376–78

London Symphony (Vaughan Williams), 814, 817–18

"London to Thee I Do Present" (Britten), 149

Long, John Luther, 596

Lotario (Handel), 334

"*Lotosblume, Die*" (Schumann), 713

Louise (Charpentier), 259, 462

Love for Three Oranges, The (Prokofiev), 578

"Love Song of an Idiot, The" (Mussorgsky), 557

Love, the Magician (Falla), 260, 262–64

Lucia di Lammermoor (Donizetti), 221, 224–25

Luciani, G. A., 622

Lucifer (Carissimi), 8

Lucrezia (Respighi), 624

"Lullaby" (Brahms), 139

Lully, Jean Baptiste, 8, 468, 502

Lulu (Berg), 78–79, 80

Lulu (Wieland), 529

Lux Aeterna (Hanson), 348

Lyric Pieces (Grieg), 322, 326

Lyric Suite (Berg), 78, 80

Macbeth (Bloch), 102, 104

Macbeth (Strauss), 761, 771

Macbeth (Verdi), 829–30

Machaut, Guillaume de, 4

Macht der Liebe und des Weins, Die (Weber), 889

Madama Butterfly (Puccini), 591–92, 595–97

Madona, Poema sinfonico (Villa-Lobos), 843

Madrigal, 4, 5

Maeterlinck, Maurice, 191–93, 201, 228, 270, 398

Magdalene (Prokofiev), 576

"Magic Fire Music, The" (Wagner), 875

Magic Flute, The (Mozart), 522, 523, 524, 525, 529–31

Magic Fountain, The (Delius), 208

Mahler, Gustav, 63, 81, 153, 448–59, 669

Maid of Pskov, The (Rimsky-Korsakov), 631, 632

"Mainacht, Die" (Brahms), 139

Maine, Basil, 243

Maleden, Pierre, 654

Malfatti, Therese, 51

Maligny, Bernier de, 423

"Malinconia, La" (Beethoven), 69

Malko, Nicolas, 727

Mallarmé, Stéphane, 190, 197

Mälzel, Johann Nepomuk, 61

Ma mère l'oye (Ravel), 612, 615, 618

Mamoulian, Rouben, 291

"Mandoline" (Debussy), 189

Manet, Edouard, 190, 195

Manfred (Schumann), 712

Mann, Thomas, 665

Manon (Massenet), 268, 466, 467, 468–69, 588

Manon Lescaut (Puccini), 588, 592

Manuel Venegas (Wolf), 902

Manzoni, Alessandro, 827, 839

Maometto II (Rossini), 646

Marchand, Louis, 18

Marche slave (Tchaikovsky), 809

Maria Egiziaca (Respighi), 624

Marie-Magdaleine (Massenet), 465

Mariés de la tour Eiffel, Les, 399, 506

Marker, Leonard, 79

"Marks, G. W.," 118

Marmontel, Antoine, 94, 188, 406

Maria Golovin (Menotti), 489, 497

Marriage, The (Mussorgsky), 549, 552

Marriage of Figaro, The (Beaumarchais), 648

Marriage of Figaro, The (Mozart), 521, 525–27, 529

Marschner, Heinrich, 706

Marsick, Martin, 252

Martini, Padre, 516

Martinu, Bohuslav, 753

Martucci, Giuseppe, 623

Marxsen, Eduard, 118

Mascagni, Pietro, 429, 431, 460–63, 588

Mason, Daniel Gregory, 136

Mass, 4

Massenet, Jules, 252, 268, 464–70, 588

Mass in B minor (Bach), 20, 23, 24–25, 74

Mass of Life, A (Delius), 209, 210

Mathis der Maler (Hindemith), 386, 391–92

Mattheson, Johann, 330

Maupassant, Guy de, 146

Maurel, Victor, 429 430

Ma Vlast (Smetana), 752, 755–56

May, Florence, 123

May Day Symphony (Shostakovich), 728

May Night (Rimsky-Korsakov), 633

Mayrhofer, Johann, 679

Mazeppa (Liszt), 442–43

Mazurka, 178

Measure for Measure (Shakespeare), 850

Meck, Nadezhda Filaretovna von, 189, 798, 799, 800, 801, 802, 804

Médecin malgré lui, Le (Gounod), 309

Médée (Milhaud), 507

Medici, I (Leoncavallo), 429, 430

"Meditation" (Bartók), 44

"Méditation" (Gounod), 311

"Méditation" (Massenet), 470

Medium, The (Menotti), 492, 496

Mefistofele (Boïto), 312, 588

Méhul, Etienne Nicolas, 891

Meistersinger, Die (Wagner), 137, 206, 855, 856, 868–70

Melody in F (Rubinstein), 286

Melville, Herman, 147

Mendelson, Myra, 579

Mendelssohn, Arnold, 387

Mendelssohn, Felix, 22, 114, 167, 246, 248, 450, 471–88, 685, 895

Mengelberg, Willem, 454

Menotti, Gian-Carlo, 34, 36, 489–97

Menuhin, Yehudi, 570, 884

Mephisto Waltz (Liszt), 312, 444–45

Mer, La (Debussy), 198–99

Meral, Paul, 398

Mérimée, Prosper, 95

"Merry Cuckoo, The" (Britten), 148

Merry Mount (Hanson), 349

Mesmer, Dr. Franz Anton, 515

Messiah (Handel), 246, 335–37, 338, 339, 340–43, 383

Metamorphosen (Strauss), 763

Metastasio, Pietro, 298, 302, 366

Meyerbeer, Giacomo, 97, 110, 276, 311, 498–504, 558, 640, 851

Miaskovsky, Nikolai, 573

Midi, Le (Haydn), 375

Midsummer Night's Dream, A (Mendelssohn), 475–76, 479, 485–86, 895

"Mighty Five, The," 111, 547, 612, 627–28, 802–3

Mikrokosmos (Bartók), 43–44

Milhaud, Darius, 292, 398–99, 505–11

Military Polonaise (Chopin), 178

Military Symphony (Haydn), 377

Miliukova, Antonina, 797

Milton, John, 149

"Minuet of the Will-o'-the-Wisps" (Berlioz), 92

Minute Waltz (Chopin), 177

"*Mir ist so wunderbar!*" (Beethoven), 73

Mireille (Gounod), 310

Miroirs (Ravel), 610, 615, 616

Miserere (Allegri), 516

Missa Papae Marcelli (Palestrina), 4

Missa Solemnis (Beethoven), 52, 55, 72, 73–75

Mitridate, Rè di Ponto (Mozart), 516

Mitropoulos, Dimitri, 284

Mlada (Rimsky-Korsakov), 634

Moïse (Rossini), 644

Moke, Camille, 84, 85

Moldau, The (Smetana), 755–56

Molinari, Bernardino, 33, 623

Moments musicaux (Schubert), 694

Monet, Claude, 195

Monodic style, 6

Montagu-Nathan, M., 627

Monteverdi, Claudio, 5, 6–7, 33, 304

Moonlight Sonata (Beethoven), 51, 68

"Moon Love," 805

"*Morgen*" (Strauss), 761, 774

Mörike, Eduard, 900

Morley, Thomas, 5

"Morning Star" (Britten), 149

Mors et Vita (Gounod), 310

Moscheles, Ignaz, 316, 475

Moses und Aron (Schoenberg), 664

Motet, 4

Mother Goose Suite (Ravel), 612, 615, 618

Mottl, Felix, 155, 306, 900

Mozart, Wolfgang Amadeus, 21, 46, 47, 54, 56, 65, 69, 140, 218, 270, 362, 369, 370, 512–43, 695, 888

Mozart and Salieri (Rimsky-Korsakov), 634

Muck, Karl, 103, 155, 900

Mühlfeld, Richard, 135

Müller, Wilhelm, 696, 697

"*Müller und der Bach, Der*" (Schubert), 697

Muradeli, Vano, 573

Murder, Hope of Women (Hindemith), 387

Murger, Henri, 430, 589

Musical America, 103

Music for Radio (Copland), 182

Music for the Theatre (Copland), 181, 182

Musical Offering, The (Bach), 20

Music for a Scene from Shelley (Barber), 33, 35

Mussolini, Benito, 461, 491

Mussorgsky, Modest, 41, 70, 111, 544–57, 627, 628, 632, 633

My Country (Smetana), 752, 755–56

My Home (Dvořák), 237

"My Saviour Now is Dying from Love Unbounded" (Bach), 24

Nabucco (Verdi), 823, 829

Napoleon Bonaparte, 56–57

Napravnik, Edouard, 112

Nashe, Thomas, 149

National Music (Vaughan Williams), 814, 815

Neefe, Christian Gottlob, 47

Neri, Filippo, 8

Nero (Handel), 330

Nerone (Mascagni), 461

Netherlands school, 4

Neue krumme Teufel, Der (Haydn), 366

Neue Liebeslieder waltzes (Brahms), 134

Neues vom Tage (Hindemith), 386

Neumann, Angelo, 450

Newman, Ernest, 897

New World Symphony (Dvořák), 235–36, 237, 238–39

New York City Ballet Company, 100

Niedermeyer, Abraham Louis, 267

Niemann, Walter, 133, 137

Nietzsche, Friedrich, 94

"Night" (Mussorgsky), 549

Night on Bald Mountain, A (Mussorgsky), 548, 549, 555

Nights in the Gardens of Spain (Falla), 259–60, 264–65

Nijinsky, Waslaw, 779

Nikisch, Artur, 155

Nobilissima Visione (Hindemith), 388, 391, 395

Noces, Les (Stravinsky), 781, 784

Noches en los Jardines de España (Falla), 259–60, 264–65

"None But the Lonely Heart" (Tchaikovsky), 800

Nonne sanglante, La (Gounod), 309

Nordic Symphony (Hanson), 347, 348, 350, 351

Nordraak, Rikard, 317, 318

Norfolk Rhapsodies (Vaughan Williams), 813, 814, 815

Norma (Bellini), 222

North and West (Hanson), 347

Norwegian Rhapsody (Lalo), 424

Nose, The (Shostakovich), 728

"Now Is the Month of Maying" (Morley), 5

Nozze di Figaro, Le (Mozart), 521, 525–27, 529

Nozze de Teti, Le (Cavalli), 7

"*Nuages*" (Debussy), 198

Nuove musiche, 6, 8, 9,

Nursery Songs (Mussorgsky), 557

Nuschi-Nuschi (Hindemith), 387

"*Nussbaum, Der*" (Schumann), 713

Nutcracker Suite (Tchaikovsky), 810–11

Oberon (Weber), 892–93, 895

Oberto (Verdi), 823

Obey, André, 146

Ode (Stravinsky), 782

Ode to Consonance (Harris), 352

Odero, Alejandro, 258

Ode to Joy (Schiller), 61, 63

Ode to Napoleon (Schoenberg), 665

Ode to Sainte-Cecile (Saint-Saëns), 654

Oedipus (Enesco), 253

Oedipus (Sophocles), 128

Oedipus Rex (Stravinsky), 782, 785, 790–91

O Ewigkeit, du Donnerwort (Bach), 81

Offenbach, Jacques, 558–64

Of Thee I Sing (Gershwin), 289–90

"O Grief, There Throbs the Racked and Bleeding Heart" (Bach), 24

Oiseau de feu, L' (Stravinsky), 779, 784, 785–86

Okeghem, Jean de, 4

Old Airs and Dances for the Lute (Respighi), 625

Old Maid and the Thief, The (Menotti), 491

Olympic (Spontini), 891

"*O nemenlose Freude*" (Beethoven), 73

"*Ondine*" (Debussy), 203

135th Street (Gershwin), 289, 294

On Guard for Peace (Prokofiev), 574

On Hearing the First Cuckoo in Spring (Delius), 209, 212–13

On the Steppes of Central Asia (Borodin), 112, 115

Opera, 5–8

Opera-scenica, 7

Oratorio, 5, 8–9, 23

Orchestral Variations (Copland), 179

Orfeo (Monteverdi), 6, 33, 304

Orfeo ed Euridice (Gluck), 299, 300, 304

Organum, 3

Orlando de Lasso, 4

Ormandy, Eugene, 601, 603

Orpheus (Stravinsky), 782, 785

Orpheus in the Underworld (Offenbach), 561, 563, 660

Otello (Rossini), 642

Otello (Verdi), 827–28, 829, 830, 836–37

Ottone (Handel), 334

"Our Love," 809

Outdoor Overture (Copland), 182

"Out on the Lawn" (Britten), 149

O versenk' dein Leid (Brahms), 119

"*O welche Lust!*" (Beethoven), 73

Oxford Symphony (Haydn), 376–77

Pacific 231 (Honegger), 399, 400–1

Paderewski, Ignace Jan, 45, 46, 165

Padilla, Mariano, 797

Paër, Ferdinando, 435, 567

Paganini, Niccolò, 86, 436, 565–71

Paganini Etudes (Schumann), 700

Pagliacci (Leoncavallo), 429–30, 431–32, 460

"*Pagodes*" (Debussy), 203

Paisiello, Giovanni, 642

Palestrina, Giovanni Pierluigi da, 4, 308

Pannain, Guido, 416

Papillons (Schumann), 700

Pardon de Ploërmel, Le (Meyerbeer), 501

Paride ed Elena (Gluck), 299

Paris Symphony (Mozart), 531

Parsifal (Wagner), 150, 484, 859, 864, 878–80

Partenope (Handel), 334

Partita, 10

Pas d'acier, Le (Prokofiev), 573

Pasquini, Bernardo, 625

Passacaglia, 10, 31

Passacaglia and Fugue in C minor (Bach), 31

Passion, 8–9, 23

Passion According to St. John, The (Bach), 19, 22, 23, 24

Passion According to St. John (Handel), 330

Passion According to St. Matthew, The (Bach), 22, 23, 24, 476, 477

Passo, Susana Gil, 884

"Pas sur la neige, Des" (Debussy), 202

Pastoral Symphony (Beethoven), 60

Pastoral Symphony (Vaughan Williams), 814, 818–19

Pathétique Sonata (Beethoven), 68

Pathétique Symphony (Tchaikovsky), 777, 801, 802, 806–8

Patrie (Bizet), 95

Paul Bunyan (Britten), 141–42

Pavane pour une Infante défunte (Ravel), 609, 612, 620

Pax Vobiscum (Schubert), 684

Pearl Fishers, The (Bizet), 95, 97

"Peasant's Lullaby, The" (Mussorgsky), 548

Pêcheurs de perles, Les (Bizet), 95, 97

Pedrell, Felipe, 257, 258–59, 261–62

Peele, George, 149

Peer Gynt (Grieg), 319–20, 322, 324

Pélissier, Olympe, 644

Pelléas et Mélisande (Debussy), 191–93, 201–2, 228, 259

Pelléas et Mélisande (Fauré), 270

Pelleas und Melisande (Schoenberg), 668, 669, 672

Penelope (Fauré), 269

Penthesilea (Wolf), 900

Pepusch, Johann Christoph, 332

Pergin, Marianne, 298

Pergolesi, Giovanni Battista, 782, 913

Peri, Jacopo, 6, 7, 304

Péri, La (Dukas), 227, 228

Périchole, La (Offenbach), 562

Perotinus, 4

Perrin, Emile, 423

Pessard, Emile, 611

Peter and the Wolf (Prokofiev), 578, 583–84

Peter Grimes (Britten), 140, 142–43, 144, 145–46

Peter Schmoll und seine Nachbarn (Weber), 889

Petite suite (Bizet), 95

Petrouchka (Stravinsky), 779, 784, 785, 786–87

Pfeiffer, Tobias, 46

Philipp, Isidor, 466

Phoebus and Pan (Bach), 22

Piano, 28

Piano concerto, 27

Piano Fantasy (Copland), 179

Piano sonata, 11, 12

Piano Variations (Copland), 182

Piave, Francesco, 831, 834

Picasso, Pablo, 265

Piccini, Nicola, 300

Pictures at an Exhibition (Mussorgsky), 550, 555–56

Pièces de clavecin (Couperin), 11

Pièces espagnoles (Falla), 259

Pierné, Gabriel, 188, 466, 779

Pierrot lunaire (Schoenberg), 669, 672

Pietra del paragone, La (Rossini), 641, 647

Pilgrim's Progress, The (Vaughan Williams), 814

Pinelli, Ettore, 319

Pines of Rome (Respighi), 623, 625, 626

Pizzicato, 7

Plaidy, Louis, 316

Planer, Minna, 850

Poem (Chausson), 161, 163

Poème roumain (Enesco), 252

Poèmes d'automne (Bloch), 102

Poem of Ecstasy (Scriabin), 714, 715–16, 719, 722

Point Counterpoint (Huxley), 70–71

"Poissons d'or" (Debussy), 204

Poliuto (Donizetti), 221

Pollitzer, Adolf, 244

Polonaise, 178

"Polovtsian Dances" (Borodin), 115–16, 633

Polyeucte (Corneille), 221

Polyeucte (Dukas), 227

Polyphony, 3, 21, 372

Pomp and Circumstance (Elgar), 250

Ponchielli, Amilcare, 587

Pons, Lily, 284

Ponte, Lorenzo da, 522, 525, 527

Popper, David, 175

Porgy and Bess (Gershwin), 285, 290, 294–96

Poro (Handel), 328, 334

Porpora, Niccolò, 366

Portsmouth Point (Walton), 885, 886–87

"*Post, Die*" (Schubert), 697

Poulenc, Francis, 140, 398, 399

Prague Symphony (Mozart), 531

Prayers of Kierkegaard (Barber), 32, 34

Prelude, Aria, and Finale (Franck), 279

Préludes, Les (Liszt), 442, 443

Prévost, Abbé, 468, 588

"Pride" (Mussorgsky), 557

Prince Igor (Borodin), 112, 115–16, 633

Prince of the Pagodas, The (Britten), 140, 144

Princesse jaune, La (Saint-Saëns), 656

Printemps (Bloch), 102

Printemps (Debussy), 190

"Prize Song" (Wagner), 137

Program music, 11, 88

Prokofiev, Serge, 572–85

Proksch, Joseph, 750

Promesi sposi, I (Manzoni), 827

Prometheus (Scriabin), 714, 715, 721, 722–23

Prophète, Le (Meyerbeer), 500, 501

"*Propylaea*" (Scriabin), 715

Prose lyriques (Debussy), 191

Protée (Milhaud), 506, 509–10

Protopopova, Catherine, 111, 113–14

Provesi, Ferdinando, 822

Prunières, Henri, 187, 397

Psalmus Hungaricus (Kodály), 418

Puccini, Giacomo, 430, 462, 586–97

"*Puerto del Vino, La*" (Debussy), 203, 262

Purcell, Henry, 5, 8, 11, 148, 243

Quest, The (Walton), 884

Quinten Quartet (Haydn), 382

"*Qui tollis*" (Beethoven), 75

"*Qui tollis peccata mundi*" (Bach), 25

"*Quoniam tu Solus Sanctus*" (Beethoven), 75

Rabaud, Henri, 466

Rachmaninoff, Serge, 137, 598–608

Radamisto (Handel), 333

Raindrop Prelude (Chopin), 176

Rain Sonata (Brahms), 136–37

Rake's Progress, The (Stravinsky), 782–83, 785

"*Rákóczy March*" (Berlioz), 92–93

Ramann, Lina, 444

Rameau, Jean Philippe, 270, 338, 502, 625

Rape of Lucretia, The (Britten), 143, 146

Rappresentazione di anima e di corpo, La (Cavalieri), 8

Rapsodie espagnole (Ravel), 610, 612, 615, 616

Rasoumovsky, Count, 60

Rasoumovsky Quartets (Beethoven), 55, 69–70, 539

Rasse, François, 101

Ravel, Maurice, 259, 268, 289, 505, 555, 609–21, 781, 813

Read, Gardner, 349

Recio, Marie, 86

Rédemption (Franck), 277, 279

Rédemption, La (Gounod), 310

Re Enzo (Respighi), 623

"*Reflets dans l'eau*" (Debussy), 203–4

Reformation Symphony (Mendelssohn), 484

Reicha, Anton, 84, 275, 435

Reichmann, Theodor, 449

Reincken, Jan Adams, 17, 18

Reinecke, Karl, 121, 208, 316

Reiner, Fritz, 491

Rellstab, Heinrich Friedrich Ludwig, 68, 697

Reményi, Eduard, 118, 138

"Rencontre" (Fauré), 272

Renoir, Pierre Auguste, 190

Requiem (Bruckner), 151

Requiem (Delius), 210

Requiem (Fauré), 269

Requiem (Mozart), 171, 521–22, 537–39

Requiem (Verdi), 838–39

Respighi, Ottorino, 622–26

Resurrection Symphony (Mahler), 456–58

Resurrezione, La (Handel), 331, 335

Retablo de Maese Pedro, El (Falla), 261

Reutter, Karl Georg, 365

Revolutionary Etude (Chopin), 165, 167, 176

Rey, Louis, 101

Rhapsody in Blue (Gershwin), 285, 289, 292–93

Rhapsody on a Theme of Paganini (Rachminoff), 137, 571, 603, 606

Rheingold, Das (Wagner), 854, 856, 872, 873

Rhenish Symphony (Schumann), 709–10

Rhinegold, The (Wagner), 854, 856, 872, 873

Richard III (Smetana), 751

Richter, E. F., 316

Richter, Hans, 39, 123, 127, 155, 234, 245, 900

"Ride of the Valkyries" (Wagner), 875

Riemann, Hugo, 498

Rienzi (Wagner), 439, 501, 851, 852

Ries, Ferdinand, 51

Rigaudon, 621

Rigoletto (Verdi), 824, 830–32

Rimsky-Korsakov, Nicolas, 41, 111, 112, 114, 545, 547, 549, 552, 554, 555, 575–76, 627–38, 777, 778, 784

Rinaldo (Handel), 331, 339

Ring des Nibelungen, Der (Wagner), 853, 856, 858, 871–78

"Rire du diable, Le" (Paganini), 571

Rite of Spring, The (Stravinsky), 780, 784, 785, 787–88

Ritter, Alexander, 760, 766

"Ritual Fire Dance" (Falla), 263

Robert le Diable (Meyerbeer), 110, 500

Roberts, Caroline Alice, 244

Rodeo (Copland), 182

Rodgers, Richard, 34

Rodrigo (Handel), 331

Rodzinski, Artur, 33, 34, 284

Roger-Ducasse, 268, 612

Rogers, Bernard, 349

Roi David, Le (Honegger), 399, 400

Roi de Lahore, Le (Massenet), 465

Roi d'Ys, Le (Lalo), 202, 424, 427

Roi s'amuse, Le (Hugo), 831

Roland (Gluck), 300

Roland-Manuel, 609, 781

Rolla, Alessandro, 567

Rolland, Romain, 57, 102, 301, 609, 652

Roman Carnival Overture (Berlioz), 92

Roman Festivals (Respighi), 625

Roman school, 4, 9

Romantic Symphony (Bruckner), 155, 157–59

Romantic Symphony (Hanson), 349, 350–51

Romeo and Juliet (Berlioz), 87, 93

Romeo and Juliet (Tchaikovsky), 797, 808–9

Roméo et Juliette (Gounod), 310

Romilda e Costanza (Meyerbeer), 500

"*Rondes de printemps*" (Debussy), 200

Rondine, La (Puccini), 592

Rondo capriccioso (Mendelssohn), 488

Ropartz, Guy de, 273

Rosamunde (Schubert), 682, 686, 691

Rosen, Jelka, 209

Rosenfeld, Paul, 101

Rosenkavalier, Der (Strauss), 765, 773–74

"*Roses d'Ispahan, Les*" (Fauré), 272

Rosier de Madame Husson, Le (Maupassant), 146

Rossetti, Dantee Gabriel, 190, 214

Rossini, Gioacchino, 219, 220, 222, 223, 512, 558, 639–51, 892

Rouet d'Omphale, Le (Saint-Saëns), 656

Rousseau, Jean Jacques, 49, 54, 300

Roussel, Albert, 259, 405

Rowlandson, Thomas, 886

Rubinstein, Anton, 286, 547, 655

Rubinstein, Artur, 284, 842

Rubinstein, Beryl, 288

Rubinstein, Ida, 613

Rubinstein, Nicholas, 796, 797

"*Rückblick*" (Schubert), 697

Rudepoêma (Villa-Lobos), 842

Rudolph, Archduke, 52, 73

"*Ruhe, meine Seele*" (Strauss), 775

Ruins of Athens (Beethoven), 543

Rumanian Rhapsodies (Enesco), 252, 253, 254–55

Russalka (Dargomyzhsky), 547

Russian Easter Overture (Rimsky-Korsakov), 634, 635, 637–38

"Russian Five, The," 111, 114, 547, 612, 627–28, 802–3

Russian Quartets (Haydn), 381–82

Russlan and Ludmila (Glinka), 547, 627, 629, 777

Ruth (Franck), 276

Ruy Blas Overture (Mendelssohn), 486

Sabaneyev, Leonid, 572, 577

"Saber Dance" (Khatchaturian), 415

Sacred Service (Bloch), 103, 104

Sacre du printemps, Le (Stravinsky), 780, 784, 785, 787–88

Sadko (Rimsky-Korsakov), 634, 635

Sadness (Barber), 32

Saint-Cricq, Caroline de, 436

St. Elizabeth (Liszt), 440

Saint Francis (Hindemith), 388, 395

St. John Passion (Bach), 19, 22, 23, 24

St. John Passion (Handel), 330

St. Matthew Passion (Bach), 22, 23, 24, 476, 477

St. Nicolas (Britten), 143

Saint of Bleecker Street, The (Menotti), 489, 497

St. Paul (Mendelssohn), 450, 478

Saint-Saëns, Camille, 95, 268, 652–63, 781

Salieri, Antonio, 49, 434, 499, 519, 520, 521, 523, 676, 678

Salome (Strauss), 762, 771–72

Salomon, Johann Peter, 370, 383

Salón México, El (Copland), 181, 183–84

Saltarello, 92, 483

Sammartini, Giovanni Battista, 298

Samosud, Samuel, 730

Samson (Handel), 337, 339, 344

Samson et Dalila (Saint-Saëns), 268, 653, 656, 662–63

Sancta Civitas (Vaughan Williams), 814

"*Sanctus*" (Bach), 25

"*Sanctus*" (Beethoven), 75

Sand, George, 168, 169–70, 172

Sanroma, Jesus Maria, 284
Sapho (Gounod), 309
Sapho (Massenet), 466
Sarasate, Pablo de, 175, 424, 426
Sardanapale (Berlioz), 85
Sardou, Victorien, 589, 590
Sarti, Federico, 623
Satie, Erik, 191, 196, 291, 405, 611, 776
Satin, Natalia, 601
Saul (Handel), 335, 339, 344
Scalero, Rosario, 33, 490
Scapino (Walton), 884, 887
Scarlatti, Alessandro, 7, 12
Scarlatti, Domenico, 7, 12, 331, 622
Scenes from Childhood (Schumann), 708
Scenes from Goethe's Faust (Schumann), 312
Scenes from Peasant Life (Grieg), 322
Schalk, Franz, 901
Schalk, Joseph, 901
Schauffler, Robert Haven, 68
Scheherazade (Rimsky-Korsakov), 634, 635, 636–37
Schelble, Johann, 475
Schelomo (Bloch), 103, 105, 106
Schenk, Johann, 49
Scherzo, 56
Scherzo fantastique (Bloch), 103
Scherzo fantastique (Stravinsky), 778
Schikaneder, Emanuel, 522, 529
Schiller, Johann Christoph Friedrich von, 61, 63
Schindler, Anton, 53, 59
Schloezer, Boris de, 714
Schmitt, Florent, 259, 268, 271, 466, 612
Schober, Franz von, 679
Schoenberg, Arnold, 76, 77, 79, 80, 448, 449, 454, 664–74
Schöne Mullerin, Die (Schubert), 683, 696–97

School for Scandal, The (Barber), 33, 35
Schorr, Daniel L., 143
Schubert, Franz, 54, 171, 237, 285, 447, 675–97
Schumann, Clara, 119–20, 122, 125, 479, 701, 702, 703, 704, 713
Schumann, Robert, 111, 119–20, 131, 312, 447, 479, 675, 685, 698–713
Schuppanzigh, Ignaz, 49, 55
Schütz, Heinrich, 7–8, 9, 23
Schwanendreher, Der (Hindemith), 388, 395
Schwanengesang (Schubert), 683, 697
Schweigsame Frau, Die (Strauss), 763
Schweitzer, Albert, 27
Schwerké, Irving, 840
Scotch Symphony (Mendelssohn), 477–78, 479, 482
Scott, Sir Walter, 224
Scriabin, Alexander, 714–24
Scribe, Eugène, 500, 501
Scythian Suite (Prokofiev), 576–77, 579
Sea, The (Debussy), 198–99
Sea Drift (Delius), 209, 210
Seasons, The (Haydn), 371, 372, 382–84, 646
Sechter, Simon, 151
Second Hurricane, The (Copland), 182
Seidl, Anton, 236, 697
Sekles, Bernhard, 387
Semele (Handel), 337, 344
Semiramide (Rossini), 643, 650–51
Semiramide riconosciuta (Gluck), 298
Senefelder, Aloys, 889
Serafin, Tullio, 490
"Serenade for a Doll" (Debussy), 204
Serly, Tibor, 41
Seroff, Victor I., 113
Serov, Alexander, 631
Serse (Handel), 328, 339, 344

Serva Padrona, La (Pergolesi), 913

Servetto, Giovanni, 566

Seven Last Words of Christ (Haydn), 258, 368, 371

Sgambati, Giovanni, 319

Shaw, Bernard, 246

Shaw, Carlos Fernandez, 259

Shebalin, Vissarion, 573

Shéhérazade (Ravel), 612

Shepherds of the Delectable Mountains (Vaughan Williams), 814

Sheridan, Richard Brinsley, 35

"Shine Out, Fair Sun, with All Your Heat" (Britten), 148

Shostakovich, Dmitri, 412, 573, 725–37, 793

"Shower, The" (Britten), 149

Sibelius, Jean, 350, 738–48

Siebold, Agathe von, 120

Siège de Corinthe, Le (Rossini), 644

Siegfried (Wagner), 854, 858, 873, 875–77

Siegfried Idyl (Wagner), 858, 881

"Siegfried's Death Music" (Wagner), 878

"Siegfried's Rhine Journey" (Wagner), 877

Sierra, Gregorio Martinez, 262, 265

Silent Woman, The (Strauss), 763

Silvana (Weber), 890

"Silver Swan, The" (Gibbons), 5

Simon Boccanegra (Verdi), 824

Simple Symphony (Britten), 141, 144

Sinfonia antartica (Vaughan Williams), 812, 820

Sinfonia breve (Bloch), 101

Sinfonia da Requiem (Britten), 142, 147–48

Sinfonia domestica (Strauss), 762

Sinfonia sacra (Hanson), 347, 351

Singspiel, 525, 529

"Sing We and Chant It" (Morley), 5

"*Sirènes*" (Debussy), 198

Sites auriculaires (Ravel), 612

Sitt, Hans, 208

Sitwell, Edith, 883

"Six, The French," 399, 400, 506, 507

Slater, Montagu, 145

Slavonic Dances (Dvořák), 234, 240–41

Slavonic Rhapsodies (Dvořák), 241

"Sleepers Awake" (Bach), 26

Smallens, Alexander, 291

Smetana, Bedřich, 41, 232, 749–57

Smithson, Henrietta, 84, 85, 86, 87, 89

"Snow is Dancing, The" (Debussy), 204

Snow Maiden (Rimsky-Korsakov), 633

Société des apaches, 612

"*Soir*" (Fauré), 272

Soirée dans Grenade (Debussy), 203, 262

Solomon (Handel), 337, 339

Sombrero de Tres Picos, El (Falla), 261, 265–66, 902

Sonata, 10, 21

Sonata, piano, 11, 12

Sonata da camera, 10

Sonata da chiesa, 10

Sonata quasi una fantasia (Beethoven), 51, 68

"*Sonetto 104 del Petrarca*" (Liszt), 446

Song of Democracy (Harris), 347

Song of Summer, A (Delius), 211

"*Song of the Flea*" (Mussorgsky), 557

Song of the Forest (Shostakovich), 731

Song of the Nightingale, The (Stravinsky), 781, 784

Songs and Dances of Death (Mussorgsky), 550, 557

Songs of Farewell (Delius), 211

Songs of Sunset (Delius), 209

Songs Without Words (Mendelssohn), 487–88

Sonnleithner, Joseph, 72

"Sonntag" (Brahms), 139

Sophocles, 128

Sorcerer's Apprentice, The (Dukas), 227, 228–29, 259

Sosarme (Handel), 334

Soudeleikine, Vera, 782

"Sound the Flute" (Britten), 149

Spalding, Albert, 34

Spanisches Liederbuch (Wolf), 904

Spanish Dance No. 1 (Falla), 266

Spartacus (Khatchaturian), 411

Spaun, Josef von, 677, 679

Specht, Richard, 137

Spectre's Bride, The (Dvořák), 234

Speidel, Ludwig, 150

Spender, Stephen, 35

Spenser, Edmund, 148

Spitz, Joseph, 231

Spohr, Ludwig, 475

Spontini, Gaspare, 502, 891

"Spring, the Sweet Spring" (Britten), 149

"Spring Song" (Mendelssohn), 487

Spring Symphony (Britten), 143, 144, 148–49

Spring Symphony (Schumann), 708–9

Stabat Mater (Rossini), 644, 645

"Stadt, Die" (Schubert), 697

Stalingrad Sonata (Prokofiev), 578

Stamaty, Camille-Marie, 654

Stamitz, Johann Wenzel, 373, 374

"Ständchen" (Brahms), 139

"Ständchen" (Schubert), 697

"Ständchen" (Strauss), 775

"Ständchen, Das" (Wolf), 905

Stassov, Vladimir, 109, 116

Statements (Copland), 182

Steele, Sir Richard, 331

Stefan, Paul, 230, 664

Steffani, Agostino, 331

Steinberg, Maximilian, 726

Stephens, James, 35

Stirling, Jane, 170

Stockhausen, Elisabeth von, 120

Stokowski, Leopold, 103, 727

Stone Flower, The (Prokofiev), 579

"Storchenbotschaft" (Wolf), 905

Story of a Soldier, The (Stravinsky), 782

Strauss, Johann, 176, 177, 895

Strauss, Richard, 42, 139, 388, 452, 454, 668, 758–75

Stravinsky, Igor, 292, 612, 776–92

Strepponi, Giuseppina, 826

Suggestion diabolique (Prokofiev), 576

Suite, 10

Suite bergamasque (Debussy), 203

Suite for Orchestra (Dohnányi), 217

Suite provençale (Milhaud), 509

Suite symphonique (Bloch), 103

Suk, Joseph, 753

Sullivan, Arthur, 316

Sullivan, J. W. N., 70

"Summer is Icumen-In" (Britten), 149

Summer Night on the River (Delius), 209, 212, 213

Sunken Bell, The (Respighi), 624

Sunless (Mussorgsky), 550, 557

Sun Quartets (Haydn), 380–81

Suor Angelica (Puccini), 592

Sur le Borysthène (Prokofiev), 578

Surprise Symphony (Haydn), 371, 377

Survivor from Warsaw, A (Schoenberg), 671

Susanna (Handel), 344

Swan of Tuonela, The (Sibelius), 747

Swarthout, Gladys, 284

Sweelinck, Jan, 9

Swieten, Baron van, 49

"Swing Low, Sweet Chariot," 238

Sylphides, Les (Chopin), 176

Symbolism, 195

Symphonic Metamorphoses (Hindemith), 391

Symphonic Ode (Copland), 181, 182

Symphonic Variations (Franck), 281

Symphonie espagnole (Lala), 424, 426

Symphonie fantastique (Berlioz), 85, 88, 89–91

Symphonie funèbre et triomphale (Berlioz), 87

Symphony, 21

Symphony on a French Mountain Air (D'Indy), 407, 408, 409

Symphony of Psalms (Stravinsky), 782, 785, 791–92

Szenkar, Eugene, 412

Szorlich, Paul, 78

Tabarro, Il (Puccini), 592

Tailleferre, Germaine, 398, 399

Tale of a Real Man, A (Prokofiev), 574

Tales of Hoffmann, The (Offenbach), 562–64

Tallis, Thomas, 816

Tancredi (Rossini), 641–42

Tannhäuser (Wagner), 152, 439, 852, 856, 861–63

Tapiola (Sibelius), 748

Tartini, Giuseppe, 622

Tasso (Liszt), 442–43

Taylor, John, 20

Tchaikovsky, Peter Ilitch, 46, 189, 422, 655, 777, 793–811

Tchang-Tsi, 459

Tcherepnin, Nicholas, 576

Te Deum (Bruckner), 154, 156

Te Deum (Kodály), 418

Telemann, Georg, 11

Telephone, The (Menotti), 492, 496

Temperament, 29–30

"*Terrasse des audiences au clair de lune, La*" (Debussy), 203

Terry, Charles Sanford, 23

Texier, Rosalie, 191

Thaïs (Massenet), 466, 467, 469–70

Thalberg, Sigismond, 437

Theme and Variations on the Name Abegg (Schumann), 700

Theodora (Handel), 337, 344

Thieving Magpie, The (Rossini), 651

Thomán, Stéphan, 39

Thomas, Ambroise, 87, 465, 466

Thomas, Theodore, 227, 760

Thomson, Virgil, 505

Three-Cornered Hat, The (Falla), 261, 265–66, 902

Three Jewish Poems (Bloch), 103

Threni (Stravinsky), 776, 783, 785, 792

Thuille, Ludwig, 101

Thun Sonata (Brahms), 136–37

Thurber, Jeanette, 235

Thus Spake Zarathustra (Strauss), 761, 762, 768

Tibbett, Lawrence, 284

Tiersot, Julien, 267

Till Eulenspiegels lustige Streiche (Strauss), 761, 767–68

Timbre d'argent, Le (Saint-Saëns), 656

"'Tis Finished" (Bach), 24

Titan Symphony (Mahler), 455–56

Toccata, 10, 31

Toccata (Schumann), 700

Toccata and Fugue in D minor (Bach), 31

Toccata in C major (Bach), 31

"*Tod das ist eine Kühle Nacht, Der*" (Brahms), 139

"*Tod und das Mädchen, Der*" (Schubert), 696

Tod und Verklärung (Strauss), 761, 766–67, 771

Tolstoy, Leo, 71

Tombeau de Couperin, Le (Ravel), 620–21

"Tonight We Love," 808

Torchi, Luigi, 623

Tosca (Puccini), 589–90, 594–95

Toscanini, Arturo, 33, 34, 284, 350, 356, 430, 461, 493, 589, 591, 592, 613, 623, 624, 730, 763, 829

Tovey, Sir Donald Francis, 129

Toward the Unknown Region (Vaughan Williams), 813

Toye, Francis, 586

Toy Symphony (Haydn or Leopold Mozart), 378

Tragic Overture (Brahms), 129, 130

Tragó, José, 258

Train bleu, Le (Milhaud), 507

Transfigured Night (Schoenberg), 668, 672, 673

"Traum durch die Dämmerung" (Strauss), 761, 771, 775

Traviata, La (Verdi), 824, 825, 834–35

Tremolo, 7

Tristan und Isolde (Wagner), 152, 204, 304, 440, 758, 855, 856, 866–68

Triumphsymphonie (Smetana), 751

Troilus and Cressida (Walton), 884, 887

Trout Quintet (Schubert), 688, 693

Trovatore, Il (Verdi), 824–25, 832–34

Truffot, Marie-Laure, 656

Turandot (Puccini), 592–93

Turgenev, Ivan Sergeevich, 268

"Turkish March" (Beethoven), 543

"Turkish March" (Mozart), 537, 542

Turn of the Screw, The (Britten), 140, 144, 147

Twain, Mark, 285

Twelve-tone system, 80, 672

Twilight of the Gods, The (Wagner), 858, 873, 877–78

"Two Grenadiers, The" (Schumann), 713

Two Nephews, The (Mendelssohn), 475

Two Portraits (Bartók), 39

Ulysse (Gounod), 309

Unaufhörliche, Das (Hindemith), 386

Unfinished Symphony (Schubert), 683, 687, 688–89

"Ungeduld" (Schubert), 697

Ungher, Caroline, 53

Unicorn, the Gorgon, and the Manticore, The (Menotti), 489

Valet de ferme, Le (Franck), 277

Valkyrie, The (Wagner), 854, 856, 872, 873–75

Valse, La (Ravel), 613, 615, 618–19

Valses nobles et sentimentales (Ravel), 613, 615, 620

Valse Triste (Sibelius), 741

Van Dieren, Bernard, 206

Vanessa (Barber), 32, 36, 494

Variations on Mozart's "Là ci darem" (Chopin), 166

Variations on a Nursery Theme (Dohnányi), 216, 218

Variations on an Original Theme (Elgar), 243, 245, 247–49

Variations on a Theme of Frank Bridge (Britten), 141, 147

Variations on a Theme by Handel (Brahms), 121, 137

Variations on a Theme by Haydn (Brahms), 121, 124–25, 217

Variations on a Theme by Paganini (Brahms), 137–38, 571

Variations sérieuses (Mendelssohn), 488

Variations symphoniques (Franck), 281

Vasco di Gama (Bizet), 95

Vaterländische Künstlerverein, 435

Vaughan, Henry, 149

Vaughan Williams, Ralph, 5, 812–20

Vaurabourg, Andrée, 398

Vecchi, Orazio, 5

"Veilchen, Das" (Mozart), 695

Velleda (Dukas), 226
Venetian school, 4, 6
Vengerova, Isabella, 33
"Verborgenheit" (Wolf), 905
Verdaguer, Jacinto, 261
Verdi, Giuseppe, 222, 587, 821–39
Verga, Giovanni, 462
"Vergebliches Ständchen" (Brahms), 139
"Verismo," 431, 462
Verklärte Nacht (Schoenberg), 668, 672, 673
Verlaine, Paul, 268, 272
"Verrat" (Brahms), 139
"Verschwiegene Liebe" (Wolf), 905
Vespri Siciliani, I (Verdi), 824
Vetrate di chiesa (Respighi), 624, 625
Viardot, Pauline, 268, 308–9
Victoria, Tomás Luis de, 4–5
Vida Breve, La (Falla), 259, 260, 266
Vidal, Paul, 180, 227
Vie parisienne, La (Offenbach), 562
Vier ernste Gesänge (Brahms), 139
Village Romeo and Juliet, A (Delius), 209, 210
Villa-Lobos, Heitor, 840–46
Villi, Le (Puccini), 588
Viñes, Ricardo, 260, 611, 612
Vitry, Philippe de, 4
Vittoria, Tomás Luis de, 4–5
Vivaldi, Antonio, 11, 28, 622
Vltava (Smetana), 755–56
Voces Intimae Quartet (Sibelius), 741, 745–46
Vogl, Johann, 679, 680, 681, 682, 693
Vogler, Abbé, 499, 890
Voice in the Wilderness, A (Bloch), 103, 104
Voivode, The (Tchaikovsky), 797
Voltaire, François Marie Arouet, 54
Von Breuning, Stephan, 52
Von Meck, Nadezhda Filaretovna, 189, 798, 799, 800, 801, 802, 804

Wachet auf (Bach), 26
Wagenseil, Georg Christoph, 514
Wagner, Richard, 15, 16, 45, 46, 60, 61, 62, 77, 87, 88–89, 96, 97, 111, 123, 124, 137, 150, 151, 152, 153, 154, 155, 156, 160, 190, 196, 204, 206, 233, 246, 254, 304, 305, 312, 407, 437, 439–40, 468, 484, 500, 501, 722, 758, 836, 847–81, 888, 893, 899, 900
Waldmädchen, Das (Weber), 889
Waldstein, Count, 49, 68
Waldstein Sonata (Beethoven), 51, 68
Walküre, Die (Wagner), 854, 856, 872, 873–75
Wallenstein's Camp (Smetana), 751
Walter, Benno, 759
Walter, Bruno, 34, 449, 727, 763
Walton, William, 289, 882–87
"Wandern, Das" (Schubert), 697
War and Peace (Prokofiev), 578
Ward, Thomas F., 207, 208
Wasielewsky, Joseph von, 74
Water Music (Handel), 332, 338, 345–46
Weber, Aloysia, 517, 518, 520
Weber, Anselm, 498
Weber, Constanze, 519
Weber, Karl Maria von, 473, 474, 499, 500, 501, 682, 860, 888–96
Webern, Anton, 667, 668
Wedding, The (Stravinsky), 781, 784
Wedekind, Frank, 78
Wegelius, Martin, 740
Weill, Kurt, 289
Weinlig, Theodor, 850
"Welcome Maids of Honor" (Britten), 149
Well-Tempered Clavier, The (Bach), 29–30, 311
Wenzel, Ernst, 316
Werckmeister, Andreas, 29
"Wer ein holdes Weib errungen" (Beethoven), 73

Werfel, Franz, 639
Werther (Massenet), 466
Wesendonck, Mathilde, 854
Wetzler, Hermann, 762
Wharton, Edith, 285
"When as the Rye" (Britten), 149
"When Will My May Come" (Britten), 149
Whiteman, Paul, 289, 292
Whitman, Walt, 813
"Widmung" (Schumann), 713
Widor, Charles Marie, 398, 506
Wieck, Clara, 119–20, 122, 125, 479, 701, 702, 703, 704, 713
Wieck, Friedrich, 699, 700, 702, 849
"Wiegenlied" (Brahms), 139
"Wiegenlied" (Strauss), 761, 774
Wilbye, John, 5
Wilde, Oscar, 76, 79, 771
Wilhelmj, August, 26, 570
Willaert, Adrian, 4
Williams, Ralph Vaughan. *See* Vaughan Williams, Ralph
Williams, Stephen, 144
William Tell (Rossini), 639, 644, 645–46, 649–50
Wilson, Edmund, 143
Winter Bonfire (Prokofiev), 574
Winter Dreams Symphony (Tchaikovsky), 796
Winterreise, Die (Schubert), 683, 684, 697
Winter Wind Etude (Chopin), 176
Wir hatten gebauet ein stattliches Haus, 129
Wirth und Gast (Meyerbeer), 409
"Wirtshaus, Das" (Schubert), 697

Wise Virgins, The (Walton), 884
Wodzinska, Maria, 168
"Wohin" (Schubert), 697
Wolf, Hugo, 139, 265, 897–905
Wood, Henry J., 210
Woods, Ursula, 815
Woyciechowski, Titus, 167
Wozzeck (Berg), 77, 80–81
"Würth, Karl," 118
Würzburg, Conrad von, 864

Yeats, William Butler, 35
Yonge, Nicholas, 5
Young Person's Guide to the Orchestra, The (Britten), 143, 148
Yradier, Sebastian, 98
Ysaÿe, Eugène, 101, 161, 163, 282

Zachow, F. W., 329
Zaremba, Nicholas, 795
Zauberflöte, Die (Mozart), 522, 523, 524, 525, 529–31
Zauberharfe, Die (Schubert), 681–82, 691
Zauberlehrling, Der (Goethe), 228
Zaza (Leoncavallo), 430
Zelter, Karl Friedrich, 472, 473, 474, 475, 476, 498
Zemlinsky, Alexander, 667
Zemlinsky, Mathilde, 668
Zoraide de Granata (Donizetti), 220
"Zueignung" (Strauss), 774
Zuléima (Debussy), 190
Zverev, Nikolai, 599
Zweig, Stefan, 763
Zwillingsbrüder, Die (Schubert), 681
Zwyny, Adalbert, 166